Garner on Language and Writing

Selected Essays and Speeches
of Bryan A. Garner

BRYAN A. GARNER

Garner on Language and Writing

Selected Essays and Speeches of Bryan A. Garner

With a foreword by Ruth Bader Ginsburg
Associate Justice, Supreme Court of the United States

Defending Liberty
Pursuing Justice

American Bar Association
Chicago

American Bar Association policy statement: The materials contained herein represent the opinions and views of the author, and should not be construed to be the views or opinions of the law firms or companies with whom such persons are in partnership with, associated with, or employed by, nor of the American Bar Association, unless adopted pursuant to the bylaws of the Association. Nothing contained in this book is to be considered as the rendering of legal advice for specific cases, and readers are responsible for obtaining such advice from their own legal counsel. This book and any forms and agreements herein are intended for educational and informational purposes only.

How Bryan Garner wanted the statement to read: The essays in this volume represent the author's views—not those of the American Bar Association.

Printed in the United States of America.
12 11 10 09 08   5 4 3 2 1

Library of Congress Cataloging-in-Publication Data

Garner, Bryan A.
   Garner on language and writing : selected essays and speeches of Bryan A. Garner / Bryan A. Garner. Foreword by Justice Ruth Bader Ginsburg.—1st ed.
     p. cm.
   Includes bibliographical references and index.
   ISBN-13: 978-1-59031-588-0
   ISBN-10: 1-59031-588-X
   1. Law—United States—Language. 2. Law—United States—Terminology.
3. Legal composition. 4. English language—Usage. I. Title.
   KF250.G376   2008
   808'.06634—dc22

                                    2007052265

Excerpts from previously published works are reprinted by permission of the publishers.

Discounts are available for books ordered in bulk. Special consideration is given to state bars, CLE programs, and other bar-related organizations. Inquire at Book Publishing, ABA Publishing, American Bar Association, 321 N. Clark, Chicago, Illinois 60610-4714.

www.ababooks.org
See also: www.lawprose.org

This book is dedicated
to the memory of my grandparents

Eleanor Sykes Griffin

(1896–1982)

whose passion for books and learning—and whose loving kindness—
will always be an inspiration

Dorothy Porter Griffin

(1902–1985)

who opened so many doors to the offices of judges and political officials,
and who generously supported my education

Meade F. Griffin

(1894–1974)

who, as a longtime justice of the Supreme Court of Texas,
inspired me to pursue law

Madge Garner

(1905–1983)

whose generosity made it possible for me, as an undergraduate,
to study literature for two summers at Oxford University,
where I made enduring friendships

Benjamin Franklin Garner

(1894–1977)

whose wry wit, sardonic humor, and intense interest in English taught me
that language can be both absorbing and entertaining

Books Written or Edited by Bryan A. Garner

Black's Law Dictionary
  (all current editions)

Garner's Modern American Usage

A Dictionary of Modern Legal Usage

The Redbook: A Manual on Legal Style

The Elements of Legal Style

The Winning Brief

The Winning Oral Argument

Legal Writing in Plain English

Guidelines for Drafting and Editing Court Rules

Securities Disclosure in Plain English

A Handbook of Basic Law Terms

A Handbook of Business Law Terms

A Handbook of Criminal Law Terms

A Handbook of Family Law Terms

The Oxford Dictionary of American Usage and Style

Making Your Case: The Art of Persuading Judges
  (with Justice Antonin Scalia)

Garner on Language and Writing

The Rules of Golf in Plain English
  (with Jeffrey S. Kuhn)

A New Miscellany-at-Law
  (by Sir Robert Megarry)

Texas, Our Texas: Reminiscences of The University
  (an anthology of autobiographical essays)

Contents

CHAPTER SIX

Legal Language   287

CHAPTER SEVEN

Legal Lexicography   333

Foreword

LAWYERS SERVE THEIR CLIENTS best when their readers can quickly and firmly grasp their points. Readers of legal writing, on and off the bench, often work under the pressure of a relentless clock. They may lack the time to ferret out bright ideas buried in complex sentences, overlong paragraphs, or too many pages. Strong arguments can escape attention when embedded in dense or Delphic prose. Lucid, well-ordered writing can contribute immeasurably to a lawyer's success as an advocate and counselor.

Bryan Garner has made the promotion of good legal writing—prose both comprehensible and engaging—his lifelong endeavor. Along with countless other lawyers and judges, I have benefited from the wise and practical aid afforded by his style manuals, usage dictionaries, and other works.

Garner on Language and Writing arranges his shorter commentary into an informative and entertaining whole. The pieces address topics ranging from the basics of expository prose to the finer points of crafting judicial opinions. Included in the collection are book reviews and interviews, as well as more reflective writing. In the latter category, I note his eloquent tributes to Charles Alan Wright, revered teacher, friend, and "godfather of [Garner's] career." Garner's essays not only instruct by prescription; they also teach by example. His prose is a model of precision, elegance, and clarity.

I am glad to add *Garner on Language and Writing* to the collection of Garner's works kept within arm's reach of my writing table. My colleagues at the Bar and on the Bench, I am certain, will find in the book's pages cues to effective expression in doses both delectable and easily digestible. Indeed, even in manuscript form, this latest production by Garner has become a "must read" primer for my law clerks.

Ruth Bader Ginsburg
Associate Justice
Supreme Court of the United States
October 2007

ॐ

Acknowledgments

MY COPIOUS GRATITUDE flows in many directions. To ABA Publishing for making this book possible, and especially to Timothy Brandhorst, who originally proposed it. To J.P. Schmelzer, whose caricatures put unforgettable faces on each chapter. To my book publishers—Thomson/West, Oxford University Press, the University of Chicago Press, and CCH—for allowing me to reprint the essays collected here. To book publishers that have anthologized or included various essays: the American Dialect Society, the University of California Press, the Lawbook Exchange, and the Texas Law Review Association. To the magazines and journals that have published my essays over the years—*ABA Journal*, *The Appellate Advocate*, *Bookman's Weekly*, *Copy Editor*, *Court Review*, *Dallas Bar Headnotes*, *English Today*, *Essays in Criticism*, *For the Defense*, *Gleanings of the H.W. Fowler Society*, *The Green Bag*, *The Law Librarian*, *Lawyer Hiring and Training Report*, *Litigation*, *Michigan Bar Journal*, *The New York Times*, *The Record*, *The Review of Litigation*, *The Scribes Journal of Legal Writing*, *The Scrivener*, *Student Lawyer*, *Texas Law Review*, *Trial*, and *The Wall Street Journal*. And to the editors of all these publications, who long ago burnished these essays before they originally appeared in print.

My special thanks go to the late Roy M. Mersky and his staff at the Tarlton Law Library in Austin, Texas; over the years, Roy greatly eased the labor of research by making whatever materials I asked for magically appear within hours. To my dear friend and favorite teacher of writing, John R. Trimble, whose deft editorial hand contributed enormously to whatever luster these essays may have. To my favorite proofreader, Karen Magnuson, who always protects me against my ever-present fallibility.

To my LawProse colleagues, Jeff Newman, Tiger Jackson, and Caroline B. Garner (as a summer intern), who did so much to prepare the manuscript and the index. To Jeffrey A. Lachina and his expert staff at Lachina Publishing Services in Cleveland, whose design and typesetting give new meaning to the word *painstaking*. And to Justice Ruth Bader Ginsburg, for contributing her gem of a foreword.

And to my readers, whose steadfast interest both delights and mystifies me. Thank you all.

Bryan A. Garner
Dallas, Texas
June 2008

MEADE FELIX GRIFFIN

Introduction

SIX VIGNETTES.

1962: "No, Bryan doesn't sit in a high chair anymore," my mother said to my grandfather.

"But he's not big enough!" insisted my grandfather. "Let's get out the dictionary." And so he did: *Webster's Second New International Dictionary*, published in 1934, perhaps the thickest one-volume dictionary ever produced. I sat on that, beside my Papa. He was Meade F. Griffin, for 19 years a justice on the Supreme Court of Texas. From my earliest memories, I was proud to be his grandson. He introduced me to the unabridged dictionary, among other things. The dictionary was my booster seat. Figuratively, it still is: I now own and frequently consult that very copy.

1968: In Mrs. Pearcy's fourth-grade class, we had a student teacher, Miss Phillips (no one used *Ms.* in West Texas in those days). Miss Phillips was dour and stern. After observing our class for two weeks, she got to teach under the supervision of a university professor of education.

"Today, children, I'm going to teach you about contractions. Can anyone name a contraction?"

The whole idea seemed absurd to me. We'd learned about contractions in third grade. But my hand shot up into the air. She called on me:

"Bryan."

"*Shan't!*"

"No, that's not a word."

"Oh, it is, Miss Phillips! It's a contraction for *shall not.*"

"No, that's not a word. Can anyone name a contraction?"

"*Won't!*" shouted Craig Howard, sitting beside me.

"Good, Craig. That's a contraction for *will not*. Excellent, Craig."

Other pupils shouted *can't* and *don't* and *isn't*, all to Miss Phillips's approval. I grew silent for the rest of class. I listened but didn't participate.

Then came recess. I went over to the dictionary stand and turned the pages of the big, thick *Webster's Third New International Dictionary*. There it was: "**shan't** [by contr.]: shall not."

I lugged the huge book over to Miss Phillips. "Look, Miss Phillips! The dictionary says that *shan't* is a contraction for *shall not*. Look! It's a word!"

She wouldn't look. She turned away.

"But look!"

She still wouldn't look. "Bryan, that's not a word. Now go run and play." I slunk away.

1969: Upon retiring from the Supreme Court of Texas, and after sitting as a special judge on the Texas Court of Criminal Appeals, my grandfather took a position as special assistant to Texas Attorney General Crawford Martin. On a family visit, my grandfather said, "The assistant AGs need help with their briefs, and I'm there to help them." I was ten years old. "They need help with their briefs," he had said. And so the seed was planted.

1974: A girl I much admired said offhandedly, "You have a really big vocabulary." She liked that. I figured I could make it even bigger—and that's what I spent the next several years doing.

"Bryan's upstairs reading the dictionary again," my older brother Brad told my parents that year. "Why does he always do that?"

No one would have guessed that it was a misplaced effort to attract females. But that was indeed the conscious origin of my interest in dictionaries and the English language. The fact that the scheme never really worked on females took a long time to register in my mind. By then I was a serious lexicologist.

1994: "Now, that's the law school. It's famous." The cabbie was driving me down 26th Street, past the University of Texas campus, toward the Austin airport. "They're working on the *Oxford Law Dictionary* there."

"Really?" I said.

"That put the law school on the map. When Oxford University was looking for a law school to team up with for a law dictionary, it chose UT Law. It's a great law school. Oxford could have gone anywhere."

"Wow."

Yes, wow. Four years earlier, the dean at UT Law School, Mark Yudof, had canceled the joint venture that I had brought to the university. By August 1990, the *Oxford Law Dictionary* was no more. We hadn't raised enough money—only about a third of the $2 million needed—and the university hadn't wanted to undertake the project if it might have to foot part of the bill. And here I was, in 1994, hearing a cab driver brag about the project as if it were still going on.

I asked: "Do you ever drive the dean of the law school?"

"I did once."

"If you ever do it again, be sure to tell him what you've told me. Would you? Tell him how proud you are of the Oxford connection. I'm sure he'll appreciate that."

2000: "Why are you going to a used-book store?" the cab driver asked. We were on our way to my favorite bookstore in Sacramento.

"I'm a book collector," I responded.

"What do you collect?"

"Law dictionaries."

"Me too!" I was surprised, and I didn't really believe him. But he continued, "I like Bouvier's law dictionary." I began to believe him: few people know the legal lexicographer John Bouvier.

"Why do you collect law dictionaries?" I asked.

"Because I'm fascinated by law. The *real* law. The *original* law. We've gotten away from that. Most of the law today is bogus. So you have to go to Bouvier to get the real law. Law dictionaries today are no good. *Black's Law Dictionary*, for example. The editors have been bought off. There's a conspiracy to get people to think that the Internal Revenue Code is valid, when in fact it's unconstitutional. The government has paid off the editors of *Black's* to support the idea that there's a legal basis for the IRS. That's a documented fact."

"Really?" I was incredulous.

"Whoever is responsible for *Black's Law Dictionary* should be shot. If I could find the editor, I'd do it myself."

Just then, we arrived at Beer's Books, down the street from California's capitol. I paid and started getting out of the cab.

"Why do you collect law dictionaries?" the cabbie asked as I was getting out.

"Just a hobby."

I've long since been disabused of the notion that a lexicographer must necessarily be, in Samuel Johnson's words, a "harmless drudge." Harmless, perhaps—but not always a drudge.

Readers may wonder what would possess someone to write the kinds of essays collected here. To me, once you understand the second vignette, it's self-explanatory. You might consider this whole book—and all my writing—a perverse, psychologically stultified attempt to get even with Miss Phillips.

It's pretty straightforward. In college I wrote papers on Shakespearean linguistics, and they were published in scholarly journals. Then I wrote a dictionary of legal usage in law school. Then a book on legal style. Then related books. I became a full-time legal lexicographer in 1988—four years after graduating from law school. When the *Oxford Law Dictionary* was canceled in 1990, I started a company—LawProse, Inc.—to train lawyers and judges in the art of writing. A noncompetition covenant prevented me from undertaking a new law dictionary for three years. Then, out of the blue, West wrote to me in 1994 asking whether I'd take on *Black's Law Dictionary*. LawProse and *Black's* have kept me occupied ever since.

Along the way, I've written lots of articles and columns—more than I'd have thought. The ABA asked me to collect the best ones for an anthology. Hence this book. With luck, you'll find something here to pique your interest. That's my earnest hope.

Bryan A. Garner
Dallas, Texas

THOMAS M. REAVLEY • FRANK H. EASTERBROOK • THOMAS GIBBS GEE

ba ba ba

The Mad, Mad World of Legal Writing

This speech was delivered at the banquet of the Texas Law Review *in April 2000. Mr. Garner was introduced by Dean William Powers of the law school—who is now president of the University of Texas.*

Thank you, Professor Powers. The last time I spoke at a *Texas Law Review* event, the editor in chief introduced me. Somebody told him to keep the intro brief. And so he began: "The less said about Bryan Garner, the better."

I take as my title "The Mad, Mad World of Legal Writing." This might lead you to believe that I'll be going for easy laughs. That's not so, although it's true enough that laughable things are hardly scarce in the world of legal writing.

- Think of the Fifth Circuit brief that Judge Thomas Gibbs Gee used to cite—the one that said, on page 32: "At the outset of this brief, the court will find an exhaustive copulation of authorities on the subject."

- Or consider my other favorite typographical error, a rather embarrassing one that occurs sometimes with the Latinism *per annum*. A friend of mine, leaving the Classics department at a major university, came to me with the employment contract he had received from a major corporation. He said, "Bryan, you're never going to believe this. Look: it says they're going to pay me $65,000 per anum." We were both dumbfounded. And he added: "I don't want to make them pay that way. I'd rather make them pay the traditional way—through the nose."

- Or think of the insensitivity to metaphor. I'm not just speaking of apocryphal stories, such as the one about the scholar who referred to hedonic damages as "a virgin field pregnant with possibilities." No, I'm talking about published writing—such as the Fifth Circuit opinion, in an employment-law case, that refers to the necessity for creating "a prophylactic against a wrongful discharge."[1]

All these things I've documented in various books and articles.

---

[1] *Findelsen v. N.E. Indep. Sch. Dist.*, 749 F.2d 234, 238 (5th Cir. 1984).

But in discussing the madness that pervades the world of legal writing, I prefer to take more dignified subjects. Let's talk about what actually goes on in legal writing—in law schools, in transactional practice, and in litigation.

First, the Law Schools

Now, before I say anything critical about the way law schools fund and operate their legal-writing programs, I should say that I've never been a part of one. Although I've taught upper-division courses both here at UT and at Southern Methodist University, I've never taught as part of the basic writing program. This is no accident. A decade ago, when I told Mark Yudof that I wanted to pursue legal writing full-time, he warned me not to try it in a law school. "You'll never be taken seriously by the faculty," he said. That comment—made over dinner in Chicago in August 1990—spurred me to create LawProse and to engage in what has become the core of my career since 1990: continuing legal education.

But back to law schools. The first curious thing is that those who teach legal writing, at most law schools, are the least-well-compensated members of the faculty—and often aren't really counted as full-fledged members of the faculty. Some earn less than the regular faculty members' secretaries. Yet what they teach, in the eyes of legal employers, is the single most important skill for law graduates to have. I'm not just making this up: an American Bar Foundation study found in 1992 that employers believe that the biggest problem with recent law graduates is that they don't know how to write.[2] And the graduates themselves say that writing is the part of their jobs that their legal education has least equipped them to do competently (let alone artfully, easily, beautifully).

Until recently, most American law schools capped appointments for full-time legal-writing instructors at two years—almost as if we wanted to keep the instructors from getting very good at what they do. This has gradually changed, but only as a result of massive lobbying and something approaching collective bargaining. And still, many schools that have lifted the caps put their writing instructors on nothing more than year-to-year contracts—as UT does.

The second curious thing is the relation between a law school's general reputation and the reputation of its legal-writing program. Generally, the schools that are commonly held up as having the best legal-writing programs—I'd better not cite one, given what I'm about to say—are

---

[2] Bryant G. Garth & Joanne Martin, *Law Schools and the Construction of Competence* 21 (American Bar Foundation Working Paper No. 9212, 1992).

among those in the bottom half of the national rankings of law schools. It's hardly an exaggeration to say that the more highly ranked a law school is, the more likely the school is to have a legal-writing program that's on an unstable footing—or in a mess.

The problems stem in large part from a lack of imagination. Those who see legal writing as being simply a matter of cleaning up grammar and punctuation, as well as learning citation form, grossly misunderstand what the field should be. Good writing results from good, disciplined thinking. To work on your writing is to improve your analytical skills. Grammar and punctuation and citation form are to writing what dribbling is to basketball. Nothing more. And you haven't learned to play basketball when you've learned how to dribble.

We have a long way to go in legal education. It's not just a matter of having a writing program. It's a matter of putting legal writing on a par with Property and Evidence and Civil Procedure. And if we can't do that because our legal-writing program consists only of teaching dribbling, then we'll need to find a way of deepening and strengthening our writing programs.

Now consider what's happening in law practice. It won't surprise you to learn that there's a direct correlation between what's happening in law practice and what has long been happening in our law schools.

The Transactional Practice

Way back in 1940, the president of the ABA—Charles Beardsley—gave a speech in San Antonio. It was published in *Texas Law Review*. As part of that speech, he criticized the lack of instruction in transactional drafting in our law schools. He said: "Learning draftsmanship in the school of experience exclusively is costly to clients, it is costly to the public, and it is costly to the lawyer. It is like learning surgery by experience. It is possible, but it is tough on the patient and tough on the reputation of the surgeon."[3]

In the more than 60 years since Beardsley said those words, little has changed. Transactional lawyers still generally learn whatever techniques of drafting they acquire, not in law school but in the school of experience. A majority of law schools today don't even offer a course in the techniques of legal drafting. And those that do typically offer only seminar courses, elective courses, that reach only a tiny minority of the student population.

---

[3] Charles Beardsley (as quoted in *Proceedings: State Bar of Texas and Texas Bar Association*, 20 Tex. L. Rev. 24, 42–43 (1940)).

The result of this is widespread ignorance of the techniques of good drafting. This is true of partners at major firms—people who've been producing documents for 30 and 40 years. That's quite a charge, so let me make good on it. I'll cite four facts in support of it.

- First, some 98% of transactional lawyers can't even name a book on the subject of legal drafting. I know this, having polled many large CLE audiences. This is shocking, in a way. Virtually all journalists could name a book on journalistic writing, and most litigators could name a book on brief-writing. But if you ask a roomful of transactional lawyers to name a book on drafting, they'll simply shrug. They don't know Reed Dickerson's classic book *The Fundamentals of Legal Drafting* or Barbara Child's *Drafting Legal Documents.* The literature on legal drafting is largely unknown to the bar.

- This leads to the second point: many of the principles of good drafting are widely and unknowingly violated. This makes CLE in legal drafting quite some fun because it means that the lawyers will hear many shocking things about the discipline.

  An example: provisos. If you look at the literature on legal drafting—and by that I mean modern legal drafting, and by that I mean post-1842 books and articles on legal drafting—you'd come away with the idea that no self-respecting drafter would ever be caught using the phrase *provided that.* You'd gather that everyone knows that provisos are horrible, horrible form. Embarrassing blemishes. How so?

  Provisos have three serious problems. First, what does *provided that* mean? Some courts have held that it means "if," that it creates a condition; others have held that it means "except," that it creates an exception; still others have held that it means neither "if" nor "except," but instead means "also," that it simply introduces an additional thought. Every time you use a proviso, there's this question of what it means. But that's only the first of the problems. The second is, what does it modify? Does it reach back 3 words, 10 words, 50 words, 500 words? How long is the sentence in which it appears? There's even a canon of construction about provisos. Listen to this: provisos modify "only the immediately preceding language." That's the canon. But there's a gaping exception: "they modify only the immediately preceding language unless it is necessary to go back further to effectuate the manifest intention of the parties." Not exactly a clear guide, is it? Finally, the third problem with provisos is that every time you use one, you're letting the text sprawl and become one long, imposing block of verbiage. Provisos create unreadable pages.

Despite these three serious drawbacks—well documented in the literature on legal drafting—American lawyers use provisos left and right. They've never heard that there's anything wrong with provisos. How can this be—that one of the most basic principles of good drafting would be so widely unknown? You guessed it: we never hear anything about this in our law schools.

- The third point in support of my charge about transactional lawyers is a damning one. And I wouldn't say it if I didn't have unassailable proof. Whereas most writers know the meanings of the words that they use, legal drafters commonly don't. They'll use *remise* in a general release because it's part of the form, without ever troubling themselves to look it up in a dictionary. They'll use *indemnify and hold harmless* in hundreds of contracts throughout their careers, without ever bothering to find out whether there's a difference between them and what that difference might be. If a colleague spouts the nonsense that you *indemnify* against third-party liabilities but *hold harmless* if you, the indemnitor, have a claim against the indemnitee, they'll accept that explanation uncritically without ever cracking a book. That is a common misconception. In fact, there is ample authority that *indemnify* and *hold harmless* are precisely synonymous—that this is just another doubled-up redundancy like *various and sundry* or *separate and distinct*.

Not long ago, I put the question to a group of 600 lawyers in Houston—learned Texas lawyers. Did anyone know with any confidence what the distinction is between *indemnify* and *hold harmless*, if there is any distinction? Not a single hand went up. I can assure you it would be no different in Los Angeles or New York.

This is merely a symptom of what I call the hocus-pocus theory of legal drafting: I don't know why we say it this way, but you just use these words and it works. At least I hope it works! I mean it had better work because we've done it that way hundreds of times. But don't ask me the specifics of why we say it that way. We just do.

This is a sad state of affairs for a learned profession to be in. If we deserve the name "learned profession"—and I believe that law does—we must know why we say what we say.

We shouldn't adopt John Fortescue's mode of reasoning, even though it's quite old. In 1475, Chief Justice Fortescue (an English judge) said: "We have several set forms of law, which are held as law, and so held and used for good reason—though we cannot remember that reason."[4] I prefer Justice Holmes's reasoning: "It is

---

[4] Y.B. 36 Hen. VI pl. 21 (pp. 25–26) (translated in Holdsworth, *A History of English Law* vol. 3, 626 (3d ed. 1923)).

revolting to have no better reason for a rule of law than that it was laid down in the time of Henry IV. It is more revolting still if the reason for that rule has long since disappeared."[5]

- Finally, my fourth illustrative point in support of my charge about the transactional practice. You've noticed the odd way that drafters commonly use word-numeric doublets: *ten thousand and no/100 dollars ($10,000.00).* Only one in five lawyers knows the reason for this doubling up. Some say it's a guard against typographical errors. It isn't. Some say it was historically a precaution against illegible handwriting. Not so. Some have actually suggested that it's a way of preventing discrepancies! That's an amazing assertion, given that there's no possibility of a discrepancy until you double up.

  Actually, the reason for the doubling up is to prevent fraudulent alterations. In the days of scribes, it would have been too easy, if you were using numerals alone, to change zeros to eights or nines. But you can't make the corresponding alterations in the words—at least, not without betraying the fraud. That's why, in cases of discrepancy, the words prevail over the numerals.

  But the practice of doubling up has little justification in most modern drafting. There's no good reason for having it in statutes or in most contracts. (An exception I'd make is negotiable instruments.) One significant danger to doubling up is that, when you review your work, the numerals jump off the page at you—they're what you'll review most closely. Yet the words will control in cases of discrepancy.

  I was leading a drafting workshop for the general counsel's office in a Fortune 500 company in California when I saw the most severe discrepancy I've ever found—the numerals were correct and the words were wrong, yet the words governed. Page 4 of the contract said: "sixty-thousand and no/100 dollars ($80,000)." This amount, sadly, was what the corporation was to receive *quarterly* under one of its contracts. (I immediately regretted bringing this to the lawyers' attention: after an otherwise lively and enjoyable day, a pall temporarily descended over the room. And in one little corner of the room, the pall never lifted.) Anyway, these lawyers told me that this was a contract they prepared quite frequently: the only things that changed from deal to deal were the numbers. There were 23 numbers in the contract: this meant 46 changes, since they were doubling up. Getting 45 out of 46 right is a great percentage, but it simply isn't good enough.

---

[5] Oliver Wendell Holmes, *The Path of the Law*, 10 Harv. L. Rev. 457, 469 (1897).

These are the kinds of things that you never hear about in most law schools. And they're only the slightest hint of the fascinating things to be learned about many other drafting techniques: how and when to use *shall* and *may* (another subject on which ignorance is widespread), the trouble with *and/or* and *herein*, the proper use of recitals and of definitions, and many another subject.

But I've been hard enough on transactional lawyers, so let's turn our focus now to litigators.

The Litigation Practice

Before I get into the really serious problems that litigators have, I'll mention that many of the transactional lawyers' bad habits have migrated into litigators' writing. Some lawyers actually file briefs stating that their opponents didn't answer their discovery requests "until forty-eight (48) days after they were served." I'm curious about the implications of this. Did the lawyers actually believe that the judge, or perhaps a law clerk, might fraudulently alter the number? True story: Some years ago I received a letter from a friend of mine—a fellow Dallas lawyer—and I know it was no joke because this friend has a badly underdeveloped sense of humor. The letter said: "Dear Bryan: It was a real pleasure running into you and your two (2) daughters last week at the supermarket." This unnerved me. Did he think I was going to alter the number in his letter? Was he trying to estop me from having any more children?

Well, if transactional lawyers flout the basic principles of drafting, the vast majority of litigators commonly flout the most basic principle of good expository prose. Aristotle was the first to enunciate this principle, and though we now take it for granted, it was a very great insight when he first said it: Every piece of writing has three parts—a beginning, a middle, and an end. My two daughters both learned this in first grade. Just last year, I heard my younger daughter's teacher say to a group of parents: "We've been teaching your children that every story has three parts: a beginning, a middle, and an end." I was amazed at this revelation, since I've devoted a large part of my career to reteaching this principle to lawyers.

You see, litigators typically make their writing all "middle"—either by never stating the issues or by stating them in a highly superficial, uninformative way. I'm not talking primarily about appellate briefs—although the problem is tremendous there. No. I'm talking about run-of-the-mill submissions to trial courts.

Whereas journalists grunt and sweat over their opening words—what they call the "lead"—litigators typically begin with formulaic verbiage: "To the honorable judge of said court: Now comes Pantheon Corporation

('Pantheon'), by and through its attorneys of record, Twilbank, Del Deo, Farrington & Blumpy, 4400 First United Tower, Houston, Texas 77002-4914, and files this Pantheon's Motion for Summary Judgment, and in support thereof respectfully states as follows." And then to the facts—the middle. That's the full extent of the opener.

It's bad enough when there's a typo in that opener—I recently saw one that erroneously collapsed *respectfully* into *rectfully*—but even without typos that stuff is wasteful gibberish. It simply reiterates the title: it says that this is in fact Pantheon's motion for summary judgment, as the caption said. Yet this is how more than 90% of Texas motions begin—in fact, brief-writers throughout the United States use some variation of it.

Even the few who try to state an issue will typically do it incomprehensibly: "Whether there was a transfer or delivery of the equipment under the joint services agreement." The next sentence then says, "For all the following reasons, we contend that there was." What is that? "For all the following reasons"? That's a not-so-subtle way of telling the judge: "We're not going to make this easy for you, Judge. We're not going to tell you how many reasons there are, or what they are. Read on!"

To litigators, you see, the opener is a vestigial organ. Maybe it once served some purpose, but today it's nothing. And so judges plod through submissions that plunge straight into the middle—a 12-page statement of facts, before then getting to the standards for granting a motion for summary judgment. (Just two and a half pages on that—boilerplate that you put into each motion because trial judges in these parts are constantly forgetting the standard.) Finally, in desperation, the judge skips to the end. And what does it say, on page 37? "For all the foregoing reasons, ..." It takes the reader back to the middle.

This is what American litigators have done to judges. They've made the two most important parts of their writing into meaningless vestiges. Openers and closers are generally entirely nonsubstantive: we make the judges read the whole piece and concentrate really hard to get our messages. You can justify this, of course, on the principle that judges are paid to read what we write. It's their constitutionally sworn duty to read what we file in court. So let them earn their pay.

If you want to know what litigators have done to judges, we've taken these three parts of writing, and we've systematically, and as a class, lopped off the opener. (Holding three fingers in the air and taking down the first.) And as for the closer, we've systematically, and as a class, lopped it off. (Pretending to take down the third finger.) No, I guess I'd better not do that. But this, essentially, is what lawyers have done to judges.

This takes me to a principle laid down by John Trimble, a UT English professor and a colleague of mine at LawProse. Trimble, of course, is one of the most famous writing professors in the country, the author of *Writing with Style*, which has just appeared in a silver-anniversary second edition. Anyway, Trimble has coined a couple of maxims that express a fundamental truth about readers. He tells his students: "Readers are impatient to get the goods, and they'll resent having to work any harder than necessary to get them."

This principle led me, in the early 1990s, to develop Garner's corollary to Trimble's maxims: a brief should deliver the goods to a judicial reader within 90 seconds of the time when the judge first picks it up. And what are the goods that you're delivering? They're essentially three things: the principal question, the answer to that question, and the reason for that answer. The question is the most important thing: judges, after all, are professional question-answerers. Any competent judge who picks up a brief immediately wants to know what the question is.

Yet lawyers are frightened by questions. They like answers to unspecified questions. That's why your typical motion to dismiss reads something like this: "Dismiss, dismiss, dismiss. Talk, talk, talk." Ad nauseam. The reading that judges do is the most frustrating part of the job.

You see, it's a very rare lawyer who sums this stuff up in a tidy preliminary statement on page one—a statement that would be immediately comprehensible to any generalist. Nationally, we're talking about less than 1% of briefs that do this effectively.

And I'm not making this up. I spend a lot of time with judges—in half a dozen judicial-writing seminars each year. I always ask judges the question: How good are the briefs that you see? I first put the question to Judge Thomas Gibbs Gee at a LawProse seminar back in 1991. Judge Gee, one of the finest writers ever to sit on the federal bench, had been editor in chief of *Texas Law Review* back in 1953. I asked him, "Judge, how good is the brief-writing in the Fifth Circuit?" He answered in one word: "Execrable." Then he translated: "Horrible."

I then put the question to Judge Thomas M. Reavley, for whom I clerked after law school. I had some sense of what Reavley might say, because I could remember preparing for my clerkship thinking, What a wonderful learning experience this will be—to see advocacy at its finest, at the level just below the U.S. Supreme Court. But I was appalled by the number of briefs that really should have said at the end, "Dictated but not read." Anyway, in response to my question about the quality of brief-writing in the Fifth Circuit, Judge Reavley said: "I'm not going to answer in terms of grammar or style. I don't particularly care about grammar. I'm more interested in how helpful the brief is to the court in the decision-making process. We do get some well-written briefs in the Fifth Circuit—some genuinely helpful briefs. It's in the range of 5 to 10%."

In the ensuing years, I've learned that this is the most common answer: 5 to 10%. If you ask Judge Frank Easterbrook of the Seventh Circuit, he'll change the issue. A couple of years ago, he told me, "I'd rather answer a different question: How many of the briefs are of a high professional caliber?" Then he said it would be extravagant to say that 3% of the briefs are of a high professional caliber.

The biggest part of the deficiency, I'm convinced, is that lawyers fear synopsizing. They fear saying, on page one, precisely—and in plain English—why their clients should prevail. Even when a maverick lawyer tries to put this up front, colleagues will try to take it off. It's unconventional—far better to begin with what judges expect to see: "Now comes Pantheon Corporation ('Pantheon'), by and through its attorneys of record . . . ."

Lawyers commonly tell me that if they followed my advice in briefing, it wouldn't be what judges expect to see. My answer is: precisely. You don't want to give judges what they expect. They expect boring word-gravel. They expect meandering, aimless briefs that take seemingly forever to get through. I say that you shouldn't give judges what they expect; instead, give them a pleasant surprise.

Conclusion

One might wonder how things will be 50 years from now. You could make the case that things won't get any better. Fifty years from now, legal writing might not have the status of Property or Evidence or Civil Procedure in our law schools. Transactional lawyers might still be doubling up words and numerals—and doing all sorts of other unnecessary things—with no idea why they do it. Litigators might still use meaningless drivel at the beginnings and ends of their documents, and they'll oppose spilling the beans on page one.

But maybe things *will* get better. If that's going to happen, it'll require much effort from the people in this room.

Even in the worst case, my teaching life will remain interesting. You see, in my CLE classes I don't so much teach as unteach. As a result, the most fundamental laws of expository prose, when applied to legal writing, are often viewed as brilliant, eye-opening revelations that would revolutionize what lawyers do when putting words to paper.

But we can grow past all that. I'd be thrilled if legal writing evolved to the point where gross errors became rarities, so that we could focus on the truly finer points of reasoning and argumentation. We could sharpen our pens, our wits, and our language to tools of surgical precision.

What stands in the way at the moment is unrealistic self-assessment. Most lawyers seem to think they *are* using tools of surgical precision. It's a big problem and an all-too-human foible: a supermajority of lawyers— even law professors—grossly overestimate their writing skills, and underestimate the importance of those skills. If we move toward more realistic assessments, and heighten our goals, the path toward real improvement will become much clearer.

CHIEF JUSTICE JOHN G. ROBERTS JR.

Learning to Write

Using the Flowers Paradigm to Write More Efficiently

MOST WRITING ADVICE focuses on the end product. But we shouldn't neglect the process by which we produce our words. In important ways, the process affects the product.

Now, I can't tell you what type of pen to use or what to sip on while you're working. No one can teach the *physical* aspects of writing. But I've learned that it's quite possible to teach the *mental* aspects of writing.

Before we get to that, though, think of the ways in which legal writers so frequently get mired:

- By starting to write in earnest before they fully understand what they're writing about—and then treating that draft as something sacrosanct.
- By sidestepping the creative stage altogether, so that the final product isn't nearly as imaginative as it could be.
- By writing and sharpening sentences before knowing what the overall structure will be—and thereby wasting valuable time. When structural changes later emerge, as they inevitably will, much of this early work will have to be either scrapped or modified.
- By allowing their critical side to interrupt throughout the process.

How can you avoid these pitfalls?

Adapted from *Trial* (May 1997).

The Flowers Paradigm:
Madman–Architect–Carpenter–Judge

Several years ago Dr. Betty S. Flowers, a LawProse instructor who teaches in the University of Texas English Department, devised a shrewd new way of dramatizing the writing process. Her approach helps minimize common problems and maximize both efficiency and effectiveness.

It breaks down the writing process into four sequential steps—each one based on a "character" or personality that we all have within us: Madman, Architect, Carpenter, and Judge.[1]

The Madman "is full of ideas, writes crazily and perhaps rather sloppily, gets carried away by enthusiasm and desire, and if really let loose, could turn out ten pages an hour."[2] Typically, the legal writer doesn't really "write" at all during this stage, but instead takes copious notes, jotting down ideas and possible approaches to a problem.

The Madman's nemesis is the Judge—one's skeptical, hypercritical self, who must be reined in until the final step. But many of us have an out-of-control Judge, who is easily recognizable. As Flowers describes the Judge,

> He's been educated and knows a sentence fragment when he sees one. He peers over your shoulder and says, "That's trash!" with such authority that the madman loses his crazy confidence and shrivels up. You know the judge is right; after all, he speaks with the voice of an English teacher. But for all his sharpness of eye, he can't create anything.[3]

The key to defusing this battle between Madman and Judge is to keep the Judge at bay until the end of the writing process. Otherwise, the Judge will stifle the Madman altogether.

But what about the other two steps?

Once the Madman has generated lots of ideas, the Architect takes them, makes connections between them, and starts planning their structure. Initially, the Architect's work is nonlinear, but it will end up as an outline, possessing an arrangement that seems obvious to most people today but was a great insight when Aristotle devised it: a beginning, a middle, and an end. And if the Architect functions satisfactorily, you'll know each intermediate point—step by step—while writing the middle parts of the piece. In fact, the more explicit the architecture, the better.

Then comes the Carpenter, who starts actually building the draft. Here, the writing begins in earnest. And because the draft has a logical

---

[1] Betty S. Flowers, *Madman, Architect, Carpenter, Judge: Roles and the Writing Process*, 44 Proceedings of the Conference of College Teachers of English 7–10 (1979).

[2] *Id.* at 7.

[3] *Id.*

plan, the Carpenter's work is greatly eased: it's like filling in the blanks. You simplify the process of building when you have the Architect's specifications laid out before you.

Charles Alan Wright, the eminent legal scholar and outstanding writer, made this very point in a *Scribes Journal* essay in which he described his writing process:

> For my kind of nonfiction it is necessary first to have a complete grasp of whatever subject it is I am going to be writing about. This we can take for granted, though the research is often long and tedious. The next stage, and to me the hardest of all, is organization. I never sit down to the keyboard—in the old days it was a typewriter, then an electronic typewriter, and in recent years it has been a computer—until I am clear in my mind how I am going to organize whatever it is that I am doing.[4]

That's why, earlier in his essay, Wright said that writing is easy—it's the preparation that's difficult.

The most important thing about the Carpenter stage is to write freely, simply filling in the details according to the architectural specs. If you stop to edit, you open the door for the Judge, and this is just the type of interference your Carpenter doesn't need. But suppose you get stuck in a certain part. Just move on to the next section: you may have to leave a little hole here and there.

Understand that the carpenter has some discretion—deciding how to finish off a corner, how to build the passage from one room to the next. Some architectural details, in other words, are left to the Carpenter.

Once your Carpenter has built a draft, you can call in your Judge, who will look for problems as well as ways to refine the draft. The Judge will check for many things: whether there are transitions between paragraphs, whether the verbs need strengthening, and so on. And the Judge will check many grammatical points, too—everything from comma splices to misplaced modifiers to subject–verb agreement problems. The Judge is an inspector for quality control.

Each of these four characters needs time alone on the stage. If you shortchange any of them, your writing will suffer.

Two Qualms Answered

Is it possible, in the hurly-burly of a busy law practice, to go through these four steps with every writing project? Perhaps not with every one. But surely in the space of an hourlong writing project, you can spend 10 minutes on Madman, 5 on Architect, 25 on Carpenter, and 10 on

---

[4] Charles Alan Wright, *How I Write*, 4 Scribes J. Legal Writing 87, 88 (1993).

Judge. The rest of the time you need for short breaks in between, both to step back from the project and to put yourself in the mind of another character.

But isn't it true that we all approach problems differently? Isn't that the lesson of Myers–Briggs and other personality tests? Yes, and Flowers designed the paradigm with this in mind. You see, everyone is most comfortable working in a particular compartment of the brain. The Flowers approach ensures that you benefit from all that your brain has to offer, not just from the mental realm you're most comfortable with.

I, for example, spent years neglecting the Architect. I wrote highly polished sentences and paragraphs, and people who read my stuff generally thought of me as a good writer. But as I now look at what I wrote in those days, it seems a highly polished mishmash. The organization was unpredictable. Now that has changed—and writing has become relatively painless for me, and much quicker. I do what Professor Wright mentioned: I plan every writing project.

The Advantages of the Flowers Paradigm

Flowers mentioned eight advantages to using her paradigm.[5] Let me paraphrase them:

1. It's easy to remember.
2. It stresses the sequential nature of the writing process—that you're likely to get better results if you work through the Madman stage first rather than returning to it after you've spent three hours crafting sentences.
3. It dramatizes the need for rewriting—the Judge stage—and gives a sense of individual purpose to every draft.
4. It separates the writing task into manageable steps and lets you enjoy each stage, since you can focus on it alone.
5. It defuses the conflict that often arises when you try to write for an authority figure. When writing cautiously, we'll often produce dry, technically correct prose that is devoid of creativity, naturalness, and flow.
6. It offers a way to deal with self-image problems that sometimes interfere with the writing process. If, for example, you see yourself as a creator, you might be impatient with the polishing and careful proofing that the Judge can supply—and that every draft needs. Similarly, if you see yourself as a consummate critic, you may have a highly "repressed" style characterized by dry but technically correct prose.

---

[5] Flowers, note 1, at 9.

7. It gives everyone a new language for critiquing drafts, one that doesn't shove the editor exclusively into the role of Judge. Now an editor can look at a colleague's brief and say, "Try playing the Madman more with this section," rather than just picking up a red pen and marking away.

8. It clarifies what you can and can't teach about writing. The Madman stage is personal and subjective, a private area left almost exclusively to the writer. The Judge can be taught from good writing texts. But in the Architect and Carpenter stages—where many writers are least experienced and usually least well trained— a teacher can be very helpful.

Many writers need more help with their writing process than with anything else. For them, the Flowers paradigm can be invaluable.

ਣ ਣ ਣ

From Mush to Masterpiece

WHAT'S YOUR BIGGEST challenge as a writer? It's figuring out, from the mass of things you might possibly mention, precisely what your points are—and then stating them cogently, with adequate support. Although this might seem obvious, legal writers constantly overlook it. The result is a diffuse, aimless style. And even with your point well in mind, if you take too long to get there, you might as well have no point at all. Only those readers with a high incentive to understand you will work to grasp your meaning.

That's certainly true of law-school reading. Every law student reads plenty of diffuse writing and is expected to distill the main points. You read old cases that take forever to make a fairly straightforward point. Or you read law-review articles that take 50 pages to say what might be said more powerfully in 3. And as you read, your incentive for gleaning their main points is high: your future in law depends on it. In other words, you work as hard as any reader to break through opaque prose. You simply must.

Typical Reading

Consider a California judicial opinion issued just after the turn of the 20th century, a period still heavily represented in casebooks. See if you can follow the point:

> And in the outset we may as well be frank enough to confess, and, indeed, in view of the seriousness of the consequences which upon fuller reflection we find would inevitably result to municipalities in the matter of street improvements from the conclusion reached and announced in the former opinion, we are pleased to declare that the arguments upon rehearing have convinced us that the decision upon the ultimate question involved here formerly rendered by this court, even if not faulty in its reasoning from the premises announced or wholly erroneous in conclusions as to some of the questions incidentally arising and necessarily legitimate subjects of discussion in the decision of the main proposition, is, at any rate, one which may, under the peculiar circumstances of this case, the more justly and at the same time, upon reasons of equal cogency, be superseded by a conclusion whose effect cannot be to disturb the integrity of the long and well-

---

Adapted from *Student Lawyer* (Dec. 1999).

established system for the improvement of streets in the incorporated cities and towns of California not governed by freeholders' charters.[1]

Translation: "We made a mistake last time."

That one sentence proved daunting enough, but if you add several dozen more in the same vein, you end up with hopelessly impenetrable bafflegab. The only readers who will bother to penetrate it are those who are paid, probably handsomely, to do so.

However needful you as a reader might be to pierce through others' obscurity, you must as a writer insist on never putting your own readers to that trouble. On the one hand, then, you'll need a penetrating mind as a reader: you'll need to be able to cut through overgrown verbal foliage. On the other hand, you'll need a focused mind as a writer: you'll need to leave aside everything that doesn't help you convey your ideas readily.

That's the key to becoming an effective legal writer.

Once you have your points or ideas in mind—even if they're not fully formed—you're ready to begin. And how best to begin? With an outline.

Planning Your Writing Projects

Although writers work differently—and you'll experiment with many methods before you settle into certain habits—one thing you'll need is a way of putting down your yet-unformed ideas in some way other than a top-to-bottom order. It can be stifling to try to order ideas while they're aborning.

It's useful to think of writing as a four-step process. First, you think of things that you want to say—as many as possible as quickly as possible. Second, you figure out a sensible order for those thoughts; that is, you outline. Third, with the outline as your guide, you write out a draft. Fourth, after leaving the draft aside for a matter of minutes or days or months, you come back and edit it.

My LawProse colleague Dr. Betty S. Flowers has named each of these four steps: (1) Madman, (2) Architect, (3) Carpenter, and (4) Judge.[2] Each of those characters inside your brain has a role to play, and to the extent that you slight any of them, your writing will suffer.

If you believe, for example, that you can "rough out" a draft by simply sitting down and writing it out, you're starting at the Carpenter phase.

---

[1] *Chase v. Kalber*, 153 P. 397, 398 (Cal. Dist. Ct. App. 1915).

[2] These characters and their roles are fully described in the preceding essay, *Using the Flowers Paradigm to Write More Efficiently*.

You're asking the Carpenter to dream up the ideas, sequence them, and verbalize them simultaneously. That's a tall order. People who write this way tend to procrastinate.

If you believe that you can begin with Roman numeral I in an outline, you're still asking a lot: the Architect will have to dream up the ideas and sequence them simultaneously. And whatever your I–II–III order happens to be will probably become ossified in later drafts. Most writers' minds aren't supple enough to allow IV to become I in a later draft, even if logic dictates that it should come first. It's hard to see this if it's already been tagged "IV."

That's why it's so critical to allow the Madman to spin out ideas in the early phases of planning a piece. In a perfect setting, the ideas will come to you so rapidly that it's hard to get them all down as your mind races.

One way of doing this—and of getting yourself into this anything-goes frame of mind—is to use nonlinear outlining. Among lawyers, the most popular type of nonlinear outline is the whirlybird, or whirligig. It starts out looking like this:

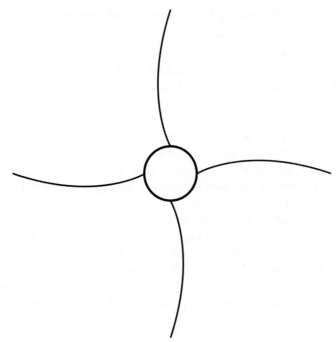

First, you fill in the blank in the center with a shorthand name for your writing project. Then you begin thinking of ideas: the more the better. For every major idea you have, you make a major branch off the center circle. For supporting ideas, try branching off from the main branch.

Everything you might want to mention goes into the whirlybird, which has no top or bottom, and no branch has priority. You're striving for copious thoughts, not ordered ones.

Once you've finished a whirlybird—whether it takes you ten minutes or ten days—you'll probably find it easy to work your ideas into a good linear outline. You'll know all the materials. It will just be a matter of organizing them sensibly.

And once the Architect has finished working, the Carpenter's job—the one that writers most often procrastinate on—becomes relatively easy. It's just a matter of filling in the blanks. Further, the Judge will be able to focus on tiny matters of form, and that's what the character is best suited to. The Judge shouldn't be having to think on several levels simultaneously, as when not only the citation form but also the overall structure is flawed.

If you give me a pile of writing samples, I'll critique them according to this paradigm. A writer who allows typos in the final draft needs to leave more time for the Judge. A writer who uses no headings, and for whom it would be difficult to devise headings once a draft is done, needs to develop the Architect. A writer whose prose is "correct" but pedestrian needs to work on the Madman.

Each character must have its time in the lead. What you don't want is to have one dominate so much that the others get squeezed out. The writing will suffer.

Perhaps the most important phases—because they're the most unpredictable and mysterious—are the first two: Madman and Architect. They will determine how original and insightful the writing is.

So, as you can see, writing well is much more than getting the grammar, spelling, punctuation, and word choice right. Those are matters for the Judge, who, in the end, will tidy things up. But remember that the Judge part of your brain won't contribute many interesting or original thoughts.

Increased Efficiency

Although you might fear that you wouldn't have time to go through all four phases, try it: it's one of the surest ways to good writing. In a one-hour span, you might spend 10 minutes on Madman, 5 minutes on Architect, 25 minutes on Carpenter, and 10 minutes on Judge—with short breaks in between. That's a great way to spend an hour. But it won't simply happen. You have to plan how you're going to transform mushy thoughts into something you can be proud of.

The Stuttering Writer

WHY DO PEOPLE STUTTER? No one knows for sure. Scientists believe that it may in part have a neurological basis. But not surprisingly, there is also evidence that environment plays a role. More about the environmental factors in a moment.

The known facts are that about 90% of stutterers are male, and that about 1 in 30 males is a stutterer. The condition is not at all uncommon. But what causes it?

Well, virtually all children stammer when they're first learning to form sentences. And the one common environmental characteristic of stutterers is a nervous adult, usually a parent, who won't let the stammering child finish a thought without imposing negative emotional pressure: "Out with it, Johnny! Come on!" And poor Johnny can't get it out— sometimes for the rest of his life.

So what does all this have to do with writing?

I suggest that, throughout the United States, we've bred several generations of writing-stutterers. You see, writing instruction has too often been of the don't-do-this-and-don't-do-that school. Too many schoolchildren learn writing in an environment in which they feel as if the teacher is standing over them with a ruler, ready to rap their knuckles. They pick up a pencil and freeze.

Too many of us learned to write at the hands of someone who, essentially, took all the fun out of it. Although many junior-high and high-school teachers in this country do much good, many others do much harm.

There's a balance to be struck. On the one hand, it's important to learn to express yourself freely. That's why many experts in child development recommend not correcting children's language much at all until they're speaking in complete sentences—maybe not even until fourth or fifth grade. On the other hand, we do need to instill a sense of linguistic standards in our children.

Among teachers in the early grades, this balance plays out in the debate between those who support the whole-language approach and those who support phonics. Whole-language adherents have kids write out stories however they like, without correcting much if anything: creative spellings are fine. The idea is to cultivate the students' creativity, not

Adapted from *Student Lawyer* (Feb. 2001).

stifle it with rules. Proponents of phonics have children learn spelling through sounding out syllables: then they can read sentences aloud even if they don't yet understand them. And soon enough they'll be able to write out their own sentences—and spell correctly.

Among college teachers, the balance plays out somewhat differently. We want students to use their creativity and develop imaginative approaches to their subject matter. But we also want them to know and respect idiomatic English—with good punctuation, good grammar, and sound word choices. We want both.

Yet traditional teaching methods have emphasized the latter: correctness over creativity, idiomatic rigor over imagination. And from the teacher's perspective, it's easier to mark papers by focusing exclusively on the small points: misspelled words, misplaced commas, dangling participles, and split infinitives. To mark a paper for these, the teacher needn't think much about the whole. It's easy enough to spill ink on the paper by pouncing on the peccadilloes.

As Sir Walter Scott once put it, "Many a clever boy has been flogged into a dunce, and many an original composition corrected into mediocrity." Even back in his time (the early 1800s), we were creating writing-stutterers.

One of the most interesting points about writing is that those who pounce on "errors," especially in the United States, don't know what they're talking about. Their negativity is misplaced. They never bother to check what the authorities say.

And one of the most common manifestations of this problem is their stricture against beginning sentences with *And* and *But*. (Have you noticed that I've now done it 8 times in this essay? That's 8 out of 43 sentences so far.) Did you know that professional writers do this in about 10% of their sentences? And did you know that grammarians have long said that this is perfectly proper?

Let me cite chapter and verse, with just a few examples through the years:

- **1896:** "Objection is sometimes taken to employment of *but* or *and* at the beginning of a sentence; but for this there is much good usage."[1]

- **1938:** "Next to the groundless notion that it is incorrect to end an English sentence with a preposition, perhaps the most widespread of the many false beliefs about the use of our language is the equally groundless notion that it is incorrect to begin one with

---

[1] Adams Sherman Hill, *The Principles of Rhetoric* 88 (rev. ed. 1896).

'but' or 'and.' As in the case of the superstition about the prepositional ending, no textbook supports it, but apparently about half
of our teachers of English go out of their way to handicap their
pupils by inculcating it. One cannot help wondering whether
those who teach such a monstrous doctrine ever read any English
themselves."[2]

- **1965:** "That it is a solecism [mistake] to begin a sentence with
  and is a faintly lingering superstition. The *OED* [*Oxford English
  Dictionary*] gives examples ranging from the 10th to the 19th century; the Bible is full of them."[3]

- **2000:** "*But* and *And* are absolutely valid ways to begin a sentence.
  Not only valid ways, but *excellent* ways. And all seasoned writers
  know it."[4]

I could multiply examples. If anybody ever told you that it's a mistake to
begin a sentence with *And* or *But*, that person was wrong when making
the statement. It's not that grammatical standards have changed on this
point. The standards have stayed constant: it's just that too many "correc-
tors" have believed a myth—no, a superstition.

If you think I've slanted the authorities, please look up the point in
any text you like.

And then think of the times you've been "corrected" on this point. If
you've been unfortunate enough to experience this, you may be among
the writing-stutterers. You're among the unfortunate many who have
learned writing at the hands of a martinet.

If you want true proficiency in writing, you'll need to unlearn many
such dogmas. Get a good book on writing and relish it. A great place to
start, for any writing-stutterer, is John Trimble's *Writing with Style* (2d ed.
2000). If you want to know what it's like to learn at the hands of an
unintimidating master—an encouraging mentor—try Trimble.

And if you want an enlightened guide to grammar, a slender and
entertaining handbook by a legal editor, try *The Miss Grammar Guidebook*,
by Karen Larsen.[5] She's full of reliable information.

Meanwhile, work on your expressiveness. Learn to polish your writing at the end, but first try to relax and convey your thoughts forcefully.
Avoid starting a writing project with dos and don'ts. Carried to an
extreme, those things would make writing-stutterers of us all.

---

[2] Charles Allen Lloyd, *We Who Speak English: And Our Ignorance of Our Mother Tongue* 19
(1938).

[3] Ernest Gowers, ed., *A Dictionary of Modern English Usage* 29 (2d ed. 1965).

[4] John R. Trimble, *Writing with Style* 85 (2d ed. 2000).

[5] Oregon State Bar, 1994.

❧ ❧ ❧

The Importance of Attentive Reading

THE COMPANY WE KEEP is crucial to who we are—in all sorts of ways. For example, imagine that you aspire to be a first-class figure skater, but you don't ever see one perform, much less skate with one. If you aspire to master any challenging skill at all, your progress will suffer if you don't learn from others who've already become proficient. Left to your own devices, you could stay mired in mediocrity.

When it comes to writing, there's a community of writers that you needn't know personally. You must simply observe what they do to make their writing so readable and effective. Some people actually teach themselves by resorting to good models. For example, when Robert Louis Stevenson decided that he wanted to learn to write—really write—he invented an exercise. He'd take a passage from a writer of acknowledged standing, he'd read it twice, and then he'd turn it over and try to replicate what he'd just seen—word for word, punctuation mark for punctuation mark. He'd fail to come very close at first, and so he'd repeat the exercise. Over time, he got better and better. And he seems to have been motivated enough to have continued that exercise for many years.

So what would that exercise have taught him? Undoubtedly he (1) cultivated a keen ability to remember and imitate, (2) found that he often fell short by using more words than necessary, (3) learned a good deal about word choice, (4) developed a pleasing variability in syntax, (5) acquired a better understanding of building paragraphs, and (6) internalized the tools that writers use to link their paragraphs for better flow. With time, he must have found more and more instances in which his own work outshone the passage that he was trying to replicate. That is, there were times when his rewritten passage was shorter, bolder, more striking, and altogether more pleasing.

Part of what Stevenson can teach us—and most people have already figured this out—is that learning a skill begins by imitation. Hand a young girl some golf clubs, let her watch good golfers on a practice range, and soon she'll be making a pretty good swing. Do it again and again, day after day, and people will marvel at the move she makes when striking the ball. Much learning occurs by osmosis.

And although you begin by imitating, by the time you master a skill you develop your own distinctive technique—based in part on what

Adapted from *Student Lawyer* (Sept. 2007).

you've admired in your predecessors. That's true of writing, painting, playing a musical instrument, or whatever the endeavor might be.

I was reminded of this truth recently while interviewing three federal judges at each level of our judicial system—Chief Justice John G. Roberts of the U.S. Supreme Court, Chief Judge Frank H. Easterbrook of the Seventh Circuit Court of Appeals in Chicago, and Chief Judge James M. Rosenbaum of the District of Minnesota. I asked, as I usually do in my judicial interviews, "How does a law student or lawyer who wants to improve actually do it?" In their separate interviews, all three emphasized the importance of reading more attentively.

Chief Justice Roberts responded: "You develop a lot as a writer the more you read . . . . People lose a lot of writing ability when they get to law school because they tend to read a lot of stuff that isn't well written, and they tend to stop reading other stuff that is well written because they don't have the time. They're focused on some badly written cases, from whenever, or some badly written statute. And they're not reading anything good."

The phrase "badly written cases, from whenever" stuck with me. Even today, the most heavily represented period in our casebooks is 1880 to 1920, which was the nadir of judicial writing in this country. That was the period in which opinions were most abstruse, diffuse, and verbose. The students forced to read those cases have their style polluted.

Chief Judge Easterbrook suggested remedies. He was discussing what second-year lawyers, as opposed to law students, could do to improve. His diagnosis was similar to the Chief Justice's, and he followed it with a prescription: "Spend more time reading. And stop reading what lawyers are writing, because mostly lawyers read what other lawyers are writing . . . and that's mostly bad. Start reading Hemingway and Faulkner. Their styles are different, but they're both wonderful writers. Read the Saul Bellows of the world. There's a lot of good and interesting writing out there."

But Judge Easterbrook went further, perhaps for those who don't have a literary bent and would prefer not to make the leap of adapting a novelist's style to what legal writers do. He touted good modern journalism: "Start reading good magazines. Pick up a copy of *The Atlantic* or *Commentary*, where people write intelligently about important issues in short compass, using real English sentences. The magazines have good editors who edit down the pieces, but generally they choose good writing."

Then came his most pointed observation: "The best way to become a good legal writer is to spend more time reading good prose. And legal prose ain't that! So read *good* prose. And then when you come back and start writing legal documents, see if you can write your document like a good article in *The Atlantic*, addressing a generalist audience. That's how you do it: get your nose out of the lawbooks and go read some more."

And what does an eminent trial judge say? In his off-the-cuff response, Chief Judge Rosenbaum evoked shades of Robert Louis Stevenson: "One of the ways you learn to be a painter is to study paintings. It's not for nothing that when you go to the Louvre or the Metropolitan Museum of Art there will be art students sitting there copying. Nobody is going to mistake what they're doing for Matisse or Picasso or Delacroix. What they're doing is learning the techniques that the artists used."

How does that relate to legal writers? "Language," he said, "is the tool that we use. And learning to write takes work. When you read really well-written, beautiful prose, it leaves an impression. And that impression can matter."

A good writing style is rewarded so automatically that you hardly notice what's going on. You think that it's the merits of the case or the soundness of the thought that matters, and that's true as far as it goes. But it's the style, the technique, that makes the thought so transparently powerful. The same thought, in shabby dress, appears much less compelling.

So read widely and attentively. My own highest recommendations for newsweeklies go to *The New Yorker* and *The Economist*. Reading through them will be a tonic for your style. And if you've been researching legal points and you're preparing to write something, take a few minutes first to read a short piece in one of those magazines. Over time, your writing will benefit enormously.

2a 2a 2a

Telling the Good from the Bad

SOME WRITING IS GOOD; some is bad. It's pretty easy to evaluate. Below
are eight passages. Four are good, and four are bad. You'll probably readily see which ones fall into each category. In some the meaning will be
immediately clear to you; others will baffle you with their obscurity. Some
will appeal to your ear; others you'll find repugnant. You be the judge. In
the margin, mark the good ones with a G, the bad ones with a B:

1. A signature on a pleading constitutes a certificate by the signator
   that the instrument is not groundless or brought in bad faith or
   for the purpose of harassment, except that a signature on a general
   denial will not provide a basis for a violation on these grounds.

2. This case squarely presents questions of exceptional importance.
   The Eighth Circuit's opinion retroactively imposes an unconstitutional punishment without the kind of fair notice mandated
   by the Due Process Clause. While purporting to uphold an arbi-
   tration agreement that expressly precluded punitive damages, the
   Eighth Circuit reinstated an award of punitive damages 3000
   times greater than Stark's actual damages. This holding contra-
   venes three important federal policies, each of which would
   independently warrant this Court's protection. First, ...

3. In the case of a consignment that is not a security interest when
   the filing and notification requirements have not been met, the
   interests of a person delivering goods to another is subordinate
   to a person who would have a perfected security interest in the
   goods if they were the property of the debtor.

4. Nevertheless, the fact that the Named Plaintiffs likely cannot
   also be members of the Repair Fee Subclass or the Recent Purchaser Subclass does not mean that their claims are not typical
   of the claims of the members of these proposed subclasses.

5. Constitutional guarantees have real meaning to those accused of
   crime: the shields raised by the Constitution do not dissolve
   upon the utterance of ritualistic words, and its promises mean
   what their plain language conveys.

Adapted from *Student Lawyer* (Nov. 2005).

6. Here we have more than the inconceivably slow unfolding of a "conspiracy." These two years saw a continuing struggle for customers between Interborough and the 13 new wholesalers. At times Interborough gained; at others it lost. During the last year, the struggle was intensive enough for Meyer to characterize it as a "dogfight." That someone may lose this sort of struggle is perhaps a regrettable feature of the free-enterprise economy. But the word for what happened is not "conspiracy." It is "competition."

7. The question whether a product accused of infringement is an "equivalent" of the claimed invention is an issue of fact, and this Court gave specific guidance to the Federal Circuit on how to review such a factual determination. But the Federal Circuit balked, threw up its hands, and instead, in Judge Michel's words, "by-passed the all-elements rule altogether." This is profoundly wrong in law, in logic, and in policy.

8. Of even greater significance, would be the plaintiff who claims he has lung cancer and is a member of a trial group that is comprised of himself and four other plaintiffs complaining of pleural plaques compared to another plaintiff who also complains of lung cancer but is joined in a trial group of himself and four other plaintiffs complaining of mesothelioma.

In my experience, most law students and lawyers have little trouble distinguishing the good prose from the bad. But they have a hard time providing concrete reasons for their preferences—apart from using adjectives such as *unclear, confusing,* and *incoherent,* or *clear, straightforward,* and *interesting.* One major purpose of writing instruction is to enhance your ability to analyze the stylistic qualities that make some writing good and other writing bad.

Of course, no writer produces bad work on purpose. The writer just doesn't know how to do better. Offering advice and suggestions—such as eliminating redundancy, replacing fancy expressions with simple ones, and introducing signposts—makes little if any impression if the writer can't recognize redundancy, see opportunities to simplify, or see the need for signposts. All these things require judgment.

And while rules can be taught, judgment is a trickier matter: judgment is a matter of *when* to apply the rules. That's not something that you can memorize. Judgment isn't so much something that you can be taught as it is something that you can develop, perhaps by yourself and perhaps with the help of training.

If you want to improve your style, you must develop stylistic judgment. You must learn to distinguish good writing from bad. (Accept that in law, you'll see much more bad writing than good.) You must become sensitized to bad writing. And you must keep this critical sense active in all your reading, whether it's a newspaper, a law journal, a biography, a novel, or a treatise on eminent domain.

Again and again, whatever the genre, you'll see that good writing is easy to read, while bad writing is hard to read. If you can't understand something you're reading, you shouldn't assume that you're dull-witted or that the subject is simply over your head. Instead, you can safely assume that the writer isn't or wasn't much of a writer. A good writer who knows a subject well can make almost any point seem readily intelligible, even with an arcane topic.

There are only two things lawyers get paid for: writing persuasively and speaking persuasively. It's not as if those are two important things among many. They are the *only* two things. That's it. And your writing comes first. When you improve your writing, your speaking will automatically become better. The contrary isn't necessarily true at all.

Now let's return briefly to those eight passages. Of the four good passages, one was written by Theodore B. Olson of Washington, D.C. (#2); two by Jay Topkis of New York City (#5, #6); and one by Robert H. Bork, of Washington, D.C. (#7). What these writers have in common is a knack for clear, bright exposition and argument. In that, of course, they stand well above the crowd.

And what exactly is the crowd like? Having spent over two decades closely studying legal writing, particularly that of practicing lawyers, I'd say that 80% of lawyers have a style akin to that of the four bad passages. (Most in that number actually believe that they're good writers.) Perhaps only 2% can produce prose similar to that of the four good passages. And perhaps 18% are somewhere in between.

The habit of writing clearly and persuasively isn't one you're born with. Almost anyone can cultivate it to a significant degree. It's true that not everyone can become a masterly stylist. Not everyone has the patience and fortitude to develop the necessary knowledge and skill. But almost everyone can become competent, most can become better than competent, and a few will become true experts.

A big part of competence is attitude. To do a job well, you must take pride in what you're doing. If you believe that, then you'll probably come to believe in the importance of doing things better than they've customarily been done.

ঌ ঌ ঌ

Finding Good Models of Writing

To LEARN ANY SKILL, you need good models. For example, you can't learn to paint well without studying the work of good painters. You can't learn to play the piano well without watching and listening to good pianists. You can't learn to hit a golf ball well without seeing good golfers. And you can't learn to write well without closely observing the work of good writers. Mere observation isn't enough, of course—copious practice is also necessary—but it's surely a prerequisite.

In legal writing, there are special hurdles not faced by artisans in other endeavors. It's no trouble to find out where to find good paintings, good pianists, and good golfers. No one is likely to be misled. And it's not hard to find good writers. But in *legal* writing, things get tricky. If you're looking for a model research memo, motion, brief, or contract, where do you go? If you go to just any senior lawyer, even in a major firm, and ask for an example of the last such document the lawyer prepared, odds are slim that you'd get a model worth following. More likely, you'd see a document with many blunders that expert legal writers would disapprove.

Why? Because we've had bad models for a long time, and in our precedent-bound field they tend to be perpetuated. Even our very method of legal education—using the casebook method of teaching mostly from old, badly written judicial opinions—tends to send lots of bad signals to each new generation of law students about what a legal document should look like. That's a pervasive problem.

And then finding particular models of excellence can also be a problem. Some years ago, one of my professorial colleagues at a law school where I was teaching audited my upper-division course and saw that I showed my students examples of first-rate research memos. He also noted that I was critical of the sample memos in most first-year legal-writing texts. He took me aside and said that in the first-year program at that particular law school, the legal-writing professors were carefully avoiding showing the students examples of good memos for fear that they'd slavish copy the format. The advice to first years was: research well, think clearly, and write it up clearly. Now go do a research memo!

Adapted from *Student Lawyer* (March 2008).

That's hardly useful advice. Law students need models. They need to
see what a good executive summary looks like, with a question presented and a brief answer—not the typical question presented but one
that can actually be read and understood by any intelligent reader in one
reading. They need to see a statement of facts that is neither too sparse
nor too detailed. They need to see how the body of the memo states the
law, develops the analysis, and applies the law to the facts at hand to
prove the conclusion that was stated clearly on page one. And they need
to see several strategies for closing well. Summer associates need the
same thing.

And newly minted lawyers need to see samples of good motions and
briefs. But as I say, looking in files in a law office is likely to turn up
nothing but mediocrities—documents with a fair amount of credibility-
destroying legalese, slow windups, slow deliveries, confusing factual statements, weak analyses, and rote conclusions. I know this because I see these
documents week in and week out in law firms and legal departments all
across the nation.

On the transactional side, the problem is even worse. Most forms are
riddled with elementary mistakes that can have serious consequences down
the line: poor organization, inconsistently stated duties, insufficient headings, prodigious amounts of vague and ambiguous legalese, improper
punctuation, confusing design, and so on. All these things detract from
the substance of contracts and other types of legal instruments.

The problem, then, is finding good models. I've been aware of the
problem for a long time, and I've tried to remedy it in my own books,
especially in *Legal Writing in Plain English* and in *The Redbook: A Manual
on Legal Style*, both of which contain plentiful examples that it has taken
a career to collect from some of the best legal writers around the country. But let's assume you want more examples than can be found in those
two books. Where should you look? Here are my recommendations.

Let's begin with legal scholarship. The answer here is pretty easy: get
a subscription to the *Green Bag* (www.greenbag.org). Here you'll find
some of the best, most interesting legal scholarship to be found anywhere. It's a law review that defies most law-review conventions. Your
subscription will get you not just a quarterly journal at a reasonable cost,
but also a yearly almanac of good writing.

For several other types of legal writing, the *Green Bag Almanac* is
your best choice. Published since 2006, it gives awards for excellent legal
writing of various kinds, including short pieces in law reviews, long
pieces in law reviews, op-ed pieces, judicial opinions, briefs, motions, and
books. Most of the award-winners are reproduced in full. It's an extraor-

dinarily useful compendium of good legal writing—and it comes free with your subscription to the *Green Bag*.

For briefs, there are outlets many legal writers hardly ever think of, such as the Solicitor General's website (www.usdoj.gov/osg/briefs/search.html), which contains every brief that the SG has filed in the federal appellate courts since July 1998 and selected briefs going back to 1982. Mostly, the briefs are astoundingly good—on the whole, markedly superior to what other lawyers are filing in those courts. Also worth reading are any Supreme Court briefs you can find by Walter Dellinger, Clifton Elgarten, Miguel Estrada, Theodore B. Olson, Evan M. Tager, or Charles Alan Wright.

The documents for which finding standout exemplars is especially difficult are research memos, motions, and contracts—and I mean actual examples prepared by practicing lawyers, as opposed to law-school exercises. And remember that these are the types of documents that new lawyers are most likely to need to prepare.

For these types of documents, books are the best resources.

Oh, and law students will need some good models of exam answers for law-school courses. The best resource I know is Charles R. Calleros's *Law School Exams: Preparing and Writing to Win* (2007). Get it and study it.

꙾ ꙾ ꙾

_____

The Third and Fourth Levels
of Competence

THERE ARE TWO—and only two—major skills that you need as a lawyer: people skills and writing skills. If you have them, you're pretty well assured of success in the legal profession. Although some people who excel in people skills don't write well, it's all but impossible to write well if you don't understand people. They're your readers, after all, and you must think about them constantly when you write. Understanding readers is, in legal terms, a condition precedent to good writing.

If you doubt that, consider for a moment the two or three most irritating e-mail messages (apart from spam) that you've received lately. Now think about the writers of those messages. They have irritating personalities, don't they? Irksome people write irksome e-mail messages and letters. They probably don't understand themselves very well—much less their readers.

No one wants to be that type of person or that type of writer. But that's how anyone who doesn't toil at honing these all-important skills might end up. Let's focus on how you can sharpen them.

In the mid-20th century, the American psychologist Abraham Maslow (1908–1970) developed a four-stage analysis of how people master a skill. First comes unconscious incompetence: you have no idea how little you know, and what you don't know doesn't faze you. Second comes conscious incompetence: you've learned enough to sense how little you really know, and this incompetence has begun to bother you. Third comes conscious competence: you've learned a good deal and you're getting the hang of it, but you have to concentrate to get it right. Then, finally, comes unconscious competence: your skill has become a matter of habit, and you write well without thinking about technique.

Maslow's categories apply quite well to legal writers. Consider what each type is like.

Unconsciously incompetent (UI) writers: These are the people who think they know the rules but never bother checking up on their "knowledge." They're fond of saying things like this: "You shouldn't split a verb phrase with an adverb." "You can't have a one-sentence paragraph." "It's bad grammar to begin a sentence with _but_." And worst of all: "I'm concerned with substance, not with style." They like phrases such as _above-_

_____

Adapted from _Student Lawyer_ (Sept. 2004).

referenced cause, *as per*, *enclosed please find*, and *pursuant to*. They think they learned how to write well in high school, and many of them have grown fond of legalese. These writers are clueless about their own cluelessness. They're not stupid—they're just deluded.

Consciously incompetent (CI) writers: As you might suspect, relatively few legal writers are in this category because they either repress their awareness (reverting to unconscious incompetence) or work to remedy their deficiencies (progressing to conscious competence). Writers in this category may say things like this: "I don't know grammar very well." "I'm not nearly as good a writer as my colleagues." But not many lawyers own up to the need to improve. Also, this is a maddening phase because you feel uncertain about how to improve.

Consciously competent (CC) writers: These are the ones who trouble themselves to find out what respected authorities say about writing. They don't leave readily answerable questions unanswered. They'll be heard saying things like this: "Although the *AP Stylebook* rejects the consistent use of the serial comma, I looked and found that all the other punctuation authorities, including *The Chicago Manual of Style*, favor its uniform use." "According to Bernstein, careful writers don't use *fortuitous* as a synonym for *fortunate*." "What's your authority for stigmatizing split infinitives?" These writers have intellectual curiosity, and they know where to find reliable answers. (*The Chicago Manual of Style* is always at their desk, and Theodore Bernstein is a household name.)

Unconsciously competent (UC) writers: These writers have passed through the stage of conscious competence. They have integrated their years of learning so thoroughly into their writing that their accumulated knowledge is like muscle memory. They would never think of writing *Enclosed please find*. In fact, they'd be embarrassed if someone suggested it. If they're litigators, they've learned to torpedo obvious counterarguments *before* their adversaries have a chance to write about them. If they're transactional lawyers, they've long since learned to avoid the phrase *provided that* because it typifies poor drafting and causes needless ambiguities (and therefore needless litigation).

While thinking through this column, I found myself on an airplane next to Evan M. Tager, an appellate lawyer who's a partner at Mayer, Brown & Platt in Washington, D.C. By any measure, he's a successful legal writer. After telling him about Maslow's categories, I asked him how he'd assess the bar as a whole. His answers:

UI: 65%
CI: 20%
CC: 14.8%
UC: .2%

The next day, I taught a seminar in Washington at Swidler & Berlin. I asked the lawyers—a mix of partners and associates—how they'd assess the bar as a whole. Their answers:

UI: 56%
CI: 22%
CC: 15%
UC: 7%

The day after that, in a Boston seminar, the lawyers at Ropes & Gray—again partners and associates—gave virtually identical answers.

That's enough surveying to satisfy me (as if I weren't already convinced) that something is seriously amiss in our *literary* profession. Remedying the problem will require monumental efforts by thousands of people. Then again, maybe half of us would be happier simply to repress the thought.

The five keys to moving toward competence are these: (1) do lots of writing regularly over many, many years; (2) teach yourself everything you can by closely analyzing how good writers do what they do; (3) monitor your reactions to whatever you read, and analyze exactly what irritates or delights you; (4) learn as much as you can by reading good books about writing techniques; and (5) be as self-critical as you can stand being (but no more).

❧ ❧ ❧

The Benefits of Keeping a Daily Journal

Sir David Williams, an eminent British law professor who rose to become the chief executive officer of Cambridge University, recently told me he keeps a daily journal. It's nothing pretentious—just a record of the notable events that occur each day. He's been keeping it pretty steadily since the 1940s. Imagine the record of facts, anecdotes, and thoughts he has compiled.

You can, and should, do the same. Take just ten minutes a day to jot down what happened. You'll benefit in four salient ways:

- First, you're going through an important phase in your life, and it'll all be a blur to you later if you haven't kept a running account.

- Second, every day you're learning things about people, about books, about methods of thinking, about all sorts of things. Recording your perceptions will help them take hold in your brain. It'll even improve your perceptions.

- Third, keeping a daily journal is a great exercise in concrete thinking. Many immature writers sit down and immediately try to think big thoughts—and they get stuck. Mature writers habitually move from concrete bits of experience to larger, more abstract implications; a journal will help you develop this skill.

- Fourth, your fluency will improve tremendously if writing is an everyday activity for you.

Essentially, what you're doing with a journal is "freewriting," also known as "automatic writing" or "babbling." Don't allow yourself to edit for punctuation, grammatical errors, and the like. The goal is to write down your thoughts as they come to you. Get down as much as you can in ten minutes. Occasionally, if you need to, you can expand this to 15 or 20 minutes—but remember, this should not become a burden to you. It should be a cathartic habit.

Imagine how a law student's entry might look:

September 25

This morning, in Contracts, Professor Fussell asked Jill Rotsky (he called her "Miss Rotsky" even though she's married) to recite the facts of

---

Adapted from *Student Lawyer* (Sept. 2004).

Hadley v. Baxendale. *She looked down and didn't respond. After about 45 seconds of embarrassing silence, he asked Robert Stinson, who responded that a doctor had promised to graft skin from the plaintiff's chest onto the palm of the plaintiff's hand. Stinson had confused* Hadley *with the "hairy hand" case* (Hawkins v. McGee).

At that point, Professor Fussell asked for anyone in the class to recite the facts of Hadley. *I could have done it, but I remained silent. I've been terrified of Professor Fussell since I first arrived on campus. He's legendary for his monumental four-volume treatise on contracts, and I find him more intimidating than anyone else I've seen. Many of my classmates feel the same way. We've talked about this from the very first day of class.*

Anyway, no one made a sound. Professor Fussell waited in silence about 30 seconds, looked at his watch, and calmly said: "So no one is prepared to recite the facts of Hadley v. Baxendale. *You can expect to see a question about it on the final, but you've now wasted a class period. On Wednesday, please be prepared—all of you—to explain the facts of* Balfour v. Balfour. Hadley *is not to be mentioned in this class for the rest of the semester." He then strode out of class, only five minutes after the period had begun.*

There wasn't a stir in the room until well after he'd left. Bill Jenkens, sitting beside me, was the first to react, exclaiming, "This sucks!" I heard someone call Professor Fussell a "pompous ass," but I don't think that's the prevailing opinion. Several of us went across the street to Harold's for coffee and talked about what had happened. Three of us thought that this had been a learning experience (vowing that we'd never fail to speak up again in such a situation), and two said essentially that it was all an ego trip for Fussell. Maybe time will tell.

Notice that it's pretty dispassionately descriptive. This is the kind of law-school experience that ends up being exaggerated in the retelling. By the third year, eyewitnesses will be quoting Professor Fussell as berating the students and saying that none of them would ever pass the bar. When you look back at your journal, you may recognize some valuable lessons about witnesses, memories, and perceptions.

From time to time, you may end up recording impressions more than particular events:

I'm finding that the judges who hear criminal cases are markedly different in their courtroom styles.

Judge Hinojosa, who presides over Criminal Court 1, expects everyone to dress conservatively and behave professionally. He once ordered a female attorney wearing a mini-skirt to go home and change. And he repeatedly warned a male attorney to stop belittling a hostile witness before holding the attorney in contempt. Hinojosa won't allow what he calls "courtroom histrionics," which includes gestures, raised voices, and sarcasm. He doesn't tolerate bad behavior by witnesses either. Once when a witness got angry and started shouting and waving his fist, the judge ordered him to calm down or the bailiffs would take him into custody. He often asks advocates to explain their objections, but when he overrules them, he usually says why he's doing so, which certainly must make appeals easier. Hinojosa constantly takes notes during the trial and only occasionally asks questions.

Then there's Judge Muies, the youngest criminal-court judge in the county. He was a criminal practitioner for only six years, but the governor appointed him to the bench when Judge Vanden retired. He usually wears flamboyant ties and always seems relaxed, even laid back. He often doesn't seem to be paying a lot of attention to the arguments, and when someone objects, it can take several seconds for him to respond. Clerks often slip into the court and deliver stacks of papers. When that happens, his pen gets busy, signing things perhaps. I saw it happen during a bench trial; I can't help wondering whether he heard all the evidence, although I agreed with his decision. Several cases tried in his court have been appealed, but since he hasn't been a judge for very long, the Court of Appeals hasn't released any opinions yet.

I hope I don't have to argue anytime soon before Judge Hernshorn of the Court of Appeals. He always seems to be impatient. He limits how much time each side has to make an opening and closing statement and uses a timer to enforce it. He interrupts speakers frequently with questions, almost always pointed ones, usually about things the attorneys don't seem to want to talk about because it won't help their clients. He reminds me of Professor Kaga in law school; you always had to be thoroughly prepared for anything he might ask. Hernshorn really dislikes attorneys who simply recite what they wrote in the brief; he berates them for wasting the court's time (I suppose he's right about that). He also takes notes; I've watched his pencil and it moves furiously fast, so he might be using shorthand.

Judge Milroy of the Court of Appeals is very different. She radiates patience and encourages speakers to make their case as well as possible. She agrees with Hernshorn that wooden recitation is a waste of time, but says that sometimes a good oral delivery can convey something that didn't come across in writing, so she wants to hear it. She must be very well-read, because she's always coming up with apt quotations from literature and great speeches and the like. She's a gifted speaker, too, so when she explains to an attorney why an argument in the brief needs clarification, the reason is always clear.

In your journal, you should be honest and candid. It's a safe place for you to chronicle your thoughts. After all, unless you decide otherwise, it's for your eyes only.

You may think that a journal like this is simply too far removed from "legal" writing to do you much good. Don't make this mistake. In chronicling your daily routine, you'll be drawing on your powers of description and analysis. The better you become at it, the better you'll become at writing legal memos, client letters, briefs, and even contracts. You'll be developing deftness with the written word.

Your journal will also become an odyssey of discovery and self-discovery. As Joyce Carol Oates, the noted writer of both fiction and nonfiction, has said: "All of us who keep journals do so for different reasons, I suppose, but we must have in common a fascination with the surprising patterns that emerge over the years—a sort of arabesque in which certain elements appear and reappear, like the designs in a well-wrought novel."

The biggest challenge you face is simply to decide to begin writing, and then do it. A life of writing is a life of action. The best way to learn to write well—really well—is to write regularly. For an investment of ten minutes a day, you'll reap profits for the rest of your life.

ॐ ॐ ॐ

Why You Should Start a Writing Group

FEEDBACK. You can never get enough of it on your writing. It's essential to your growth as a lawyer. But associates and summer associates rarely get much from senior lawyers. That's why you should make your own feedback by forming a writing group while in law school, or soon after you graduate. I wish I'd done it when I was starting out.

Here's how a writing group should work.

Organize a group of four to five who'll agree to meet periodically, maybe once a month for an extended working lunch of 90 minutes or so. Four seems to be the minimum number, and five seems optimal.

Everyone should bring a brown-bag lunch and—more important— five copies of a polished draft of a memo, letter, motion, brief, or other project that involves original research and writing. (Form interrogatories or some other stock document won't do.) It can be anything from a 2-page letter to a 50-page brief.

Begin by setting out some ground rules. First, stress the importance of tact. There are many ways to give critical feedback. Choose one that's honest but not spiteful. Second, give good comments with the bad. An editor who's unduly harsh—or entirely uncritical—helps no one. Sometimes what writers need most is a little encouragement. Third, devote the time you have together to each other. Turn off your cell phones and other gadgets.

We'll say that you form a group with Bill, Frances, Gary, and Stephanie. Bill goes first, and Frances is assigned to take the lead in discussing Bill's writing. Bill doesn't say anything about the project. He simply passes out a copy and watches the time as the others silently read and edit for five minutes. At the five-minute mark, Bill calls time, and anyone can ask for an additional 90 seconds. Then Bill calls time again, and Frances begins the discussion with general comments about the piece, noting what she likes and dislikes. Gary, Stephanie, and you then contribute your thoughts. All must contribute to the discussion. At the end of that discussion, everyone hands Bill the marked version of his paper. He can do with these copies what he will. One hopes that he'll use them in preparing a final draft. All told, the discussion of Bill's paper lasts about ten minutes.

Adapted from *Student Lawyer* (Jan. 2006).

Next, Frances becomes the timekeeper as we repeat the exercise. Gary takes the lead in discussing this second piece, and the same ground rules apply.

A good sample discussion might go like this, after the group has had five minutes of editing Gary's research memo.

Stephanie: I like your instincts of beginning with an issue and answer, but I can't understand the issue you posed. I've read it over and over, yet your answer doesn't seem to address that question squarely. You seem to be answering a different question.

You: I spent too much time puzzling over those first two paragraphs, and in six minutes got only as far as the second line of page two. The framing of the issue may reflect your assignment, but you've written an insider memo that only a few people have a chance of understanding. And as time passes nobody will understand much of it. Your research and analysis won't be useful anymore.

Bill: I skipped ahead to page five, where I think you've reframed the question more understandably. Look at the second paragraph on that page. That's the first time you've crystallized the client's problem, but then you don't answer the question until page eight. I'd take the second paragraph on page five and the fourth paragraph on page eight and make that your issue and answer.

Frances: I noticed that you use apostrophes inconsistently. On page one, the first time you use *attorneys' fees*, it's a plural possessive, but then in the next sentence you made it singular, and then the third time you lost the apostrophe altogether. I line-edited the first page and a half to clean up several little inconsistencies like that and remove some of the verbose phrasing. For example, you wrote *prior to the time when* where you could have simply written *before*. And because you're in federal court, you shouldn't use *cause of action*; the correct word is *claim*.

If Gary receives this critique with the proper degree of humility and openness—in other words, with an unneurotic attitude—he will benefit tremendously from these comments.

Let's say that, after the group has been going for a while, Stephanie brings a draft brief that shows real virtuosity. The comments might go like this:

Frances: You've succinctly summarized a complex problem on page one, and your opener is a real grabber.

You: I felt pretty much persuaded by the time I'd finished the second paragraph. It's really clean, and I thought it was a pleasure to read.

Gary: When I read the first page, I felt skeptical about your probable-cause argument. So I skipped to the part where you addressed that point, and you pretty well dispelled my skepticism. If I were the judge, I'd be curious how the other side is going to respond because your points seem difficult to refute.

Bill: Yes, the logic is plainly laid out for the judge. What I liked was your relaxed, confident, natural tone. This is the best writing sample you've ever brought us.

Imagine what a boost these comments would be to Stephanie's confidence, especially if she's already gone through some difficult sessions in which her writing didn't draw such praise.

One great by-product of being part of a writing group is that you'll become a better editor. And you'll develop a more finely tuned sensibility as a reader, both by learning to react frankly and helpfully to others' writing and by watching your colleagues' reactions. You'll be amazed how one of your colleagues will catch things that you missed—a misplaced apostrophe, a misspelled word, or a subtle grammatical problem. Meanwhile, another colleague will point out a structural flaw that everyone else missed, by showing, for example, that the first paragraph should be omitted and the second and third paragraphs transposed. You'll see in almost every session how a piece of writing can be analyzed on many levels. And you'll begin to analyze on those levels yourself.

Another great by-product is the friendships that you'll develop and strengthen. You'll be working collaboratively with people who might not otherwise have the opportunity to work with you. Over time, you'll develop a certain level of reciprocal trust.

Unfortunately, you'll always have a thousand excuses *not* to form a writing group. Many people would no sooner join such a group than they'd join a breath-testing group (with sessions first thing each morning). The whole purpose of a writing group is to solicit criticism, and many people can't bear being criticized.

Ultimately, though, receiving and accepting criticism is the only way to grow and flourish as a writer. And a writing group helps ensure high-quality, trustworthy criticism.

LORD DENNING • CLARENCE DARROW • LEARNED HAND

Style

The Letters of the Law

WHY SHOULD WE TALK OF *legal* style? After all—above all—good legal
style is good English style, isn't it? Take the opinions of Justice Oliver
Wendell Holmes, Justice Robert H. Jackson, or Judge Learned Hand; the
commentary of William Prosser or Fred Rodell; or the advocacy of
Clarence Darrow. These lawyers wrote superb prose. If that's your aim as
well, then a thorough understanding of Strunk and White's *The Elements
of Style* might arguably be all you need.

Since law is a literary profession, lawyers and judges have much to
learn from that book, but we also sense that something is lacking. When
we come upon rules such as "Do not use dialect unless your ear is good,"
and "Make sure the reader knows who is speaking," we conclude that the
authors of *The Elements of Style* address primarily novelists, not us. We feel
uneasy about their warning, "Do not explain too much"; for the legal
writer, explaining too little all but ensures failure. However much we
might like to "Avoid foreign languages," we cannot do without *voir dire,
res ipsa loquitur, de minimis,* and dozens of other Latin and French phrases.

Like authors of other general style manuals, Strunk and White really
don't address the specialized world of legal writers. True, our goals are
often similar to those of other writers, but we face special problems. For
example, we constantly struggle to distinguish terms of art from highfalutin jargon, and that from useful professional shorthand. (Avoid foreign
languages, yes—but when and how?) We use ordinary English words in

---

From *The Elements of Legal Style* (2d ed. 2001).

extraordinary senses, and extraordinary English words in senses ordinary only to us. We use and cite authorities in peculiar ways.

But the most bedeviling problem we face is of a different order: we have a history of wretched writing, a history that reinforces itself every time we open the lawbooks. It would take hundreds of prolific Holmeses and Prossers and Darrows to counterbalance all the poor models that continually reinforce the lawyer's bad habits.

Daily encountering these models, many of us set legal writing apart from other literary endeavors, just as we delude ourselves into believing that good legal reasoning differs from good reasoning in general. We persist in making our profession exclusive, all the while rationalizing our inability to write well by invoking the age-old legal standards. If Strunk and White did not address us directly—to the exclusion of the rest of humanity ("nonlawyers," as we say)—then of what use is their book? Not being lawyers, they did not understand our special circumstances.

In truth, though, our circumstances aren't so very special. Legal writers must recognize what the rest of the literary world already knows: a good style powerfully improves substance. Indeed, it largely *is* substance. Good legal style consists mostly in figuring out the substance precisely and accurately, and then stating it clearly and forcefully.

Too many of us equate artful writing, or "style," with the warrior's cumbersome headdress, pleasing to the eye but irrelevant (perhaps even a hindrance) to the conquest. Music provides the better analogy. Does anyone fail to recognize that a Beethoven symphony becomes a different piece when played by an ensemble of kazoos instead of a major symphony orchestra? The medium is the music. Why should we find it difficult to accept the parallel truth in writing?

Take two lines from Samuel Taylor Coleridge's "Rime of the Ancient Mariner":

> Alone, alone, all, all alone
> Alone on a wide, wide sea![1]

We can capture the information contained in these lines by saying, "Alone on the ocean." But we have lost much of the meaning and impact—the desolate voice and tone and mood. We have obliterated the special way in which the poet expressed himself.

Writers meet constantly with choices in expression. Word choice, sentence structure, sequences of thought—these may all vary while the message remains the same. But each variation gives the reader a different impression. A sure sense of style guides you to the better, more effective choices, which evoke from readers precisely the desired impressions.

---

[1] Part 4, stanza 1 (1798).

What Is Style?

We can hardly improve on Jonathan Swift's formulation of style: "proper words in proper places." That focuses on the right level of detail, but it begs questions of propriety. What are proper words? And how do you know where their proper places are?

In judging words and their placement, remember that the character of the writer determines the character of the prose. Even when the subject is as alien from everyday life as the Rule in Shelley's Case, style reveals self as surely as anything else. What you say and how you say it reflects your mental habits and your personality. In trying to write your best, you may strive to proportion one part to another and to the whole, to accent what matters most, to cut out what is useless, and to keep an appropriate tone throughout. But even with these goals in mind, different writers—however skilled—will approach a topic differently, often quite differently.

Style embodies the message, delivers it for circulation. When style suffers—because of poor organization, sloppy paragraphing, clumsy rhythms, thoughtless jangles, or other befogging lapses—the content also suffers. When the style is good, the content benefits.

Though all lawyers pay lip service to the importance of good legal writing, few seem to appreciate the capacity of style to influence results. Listen to Lord Denning, probably the greatest of Britain's judicial stylists:

> [Y]ou must cultivate a style [that] commands attention. No matter how sound your reasoning, if it is presented in a dull and turgid setting, your hearers—or your readers—will turn aside. They will not stop to listen. They will flick over the pages. But if it is presented in a lively and attractive setting, they will sit up and take notice. They will listen as if spellbound. They will read you with engrossment.[2]

So convinced was Lord Denning of the importance of style that he attributed the British role in winning World War II as much to Winston Churchill's manner of speaking and writing as to Churchill's strategy or intelligence.[3]

For the sake of lesser battles, you need guidance to develop an effective legal style. As used here, the phrase *legal style* refers generally to expository prose about legal subjects, whether in the form of persuasion, narration, description, or analysis. Most forms of legal writing fall within those realms: judicial opinions, advocacy, scholarly commentary, opinion letters, and other writing in and about law. Legal drafting—for instance,

---

[2] Lord Denning, *The Family Story* 216 (1981; repr. 1982).
[3] *Id.*

of legislation, rules, and contracts—requires separate treatment and has received it in some excellent works.[4]

The chief aim of style is clarity. But achieving clarity is only the first step; much remains—brevity, for example, and accuracy. Variety, elegance, imagination, force, and wit can make your prose interesting as well as clear. Often you must do more than simply communicate; you must persuade or even delight.

Don't confuse the negative with the positive virtues of writing: avoiding grammatical and rhetorical gaffes won't make you an exemplary stylist. Despite what some writing texts might have you believe, there are no real formulas for a good prose style. Removing needless passive-voice verbs, keeping sentences short, and using "action" verbs usually improve a piece of writing, but they still may not result in a good style.

Everything hangs on context and purpose. We value simplicity, but writing as simply as possible does not always mean writing simply. Complicated language occasionally proves unavoidable. Take the legislative jungle that is the tax code: "It can never be made simple, but we can try to avoid making it needlessly complex."[5] We can try to say it in plain language.

But what is "plain language"? I define it as the idiomatic and grammatical use of language that most effectively presents ideas to the reader. By that definition, plain language may be, in some sense, unplain. Who would call Immanuel Kant's categorical imperative plain, despite the seeming simplicity of the words? "Act as if the maxim on which you act were to become, through your will, a universal law." On the other hand, who would volunteer to simplify it?

Still, most of us aren't framing Kantian thoughts. We should stick to a plain approach. Our age prefers it.

Two Rhetorical Traditions

If we look to the history of rhetoric, we find that our Western legacy contains more than plain bequests. From classical Greek and Roman times, two literary traditions have grown alongside each other. One, a

---

[4] *See, e.g.*, Reed Dickerson, *The Fundamentals of Legal Drafting* (2d ed. 1986); Janice C. Redish, *How to Write Regulations and Other Legal Documents in Clear English* (1991); Barbara Child, *Drafting Legal Documents* (2d ed. 1992); Scott J. Burnham, *The Contract Drafting Guidebook* (1992); Garner, *Guidelines for Drafting and Editing Court Rules* (1996); *see also* Garner, *Legal Writing in Plain English* 119 (2001).

[5] *Dobson v. C.I.R.*, 320 U.S. 489, 495 (1943) (per Jackson, J.).

florid oratorical style called Asiatic prose, sports elaborate antitheses, complicated syntax, and correspondences in sense and sound. The other, Attic prose, is refined conversation: concise, restrained, shorn of intricacy.

Both styles came naturally to Cicero, one of the great lawyers of antiquity. Immensely articulate, he began his career with a strong Asiatic bent, which he relaxed as he matured. Fortunately, he left a record of his thoughts about forensic style. An eloquent lawyer, wrote Cicero, must prove, must please, and must sway or persuade:

> For these three functions of the orator there are three styles, the plain [Attic] style for proof, the middle style for pleasure, the vigorous [Asiatic] style for persuasion . . . . Now the man who controls and combines these three varied styles needs rare judgment and great endowment; for he will decide what is needed at any point, and will be able to speak in any way which the case requires.[6]

Cicero concluded that an eloquent speaker "can discuss trivial matters in a plain style, matters of moderate significance in the tempered style, and weighty affairs in the grand manner."[7]

English-speaking lawyers reach too often for weighty grandeur. We find oratory and brief-writing about slip-and-fall cases that, by implication, would put them on a par with the most important constitutional issues. The style, we might say, inflates the subject matter. Or, as Swift might have put it, improper words have been put in improper places, or improper words in proper places, or proper words in improper places. In that confusion lies the rhetorical origin of legalese, a bastardized Asiatic style.

Whatever claims legalese may have to legal tradition, modern readers—even of lawbooks—prefer the Attic style. We like what is plain; we grow impatient with what is fancy. Legal readers tend to admire directness and scorn baroque curlicues.

In other periods, Asiatic writers have reached great heights. The Asiatic style may not be to your taste or mine, but it has produced some great literature. One thinks of the prose of John Milton, Samuel Johnson, Edmund Burke, or Thomas De Quincey. A one-sentence extract from *The Rambler* illustrates Johnson's style:

> Among other opposite qualities of the mind which may become dangerous, though in different degrees, I have often had occasion to consider the contrary effects of presumption and despondency; of heady

---

[6] Cicero, "Orator" §§ 69–70, at 357, in *Brutus, Orator* (H.M. Hubbell trans., 1939; rev. & repr. 1962).

[7] *Id.* § 101, at 379.

confidence, which promises victory without contest, and heartless pusillanimity, which shrinks back from the thought of great undertakings, confounds difficulty with impossibility, and considers all advancement towards any new attainment as irreversibly prohibited.[8]

Few 20th-century writers—not even Benjamin Cardozo—would choose Johnson's high-flown words. True, Cardozo went as far as to write, "The decree under review protects the petitioner with sedulous forethought against an oppressive inquisition";[9] but Johnson might well have gone further, as by substituting *prepense* for *forethought.*

Cardozo best exemplifies the refined Asiatic style in modern legal writing, as when he described this very style in judicial opinions. He called this style

> the refined or artificial, smelling a little of the lamp. With its merits it has its dangers, for unless well kept in hand, it verges at times upon preciosity and euphuism. Held in due restraint, it lends itself admirably to cases where there is need of delicate precision. I find no better organon where the subject matter of discussion is the construction of a will with all the filigree of tentacles, the shades and nuances of differences, the slender and fragile tracery that must be preserved unmutilated and distinct.[10]

More than anything else, Cardozo's Asiatic indulgences differentiate his style from that of Holmes. When commentators contrast Holmes's style with Cardozo's—usually extolling the one and inveighing against the other—what they unwittingly observe is that Holmes inclined toward the Attic, Cardozo toward the Asiatic style.

Conversation vs. Contrivance

Holmes's Attic style moves more swiftly than Cardozo's Asiatic style. Even the long sentence in the following extract reads like recorded conversation:

> Persecution for the expression of opinions seems to me perfectly logical. If you have no doubt of your premises or your power and want a certain result with all your heart you naturally express your wishes in law and sweep away all opposition. To allow opposition by speech seems to indicate that you think the speech impotent, as when a man says that he has squared the circle, or that you do not care wholeheartedly for the result, or that you doubt either your power or your premises.

[8] Samuel Johnson, *The Rambler,* No. 25, 12 June 1750, in *Samuel Johnson & Periodical Literature: The Rambler* vol. 1, 145, 147 (1978).

[9] *Sinclair Refining Co. v. Jenkins Petroleum Process Co.,* 289 U.S. 689, 697 (1933).

[10] Benjamin N. Cardozo, *Law and Literature,* 52 Harv. L. Rev. 472, 481 (1939).

But when men have realized that time has upset many fighting faiths, they may come to believe even more than they believe the very foundations of their own conduct that the ultimate good desired is better reached by free trade in ideas—that the best test of truth is the power of the thought to get itself accepted in the competition of the market, and that truth is the only ground upon which their wishes safely can be carried out. That, at any rate, is the theory of our Constitution. It is an experiment, as all life is an experiment. Every year, if not every day, we have to wager our salvation upon some prophecy based upon imperfect knowledge.[11]

Even without knowing the Attic and Asiatic styles, jurists have recognized the differences between Holmes's style and Cardozo's. Take three typical statements from legal literature. First: "Holmes could put in a sentence a thought that would take Cardozo a page, and yet Cardozo's graceful, old-fashioned English is a delight to read, and in its own gentle way, it is as unique as Holmes's."[12] Conceding that "Cardozo's style had certain charms," another commentator remarks: "His style, cold and smooth and at times irritatingly precious, was a mere adornment for fairly conventional ideas. In contrast to the spontaneity and fire of Holmes's best pages, those of Cardozo are artificial and lifeless."[13] And this, from one recalling his legal schooling: "[A]nother professor [at Harvard], whom we called 'Bull' Warren . . . , would get absolutely apoplectic in discussing the opinions of Justice Cardozo, whom we students most admired for his lucidity and flowing style. His objections were centered mainly, as we gathered, on Cardozo's style of putting the subject last."[14]

So offensive was Cardozo's Asiatic style to Jerome Frank that he accused Cardozo of retreating from the 20th century and reemerging "disguised as an 18th-century scholar and gentleman."[15] Frank said that

---

[11] *Abrams v. United States*, 250 U.S. 616, 630 (1919) (Holmes, J., dissenting).

[12] Ray Henson, *A Study in Style: Mr. Justice Frankfurter*, 6 Vill. L. Rev. 377, 378 (1961).

[13] David Weissman, *"Supremecourtese": A Note on Legal Style*, 14 Law. Guild Rev. 138, 139 (1954).

[14] Philip Goodheim, *Literary Style and Legal Writing, or, Why Not Throw Some Literary Effort into Preparing Mr. Blackstone's Chowder?* 37 N.Y. St. B.J. 529, 529–30 (1965). Note that Cardozo has also been much praised, as by Judge Charles E. Clark, who said that Cardozo's "own standard of literary effort was so high as to make our lesser attempts seem feeble indeed." *State Law in the Federal Courts*, 55 Yale L.J. 267, 268 (1946). And by Justice Frankfurter: "The bar reads [Cardozo's] opinions for pleasure, and even a disappointed litigant must feel, when Judge Cardozo writes, that a cause greater than his private interest prevailed." Felix Frankfurter, *Law and Politics* 103, 106 (1939).

[15] Jerome Frank, *The Speech of Judges: A Dissenting Opinion*, 29 Va. L. Rev. 625, 630 (1943) (published anonymously). For Frank's acknowledgment of authorship of that essay, see Frank, *Some Reflections on Judge Learned Hand*, 24 U. Chi. L. Rev. 666, 672 n.18 (1957).

Cardozo wrote "of 20th-century America not in the idiom of today but in a style that employed the obsolescent 'King's English' of two hundred years ago." Thus Cardozo's Asiatic habits: "inverted expressions [what Professor Warren detested], negative constructions, sinuous turns of phrase, elaborate metaphors." Frank, a confirmed Atticist (without so phrasing it), preferred the writings of Thoreau and Justice Holmes, which he said "are full of native idioms; are made of the American speech of their day, heightened and polished."[16]

Deciding What's Good

Frank's statements lead us to important questions. What is it that makes us say, "This is good legal writing"? Why do we decide that a brief or judicial opinion is well written? What do we value in writing? When we habitually ask these questions, we awaken the critical faculty. We come to recognize that style often differentiates the workaday from the great judge. To contemplate a contradiction, imagine if Holmes had been just as brilliant a jurist but devoid of stylistic genius: would American law have taken quite the same course?

We remember and reread great opinions largely because they are well written. Leading cases have likely become so by virtue of memorable opinions. We may be less interested in the subject matter than in how the judge has dealt with it. By contrast, even the best material can be spoiled by an inept hand.

"Fine," you may say, "but what do masters like Holmes and Cardozo have to do with me, an average writer without literary aspirations?" Analyzing their prose may be no more helpful to you than showing films of Ben Hogan or Babe Zaharias to a novice golfer. Perhaps you cannot learn to write greatly—only to avoid writing poorly.[17] But whatever your individual abilities, the masters provide the best models.

More particularly, the *Attic* masters provide good models. They suit our time. We can admire an Asiatic writer like Cardozo from afar, appreciating his style without trying to imitate it. But those of us less talented than Cardozo will stumble—or plunge—when we try it. (Even he did not always succeed.) Before experimenting with the showier qualities in writing, let's master the art that conceals art: let's try to be direct, simple, lucid, and brief.

---

[16] 29 Va. L. Rev. at 629.

[17] *See* Richard A. Posner, *Law and Literature: A Misunderstood Relation* 297 (1988).

To be sure, Cardozo's style was sometimes all of those things, especially in factual narrative. Indeed, his statement of the facts in *Palsgraf v. Long Island Railroad*[18] has been hailed as a model of plain language.[19] But his literary flair was not plain, and it sometimes betrayed him when he attempted to elevate the mundane. He once wrote, for example, in an opinion addressing whether a man who paid his employer's debts could take a tax deduction: "Life in all its fullness must supply the answer to the riddle."[20] Did anyone ever write an emptier sentence?[21]

In the judgment of Karl Llewellyn, that great analyst of judicial opinions, it is where Cardozo "is off-base that the creaking ornament and oversubtle phrasing chiefly flourish."[22] How, then, do we find ornaments that don't creak and phrases that have just the right degree of subtlety? For most of us, it's best to be wary of ornament and subtlety. Still, we need not forswear them altogether. How much less engaging, for example, Llewellyn's own writing would have been without them!

In every context, we must weigh what is appropriate. We need not—should not—suppress all the literary devices at hand. Even the Attic style uses them. Nor should we seek one style as the ideal for all legal writing, any more than we should force on society an absolute dress code. A formal dinner may require evening clothes, but they would look absurd on the beach. The law has its beaches as well as its stately ceremonies, and much in between. We should not try to make it always solemn.

Fluffy Speech Not Required

Holmes once found himself the object of censure by Chief Justice William Howard Taft for writing that amplifications in a statute would "stop rat holes" in it. Hughes thought the phrase too racy. Holmes recalled his answer to that charge: "I said our reports were dull because we had the notion that judicial dignity required solemn fluffy speech, as, when I grew up, everybody wore black frock coats and black cravats."[23] That "fluffy speech" is the source to this day of the monotone we hear upon opening virtually any volume of American judicial opinions.

---

[18] 162 N.E. 99, 99 (N.Y. 1928).

[19] *See* Richard C. Wydick, *Plain English for Lawyers* 5–6 (4th ed. 1998).

[20] *Welch v. Helvering*, 290 U.S. 111, 115 (1933).

[21] *See* Erwin N. Griswold, *Foreword: The Supreme Court 1959 Term*, 74 Harv. L. Rev. 81, 90 (1960).

[22] Karl Llewellyn, *The Common Law Tradition: Deciding Appeals* 37 n.29 (1960).

[23] *Holmes–Pollock Letters* vol. 2, 132 (Mark D. Howe ed., 1941) (adding, in reference to the latter phrase, "I didn't say that to them.").

We are right to judge what is good and bad in writing, what is effective and ineffective. Ultimately, everything is good that is "conceived with honesty and executed with communicative ardor."[24] Or, as Voltaire said, "Every style is good save that which bores."[25]

So never bore your readers. Legal writing shouldn't be lethal reading. Your readers are the ones, finally, who matter: you have invited them to attend to your words, you seek their precious time, and you may even expect to be paid for your efforts. Courtesy requires that you show your readers some grace and consideration.

Don't just expect their interest. Arouse it. That dictum (if only we could make it a mandate!) runs counter to everything that legal writing is about. Judges are paid to evaluate lawyers' writing, whether in a brief or in a simple court paper. To thwart their opponents' work, lawyers must read and understand it, and (of course) must analyze judicial opinions. There can be no doubt: we're not in the business of pleasure reading.

Then why make someone else's task more enjoyable by increasing your own effort? The answer lies in success, in results: Holmes did it; Cardozo did it; Jackson and Hand did it; so did Prosser and Rodell and Darrow. If, as an advocate, you do it, you may make your opponent's reading easier; but you also upset your opponent because you reduce the judge's work and increase your likelihood of winning. If you do it as a judge, you add distinction to the judiciary as well as to your opinions, which will fare better in the esteem of your fellow lawyers; you're stating the law better for the present and the future.

Whenever you do it, in whatever capacity, you add luster to the letters of the law.

---

[24] Robert Louis Stevenson, *Learning to Write* 30 (1888; repr. 1920).

[25] "[T]outs les genres sont bons, hors le genre ennuyeux." Voltaire, Preface to *L'Enfant Prodigue*, in *Oeuvres Complètes de Voltaire* vol. 3, 442, 445 (1877) (*genre* meaning "le style de l'auteur" [Littré]).

ɞ ɞ ɞ

On Legal Style

"TAKE CARE OF THE PENNIES," says the thrifty old proverb, "and the pounds will take care of themselves." In like manner we might say, "Take care of the individual words and sentences, and the paragraphs will take care of themselves."

At the sentence level, the oversimplification is but a slight one. What most legal writing today lacks is a fastidious attention to words, the very tools of our trade. By handling words and phrases carefully, you'll sharpen your tools, for the sake not just of making yourself understood, but of winning allies.

Though legal writing for centuries has been largely unreadable, nothing in the nature of writing about law requires that it be murky or obscure. Holmes, Cardozo, and Hand give proof enough to that proposition.

A great part of the problem in the battle to improve legal style is to convince legal writers that style is more than the glossy varnish on a piece of writing, an optional coating that one may as well do without. The fallacy that style is merely a patina on prose has done much harm. Literary critics have long known that style and content, form and substance, are inseparable. Until legal writers recognize this fundamental truth, we will have to wade through a great deal more legal pishposh.

The fallacy of "style-less" legal writing most commonly takes the form of judges' and lawyers' believing they need not strive for style in their prose, since the facts and the law are all that matter. In truth, however, one cannot escape having a style.

To paraphrase Susan Sontag, the antipathy to "style" is always an antipathy to a given style; there is no style-less legal writing, only writing of more or less grace and adeptness, and belonging to different stylistic traditions and conventions.

The polestar of style has long been agreed on: clarity. Beyond that, much else is possible: simplicity, allusiveness, directness, forcefulness, irony, wit, and so forth. The particular makeup of a piece of writing depends on the writer's own makeup, as well as the writer's purpose. One's style reveals oneself as surely as any other index.

An essay on style might appropriately set out to be a homily, if we believed, as Norman Mailer does, that style is character, and that "a good

---

Adapted from *ABA Journal* (1 Oct. 1988).

style cannot come from a bad, undisciplined mind." Ah, you might fallaciously say, thinking of all those proverbs about lawyers: So that is why legal writing has historically been so bad! Well, seriously, who among us would argue that legalese—the scourge of our profession—is the product of a good, disciplined mind?

Despite the individuality of any given style and its dependence on the personality of the writer, there are certain requisites to the attainment of a good writing style. Clarity is chief among these, as writers since the time of Aristotle have recognized: "Style to be good must be clear, as is proved by the fact that speech that fails to convey a plain meaning will fail to do just what speech has to do."

Context and Purpose

Despite the myth to the contrary, no one formula unfailingly produces a good prose style. Much hangs on the context and the purpose. So the "plain English" movement in the law—a salutary force in almost every respect—would be misguided to the extent that some of its advocates might believe that every notion can be simply expressed. Though it is true that lawyers have often obscured simple thoughts by using murky language, it is also true that complex expressions are sometimes unavoidable.

In all writing, the ideas are paramount. The careful writer structures ideas for logical presentation. Beyond that abstract principle, however, are the individual words by which we convey ideas. It's not enough to structure ideas. We must develop a keen sensitivity to the nuances of individual words, and then to the juxtaposition of words into sentences.

Developing that sensitivity calls for curiosity and meticulousness. To give a rather elementary example, if we never check the difference between "continual" and "continuous," we might one day lose a claim of adverse possession.

Or say you're alleging "contribution and indemnity." Do you know the difference between the two words, and do they both fit your context? Why, in a brief addressing an admiralty question, have you used "collision" in one paragraph and "allision" in the next? Is there a distinction? (Of course there is.)

Smart lawyers wrestle daily with questions of this kind—I almost wrote "niggling questions of this kind," but they are anything but niggling.

"Exactness in the use of words," wrote Felix Frankfurter, "is the basis of all serious thinking. You will get nowhere without it. Words are clumsy tools, and it is very easy to cut one's fingers on them, and they need the closest attention in handling. But they are the only tools we have, and imagination itself cannot work without them."

◖ ◖ ◖

In Praise of Simplicity

ONE QUALITY THAT great legal writers share is the ability to express difficult legal ideas as simply and directly as possible. That's what Max
Radin did in the early 20th century, what Grant Gilmore did in mid-
century, and what Charles Alan Wright did in the latter part of the century. Simplicity, as Irving Younger once observed, is a great virtue.

But there have always been writers who oversimplify, and their writings are worrisome. For example, I have a book by one of Max Radin's
contemporaries, an author named Ira H. Ruben. The title of this 72-page
treatise is *Law Guide for All*.

Though the book was first published in 1938, my copy is from the
ninth printing of 1959. The introduction explains its ambitious approach:
"In [the book's] brevity and simplicity, . . . authoritative exactness has
not been sacrificed. *Correct* legal principles have been rigidly adhered to
in a way that permits their *complete* understanding by the average person
of average intelligence."[1]

I wonder just how complete the average person's understanding
would have been after reading the following explanation of curtesy:

> Conversely, the husband has a right of "curtesy" in his wife's real estate
> of which she may be possessed *at the time of her death*. There is no incho-
> ate right of curtesy and therefore, it only attaches to such real property
> which she owns at the time of her death. Curtesy is a full right for life
> in all the income from such property but not in the property itself.[2]

With that paragraph, curtesy is dispatched and we're off to the next topic—
with "complete understanding," as Ruben would have it.

So what distinguishes a Ruben from a Radin? Both were popularizers, for Radin wrote an excellent little book entitled *The Law and You*—
190 pages long—published in 1948 (and dedicated to William O. Douglas).
The chief difference is that Radin simplified without oversimplifying; he
acknowledged how complex much of the law is—especially as it inter-
sects with real life. And Radin displayed more than a hint of impatience
that things have become so needlessly complex.

Adapted from *The Scribes Journal of Legal Writing* (1993).
[1] Ira H. Ruben, *Law Guide for All* iii (1938; repr. 1959).
[2] *Id.* at 15.

So in Radin, one reads about what happens to the property of a person who hasn't made a will: "The rules for this distribution are quite complicated. In what order the relatives take if there are no children or grandchildren, and who excludes whom, are matters which give rise to a great many questions and perplexities."[3] In many passages, one hears the call for law reform:

> One of the difficulties of the inheritance tax system is its complexity, especially in the United States, where there is a federal tax, and in many states, a state tax as well. This requires a great deal of computation which can scarcely be done by such untrained and inexperienced persons as most heirs. Expert guidance is needed and adds to the annoyances and anxieties of people . . . at a time when they are least capable of bearing them.[4]

Radin's voice is that sensible throughout, especially in the preface, which reads rather differently from Ruben's:

> All that the book hopes to do is to rid anyone of the notion that law is something with which he has no relation except when he gets into what is called "trouble." If, incidentally, he gets a slight acquaintance with legal terms and concepts, with how the law operates and why it takes the form with which it confronts him, it is hard to suppose that this knowledge will do the ordinary ingenuous and peaceful citizen any harm.[5]

No harm? Radin's phrasing is unduly modest: the book still pays dividends to those who trouble to read it. What an admirable thing Radin did, making law more accessible to nonlawyers without oversimplifying.

Many more scholars ought to consider this type of effort worthwhile. But few seem to write such books. Among the few others who come to mind is Lon Fuller, whose *Anatomy of the Law* (1968) is an undervalued classic.

If the Radins and the Fullers of the legal world don't step forward to do this important work, there are always plenty of Rubens who would be happy to try their inept hands at stating "correct" legal principles that any person on the street can "completely understand."

---

[3] Max Radin, *The Law and You* 72 (1948).

[4] *Id.* at 73.

[5] *Id.* at 9.

&❧ &❧ &❧

Putting the Action in Your Verbs,
and Your Verbs in Active Voice

ONE THING YOU'RE CERTAIN to be doing in a law-related job is writing.
So take every word you write seriously. You'll be judged by your words.

At the sentence level, two perils can spoil your writing: buried verbs
and passive voice. You need to be thoroughly familiar with them, or else
they're unavoidable.

The first consists of burying the action in abstract nouns. Linguists
call this "nominalization" (itself a long abstract noun) because to nomi-
nalize is to form a noun. I call the result of this process a "buried verb"
because it's a word in which an action verb has been buried. You can
make a contribution (worse) or you can *contribute* (better). You can *have a
discussion about the issues* (worse) or you can *discuss the issues* (better). You
can *make provision for indemnification of someone* (worse) or you can *indemnify someone* (better). Look especially for words ending in *-ion*. Examples
are endless.

Buried verbs are actually more harmful to your style than passive
voice. They mark plodding prose. How? Three ways.

First, they're longer than the verbs they displace—by at least one syllable (e.g., *know* becomes *knowledge*), and often by two (e.g., *interpret*
becomes *interpretation*). Longer words weigh down prose. Instead of tight-
ening sentences, you are padding them. Plus, when you change the long
noun back into a shorter verb, you often eliminate a prepositional phrase:
authorization by the board may become *the board authorized*. Uncover those
buried verbs and your writing will be snappier.

Second, they reflect muddy thinking. Writers hide behind buried
verbs because the long nouns seem more technical and less subjective. To
charge a party with being *in violation of* an agreement seems less personal
than saying the party *violated* the agreement. The wordier form is less
concrete, less focused on the issue at hand. Uncover those buried verbs
and your writing will be clearer.

Third, buried verbs are stagnant and dull. They don't *do* anything. To
liven up the sentence, give it more action. Just liberate the inner verb in
one that's been buried. When you read that police are *conducting an examination of* physical evidence, you don't visualize what's going on—it sounds

Adapted from *Student Lawyer* (May 2003).

like something that goes on behind closed doors. But when you read that the police are *examining* that evidence, you get a mental picture of the action itself. Uncover those buried verbs and your writing will have more impact.

Consider a sentence from a brief: "There was a disagreement between the parties about whether there had been a final resolution by Judge Bertelsman of Fannin Corporation's request." Cut that 22-word sentence down to 13 words—and make it sharper, clearer, and stronger—just by uncovering the buried verbs: "The parties disagreed about whether Judge Bertelsman had finally resolved Fannin Corporation's request." Some people would erroneously diagnose the problem with the original as being passive voice.

That's the other major peril: regularly putting your verbs in the passive voice. You've heard this one before, of course. *Don't use passive voice.* That advice may resonate in your mind. But how well can you identify passive voice? Count the examples in the following passage:

> In *Reich v. Chez Robert, Inc.,* the court found that § 203(m) required three conditions to be met before an employer can lawfully reduce the amount paid to an employee by a tip credit: (1) the employer must inform each employee that a minimum wage is required by law; (2) the employer must inform each employee of the dollar amount of the minimum wage; and (3) the employee must actually keep the tips received. It is clear under the law that vague assertions of the restaurant's compliance with the notice provision of § 203(m) do not constitute compliance. Instead, testimony regarding specific conversations where the provisions of the Act were explained to an employee must be provided.

Guess what. Few law-review editors could accurately spot every passive-voice construction in that passage. Let's come back to the answer after fixing in our minds exactly what the passive voice is.

It all has to do with the difference between acting and being acted on: in active voice the subject acts, while in passive voice the subject is acted on. From a mechanical point of view, passive voice has two parts: a *be*-verb (e.g., *is, are, was, were*) and a past participle (e.g., *broken, sued, considered, delivered*). Contrary to popular belief, a *be*-verb alone isn't passive voice at all: there must be a past participle as well.

Watch for two things when trying to spot passive voice. First, some constructions that appear passive really just involve a past-participial adjective: *He was embarrassed.* Now, if you make that *He was embarrassed by Jane,* then it is passive (because *embarrassed* then functions as a verb); but with *embarrassed* alone at the end, it's just a participial adjective. That's a subtle point to some, but experts will recognize it. Second, the *be*-verb may not actually appear in the sentence. It may be what grammarians call an "understood" word, as in *the amount charged will vary* (the full sense of the phrase is *that is charged*) or *the fee set by the trustees* (the complete relative clause is *that is set*). These constructions with implied *be*-verbs are indeed passive.

What's wrong with passive voice? Stylists agree that it's generally weaker than active voice. It requires two extra words, and the subject of the sentence isn't performing the action of the verb—you're backing into the sentence with the recipient of the action. And the actor either is identified in a prepositional phrase or is missing altogether.

Politicians are often said to love passive voice because they don't have to fess up to anything: they can just say, "Mistakes were made." Notice that I used it in the preceding sentence (*are said*) so I didn't have to personally smear politicians: *I* didn't say it, but some unspecified accusers have said it.

The usual advice that people remember about passive voice is overdrawn: there's no absolute prohibition, only a strong presumption against it. Passive voice does have its place. The recipient of the action may be more important than the actor (e.g., *the defendant was convicted*) or the actor may be unknown (e.g., *the building was vandalized*). And sometimes passive voice simply sounds better. It may be handy, for example, to move a punch word to the end of a sentence for impact (e.g., *our client's bail has been revoked*).

Now back to that challenge passage. How many passive-voice verbs are in the passage quoted earlier? There are six: (1) *to be met*, (2) *paid*, (3) *is required*, (4) *received*, (5) *were explained*, and (6) *be provided*. If you found four, you know the basics of passive. If you spotted the others (#2 and #4), take some extra credit: they have understood *be*-verbs, *to be paid* and *that are received*.

Now consider the passage revised. I've stripped out the buried verbs, changed passive-voice constructions to active, and slightly reorganized the ideas:

> In *Reich v. Chez Robert, Inc.*, the court found that § 203(m) requires an employer to meet three conditions before reducing the employee's tip credit. First, the employer must inform each employee that the law imposes a minimum wage. Second, the employer must say what that wage is. It isn't enough for the restaurant to assert vaguely that it has complied with either requirement; the court will require clear testimony about specific conversations in which the employer explained the Act. Third, the employee must actually keep the tips.

Once the buried verbs and passive-voice constructions are gone, the reader's job gets easier. Without necessarily knowing why, the reader will have a better impression of the writer.

If you want to be a good writer, you must know how to handle sentence parts. Although you can acquire this knowledge only through hard work and constant vigilance, knowing about the two pitfalls discussed here will take you a long way.

ટેન ટેન ટેન

Colloquiality in Law

WITHIN THE BOUNDS of modesty and naturalness, colloquiality ought to be encouraged—if only as a counterbalance to the frequently rigid and pompous formalities that generally pervade legal writing.

Many people, however, misunderstand the meaning of colloquiality. The term is not a label for substandard usages; rather, it means "a conversational style." The best legal minds, such as Learned Hand, tend to look kindly upon colloquiality: "[A]lthough there are no certain guides [in the interpretation of a statute], the *colloquial* meaning of the words [of the statute] is itself one of the best tests of purpose . . . ."[1] Nearly 30 years earlier in his career, Hand wrote, as a trial judge: "The courts will not be astute to discover fine distinctions in words, nor scholastic differentiations in phrases, so long as they are sufficiently in touch with affairs to understand the meaning which the man on the street attributes to ordinary everyday English."[2]

In formal legal writing, occasional colloquialisms may give the prose variety and texture; in moderation, they are entirely appropriate even in judicial opinions. Still, the colloquial touches should not overshadow the generally serious tone of legal writing, and should never descend into slang.

Good writers do not always agree on where to draw that line. Some judges feel perfectly comfortable using a picturesque verb phrase such as *squirrel away*: "This sufficed, in the absence of any record-backed hint that the prosecution . . . squirrelled the new transcript away . . . ."[3] Others would disapprove. Some, like Justice Douglas, would use *pell-mell*: "The Circuits are in conflict; and the Court goes pell-mell for an escape for this conglomerate from a real test under existing antitrust law."[4] Others would invariably choose a word like *indiscriminately* instead. Some, like Chief Justice Rehnquist, would use the phrase *Monday morning quarterbacking*.[5] And some would use *double-whammy*.[6]

Adapted from *The Scribes Journal of Legal Writing* (1992).

[1] *Brooklyn Natl. Corp. v. C.I.R.*, 157 F.2d 450, 451 (2d Cir. 1946) (Hand, J.) (emphasis added).

[2] *Vitagraph Co. of Am. v. Ford*, 241 F. 681, 686 (S.D.N.Y. 1917).

[3] *United States v. Chaudhry*, 850 F.2d 851, 859 (1st Cir. 1988).

[4] *Missouri Portland Cement Co. v. Cargill, Inc.*, 418 U.S. 919, 923 (1974) (Douglas, J., dissenting).

[5] *See Vermont Yankee Nuclear Power Corp. v. Nat. Resources Defense Council, Inc.*, 435 U.S. 519, 547 (1978).

[6] *See American Bankers Assn. v. S.E.C.*, 804 F.2d 739, 749 (D.C. Cir. 1986).

For my part, I side with the colloquialists. In a profession whose writing suffers from verbal arteriosclerosis, some thinning of the blood is in order.

But progress comes slowly. The battle that Oliver Wendell Holmes fought in 1924 is repeated every day in law offices and judicial chambers throughout this country. Holmes wanted to say, in an opinion, that amplifications in a statute would "stop rat holes" in it. Chief Justice Taft criticized, predictably, and Holmes answered that law reports are dull because we believe "that judicial dignity require[s] solemn fluffy speech, as, when I grew up, everybody wore black frock coats and black cravats . . . ."[7] Too many lawyers still write as if they habitually wore black frock coats and black cravats.

---

[7] *Holmes–Pollock Letters* vol. 2, 132 (Mark D. Howe ed., 1941).

ﻬﻬﻬ

Judges on Effective Writing

LAWYERS ARE NOTORIOUSLY POOR at gauging what judges prefer in legal writing. Too many of us believe, for example, that judges expect us to use legalese. In 1991, when the Texas Plain-Language Committee surveyed all the state district and appellate judges in Texas, we found that more than 80% prefer plain language (*Plaintiff complains of Defendant and says*) over legalese (*Now comes the Plaintiff, by and through his attorneys of record, Darrow and Holmes, and for his Original Petition in this cause would respectfully show unto the Court the following*). Indeed, several judges responded to the survey with a plea that we stamp out legalese once and for all.

The results of that survey surprised many Texas litigators—and many changed the form of their court papers. But many more have persisted in the old, legalistic style—perhaps out of a fondness akin to what some people feel for the language of the King James Version of the Bible. Judge Lynn Hughes of Houston speaks directly to those litigators: "Anyone who thinks *Comes now the Plaintiff* is anything like the King James Version has no sense of poetry."

Literary tastes may differ, of course, but it's worth knowing what judges say—and have been saying for a long time—about the language we lawyers use. Following are some choice quotations I've collected.

Judicial Diagnoses

"Lawyers spend a great deal of their time shoveling smoke."

—Hon. Oliver Wendell Holmes[1]
U.S. Supreme Court

"[Too many lawyers believe that] it is essential to legal English that one write as pompously as possible, using words and phrases that have long since disappeared from normal English discourse."

—Hon. Antonin Scalia[2]
U.S. Supreme Court

Adapted from *Michigan Bar Journal* (Feb. 2005).

[1] Oral remark frequently attributed to Justice Holmes.

[2] Oral remarks delivered to Colorado Bar Association, September 1990 (as quoted in *USA Today*, 17 Sept. 1990).

"The reason legal writing has gotten to such a low point is that we have had very bad teachers—judges who wrote years ago and wrote badly. We learned bad habits from them and their opinions in law school."

—Hon. William Bablitch[3]
Supreme Court of Wisconsin

Stick to the Mother Tongue

"[The advocate] will stock the arsenal of his mind with tested dialectical weapons. He will master the short Saxon word that pierces the mind like a spear and the simple figure that lights the understanding. He will never drive the judge to his dictionary. He will rejoice in the strength of the mother tongue as found in the King James version of the Bible, and in the power of the terse and flashing phrase of a Kipling or a Churchill."

—Hon. Robert H. Jackson[4]
U.S. Supreme Court

"[A]void as much as possible stilted legal language, the thereins, thereofs, whereinbefores, hereinafters, and what-have-yous. Use English wherever you can to express the idea as well and as concisely as in law or Latin. A healthy respect for the robust Anglo-Saxon appeals more than does the Latin, whether or not it is Anglicized. The home-grown product in this case is better than the imported, not to say smuggled, one."

—Hon. Wiley B. Rutledge[5]
U.S. Supreme Court

"Write so that you're understood. English is a hard language to learn, but it's an easy language to communicate in. There's no reason to put Latin in your brief."

—Hon. Craig T. Enoch[6]
Fifth Court of Appeals, Dallas

---

[3] Quoted in Mark Rust, *Mistakes to Avoid on Appeal*, ABA J., 1 Sept. 1988, at 78, 80.

[4] *Advocacy Before the United States Supreme Court*, 37 Cornell L.Q. 1 (1951).

[5] "The Appellate Brief," in *Advocacy and the King's English* 429, 438–39 (George Rossman ed., 1960).

[6] Oral remarks delivered at Appellate Practice Conference, sponsored by the University of Texas, Austin, Texas, 5 June 1992.

"Don't use legalese. It causes you to put your contentions in stale ways."

—Hon. Thomas Gibbs Gee[7]
U.S. Court of Appeals
for the Fifth Circuit, 1974–1991

"Legalese is an impediment to clear, logical thinking."

—Hon. F. Lee Duggan[8]
First Court of Appeals, Houston

"It's easier for a judge when you're using common usage.
Judges are only human, after all."

—Hon. Carolyn Wright[9]
Family District Court, Dallas

Simplify, Simplify!

"For a hundred years, good lawyers have been writing without
all the garbage and in a simple, direct style."

—Hon. Lynn N. Hughes[10]
U.S. District Court, Houston

"A lawyer should write the brief at a level a 12th grader could
understand. That's a good rule of thumb. It also aids the writer.
Working hard to make a brief simple is extremely rewarding because
it helps a lawyer to understand the issue. At the same time, it scores
points with the court."

—Hon. William Bablitch[11]
Supreme Court of Wisconsin

---

[7] Oral remarks delivered at Advanced Litigation Drafting seminar, sponsored by LawProse, Inc., Houston, Texas, 26 Sept. 1991.

[8] Oral remarks delivered at Advanced Litigation Drafting seminar, sponsored by LawProse, Inc., Houston, Texas, 26 Mar. 1992.

[9] Oral remarks delivered at Advanced Litigation Drafting seminar, sponsored by LawProse, Inc., Dallas, Texas, 10 Oct. 1991.

[10] Oral remarks delivered at Advanced Litigation Drafting seminar, sponsored by LawProse, Inc., Houston, Texas, 26 Sept. 1991.

[11] Quoted in Mark Rust, *Mistakes to Avoid on Appeal*, ABA J., 1 Sept. 1988, at 78, 80.

"When a judge finds a brief which sets up from twelve to twenty
or thirty issues or 'points' or 'assignments of error,' he begins to look
for the two or three, perhaps the one, of controlling force. Somebody
has got lost in the underbrush and the judge has to get him—or the
other fellow—out. That kind of brief may be labeled the 'obfuscating'
type. It is distinctly not the kind to use if the attorney wishes calm,
temperate, dispassionate reason to emanate from the cloister. I strongly
advise against use of this type of brief, consciously or unconsciously.
Though this fault has been called overanalysis, it is really a type of
underanalysis."

—Hon. Wiley B. Rutledge[12]
U.S. Supreme Court

"The key is to make the brief easy for the judge to follow."

—Hon. Lloyd Doggett[13]
Supreme Court of Texas

Cut the Verbiage

"You want your brief to be as readable as possible . . . . If I pick up a
brief of 49 and a half pages, it has a little less credibility than one that
succinctly argues its points in 25 pages . . . . There's nothing better to
read than a well-written brief from a really good lawyer."

—Hon. Jerry E. Smith[14]
U.S. Court of Appeals
for the Fifth Circuit

"Eye fatigue and irritability set in well before page 50."

Hon. Patricia M. Wald[15]
U.S. Court of Appeals
for the D.C. Circuit

---

[12] "The Appellate Brief," note 5, at 434.

[13] Oral remarks delivered at Appellate Practice Conference, sponsored by the University of Texas, Austin, Texas, 5 June 1992.

[14] Oral remarks delivered at Appellate Practice Conference, sponsored by the University of Texas, Austin, Texas, 5 June 1992.

[15] Quoted in Mark Rust, *Mistakes to Avoid on Appeal*, ABA J., 1 Sept. 1988, at 78, 78.

"A brief should manifest conviction . . . . [That] is virtually impossible
. . . if it contains an excessive number of quotations or is larded with
numerous citations to the authorities. Short quotations sometimes
clinch a point, but long ones fail in that objective."

—Hon. George Rossman[16]
Supreme Court of Oregon

"Start in the very first sentence with the problem in this case. Put it
right up front. *Start early.* Don't bury it under a lot of verbiage and
preliminaries."

—Hon. Nathan L. Hecht[17]
Supreme Court of Texas

Does Style Matter?

"Style must be regarded as one of the principal tools of the judiciary
and it thus deserves detailed attention and repeated emphasis."

—Hon. Griffin B. Bell[18]
U.S. Court of Appeals
for the Fifth Circuit

"Lawyers are excused from the necessity of interesting their readers,
and all too often—let's face the evidence—they take advantage of this
enviable exemption."

—Hon. Jerome Frank[19]
U.S. Court of Appeals
for the Second Circuit

---

[16] "Appellate Practice and Advocacy," in *Advocacy and the King's English* 241, 246 (George
Rossman ed., 1960).
[17] Oral remarks delivered at Advanced Litigation Drafting seminar, sponsored by
LawProse, Inc., Dallas, Texas, 10 Oct. 1991.
[18] *Style in Judicial Writing*, 15 J. Pub. Law 214, 214 (1966).
[19] Quoting John Mason Brown, a literary critic, in "Some Reflections on Judge Learned
Hand," in *Advocacy and the King's English* 858, 865-66 (George Rossman ed., 1960).

"Is good writing rewarded? I used to think it doesn't matter much,
in comparison with legal authority, justice, and the like. Now I know
better: Good writing is rewarded so automatically that you don't even
think about it."

—Hon. Murry Cohen[20]
Fourteenth Court of Appeals, Houston

---

[20] Oral remarks delivered at Appellate Practice Conference, sponsored by the University of Texas, Austin, Texas, 5 June 1992.

꙳ ꙳ ꙳

On Conjunctions as Sentence-Starters

IT IS WELL KNOWN that Jonathan Swift (1667–1745), the author most famously of *Gulliver's Travels* (1726) and the satirical essay "A Modest Proposal" (1729), was a master stylist.[1] In language circles, it is also well known that Swift wanted to establish an English Academy—comparable to the Académie Française—to regulate the English language.[2] He cared deeply about English grammar and usage.[3] What is not so well known is that he began more than one-fifth of his sentences with conjunctions such as *and*, *but*, and *so*.[4]

At more than 20%, Swift's conjunction-led sentences were much more numerous than those of most modern writers. A study of noted American and British authors of the 1950s found that 7.5% of their sentences began with *and* or *but*.[5] (Adding *so*, *yet*, *or*, and *nor* to the list would undoubtedly boost the figure.) A 1963 study found that 8.75% of the sentences in the work of first-rate 20th-century writers began with conjunctions.[6] My own study suggests that in contemporary journalism, the figure is closer to 15%.

Adapted from *Advanced Legal Writing & Editing* (2008).

[1] *See* Antony Kamm, *Collins Biographical Dictionary of English Literature* 457 (1993) (noting that "Swift's distinction is his prose—simple, controlled, and concrete"); *British Authors Before 1800* 504, 506 (Stanley Kunitz & Howard Haycroft eds., 1952) (calling Swift "the greatest satirist of our tongue" and remarking on his "magnificent talent for clear, strong prose").

[2] Paul Harvey, *The Oxford Companion to English Literature* 755, 757 (2d ed. 1932); *Dictionary of National Biography* vol. 19, 204, 213 (1917); *see* David Crystal, *The Cambridge Encyclopedia of the English Language* 73 (1995) (noting Swift's prediction that "if it [English] were once refined to a certain Standard, perhaps there might be ways found out to fix it forever"); Raymond Chapman, "Swift, Jonathan," in *The Oxford Companion to the English Language* 1011 (Tom McArthur ed., 1992) (noting that "Swift expressed strong opinions in the contemporary debate about good English").

[3] *See, e.g.*, Robert McCrum, William Cran & Robert MacNeil, *The Story of English* 131 (1986) (calling Swift's writings on the condition of the language "the greatest conservative statement for English ever put forward"); Albert C. Baugh & Thomas Cable, *A History of the English Language* 257 (3d ed. 1978) (noting that "[i]n matters of language Swift was a conservative"); *Chambers's Encyclopedia of English Literature* vol. 2, 122, 126 (David Patrick ed., 1903) (noting that "Swift was a great purist, as is shown in his early and excellent rebuke . . . of the slipshod vulgarity [that] threatened English at the close of the seventeenth century").

[4] *See* Louis T. Milic, "Connectives in Swift's Prose Style" (1967), in *Linguistics and Literary Style* 243, 255 n.12 (1970).

[5] William Carl, "Frequencies of Some Sentence Connectors," in *Studies in Honor of Raven I. McDavid Jr.* 251, 255–56 (Lawrence M. Davis ed., 1972).

[6] Francis Christensen, "Notes Toward a New Rhetoric," 25 *College English* 9 (1963).

These figures don't surprise anyone who has really studied English style or the literature on writing well. Harvard writing professor Richard Marius, for example, notes how common *and* and *but* are as sentence-starters:

> Any glance at a newspaper or magazine shows that professional writers frequently begin sentences with conjunctions. John F. Kennedy used conjunctions to begin fifteen sentences in his short inaugural address. E.B. White, one of the finest essayists of our time, uses conjunctions to begin many of his sentences. So does Lewis Thomas, one of our best writers about science. So the false rule would seem to have little validity among those who write English best.[7]

That view reflects what has long been an overwhelming consensus.[8]

But can't you achieve the same effect with *however?* you might wonder. No, unfortunately. That word is relatively infrequent in polished writing: it appears only once every 2,000 words or so[9]—usually not at the beginning of a sentence. (In mediocre student writing, it can occur several times on a single page,[10] frequently as a sentence-starter.) Hence the many well-taken recommendations to avoid beginning a sentence with *however*.[11] It's slow at three syllables; the accent is on the middle syllable, and then the word falls off in the unaccented final syllable; it requires

---

[7] Richard Marius, *A Writer's Companion* 112 (1985).

[8] *See, e.g.,* John R. Trimble, *Writing with Style* 85 (2d ed. 2000) (stating that "*But* and *And* are absolutely valid ways to begin a sentence," adding: "Not only valid ways, but *excellent* ways"); William Zinsser, *On Writing Well* 74 (6th ed. 1998) (calling it impossible to overstate the value of *but* as a sentence-starter, adding that "there's no stronger word at the start"); Kingsley Amis, *The King's English* 14 (1997) (noting that *and* and *but* "can give unimprovably early warning of the sort of thing that is to follow"); R.W. Pence & D.W. Emery, *A Grammar of Present-Day English* 106 n.15 (2d ed. 1963) (noting that the construction is "widely used today and has been widely used for generations"); Adams Sherman Hill, *The Principles of Rhetoric* 88 (rev. ed. 1896) (noting that although "objection is sometimes taken to employment of *but* or *and* at the beginning of a sentence," in fact "there is much good usage" supporting the habit); Alexander Bain, *English Composition and Rhetoric* 110 (4th ed. 1877) (noting the great utility of *but* as a sentence-starter).

[9] William Carl, "Frequencies of Some Sentence Connectors," in *Studies in Honor of Raven I. McDavid Jr.* 251, 256 (Lawrence M. Davis ed., 1972).

[10] *Id.*

[11] *See, e.g.,* Christopher Lasch, *Plain Style* 101 (Stewart Weaver ed., 2002) (stating that "[i]f you want to begin a sentence by contradicting the last, use *but* instead of *however*"); William Zinsser, *On Writing Well* 74 (6th ed. 1998) (warning not to start a sentence with *however* because "it hangs there like a wet dishrag"); William Strunk Jr. & E.B. White, *The Elements of Style* 48–49 (3d ed. 1979); Lucille Vaughan Payne, *The Lively Art of Writing* 85–86 (1965) (calling the awkwardness of the initial *however* "one of those stylistic mysteries that can't really be explained"); Sheridan Baker, *The Practical Stylist* 16–17 (1962) (stating that "*however* is always better buried in the sentence between commas").

a comma (unlike *but*). The word is rhythmically flat-footed at the head of a sentence.

Let's get back, though, to the main point: the legitimacy and importance of beginning with a conjunction. You may well wonder why almost every native speaker of American English (and British English too, for that matter) learns at some point that it's an error to begin a sentence with *and* or *but*. It's a baffling question. Some writers suggest that it's a mystery.[12] Others suggest, probably correctly, that the prohibition begins "in grade school, where the overabundance of initial *and*s is a problem for the teacher."[13] John Trimble, the noted writing guru at the University of Texas, cites three possible reasons why English teachers perpetuate the myth: (1) English teachers themselves learned it at an impressionable age and never questioned its legitimacy; (2) they condemn anything that looks informal; and (3) they're trying to teach compound as opposed to simple sentences.[14]

The idea that an initial conjunction is bad grammar or poor style finds no support in grammar books—even old ones. The playwright Ben Jonson, Shakespeare's contemporary, mentioned the sentence-starting *and* in his 17th-century *English Grammar*.[15] Although many other English grammars over the next few centuries omitted the point, none disapproved. In their 1906 book *The King's English*, the Fowler brothers (H.W. and F.G.) wrote, in passing: "After *for* and *and* beginning a sentence commas are often used that are hardly ever correct."[16] Even so, by 1938, the modern fuss had boiled up to such a point that Charles Allen Lloyd, an American grammarian, felt sufficiently provoked to pen this trenchant rebuke:

> Next to the groundless notion that it is incorrect to end an English sentence with a preposition, perhaps the most widespread of the many false beliefs about the use of our language is the generally groundless notion that it is incorrect to begin one with 'but' or 'and.' As in the case of the superstition about the prepositional ending, no textbook supports it, but apparently about half of our teachers of English go out of their way to handicap their pupils by inculcating it. One cannot

---

[12] *See, e.g.*, Marius, note 7, at 112.

[13] William Carl, "Frequencies of Some Sentence Connectors," in *Studies in Honor of Raven I. McDavid Jr.* 251, 256 (Lawrence M. Davis ed., 1972).

[14] Trimble, note 8, at 85.

[15] Ben Jonson, *The English Grammar* [1640], in *Ben Jonson* vol. 8, 463, 549 (C.H. Herford et al. eds., 1947) (noting that "*and*, in the beginning of a sentence, serveth in stead of an Admiration [i.e., an exclamation mark]").

[16] H.W. Fowler & F.G. Fowler, *The King's English* 242 (3d ed. 1931).

help wondering whether those who teach such a monstrous doctrine
ever read any English themselves.[17]

All the acknowledged authorities agree that the prohibition of initial
*and*s and *but*s is nonsense. It's been called everything from "a faintly lingering superstition"[18] to Lloyd's "monstrous doctrine."[19] One English
teacher who has pondered the problem has aptly asked, "[W]hy should
we . . . teach any grammar at all if what we teach happens to be false?"[20]
Why indeed?

Saying all this in the abstract is one thing. But seeing is believing. So
the following pages will show you what all the fuss is about. It's important
because this principle will affect virtually every paragraph you write—
certainly every page you write. It will give your writing much more
force, verve, smoothness, fluency, simplicity, and pleasing directness. See
for yourself how writers have long been connecting their sentences and
paragraphs to each other. But notice that the writers use other sentence-
starting techniques as well, for they know that initial conjunctions can
certainly be overdone—just as any good thing can be overdone.

But this can't mean that you shouldn't acquire the good habit. It's
fair to say that you'll never progress as far as you should until you get in
the habit.

---

[17] Charles Allen Lloyd, *We Who Speak English: And Our Ignorance of Our Mother Tongue*
19 (1938).

[18] H.W. Fowler, *A Dictionary of Modern English Usage* 29 (Ernest Gowers., ed., 2d ed.
1965).

[19] Lloyd, note 17, at 19.

[20] T.W.H. Holland, *The Nature of English* 135 (1967).

Geoffrey Chaucer, *The Parson's Tale*

(ca. 1393–1400)

258   *The Canterbury Tales* |X (I) 901-923

apayed of roosted flessh and sode flessh, with which the peple feden hem in greet reverence, but they wole have raw flessh of folkes wyves and hir doghtres./ [And] certes, thise wommen that consenten to hire harlotrie doon greet wrong to Crist, and to hooly chirche, and alle halwes, and to alle soules; for they bireven alle thise hym that sholde worshipe Crist and hooly chirche, and preye for Cristene soules./ [And] therfore han swiche preestes, and hire lemmanes eek that consenten to hir leccherie, the malisoun of al the court Cristien, til they come to amendement./ The thridde spece of avowtrie is somtyme bitwixe a man and his wyf, and that is whan they take no reward in hire assemblynge but oonly to hire flesshly delit, as seith Seint Jerome,/ and ne rekken of nothyng but that they been assembled; by cause that they been maried, al is good ynough, as thynketh to hem./ [But] in swich folk 905 hath the devel power, as seyde the aungel Raphael to Thobie, for in hire assemblynge they putten Jhesu Crist out of hire herte, and yeven hemself to alle ordure./ The fourthe spece is the assemblee of hem that been of hire kynrede, or of hem that been of oon affynytee, or elles with hem with whiche hir fadres or hir kynrede han deled in the synne of lecherie. This synne maketh hem lyk to houndes, that taken no kep to kynrede./ [And] certes, parentele is in two maneres, outher goostly or flesshly; goostly, as for to deelen with his godsibbes./ For right so as he that engendreth a child is his flesshly fader, right so is his godfader his fader espiritueel. For which a womman may in no lasse synne assemblen with hire godsib than with hire owene flesshly brother./ The fifthe spece is thilke abhomynable synne, of which that no man unnethe oghte speke ne write; nathelees it is openly reherced in holy writ./ This cur- 910 sednesse doon men and wommen in diverse entente and in diverse manere; but though that hooly writ speke of horrible synne, certes hooly writ may nat been defouled, namoore than the sonne that shyneth on the mixne./ Another synne aperteneth to leccherie, that comth in slepynge, and this synne cometh ofte to hem that been maydenes, and eek to hem that been corrupt; and this synne men clepen polucioun, that comth in foure maneres./ Somtyme of langwissynge of body, for the humours been to ranke and to habundaunt in the body of man; somtyme of infermetee, for the fieblesse of the vertu retentif, as phisik maketh mencion; somtyme for surfeet of mete and drynke;/ and somtyme of vileyns thoghtes that been enclosed in mannes mynde whan he gooth to slepe, which may nat been withoute synne; for which men moste kepen hem wisely, or elles may men synnen ful grevously./

Remedium contra peccatum luxurie.

Now comth the remedie agayns Leccherie, and that is generally chastitee and continence, that restreyneth alle the desordeynee moevynges that comen of flesshly talentes./ [And] evere the gretter merite shal 915 he han, that moost restreyneth the wikkede eschawfynges of the ardour of this synne. [And] this is in two maneres, that is to seyn, chastitee in mariage, and chastitee of widwehod./ Now shaltow understonde that matrimoyne is leefful assemblynge of man and of womman that receyven by vertu of the sacrement the boond thurgh which they may nat be departed in al hir lyf, that is to seyn, whil that they lyven bothe./ This, as seith the book, is a ful greet sacrement. God maked it, as I have seyd, in paradys, and wolde hymself be born in mariage./ [And] for to halwen mariage he was at a weddynge, where as he turned water into wyn; which was the firste miracle that he wroghte in erthe biforn his disciples./ Trewe effect of mariage clenseth fornicacioun and replenysseth hooly chirche of good lynage; for that is the ende of mariage; and it chaungeth deedly synne into venial synne bitwixe hem that been ywedded, and maketh the hertes al oon of hem that been ywedded, as wel as the bodies./ This is verray mariage, that 920 was establissed by God, er that synne bigan, whan natureel lawe was in his right poynt in paradys; and it was ordeyned that o man sholde have but o womman, and o womman but o man, as seith Seint Augustyn, by manye resouns./ First, for mariage is figured bitwixe Crist and holy chirche. [And] that oother is for a man is heved of a womman; algate, by ordinaunce it sholde be so./ [For] if a womman hadde mo men than oon, thanne sholde she have moo hevedes than oon, and that were an horrible thyng biforn God; and eek a womman ne myghte nat plese to many folk at oones. [And] also ther ne sholde nevere be pees ne reste amonges hem; for everich wolde axen his owene thyng./ [And] further over, no man ne

Of the 28 sentences that begin on this page, 11 begin with conjunctions.

39%

William Shakespeare, *Hamlet*
(ca. 1601)

Act 2 Scene 2   HAMLET

460 With blood of fathers, mothers, daughters, sons,
Baked and impasted with the parching streets,
That lend a tyrranous and damnèd light
To their vile murders. Roasted in wrath and fire,
And thus o'er-sizèd with coagulate gore,
465 With eyes like carbuncles the hellish Pyrrhus
Old grandsire Priam seeks.'
So, proceed you.
POLONIUS Fore God, my lord, well spoken, with good
accent and good discretion.
470 FIRST PLAYER   'Anon he finds him,
Striking too short at Greeks. His antique sword,
Rebellious to his arm, lies where it falls,
Repugnant to command. Unequal match,
Pyrrhus at Priam drives, in rage strikes wide;
475 But with the whiff and wind of his fell sword
Th'unnervèd father falls. Then senseless Ilium,
Seeming to feel his blow, with flaming top
Stoops to his base, and with a hideous crash
Takes prisoner Pyrrhus' ear. For lo, his sword,
480 Which was declining on the milky head
Of reverend Priam, seemed i'th' air to stick.
So, as a painted tyrant, Pyrrhus stood,
And, like a neutral to his will and matter,
Did nothing.
485 But as we often see against some storm
A silence in the heavens, the rack stand still,
The bold winds speechless, and the orb below
As hush as death, anon the dreadful thunder
Doth rend the region: so, after Pyrrhus' pause,
490 A rousèd vengeance sets him new a-work;
And never did the Cyclops' hammers fall
On Mars his armour, forged for proof eterne,
With less remorse than Pyrrhus' bleeding sword
Now falls on Priam.
495 Out, out, thou strumpet Fortune! All you gods,
In general synod, take away her power,
Break all the spokes and fellies from her wheel,
And bowl the round nave down the hill of heaven,
As low as to the fiends!'
500 POLONIUS This is too long.
HAMLET It shall to the barber's, with your beard. (*To First
Player*) Prithee, say on. He's for a jig or a tale of
bawdry, or he sleeps. Say on, come to Hecuba.
FIRST PLAYER
'But who, O had seen the mobbled queen'—
505 HAMLET 'The mobbled queen'?
POLONIUS That's good; 'mobbled queen' is good.
FIRST PLAYER
'Run barefoot up and down, threat'ning the flames
With bisson rheum; a clout upon that head
Where late the diadem stood, and for a robe,
510 About her lank and all o'er-teemèd loins,
A blanket in th'alarm of fear caught up—
Who this had seen, with tongue in venom steeped,
'Gainst Fortune's state would treason have pronounced.
But if the gods themselves did see her then,

When she saw Pyrrhus make malicious sport   515
In mincing with his sword her husband's limbs,
The instant burst of clamour that she made—
Unless things mortal move them not at all—
Would have made milch the burning eyes of heaven,
And passion in the gods.'   520
POLONIUS Look whe'er he has not turned his colour, and
has tears in 's eyes. (*To First Player*) Prithee, no more.
HAMLET (*to First Player*) 'Tis well. I'll have thee speak out
the rest soon. (*To Polonius*) Good my lord, will you see
the players well bestowed? Do ye hear?—let them be   525
well used, for they are the abstracts and brief chronicles
of the time. After your death you were better have a
bad epitaph than their ill report while you live.
POLONIUS My lord, I will use them according to their
desert.   530
HAMLET God's bodykins, man, much better. Use every
man after his desert, and who should scape whipping?
Use them after your own honour and dignity—the less
they deserve, the more merit is in your bounty. Take
them in.   535
POLONIUS (*to Players*) Come, sirs.   *Exit*
HAMLET (*to Players*) Follow him, friends. We'll hear a play
tomorrow. Dost thou hear me, old friend? Can you play
the murder of Gonzago?
⌐PLAYERS⌐ Ay, my lord.   540
HAMLET We'll ha't tomorrow night. You could for a need
study a speech of some dozen or sixteen lines which I
would set down and insert in't, could ye not?
⌐PLAYERS⌐ Ay, my lord.
HAMLET Very well. Follow that lord, and look you mock   545
him not.   ⌐*Exeunt Players*⌐
My good friends, I'll leave you till night. You are
welcome to Elsinore.
ROSENCRANTZ Good my lord.
HAMLET
Ay, so. God b'wi' ye.   *Exeunt all but Hamlet*
Now I am alone.   550
O, what a rogue and peasant slave am I!
Is it not monstrous that this player here,
But in a fiction, in a dream of passion,
Could force his soul so to his whole conceit
That from her working all his visage wanned,   555
Tears in his eyes, distraction in 's aspect,
A broken voice, and his whole function suiting
With forms to his conceit? And all for nothing.
For Hecuba!
What's Hecuba to him, or he to Hecuba,   560
That he should weep for her? What would he do
Had he the motive and the cue for passion
That I have? He would drown the stage with tears,
And cleave the general ear with horrid speech,
Make mad the guilty and appal the free,   565
Confound the ignorant, and amaze indeed
The very faculty of eyes and ears. Yet I,
A dull and muddy-mettled rascal, peak
Like John-a-dreams, unpregnant of my cause,

752

Of the 58 sentences that begin on this page, 6 begin with conjunctions.

10%

Jonathan Swift, *A Letter of Advice to a Young Poet*
(1720)

---

118   **JONATHAN SWIFT**

Arbiter, going upon the same mistake, has confidently declared, that one ingredient of a good poet, is, "*mens ingenti
literarum flumine inundata;*"[a] I do, on the contrary, declare,
that this his assertion (to speak of it in the softest terms) is
no better than an invidious and unhandsome reflection on
all the gentlemen-poets of these times; for, with his good
leave, much less than a flood, or inundation, will serve the
turn; and, to my certain knowledge, some of our greatest
wits in your poetical way, have not as much real learning as
would cover a sixpence in the bottom of a basin; nor do I
think the worse of them.

For, to speak my private opinion, I am for every man's
working upon his own materials, and producing only what
he can find within himself, which is commonly a better stock
than the owner knows it to be. I think flowers of wit ought
to spring, as those in a garden do, from their own root and
stem, without foreign assistance. I would have a man's wit
rather like a fountain, that feeds itself invisibly, than a
river, that is supplied by several streams from abroad.

Or if it be necessary, as the case is with some barren wits,
to take in the thoughts of others, in order to draw forth
their own, as dry pumps will not play till water is thrown
into them; in that necessity, I would recommend some of the
approved standard authors of antiquity for your perusal, as a
poet and a wit; because maggots being what you look for, as
monkeys do for vermin in their keepers' heads, you will find
they abound in good old authors, as in rich old cheese, not
in the new; and for that reason you must have the classics,
especially the most worm-eaten of them, often in your hands.

But with this caution, that you are not to use those an-
cients as unlucky lads do their old fathers, and make no
conscience of picking their pockets and pillaging them. Your
business is not to steal from them, but to improve upon them,
and make their sentiments your own; which is an effect of
great judgment; and though difficult, yet very possible, without the scurvy imputation of filching. For I humbly conceive,
though I light my candle at my neighbour's fire, that does
not alter the property, or make the wick, the wax, or the
flame, or the whole candle, less my own.

        [a] " A mind flooded with a vast river of learning."

Of the 7 sentences that begin on this page, 4 begin with conjunctions.

57%

James Madison, *The Federalist No. 52*
(1788)

this branch. In order to decide on the propriety of this article, two questions must be considered: first, whether biennial elections will, in this case, be safe; second, whether they be necessary or useful.

First. As it is essential to liberty that the government in general should have a common interest with the people, so it is particularly essential that the branch of it under consideration should have an immediate dependence on, and an intimate sympathy with, the people. Frequent elections are unquestionably the only policy by which this dependence and sympathy can be effectually secured. But what particular degree of frequency may be absolutely necessary for the purpose does not appear to be susceptible of any precise calculation, and must depend on a variety of circumstances with which it may be connected. Let us consult experience, the guide that ought always to be followed whenever it can be found.

The scheme of representation as a substitute for a meeting of the citizens in person being at most but very imperfectly known to ancient polity, it is in more modern times only that we are to expect instructive examples. And even here, in order to avoid a research too vague and diffusive, it will be proper to confine ourselves to the few examples which are best known, and which bear the greatest analogy to our particular case. The first to which this character ought to be applied is the House of Commons in Great Britain. The history of this branch of the English Constitution, anterior to the date of Magna Charta, is too obscure to yield instruction. The very existence of it has been made a question among political antiquaries. The earliest records of subsequent date prove that parliaments were to *sit* only every year; not that they were to be *elected* every year. And even these annual sessions were left so much at the discretion of the monarch, that, under various pretexts, very long and dangerous intermissions were often contrived by royal ambition. To remedy this grievance, it was provided by a statute in the reign of Charles II that the intermissions should not be protracted beyond a period of three years. On the accession of William III, when a revolution took place in the government, the subject was still more seriously resumed, and it was declared to be among the fundamental rights of the people that parliaments ought to

Of the 13 sentences that begin on this page, 3 begin with conjunctions.

23%

Benjamin Franklin, *Autobiography*
(1793)

---

conversation, every thing being studied in our rules which might prevent our disgusting each other. From hence the long continuance of the club, which I shall have frequent occasion to speak further of hereafter.

But my giving this account of it here is to show something of the interest I had, every one of these exerting themselves in recommending business to us. Breintnal particularly procur'd us from the Quakers the printing forty sheets of their history, the rest being to be done by Keimer; and upon this we work'd exceedingly hard, for the price was low. It was a folio, pro patria size, in pica, with long primer notes. I compos'd of it a sheet a day, and Meredith worked it off at press; it was often eleven at night, and sometimes later, before I had finished my distribution for the next day's work, for the little jobbs sent in by our other friends now and then put us back. But so determin'd I was to continue doing a sheet a day of the folio, that one night, when, having impos'd my forms, I thought my day's work over, one of them by accident was broken, and two pages reduced to pi, I immediately distributed and compos'd it over again before I went to bed; and this industry, visible to our neighbors, began to give us character and credit; particularly, I was told, that mention being made of the new printing-office at the merchants' Every-night club, the general opinion was that it must fail, there being already two printers in the place, Keimer and Bradford; but Dr. Baird (whom you and I saw many years after at his native place, St. Andrew's in Scotland) gave a contrary opinion: "For the industry of that Franklin," says he, "is superior to any thing I ever saw of the kind; I see him still at work when I go home from club, and he is at work again before his neighbors are out of bed." This struck the rest, and we soon after had offers from one of them to supply us with stationery; but as yet we did not chuse to engage in shop business.

I mention this industry the more particularly and the more freely, tho' it seems to be talking in my own praise, that those of my posterity, who shall read it, may know the use of that virtue, when they see its effects in my favour throughout this relation.

Of the 9 sentences that begin on this page, 3 begin with conjunctions.

33%

Percy Bysshe Shelley, *A Defence of Poetry*
(1821)

---

360   **SHELLEY**

distributes itself thence as a paralyzing venom, through the
affections into the very appetites, until all become a torpid
mass in which hardly sense survives. At the approach of
such a period, poetry ever addresses itself to those faculties
which are the last to be destroyed, and its voice is heard,
like the footsteps of Astræa, departing from the world.
Poetry ever communicates all the pleasure which men are
capable of receiving: it is ever still the light of life; the
source of whatever of beautiful or generous or true can
have place in an evil time. It will readily be confessed that
those among the luxurious citizens of Syracuse and Alex-
andria, who were delighted with the poems of Theocritus,
were less cold, cruel, and sensual than the remnant of their
tribe. But corruption must utterly have destroyed the fabric
of human society before poetry can ever cease. The sacred
links of that chain have never been entirely disjoined, which
descending through the minds of many men is attached to
those great minds, whence as from a magnet the invisible
effluence is sent forth, which at once connects, animates, and
sustains the life of all. It is the faculty which contains
within itself the seeds at once of its own and of social
renovation. And let us not circumscribe the effects of the
bucolic and erotic poetry within the limits of the sensibility
of those to whom it was addressed. They may have perceived the beauty of those immortal compositions, simply as
fragments and isolated portions: those who are more finely
organized, or born in a happier age, may recognize them as
episodes to that great poem, which all poets, like the co-
operating thoughts of one great mind, have built up since
the beginning of the world.
        The same revolutions within a narrower sphere had place
in ancient Rome; but the actions and forms of its social life
never seem to have been perfectly saturated with the poetical
element. The Romans appear to have considered the Greeks
as the selectest treasuries of the selectest forms of manners
and of nature, and to have abstained from creating in measured language, sculpture, music, or architecture, anything
which might bear a particular relation to their own condition, whilst it should bear a general one to the universal
constitution of the world. But we judge from partial evi-

Of the 11 sentences that begin on this page, 3 begin with conjunctions.

27%

Lindley Murray, *An English Grammar*
(1824)

Murray was known as "the father of English grammar."

---

174   ETYMOLOGY.

were formed gradually, and without plan or method, why should we believe, that the Classic tongues were otherwise formed? Are they more regular than the modern? In some respects they may be so; and it is allowed that they are more elegant: for, of two towns that are built without a plan, it is not difficult to imagine, that the one may be more convenient and more beautiful than the other. ⎡But⎤ every polite tongue has its own rules; and the English that is according to rule, is not less regular than the Greek that is according to rule; and a deviation from the established use of the language, is as much an irregularity in the one as in the other: nor are the modes of the Greek tongue more uniform in Xenophon and Plato, or of the Latin in Cicero and Cæsar, than those of the English are in Addison and Swift, or those of the French in Rollin, Vertot, and Fenelon. ⎡But⎤ why should the Inflections of language be considered as a proof of refinement and art, and the substitution of auxiliary words as the work of chance and of barbarism? Nay, what evidence can be brought to show, that the Inflections of the Classic tongues were not originally formed out of obsolete auxiliary words prefixed, or subjoined, to nouns and verbs, or otherwise incorporated with their radical letters? Some learned men are of opinion, that this was actually the case. ⎡And⎤ though the matter does not now admit of a direct proof, the analogy of other languages, ancient as well as modern, gives plausibility to the conjecture.

The inflections of Hebrew nouns and verbs may, upon this principle, be accounted for. The cases of the former, are marked by a change made in the beginning of the word; and this change is nothing more than a contracted preposition prefixed, answering to the English *of, to, from*: as if, instead of *animal, of animal, to animal, from animal*, we were to pronounce and write *animal, fanimal, tanimal, franimal;* which, if we were ac-

---

Of the 9 sentences that begin on this page, 3 begin with conjunctions.

33%

Thomas Carlyle, *Sir Walter Scott*
(1838)

---

the pen in his hand. But indeed the most unaccountable
ready-writer of all is, probably, the common Editor of a Daily
Newspaper. Consider his leading articles; what they treat
of, how passably they are done. Straw that has been thrashed
a hundred times without wheat; ephemeral sound of a sound;
such portent of the hour as all men have seen a hundred times
turn out inane: how a man with merely human faculty,
buckles himself nightly with new vigour and interest to this
thrashed straw, nightly thrashes it anew, nightly gets-up new
thunder about it; and so goes on thrashing and thundering
for a considerable series of years; this is a fact remaining
still to be accounted for, in human physiology. The vitality
of man is great.
Or shall we say, Scott, among the many things he carried
towards their ultimatum and crisis, carried this of ready-
writing too, that so all men might better see what was in it?
It is a valuable consummation. Not without results;—results,
at some of which Scott as a Tory politician would have
greatly shuddered. For if once Printing have grown to be as
Talk, then DEMOCRACY (if we look into the roots of things)
is not a bugbear and probability, but a certainty, and event as
good as come! 'Inevitable seems it me.' But leaving this,
sure enough the triumph of ready-writing appears to be even
now; everywhere the ready-writer is found bragging
strangely of his readiness. In a late translated *Don Carlos,*
one of the most indifferent translations ever done with any
sign of ability, a hitherto unknown individual is found assur-
ing his reader, 'The reader will possibly think it an excuse,
when I assure him that the whole piece was completed within
the space of ten weeks, that is to say, between the sixth of
January and the eighteenth of March of this year (inclusive
of a fortnight's interruption from over-exertion); that I
often translated twenty pages a-day, and that the fifth act
was the work of five days.'[14] O hitherto unknown individual,
what is it to me what time it was the work of, whether five
days or five decades of years? The only question is, How
well hast thou done it?
So, however, it stands: the genius of Extempore irresistibly

[14] *Don Carlos,* a Dramatic Poem, from the German of Schiller. Mann-
heim and London, 1837.

Of the 15 sentences that begin on this page, 4 begin with conjunctions.

27%

Mark Twain, *Taming the Bicycle*
(ca. 1880)

opposite thing—the big wheel must be turned in the direction in which you are falling. It is hard to believe this, when you are told it. And not merely hard to believe it, but impossible; it is opposed to all your notions. And it is just as hard to do it, after you do come to believe it. Believing it, and knowing by the most convincing proof that it is true, does not help it: you can't any more *do* it than you could before; you can neither force nor persuade yourself to do it at first. The intellect has to come to the front, now. It has to teach the limbs to discard their old education and adopt the new.

The steps of one's progress are distinctly marked. At the end of each lesson he knows he has acquired something, and he also knows what that something is, and likewise that it will stay with him. It is not like studying German, where you mull along, in a groping, uncertain way, for thirty years; and at last, just as you think you've got it, they spring the subjunctive on you, and there you are. No—and I see now, plainly enough, that the great pity about the German language is, that you can't fall off it and hurt yourself. There is nothing like that feature to make you attend strictly to business. But I also see, by what I have learned of bicycling, that the right and only sure way to learn German is by the bicycling method. That is to say, take a grip on one villainy of it at a time, and learn it—not ease up and shirk to the next, leaving that one half learned.

When you have reached the point in bicycling where you can balance the machine tolerably fairly and propel it and steer it, then comes your next task—how to mount it. You do it in this way: you hop along behind it on your right foot, resting the other on the mounting-peg, and grasping the tiller with your hands. At the word, you rise on the peg, stiffen your left leg, hang your other one around in the air in a general and indefinite way, lean your stomach against the rear of the saddle, and then fall off, maybe on one side, maybe on the other; but you fall off. You get up and do it again; and once more; and then several times.

By this time you have learned to keep your balance; and also to steer without wrenching the tiller out by the roots (I say tiller because it *is* a tiller; "handle-bar" is a lamely descriptive phrase). So you steer along, straight ahead, a little while, then you rise forward, with a steady strain, bringing your right leg, and then your body, into the saddle, catch your breath, fetch a violent hitch this way and then that, and down you go again.

But you have ceased to mind the going down by this time; you are getting to light on one foot or the other with considerable certainty. Six

Of the 20 sentences that begin on this page, 5 begin with conjunctions.

25%

Richard Grant White, *Words and Their Uses*
(1899)

---

46   WORDS AND THEIR USES

But although the written speech of these people would be to this degree indistinguishable, an ear at all nice in its hearing would be able to separate the sheep from the goats by their bleat. The difference would be one not of pronunciation (for the standard of pronunciation is also the same in both countries, and well-educated people in both conform to it with like habitual and unconscious ease), but of pitch of voice, and of inflection. Among those of both countries who had been from their birth accustomed to the society of cultivated people, even this distinction would be made with difficulty, and would, in many cases, be impossible. But the majority of one half hundred could thus be distinguished from the majority of the other; and the superiority would be greatly on the side of the British fifty. The pitch of the British Englishman's voice is higher and more penetrating than the American Englishman's, and his inflections are more varied than the other's, because they more frequently rise. The voice of the former is generally formed higher in the throat than that of the latter, who speaks from the chest with a graver monotone. Thackeray and Goldwin Smith are characteristic examples on the one side, Daniel Webster and Henry Ward Beecher on the other. The distinction to a delicate ear is very marked; but other difference than this of pitch and inflection there is none whatever. Pronunciation is exactly the same. And even in regard to pitch and inflection, there is not so much difference between the average British Englishman of culture and the average American Englishman of like training, as there is between the Yorkshireman and the Norfolkman; and there is very much more difference between the pronunciation and the idiom of the

---

Of the 10 sentences that begin on this page, 3 begin with conjunctions.

30%

Will Durant, *The Story of Philosophy*
(1926)

---

14   THE STORY OF PHILOSOPHY

It was his reply to these questions that gave Socrates death and immortality. The older citizens would have honored him had he tried to restore the ancient polytheistic faith; if he had led his band of emancipated souls to the temples and the sacred groves, and bade them sacrifice again to the gods of their fathers. But he felt that that was a hopeless and suicidal policy, a progress backward, into and not "over the tombs." He had his own religious faith: he believed in one God, and hoped in his modest way that death would not quite destroy him; [1] but he knew that a lasting moral code could not be based upon so uncertain a theology.   If one could build a system of morality absolutely independent of religious doctrine, as valid for the atheist as for the pietist, then theologies might come and go without loosening the moral cement that makes of wilful individuals the peaceful citizens of a community.

If, for example, *good* meant *intelligent,* and *virtue* meant *wisdom;* if men could be taught to see clearly their real interests, to see afar the distant results of their deeds, to criticize and coördinate their desires out of a self-cancelling chaos into a purposive and creative harmony—this, perhaps, would provide for the educated and sophisticated man the morality which in the unlettered relies on reiterated precepts and external control.   Perhaps all sin is error, partial vision, foolishness? The intelligent man may have the same violent and unsocial impulses as the ignorant man, but surely he will control them better, and slip less often into imitation of the beast.   And in an intelligently administered society—one that returned to the individual, in widened powers, more than it took from him in restricted liberty—the advantage of every man would lie in social and loyal conduct, and only clear sight would be needed to ensure peace and order and good will.

But if the government itself is a chaos and an absurdity, if it rules without helping, and commands without leading,—

[1] Cf. Voltaire's story of the two Athenians conversing about Socrates: "That is the atheist who says there is only one God." *Philosophical Dictionary,* art. "Socrates."

Of the 10 sentences that begin on this page, 3 begin with conjunctions.

30%

Albert Einstein, *The Mechanics of Newton*
(1927)

reasons he deserves our deepest reverence. The figure of Newton has, however, an even greater importance than his genius warrants because destiny placed him at a turning point in the history of the human intellect. To see this vividly, we have to realize that before Newton there existed no self-contained system of physical causality which was somehow capable of representing any of the deeper features of the empirical world.

No doubt the great materialists of ancient Greece had insisted that all material events should be traced back to a strictly regular series of atomic movements, without admitting any living creature's will as an independent cause. [And] no doubt Descartes had in his own way taken up this quest again. [But] it remained a bold ambition, the problematical ideal of a school of philosophers. Actual results of a kind to support the belief in the existence of a complete chain of physical causation hardly existed before Newton.

Newton's object was to answer the question: is there any simple rule by which one can calculate the movements of the heavenly bodies in our planetary system completely, when the state of motion of all these bodies at one moment is known? Kepler's empirical laws of planetary movement, deduced from Tycho Brahe's observations, confronted him, and demanded explanation.* These laws gave, it is true, a complete answer to the question of *how* the planets move round the sun: the elliptical shape of the orbit, the sweeping of equal areas by the radii in equal times, the relation between the major axes and the periods of revolution. [But] these rules do not satisfy the demand for causal explanation. They are three logically independent rules, revealing no inner connection with each other. The third law cannot simply be transferred quantitatively to other central bodies than the sun (there is, e.g., no relation between the period of revolution of a planet round the sun and

---

* Today everybody knows what prodigious industry was needed to discover these laws from the empirically ascertained orbits. [But] few pause to reflect on the brilliant method by which Kepler deduced the real orbits from the apparent ones—i.e., from the movements as they were observed from the earth.

Of the 14 sentences that begin on this page, 4 begin with conjunctions.

29%

Oliver Wendell Holmes, *U.S. v. American Livestock Commission Co.*, 279 U.S. 435, 437–438
(1929)

ON TRADE COMBINATIONS AND BOYCOTTS

ducers Commission Association bought or sold or attempted to buy or sell upon the Oklahoma City Stockyards was or was not the live stock of its members." It is said so far as appears all the sales were *ultra vires* and that the appellees should not be enjoined from refusing to cooperate in an illegal act. But apart from the presumption that the corporation was acting only within its powers and from the burden resting on the doer of a *prima facie* illegal act, the boycott, to justify it, we agree with the Government that it would be absurd to suppose that a cooperative society organized for the special purpose of aiding its members should confine its business to the illegal sale of the products of nonmembers. If not all, we must assume that some at least of its business was legitimate and that to some extent it might sell live stock that its members produced. But the boycott was general, intended, it would seem, to drive the Producers Commission Association out of business. That association was a competitor of the appellees and the suggestion that it was acting *ultra vires* sounds like an afterthought and cannot be supposed to have been the motive for the act. It is said that motive does not matter, but motive may be very material when it is sought to justify what until justified is a wrong. But, whatever the motive, nothing is shown or suggested by the evidence to justify the general boycott that the Secretary's order forbade. The Secretary's order should be enforced, but without prejudice to the right of the appellees to refuse to deal with the Producers Commission Association in matters beyond its power.

A suggestion was made that the last named association was not within the protection of the Act of Congress. We see nothing in the limitation of its powers to prevent it, the statute seems to recognize it, § 306 (f), and the corporation was found by the Secretary to be a market agency duly registered as such.

Decree reversed.

United States v. American Livestock Commission Co., et al.
279 U. S. 435

[167]

Of the 9 sentences that begin on this page, 3 begin with conjunctions.

33%

Theodore H. White, *The Making of the Preisdent 1968*
(1969)

little dreams," and persuaded the city fathers to reserve the entire lake front for green and parks. Today there rises along the shore, a clifflike ridge of great buildings, extravagantly designed apartment towers, imposing hotels, glistening luxury shops, all looking down on gardens, flowers and trees to present to visitors one of the most majestic façades of any city in the world. Culture has passed through this town, flirted with the city, touching it in the past with poetry, leaving behind a great art museum, a great university, two great newspapers. But the city's image was caught best and forever by its poet laureate, Carl Sandburg, who put the gloss on Chicago—"Hog Butcher for the World, Tool Maker, Stacker of Wheat, Player with Railroads and the Nation's Freight Handler; Stormy, husky, brawling, City of the Big Shoulders." For Chicago is a working-man's city—like Detroit, or Brooklyn, or Pittsburgh, only larger and more powerful. New York may be Cosmopolis; Chicago is what America is all about.

Chicago is industry—people who make things, get things done. Sandburg's Chicago is, of course, dead: though the stockyards still stank of death and offal in the summer of 1968, the meat industry is moving away and hog-butchering declines. Railways shrivel in Chicago as they do everywhere in America; wheat and corn move from the great plains to the outer world by more convenient lake outlets. But the essence of what Sandburg caught is still there: muscle. From the new towers one can look south through the smog over the greatest steel-making complex in the world—from South Chicago through Gary, the great mills pour more steel (25,000,000 tons annually) than the Ruhr of Germany, than the British Midlands, than all of France. Chicago beats and twists this steel into tractors, trucks, freight cars, heavy equipment. And Chicago does far more than process brute metal. In the stadium of the University of Chicago is a plaque that notes that here the first continued fission of the atom was achieved—and an enormous electronics industry now employs scores of thousands; so does the printing industry; so do food industries; so do the wholesale and banking establishments. No one who wants work in Chicago is unemployed. But it is a hard-knuckled city, a union town, friendly if one knows how to make friends, uptight to strangers.

Chicago sorts itself out neatly on a map. Behind Burnham's magnificent lake front the beauty quickly crumbles into endless stretches of one-family or two-family homes of working people, their factories and shops dreary concrete patches among undistinguished wood-frame or red-brick huddles. North of the Chicago River—which bisects the town—and in a great swath to the west live those called by sociologists the "ethnics"—Germans, Poles, Italians, Irish, Jews of the working class. In the suburbs, and chiefly to the north, live the white Protestant middle class and those of the "ethnics" who seep upward toward the sun, the

Of the 18 sentences that begin on this page, 5 begin with conjunctions.

28%

William Strunk Jr. & E.B. White, *The Elements of Style*
(3d ed. 1979)

the end, sometimes it is more effective in that spot than anywhere else. "A claw hammer, not an ax, was the tool he murdered her with." This is preferable to "A claw hammer, not an ax, was the tool with which he murdered her." Why? Because it sounds more violent, more like murder. A matter of ear.

[And] would you write "The worst tennis player around here is I" or "The worst tennis player around here is me"? The first is good grammar, the second is good judgment—although the *me* might not do in all contexts.

The split infinitive is another trick of rhetoric in which the ear must be quicker than the handbook. Some infinitives seem to improve on being split, just as a stick of round stovewood does. "I cannot bring myself to really like the fellow." The sentence is relaxed, the meaning is clear, the violation is harmless and scarcely perceptible. Put the other way, the sentence becomes stiff, needlessly formal. A matter of ear.

There are times when the ear not only guides us through difficult situations but also saves us from minor or major embarrassments of prose. The ear, for example, must decide when to omit *that* from a sentence, when to retain it. "He knew he could do it" is preferable to "He knew that he could do it"—simpler and just as clear. [But] in many cases the *that* is needed. "He felt that his big nose, which was sunburned, made him look ridiculous." Omit the *that* and you have "He felt his big nose. . . ."

15. *Do not use dialect unless your ear is good.*

Do not attempt to use dialect unless you are a devoted student of the tongue you hope to reproduce. If you use dialect, be consistent. The reader will become impatient or confused if he finds two or more versions of the same word or expression. In dialect it is necessary to spell phonetically, or at least ingeniously, to capture unusual inflections. Take, for example, the word *once*. It often appears in dialect writing as *oncet*, but *oncet* looks as though it should be pronounced "onset."

A better spelling would be *wunst*. [But] if you write it *oncet* once, write it that way throughout. The best dialect writers, by and large, are economical of their talents, they use the minimum, not the maximum, of deviation from the norm, thus sparing the reader as well as convincing him.

16. *Be clear.*

Clarity is not the prize in writing, nor is it always the principal mark of a good style. There are occasions when obscurity serves a literary yearning, if not a literary purpose, and there are writers whose mien is more overcast than clear. [But] since writing is communication, clarity can only be a virtue. [And] although there is no substitute for merit in writing, clarity comes closest to being one. Even to a writer who is being intentionally obscure or wild of tongue we can say, "Be obscure clearly! Be wild of tongue in a way we can understand!" Even to writers of market letters, telling us (but not telling us) which securities are promising, we can say, "Be cagey plainly! Be elliptical in a straightforward fashion!"

Clarity, clarity, clarity. When you become hopelessly mired in a sentence, it is best to start fresh; do not try to fight your way through against the terrible odds of syntax. Usually what is wrong is that the construction has become too involved at some point; the sentence needs to be broken apart and replaced by two or more shorter sentences.

Muddiness is not merely a disturber of prose, it is also a destroyer of life, of hope: death on the highway caused by a badly worded road sign, heartbreak among lovers caused by a misplaced phrase in a well-intentioned letter, anguish of a traveler expecting to be met at a railroad station and not being met because of a slipshod telegram. Usually we think only of the ludicrous aspect of ambiguity; we enjoy it when the *Times* tells us that Nelson Rockefeller is "chairman of the Museum of Modern Art, which he entered in a fireman's raincoat during a recent fire, and founded the

Of the 43 sentences that begin on this page, 5 begin with conjunctions.

12%

Sheridan Baker, *The Complete Stylist and Handbook*
(2d ed. 1980)

Believe in your thesis.

Notice how your assertion about welfare mellowed as you revised. And not because you have resorted to cheap tactics, though tactics may get you to the same place, but rather because you brought it under critical inspection, asking what is true in it: what can (and cannot) be assumed true, what can (and cannot) be proved true. And you have asked yourself where you stand.

You should, indeed, look for a thesis you believe in, something you can even get enthusiastic about. Arguing on both sides of a question, as debaters do, is no doubt good exercise, if one can stand it. It breaks up old ground and uncovers what you can and do believe, at least for the moment. But the argument without the belief will be hollow. You can hardly persuade anyone if you can't persuade yourself. So begin with what you believe, and explore its validities.

Conversely, you must test your belief with all the objections you can think of, just as you have already tested your first proposition about welfare payments. First, you have acknowledged the most evident objection—that the opposition's view must have some merit—by starting your final version with "Despite their immediate benefits . . . ." Second, you have gone a little deeper by seeing that in your bold previous version you had, with the words *are eroding*, begged the question of whether responsibility is in fact undergoing erosion; that is, you had silently assumed that responsibility *is* being eroded. This is one of the oldest fallacies and tricks of logic. To "beg the question," by error or intent, is to take for granted that which the opposition has not granted, to assume as already proved that which is yet to be proved. But you have saved yourself. You have changed *are eroding* to *may be eroding*. You have gone farther in deleting the *perhaps more than anything else*. You have come closer to the truth.

You may wonder if it is not astoundingly presumptuous to go around stating theses before you have studied your subject from all angles, made several house-to-house surveys, and read everything ever written. A natural uncertainty and feeling of ignorance, and a misunderstanding of what truth is, can well inhibit you from finding a thesis. But no one knows everything. No one would write anything if he waited until he did. To a great extent, the writing of a thing is the learning of it—the discovery of truth.

So, first, make a desperate thesis and get into the arena. This is probably solution enough. If it becomes increasingly clear that your thesis

---

Of the 25 sentences that begin on this page, 7 begin with conjunctions.

28%

Richard A. Posner, *Cardozo: A Study in Reputation*
(1990)

CHAPTER FOUR

62

on their side; and he is not thought a great man *because* his voluminous writings do not compose a coherent whole. Indeed, ambiguous and equivocal expression—not to mention diffusion of
effort (the strategy of the fox, in contrast to the concentration of
the hedgehog)—makes it harder to achieve fame. But once the
world is convinced of a writer's or thinker's merit despite the
ambiguities and equivocations of his work, those attributes enhance his fascination, provide occasions for research and debate,
and magnify his following.

2. Luck plays a great role in reputation. Abraham Lincoln died
at the right moment—and in the right manner—from the
standpoint of posthumous fame. The manner of his death was
consistent with martyrdom, and the timing ensured that his
achievement in preserving the union and in freeing the slaves
would not be shadowed by the subsequent failures—failures one
man could not have avoided—in the period of reconstruction.
And so with Orwell. Had he lived to a ripe old age (he was born
in 1903 and died in 1950, so with better health he might be
alive today), he would have taken a position on contemporary
political events, and then either the neoconservatives or the so-
cialists would have had to disown him—he would have lost half
his adulators! He *might* have offset this loss by creating additional
works of the resonance of *Nineteen Eighty-Four,* but the regression
phenomenon suggests that this is unlikely. And since, as Samuel
Johnson remarked, people are judged by their worst work when
they are living and by their best work when they are dead, producing works below one's top level hurts one in one's lifetime and
does not help one after death.

3. But luck is rarely the whole story, contrary to the impression a reader might take away from Gary Taylor's fascinating
study of Shakespeare's reputation.[9] Taylor belongs to the school
of literary critics that is vigorously debunking canonical works of

9. *Reinventing Shakespeare: A Cultural History, from the Restoration to the Present*
(1989).

Of the 10 sentences that begin on this page, 4 begin with conjunctions.

40%

William Zinsser, *On Writing Well*
(6th ed. 1998)

---

26   ON WRITING WELL

tion or sleep. Now I'm saying you must write for yourself and not be gnawed by worry over whether the reader is tagging along.

I'm talking about two different issues. One is craft, the other is attitude. The first is a question of mastering a precise skill. The second is a question of how you use that skill to express your personality.

In terms of craft, there's no excuse for losing readers through sloppy workmanship. If they doze off in the middle of your article because you have been careless about a technical detail, the fault is yours. But on the larger issue of whether the reader likes you, or likes what you are saying or how you are saying it, or agrees with it, or feels an affinity for your sense of humor or your vision of life, don't give him a moment's worry. You are who you are, he is who he is, and either you'll get along or you won't.

Perhaps this still seems like a paradox. How can you think carefully about not losing the reader and still be carefree about his opinion? I assure you that they are separate processes.

First, work hard to master the tools. Simplify, prune and strive for order. Think of this as a mechanical act, and soon your sentences will become cleaner. The act will never become as mechanical as, say, shaving or shampooing—you will always have to think about the various ways in which the tools can be used. But at least your sentences will be grounded in solid principles, and your chances of losing the reader will be smaller.

Think of the other as a creative act: the expressing of who you are. Relax and say what you want to say. And since style is who you are, you only need to be true to yourself to find it gradually emerging from under the accumulated clutter and debris, growing more distinctive every day. Perhaps the style won't solidify for years as *your* style, *your* voice. Just as it takes time to find yourself as a person, it takes time to find yourself as a stylist, and even then your style will change as you grow older.

But whatever your age, be yourself when you write. Many old men still write with the zest they had in their twenties or

---

Of the 24 sentences that begin on this page, 4 begin with conjunctions.

17%

The Economist

(2004)

▸ conditions at other plants under threat.

The 35-hour week, established in western Germany in the late 1980s and early 1990s, is still insisted on publicly by IG Metall and Verdi, the biggest white-collar union. But threatened plant closures and other hard-luck stories have forced concessions at, for example, Continental, a tyre company, and ThyssenKrupp, a steelmaker. Volkswagen is preparing for a showdown over how to cut labour costs by 30%.

Germans work fewer hours per year than workers in any other rich country except the Netherlands and Norway, according to the OECD. At DaimlerChrysler's Sindelfingen plant the workers get a five-minute break every hour. With that and local holidays they work 72 hours less per year than colleagues in Bremen. Lengthening the working week is a less painful way of cutting costs than trimming wages, even if it makes it little easier to find jobs for Germany's 4.4m unemployed.

That challenge is the focus of another labour-market reform that has just passed into law. Hartz IV, as it is called, merges social-security payments with the unemployment-benefit system. That may sound like paper-shuffling but it is, claims Matthias Platzeck, premier of Brandenburg, "the biggest social revolution in Germany since the second world war." From January, the long-term unemployed, whose lives have been too cushy, will find the tap turned off if another household member is in work, or they have too many assets, or they are unwilling to take jobs offered.

It will be hard for any of these measures to make a big difference in places with high unemployment: in eastern Germany, for instance, average unemployment is 18.5% and there are areas where it is closer to 30%. But everywhere, say the polls, there is a growing readiness to be flexible to save jobs, including working longer hours. Perhaps not as long as Jürgen Kluge, who heads the German arm of McKinsey, and recently claimed to work between 70 and 80 hours a week. But the relentless fall in hours worked in Germany seems likely to be reversed over the next few years. ∎

The European Union's troubles

Stability and instability

BRUSSELS AND PARIS
Fights loom over the constitution, the budget and the stability pact

PRESIDENT JACQUES CHIRAC chose July 14th to announce that France would, after all, hold a referendum on the draft European Union constitution, probably in the second half of 2005. It was time, he said, to "bet on Europe". With an unpopular government and uncertainty in France about today's EU of 25, this could be a big gamble. But in truth Mr Chirac had little choice. He was cornered abroad, notably by Tony Blair's decision to have a referendum in Britain, a move that hugely upset Paris. At home, he was under pressure from his own party. The prime minister, Jean-Pierre Raffarin, and the finance minister, Nicolas Sarkozy, had both come out for a referendum. Besides, direct consultation is a fifth-republic tradition: there have been nine referendums since 1958.

The risk, as with all referendums, is that the French may not answer the question. In 1992, they almost sank the Maastricht treaty, backing it by a wafer-thin 51-49%, mainly because of discontent with the Mitterrand government. Mr Chirac's government is also unpopular. And the opposition Socialist Party is split on whether to back the constitution. Mr Chirac's best hope is that the French might prove more enthusiastic than they seem. A TNS-Sofres poll in May suggested that 72% of voters backed the idea of a European constitution, and 67% were positive about Europe.

Even so, a referendum in France must increase the odds that the constitution will never be ratified. At least nine other countries are holding votes. The trickiest may be in Poland and Britain. And a further development this week may make a British referendum even harder to win: the European Commission's confirmation of its

proposals to phase out the British EU budget rebate. Britain immediately declared that the rebate, famously negotiated by Margaret Thatcher in 1984, was "unnegotiable". Since any change requires a unanimous vote, the British may be able to prevail. But they will be in a minority of one against 24–and the fight is likely to be going on at the same time as a vote on the constitution, encouraging a no vote.

Yet another problem for the constitution may stem from the EU's notoriously misnamed stability and growth pact, which supposedly limits budget deficits of euro-area members to below 3% of GDP. Last November, to the great irritation of smaller countries, the French and Germans persuaded a qualified majority of their fellow governments in the Council of Ministers to reject the commission's proposal to threaten sanctions against the pair, and instead to put the entire pact into abeyance. But this week the European Court of Justice ruled that the council had exceeded its powers.

The judgment, which had been sought by the commission, was hailed as a victory for Brussels over national governments. But that interpretation merits closer scrutiny. It has long been a truism of European politics that, when the commission gets into a fight with national governments, it is the commission that comes off worse. And although the judges annulled the decision to put the pact in abeyance, they also said that the council's failure to adopt the commission's recommendations was not something they either could or should overrule. Thus the court's decision is unlikely actually to change French or German fiscal policy: it will remain possible for the council to ignore any new recommendations for sanctions that the commission may make.

More likely than a fresh proposal for sanctions is a fresh set of negotiations. The commission will discuss with governments some form of revised recommendations with which all can live. In short, a purist interpretation of the pact will be displaced by the real world of political fudge. And further ahead, the terms of the pact itself may yet be watered down. The commission plans to make proposals for revising the pact in September.

How, one might ask, could any of this affect the EU constitution? The answer lies in the Dutch referendum that will be held early next year. The Dutch were by far the angriest at the let-off for France and Germany. When they realise that, even after the court ruling, the French and Germans are unlikely to suffer sanctions, the feeling that there is one rule for the big and another for the small may strengthen Dutch Euroscepticism (see page 55).

In short, it has been a bad week for the EU constitution–and maybe for the future of the EU itself. ∎

Of the 54 sentences that begin on this page, 12 begin with conjunctions.

22%

U.S. News & World Report
(2004)

"Howard Dean never believed in the movement. Never."

JOE TRIPPI, *former Dean campaign manager*

him the subject of intense scrutiny by the media and starting his downfall. But Gore's endorsement didn't *make* Dean the front-runner. Gore endorsed Dean because Dean already *was* the front-runner. Dean had received the endorsement of AFSCME and SEIU, with their 3 million members, three weeks before Gore endorsed Dean. To many in the media, it was that and not the endorsement of a losing presidential candidate that cemented Dean's front-runner status. Trippi disagrees. "We became the front-runner, but we weren't built for that," Trippi said in an interview after the campaign. But what was the campaign built for? Failure? True, people may have had different expectations of Dean after he became the front-runner. He wasn't just a protest candidate anymore. Now he had to demonstrate that he could broaden his base, be presidential, and beat George Bush. He needed a Plan B. But the Dean campaign had no Plan B, because it could barely execute Plan A. Plan A—building an insurgent campaign based on a message of empowerment, opposition to the war in Iraq, and a considerable amount of Bush bashing—had, coupled with a truly impressive use of the Internet to raise funds, gotten Dean further than he had ever hoped to get. But Dean could not move beyond that point. He could not pivot from being an insurgent to being something broader. The Internet did not fail Dean—it got him as far as he got—but as Mike Ford pointed out, the Internet built a base of 600,000 people while Dean was going to need 54 million people to win the presidency.

"Dated Dean, Married Kerry," the bumper stickers in Iowa read, and for many it was true. Dean had excited them, energized them, made them believe it was possible to beat Bush. But once they thought it was possible, they started wondering whether Dean was the best vehicle for their hopes, whether he was truly presidential. Dean's Iowa director, Jeani Murray, said: "We did a focus group in August that said if the message moves from change to electability, Kerry was going to win in Iowa."

Which he did. But what happened to all those Dean voters identified as Ones, the voters who would vote for Dean without fail? The most likely explanation is that thousands of them never really existed, thousands did not show up at the caucuses, and thousands showed up and voted for someone else. "Would we have done better with a better organization?" Mike Ford asked. "Yes. But we wouldn't have won. What you want in a campaign is people feeling increasingly better about your candidate so you top out at the end. In our case, the better the voters knew Dean, the less they liked him. Organization could not have saved this one."

That is the opinion, of course, of someone who was partly responsible for the organization. Others have a different point of view. "This was a campaign that ill-served its candidate," one top Dean aide said. "We let him down." Some of Dean's former aides say Dean remained a powerful and appealing candidate to the end but was doomed by an organization without, in the words of Tom Harkin, "any structural integrity." Then there are those who say, yes, the campaign was awful, but it was awful because of the "insurgent/empowerment" philosophy that Dean and Trippi stubbornly clung to, even at the expense of building an efficient campaign organization. "We were supposed to be insurgents, outsiders, free-form," Ochs said. "Experience was seen somehow as a negative. It was hubris, the hubris of believing that anything new and different was good. Mundane, traditional campaign tasks were not valued. The campaign often operated in a head-scratching, mind-numbingly ridiculous manner."

While losing campaigns are rarely as bad as they look and winning campaigns are rarely as good, there were dramatic differences between the Dean and Kerry campaigns in Iowa: The Kerry campaign acted decisively and sent an Iowa expert to Iowa when things looked bad, something the Dean wanted to do by sending Joe Trippi but could not manage. The Kerry campaign coordinated the needs of Iowa with the candidate's message and appearances, which the Dean campaign often could not manage. And the Dean campaign was obsessed with its political philosophy and Internet movement, while the Kerry campaign was obsessed only with making John Kerry the Democratic nominee. Kerry won Iowa and Dean lost, and that was the whole campaign. Democrats wanted a standard-bearer, one who could beat George W. Bush, and they wanted him fast. And once they had a true front-runner, one who had actually won a state, they were going to stick with him.

Sitting on his campaign plane a few weeks before he was due to accept the Democratic nomination for president, John Kerry looked back at Iowa. "There was a media perception that our campaign was written off," he said. "People had all but handed the nomination to Howard Dean. So we had to win Iowa or come in a very strong second. Very early on, in January of 2003, things were going well for Kerry. Then, the ground shifted, and Howard Dean shifted it. "What we couldn't control was the war in Iraq," Kerry said. "Basically, I was moving very effectively and very well until the war in Iraq stopped the debate and changed the dynamic. It just didn't matter what you were doing and what you said; there was just one angry topic. Dean didn't have to vote on the war, and he moved in and created a different dynamic." Nothing

Of the 51 sentences that begin on this page, 9 begin with conjunctions.

18%

Starting sentences with conjunctions isn't restricted to nonlegal literature. Look at opinions written by the best living legal writers on the United States Supreme Court—Chief Justice John G. Roberts, Justice Antonin Scalia, Justice Ruth Bader Ginsburg, and Justice Stephen G. Breyer. All of them use sentence-starting conjunctions gracefully and effectively, and restrict *however* to occasional midsentence appearances. From their opinions, you can learn much about style as well as law. So cast off superstition. And adopt a stylistic technique used by the best writers.

ن& ن& ن&

Genteelisms, Officialese, and Commercialese

MOST OF US NEED to work hard at being plainspoken. Oddly, achieving a natural style takes a lot of effort because of an unconscious tendency toward verbal inflation. When it comes to word choice, we should follow the advice of H.W. Fowler and F.G. Fowler: prefer simple words over fancy ones (*house*, not *residence*), concrete words over abstract ones (*pay*, not *remuneration*), and Anglo-Saxon words over Latin derivatives (*end* or *fire* over *terminate*).[1]

Three related linguistic viruses discourage plainspokenness: genteelisms (words and phrases by which insecure people try to raise their social status), officialese (words and phrases that many people consider "official-sounding"), and commercialese (words and phrases commonly found in formulaic business correspondence). The *-ese* suffix found in *officialese* and *commercialese*, as in *legalese*, denotes a caricatured literary style. Other types include academese and journalese. But officialese and commercialese—together with genteelisms—make up a peculiar overlay for lawyers' language.

Genteelisms: U vs. non-U

One fascinating aspect of sociolinguistic study involves the relationship between language and social class. Social insecurity leads people to inflate their word choice, as if that might enhance their social position. They feel more "professional." So proles adopt what they think are "middle class" words (virtually always getting it wrong, as it happens); lower-middle-class people adopt what they think of as upper-middle-class refinements (again getting it wrong), and their attempts backfire. This age-old, much-studied use of genteelisms rigidifies social stratification. Instead of pro-

---

Adapted from *Advanced Legal Writing & Editing* (2008).

[1] *See* H.W. Fowler & F.G. Fowler, *The King's English* 11 (3d ed. 1931).

viding people with social uplift, pretentious word choices help keep them down.[2]

Linguists have studied this phenomenon for decades, and have tagged it with some jargon of their own: *non-U* (the *U* stands for *upper class*). Here's what a sampling of these scholars have to say about the phenomenon:

- "Differences between U and non-U word choice are fairly well known . . . . One salient characteristic of U [is] the preference for plain and forthright terms instead of euphemistic ones, particularly when the latter are voguish terms smacking of advertising or social uplift."[3]
- "It is only people who are uncertain of their native tongue who call a napkin by the grotesque name of 'serviette.'"[4] (This *napkin/serviette* choice is the most famous class marker in British English.)
- "A U person never uses words that are longer or more complicated than necessary . . . [A] statement like, 'As of this moment in time, it was deemed necessary to escalate before finalizing . . . .' [is] not only ugly, but definitely non-U."[5]

As it happens, every language has two types of dialects: regional dialects and class dialects. Those who speak the standard speech of the nation (Standard American English, in this case) are automatically sorted by their class dialect.[6] It's not a caste system or even an explicit class

---

[2] Dwight Bolinger, *Are You a Sincere H-Dropper?* 50 Am. Speech 313 (1975) (quoting Ralph B. Long as writing that "[p]eople who really know little or no English grammar . . . , when in doubt between two constructions, pick the less usual and presumably more elegant"); Otto Jespersen, *Mankind, Nation, and Individual from a Linguistic Point of View* 94 (1946) ("The lower class—or part of the lower class, or, we should say, perhaps, some of the lower classes—strive to a great extent to copy their 'betters,' and to seek to become more refined, or at least appear more refined, than they actually are."); James Bradstreet Greenough & George Lyman Kittredge, *Words and Their Ways in English Speech* 317 (1901) ("Vanity and social ambition . . . combine with courtesy and servility . . . to support this natural bent, and the disposition to 'magnify one's office' contributes its share in producing the final result.").

[3] Thomas Pyles, "The Auditory Mass Media and U," in *Studies in Honor of Raven I. McDavid Jr.* 425, 427 (Lawrence M. Davis ed., 1972).

[4] S.P.B. Mais, *The Writing of English* xiii (1935).

[5] H.B. Brooks-Baker, Foreword, *U and Non-U Revisited* xvii (Richard Buckle ed., 1978).

[6] Paul Fussell, *Class* 177 (1983) (noting that because the United States is a democracy, class distinctions have developed with greater rigor than elsewhere, and language, far from coalescing into one great central mass without social distinctions, has developed even more egregious class signals than anyone could have expected).

system, as it is in other countries. But it certainly exists, and we all participate:

> The existence of different manners of speech for persons in various ranks is a familiar fact. We are constantly sorting and classifying people according to them. A variation of any national language according to social levels is called *class dialect* . . . . When we talk, then, we tell much more about ourselves than the factual statements we are making. The sum total of small nuances will indicate much about our training, environment, economic position, and even profession. In conversation we are unconsciously providing a rich commentary about ourselves.[7]

Linguists have called genteelisms "middle-class pseudo-elegant style,"[8] "the magniloquence of vulgar display,"[9] and "vulgarly genteel."[10] Stylists have almost universally condemned their use; Eric Partridge called them "those words and phrases [that] the semiliterate and far too many of the literate believe to be more elegant than the terms they displace."[11] Even Emily Post, the 20th century's leading adviser to Americans on matters of etiquette, scorned genteelisms as "pseudo-eloquence . . . on a par with curled up third and little fingers holding a teacup."[12]

The classic statement is that of H.W. Fowler, who wrote that genteelisms are "thought to be less soiled by the lips of the common herd, less familiar, less plebeian, less vulgar, less improper, less apt to come unhandsomely betwixt the wind and our nobility."[13] Of course, Fowler made clear that genteelisms abound in the speech of vulgar plebeians.

The class of common genteelisms covers a range of stylistic missteps. Most of them involve reaching for a high-sounding phrase when a single word would do (*on an annual basis* for *yearly*) or a pompous word when a simple one is available (*utilization* for *use*). Many involve euphemisms (*expecting* for *pregnant*). Others involve hypercorrection, a grammatical error made while trying too hard to avoid making one (*between you and I* for *between you and me*, or *feel badly* for *feel bad*).

[7] Margaret Schlauch, *The Gift of Tongues* 261 (1943; repr. 1960).

[8] Fussell, note 6, at 184.

[9] Greenough & Kittredge, note 2, at 322.

[10] Bergen Evans & Cornelia Evans, *A Dictionary of Contemporary American Usage* 161 (1957).

[11] Eric Partridge, *Usage and Abusage* 104 (1947).

[12] Emily Post, *Etiquette: The Blue Book of Social Usage* 30 (rev. ed. 1947).

[13] H.W. Fowler, *Modern English Usage* 222 (Ernest Gowers ed., 2d ed. 1965).

Consider this short list of common genteelisms. Do you see any that you yourself often use? Teach yourself to delight in the plainspoken alternative.

Genteel & Non-U	Plainspoken U
approximately	about
assistance	help
at this time	now
beverage	drink
cease	stop
corridor	hall
depart	leave; go
endeavor	try
I desire to purchase	I'd like to buy
indicate	say; show
individual	person
inquire	ask
in regard[s] to	about
irregardless	regardless
pass away	die
perspire	sweat
peruse	read
place	put
previous to	before
prior to	before
proceed	go
purchase	buy
real classy; class act	[nothing]
reside	live
residence	house
retire	go to bed
send it to my partner or I	send it to my partner or me
soiled	dirty
subsequently	later
subsequent to	after
sufficient	enough
transpire	happen

Airlines, restaurants, and other public accommodations are full of genteelisms.[14] Hotels are among the worst offenders. A typical check-in goes something like this:

Clerk: How may I be of assistance?
Traveler: I'd like to check in, please.
Clerk: May I please have your name?
Traveler: Leslie Brown.
Clerk: I have your reservation here, Mr. Brown. Do you require one evening or two?
Traveler: Just one night.
Clerk: Do you require a single accommodation, or double?
Traveler: A single room would be fine. We have a conference here tomorrow. I should have some boxes in storage.
Clerk: The notification on your reservation informs me that we have previously secured them in the conference area.
Traveler: Good. Are there any restaurants nearby?
Clerk: We have several dining establishments in the immediate vicinity. Please see the concierge [pronounced, in non-U, "con-see-air" or (worse) "con-see-ay"], who can assist you momentarily.
Traveler: Thank you.
Clerk: Do you require any assistance with your luggage at this time?
Traveler: Yes, thank you.
Clerk: George, our bellman, will accompany you to your sleeping accommodation. The elevators are down the corridor to the right. George, we need luggage assistance, please.

Similarly, people who answer business phone calls often go into a long spiel: "Good afternoon. Hendrickson, Pinsky & Samuelson. This is Doris speaking. How may I be of assistance?" All before the caller has gotten a word in.

Officialese: What It Supposedly Means to "Be Professional"

Closely related to genteelisms is "officialese." When you get off the airplane—er, "deplane"—in Los Angeles, you're greeted with endless repeats of the following message: "Please maintain visual contact with your personal property at all times." Not *watch* but *maintain visual contact.*

---

[14] *See, e.g.*, Fussell, note 6, at 184–86; Garner, *Garner's Modern American Usage* 31–32 (2d ed. 2003) (s.v. "Airlinese").

Not *closely* but *at all times*. Not *belongings* but *personal property* (presumably, your realty is exempt).

Like genteelisms, officialese is puffed-up language meant to elevate the user's status. Whereas genteelisms are intended to project an elevated social status, officialese is intended to project an air of authority supposedly fitting a "professional." But the result in either case can be ludicrous. Police-talk, to take an extreme example, is an easy target for satirical jabs: "The white males proceeded at a high rate of speed to the intersection of State Highway 37, where they exited the vehicle. The officers then exited their vehicles and engaged in foot pursuit of the white males."

Ernest Gowers saw the root of officialese in the official's role as an intermediary between the law and the public. That role often requires the official to approximate legal language. "And our system of government imposes on them the need always of being cautious and often of avoiding a precision of statement that might be politically dangerous. Moreover, officials do not easily shake off the idea that dignity of position demands dignity of diction."[15] In later years, Gowers further refined his analysis of the causes: "a feeling that plain words sort ill with the dignity of office, a politeness that shrinks from blunt statement, and, above all, the knowledge that for those engaged in the perilous game of politics, and their servants, vagueness is safer than precision."[16]

The use of officialese results in prose that is stilted, convoluted, and sometimes even indecipherable. Consider this selection from a City of Detroit publication, along with my plain-English translation:

Before:

It is our hope that this guide will be of some aid to you, and will help ease some of the frustrations that may occur during the Building Permit process. It is of our utmost concern that your project be reviewed in the most complete, timely, and expeditious fashion. We want to provide you a service that is professional and most importantly reliable. If there are any other questions that may not have been covered, please feel free to contact one of the Structural Plan Reviewers listed below.

After:

We hope this guide makes getting your building permit easier. We want your project's review to be as fast and trouble-free as possible, and our service to you to be professional and reliable. For answers to any other questions about your project, call one of these structural-plan reviewers: [list].

---

[15] Ernest Gowers, *The Complete Plain Words* 270 (1948, rev. 1988).
[16] Fowler, note 13, at 411.

Officialese may be thought of as having its own set of "rules," each being the opposite of advice that any good stylist would give aspiring writers. Here are a few examples:

- Prefer longer sentences over shorter ones. Make them wordy. Never use a word when a phrase is available (make it *take a lease*, not *rent*; *make recommendations*, not *recommend*). Never use a short phrase when a longer one is available (make it *voluntarily enter into a binding lease agreement*, not *take a lease*; *compile a detailed report containing multiple recommendations and suggestions*, not *recommend*).
- Prefer fancy words over plain ones. Make it *obtain* or *acquire*, not *get*; *utilization*, not *use*; *facsimile transmittal*, not *fax*.
- Prefer vagueness over directness. Make it *initiate the application process*, not *apply*; *effectuate the successful administration of*, not *carry out*.
- Prefer the passive voice over the active voice. Make it *when the forms have been submitted, a hearing will be set*, not *when you submit the forms, we'll set a hearing*.
- Prefer buzzwords over traditional words. Make it *incent*, not *encourage*; *impact*, not *affect*; *strategize*, not *plan*.

Commercialese: It's Bad for Business

Good business letters get right to the point and strike the right tone. Commercialese defeats both goals, especially the one about tone.

Do you sound like a machine or a person? A self-important bureaucrat or a thoughtful counselor? A faceless lawyer or an individual? Your correspondence should reflect that you're direct, pleasant, and unpretentious.

Often, a poor tone in legal and other business correspondence stems from laziness. The classic excuse for using an unduly formal style—"we've always done it that way"—can be hard to stand against. After all, formulas for writing poorly abound, especially in routine correspondence: you just mimic those ancient (and often meaningless) words and phrases that you've seen other people use so often.

If you want to write a bad letter, start with *Enclosed please find*, not *Here is* or *Enclosed is*. Business-writing authorities have universally condemned *Enclosed please find* for well over a century:

- "[*Please find enclosed*:] A more ridiculous use of words, it seems to me, there could not be."[17]
- "All stereotyped words [that] are not used in talking should be avoided in letter writing. There is an idea that a certain peculiar

---

[17] Richard Grant White, *Every-Day English* 492 (1880).

commercial jargon is appropriate in business letters. The fact is, nothing injures business more than this system of words found only in business letters. The test of a word or phrase or method of expression should be, 'Is it what I would say to my customer if I were talking to him instead of writing to him?' "[18]

- "*Inclosed herewith please find. Inclosed* and *herewith* mean the same thing. How foolish to tell your reader twice exactly where the check is, and then to suggest that he look around to see if he can find it anywhere. Say, 'We are inclosing our check for $25.50.' "[19]

- "**Please Find Enclosed.** This worn-out formula is not in good use in letters, either business or personal."[20]

- "*Enclosed please find* [should be] *Enclosed is* or *are* or *We are enclosing*. '*Enclosed please find* our check' . . . is better expressed as '*Enclosed is* our check.' *Find* means to meet with, or light upon, accidentally; to come upon by seeking."[21]

- "*Enclosed please find*. Needless and faulty phraseology. The word *please* has little meaning in this instance, and the word *find* is improperly used. POOR: *Enclosed please find* sample of our #1939 black elastic ribbon. BETTER: *We are enclosing* (or *We enclose*) a sample of our #1939 black elastic ribbon."[22]

- "You have seen how whisker-talk tends to hide personality and mechanize letters . . . . The reader is chilled by a conglomeration of words [that] sound more as if they came from robot than from man.

  "So much for the worn-out, hackneyed expressions so often seen in business letters—whiskers, rubber-stamps, chestnuts, call them what you please. They are sleeping pills [that] defeat the aim of making every letter a warm, *personal contact* with the reader.

  "The following list includes some of these bromides; make sure you avoid them: [the list includes *enclosed find, enclosed herewith, enclosed please find*, and *herewith please find*]."[23]

- "Business words and expressions borrowed from an earlier generation can make your writing sound artificial and pedantic. Every letter will read like a form letter, and you will sound bored or, even worse, boring. Thinking up substitute phrases is easy if you

---

[18] Sherwin Cody, *How to Do Business by Letter* 20 (19th ed. 1908).

[19] Wallace E. Bartholomew & Floyd Hurlbut, *The Business Man's English* 153 (1924).

[20] Maurice H. Weseen, *Crowell's Dictionary of English Grammar* 470 (1928).

[21] P.H. Deffendall, *Actual Business Correspondence* 42 (1929).

[22] A. Charles Babenroth, *Modern Business English* 108 (Charles C. Parkhurst ed., 3d ed. 1942).

[23] L.E. Frailey, *Handbook of Business Letters* 32–33 (2d ed. 1965).

put your mind to it. Consider some of these revisions: . . . *Enclosed please find* [becomes] *I am enclosing.*"[24]

- "Business writing is often filled with overly formal, antiquated, and stiff phrases like 'Enclosed please find,' 'As per your request,' and 'Pursuant to our conversation.' Such usage is a holdover from times gone by and does not belong in contemporary business writing . . . . As a rule, the conversational test will help you identify language that needs modernization."[25]
- "Using unnecessarily formal words (such as *herewith*) and outdated phrases (such as *please find enclosed*) is another cause of affectation."[26]
- "[I]n any business letter, certain principles are universal. 'Inure to the benefit of' is four words too long, 'enclosed please find' sounds pompous and silly, and 'I am writing this letter to inform you that . . .' is a thoughtless statement of the obvious."[27]

The phrase has no defenders—at least none who are willing to go on the record.

If you want to write effective letters, put down the words that you would say to the recipient if he or she were with you in your office. Be conversational. Be real.

But *enclosed please find* has many aged companions that letter-writers keep on life support. Below are some examples. See how much more agreeably natural the plain English equivalents are:

Instead of This:	Write This:
at your earliest convenience	as soon as you can
beg	ask
deem it necessary	find it necessary; think it's needed
in light of the fact that	because
we are in receipt of	we've received
as per our telephone conversation of this date	as we discussed this afternoon
pursuant to your instructions	as you requested
same (pron.)	it

---

[24] Maryann V. Piotrowski, *Effective Business Writing* 53 (1989).

[25] Gary Blake & Robert W. Bly, *The Elements of Business Writing* 50 (1991).

[26] Charles T. Brusaw et al., *The Business Writer's Handbook* 30 (4th ed. 1993).

[27] Kelly Cannon, "Lawyers vs. Language," in *Vocabula Bound* 13, 15 (Robert Hartwell Fiske ed., 2004).

A Summary of Tips

- Keep your prose plainspoken. You'll appear more confident and more genuine.

- Genteelisms are "pseudo-elegant" alternatives to simple words or phrases. Though socially insecure people inflate their language to sound more eloquent, it invariably backfires on them.

- Officialese is puffed-up language like *maintain visual contact* instead of *watch*. It's meant to sound more "professional" and to be more precise. In fact, it sounds pseudo-fancy and bureaucratic.

- Commercialese is the boilerplate most commonly found in business correspondence, such as *enclosed please find*. Relying on formulaic phrases like that makes us sound more robotic than human.

- In business correspondence, aim to be concise, conversational, and personable. Get right to your point and lead with a summary.

ℯℴ ℯℴ ℯℴ

The Aesthetics of Your Pages

FEDERAL DISTRICT JUDGE Lynn N. Hughes of Houston says that he can
reject more than half the applications he receives for various positions,
including judicial clerkships, just by looking at the résumé from across
the room. How? By the appearance of the type on the page. Some people have such poor aesthetic judgment that there's no use for them in an
office that prides itself on high-quality work product.

The lawyer's aesthetic judgment is more on the line today than ever
before. Take how we indicate emphasis, for example. In the days of typewriters, there were two ways to highlight text: capitalizing and underlining. Now we have many more devices available, such as typeface, type
size, boldface, italics, and the judicious use of white space.

Yet the legal profession is still largely unaware of how important
page layout can be. On the whole, we're still stuck in the ugly typewriting
mode: we still tend to rely on all-caps text and underlining as means of
emphasis. Professional typographers I've spoken with are bewildered by
our naiveté about the importance of not just what words appear on the
page, but *how* they appear.

Here, then, are a few tips on how to create readable pages that won't
cause your readers to think less of your writing. Failing to use document
design knowledgeably puts you at a disadvantage because readers have
mostly become accustomed to well-designed documents.

1. Choose a readable typeface. For text, a readable typeface usually
means a serif typeface, such as the one used throughout this book, as
opposed to a sans serif (/sanz **ser**-if/, it's pronounced in English). Serifs
are the "feet" and other short strokes that project from the ends of the
main strokes that make up a character. A sans serif typeface is literally
"without serifs."

This is a serif typeface: Century Schoolbook.

This is a sans serif typeface: Arial.

Although sans serif typefaces often work well in headings and the like,
they can be tiresome to read in lengthy blocks of text. That's why publishers everywhere tend to put the body of an article or book in a serif
typeface. Among the better ones are Bookman, Caslon, Garamond,
Goudy, Palatino, and Times Roman. One typeface, Courier, long pre-

---

Adapted from *Student Lawyer* (May 2008).

dominated in American legal writing, but only because writers had only that choice on a typewriter. Avoid it at all costs—it's an eyesore.

2. Use white space meaningfully. Ample white space makes a page more inviting. The primary ways to create white space on the page are to use generous margins (more than one inch where possible, preferably 1.2 inches), to supply ample headings and subheadings, and to enumerate items in vertical lists. Cramming type onto a page is always a blunder.

3. Supply headings as needed. The more complicated the document, the simpler and the more overt you should make the structure. The best way to do this is to use informative, easily accessible headings. Good headings and subheadings make a document much easier to follow. Not only do they serve as navigational aids for readers, but they'll also help you organize thoughts logically.

4. Put more space above headings than below. It makes perfect sense to group closely related things together. So why should headings and subheadings be equidistant from the bottom of one segment of text and the top of the next? Though it's a common practice, it makes no sense at all. And professional typographers know better. Start looking at books, magazines, even advertisements. There's a lot to be learned from examining how professionals use type.

5. Avoid all-caps and initial-caps text. What's the problem with using all capitals? Because all the characters are uniform in height, it's hard to distinguish one from the next. The text letters don't have what typographers call "ascenders" and "descenders," the parts of letters that go above the baseline (as does *b*) and below it (as does *p*). All-caps text causes reading difficulties that are largely a physiological matter, not a mere question of taste. The ascenders and descenders give words distinct shapes that help us recognize them more efficiently. Even initial-caps text can be distracting, especially in an argumentative heading that consists of a complete sentence. Try using ordinary capitalization (mostly lowercase), with boldface, in any heading that's a complete sentence.

Although some statutes require certain types of language—such as warranty disclaimers—to be conspicuous, they typically don't mandate all-caps text. And think about this: the purpose of such a statute is to make sure the reader sees and understands the contract term, but the *effect* of using all-caps is to make the text *harder* to read and understand. There's always a better way, such as using boldface type or putting the highlighted text in a box.

6. Use boldface type appropriately. That is, use boldface exclusively in headings, *never* in text. Many lawyers, unfortunately, have fallen into the habit of boldfacing any word that seems important to them, either in their own text or in quoted matter. Think to yourself: how do professional writers and editors achieve emphasis without resorting to such crude mannerisms? It's usually by placing the important words toward the end of the sentence—at the climactic point.

7. Avoid underlining. Generally, italicizing is preferable to underlining, which was traditionally (on a typewriter) nothing more than a poor substitute for italics. The effect of underlining is to take up white space between lines, thereby making the lines harder to read. And on most computer-set type, the underline obscures the letters' descenders, making the text less legible. Here's what Justice Scalia and I say about the subject in our book *Making Your Case*: "As for underlining, it's a crude throwback: that's what writers used in typewriting—when italics weren't possible. Nobody using a computer in the 21st century should be underlining text. To the extent that the *Bluebook* suggests otherwise, it should be revised."

8. Use vertical lists when possible, with hanging indents. Enumerate items whenever possible by breaking down lists into paragraphs and subparagraphs, especially in legal drafting. Using a tabulated list allows the writer not only to display the points better but also to improve the sentence structure. Make sure that the list falls at the end of a sentence—not at the beginning or in the middle. And use hanging indents. That is, don't let the second line of an enumerated item wrap around to the left margin; instead, make the first character of the second line fall right below the first character, like this:

(a) The good thing about hanging indents is that progressively indented text cascading from the lefthand side of the page immediately displays the levels of hierarchy.

(b) In narrow columns (as in a magazine), the look isn't terrific, but it's crucial in full-page-size legal documents.

9. Use bullets for lists as needed. When you want to highlight important ideas in a list, there's hardly a better way than to use a series of bulleted list items, as below. They effectively take the reader's eye from one point to the next. Although legal writers seem to fear that bullets characterize the breezy journalist's style, in fact they contribute to efficient communication. That's why journalists use them, and it's why you should consider using them. But keep some points in mind:

• End your introduction to the bulleted list with a colon.
• Always use a hanging indent with bulleted items.
• Be sure that the bullets are proportional to the type size (about the size of an "o").

- Make a short left tab indent after the bullet, so that only a small space (perhaps the width of one or two forward spaces) appears between the bullet dot and the text.
- Single-space bulleted text, perhaps with an extra half space between items.
- Capitalize the first word in each bulleted item if that item ends with a period.
- Keep your items grammatically parallel.
- Resist the temptation to play with computer-generated boxes, arrows, and cutesy smiley-faces.

10. Don't create "fine print" or wall-to-wall type. Ideally, a line of type should accommodate 45 to 70 characters, but the fine print that characterizes so many legal documents often spans 150 characters to the line. In text of that kind, the reader's eye tends to get lost in midline or in moving from the end of one line to the beginning of the next. One way to improve a document with a large block of text—and, typically, small margins on each side—is to use a double-column format. That design can be extremely helpful, for example, in consumer contracts such as warranties and residential leases.

For more information on this important subject, my own favorite sources are Colin Wheildon's *Type & Layout* (1995), Philip Brady's *Using Type Right* (1988), and Robert Bringhurst's *The Elements of Typographic Style* (1992). Consult them and learn all you can. And pay attention to well-designed magazines and books that you read. You'll need a sense of typographic design for the rest of your working life—or else you might discover that you've been judged negatively from across the room.

JUSTICE OLIVER WENDELL HOLMES

Persuasive Writing

Briefs to the U.S. Supreme Court

A BRIEF IS A WRITTEN STATEMENT setting forth the factual background and legal contentions of a party in appellate litigation.

It is chiefly through written briefs that counsel persuade the Supreme Court. Justice Oliver Wendell Holmes, for example, was rarely influenced by oral argument—usually, instead, by the record and the briefs. That is not surprising, since oral argument is fleeting, whereas briefs are permanent. A brief may be referred to in the seclusion of chambers, before and after argument. Whether in forming a justice's initial impression of the case, or in answering questions about a party's position during the writing of an opinion, the briefs alone speak for the parties.

Not always have advocates briefed the Court. It was not until 1821 that the Supreme Court rules first required all parties to submit written briefs:

> After the present term, no cause standing for argument will be heard by the Court, until the parties shall have furnished the Court with a printed brief or abstract of the cause containing the substance of all the material pleadings, facts, and documents, on which the parties rely, and the points of law and fact intended to be presented at the argument.[1]

Adapted from *The Oxford Companion to the Supreme Court of the United States* (2d ed. 2005).

[1] 19 U.S. v, rule XXX, Feb. term 1821.

Half a century later, the rule on briefing was amended and expanded,[2] and it has undergone several changes in this century, but the crucial parts remain the same: (1) a succinct statement of the case and of the questions involved; and (2) the argument, specifically citing the authorities relied on.

Today's Supreme Court rules emphasize that a brief should be what its very name suggests: "A brief must be compact, . . . concise, and free from burdensome, irrelevant, immaterial, and scandalous matter."[3] It was not just an abstract fear of lawyerly verbosity but experience that demanded such a rule. Early in the 20th century, when there were no page limits on briefs, Justice John H. Clarke complained of briefs with more than a thousand pages. Under the current rule 24.6, such a brief would be "disregarded and stricken by the Court."[4]

Effective advocates today put what they need into well under 50 pages. In the mid-1970s, Chief Justice Warren Burger suggested a 50-page limit, and in 1980 the revised rules established that limit.

Most of the briefs submitted to the Court are not written by advocates experienced in Supreme Court practice, and the justices must contend with the "diffuseness" that Chief Justice Charles Evans Hughes lamented. In many dozens of cases every year, lawyers reveal in their briefs little awareness of what the Court finds persuasive. In short, the average written argument is inadequate.

Too many advocates approach briefing with the view merely of setting down the facts and the law on the page. They fail in imagination and tight analytical rigor. As a result, briefs are too often uninteresting as well as unpersuasive. And an inadequate brief hurts a party's chances of prevailing. In a 1942 article in the *ABA Journal* on appellate briefing, Justice Wiley B. Rutledge advised: "[M]ake your briefs clear, concise, honest, balanced, buttressed, convincing and interesting. The last is not the least. A dull brief may be good law. An interesting one will make the judge aware of this."[5]

That an unfocused brief may lose a case, even with good law behind it, may shock some. Given the great burdens on the Court's time, however, an effective brief concisely brings home the nub of why the case ought to occupy the justices' attention.

---

[2] 14 Wall. xi.

[3] Rule 24.6.

[4] *Huffman v. Pursue*, 419 U.S. 892, 892 (1974).

[5] Wiley B. Rutledge, *The Appellate Brief*, 28 ABA J. 251, 255 (1942).

Although the rules about briefing have become more and more specific with time, the qualities that go into a good brief have remained the same. In the early 19th century, Justice Joseph Story described the "eloquence of the bar"—written as well as oral—as "plain, direct, and authoritative . . . . It forbids declamation, and efflorescence of style."[6]

---

[6] *Selections from the Works of Joseph Story*, 186–87, 188 (1839).

ठ& ठ& ठ&

The Three Parts of a Brief

A GOOD BRIEF HAS THREE PARTS: an introduction, a middle, and a conclusion. You'd think everyone knows this. Not so: the orthodox way of writing a brief is to give only one part—a middle.

How so? Well, formbook-style openers typically just restate the title. For example: *Plaintiff Pantheon Corporation, by and through its attorneys of record, files this Pantheon's Memorandum in Support of Its Motion for Summary Judgment.* Hence the title. That's why it's called "Pantheon's Memorandum in Support" just an inch above this wasteful sentence. In some briefs, the hence-the-title sentence starts with *Now comes* . . . .

The conclusion, meanwhile, is equally formulaic: *For all the foregoing reasons* . . . or (in antique language) *Wherefore, premises considered,* . . . . These concluding refusals to summarize are every bit as common as pointless openers.

If you're writing that way, you're not thinking about the most critical parts of the brief: the beginning and the end.

A Proper Opener

The ideal introduction concisely states the exact points at issue. Stripped of all extraneous matter, the intro serves as an executive summary: it places the essential ideas before the judge.

Fortunately, you're always able to put a preliminary statement on the first page of a brief, even if the rules don't call for it. Just stick it there— as far up front as you can. In two jurisdictions I know of—New York and New Jersey—including a preliminary statement is the norm. (Of course, some are much better than others.) In most jurisdictions, very few lawyers use them. But it's always advisable.

How do you decide what goes into the preliminary statement? Figure out how many arguments you want to make, and then turn each into an issue statement. There's a one-to-one correspondence between issues and arguments.

Adapted from *Trial* (Mar. 1999).

Let's say you have a single issue. You might begin this way:

Motion for Summary Judgment
Preliminary Statement

In ruling on this motion, the Court is presented with the following issue:

> Section 7300 of the Internal Revenue Code prohibits the un-authorized disclosure of a taxpayer's tax audit by an IRS agent. While drinking at a hotel bar, IRS Agent Harold Collins confronted Susan Jones, who was dining with her family in an adjoining restaurant, and shouted, "Ms. Jones, if I had your audit case, I'd have you in jail by now." Did Agent Collins make an unauthorized disclosure of Susan Jones's tax audit?

That type of opener uses the so-called deep-issue technique—in which the issue is framed in separate sentences totaling fewer than 75 words.[1]

Although the deep issue is hard to beat, you can also state the issue less formally in the preliminary statement. Here's an example of how Stephen M. Shapiro of Chicago did it. He begins with the larger context and then moves quickly to a focused legal question:

Preliminary Statement

> Like all other states, Pennsylvania requires funds to finance the construction, maintenance, and repair of its roads, bridges, and tunnels. Also like other states, Pennsylvania raises the funds largely through taxes and fees levied on the users of its highways. A substantial proportion of these taxes is paid by interstate motor carriers. Appellant American Trucking Associations, Inc., as their representative, has brought this suit not because of any objection to the raising of revenues by highway-user charges or to the level of revenues Pennsylvania seeks to raise, but solely because the discriminatory nature of the two highway-use taxes Pennsylvania has adopted—the marker fee and its successor, the axle tax—favors local interests at the expense of interstate commerce.

In short, don't depend on a rule to tell you to put the issues up front. True, the better rules require them at the outset, as Rule 14 of the U.S. Supreme Court does. But many sets of rules, especially for trial courts, don't require them at all. And even on appeal, various state-court rules

---

[1] *See* Garner, *Issue-Framing: The Upshot of It All*, Trial, Apr. 1997, at 74 (reprinted here as next essay).

merely require "Points Relied On" or "Points of Error"—something rather different from a true issue.

Regardless of these requirements, always open with a preliminary statement that highlights the issues. Your judicial readers will be grateful.

A Satisfactory Middle

The middle should, with a series of headings and subheadings, develop the reasoning by which you seek to prove the affirmative or the negative of the issues stated in your introduction. To do that, you must select the main ideas that prove your conclusion. Then you arrange them in a way that shows the relations they naturally bear to one another and to the essential idea or group of ideas. All the main headings and subheadings should drive the reader toward your conclusion.

Let's say you have three issues. If so, you'll have three parts in the body of the brief, typically proceeding from the strongest to the least strong. (Forget the lame arguments.) Each part will be organized more or less as follows:

- Elaborate the legal premises embedded in the issue statement.
- Show how the factual points fit into the legal premises.
- Rebut counterarguments.
- Drive the point home with an additional reason or set of reasons.

That's the basic way of organizing the discussion of each issue.

The trickiest part is dealing with counterarguments. You must demolish all serious ones, and the dialectical method of arguing (at the end of this essay) is the best tool for this. A dialectic is something like a pendulum through time. At its simplest, it's in the form thesis–antithesis–conclusion; or, you might say, position–counterposition–resolution.

Let's assume that, in a given section of the brief, you've made your main point. Then you'll need to ask yourself, "Why would a judge decide against me?" Deal with any possible snags in your argument. That way, you'll show yourself to be both thorough and frank.

In using the dialectical structure, though, never set out the opponent's points at great length before supplying an answer. Your undercutting needs to be swift and immediate.

Try addressing the counterarguments in the middle part of each argument—not at the beginning and not at the end. Then quickly knock each one down.

A Strong Closer

Your conclusion should briefly sum up your argument, reminding us of its key points and showing clearly why the decision you seek is correct. A good way to do this is to answer the questions posed on page one.

Like your opening words, your closing words are critical. They're your leave-taking. You should no more use a formulaic closer than you should send off a trusted ally on an important mission with a perfunctory "See ya."

Yet the classic *Wherefore, premises considered, . . .*—a form with regional variations throughout the country—is just that type of closer.

To conclude strongly, capsulize your very best reasons—maybe three or four—why the court should do what you urge. And leave it at that. But put it in a nutshell, without any reference to "foregoing reasons" (which few ever bother to name). Count the reasons. List them. Then your argument will look substantial.

Here's an example of a closer in a successful motion for rehearing that I wrote. The quotation from Justice Robert H. Jackson strategically appeals to the best judicial instincts:

Conclusion and Prayer

We are asking this Court to change its mind. We think this to be not only possible, but necessary. And there is a long tradition of great judges who have thought better on second thought, as Justice Jackson once observed when doing an about-face:

Precedent . . . is not lacking for ways by which a judge may recede from a prior opinion that has proven untenable and perhaps misled others. See Chief Justice Taney, *License Cases*, 5 How. 504, recanting views he had pressed upon the Court as Attorney General of Maryland in *Brown v. Maryland*, 12 Wheat. 419. Baron Bramwell extricated himself from a somewhat similar embarrassment by saying, "The matter does not appear to me now as it appears to have appeared to me then." *Andrews v. Styrap*, 26 L.T.R., N.S. 704, 706. And Mr. Justice Story, accounting for his contradiction of his own former opinion, quite properly put the matter: "My own error, however, can furnish no ground for its being adopted by this Court . . . ." *United States v. Gooding*, 12 Wheat. 460, 478. Perhaps Dr. Johnson really went to the heart of the matter when he explained a blunder in his dictionary—"Ignorance, sir, ignorance." But an escape less self-depreciating was taken by Lord Westbury, who, it is said, rebuffed a barrister's reliance upon an earlier opinion of his Lordship: "I can only say that I am amazed that a man of my intelligence should have been guilty of giving such an opinion." If there are other ways of gracefully and good-naturedly surrendering former views to a better considered position, I invoke them all. [Footnoted citation to *McGrath v. Kristensen*, 340 U.S. 162, 177–78 (1950) (Jackson, J., concurring).]

Reynolds prays for even one such invocation.

In particular, Reynolds asks the Court to grant this motion for rehearing and provide the following relief (in the alternative):

- affirm the trial court's judgment against Fuller Indemnity; or
- reverse the judgment and render judgment for a lesser amount; or
- reverse the judgment and remand the case to the trial court.

Respectfully submitted, [etc.]

A Sea Change

All this may sound obvious. But judging from what lawyers actually file, it's little known. Go down to the courthouse and look at the filings: you'll see that more than 80% of them have boilerplate openers and closers. So, in effect, they're all middle. I'm convinced that this syndrome, more than anything else, explains why most briefs are inadequate.

Lawyers fear true openers and closers because they fear summarizing. They know that doing it properly takes a lot of work. So they opt for boilerplate.

But remember what Samuel Johnson once said: "What is written without effort is in general read without pleasure."[2] Talk to judges, as I often do, and they'll tell you that they generally read briefs without the remotest hint of pleasure. It need not be so.

---

[2] As quoted in George Birkbeck Norman Hill, *Johnsonian Miscellanies* vol. 2, 309 (1897).

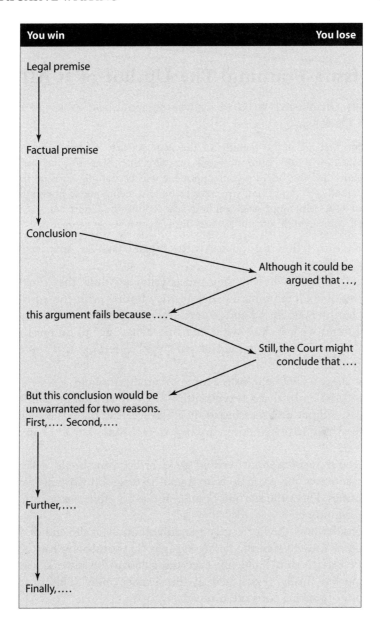

❧ ❧ ❧

Issue-Framing: The Upshot of It All

PERHAPS THE WISEST WORDS ever written about brief-writing are these of Karl Llewellyn:

> [T]he first art is the framing of the issue so that if your framing is accepted, the case comes out your way. Got that? Second, you have to capture the issue, because your opponent will be framing an issue very differently. . . . And third, you have to build a technique of phrasing of your issue which not only will help you capture the Court but . . . will stick your capture into the Court's head so that it can't forget it.[1]

The failure to follow this advice is the biggest fault in American brief-writing today.

Brief-writers rarely state their issues well. They think they can "knock out some of the preliminaries" before they bother with the core of the brief. Then they go ahead and "knock out" the first section because they have in mind what it deals with. And then what's left to do but the final section or two? With this kind of start, they're feeling as if the draft is virtually done.

For these writers, the issues come as an afterthought.

The problem is that a brief written that way will simply talk around the issues without ever piercing to their essence. And the writer will think that everything has been covered when in fact some key links are apt to be missing.

If you're serious about writing good briefs, you should delay composing sentences and paragraphs until you have a good working statement of the issues. That's the starting point—not, as so often seems to happen, the ending point.

Consider how the key issue often emerges only at the end of a briefing project. You see it in the flash of insight that somebody has the night before a brief is due. Suddenly, everything has to be reworked because the issue has finally crystallized in the writer's mind. This is a prime symptom of starting to write too early.

How common is the problem? My guess—based on the hundreds of writing samples I review each year—is that more than half of American briefs suffer from this fault.

To avoid it, try the following tips.

Adapted from *Trial* (Apr. 1997).

[1] Karl N. Llewellyn, *A Lecture on Appellate Advocacy*, 29 U. Chi. L. Rev. 627, 630 (1962).

Satisfy the 90-Second Test

Every brief should make its key point within 90 seconds. But probably only 1% of American briefs actually do that. The ones that do are spectacularly quick reads: though barely into the brief, the judge already has the desired overview—understands the basic question, the answer, and the reasons for that answer.

The trick is to cultivate a knack for framing issues well. To do this, you'll probably need to forget much of what you learned in law school about framing legal issues. Forget the idea that you should begin with *Whether*. Forget the notion that you should load it all into one sentence (a format that ensures an unchronological presentation). Forget making the issue as abstract as possible.

What does a good persuasive issue look like? Here's one:

> As Hannicutt Corporation planned and constructed its headquarters, the general contractor, Laurence Construction Co., repeatedly recommended a roof membrane and noted that the manufacturer also recommended it. Even so, the roof manufacturer warranted the roof without the membrane. Now that the manufacturer has gone bankrupt and the roof is failing, is Laurence Construction jointly responsible with the insurer for the cost of reconstructing the roof?

Some briefs wouldn't deliver that information up front or even in the first few pages. And you wouldn't find a concise statement anywhere. All the facts—important, relevant, or not—would be mixed together and sprinkled throughout the statement of facts and possibly even the arguments. This diffuse style forces a judge to scrutinize every sentence and—eventually—piece together enough facts to figure out what the issues are. Brief-writers may believe that if a judge devotes a lot of time to understanding the brief, the judge will thoroughly understand the case. But even if that were true, it isn't realistic. Besides, it isn't reasonable or fair to impose on a busy judge's limited time. And it won't serve the client's best interests.

Some brief-writers may fear that they will put their case in jeopardy by presenting a straightforward issue or issues because the judge might disagree and declare the real issue to be something else. So they avoid stating an issue and simply discuss every aspect of the case, assuming that the judge can sift out what is and isn't important. But this style is likely to backfire.

A judge wants to know immediately what question he or she is supposed to answer. That's what matters to the judge. But the shotgun approaches suggest that there are multiple issues without making clear what they are or how many there are. So a judge must search for the hidden questions before attempting to find answers. And the judge may discover and address issues the brief-writer didn't intend to raise. Instead of forcing the judge to guess what you want, tell the judge up front with disarming lucidity.

I'm not much inclined to formulas. But if there's a good formula for beginning a court paper, I think it's this: "In deciding this [motion, etc.], the Court need address only the following [two, three, etc.] issues: . . . ." What comes after the colon will be the most challenging thing you'll have to write.

Phrase the Issues in Separate Sentences

The one-sentence version of an issue doesn't seem to be required anywhere, but it's a widely followed convention. And it's ghastly in its usual form because it leads to unreadable issues that are deservedly neglected. Either they're surface issues that are too abstract, or else they're meandering, unchronological statements that can't be understood without being laboriously reconstructed.

How would most brief-writers state the following issue?

> Is Handy Vehicle Repairs liable for the hail damage suffered by Michael Dodson's Jaguar in April 2006 when Dodson dropped off the car for repairs in November 2005, and Handy Vehicle Repairs has a plainly visible sign warning that unclaimed vehicles will be parked outdoors after 30 days, and when Handy moved the car to an outside parking space in February 2006 after Dodson didn't respond to messages left in December 2005 and January 2006 on voice-mail and with his secretary for him to pick up his car? [89 words]

A sensible writer wouldn't want this muddled 89-word version, but instead would produce something like this:

> Whether Handy Vehicle Repairs is liable for the damage to Dodson's Jaguar?

Readable, yes, but hardly informative. One would need to plow through the whole brief to feel comfortable answering that question. It's a classic *surface issue*.

But if the choice is between that 12-word version and the 89-word version, most would probably take the shorter one.

Anyone making that choice, however, ignores the true problem: we've simply started off with a miserably bad premise—that an issue needs to be cast in a single sentence. And where did we get this premise? It seems to come from a well-intentioned attempt to get issue-writers to be succinct. "By golly," the idea went, "we'll just force them to say it all in one sentence."

But you're much better off framing the issue in separate sentences. Tell a miniature story by presenting the facts in chronological order, and use a statement–statement–question format. Thus:

> Handy Vehicle Repairs has a plainly visible sign warning that unclaimed vehicles will be parked outdoors after 30 days. Dodson brought his Jaguar to be repaired. Handy fixed the car and left Dodson several messages to pick it up. Dodson didn't reply, so after 60 days Handy parked the car outdoors, where it was damaged by hail a few months later. Is Handy liable for the damage? [67 words]

Instead of one convoluted sentence or one empty sentence, we have four sentences laying out for us a developing story. The information is presented in a way that readers can easily understand.

There are far better ways to enforce brevity than limiting an issue to a single sentence. But that brings us to another point.

Limit the Issues to 75 Words Apiece

About 98% of the time, if you can't phrase your issue in 75 words, you probably don't know what the issue is. It's that simple.

Believe me, it takes hard work. I've seen people take a day to frame one question. But it's well worth the effort. Why? Well, you're more likely to spot problems in your logic, and you're more likely to spark your judicial reader's interest. More than that, though, you'll be satisfying a yearning that almost every judge feels: you'll be reducing the question to bite-size form.

Typically, you need 50 to 75 words to state an issue well. Some examples:

- Section 305 of the Government Code makes it a crime for a lobbyist to enter into a contingency-fee lobbying contract. Smith has agreed to lobby for water legislation on behalf of the Guernsey Corporation; if the legislation passes, Guernsey will pay Smith $1 million. Has Smith committed a crime? [50 words]

- For over 30 years, Texas courts have held that the term "single-family dwelling" imposes a use restriction unless the term appears in a section of the restrictive covenants solely governing the architectural form of dwellings. The Beautiful Valley covenants contain the term "single-family dwelling" in a section containing both use and architectural restrictions. Do the Beautiful Valley restrictive covenants prevent Mr. Johnson from running a boarding house in his home? [72 words]

I could proliferate examples—and commonly do when teaching the subject of issue-framing. Suffice it to say that although the issue may exist
that would defy a 75-word treatment, I haven't encountered it.

Weave Facts into the Issues to Make Them Concrete

Unfortunately, some court rules actually require you to write "a concise
statement, not exceeding two pages, of the questions involved *without
names, dates, amounts or particulars*, with each question numbered, set forth
separately and followed immediately by the answer, if any, of the court
from which the appeal is taken."[2] If you're bound by such a rule, follow
it. You can still follow most of the advice given here about issue-framing.
You'll just have to do everything more abstractly.

The better approach is to weave facts into your issue statements, so
that you tell a story in miniature, with names and all. But remember that
you want only key particulars—the ones that help the reader understand
the problem. Some good examples:

- Under Minnesota law, a claim for an injury resulting from an improvement to real property must be commenced within two years
  of the time when the injury was or should have been discovered.
  The Johnsons built a home in 2001, first noticed mold growing in
  their home on July 1, 2001, and filed this lawsuit on July 3, 2004. Is
  the Johnsons' claim barred by the two-year statute of limitations?
  [71 words]

- Spoliation may be used to establish that evidence was unfavorable
  to the party responsible. Oscar Waste Disposal dumped asbestos-
  containing soil on top of suspected asbestos-containing soil removed
  from Valley Fair Amusement Park, preventing accurate testing of the
  suspect soil. Is Valley Fair entitled to an inference that the suspect
  soil did not contain asbestos? [56 words]

Were the particulars omitted there, the issues would still be understandable, but they'd lack the human element, so they'd be far less involving
and memorable.

---

[2] N.Y.C.P.L.R. § 5528(a) (McKinney 1996) (emphasis added).

Write Fair but Persuasive Issues
That Have Only One Answer

An issue is essentially a *question*, and the best issue ends with a question mark. Why? Because a bona fide question looks and sounds objective even when it's slanted. You promote your answer by putting a question on the table.

In any event, the judicial reader won't accept any answers until figuring out the question. If you supply it ready-made, the chances are greater that the judge will see the question as you see it. If you don't supply an explicit question, the judge's formulation is more likely to differ from what you'd like it to be.

And remember: this formulation is inevitable because judges are impatient to understand exactly what questions they're being asked to answer.

Highlight the Reasons
for the Conclusion You're Urging

If you follow the advice in the preceding sections, writing your conclusion—your statement of what you want the court to do—should be straightforward: it will be the answer to the question posed by your issue. And the answer will always include a good reason. If you omit the reasons for your conclusion, you'll seem to be hiding something. But if you supply a good reason, you're likely to seem both thoughtful and sensible, making your argument all the more persuasive.

This tip is key to both your opening words and your closing words: succinctly tell the court *why* it should do what you ask.

Try following this formula: "Because _____, [my position is] _____." Your brief will instantly gain both clarity and persuasiveness.

Many briefs in this country never clearly state why the court should do what the brief-writer asks. Think of all the briefs you've seen that can be boiled down to something like this: "[Proposition 1.] [Citation.] [Proposition 2.] [Citation.] [Proposition 3.] [Citation.] For the foregoing reasons, judgment should be entered for the plaintiff." Or, if a brief does mention reasons, they're often buried somewhere in the middle of a long, jumbled paragraph.

So make your conclusion clear, and make your reasons explicit. But most important, make the *issues* the focal point of your brief by framing them well and putting them up front. If you do that, you're likely to write a brief that is focused, lucid, and persuasive.

ࢬ ࢬ ࢬ

The Deep Issue: A New Approach to Framing Legal Questions

Introduction

THOUGH CRITICAL TO good legal writing, issue-framing is a subject mired in confusion. In fact, anyone seeking to learn how to frame a legal issue is sure to hear some inane pronouncements such as, "Phrase it in a single sentence," or "Start with the word *whether*," or "Omit all particulars." No wonder many lawyers' memos and briefs, as well as judges' opinions, read like windy impromptu sermons in search of a point. Indeed, poor issue-framing is the most serious defect in modern legal writing.

Let me offer a new paradigm. The well-written issue—what I call a "deep" issue—should:

- Consist of separate sentences.
- Be limited to 75 words.
- Incorporate enough detail to convey a sense of story.
- End with a question mark.
- Appear at the outset of a memo, brief, or judicial opinion, not after a statement of facts.
- Be simple enough that even a nonlawyer can read and understand it.

This model leads to tighter, more cogent writing by providing the reader with a context for the details to follow. And it helps test how sound the ideas are.

A Neglected Art

Why the concern with issues? Because no element is more important in persuasive and analytical writing. If you have crystallized the key question you're addressing, your writing will inevitably be much clearer.

Unfortunately, very few legal writers frame their issues well. As a result, legal memos, briefs, and judicial opinions are often diffuse, repetitive, and poorly organized. Sometimes these documents never reveal precisely what question they purport to answer, even to the reader who works hard to identify it.

Adapted from *The Scribes Journal of Legal Writing* (1994–1995).

Any piece of persuasive or analytical writing must deliver three things: the question, the answer, and the reasons for that answer. The better the writing, the more clearly and quickly those things are delivered. All of us should insist that our writing enable the reader to identify those things within 90 seconds of picking up the document.

To do this consistently, we need to open our discussion with a factually specific issue that captures the essence of the problem. Here is how a lawyer did just that back in 1835:

> A Turk, having three wives, to whom he was lawfully married, according to the laws of his own country, and three sons, one by each wife, comes to Philadelphia with his family, and dies, leaving his three wives and three sons alive, and also real property in this State to a large amount. Will it go to the three children equally, under the intestate law of Pennsylvania?[1] [67 words]

Anyone of moderate legal sophistication can understand that question. And most of us, having seen the question, would probably like to know the answer.

But six lawyers in ten would probably build up to the question with at least two pages of facts explaining how the Turk came to the U.S., when and where the marriages were solemnized, what the names and birthdates of the sons are, and so on. In other words, those six writers would open with a badly overparticularized statement of facts—a statement that would leave us bewildered about the upshot of it all.

Three more of the ten would probably assume that we already know the facts and so dispense with them altogether. If they were writing analytical memos, the so-called issues framed by these three lawyers would read something like this: "Is our client entitled to take one-third under Pennsylvania law?" Then the writing would launch into a legal discussion of the intestacy laws. Never mind that the intended reader and the writer don't have an identical understanding of the facts—something that will likely never emerge if the memo is written in this way. Further, a reader who later comes across the memo will remain none the wiser even after reading it in full; as a result, the memo can never be useful in future research.

Perhaps the one other lawyer would write an issue more like the 1835 version than either the overparticularized or the overvague approach, but hardly one in a hundred would frame it with equal compactness and clarity.

Those are the two goals of the deep issue: compactness and clarity.

---

[1] *A Question of the Conflict of Laws*, 14 Am. Jurist 275, 275 (1835).

The Clarity of a Deep Issue

A "deep" issue, always very tangible, sums up a case in a nutshell, and so is hard to frame but easy to understand. By contrast, a "surface" issue is abstract: it requires the reader to know everything about the case before it can be fully comprehended, and so is easy to frame but hard to understand.

Say a defendant is moving for summary judgment. Which of the following statements is more helpful?

1. Can Jones maintain an action for fraud?

2. To maintain a cause of action for fraud under California law, a plaintiff must show that the defendant made a false representation. In his deposition, Jones concedes that neither Continental nor its agents or employees made a false representation. Is Continental entitled to summary judgment on Jones's fraud claim? [49 words]

The shorter version sends us elsewhere to learn what, precisely, the issue is; the longer version asks us to do considerably less work. Whereas the surface issue says next to nothing about what the court is really being asked to decide, the deep issue explains precisely what that something is. To put it differently, the surface issue does not disclose the decisional premises; the deep issue makes them explicit. It yields up what Justice Oliver Wendell Holmes called the "implements of decision."[2]

The goal is ease of understanding. Generally speaking, the more abstract the issue, the more superficial it is: the reader must learn much more to make any sense of it. The more concrete the issue, the deeper it is: the reader need hardly exercise the brain to understand.

Consider another set of examples—different versions of the same issue considered from the same side of the case:

1. Does the cessation-of-production clause modify the habendum clause in an oil-and-gas lease?

2. Since first considering the issue 30 years ago, this Court has consistently held that the word "produced"—as used in the habendum clause of an oil-and-gas lease—means "*capable* of being produced in paying quantities." Should this Court now adopt a novel interpretation that would cast doubt on the validity of tens of thousands of leases in the State? [61 words]

---

[2] Quoted in John W. Davis, "The Argument of an Appeal," in *Advocacy and the King's English* 212, 216 (George Rossman ed., 1960).

The first is a dry legal question seemingly devoid of any real interest to anyone but oil-and-gas experts. The second, in addressing what are probably the judges' true concerns, defines the issue in a way that anyone can understand: its premises are explicit.

The Brevity of a Deep Issue

Besides being clear, a deep issue must be stated briefly—somewhere in the range of 50 to 75 words. Past 75 words or so, the writer loses focus and the reader loses interest. If you can't frame your issue in 75 words, you probably don't know quite what the issue is.

Working out a compact statement of the issue can be excruciatingly difficult. Sometimes, with a complex piece of litigation, it can take days. But it's well worth the effort because we're more likely to spot problems in the logic, and we'll certainly write more cogently.

But is the 75-word limit always achievable? In my experience, yes. In fact, all the memo examples and briefing examples in this essay—and thousands of other issues I've looked at—have met this standard. And I have yet to encounter the legal issue that couldn't be framed in 75 words. It may exist, but I haven't found it.

How Deep Issues Work in Memos

Almost all the examples so far have been persuasive issues—written to advance an advocate's point of view. But we should back up to the pretrial stage, when the lawyer is first analyzing a problem. For the analytical issue differs markedly from the persuasive issue.

The analytical issue is open-ended. It doesn't have an implicit answer. Still, it makes the reader yearn to know the answer—e.g.:

1. Section 273 of the Immigration Act makes it a crime to bring an illegal alien to the U.S. Meanwhile, section 2304 of the Maritime Act makes it a crime for the master of a vessel to fail to rescue persons aboard a vessel in distress. Does a master commit a crime under the Immigration Act when he rescues illegal aliens aboard a ship in distress and brings them to the U.S.? [71 words]

2. Mr. and Mrs. Zephyr were killed in the crash of an airplane negligently piloted by Mr. Zephyr. Their daughter, Kate, has sued the estate of her deceased father for the wrongful death of her mother. Does the doctrine of interspousal immunity bar Kate's recovery when there is no marital harmony to preserve? [52 words]

3. Appleseed School District, a public employer, has uncovered evidence that an employee in one of its school cafeterias is stealing money from the register. Appleseed wishes to confirm its suspicions so that it may fire the suspected employee. Is it legal under California and federal law for Appleseed to covertly videotape the employee at her workstation? If it is legal, do any restrictions apply? [64 words]

4. The Internal Revenue Service requires all persons who receive more than $10,000 in cash in a trade or business to report the payment and provide the name of the payor. Paul Smith, an attorney, receives $14,000 in cash from a client and reports the payment but omits the client's name in the belief that disclosure would violate the attorney-client privilege. Is there an attorney-client-privilege exception to the IRS disclosure requirements? [73 words]

5. Georgette Frye, Mayor of Monrovia, California, owns two office buildings in downtown Monrovia. The California Political Reform Act prohibits a public official from participating in a decision in which he or she has a material financial interest. Is Frye prohibited from voting on a Council resolution to provide a new sewer system for downtown Monrovia? [55 words]

6. Johnson was convicted of aggravated robbery in 1988 at the age of 16. Five years later, the Kansas Legislature enacted the Sentencing Guidelines Act, requiring that prior juvenile convictions be used to enhance the sentence of an adult convicted of a crime. After Johnson was convicted of criminal damage to property in 1994, the court used his 1988 conviction to enhance the sentence. Does this procedure violate the U.S. Constitution's ex post facto clause? [74 words]

7. Missouri law provides that a party to a contract cannot tortiously interfere with its own contract. Dr. Borstead claims that St. Anthony's Hospital tortiously interfered with a lease between himself and St. Anthony's Properties, Inc., the hospital's wholly owned subsidiary. Can St. Anthony's Hospital tortiously interfere with the lease of its wholly owned subsidiary? [54 words]

And precisely because we want to know the answer to an analytical issue, there is no better way to capture our interest.

In an analytical memo, the deep issue should be followed immediately by a brief answer (with reasons stated explicitly within it). Thus, the question and the answer amount to something resembling an executive summary: the reader understands the gist of the memo merely by reading the first few lines.

"But isn't that how most legal memos read?" you might ask. Actually, no. Not at all. Were you to sample hundreds of memos in major law firms and corporate law departments throughout the country, you'd find, as I have, that only about 1% of them begin with a deep issue and a short answer.

Let's take an example. Harry, a first-year associate at a law firm, writes a memo for Sarah, his supervisor, addressing a matter that they've worked on together for six months. The memo begins this way:

Does 29 F.C.F.R. § 181.009 apply to the Photostat transactions?

The follow-up discussion for this memo, under the heading "Discussion," is inevitable:

29 C.F.R. § 181.009 states in pertinent part: . . . .

Then a block quotation, and we're off to the tortoise races.

On a better day, Harry would have followed his surface issue with a short answer, but still the memo would be unsatisfactory. Why? First, because Sarah wouldn't know whether she and Harry had an identical understanding of what he refers to as "the Photostat transactions." Were there no nuances there? And what are the prominent aspects of those transactions? Second, even if Sarah and Harry once had identical understandings of "the Photostat transactions," their understandings have probably changed over time, so that six months later they think very differently about what they mean by that phrase. If the memo doesn't disclose the writer's premises, it will be impossible to assess the context in which it was written. Third, Sarah's and Harry's colleagues may wish to capitalize on Harry's research. Unfortunately, though, when they get Harry's memo, it reads like a private conversation in coded language.

Fourth—and perhaps most important—Barbara, the chair of the associates committee, reads the memo and feels none the wiser. And Barbara knows that—as writing guru John Trimble teaches—good writing makes readers feel smart, whereas bad writing makes readers feel stupid. Barbara writes an uncomplimentary comment in Harry's file. His annual review will not be pleasant.

A fanciful scenario, you say? Well, it's played out routinely in hundreds of law offices throughout the United States. It would be interesting to quantify the amount of wasted time, money, and energy that goes into producing and deciphering poorly written memos.

Before we leave Harry, it's a fair question to ask how he might have framed the Photostat issue. Here's one way:

Photostat, Inc. is a Colorado franchiser that wants to sell franchises to foreign customers who will operate their franchises in foreign countries.

FTC regulations require that franchisers disclose certain information to all prospective franchisees. Do these regulations apply to Photostat's sale of franchises to foreign franchisees? [46 words]

Once again, the issue is at least faintly interesting to most legal readers. And upon reading the short answer immediately following, the reader sees an orderly mind at work.

In sum, a memo containing a deep issue has the following advantages:

- Because the premises are explicit, the assigning attorney will be better able to spot any erroneous assumptions.
- Both primary and secondary readers will be able to read and understand the memo. It won't read like a conversation between insiders.
- The memo will be more comprehensible, even to the insiders, a year or two after it's written.
- Colleagues researching similar points in different cases will find the memo more helpful.
- The analytical issue can be readily transformed into a persuasive issue, and thus the memo into a brief.

How Deep Issues Work in Briefs

Many advocates fail to appreciate that the outcome of a case rests on how the court approaches the issues presented. As an advocate, you want to state the issue fairly, yes, but in a way that supports your theory of the case. A good persuasive issue, in other words, should answer itself.

Take *Eisenstadt v. Baird*, in which the plaintiffs attacked a state law prohibiting the sale of contraceptives to unmarried people. Here is how the Supreme Court framed the issue:

> If the right of privacy means anything, it is the right of the *individual*, married or single, to be free from unwarranted governmental intrusion into matters so fundamentally affecting a person as the decision whether to bear or beget a child.[3]

Richard A. Posner has observed that the decision might not have seemed so clear-cut if the Court hadn't "set up a straw man" (to use his words).[4] If, instead, the Court had posed the question with different premises, the outcome might have been different:

> We must decide whether the state is constitutionally obligated to allow the sale of goods that facilitate fornication and adultery by making those practices less costly.[5]

---

[3] 405 U.S. 438, 453 (1972).

[4] Richard A. Posner, *Law and Literature: A Misunderstood Relation* 305 (1988).

[5] Adapted from *id.*

How do the premises differ? The Court's premise is that the prohibition is an "unwarranted governmental intrusion"; Posner's hypothetical premise is that contraceptives "facilitate fornication and adultery."

As an advocate, you want to find the premises that will nudge the court toward your conclusion, and then make your premises explicit. If the court decides to answer the question you pose, then the court will probably reach the conclusion you urge.

A noted advocate—who, exactly, is unclear, because the quotation is variously attributed to Rufus Choate, Clarence Darrow, and John W. Davis, among others—once said that he'd gladly take either side of any case as long as he could pick the issues. If you pick the issues that will actually be decided, you're already more than halfway home.

Karl Llewellyn, one of the great legal thinkers and writers of the 20th century, well understood this truth:

> Of course, the first thing that comes up is the issue and the first art is the framing of the issue so that if your framing is accepted the case comes out your way. Got that? Second, you have to capture the issue, because your opponent will be framing an issue very differently. . . . And third, you have to build a technique of phrasing of your issue which not only will capture the Court but . . . will stick your capture into the Court's head so that it can't forget it.[6]

Llewellyn's initial point is the most powerful: the *first* art is framing the issue so that, if your framing is accepted, you win. The persuasive issue, then, implies only one answer—yours.

Still, the persuasive issue is much more than a mere statement of the conclusion. The advocate comes forward asking the court to address a straightforward question—e.g.:

1. Texas law provides that a lease predating a lien is not affected in foreclosure. Nelson's lease predates Marshall's lien, on which Marshall judicially foreclosed last month. Was Nelson's lease affected by the foreclosure? [33 words]

2. Liability-insurance coverage for directors and officers of financial institutions is universally required in order to recruit well-qualified directors and officers. When the Trew Group acquired First Eastern from the FDIC in 1987, the FDIC agreed to pay the "reasonable and necessary" operating costs of First Eastern. Is the FDIC obligated to pay the cost of directors' and officers' liability insurance for First Eastern? [65 words]

---

[6] Karl N. Llewellyn, *A Lecture on Appellate Advocacy*, 29 U. Chi. L. Rev. 627, 630 (1962).

3. On dozens of occasions over the course of a decade, United Peoria hired and paid a waste-hauler to haul its hazardous liquid waste to a landfill. In accordance with United Peoria's instructions, the hauler discharged thousands of gallons of United Peoria's waste into the landfill. Were these discharges an "accident" from United Peoria's point of view? [57 words]

4. Boskey Insurance issued an excess-insurance policy to BEC for liability exceeding $100,000. BEC represented to Boskey that it had purchased primary coverage (for the first $100,000 of liability) from Cooper Insurance. If Cooper becomes insolvent, should Boskey be required to step down and provide primary coverage when it never bargained for a role as—or contracted to be—a primary insurer, and when its premium reflected only the risk taken as an excess insurer? [75 words]

As in the first two examples, an issue often proceeds from the law to the facts. Yet, as in the third and fourth examples, it may sometimes proceed from the facts to the law. The only key to organizing the statements is to allow the whole to be readily absorbed—and this usually means putting the most challenging pieces of information at the beginning and the end (the emphatic positions), and the most easily comprehensible part in the middle. Following are still more examples:

5. Texas prohibits a person from bringing a claim for breach of implied warranty when that person knowingly purchased used goods. Paula Wheelock admitted at her deposition that she purchased a 1986 Chevrolet—the car she claims General Motors impliedly warranted—with 11,000 miles on the odometer. Should Wheelock's claim for breach of implied warranty be dismissed because the car was used when she bought it? [65 words]

6. California Civil Code § 1504 states that a duly made offer of performance stops the running of interest on an obligation. Jim mailed a refund check to Tom, but Tom failed to cash the check for several years. Is Tom now entitled to the interest that accrued on the refunded amount while the check went uncashed? [56 words]

7. At 7:30 one morning last spring, Father Michael Prynne, a Roman Catholic priest, was on his way to buy food for himself at the grocery store when his car collided with Ed Grimley's truck. The Catholic Church neither owned Michael Prynne's car nor required its priests to buy groceries as part of their priestly functions. Was Michael Prynne acting as an agent for the Church at the time of the accident? [71 words]

8. The Colorado Water Board lowered Cherry Creek's minimum stream flow from 12 cubic feet per second to 7. The Board's deci-

sion—reached after four public hearings—was based on recommendations of both the Colorado Division of Wildlife and three independent aquatic biologists, all of whom concluded that 7 cubic feet per second was the optimal minimum for Cherry Creek. Was the Board's decision arbitrary and capricious under the Administrative Procedure Act? [71 words]

9. In 1946, ABC manufactured and sold to Feldspar a hoist designed for attachment to a free-swinging trolley system. Thirty years later, without ABC's knowledge, Trubster acquired the hoist, added a new motor, pulley, and cable, and integrated the hoist into a fixed elevator dumbwaiter system. Is ABC liable for injuries resulting from integration of its hoist into a system defectively designed by Trubster? [64 words]

Occasionally, you'll need to assume that your audience knows something about some area of the law. In #10, below, the writer assumes that the reader understands comparative negligence. In #11, the writer assumes that the reader knows something about the availability of injunctions as a remedy. And in #12, the writer assumes that the reader knows basic trademark law.

10. Misunderstanding the comparative-negligence scheme in this state, the trial court erroneously instructed the jury that if Parker was 50% or more liable for the accident that injured him, he could not recover. Even so, the jury found that the defendant, Davis, was not liable for Parker's injuries. Was the erroneous instruction harmless error, when the jury never considered the degree of Parker's fault in the accident? [67 words]

11. Solsoft has granted a license to Creative Capital to use copyrighted computer software solely in support of Creative Capital's internal business operations. Creative Capital now says it will offer third parties services based on uses of that software. Under principles of copyright and breach of contract, can Creative Capital be enjoined from doing that? [54 words]

12. Nabisco uses its valuable "Shredded Wheat" trademark to identify its breakfast cereal, but the Examiner rejected Nabisco's trademark application on descriptiveness grounds. A survey conducted last month shows that most cereal consumers associate the "Shredded Wheat" trademark with a single source, and that a significant percentage of consumers know that Nabisco is that single source. Should Nabisco's "Shredded Wheat" trademark be registered on grounds that it has acquired secondary meaning? [70 words]

Some briefs would take at least ten pages to deliver the information contained in any of those formulations. And you wouldn't find a concise statement even on page ten. Instead, you would find the relevant tidbits strewn amid other facts throughout the first ten pages. To glean the issue, the judge would have to read with the most intense concentration. That's quite a demand to impose on anyone. And yet brief-writers seem to make this imposition routinely.

A big part of the problem seems to stem from fear—fear that if the judge doesn't see the issue in the same way as the advocate, the advocate is sunk. "How do I know what the judge will latch onto?" the diffident advocate asks. "I won't state the issue in a single way, but rather talk about the case and the parties in a way that gives the judge several handles on the case. But I'm not going to marry myself to a single issue or set of issues." Unfortunately, the result of this understandable fear is that the advocate has no clearly framed issues—no theory of the case.

And the judicial reader becomes frustrated. Why? Because, at first, only one thing matters to the judge: "What question am I supposed to answer in this case? If I can figure that out," thinks the judge, "I'll be ready to decide the case. But until I find out what that is, I'm just groping for it."

Framing the deep issue at the outset is a way of capturing the judicial imagination. Whoever does that well is most likely to win. Indeed, a well-framed issue can often become the starting point for the majority opinion.

Deep Issues in Judicial Opinions

It's no accident that the most readable judicial opinions invariably begin with a brief statement of the overarching issue in the case. Among the ablest practitioners of this art was Judge Thomas Gibbs Gee, of the Fifth Circuit, who enshrined it as the first principle in his style sheet for opinions: "Try to state the principal question in the first sentence."[7]

Even when the judge ignores that advice, though, an adept legal reader will usually try to deduce from the judicial opinion just what the issue is.

Let's take an example.

Probably the most famous hypothetical case ever posed is Lon Fuller's *Case of the Speluncean Explorers.*[8] In that case, a panel of five appellate judges, in the year A.D. 4300, must decide the fate of four cave explorers

---

[7] *A Few of Wisdom's Idiosyncrasies and a Few of Ignorance's: A Judicial Style Sheet*, 1 Scribes J. Legal Writing 55, 56 (1990).

[8] 62 Harv. L. Rev. 616 (1949).

who—having been trapped in a cave for 23 days, told by miners that it would take 10 more to dig them out, and advised by doctors that all would die of starvation during that additional period—killed and ate one of their companions. The murder statute reads as follows: "Whoever shall willfully take the life of another shall be punished by death."

In Fuller's fictitious opinions, no two of the five judges approach the case in the same way. They all answer different questions. Here is how I would frame those questions:

Truepenny, C.J.

If a statute unambiguously requires the death sentence—without exception—for anyone who willfully takes another's life, may judicial sympathies properly lead an appellate court to make allowances for those who violate the statute under extraordinary circumstances?

Foster, J.: 1st issue

Does the statutory law of murder apply to persons who find themselves buried and starving in a cave—their only hope being cannibalism—who, in short, have returned to a state of nature and drawn a new social compact?

Foster, J.: 2d issue

The murder statute requires the death penalty for anyone who willfully takes another's life. Yet the statute has never been thought to apply literally to every case. Must we now apply it literally in a case in which everyone agrees that the result would be grossly unfair?

Tatting, J.

Can I participate in a case in which I am repelled by either result, and in which I cannot resolve the doubts that beset me? (He decides that he cannot.)

Keen, J.

Four speluncean explorers, trapped in a cave, killed Roger Whetmore and ate his flesh. Did they not willfully take Whetmore's life?

Handy, J.

Four men, trapped in a cave, resorted to homicide and cannibalism to survive. Fully 90% of society and 90% of this court believe that these men should be pardoned or given a token punishment. They have undoubtedly already suffered more torment and humiliation than most people would endure in a thousand years. Should we now affirm their death sentences?

Consider which of those issues is best from the prosecutor's point of view, and which one from the defense lawyer's point of view. It's a matter of gauging which question most judges would want to answer—at least, assuming the judges are at all inclined to your view of the case. In my view, the best issues are clear-cut. For the prosecution, Keen's issue is best because it doesn't muddy the waters the way Truepenny's does by dragging judicial sympathies into the issue statement. For the defense, Foster's second issue is best because it's a true legal argument based on an eminently plausible interpretation of a statute.

Let's return, though, to Gee's point: "Try to state the principal question in the first sentence." In fact, his own usual practice was to state it in the first *paragraph*, and the advice would be sounder if we replaced *sentence* with *paragraph*. Still, the insight was a great one, and it provides a reliable standard by which to evaluate judicial openers.

Roughly speaking, there are a dozen types of judicial openers, which you can place on a continuum:

No Hint of Issue	**Surface Issue**	**Deep Issue**
Types 1–6		Types 7–12

The least satisfactory opener for a judicial opinion has nothing to do—from all that appears—with the question that the court is to answer. The most satisfactory, on the other end of the spectrum, puts the issue neatly up front.

Of the dozen types—ranging from worst to best—the first six fall on the left side of the continuum, and the last six fall on the right. Here they are:

Categories 1 Through 6: Unsatisfactory Judicial Openers

1. The first type of opener—very common—states how the case got to the court when that's not a determinative point. In this type, the writer just perfunctorily announces why the court has heard the case—e.g., "This is an appeal by the State under Neb. Rev. Stat. § 29-2320 (Reissue 1989)."[9] The problem is that most readers are initially uninterested in how the case got there. They want to know about the core conflict.

---

[9] *State v. Foral*, 462 N.W.2d 626, 627 (Neb. 1990).

How helpful as an opener is the following laborious treatment of procedure? Why are we being told any of this?

> This is the second appeal to this court relating to the resolution of the question of whether the plaintiff or the defendants held title to the property located at 8 Orange Street in New Haven, prior to the taking of the property by the city of New Haven by eminent domain in 1989. See *Papagorgiou v. Anastopoulous*, 23 Conn. App. 522, 582 A.2d 1181 (1990). There are two other actions involving this property presently pending in the courts. The first, which was argued with this appeal; *New Haven v. Konstandinidis*, 29 Conn. App. 139, 612 A.2d 822 (1992); is an appeal to this court from the granting of a summary process judgment of possession in favor of the city of New Haven against Angelika Papagorgiou, the plaintiff in this action. The other action, which has been stayed in the trial court pending disposition of this appeal, involves a challenge by the defendants in this action to the statement of compensation filed by the city of New Haven on August 11, 1989, in the condemnation proceeding. The plaintiff here, Angelika Papagorgiou, was permitted to intervene in the condemnation action because of her claim that she possessed equitable title to the property on the date of the condemnation.[10]

Even stripped of tedious detail, an opener in this category doesn't inspire confidence in the writer's logic:

> This case comes to us on an expedited appeal filed by the government from an order granting a motion to suppress tangible evidence. We reverse.[11]

If all the information in the first of those examples is really necessary, it ought to appear *after* the facts—and well after the issue. As for the second, are we to conclude that this court invariably reverses expedited appeals filed by the government? In fact, if the second example is read literally, it contains a rather bad miscue.

And where does this non sequitur come from? It seems to result inevitably from the well-meaning view that the court's ultimate disposition should appear in the opening paragraph. Of course, it probably should, but only if it somehow follows from whatever has already been stated. If it doesn't relate to the

---

[10] *Papagorgiou v. Anastopoulous*, 613 A.2d 853, 854 (Conn. App. 1992).
[11] *United States v. Harris*, 617 A.2d 189, 190 (D.C. 1992).

preceding statements, then placing it at the outset suggests a grotesque lapse in logic.

2. The second type of opener hardly moves any closer to the issue. It states the subject matter of the case—and gives a resolution—but doesn't disclose the issue. This opener typifies opinions that never get around to clarifying the deep issues in the case. The court merely begins with either a procedural recitation or a general statement about what type of case it is. For example, the court might say, in substance, "This is a tort case. We reverse and remand." Whether the court ever really reaches the deep issues in the case seems often a matter of chance. Some typical examples:

- This appeal from summary judgment challenges the district court's interpretation of a contract provision to require reimbursement of legal expenses incurred in litigation against a subrogated insurer. We affirm in part and reverse in part.[12]

- Otha "Buddy" Chandler, Jr. appeals his conviction on one count of causing a false entry to be made in a book, report or statement of a savings and loan association, a violation of 18 U.S.C. § 1006 (1988). We affirm.[13]

- We have for review *Murray v. State* [citation], based on conflict with *State v. Rucker* [citation]. We have jurisdiction. Art. V, § 3(b)(3), Fla. Const. We quash the district court decision in *Murray*.[14]

- Defendant Grand Properties, Ltd. appeals the judgment of the trial court awarding the sum of $18,675.81 to plaintiff Latter & Blum, Inc. We affirm.[15]

This type of opener accounts for a significant percentage of American opinions.

3. A third type of opener—still on the left side of the continuum—states some facts but omits the issue and the resolution. Sometimes facts can be interesting: the authors of the following narratives at least tried to create reader interest. The first begins with startling facts but fizzles at the end of the sentence—the position of greatest emphasis—with the word *misdemeanor*. The result is what rhetoricians call "bathos," an anticlimactic progression from something serious to something commonplace:

---

[12] *Century Indem. Co. v. Geiger-Berger Assocs., P.C.*, 1993 WL 35930, at *1 (Minn. App. 16 Feb. 1993).

[13] *United States v. Chandler*, 910 F.2d 521, 521 (8th Cir. 1990).

[14] *Murray v. State*, 616 So.2d 955, 955 (Fla. 1993).

[15] *Latter & Blum, Inc. v. Grand Props., Ltd.*, 617 So.2d 80, 81 (La. App. 1993, writ denied).

James Sumpter shot and killed his wife, Lois Sumpter, with a handgun. He was convicted by a jury of felony murder and of pointing a pistol at another, and was sentenced to life imprisonment and for a misdemeanor.[16]

The next example begins vividly—almost as if the author had attended a judicial-writing seminar and learned the wrong lessons. Note how the ending of the distress call is equated with the ending of three human lives—a rhetorical flourish whose effect seems callous at best:

"We're going over, now!" Thus ended a brief distress call on the night of February 1, 1982 from the master of the fishing vessel CHICA to the Coast Guard, and shortly thereafter, his life and that of his two crewmen.[17]

But even an opener that states interesting facts fails its job if it doesn't also focus the reader on the legal issue and how it will be resolved.

And then, of course, some openers in this category do nothing at all to interest the reader. They state facts, yes, but hardly interesting ones:

In 1975 Golden Sun Feeds, Inc. (GSF) entered into an agreement with the Chicago, Rock Island and Pacific Railroad (the predecessor of Chicago and North Western Transportation Company—CNW) to have a switch and spur track constructed to service its facility in Estherville, Iowa. GSF spent over $150,000 on this project. After 1981 GSF received a declining number of carloads over the track. In 1984, 1985, and 1986 it received no rail shipments and, in 1987, GSF received ten rail cars in order to test the cost as compared to truck shipments.[18]

4. The fourth category moves only a mite down the continuum: it states some abstract facts and the resolution of the case, but it neglects to state the issue. Often, as the following example illustrates, merely stating the facts will not lead directly to an issue:

The appellant, Lavon Guthrie, was convicted after a jury trial of the capital offense of murder committed during a robbery in the first degree, in violation of § 13A–5–40(a)(2), Code of Alabama 1975. At the sentencing phase of the trial, the jury voted unanimously to recommend that the appellant be sentenced to

---

[16] *Sumpter v. State*, 398 S.E.2d 12, 13 (Ga. 1990).

[17] *Brophy v. Lavigne*, 801 F.2d 521, 522 (1st Cir. 1986).

[18] *Chicago & N.W. Transp. Co. v. Golden Sun Feeds, Inc.*, 462 N.W.2d 689, 690 (Iowa App. 1990).

death. At the trial court's sentencing hearing held pursuant to
§ 13A–5–47, the trial court sentenced the appellant to death by
electrocution.

This case must be remanded to the circuit court for that
court to determine whether the state exercised its peremptory
challenges in a racially discriminatory manner in violation of
Batson v. Kentucky [citation] and *Ex parte Branch* [citation].
Although the appellant neither raised this issue in the trial court
nor argued it on appeal, the plain error doctrine requires our
review of this issue.[19]

Take another example:

In a civil-forfeiture action, the registered owner of a vehicle used
in the commission of a felony appeals the trial court's determination that the vehicle was owned by his stepson. We affirm.[20]

The surface issue there is ownership. The deep issue is whether
sufficient evidence overrode the legal presumption that the registered owner of a car is the true owner. The reason for the
holding was that the stepson took possession immediately upon
the stepfather's purchase; the stepson always used the car, the rest
of the family rarely; the stepson "souped up" the car in various
ways; and the stepfather made a nonverbal admission by nodding
his head when his wife said that the car had been a graduation
present to the stepson.

The court could have reached the deep issue more concisely
by opening the opinion in this way:

In this civil-forfeiture action, the registered owner of a seized
car—one involved in drug transactions—contests the trial court's
determination that his stepson owned the car. Because abundant evidence, including the stepfather's own admission to the
police, overrides the legal presumption that the registered owner
is the true owner and establishes that the stepson was the true
owner, we affirm.

The advantage of this rewrite—into a "deep issue" form—is
that, as the details are filled in later, the reader will assimilate
them through the filter that the opener provides.

5. The next type—the fifth category—brings a glimmer of an issue.
   Here, the judicial writer states what the issue "involves" without
   saying what it is. In this category belong some of the most frus-

---

[19] *Guthrie v. State*, 616 So.2d 913, 913 (Ala. Crim. App. 1992).
[20] Unpublished opinion of a state intermediate court.

trating openers that legal readers encounter. Upon seeing words such as "The issue here . . . ," the reader inevitably perks up. But with the word *involves*, the sentence typically crumbles:

- The issue here involves the rule requiring corroboration of the confession of an accused by some independent evidence of the *corpus delicti*. We return to this well plowed ground because of the contentions of the petitioner, Robert Leslie Ballard, Jr. (Ballard), who stands convicted, *inter alia*, of felony murder in an attempted robbery. Ballard contends that corroboration of the *corpus delicti* in this case requires independent proof of the attempted robbery. As explained below, this contention greatly overstates the corroboration requirement.[21]

- This case involves the transfer of assets by George Dumas to an *inter vivos* trust and a suit by his wife, appellee, alleging that the transfer of those assets constituted a fraudulent transfer and that her late husband intended to defraud her by depriving her of her elective share of his probate estate.[22]

In framing issues, the word *involves* ought to be a no-no.

6. The sixth and final unsatisfactory opener brings us to the brink of an issue. Yet because this opener states what amounts to a surface issue, the reader can't really hope to understand it until after reading much more. The question is on the order of, "Has the plaintiff stated a claim?" You're only a little wiser after reading it.

- This is an appeal from the forfeiture of two bail bonds to appellee, the State of Maryland. Appellant, Fred W. Frank Bail Bondsman, Inc., on behalf of Allegheny Mutual Casualty Company and All American Bail Bonds, has appealed from an order of the Circuit Court for Wicomico County denying its Petition to Strike Forfeiture, Set Aside Judgment, and Release Bond. On appeal, we are asked:

  Whether the Circuit Court erred in denying the Petitions to Strike Forfeiture, Set Aside the Judgments Against the Bail Bondsman and the Surety, and Release the Bonds because it was impossible for the surety to fulfill its contractual obligation to produce the defendants.

  Finding no error, we shall affirm the judgment of the circuit court.[23]

---

[21] *Ballard v. State*, 636 A.2d 474, 474 (Md. 1994).

[22] *Dumas v. Estate of Dumas*, 627 N.E.2d 978, 979 (Ohio 1994).

[23] *Fred W. Frank Bail Bondsman, Inc. v. State*, 636 A.2d 484, 485 (Md. Ct. Spec. App. 1994).

- Earl Rhymer appeals the denial of his petition for post-conviction relief. He raises five issues for our review, which we consolidate into four and restate as follows:

    I. Whether Rhymer should be granted post-conviction relief based on newly-discovered evidence.
    II. Whether the post-conviction court denied Rhymer due process and a fair hearing.
    III. Whether the post-conviction court failed to issue sufficient findings of fact and conclusions of law.
    IV. Whether Rhymer was denied the effective assistance of trial and appellate counsel.

We reverse and remand.[24]

Although the writer wisely focuses on the issue, the opener fails: far too much is being postponed. The issue statement is unedifying.

Categories 7 Through 12: Satisfactory Judicial Openers

7. The seventh type comes much closer to the deep issue: the writer gives everything but one dispositive fact. This category approaches the ideal because the reader now knows what to look for—something the writer hasn't yet been explicit about. The writer could make the reader's job easier by supplying whatever that something is. In the following examples, what's the one missing ingredient that would transform the introductory passage into a deep issue?

    - William Fraser appeals from an order dismissing his amended complaint under Super. Ct. Civ. R. 12(b)(6) for failure to state a claim upon which relief could be granted. Fraser had sued appellees Gottfried and Bush for an accounting, money damages, and other relief based on appellees' supposed breach of a partnership agreement, but the trial court ruled that the complaint failed to allege the existence of a partnership. We disagree and, accordingly, reverse and remand for further proceedings.[25]

    - Donald Smith appeals from a Workers' Compensation Board decision denying Smith's petition to commute his future benefits into a lump-sum settlement. 39 M.R.S.A. § 71–A (1989). Smith contends that there is no rational basis for the hearing officer's decision that a lump-sum settlement would not be in Smith's best interest. Because we conclude that the hearing officer had a rational basis for his decision, we affirm the decision and decline

---

[24] *Rhymer v. State*, 627 N.E.2d 822, 823 (Ind. App. 1994).
[25] *Fraser v. Gottfried*, 636 A.2d 430, 430 (D.C. 1994).

to reach the issues raised by Great Northern Paper Co. and the amicus parties.[26]

In the first of those openers, we need to know—succinctly—what the complaint alleged. In the second, we need to know just what the rational basis is. With those facts supplied, both could easily be transformed into deep issues.

8. The eighth category—already in the upper reaches of American judicial writing—provides a strong narrative setup with something approaching a deep issue. Like a brief, a judicial opinion shouldn't begin with a "statement of facts" or "factual background" section—though many opinions do just that. Instead, the opinion should set the stage for factual exposition—usually by providing a deep issue. The following examples come close to succeeding because they blend analytical language into the facts being supplied:

- Although the substantive issues raised by this appeal are fairly significant, they are not nearly as significant as the procedural quagmire that we find before us. What began as a developer's test of a newly enacted Anne Arundel County tax ordinance has brought to light an apparent anomaly in the statutory scheme that provides administrative review by both the Anne Arundel County Board of Appeals (the Board) and the Maryland Tax Court of the imposition of certain local taxes.[27]

- Arrested for feeding the pigeons and walking her dogs in the park, Anita Kirchoff recovered $25,000 from the police. The defendants gave up, but Kirchoff's lawyers did not. They wanted some $50,000 in fees under 42 U.S.C. § 1988. The district court gave them $10,000 on the ground that their contingent fee contract with the Kirchoffs entitled them to 40% of any award. The case requires us to decide whether the contingent fee is the appropriate rate under § 1988 when the case resembles private tort litigation in which contingent fees are customary. First, however, we pause for the facts.[28]

The second example states both the essential facts and the issue with elegant economy, and neatly ushers us into a narrative of what happened to cause the lawsuit. Still, we're left to wonder how the issue will be be resolved—and that may leave us feeling

---

[26] *Smith v. Great N. Paper, Inc.*, 636 A.2d 438, 439 (Me. 1994).
[27] *Crofton Partners v. Anne Arundel County*, 636 A.2d 487, 488 (Md. Ct. Spec. App. 1994).
[28] *Kirchoff v. Flynn*, 786 F.2d 320, 320 (7th Cir. 1986).

unfocused. Then again, this example may generate enough interest that the reader will be naturally inclined to read further.

9. In the ninth category, the writer frames the deep issue—ele-
gantly or inelegantly—but postpones the answer. Though most
modern judges consider it desirable to state the court's resolution up front, along with the reasoning in a nutshell, there are
exceptions. If the issue is cleanly stated and sufficiently intrigu-
ing, it might just as well stand alone in the opener, as in the
examples following. Such openers can cue us quite effectively, as
these four examples illustrate:

- This case presents the question whether certain statutes and regulations of the State of Mississippi violate our constitutional guar-
antee of freedom of speech because they effectively ban liquor
advertising on billboards and in printed and electronic media
within the state.[29]

- We have for review *Metropolitan Dade County v. Metro-Dade Fire
Rescue Service District*, 589 So.2d 920 (Fla. 3d DCA 1991), in
which the Third District Court of Appeal certified to this Court
the questions resolved by its opinion as ones of great public
importance. *Id.* 589 So.2d at 924 n.6. The district court did not
articulate a question; however, we have constructed the following question for resolution:

    Does the Dade County Commission have legislative author-
    ity over the Metro-Dade Fire and Rescue Service District
    to determine what specific governing powers the district's
    governing body may exercise when the voters of Dade
    County have passed an amendment to the county charter
    which specifically states that the County Commission shall
    not be the governing body of the district?[30]

- The issue in this case is whether a court may render a judgment
partially maintaining an exception of no cause of action when
the judgment adjudicates one or more, but less than all, of the
demands or causes of action asserted against the excepting party.
A related issue is whether the party opposing the exception
must appeal from the judgment partially maintaining the excep-

---

[29] *Lamar Outdoor Advert., Inc. v. Mississippi St. Tax Commn.*, 701 F.2d 314, 316 (5th Cir.
1983) (*per* Gee, J.) (postponing until the last page the holding that, indeed, advertisers'
constitutional rights had been violated).

[30] *Metro-Dade Fire Rescue Serv. Dist. v. Metropolitan Dade County*, 616 So.2d 966, 967
(Fla. 1993) (question put into lowercase).

tion in order to prevent the judgment from acquiring the authority of the thing adjudged. These issues implicate the concepts of
cumulations of actions and joinder of parties, partial final judgments, and appealability of partial final judgments.[31]

- The Federal Bureau of Investigation (FBI) has accumulated and
  maintains criminal identification records, sometimes referred to
  as "rap sheets," on over 24 million persons. The question presented
  by this case is whether the disclosure of the contents of such a
  file to a third party "could reasonably be expected to constitute
  an unwarranted invasion of personal privacy" within the meaning of the Freedom of Information Act (FOIA), 5 U.S.C.
  § 552(b)(7)(C) (1982 ed., Supp. V).[32]

Even so, a stall is a stall, and readers may impatiently flip to the
last paragraph to appease their wakened curiosity.

10. The tenth category—drawing ever closer to the fully deep
    issue—has all the basic ingredients, but abstract facts. Some judi-
    cial writers manage to state the key facts, the legal question pre-
    sented, and the conclusion, all with admirable succinctness. Con-
    sider the following example, from a United States Supreme Court
    opinion:

> An undercover government agent was placed in the cell of
> respondent Perkins, who was incarcerated on charges unrelated
> to the subject of the agent's investigation. Respondent made
> statements that implicated him in the crime that the agent
> sought to solve. Respondent claims that the statements should
> be inadmissible because he had not been given *Miranda* warn-
> ings by the agent. We hold that the statements are admissible.
> *Miranda* warnings are not required when the suspect is unaware
> that he is speaking to a law enforcement officer and gives a
> voluntary statement.[33]

The problem there is excessive abstractness. Such a recital feels
devoid of human interest.

Occasionally, however, the issue may be so riveting that the
concrete facts can wait for further development:

> Today we are asked to decide whether an elected judge may
> constitutionally be reprimanded for making truthful public

---

[31] *Everything on Wheels Subaru, Inc. v. Subaru South, Inc.*, 616 So.2d 1234, 1235 (La. 1993).
[32] *United States Dept. of Justice v. Reporters' Commn. for Freedom of Press*, 489 U.S. 749, 751
(1989).
[33] *Illinois v. Perkins*, 496 U.S. 292, 294 (1990).

statements critical of the administration of the county judicial
system of which he is a part. Concluding (1) that such statements address matters of legitimate public concern and (2) that
the state's interest in promoting the efficiency and impartiality
of its courts does not, under the circumstances of this case, out-
weigh the plaintiff's countervailing first amendment right to air
his views, we reverse the judgment of the district court and
remand for further proceedings.[34]

11. The eleventh category is a special one: the perfect way to handle
a messy appeal, where the best you can do is describe the issues
and their resolution. In the example below, Judge Gee fully orients
us to the concrete facts, the issue, the reasoning, and the conclusion—no small feat in a complicated case:

> Appellant Jeetendra Bhandari sued appellee First National Bank
> of Commerce after First National declined to issue him a credit
> card. First National refused Bhandari credit in part because he
> was not a citizen of the United States. The district court held
> that neither 42 U.S.C. § 1981 nor the Equal Credit Opportu-
> nity Act ("ECOA") gave Bhandari a legal remedy for private
> alienage discrimination. The court determined, however, that
> First National had violated the ECOA by not telling Bhandari
> all its reasons for denying him credit. The court awarded dam-
> ages, costs, and attorneys' fees. Bhandari appeals, contending
> that the district court erred in various respects. We hold that
> the law of this Circuit recognizes actions for private alienage
> discrimination under § 1981, but that alienage discrimination is
> not actionable under the ECOA. Accordingly, we affirm in
> part, reverse in part, and remand.[35]

To avoid getting bogged down in Bhandari's various claims, Gee
used general language at a crucial point in the paragraph: "Bhandari appeals, contending that the district court erred *in various
respects.*" In many judges' hands, that three-word phrase (*in various respects*) would be expanded into three paragraphs or even
three pages of exposition, all before the holding is announced.
But Gee understood the need for *swiftly* identifying the type of
case and the issue. Then, of course, the opener proceeds with the
bifurcated holding.

---

[34] *Scott v. Flowers*, 910 F.2d 201, 201 (5th Cir. 1990).
[35] *Bhandari v. First Natl. Bank of Commerce*, 808 F.2d 1082, 1084, *superseded*, 829 F.2d
1343 (5th Cir. 1987), *vacated*, 492 U.S. 901 (1989).

Here's another example in this category:

> This is an appeal from a jury verdict in favor of Dudley M. Maples in the Lauderdale County Special Court of Eminent Domain. The State Highway Commission ("the Commission") sought to condemn a portion of Maples' property for purposes of a highway expansion project, offering Maples fair market value for the affected tract. Maples filed a Statement of Values which included not only a claim for the fair market value of the land taken, but also for damages to the remainder resulting from diminished access. The jury awarded Maples more than the Commission proposed to pay, but substantially less than Maples demanded. Maples appeals, assigning eight errors, arguing generally that he did not receive a fair trial, that the jury award was insufficient, that Lauderdale County should not have been a named defendant, and that the court erred in not allowing him to recover expenses and attorney's fees for the defense of the suit. Finding no reversible error, we affirm.[36]

If the court tried to capsulize its reasons on each of the eight alleged errors—or on each of the four main thrusts—the opener might have been extended intolerably.

12. Now to category number twelve. Below are three openers that have all the essentials: concrete facts, a deep issue, and a clear resolution. Moreover, their wording is artful—both concise and precise. In short, they do exactly what an introduction should do: they capture our attention and leave us feeling well oriented for the discussion to come. And what follows each opener should be an elegant opinion:

- While investigating some serial murders near Kansas City, Hough, a federal undercover agent, posed as a prisoner confined in the same cell as the primary suspect in the murders, Perkins, who had been jailed on unrelated charges. On Hough's second day as Perkins's cellmate, Perkins confided that he knew where two of the bodies were buried. He now claims that his incriminating statements should be held inadmissible because he had received no *Miranda* warnings. But we disagree because the warnings are not required when a suspect, though unaware that his conversation is with a law-enforcement officer, engages in the conversation voluntarily.[37]

---

[36] *Maples v. Mississippi St. Hwy. Commn.*, 617 So.2d 265, 266 (Miss. 1993).
[37] Revision of the first example under category #10—with hypothetical concreteness supplied.

- Appellant, Frederick Ward Associates, Inc., appeals from a declaratory judgment entered in the Circuit Court for Cecil County (Cole, J.) in favor of appellees, Venture, Inc., and Charles Cupeto. The court ruled that appellant's judgment against a "Chris Walker" did not constitute a lien against land deeded to a "John C. Walker" and subsequently transferred to appellees. Appellant asks:

  > Did the court err in ruling that the judgment entered against "Chris Walker" does not constitute a lien against land owned by him, but titled in the name of "John C. Walker"?

  We answer this question in the negative and, therefore, affirm.[38]

- Congress enacted the Clean Water Act "to restore and maintain the chemical, physical, and biological integrity of the Nation's waters." 33 U.S.C. § 1251 (1988). As one means of improving water quality, Congress ordered the Environmental Protection Agency (EPA) to design pretreatment standards for industrial water discharges into publicly owned treatment works. 33 U.S.C. § 1317(b). Under the Act, someone who knowingly violates these standards and knows that he or she thereby places another person in imminent danger of death or serious injury commits a felony. 33 U.S.C. § 1319(c)(3) (1988 & Supp. II 1990). Does this criminal sanction apply when the imminent danger is not to people at the publicly owned treatment works, municipal sewers or other downcharge, but rather to employees handling the pollutants on the premises from which the illegal discharge originates? We hold that it does not.[39]

Imagine how much shorter judicial opinions might be if the deep issue were to become standard. But, of course, without better briefing, courts would find it difficult to frame deep issues consistently. Still, it can be done, as Judge Gee and various others have demonstrated.

The Vocabulary of Judicial Issues

Many examples quoted above contain phrases that every appellate judge ought to keep handy:

This case presents the question whether . . . .

The case requires us to decide whether . . . .

Today, we must decide whether . . . .

We are confronted with the question whether . . . .

---

[38] *Frederick Ward Assocs., Inc. v. Venture, Inc.*, 636 A.2d 496, 496 (Md. Ct. Spec. App. 1994).

[39] *United States v. Borowski*, 977 F.2d 27, 27 (1st Cir. 1992).

Because these phrases usually signal a deep issue, they are worth adding to the stock judicial vocabulary. If the writer can't fill in the blank, then more thought is required before the writing can begin. Concededly, though, given the state of American brief-writing, the blanks will often be devilishly hard to fill in.

For maximal clarity and rhetorical impact, the word *because* should figure prominently in most opening paragraphs. A good formula is *Because . . . , we hold that . . . .* If the *because*-clause is long, the judge could reverse the clauses: "We hold that . . . for two reasons. First, ... Second, ..."

The difference between openers that use that formula and those that don't is palpable. Consider how these two openers, by the same judge, affect you as a reader. The first gives only a conclusion, while the second couples a reason with the conclusion:

- The petitioner–appellant in this case, Martha's Vineyard Scuba Headquarters, Inc. (Mavis), took not a particle of comfort when an order was entered in a federal district court awarding title to various artifacts received from a sunken ship to a rival, Marshallton, Inc. (Marshallton). Mavis appeals. We affirm.[40]

- A disappointed faculty member, Harriet Spiegel, sued the trustees of Tufts College in the United States District Court for the District of Massachusetts following rejection of her tenure application. The district court dismissed most—but not all—of her statements of claim without requiring defendants to answer, and thereafter authorized a partial judgment in Tufts' favor . . . . Because we conclude that the judgment was prematurely entered, we dismiss the appeal.[41]

Readers' Reactions to Deep Issues

The purpose of using separate sentences and of limiting the issue to 75 words is to help the reader. A one-sentence issue of 75 or so words is difficult to follow, especially when the interrogative word begins the sentence and the end is merely a succession of *when*-clauses—e.g.:

Can Barndt Insurance deny insurance coverage on grounds of late notice when Fiver's insurance policy required Fiver to give Barndt notice of a claim "immediately," and when in May 1994, one of Fiver's offices was damaged by smoke from a fire in another tenant's space, and when 10 months later, Fiver gave notice, and when Barndt

---

[40] *Martha's Vineyard Scuba H.Q., Inc. v. Unidentified, Wrecked & Abandoned Steam Vessel,* 833 F.2d 1059, 1061 (1st Cir. 1987).
[41] *Spiegel v. Trustees of Tufts College,* 843 F.2d 38, 40–41 (1st Cir. 1988).

investigated the claim for 6 months before denying coverage and did
not raise a late-notice defense until 18 months after the claim was filed?
[81 words]

That's a muddle. Readers forget the question by the time they reach the
question mark. Part of the reason is that the time is out of joint: we begin
with a present question, then back up to what happened, and then, with
the question mark, jump back to the present.

The better strategy is to follow a chronological order, telling a story
in miniature. Then, the pointed question—which emerges inevitably
from the story—comes at the end:

> Fiver's insurance policy required it to give Barndt Insurance notice of
> a claim "immediately." In May 1994, one of Fiver's offices was damaged
> by smoke from a fire in another tenant's space. Ten months later, Fiver
> gave notice. Barndt investigated the claim for 6 months before denying
> coverage and did not raise a late-notice claim until 18 months after the
> claim was filed. Can Barndt now deny coverage because of late notice?
> [73 words]

Instead of one 81-word-long sentence, we have five sentences averaging
just 15 words each. And the information is presented in a way that we
can easily understand.

Because seasoned legal readers are always impatient to reach the
issue, opening a memo, brief, or judicial opinion with the deep issue sat-
isfies a universal need.

But is the 75-word limit a fair one? Where does it come from? It is
the result of my own experimentation and informal testing. Once you
let an issue go beyond that length, you're likely to be rambling. You lose
the rigor of a concentrated statement. And you probably lose readers,
too.

The Importance of It All

At first glance, these principles of issue-framing may seem elementary.
Yet, judging from most legal writing, they are not at all obvious. And in
any event, stylists who cultivate the ability to frame good issues know
just how difficult it is: it requires a great deal of mental energy.

It is therefore tempting to forgo the effort, and many writers do.
Legal writers everywhere seem preoccupied with answers but rarely
with the questions they are answering or the premises from which their
conclusions might follow. As a result, much of the "analysis" and advocacy that goes on is sloppy—or worse.

Even the greatest legal intellects must remain vigilant about these points. One of the most important 20th-century legal philosophers warned about how easy it is to stumble over fundamentals. H.L.A. Hart was writing about theories of punishment, but his point holds true in any field: "One principal source of trouble is obvious: it is always necessary to bear in mind, and fatally easy to forget, the number of different questions [that various theories] seek to answer."[42] Even the great philosophers, then, can benefit from giving more thought to their issues.

Charting a Course

Since 1991, teaching the importance of framing deep issues has been the cornerstone of my CLE seminars. The ideas underlying the deep issue have been tested now on thousands of lawyers throughout the United States, many of whom have helped refine these ideas. And the lawyers I deal with week by week confirm what I have long thought: the deep issue is central both to good writing and to good thinking.

Yet the idea is still considered novel: one-sentence surface issues still pervade law-school writing texts, appellate-practice texts, and collections of model briefs. In fact, Illinois appellate rules contain "model" issues that have all the classically bad qualities.[43]

But perhaps things are changing. Many advocates now use deep issues, and they report good results. Perhaps the law-school text-writers will adapt their recommended forms so that law graduates won't have to unlearn so many bad habits.

Undoubtedly the most important reform, though, must occur in court rules. If courts began to mandate deep issues, they would find it easier to handle their caseloads. Many weak cases would die because the exercise of writing a deep issue would reveal their weaknesses more palpably than anything else. Strong cases would prevail more easily because their strengths would be made plainer than they typically are today.

Perhaps the profession would gradually regain a skill that it has lost. What is that skill? Well, it is multifaceted and difficult to describe without lapsing into clichés such as these:

- Home in on the problem.
- Separate the wheat from the chaff.

---

[42] H.L.A. Hart, "Postscript: Responsibility and Retribution," in *Punishment and Responsibility: Essays in the Philosophy of Law* 210, 231 (1968).

[43] *See* Ill. Sup. Ct. R. 341(e)(3).

- See the forest, not just the trees.
- Cut to the chase.
- Go to the heart of the matter.
- Convey the big picture.
- Aim at the bull's eye.
- Zero in.

But the very fact that we have so many clichés referring to aspects of this skill demonstrates how highly we all value it, at least as readers.

If readers yearn to understand the problem and resent having to sweat unnecessarily to understand it, then most legal writers engender resentment every day. They could instead build credibility. And as far as I know, the deep issue is the best model for doing that consistently.

ஊ ஊ ஊ

The Language of Appellate Advocacy

NEVER HAS A CASE BEEN ARGUED in which some aspect of language did not play a crucial role. At a minimum, lawyers' uses of language make their arguments more or less persuasive. But lawyers and judges are often called on to muster greater linguistic sophistication: to interpret the Constitution or statutes, to construe private legal documents, or to explain the precise import of precedents. Effective litigators must be more than legal technicians; they must also be rhetoricians, semanticists, and stylists.

Skeptics should read *James v. United States*,[1] a case that called upon each of these three skills. The case arose from two separate incidents at flood-control projects used as water-sports facilities. Government employees at the facilities had, without adequate warning, opened the floodgates to drain off water while water-skiers and fishermen were nearby. Several people were haplessly sucked through the gates, and two were killed. The trial judge in one case said it went "beyond gross negligence" and "constitutes a classic classroom example of death and injuries resulting from conscious governmental indifference to the safety of the public."

The question in *James* was whether a statutory exemption from liability for "any damage from or by floods or flood waters at any place" would immunize the government from suit. The question whether "damage at any place" refers to the loss of human life implicates rhetorical concerns—why was the statute so phrased?—and semantic ones—at what level of abstraction is "damage" to be read? Making the distinction between *damage* and *damages*—which the dissenters in the Supreme Court did, but the majority failed to do—requires at least an instinctive understanding of semantics.

Alas, the Court held that Congress, by using the phrase "damage at any place," intended to immunize the government even from gross negligence—or worse—that results in human death. Congress, it seems, intended to lump loss of life, among other things, into the phrase "damage at any place." Whether members of Congress resented this imputation of callousness one can only guess.

Before turning to semantics and style, let us consider rhetoric. Many lawyers may resist thinking of themselves as rhetoricians. The word *rhetoric*

Adapted from *Litigation* (Summer 1989).
[1] 478 U.S. 597 (1986).

calls up negative images of word-mongering and verbal distortion, as in Benjamin Disraeli's reference to William Gladstone as a "sophistical rhetorician, inebriated with the exuberance of his own verbosity." But I refer to rhetoric in the older sense: "the art of adapting discourse, in harmony with its subject and occasion, to the requirements of a reader or hearer."[2] In deciding what the issues will be, for example, and in stating those issues for the court, an appellate advocate employs just such rhetorical skills. This is the type of rhetoric that helps win an appeal; the other type—that attributed to Gladstone—will doom one to failure.

Though every case is unique, certain rhetorical approaches determine success or failure for the advocate. The rhetorician knows, for example, not to argue that the court's failure to overturn the ruling below will result in a grave injustice. Every appellant believes that, and generic arguments carry no power. Better to show why and how injustice will result, without ever resorting to the abstract statement.

The most important analytical step in the appellate process—in fact in most aspects of litigation—is framing the issues. "First settle what your case is before you argue it," wrote Lord Chief Justice Robert Wright.[3] Many rhetorical considerations enter this process. It is usually unwise, for example, to heap a dozen or more issues into your brief, hoping that the court will find an appealing one. This all too common method relegates the lawyer to little better than an issue-spotter, and burdens the court deciding the issue. The seasoned, confident lawyer argues with sophistication. He or she does not pray that the 50th point of error will be that final straw that breaks the back of the lower court's judgment. "One has to strike for the jugular," wrote Oliver Wendell Holmes, "and let the rest go."[4] (Criminal cases, of course, are different: a lawyer is more obliged to raise every issue that might arguably be meritorious.)

Second, use the alembic of your mind to distill the essence of the issues. Formulate your thoughts so you express them crisply. If your arguments are shrouded in nebulous terminology, the court will very likely suspect that they are either ill-formed or wrong. As Sir Frederick Pollock observed, "A doctrine capable of being stated only in obscure or involved terms is open to reasonable suspicion of being either crude or erroneous."[5]

Even substantive issues implicate rhetoric. You must thoroughly analyze what you want the court to do. Many lawyers become confused by questions from the court about whether, for example, simple reversal is

---

[2] J.F. Genung, *The Working Principles of Rhetoric* 1 (1901).
[3] *Trial of the Seven Bishops*, 12 Howell's State Trials 193, 342 (1688).
[4] Oliver Wendell Holmes, *Speeches* 77 (1913).
[5] *Holmes–Pollock Letters* vol. 2, 38 (1941).

possible without a remand to determine a remaining issue. You cannot mold your message to an appellate audience without knowing all its dimensions, including such basics as the applicable standard of review and the relevant caselaw.

The tone of advocacy is another important element of rhetoric. More and more lawyers take the most combative tone possible, thereby giving new meaning to the antique legal phrase *brutum fulmen*. Every position of an opponent is "utterly fallacious," "a logical absurdity," "completely without support in law or in fact," or the like. Advocates who adopt this approach seem to want every case to be a knockout; they launch roundhouse punches in every argument. Judges are quickly wearied by such rhetoric. The world is more complicated than the proponents of such arguments suggest. Most cases have some merit on both sides; not every opposing argument need be ground down to absurdity. Judges faced by a bellicose advocate are more likely to suspect something amiss in that side's case than to believe that the advocate is rightly (much less righteously) indignant. Heed Laurence Sterne's observation in *Tristram Shandy*: "Heat is in proportion to the want of knowledge."[6]

One final point about rhetoric: What I have been describing is a part of a larger trend toward overstatement. Overstating the facts or the law damages your credibility as an officer of the court; if you fudge here or there, you are bound to be found out. Conscientiously avoid overstatements of any kind, lest you undermine not only your immediate client's cause, but also your own credibility and therefore the chances for future clients.

The lawyer as semanticist has a different orientation from the rhetorician. Rather than seeking to persuade, the semanticist seeks primarily to understand and remain clearheaded. This linguistic sensitivity helps the lawyer avoid arguing at length about words without knowing that verbal confusion is the basis of the dispute. The phenomenon is common. Though any practitioner might confirm Lord Mansfield's observation that "most of the disputes in the world arise from words,"[7] many seem unable to get behind the words in seeking solutions.

Words can be slippery, and the semanticist knows it. Wesley Newcomb Hohfeld used a semantic approach in showing that *property* in one sentence could refer to the rights in a thing, and then in the next sentence to the thing itself. And Holmes, a consummate judicial semanticist, observed: "The law talks about rights, and duties, and malice, and intent, and negligence, and so forth, and nothing is easier, or, I may say, more

---

[6] Vol. 1, 53 (1761).
[7] *Morgan v. Jones* [1773] Lofft 160, 176; 98 All E.R. 587, 596.

common in legal reasoning, than to take these words in their moral sense, at some stage of the argument, and so to drop into fallacy."[8]

Semantic shifts of this kind plague the law. If you can sort them out in a given case, you do your client and the court a great service. You might, for example, need to show a court the two quite different meanings of *conclusive evidence*, where application of the term will win or lose the case. The adept lawyer–semanticist knows that the phrase may mean: (1) evidence so strong as to overbear any evidence to the contrary, or (2) evidence that, though not irrebuttable, so preponderates as to oblige a fact-finder to come to a certain conclusion.[9] Both senses have strong historical support, although the latter probably began as a loose usage. The difference can be significant. Yet how easy it is to argue about "conclusive evidence" without ever knowing the ambiguity of the phrase.

The semanticist may also help the court with what appear to be simple English words, such as *intent* or *malice*. When it comes to words like these, we are all likely to be lulled into thinking, "Well, everyone knows what that means!" But as one of the founders of modern semantics, I.A. Richards, warned: "The really serious misunderstandings (from the lost point to the quarrel) concern those other words we all think we do really know—the familiar, friendly, incessantly useful key words [that occur] in every third sentence. In general the more useful a word is the more dangerous it can be."[10] As a result, semantic vigilance is essential to deal skillfully and knowledgeably with the innumerable tricky words that occur in law. Particularly is it essential in the intellectual world of the appellate court.

Such vigilance is not directed just to the character of key words in one's own argument or in precedents. The appellate advocate must be equally vigilant about an opponent's use of key words and phrases. Remember: "a word's job—what it is doing at a place in a passage—is not settled simply by its dictionary sense or senses; it is settled by what the occasion and the rest of the passage hands it to do then and there."[11] Do not let your opponent use broad legal words to perform unorthodox jobs. The judges deciding the case will benefit from your semantic keenness.

The lawyer–semanticist realizes that, because words have more than one meaning and meanings change, root senses of a term ordinarily provide little insight into its current meaning. Learned Hand cautioned against making a fortress of a dictionary. It may seem odd for a lexicog-

---

[8] "The Path of the Law," in *Collected Legal Papers* 167, 171 (1952).
[9] *Black's Law Dictionary* 596 (8th ed. 2004).
[10] I.A. Richards & C. Gibson, *Learning Basic English* 88 (1945).
[11] *Id.*

rapher to reinforce the point, but dictionaries are easily abused. Etymologies, for example, are generally of no use to courts in understanding the modern senses of legal words. Although it may not hurt to observe that *perjury* is "oath-breaking," we shed little if any light by asking whether those in a conspiracy "breathed together." Yet advocates sometimes rely on such arguments.

Semantic discipline does not just steer you away from fallacy. By sensitizing you to the uses of emotive language, it enhances your ability to persuade. In spite of the truism that jury arguments make lousy oral arguments on appeal, judges are not impervious to common human feelings, even if the effects are subliminal. In tailoring the emotive vocabulary for your side of a case, think about how your description of the parties might affect a dispassionate tribunal. Take, as an example, an appeal from a jury verdict awarding damages to a widow in a wrongful-death case. If you represent the appellee, you want to call the decedent "Bobby Whitfield" and the defendant "XYZ Corporation." But if you represent the appellant, you will want the court to hear the case on a more abstract level: *appellant* and *appellee*, or *plaintiff* and *defendant*, will do nicely.

Exceptions occasionally arise, as when Archibald Cox argued the Nixon-tapes case before Judge John Sirica. When Cox referred to the possibility that the tapes would "implicate respondent," everyone in the courtroom had a vivid picture of that certain respondent. But that was an exceptional case.

There are subtler, and more important, uses of emotive language than what you call the parties. The facts of most cases can be faithfully presented in a number of ways. But your side's characterization will naturally be slanted, and you should premeditate your slant. For example, if you seek to enforce a guaranty against a savings-and-loan association whose former CEO signed the guaranty, you might make frequent (though seemingly incidental) references to honoring one's obligations, or failing to do so; and you may, depending on the facts, use charged verbs such as *renege* and *dishonor*.

If you represent the thrift, on the other hand, and you contend that the former CEO defrauded the association in signing the guaranty, your vocabulary should portray the association as a victim. You want to distance your client from the malfeasances of its former CEO.

These observations may seem self-evident. They should be, but experience suggests they are not: All the time, advocates slip into a faceless, soporific argument in which the facts come across as lifeless data. If your opponent errs in this way, you have a much greater chance of capturing the judge's imagination and sympathy with a vivid, forceful depiction of the issues.

If you doubt the effect of emotive language on appellate judges, then note how they themselves use it. When affirming a capital conviction, appellate judges ordinarily set out at length—and, increasingly often, in gory detail—the crimes committed by the defendant. Rarely, however, do you get more than a glimpse of the crime in an opinion explaining a reversal. Usually, you must turn to the dissenting opinion to learn just how heinous the offense was.

Litigators must also be stylists. One commentator has listed several advantages of a good legal style: "[I]t develops analytical thought; it creates the necessary clarity; it subordinates the parts to the whole; it gives a sense of direction by which the necessary ground may be covered; and it brings the law and the facts into relation with each other."[12] My sole quarrel with that statement is that it suggests that "style" is the cause, rather than the effect, of careful analysis, clarity, and concinnous arrangement.

Despite the truism that words are a lawyer's stock-in-trade, the skill with which lawyers wield their words does not seem to be increasing. In the judicial ranks, we encounter fewer impenetrable opinions than two generations ago, yet it is hard to point to a literary equal of Holmes, Cardozo, or Jackson among contemporary judges. These extremes aside, however, lawyers today are generally no more fastidious in their use of language than they ever have been.

Here are three reasons why lawyers should nurture an interest in—if not a romance with—the English language. First, expression is substance. "It is not," as the novelist Martin Amis has written, "that . . . you get your content and soup it up with style; style is absolutely embedded in the way you perceive."[13] Still, many lawyers seem to believe that "style" is merely the sometimes unnecessary spit and polish of writing.

Why, after all, be concerned with the distinction between *that* and *which*? Why fret over whether to call an indictment *duplicitous* or *multiplicitous* when questioning its efficacy? The answer is that these niceties affect meaning. In criminal law, *duplicitous* means one thing (charging two separate crimes in the same count), and *multiplicitous* means quite another (charging one crime in two or more counts). It simply will not do to use both words where only one fits, or to use the wrong word. Further, the legal writer must be sensitive to the lay meaning of *duplicitous*—namely "deceitful."

---

[12] Perlie P. Fallon, *The Relation Between Analysis and Style in American Legal Prose*, 28 Neb. L. Rev. 80, 92 (1948).
[13] As quoted in *Writers on Writing* 110 (Jon Winokur ed., 2d ed. 1987).

Even minuter questions, such as the placement of a comma, affect meaning. Indeed, sometimes "men's lives may depend comma."[14] Assume, however, a situation in which the placement of a comma is purely discretionary: The basic meaning would be the same with or without it. Should one give this a moment's thought? Of course! Even if the substance of the sentence remains unaffected, a discriminating reader will draw inferences and will perceive differences in tone. For example, a sensitive reader sees the difference that a comma makes here:

> He beat his dog with a steel rod.
> He beat his dog, with a steel rod.

If you read the two versions carefully, you will notice that the comma in the second sentence conveys a tone of disgust and condemnation absent in the first. One thinks of Oscar Wilde's perfectionist statement: "All morning I worked on the proof of one of my poems, and I took out a comma; in the afternoon I put it back." Lawyers do not have the leisure to consider their punctuation at such length, but we would all be better off inching closer to Wilde's approach.

Where punctuation is merely wrong, and the meaning is unaffected, the discriminating reader draws other types of inferences—usually unfavorable ones—about the writer. Any writer wants to avoid these, for they commonly extend beyond one's grammatical knowledge to one's level of education and carefulness in general. Well-crafted writing lends credibility to what is being said. It is worth repeating: We cannot divorce style from substance.

The second reason for seeking to develop an effective writing style is that lawyers must convince, not just communicate. It is said that communication is the end of language. Perhaps. But there are higher purposes as well. We might justify all manner of clumsy, flat prose if communication were the ultimate, or only, criterion. For example:

> Your honor, for the aforesaid and above-referenced reasons, plaintiff respectfully submits to this Honorable Court that, he should prevail in the motion submitted simultaneously herewith.

The sentence may communicate, but it is unlikely to persuade.

In law, we should set for ourselves a higher standard than merely communicating. One aspect of that higher linguistic standard is a heightened sensitivity to context. In a conversation at home, you have more latitude in grammar and word choice than you do in a letter to a client.

---

[14] *United States v. Palmer*, 16 U.S. 610, 636 (1818).

And you have still less latitude in a brief that you submit to an appellate court. With your family, it is usually enough to get your point across, however rough-hewn your expression. In appellate briefs, though, you want to make your point so compellingly that the judges will not just understand it, but agree with it. The context is more formal, the language more formal. Precision, clarity, and succinctness move to the fore. Like it or not, grammar and diction are professional accoutrements that you cannot neglect or abuse with impunity.

Finally, recognize that the English language is our greatest legacy. It is a legacy not just in the sense that we have inherited it from the great writers and orators of the past, to whom it links us, but also in the sense that we will pass it on to succeeding generations. The English language provides us with an unparalleled word-hoard. It is a living organism that constantly evolves because of the ways in which people use it every day. Whether or not pop grammarians are right in bewailing the "deterioration" of the language, there are, in any given context, unquestionably better and worse uses of language. Whenever we strive for the most appropriate uses of language, we do our fellow speakers of English, and certainly the legal profession as a whole, a great favor.

The task of effective legal writing is not just reveling in the glories of the English language. It can be something as mundane as proofreading. *The New York Times* once quoted me as saying that briefs in the Fifth Circuit "were on the whole rather appalling" when I clerked there.[15] Friends asked whether that was an exaggeration. I had to say it was not. Many of the briefs seemed to have been dictated but never revised, much less proofread. Apart from the lack of thorough research and analysis, the briefs too often lacked even the most superficial indication of care.

As a result, my fellow clerks and I began collecting an all-too-lengthy list of "howlers"—statements in briefs that were unintentionally humorous. It was one thing to discover an unpersuasive contention such as, "The defense objects to the characterization that the defendant is a scumbag who imported large amounts of cocaine into the country." It was quite another to see slips of the pen, or slips of the word processor, such as these:

- The ALJ failed to acknowledge the presents of the testimony of the claimant's wife.
- The expert testified that on wet grass verses dry grass the turning circle was bigger.

---

[15] Laura Mansnerus, *Lawyer Talk? You Can Look It Up*, N.Y. Times, 11 Dec. 1987, at B8.

- When he was being questioned regarding the fact the monitoring procedures regarding Title III tape recordings had no president.
- The court cut the defendant off by sustaining non-existent objections from the prosuctors.
- On discussion now turns on the most damaging evidence in the entire record that the District court failed to give any evidence to in describing the question of retaliatory discharge for engaging in the protected activity.
- Only the musician can control the content of a liver performance.

These are only a few of the typographical horrors that appeared. I had always assumed, as a law student, that an argument before a federal court of appeals would be an occasion for utter meticulousness and professionalism. Instead, many lawyers filed what seemed to be a first draft. Too often, it was the prosuctors against the scumbags; and the typographical errors usually reflected the degree of substantive concern.

In the end, care and hard work are the keys. Few of us can pretend to be a Charles Alan Wright, turning out masterly briefs only a short time before the deadline, or writing a law-review article in 45 minutes.[16] To be effective, most of us need to begin the research and writing long before the due date, and to revise the draft several times in the light of our colleagues' comments and criticisms.

The writing process varies from person to person. Some draw inspiration from long walks in the morning, others from cups of coffee late into the night. But when the writing has properly begun, one thing is certain: You have begun to think about the problem and its complications as never before.

How much better your written thoughts are when you become accustomed to examining legal issues—as well as your own prose—from different linguistic vantages. When you acquire that ability, you are considerably closer to virtuosity. And, as an advocate, to victory.

---

[16] *See* Raymond Price, *With Nixon* 248–49 (1977).

໖ ໖ ໖

Grasping Your Nettles

YESTERDAY, WHEN I WAS teaching a seminar on advocacy for the lawyers at the Federal Deposit Insurance Corporation, one participant asked, "What do you do if there's a real weakness in your case? Do you mention it in your brief or oral argument?" Another participant chimed in, "You'd never mention it, would you? You don't want to call attention to your own weaknesses!"

In fact, the wiser strategy is a little counterintuitive: whether you're before a judge or a jury, bring out your vulnerable points and show that they don't really harm your case. If, for example, you're a prosecutor whose main witness is a convicted criminal who's been given leniency in exchange for testifying, or is a paid government informant, you must bring out that fact on direct examination. Don't let the defense lawyers squawk about it on cross-examination. If your adversary is the one who mentions your weaknesses, you don't get to control the presentation, or the "spin" that's put on the point, when the jury first hears about it.

But if you've already made the disclosure in your direct examination, then the jury is more likely to conclude that this isn't much of a weakness at all. You've inoculated your case against serious infection.

This strategy of putting forward your biggest weakness and dealing with it forthrightly, before the adversary can harp on it, has traditionally been called "grasping your nettles firmly." Like so many picturesque phrases in the language, it seems to come from Shakespeare: "Out of this nettle, danger, we pluck this flower, safety." So wrote the Bard in *Henry IV, Part 1*, alluding to the all-too-human tendency to ignore known problems in the vain hope that they won't get any worse. To grasp your nettles firmly is to act boldly in performing an unpleasant task.

Stinging nettle, by the way, is a mint-like perennial weed whose serrated leaves bear hollow hairs containing irritating chemicals. In the Middle Ages, people were occasionally flogged with nettles as punishment. The hairs break easily when brushed against, and you feel as if you've been stung by a bee. But it's the brushing that causes the sting—a firmer, bolder grasp of the weed's stem is less likely to result in a sting.

So the legal metaphor is particularly apt: if you take hold of the weaknesses in your case and handle them appropriately, they're less likely to damage you. If you ignore them, or just brush against them, your adversary is more likely to flog you with them.

Adapted from *Student Lawyer* (Jan. 2008).

Let's consider a case in point. One of the most successful litigators in the country, Brian O'Neill of Minneapolis, once represented a class of fishermen in an oil-spill case in the Gulf of Alaska. (This case preceded his brilliant work in the *Exxon Valdez* case.) Millions of fish had been killed in the oil spill, and the fishermen had sued the responsible oil company. The problem for the fishermen, though, was that they'd had a record catch that year: more fish came in during the year of the spill than they'd caught the years before or after. In various mock trials, O'Neill kept losing the case. The juries rejected the fishermen's claim for damages because, after all, they'd had a record year.

That was a huge weakness. It seemed to undercut the entire lawsuit.

But then it occurred to O'Neill and his colleagues how they might frame the argument a little differently for their 805 clients. Here was their new approach: In fishing, as in farming, there are good years and bad years, and perhaps once in a person's career there'll be a bonanza year—a year that makes life in an arduous, up-and-down industry worth the commitment. This year would have been the bonanza year for those fishermen, and they were deprived of it. Sure, they made a little more money that year than they did just before or after, but they were deprived of what would have been their year of a lifetime.

With that argument, O'Neill began winning mock trials, and then he won in 16 test-case trials tried to juries. Ultimately, the oil company settled all the claims for $51 million. In retrospect, O'Neill recounts, the argument seems pretty obvious. But it took two years of working on the case before anyone thought of the winning strategy.

Perhaps it's human nature to want to ignore one's weaknesses. Perhaps it's human nature to hope against hope that one's adversary will overlook them. But in the adversarial context, you must overcome your natural instinct to run from your weaknesses; otherwise, your client's cause can be seriously undermined.

Sometimes in a law office, colleagues will consider whether to preemptively rebut arguments sure to be made by the adversary. Consider the party filing a motion, or perhaps the party filing an appeal. The common question is whether to rebut the counterarguments when first filing or to do it in replying to the adversary's responsive brief.

"Save our answer to that point for the reply!" are words often heard in such meetings.

Again, it's typically a matter of that lawyer's not wanting to grasp the nettles firmly. The age-old advice among professional rhetoricians is to organize an argument this way: (1) make your positive case, (2) knock down the obvious counterarguments, and (3) drive your main point home.

Address the adversary's points—or what you suspect they'll be—in the middle of your argument, not at the beginning or the end. You never

want to put the opponent's points in the most prominent positions of
your brief. And demolish those points quickly, with unanswerable punches
if possible. Don't dwell on the counterarguments. The undercutting needs
to be swift and immediate.

Adopting this strategy has at least three benefits. First, you put your
adversary on the defensive. Second, if the adversary does make the argument you've already demolished, you've made it sound as if the adversary wasn't listening to you. Third, by taking on the reasons why the
court might favor a contrary decision, you've shown yourself to be an
honest, informed advocate who has thought through all sides of the case.
As you carry your points, you're managing the opposition. And when
you do it effectively, the reader or listener senses your logical and argumentative triumph.

It's all a matter of trust. You want your readers or listeners to know
that when you're vulnerable on a point—either factually or legally—
you're exposing the weakness and dealing with it forthrightly. You're
acknowledging things as they are, not pretending that they're more
favorable to you than they are. The mature advocate knows that every
case, *every* case, has its embarrassments that must be handled both frankly
and fairly.

Two final cautions: (1) Don't refute a highly subtle or nonobvious
counterargument that probably hasn't occurred to the opposition—
instead, let your opponents waive it. (2) Don't caricature the counterarguments by misstating what they really are. Be square with them.

ès ès ès

Debriefing Your Briefs

MOST APPELLATE ADVOCATES BELIEVE that mock oral arguments can be quite useful. Given that a supermajority of cases are decided on the briefs, why not focus your energies on testing your written arguments instead of your oral arguments? This means something more formal than merely walking down the hall to ask a colleague, "Could you read this over?" It means seeking a truly objective view from readers who can't possibly be predisposed.

I've done this over the years by conducting focus groups to engage in what I call "mock judicial readings." It's an eight-step process.

1. Hire five or six of the smartest lawyers you know—some women and some men, with various levels of experience and various political philosophies—to participate in the mock judicial reading. If you have a plaintiff's case, hire defense lawyers. Offer to pay a generous hourly rate for two hours of their time. Have them run a conflicts check, but don't disclose what side of the case you're on.

2. On the day of the focus group—say, from 7 to 9 a.m. (when everyone is fresh), about a week before your brief is due—have two sets of briefs ready: your opponent's and your own. If you represent the appellee, your task is easy: just be sure that your brief looks like a finished, filed product. If you represent the appellant, you'll need to prepare a mock appellee's brief based on your opponent's filings in the lower court. Again, it should look like a final product.

3. Have someone neutral run the focus group. Don't introduce the lawyers involved until after you're finished. Ensure that the brief-writers are there to watch.

4. Explain to the participants that they are playing the role of appellate judges. They should read as if they were judges, and they should try to understand the case that's being presented to them in the briefs. The moderator and others in the room are not there to answer questions but simply to observe. Any questions that participants have should be referred to the briefs.

Adapted from *The Winning Brief* (2d ed. 2004).

5. Give the participants the appellant's brief (regardless of which side you're on). Ask them to read in silence for 15 minutes. Then stop the reading and ask them questions such as these: "What's your first impression of the case?" "What are the issues you're concerned about?" "Is the brief giving you what you need to decide this case?" You'll be surprised at how quickly, through discussing the case, the participants will move toward a command of the critical issues. Keep the discussion time to 15 minutes.
6. Ask them to continue for another 10 minutes with the appellant's brief. Discuss for 10 more minutes.
7. Next, give them the appellee's brief. Repeat steps 5 and 6.
8. By now, you'll be in a position to ask which brief is more persuasive and why. Ask each participant to say how he or she would vote in the case and to explain why. Assume that the case has to be decided right then, and caution that you're asking only for an honest reaction given the limited time frame. Disallow abstentions.

This procedure is always an eye-opener for everyone involved. The "judges" find it intellectually stimulating; the lawyers involved in the case are often shocked at how rapidly the readers dissect even a complex case; and the principal brief-writer typically finds it a nerve-racking and humbling experience.

But in major cases it's well worth the time and the investment. For a relatively modest expenditure, you can simulate a conference in which judges decide your case. And you'll see why it's important to have five or six participants—as opposed to just one colleague—because the participants invariably react to one another and help one another understand the dispositive points.

I first used this technique to preserve a sizable plaintiffs' judgment back in 1993, and I've done it many times since then. In fact, I now have a regular list of mock judicial readers.

When I publicized the use of focus groups on CounselConnect (an online forum for lawyers) in 1994, lawyers throughout the country responded that they had never thought of anything like it. Presumably, these are many of the same lawyers who use jury consultants and who assemble panels of retired judges for mock oral arguments.

Sometimes when I hold focus groups, I'm not a lawyer in the case. For example, a law firm once came to me after its client had received a multimillion-dollar judgment against it. The firm was planning its appeal, and the client had approved the use of a focus group. Because the client was the appellant, the firm had to prepare a mock appellee's brief based on the filings.

As it happened, I didn't have a chance to edit the appellant's brief before the mock judicial reading. Not that a simple edit would have mattered. The appellant lost in the focus group by a 4-to-1 vote.

The client and the lawyers—having lost—were ecstatic. They had discovered how to rewrite the brief in a way that would allay the judges' concerns.

That's precisely what they did. They won their appeal in a unanimous decision. They had erased a huge judgment. And they had learned the value of mock judicial readings.

SIR JAMES FITZJAMES STEPHEN • SAMUEL WILLISTON

Legal Drafting

Transactional Apathy

AT A SCRIBES LUNCHEON some years ago, I had the pleasure of sitting next to Reed Dickerson, the longtime champion of legal drafting as a distinct discipline. By "drafting," of course, I mean the specialized brand of writing that binds people's conduct in the future, apportioning their rights and duties. Dickerson and I passed the hour talking about drafting, and about his books on the subject: *The Fundamentals of Legal Drafting* (2d ed. 1986) and *Materials on Legal Drafting* (1981). Our conversation—sadly, the only one we ever had—confirmed my impression that Dickerson felt frustrated at the lack of interest in his subject.

I share that frustration.

The disparities are real: while litigators are keen on improving their writing, most transactional lawyers simply aren't.

I see this week in and week out in two ways. First, in an online forum I once moderated called "Legal Writing," the discussions about brief-writing always sparked great interest, but discussions about drafting died quickly. Second, CLE seminars on drafting routinely draw one-fourth as many people as those on persuasive writing.

Why is this so? Is there less to learn about drafting than about persuasive writing? Are the forms already set, so that drafters don't have much discretion about wording? Or is it that drafting is enough like other types of writing that there's no reason to study it separately?

Adapted from *The Scrivener* (Winter 1998).

Although Dickerson spent his career debunking these beliefs, they unaccountably persist. And they're dangerous to the profession because they perpetuate poor drafting, which has enormous consequences.

Think about it: drafted documents—whether they're contracts, statutes, ordinances, or constitutions—have a longer shelf life than almost any other type of writing. They're interpreted and argued about for years. Often, they're argued about most strenuously years after the drafter has perished.

The consequences are economic, too. Lon Fuller of Harvard Law School once did some empirical work on this point and found that 25% of contractual litigation resulted directly from poor drafting. What do you suppose the figure might be today? And what would it be if we included other types of drafting, such as statutes or ordinances?

In my CLE seminars on legal drafting, I routinely ask audience members to answer two questions:

1. What percentage of the legal drafting that you see is of a genuinely high quality?
2. What percentage of legal drafters would claim to produce high-quality drafting?

Although there's some variation within any audience of transactional lawyers, the consensus is quite predictable: the lawyers say that 5% of the drafting they see is of a genuinely high quality, and that 95% of the drafters would claim to produce high-quality documents.

There's a big gap there. It signals that there's still a great deal of consciousness-raising needed within the profession—especially on the transactional side. Reed Dickerson said it well, though he used a metaphor more fit for the 1960s than for today: "It's hard to sell a man a new suit of clothes if he thinks he's already well accoutered."

≈♣ ≈♣ ≈♣

Legislative Drafting

DRAFTING DENOTES the specific type of legal writing dealing with legislation, instruments, or other legal documents that are to be construed by others. Statutes, rules, regulations, contracts, and wills are examples of legal drafting. The style is considerably different from that of other legal writing, such as judicial opinions and legal commentary. Many of the worst mannerisms of legalese pervade legal drafting, for the myth of precision has traditionally been one of the drafter's tenets.

A 19th-century English practitioner once delineated the style of good drafting this way:

> [It] is free from all colour, from all emotion, from all rhetoric. It is impersonal, as if the voice, not of any man, but of the law, dealing with the necessary facts. It disdains emphasis and all other artifices. It uses no metaphors or figures of speech. It is always consistent and never contradicts itself. It never hesitates or doubts. It says in the plainest language, with the simplest, fewest, and fittest words, precisely what it means. These are qualities [that] might be used to advantage more frequently than is common in literature, and unfortunately they are not to be found in many legal compositions, but they are essential to good legal composition, and are not essential to literary composition.[1]

Perhaps the most sensible approach to the broad principles of drafting statutes is that of Montesquieu, who discussed the subject in *L'Esprit des Lois*.[2] I've paraphrased his points:

- The style should be both concise and simple: whatever is grandiose or rhetorical should be omitted as distracting surplusage.
- The words chosen should be, as nearly as possible, absolute—not relative—so as to minimize differences of opinion.
- Statutes should be confined to the real and the actual, avoiding the metaphorical or hypothetical.
- They should not be subtle, but instead comprehensible to the average person.

Adapted from *A Dictionary of Modern Legal Usage* (2d ed. 1995).

[1] J.G. Mackay, *Introduction to an Essay on the Art of Legal Composition Commonly Called Drafting*, 3 Law Q. Rev. 326, 326 (1887).

[2] C. Montesquieu, *L'Esprit des Lois* 39, ch. 16, 614–17 (Thomas Nugent trans., 1752).

- They should not confuse the main issue with exceptions, limitations, and modifications, unless such devices are absolutely necessary.
- They should not be argumentative: they should not give detailed reasons for their bases. (This is not to criticize general-purpose clauses, which are quite valuable.)
- They should be maturely considered and practically useful and should not shock the public sense of reason and justice.

Those goals are extraordinarily difficult to attain, and few have succeeded in attaining them. Samuel Williston (1861–1963), the author of many Uniform Acts approved by the Commissioners of Uniform State Laws between 1905 and 1920, was among those few: "Williston was one of the best statutory draftsmen who has ever worked at that mysterious art; he was the most ingenious system-builder in the history of our jurisprudence; he wrote with lucidity and grace."[3]

In fact, complaints about mediocre to horrible statutory drafting have echoed through the decades and centuries—e.g.:

- In 1857, Lord Campbell criticized "an ill-penned enactment, like too many others, putting Judges in the embarrassing situation of being bound to make sense out of nonsense, and to reconcile what is irreconcilable."[4]

- "So unintelligible is the phraseology of some statutes that suggestions have been made that draftsmen, like the Delphic Oracle, sometimes aim deliberately at obscurity, as a disingenuous means of passing a Bill quickly through Parliament."[5]

- "Parliament has been industrious in multiplying offences, very inartistically drawn, but it is slow to remedy clear absurdities and deficiencies in the law as they come to light . . . ."[6]

- "For over a century and a half judges have railed against incomprehensible drafting, only to be met with the bland reply that the judges are themselves to blame. The existing draftsmen are not only established but entrenched. No other word than pathetic can describe Lord Gardiner's hope in 1971 to 'encourage' them to be simpler . . . ."[7]

---

[3] Grant Gilmore, *The Ages of American Law* 134 n.12 (1977).
[4] *Fell v. Burchett* [1857] 7 E. & B. 537, 539.
[5] Carleton K. Allen, *Law in the Making* 486 (7th ed. 1964).
[6] Glanville Williams, *Textbook of Criminal Law* 8 (1978).
[7] J.A. Clarence Smith, *Legislative Drafting: English and Continental*, 1980 Statute L. Rev. 14, 22.

- "[T]he ultimate style and shape of much legislation is today increasingly unsatisfactory. Many statutes emerge from the parliamentary process obscure, turgid, and quite literally unintelligible without a guide or commentary."[8]

- "The Statute Law Society criticized the language of the statutes as: 'legalistic, often obscure and circumlocutious, requiring a certain type of expertise in order to gauge its meaning. Sentences are long and involved, the grammar is obscure, and archaisms, legally meaningless words and phrases, tortuous language, the preference for the double negative over the single positive, abound.' "[9]

Perhaps the current state of affairs results mostly from the fact that "statutory drafting . . . [is] an insufficiently appreciated art."[10] That holds as true in the U.S. as it does in Great Britain. Only someone with experience and wisdom recognizes that "[t]here is no more important, exciting, and intellectually rewarding work for a lawyer than that of drafting legislation."[11] The accomplished writer who tries legislative drafting will find that it taxes one's literary abilities as much as any other type of writing.

In an important early work on the writing of statutes, George Coode laid down for the first time some important rules of drafting that have formed the basis for modern principles of drafting—and have been routinely ignored in practice.[12]

The fundamental mode of statutory expression as worked out by Coode, is to recite facts concurrent with the statute's operation as if they were present facts, and facts precedent to the statute's operation as if they were past facts.

In elaboration of that deceptively simple statement, what follows is a modernization of Coode's precepts on the use of tenses in statutes, and especially the use of *shall* and *may*.[13]

Coode recognized that much of the trouble in statute-drafting originates in the use of *shall*. Proscriptions that begin "No person *shall* . . ." are inferior to those that begin "No person *may* . . ." because *shall* can be understood in two senses: simple futurity (i.e., *will*) and obligation (i.e., *must*).

---

[8] P.S. Atiyah, *Law and Modern Society* 127–28 (1983).

[9] Michael Zander, *The Law-Making Process* 22 (2d ed. 1985) (quoting the Report of the Renton Committee entitled *Preparation of Legislation*).

[10] Rupert Cross, *Statutory Interpretation* 12 (1976).

[11] Glanville Williams, *Learning the Law* 214 (11th ed. 1982).

[12] *See* George Coode, *On Legislative Expression* (1842).

[13] This adaptation paraphrases Coode as quoted in E.A. Driedger's *The Composition of Legislation* 225–28 (1957).

The drafter should not attempt to render every action referred to in a statute in a future tense. Some drafters erroneously assume that the words *shall* and *shall not* put the enacting verb into a future tense. Yet in commanding, as in a statute that mandates a certain action, *shall* is modal rather than temporal. Thus it denotes compulsion—the obligation to act—not a prophecy that the person will or will not at some future time perform some act. The commandment "Thou shalt not kill" is not a prediction; it is obligatory in the present tense, continuously through all the time of the law's operation.

Likewise, when the verb *may* is used, the expression is not of a future possibility; instead, it is of permission and authority. The statement "The chair *may canvass* committee members" means that the chair *is authorized to canvass* the committee members.

Yet because the legal action referred to in a statute is sometimes—when *shall* is used—supposed to be in the future tense, drafters often attempt (for the sake of consistency) to express the circumstances that are required to precede the operation of the statute (i.e., all conditions) in the future or future perfect tense. Thus, in poor drafting language, one frequently finds the following expressions:

- If any person *shall give* [read *gives*] notice, he *may* appeal . . . .
- If the commissioners *shall instruct* [read *instruct*] by any order . . . .
- All elections *shall* [read *must*] hereafter, so far as the commissioners *shall direct* [read *direct*] . . . .
- In case any person *shall willfully neglect or disobey* [read *willfully neglects or disobeys*] . . . .
- When such notice *shall have been published* [read *is published*] . . . .
- If any balance *shall have been found* [read *is found*] to be due . . . .

The fear that gives rise to this use of *shall* is that, if the condition for operation of the statute were expressed in the present tense (i.e., when any person is aggrieved), the law would be contemporaneous and would operate *only* on conditions that are met at the moment when the statute is enacted. Likewise, some drafters wrongly assume that if a statute were expressed in the present perfect tense (i.e., when any person has been convicted), the law would be retrospective and would apply *only* to convictions that took place before the act was passed.

These apprehensions are mistaken. An elementary rule of statutory construction is that past tenses never give retrospective effect to a statute unless the intention for retrospectivity is clearly and distinctly framed in words to that effect. Any number of statutes are written in the present or present perfect tense but still are interpreted prospectively only.

If the law is regarded, while it remains in force, as *constantly speaking*, then a simple two-part rule will serve to guide those who draft statutes:

1. Use the *present tense* to express all facts and conditions required to be concurrent with the operation of the legal action. E.g., "If by reason of the largeness of parishes the inhabitants *cannot* reap the benefits of this Act, two or more overseers *must be chosen*." (The first clause in this conditional sentence is in the present tense; the main clause that follows contains obligatory language still in the present tense.)

2. Use the *present perfect tense* to express all facts and conditions required as precedents to the legal action. E.g., "When the justices of the peace of any county *assembled* at quarter sessions *have agreed* that the ordinary peace officers *are* not sufficient to preserve the peace, the justices *may* appoint a chief constable." (The left-branching dependent clauses contain verbs in the past perfect [*assembled, have agreed*] to indicate necessary precedent conditions that now exist [*are*] and thus make legal action possible; the main clause is in the present [permissive] tense to indicate the specific legal action that is open to the justices of the peace.)

ᔛ ᔛ ᔛ

Handling Words of Authority

FEW REFORMS WOULD IMPROVE legal drafting more than if drafters were to begin paying closer attention to the verbs by which they set forth duties, rights, prohibitions, and entitlements. In the current state of common-law drafting, these verbs are a horrific muddle—and, what is even more surprising, few drafters even recognize this fact. The primary problem is *shall*, to which we must immediately turn.

A. Shall. This word runs afoul of several basic principles of good drafting. The first is that a word used repeatedly in a given context is presumed to bear the same meaning throughout. (*Shall* commonly shifts its meaning even in midsentence.) The second principle is strongly allied with the first: when a word takes on too many senses and cannot be confined to one sense in a given document, it becomes useless to the drafter. (*Shall* has as many as eight senses in drafted documents.) The third principle has been recognized in the literature on legal drafting since the mid-19th century: good drafting generally ought to be in the present tense, not the future. (*Shall* is commonly used as a future-tense modal verb.) In fact, the selfsame quality in *shall*—the fact that it is a chameleon-hued word—causes it to violate each of those principles.

How can *shall* be so slippery, one may ask, when every lawyer knows that it denotes a mandatory action? Well, perhaps every lawyer has heard that it's mandatory, but very few consistently use it in that way. And as a result, courts in virtually every English-speaking jurisdiction have held—by necessity—that *shall* means *may* in some contexts, and vice versa. These holdings have been necessary primarily to give effect to slipshod drafting.

What, then, are the meanings of *shall*? The shadings are sometimes subtle, but the following examples—all but the last two from a single set of court rules—illustrate the more common shades:

- "The court . . . *shall* enter an order for the relief prayed for . . . ." The word imposes a duty on the subject of the sentence.
- "Service *shall* be made on the parties . . . ." The word imposes a duty on an unnamed person, but not on the subject of the sentence ("service," an abstract thing).
- "The debtor *shall* be brought forthwith before the court that issued the order." The word seems at first to impose a duty on the debtor but actually imposes it on some unnamed actor.

Adapted from *A Dictionary of Modern Legal Usage* (2d. ed. 1995).

- "Such time *shall* not be further extended except for cause shown." The word *shall* gives permission (as opposed to a duty), and *shall not* denies permission (i.e., it means "may not"). This problem—*shall* being equivalent to *may*—frequently appears also in the statutory phrase *No person shall.* Logically, the correct construction is *No person may,* because the provision negates permission, not a duty.
- "Objections to the proposed modification *shall* be filed and served on the debtor." The word purports to impose a duty on parties to object to proposed modifications, though the decision to object is discretionary. This amounts to a conditional duty: a party that wants to object must file and serve the objections.
- "The sender *shall* have fully complied with the requirement to send notice when the sender obtains electronic confirmation." The word acts as a future-tense modal verb (the full verb phrase being in the future perfect). Many readers of this sentence, however, encounter a miscue in reading the sentence, which confusingly suggests that the sender has a duty.
- "The secretary *shall* be reimbursed for all expenses." The word expresses an entitlement, not a duty.
- "Any person bringing a malpractice claim *shall*, within 15 days after the date of filing the action, file a request for mediation." Courts interpreting such a rule or statute often hold that *shall* is directory, not mandatory—that it equates with the softer word *should.*

So much for the "Golden Rule" of legal drafting, which Reed Dickerson put this way: "[T]he competent draftsman makes sure that each recurring word or term has been used consistently. He carefully avoids using the same word or term in more than one sense . . . . In brief, he always expresses the same idea in the same way and always expresses different ideas differently."[1]

One solution to the problem that *shall* poses is to restrict it to one sense. This solution—called the "American rule" because it is an approach followed by some careful American drafters—is to use *shall* only to mean "has a duty to." Under the American rule, only the first of the eight bulleted items above would be correct. The drafter might well say that a party *shall* send notice, but not that notice *shall* be sent by the party. (If this "has-a-duty-to" sense is the drafter's convention, *must* serves when the subject of the sentence is an inanimate object.) This solution leads to much greater consistency than is generally found in American drafting.

Another solution is the "ABC rule," so called because, in the late 1980s, it was most strongly advocated by certain Australian, British, and

---

[1] Reed Dickerson, *The Fundamentals of Legal Drafting* § 2.3.1, at 15–16 (2d ed. 1986).

Canadian drafters. The ABC rule holds that legal drafters cannot be trusted to use the word *shall* under any circumstances. Under this view, lawyers are not educable on the subject of *shall*, so the only solution is complete abstinence. As a result, the drafter must always choose a more appropriate word: *must, may, will, is entitled to*, or some other expression.

This view has much to be said for it. American lawyers and judges who try to restrict *shall* to the sense "has a duty to" find it difficult to apply the convention consistently. Indeed, few lawyers have the semantic acuity to identify correct and incorrect *shalls* even after a few hours of study. That being so, there can hardly be much hope of the profession's using *shall* consistently.

Small wonder, then, that the ABC rule has fast been gaining ground in the U.S. For example, the federal government's Style Subcommittee, part of the Standing Committee on Rules of Practice and Procedure—a subcommittee that since 1991 has worked on all amendments to the various sets of federal court rules—adopted this approach, disallowing *shall*, in late 1992. (This came after a year of using *shall* only to impose a duty on the subject of the verb.) As a result, the rules have become sharper because the drafters are invariably forced into thinking more clearly and specifically about meaning.

There is, of course, a third approach: to allow *shall* its traditional promiscuity while pretending, as we have for centuries, that preserving its chastity is either hopeless or unimportant. Of course, that approach breeds litigation, as attested in 107 pages of small-type cases reported in *Words and Phrases*, all interpreting the word *shall*. As long as the mass of the profession remains unsensitized to the problems that *shall* causes, this appears to be the most likely course of inaction.

A major cause of the litigation over *shall* is the relative strength of the word. That is, what are the consequences when somebody fails to honor a contractual or statutory duty? If it's a contractual duty, does a failure to honor a *shall*-provision always amount to a breach? Does it entitle the other party to rescind? If it's a statutory requirement, does a violation invalidate the proceedings? Or is it merely a directory provision? This unclarity about consequences is a continuing problem in any system that we adopt, however linguistically principled that system might be.

B. Shall not. Under the American rule, this phrasing works as long as it means "has a duty not to." Thus, "Thou *shalt not* steal" works, but not "The money *shall not* remain in the court's registry for more than 30 days." In the latter example, the proper choice is either *must not* or *may not*.

C. Must. Under the American rule, this word means "is required to" and is used primarily when an inanimate object appears as the subject of the clause. Hence, "Notice *must* be sent within 30 days."

Under the ABC rule, *must* denotes all required actions, whether or not the subject of the clause performs the action of the verb—e.g.: "The employee *must* send notice within 30 days."/"Notice *must* be sent within 30 days."

The advantage of *must* over *shall* is that its meaning is fastened down more tightly in any given sentence. Take, for example, a sentence from a widely used commercial lease: "The premises *shall* be used by the tenant for general office purposes and for no other purposes." Once one decides to follow the ABC rule, the dilemma in meaning becomes clear: are we mandating something with that sentence (use of the premises), or are we merely limiting the tenant's freedom to use the premises for other purposes? One might revise the sentence—removing the passive voice—in either of two ways: (a) *The tenant must use the premises for general office purposes*; or (b) *The tenant may use the premises only for general office purposes.* Which meaning is correct? Perhaps somebody should litigate the question so that we might all find out.

In private drafting—contracts as opposed to statutes, rules, and regulations—some drafters consider *must* inappropriately bossy. The word may strike the wrong tone particularly when both parties to a contract are known quantities, such as two well-known corporations. It seems unlikely that, for example, an American car manufacturer and a Japanese car manufacturer engaging in a joint venture would want the word *must* to set forth their various responsibilities. Indeed, it seems odd to draft one's own contractual responsibilities with *must*: a lawyer for Ford Motor Company is unlikely to write *Ford must . . . Ford must . . . Ford must . . . .* The word *will* is probably the best solution here.

On the other hand, in a consumer contract or other adhesion contract, *must* is entirely appropriate for the party lacking the bargaining power. In the 1994 revision of its form residential lease—a document signed by a million Texas residents every year—the Texas Apartment Association changed the traditional *shall* to either *must* or *will*. The landlord became *we*, and the tenant became *you*, so that the form read as follows: *You must . . . You must . . . You must . . . We will . . . We will . . . We will . . . .* Although one might think that the resulting tone would be irksome, none of the typical users on whom the form was tested expressed that thought. Indeed, the distinctive use of *must* for the tenant and *will* for the landlord is very much in keeping with the natural rhetoric of an adhesion contract. And it certainly informs the consumer precisely what his or her obligations are.

Must is a useful device to uncover client misunderstandings about obligations. Thus, some lawyers use it despite the danger of a bossy tone. And because present-tense drafting reduces the incidence of *must*, the *musts* that remain in a given document will—in many contexts—offend no one.

D. *Will.* This word, like any other, ought to bear a consistent meaning within any drafted document. Two of its possible meanings are discussed in (C): it may express one's own client's obligations in an adhesion contract (as in a residential lease), or it may express both parties' obligations when the relationship is a delicate one (as in a corporate joint venture).

There is still a third possibility: if a future tense really is needed, as to express a future contingency, then *will* is the word. But this circumstance is not common, since the best drafting should generally be in the present, not the future, tense.

E. *May.* This term, very simply, means "has discretion to; is permitted to." It should be the only term used to denote these senses. Thus, one would never write *the licensee is free to sell as many units as it desires,* as opposed to *the licensee may sell as many units as it desires.*

Sometimes, *may* should replace *shall*—e.g.: "No person *shall* [read *may*] set off fireworks without the prior authorization of the fire marshal." That sentence does not negate a duty; it negates permission.

F. *Must not; may not.* These two are nearly synonymous. *Must not* = is required not to. *May not* = is not permitted to. For those following the ABC rule, the phrase *must not* is usually the more appropriate wording.

Some drafters avoid *may not* because it is sometimes ambiguous—it can mean either "is not permitted to" or (esp. in AmE) "might not." For example, an application to a law school states: "This office *may not* consider applications received after April 30." Some readers would take that to mean that the office has discretion whether to consider applications received after April 30, whereas others would infer that some rule or regulation prohibits the office from doing so.

G. *Is entitled to.* This is the wording for expressing an entitlement. It means "has a right to." E.g., "The guardian ad litem *shall* [read *is entitled to*] be reimbursed for expenses reasonably incurred."

H. Using a Consistent Glossary. A disciplined drafter uses words of authority consistently. This involves, in part, restricting the vocabulary by which one sets forth duties, rights, prohibitions, and entitlements. The drafter who proliferates ways of wording duties, for example, flirts with the danger that somebody interpreting the document—most disastrously, in court—will presume that a difference in wording imports a difference in meaning.

Yet drafted documents are commonly riddled with inconsistencies. It is not uncommon, in American contracts, to find the following variations in paragraph after paragraph:

- "The employee *shall follow* . . . ."
- "The employee *agrees to follow* . . . ."
- "The employee *is to follow* . . . ."
- "The employee *must follow* . . . ."
- "The employee *understands her duty to follow* . . . ."
- "The employee *will follow* . . . ."
- "*It is the responsibility* of the employee *to follow* . . . ."

The better practice is this: after the lead-in (which states, "The parties therefore agree as follows: . . ."), use only words of authority. An adherent of the American rule would make each of the above items *the employee shall follow*; an adherent of the ABC rule would make each one *the employee must follow*.

The careful drafter might consider adopting either of the following glossaries, preferably the latter:

American Rule

shall	=	has a duty to
must	=	is required to [used for all requirements that are not duties imposed on the subject of the clause]
may not	=	is not permitted to; is disallowed from
must not	=	is required not to; is disallowed from; is not permitted to
may	=	has discretion to; is permitted to
is entitled to	=	has a right to
will	=	(expresses a future contingency)
should	=	(denotes a directory provision)

ABC Rule (Preferred)

must	=	is required to
must not	=	is required not to; is disallowed from; is not permitted to
may	=	has discretion to; is permitted to
may not	=	is not permitted to; is disallowed from
is entitled to	=	has a right to
will	=	[one of the following:]
		a. (expresses a future contingency)
		b. (in an adhesion contract, expresses one's own client's obligations)
		c. (where the relationship is more or less between equals, expresses both parties' obligations)
should	=	(denotes a directory provision)

❧ ❧ ❧

Purging the Dirty Dozen

WILLIAM CULLEN BRYANT, editor of the *New York Evening Post* from 1829 until 1878, created an "index expurgatorius" for his newspaper. Certain words simply weren't allowed in its pages. Likewise, James Gordon Bennett the Younger, owner of the *New York Herald* from 1867 to 1918, had his "Don't List." For example, he wouldn't allow his journalists to write *executive session* when they meant *secret session*.

This type of banned-word list is hardly unique to newspapers. The novelist Ambrose Bierce kept a "Little Blacklist of Literary Faults," published nearly a century ago. He despised *committed suicide*, preferring instead *killed himself* (or *herself*). He likewise disapproved of *decease* for *die*, *executed* for *hanged* (or *put to death*), *expectorate* for *spit*, *inaugurate* for *begin*, *prior to* for *before*, and so on. He wasn't fond of genteelisms. No real stylists are.

Legal drafters could benefit from a similar verbal blacklist—a simple list of words that do nothing but blemish the documents in which they appear. Learn them and ax them.

1. **and/or.** Is it a word? Is it a phrase? Both American and British courts have held that the phrase is not part of the English language. The Illinois Appellate Court called it a "freakish fad" and an "accuracy-destroying symbol."[1] The New Mexico Supreme Court declared it a "linguistic abomination."[2] The Supreme Court of North Carolina has accused a trial judge who used it of "murder[ing] . . . everybody's English."[3] The Wisconsin Supreme Court has denounced it as "that befuddling, nameless thing, that Janus-faced verbal monstrosity."[4] More recently, the Supreme Court of Kentucky called it a "much-condemned conjunctive-disjunctive crutch of sloppy thinkers."[5]

   And so it is. If a sign says, "No food or drink allowed," nobody would argue that it's okay to have both. (*Or* includes *and*.) And if a sign says, "No admission for lawyers and law stu-

---

Adapted from *Student Lawyer* (Sept. 2006).

[1] *Tarjan v. Natl. Sur. Co.*, 268 Ill. App. 232, 240 (1932).

[2] *State v. Smith*, 184 P.2d 301, 331 (N.M. 1947).

[3] *Brown v. Guaranty Estates Corp.*, 80 S.E.2d 645, 653 (N.C. 1954).

[4] *Employers Mut. Liab. Ins. Co. v. Tollefson*, 263 N.W. 376, 377 (Wis. 1935).

[5] *Raine v. Drasin*, 621 S.W.2d 895, 905 (Ky. 1981).

dents," would you argue that lawyers can go in without law students or that students can go in without lawyers? You'd be thrown out of court.

The real problem with *and/or* is that it plays into the hands of a bad-faith reader. Which one is favorable? *And* or *or*? The bad-faith reader can pick one or the other, or both—whatever reading is better from that reader's perspective.

I've done lots of drafting since 1987, the year when I learned how unnecessary *and/or* really is. I've drafted court rules, jury instructions, model contracts, car warranties, and many other documents. Never once have I needed *and/or*. You don't need it, either. Kill it.

2. **deem.** *The Pittsburgh Steelers are deemed to be the 2006 Super Bowl champions.* That's silly. They were the champs. The word *deem* should create a legal fiction, not state the truth. If you said, *For purposes of this agreement, the Seattle Seahawks are deemed to be the 2006 Super Bowl champions,* that would make sense. They weren't really, but we're treating them that way. Rarely will you need to create a legal fiction.

3. **herein.** Old-style drafters say they stick to their ways for reasons of precision. They like the *here-* and *there-* words—apparently unaware of the ambiguities they're creating. The problem with *herein* is that courts can't agree on what it means. In this agreement? In this section? In this subsection? In this paragraph? In this subparagraph? Courts have reached all those conclusions, and more.[6] Use ordinary English words: *in this agreement* may be two extra words, but it's more precise.

4. **know all men by these presents.** It's asinine, sexist deadwood. It's a legalistic way of saying, "Heads up!" Just cut it.

5. **provided that.** Experts in drafting—those who publish books on the subject—have long agreed that this phrase is the bane of drafters. It has three serious problems: (1) its meaning is unclear—it can mean *if, except, or also*; (2) its reach is uncertain—that is, it may modify the preceding 12 words or the preceding 200; and (3) it causes sentences to sprawl.

---

[6] *See, e.g., Lipton-U. City, LLC v. Shurgard Storage Ctrs., Inc.,* 454 F.3d 934, 937 (8th Cir. 2006) (part of section); *Alliance Ins. Co. v. Wilson,* 384 F.3d 547, 555 (8th Cir. 2004) (limited to subsection); *Sharp v. Tulsa County Election Bd.,* 890 P.2d 836, 841 (Okla. 1994) (section only); *Taylor v. Albree,* 56 N.E.2d 904 (Mass. 1944) (entire document).

A variant form is the phrase *provided, however, that*. If you see it, try this instead: Insert a period and begin a new sentence with a capitalized *But*. That's the way good drafters make an exception to something just stated. In fact, the drafters of the U.S. Constitution did it eight times, and they were grammatically unimpeachable on this score.

6. ***pursuant to.*** This is pure legalese. It makes beginners feel as if they belong to a club, but it's not a club you'd want to belong to. The rulemaking body for federal courts has been stamping it out for well over a decade. Instead of saying that something is required *pursuant to* the contract, say it's required *under* the contract. Or say that the contract requires whatever it is.

To be fair, the phrase does have one legitimate use. If you're at a cocktail party, and you want to signal to anyone within earshot that you're in the legal field, you can say, "Pursuant to . . . ." It doesn't matter what follows. People will think you're a boring lawyer, and they'll drift elsewhere. If that's your purpose, the phrase can be quite handy.

7. ***said.*** As the past tense of *say*, this word is fine. As a fancy-pants substitute for *the*, it isn't fine at all. It's foolish. It doesn't add one iota of precision. It just makes you sound like a Marx-brothers parody of law-talk.

8. ***same.*** Many lawyers use *same* as a pronoun because they think they're being precise: *Once the indemnitee receives such notice, the indemnitee shall acknowledge same*. In that sentence, is *same* really more precise than *it*? No. Period.

In fact, *same* is the source of the only ambiguity in the U.S. Constitution so severe that a constitutional amendment had to cure it. In April 1841, President William Henry Harrison, the ninth President, died after little more than a month in office. Vice President John Tyler became the tenth President. But did he really? Article II of the Constitution reads: *In case of the removal of the President from office, or of his death, resignation, or inability to discharge the powers and duties of the said office, the same shall devolve on the Vice President.*

So what devolved? The office? The powers and duties of the office? Contemporaries couldn't agree, and neither can modern presidential historians.

Notice something: if the drafters had said *it* instead of *same*, or *they* instead of *same*, the answer would be clear. You see, ordinary pronouns are better because they differentiate singular from plural—as *same* doesn't.

The passage of the 25th Amendment in 1967 resolved the ambiguity. Now if the President dies or resigns, the Vice President takes over the office. If the President is merely unable to serve but remains alive, the Vice President becomes Acting President.

We had to pass a constitutional amendment because of one sloppy word choice: *same* instead of *it*. And the constitutional history of the country will never be the same.

   9. **shall.** Judge Frank H. Easterbrook, one of the most celebrated jurists in the country, wrote in an opinion: "*Shall* is a notoriously slippery word that careful drafters avoid."[7] He's exactly right. Courts have held that *shall* can mean "has a duty to," "should," "is," "will," and even "may." The word is like a chameleon: It changes its hue sentence to sentence. Abjure it.

   10. **such.** What does *such* mean? To the educated nonlawyer, it means "of that kind." To the lawyer, it means "the very one just mentioned." I might tell you about a certain piece of property: *100 Main Street.* Then I tell you that my client bought *such property* last week. (You think my client is well-heeled.) Then I say that my client is constantly buying *such property.* (You now think that my client is a fool to pay money again and again for the same piece of property.) Like so much other legalese, *such* is inherently ambiguous. If you must use *such*, use it only as educated nonlawyers do. It's only the lawyers' use that causes trouble.

   11. **whereas.** This archetypal legalism used to be every lawyer's idea of how to begin a contract. No longer. One easy way to avoid it—and to avoid the never-ending sentence it spawns—is to use the subtitle "Background" or "Recitals," followed by short declarative sentences explaining what's about to be done and why.

   12. **witnesseth.** It's usually in all-caps text and spaced out across the line. Modern readers—even lawyers—take *witnesseth* to be a sort of command. They think it's the imperative mood of the verb. But no: it's indicative. It's a variant form in Elizabethan usage. Elizabethan—as in Shakespeare's day. Lawyers are slow to update their forms, as you can see.

Anyway, in the old days the opener read, *This Agreement witnesseth that* . . . . Drafters almost never use it correctly these days. They write, *This is an agreement between [one party and another].* *WITNESSETH:* . . . . That's risible. Just cut the *witnesseth*.

---

[7] *McCready v. White*, 417 F.3d 700, 702 (7th Cir. 2005).

The great shame, of course, is that most law students in this country have a yearlong course in Contracts and never read a contract from beginning to end. They never learn about preparing good contracts. They learn doctrines: offer, acceptance, and consideration. But they never see a full example of what they're studying. That's the way of legal academia.

So if you're going to prepare contracts, be prepared to teach yourself a thing or two about how to draft them most effectively. Start a reading program on legal drafting. There are lots of books on the subject. Two great sources for starting out are Peter Butt & Richard Castle, *Modern Legal Drafting* (2001) and Peter Tiersma, *Legal Language* (1999).

Meanwhile, start compiling blacklisted words and phrases. Keep it simple—like the list here. It'll be easier to follow, and you'll learn more that way. You'll feel as if you're making a difference in your own little niche of the world. And that's exactly what you'll be doing.

ᏍᎨ ᏍᎨ ᏍᎨ

The Abstemious Definer

Work Hard to Draft Without Definitions

KEEP TO A MINIMUM (hereinafter "Minimize") all definitional words, especially those in the form of midsentence parentheticals (hereinafter collectively "Defined Terms"). Most Defined Terms serve as shorthand forms for the person doing the writing (hereinafter "the Writer"). But they're typically roadblocks (hereinafter "Roadblocks" or "Impediments") for the people doing the reading (hereinafter "Readers"), who undoubtedly wish that the Roadblocks were Minimized. If a writer uses an Impediment such as a Defined Term without first ensuring that clarity and precision (hereinafter collectively "Accurate Readability") have been improved, the Writer is likely to seem willfully obscure to naive Readers (hereinafter "Naive Readers") and doltish to more sophisticated Readers (hereinafter "Sophisticated Readers"). The resulting mishmash (hereinafter "Mishmash") will drive all types of Readers, whether Naive Readers or Sophisticated Readers, away from the document (hereinafter "Repulsive Effect") precisely because the Mishmash and the effects relating thereto, including but not limited to the Repulsive Effect (hereinafter collectively the "Concomitant Effects"), are inconsistent with Accurate Readability.

Write that way if you will. But you needn't. And you shouldn't.

The advice contained in that initial paragraph—if you took the time to figure it out—is quite counterintuitive to most transactional lawyers, who have come to believe that the more you define terms, the better. Experts in the field of drafting have long held the opposite view:

- "[A] definition . . . often creates more problems than it solves."—Lord Reid[1]
- "[D]efinitions don't belong in a legal document. If they just echo the dictionary, they are pointless—like section 441(d) of the Internal Revenue Code, which says, 'For purposes of this subtitle, the term "calendar year" means a period of 12 months ending on December 31.' If they *don't* echo the dictionary but sneak in

---

Adapted from *Securities Disclosure in Plain English* (1999).
[1] *Brutus v. Cozens* [1972] 3 W.L.R. 521, 525.

something extra, they're a piece of trickery and should always be replaced by a straightforward explanation in the text of the document."—Rudolf Flesch[2]

• "In the realm of definitions, it is usually wise to try to be a minimalist, in other words, to try to convey everything you have to say clearly without using definitions at all."—Barbara Child[3]

The following example, taken from an actual prospectus, shows how readily you can draft clear passages without definitions. Notice how eliminating the definitions results in improved organization. Notice also that the left-hand column uses the defined term *Representative*. In the actual prospectus, it was defined 36 pages before this passage. I spent ten minutes searching in vain for the definition of *Representative*. (Would an investor spend that much time?) In the end, all the term means is *underwriters' representative*—an easy enough thing to say explicitly.

Not this:	*But this:*
3.4 Bridge Financing	**3.4 Bridge Financing**
In October 1998, the Company obtained bridge financing (the "Bridge Financing") which consisted of the issuance of Bridge Notes in an aggregate principal amount of $4 million (the "Bridge Notes") and warrants to purchasers of the Bridge Notes to purchase 400,000 shares of the Company's Common Stock, and a warrant to the Representative as selling agent to purchase 40,000 shares of the Company's Common Stock, and a warrant to the Representative as selling agent to purchase 40,000 shares of the Company's Common Stock (collectively, the "Bridge Warrants"). The Bridge Financing was used for the acquisition of capital equipment and construction of facility improvements. The Bridge Notes bear interest from the date of issue at a rate of 11.75% per annum, payable at maturity. The Bridge Notes are payable in full on the earlier of October 15, 1999, or the closing date of this Offering.	(A) In October 1998, we obtained bridge financing to purchase 400,000 shares of our common stock. We used this financing to acquire capital equipment and to improve our facilities. The financing consisted of: (1) bridge notes in an aggregate principal amount of $4 million, bearing interest from the date of issue at a rate of 11.75% per annum, payable at maturity (either October 15, 1999, or the closing date of this offering, whichever is earlier); and (2) warrants to buyers of the bridge notes. (B) As part of this financial transaction, we issued a warrant to the underwriters' representative as our selling agent to purchase 40,000 shares of our common stock.

---

[2] *How to Write Plain English: A Book for Lawyers and Consumers* 68–69 (1979).

[3] *Drafting Legal Documents* 356 (2d ed. 1992).

Define terms in only two circumstances: (1) when you need to clarify a term of uncertain meaning, or (2) when you need to avoid duplicating long strings of words for which a shorthand term is available.

It might be a bad thing to ban all defined terms. Despite Flesch's stance,[4] definitions do have their place. First, they can help you explain precisely what you mean by a term that, though necessary, might otherwise be confusing. And second, they can help you avoid repeating long swaths of verbiage.

Technical terms may be unfamiliar to the readers of some documents, especially consumer documents. If it's likely that readers won't understand a term such as *alternative dispute resolution*, then explain it.

Some terms, such as *Sarita Kenedy East Law Library* or *Pantheon Corporation's research-and-development division*, are so long that they bog down sentences and, when repeated, inflate paragraphs. Defining a shorthand name for a long term resolves the problem ("Library"; "Pantheon R&D").

If you define a term, use an everyday shorthand name for it. Avoid alien-sounding acronyms.

Remember that you're writing English—plain English—not some hybrid language full of terms you make up. And to the extent you must define terms, choose words that are both descriptive and immediately comprehensible.

In Example A, "GBFSH1" refers to the Griffin-Buck Family Steak-house #1. A similar acronym denotes each of the numbers up to 5. The result is a mishmash of *GBFSHs*. Merely by using the word *Restaurant* as opposed to *GBFSH*, you've enhanced clarity for the vast majority of readers.

Example B has two problems. First, the reader is served a huge bowl of alphabet soup: ten acronyms are introduced in a single sentence. Second, the example's first acronym, "NFL," is likely to cause a miscue with most readers—at least those who follow sports, especially in the fall. Moral: don't use an acronym that carries some other popular meaning.

One other thing about Example B. If you don't have the shorthand acronyms, how are you supposed to refer to Westbrook Marketing Corporation or Precision Dialing Services, Inc. a second time? Do you have to use the full name over and over? The answer, of course, is no. Simply say *Westbrook Marketing* and *Precision Dialing*. And do it without the heavy-handedness of saying, in your first mention, "Westbrook Marketing Corporation ('Westbrook Marketing')," etc. Give your reader an ounce of credit for having some candlepower.

---

[4] Rudolf Flesch, *How to Write in Plain English: A Book for Lawyers and Consumers* 68–69 (1979).

Example A

Not this:	*But this:*
On December 14, 1997, GBFSH1, GBFSH2, and GBFSH3 distributed all of their cash available for distribution (net of reserves) of $32,000 (or $40 per Interest), $32,000 (or $36 per Interest), and $36,000 (or $36 per Interest), respectively, to their Limited Partners. GBFSH4 and GBFSH5 had no cash available for distribution at July 31, 1998. Limited Partners in GBFSH1, GBFSH2, and GBFSH3 all have invested in the Griffin-Buck Family Steakhouse concept in a substantially earlier phase of that concept than did the Limited Partners in GBFSH4 and GBFSH5.	On December 14, 1997, Restaurants #1–3 distributed all their cash available for distribution (net of reserves) to their limited partners. Restaurant #1 distributed $32,000 (or $40 per Interest); Restaurant #2 distributed $32,000 (or $36 per Interest); and Restaurant #3 distributed $36,000 (or $36 per Interest). Restaurants #4 and #5 had no cash available for distribution on July 31, 1998. Limited partners in Restaurants #1–3 all invested in the Griffin-Buck Family Steakhouse concept at a substantially earlier phase of that concept than the limited partners for Restaurants #4 and #5.

Example B

Not this:	*But this:*
The Company's wholly owned subsidiaries and affiliated companies include National Foundation Life Insurance Company ("NFL"), National Financial Insurance Company ("NFIC"), American Insurance Company of Illinois ("AICI"), Westbrook National Life Insurance Company ("WNL") and together with NFL, NFIC and AICI (the "Insurance Subsidiaries"), Foundation Financial Services, Inc. ("FFS"), Westbrook Marketing Corporation ("WMC"), Precision Dialing Services, Inc. ("PDS"), Westbrook Printing Services, Inc. ("WPS"), Westbrook Funding Corporation ("WFC"), LifeStyles Marketing Group, Inc. ("LifeStyles Marketing"), Senior Benefits, LLC ("Senior Benefits"), American Senior Security Plans, LLC ("ASSP") and Health Care-One Insurance Agency, Inc. ("Health Care-One").	The Company's wholly owned subsidiaries and affiliated companies are as follows: • National Foundation Life Insurance Company; • National Financial Insurance Company; • American Insurance Company of Illinois; • Westbrook National Life Insurance Company; • Foundation Financial Services, Inc.; • Westbrook Marketing Corporation; • Precision Dialing Services, Inc.; • Westbrook Printing Services, Inc.; • Westbrook Funding Corporation; • LifeStyles Marketing Group, Inc.; • Senior Benefits, LLC; • American Senior Security Plans, LLC; and • Health Care-One Insurance Agency, Inc.

To the extent you define terms, collect the definitions at the back of the document.

Transactional lawyers are accustomed to putting definitions at the outset of their contracts—sometimes 2 pages but sometimes as much as 30 pages of intertwined, heavily cross-referenced, often incomprehensible definitions that would make any lexicographer blush. Businesspeople tend to detest this practice, but the lawyers say in their own defense: how can you read the document if you don't know what the terms mean?

It's not a good defense. No one—not even the lawyer—slogs dutifully through the definitions before reading a document. Not, that is, unless the reader is an expert in the field who knows precisely what to look for in a given definition. And that reader, who isn't the primary audience for disclosure documents anyway, will just as readily flip to the back of the document to consult the definition that he or she considers crucial.

A Last Word

You'll need to use definitions sometimes. But think about whether they add clarity for the reader or are merely conveniences for the drafter.

ટ્ટ ટ્ટ ટ્ટ

The Drafter's Machete for Slashing Through Density

IN LEGAL DRAFTING, it's critical that you break down parallel provisions. Put every list of subparts at the end of the sentence—never at the beginning or in the middle. Statutes and contracts typically contain lists, often long ones. These lists are the main cause of overlong sentences. Break them up—set them apart—and, for purposes of calculating readability, the pieces won't count as a single sentence.[1]

Although it's sometimes useful to have a (1)-(2)-(3) enumeration within a paragraph of ordinary expository writing, in legal drafting it's almost always better to set off the enumerated items. No one should have to trudge through this kind of marshy prose:

> In the event that by reason of any change in applicable law or regulation or in the interpretation thereof by any governmental authority charged with the administration, application or interpretation thereof, or by reason of any requirement or directive (whether or not having the force of law) of any governmental authority, occurring after the date hereof: (i) the Bank should, with respect to the Agreement, be subject to any tax levy, impost, charge, fee, duty, deduction, or withholding of any kind whatsoever (other than any change which affects solely the taxation of the total income of the Bank), or (ii) any change should occur in the taxation of the Bank with respect to the principal or interest payable under the Agreement (other than any change which affects solely the taxation of the total income of the Bank), or (iii) any reserve requirements should be imposed on the commitments to lend; and if any of the above-mentioned measures should result in an increase in the cost to the Bank of making or maintaining its Advances or commitments to lend hereunder or a reduction in the amount of principal or interest received or receivable by the Bank in respect thereof, then upon notification and demand being made by the Bank for such additional cost or reduction, the Borrower shall pay to the Bank, upon demand being made by the Bank, such additional cost or reduction in rate of return, *provided, however,* that the Borrower shall not be responsible for any such cost or reduction that may accrue to the Bank with respect to the period between the occurrence of the

---

Adapted from *Legal Writing in Plain English* (2001).

[1] *See* Rudolf Flesch, *The Art of Plain Talk* 36–37 (1946); *see also* Rudolf Flesch, *The Art of Readable Writing* 226–27 (1962).

event which gave rise to such cost reduction and the date on which notification is given by the Bank to the Borrower.

Drain the marshes, add some headings and subheadings, and you have a presentable piece of writing, even though the material is fairly complex:

8.3 Payment of Reductions in Rates of Return

(A) *Borrower's Obligations.* The Borrower must, on demand, pay the Bank additional costs or reductions in rates of return if the conditions of both (1) and (2) are met:

(1) the law or a governmental directive, either literally or as applied, changes in a way that:

  (a) increases the Bank's costs in making or maintaining its advances or lending commitments; or

  (b) reduces the principal or interest receivable by the Bank; and

(2) any of the following occurs:

  (a) the Bank becomes—with respect to the Agreement—subject to a tax, levy, impost, charge, fee, duty, deduction, or withholding of any kind whatever (other than a change that affects solely the tax on the Bank's total income);

  (b) a change occurs in the Bank's taxes relating to the principal or interest payable under the Agreement (other than a change that affects solely the tax on the Bank's total income); or

  (c) a reserve requirement is imposed on the commitments to lend.

(B) *Exceptions to Borrower's Obligations.* The Borrower is not responsible for a cost or reduction that accrues to the Bank during the period between the triggering event and the date when the Bank gives the Borrower notice.

A fix like that is mostly a matter of finding enumerated items, breaking them out into subparts, and then working to ensure that the passage remains readable.

You'll need to use this technique almost every time you see parenthesized romanettes (i, ii, iii) or letters (a, b, c) in the middle of a contractual or legislative paragraph. Spotting the problem is relatively easy in a paragraph like this one:

5.4 *Termination Fees Payable by Pantheon.* The Merger Agreement obligates Pantheon to pay to OJM an Initial Termination Fee if (a) (i) OJM terminates the Merger Agreement because of either a Withdrawal by Pantheon or Pantheon's failure to comply (and to cure such noncompliance within 30 days' notice of the same) with certain Merger Agreement covenants relating to the holding of a stockholders' meeting, the solicitation of proxies with respect to the Pantheon Proposal, and the filing of certain documents with the Secretary of State of the State of Delaware, (ii) Pantheon terminates the Merger Agreement prior to the approval of the Pantheon Proposal by the Pantheon

stockholders, upon Pantheon having received an Acquisition Proposal
by the Pantheon Board having concluded that its fiduciary obligations
under applicable law require that such Acquisition Proposal be accepted,
or (iii) either party terminates the Merger Agreement because of the
failure of Pantheon to obtain stockholder approval for the Merger
Agreement and the transactions contemplated thereby at a duly held
stockholders' meeting, and (b) at the time of such termination or prior
to the meeting of the Pantheon stockholders there has been an Acquisition Proposal involving Pantheon or certain of its significant sub-
sidiaries (whether or not such offer has been rejected or withdrawn
prior to the time of such termination or of the meeting).

Breaking down the list into parallel provisions, with cascading indents
from the left margin, makes the provision much clearer:

> **5.4 _Termination Fees Payable by Pantheon._** The Merger Agreement
> obligates Pantheon to pay to OJM an initial termination fee of
> $250 million if both of the following conditions are met:
> (A) any of the following occurs:
>> (1) OJM terminates the merger agreement because Pantheon's
>> board withdraws its support of the merger or because Pan-
>> theon fails to comply (and fails to properly cure its non-
>> compliance within 30 days of receiving notice) with its
>> merger-agreement covenants relating to the holding of a
>> stockholders' meeting, the solicitation of proxies on the
>> Pantheon proposal, and the filing of certain documents
>> with the Delaware Secretary of State;
>> (2) Pantheon terminates the merger agreement before the Pan-
>> theon stockholders approve the Pantheon proposal, upon
>> Pantheon's having received a business-combination offer
>> involving at least 15% of Pantheon's stock and the Pan-
>> theon board's having concluded that its fiduciary obliga-
>> tions under applicable law require acceptance of that pro-
>> posal; or
>> (3) either party terminates the merger agreement on grounds
>> that Pantheon has failed to obtain stockholder approval for
>> the merger agreement and the related transactions at a
>> duly held stockholders' meeting; and
> (B) at the time of termination or before the meeting of the Pan-
> theon stockholders there has been a business-combination
> offer involving at least 15% of Pantheon's stock or of its signif-
> icant subsidiaries (whether or not the offer has been rejected
> or withdrawn before the termination or the meeting).

There's another point here: you can't have the main verb come after
the list. The core parts of the English sentence are the subject and the
verb (and sometimes an object). One key to writing plain English is

ensuring that your readers reach the main verb early on. That way, the structure of the sentence becomes transparent.

One of the worst habits that drafters develop is putting long lists of items in the subject so that the main verb is delayed. This results in what linguists call "left-branching" sentences: ones with lots of complex information that branches out to the left side of the verb. The metaphor is that of a tree. As you read from left to right, and remembering that the tree's trunk is the verb, imagine a sentence configured in this way:

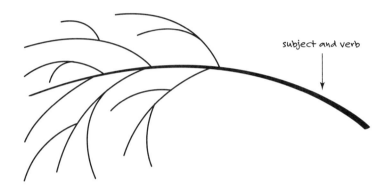

That's going to be fiendishly difficult to get through. But imagine the tree reconfigured:

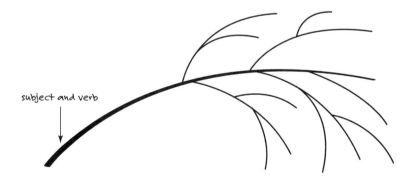

If all this talk of trees sounds too botanical, look at actual examples of sentences done both ways. Here's a typical left-brancher:

Except as may otherwise be provided in these rules—

(a) every order required by its terms to be served;

(b) every pleading subsequent to the original complaint unless the court orders otherwise because of numerous defendants;

(c) every paper relating to discovery required to be served upon a party unless the court orders otherwise;

(d) every written motion other than one that may be heard ex parte; and

(e) every written notice, appearance, demand, offer of judgment, designation of record on appeal, and similar paper

—must be served on each of the parties to the action.

The language after the enumeration—sometimes called "unnumbered dangling flush text"—is uncitable. That can be a problem. Once you put the enumeration at the end, however, the problem is cured. Here's the same sentence done as a right-brancher, with the enumeration at the end.

Notice the newly added foreshadowing language (*the following papers*):

Except as these rules provide otherwise, the following papers must be served on every party:

(a) an order required by its terms to be served;

(b) a pleading filed after the original complaint, unless the court orders otherwise because of numerous defendants;

(c) a discovery paper required to be served on a party, unless the court orders otherwise;

(d) a written motion, other than one that may be heard ex parte; and

(e) a written notice, appearance, demand, offer of judgment, designation of record on appeal, or similar paper.

Here's the upshot: find the operative verb in the sentence and move it toward the front, putting your lists at the end of the sentence. Even with fairly modest lists, this technique can make a tremendous difference in readability.

ॐ ॐ ॐ

The Art of Boiling Down:
James Fitzjames Stephen
as Drafter and Lexicographer

THE ENGLISH JURIST AND PHILOSOPHER James Fitzjames Stephen (1829–1894) has had many kindred spirits in the generations before and after he lived. Think of Lord Mansfield, who gave Stephen what almost amounted to his motto in drafting the digests of evidence[1] and criminal law[2] in the years 1875 to 1877. Mansfield wrote a sentence that typifies Stephen's thinking but goes against the current of the traditional common-law mind: "The law does not consist of particular cases, but of general principles which are illustrated and explained by those cases."[3] Making an allied point, also very much in the Stephen mold, Grant Gilmore acidly remarked in the 20th century that "the legal mind has always preferred multiplication to division."[4] Or think of Stephen's contemporary American counterpart, David Dudley Field, the leader of the New York codification movement, whose codes met with more success in various American jurisdictions than Stephen's codes met with in England.[5] Or think of Glanville Williams, who, writing about the "general part" of the criminal law in the 20th century,[6] consistently displayed the

---

Delivered as a paper at a conference on James Fitzjames Stephen in April 2005 at Boston University. Printed in an abbreviated form in *The Green Bag* (2005).

[1] Stephen, *A Digest of the Law of Evidence* (4th ed. 1881) (this, the last edition published during Stephen's lifetime, is the one quoted throughout as *Ev. Dig.*).

[2] Stephen, *A Digest of the Criminal Law* 2 (Sir Herbert Stephen & Harry Lushington Stephen eds., 5th ed. 1894) (published in the year of Stephen's death and cited here as *Crim. Dig.*).

[3] *R. v. Bembridge* (1783) 3 Doug. 332 (*per* Lord Mansfield) (quoted favorably in Stephen, Introduction, *Ev. Dig.*, note 1, at xviii. *Cf. Evi. Dig.*, at xix, where Stephen says: "I do not think the law can be in a less creditable condition than that of an enormous mass of isolated decisions, and statutes assuming unstated principles; cases and statutes alike being accessible only by elaborate indexes. I insist upon this because I am well aware . . . of the rooted belief which exists in the minds of many lawyers that all general propositions of law must be misleading, and delusive, and that law books are useless except as indexes." *Cf.* also *Evi. Dig.*, at vii–viii, where he says that the experienced practitioner learns that the law is "shorter and simpler than it looks, and . . . understand[s] that the innumerable cases which at first sight appear to constitute the law, are really no more than illustrations of a comparatively small number of principles.")

[4] Grant Gilmore, *The Death of Contract* 89 (1974).

[5] *See* Grant Gilmore, *The Ages of American Law* 119–20 n.13 (1977).

[6] *See* Glanville Williams, *Criminal Law: The General Part* (2d ed. 1961).

kind of close semantic analysis that, to a somewhat lesser extent, characterized Stephen's work.

But the closest comparison—the one recognized by Stephen's circle of friends—is to Samuel Johnson, a literary man who was enormously learned in the law. Stephen was a legal figure who was enormously learned in literary matters.[7] There was certainly a physical resemblance between the men. But there's much more. Both had undistinguished achievements in university studies.[8] Both were polymaths. Both tried their hands at lexicography. Both had penetrating intellects with sharp contours. And both left a prodigious body of influential work. So it's understandable that Stephen's brother, Leslie, would write that Fitzjames's "friends not unfrequently compared him to Dr. Johnson"[9]—and that the *Dictionary of National Biography* entry for Stephen would say that he "was pre-eminently a man of . . . Johnsonian power of mind."[10]

On a stylistic level, though, the comparison falls apart. Whereas Johnson wrote a pretty consistently elevated form of prose, at its worst known as "Johnsonese,"[11] Stephen tended to prefer a simpler, more down-to-earth style. What we'll consider here is Stephen's style as a drafter of legal digests, with a goal of understanding his strengths and weaknesses. And we'll have a look at his work in defining terms in his digests—his lexicography, if I may call it that.

Stephen the Drafter

As a teacher of writing, I've found it useful to analyze the four phases that every writer must go through: (1) coming up with ideas, (2) organizing the ideas, (3) producing a draft, and (4) critiquing the draft.[12] Dr. Betty S. Flowers of the University of Texas has given these four skills personalities and names: Madman (the creative imagination), Architect (the organizer), Carpenter (the builder of drafts), and Judge (the critic

---

[7] Sir Frederick Pollock, "Stephen, Sir James Fitzjames," in *Encyclopaedia Britannica* vol. 25, 883, 884 (11th ed. 1911) (calling Stephen a "literary lawyer").

[8] Stephen: *D.N.B.* vol. 18, 1051, 1051 (noting that "[w]ant of accurate scholarship . . . made his academical career [at Trinity College, Cambridge] unsuccessful"). *See* Leslie Stephen, *The Life of Sir James Fitzjames Stephen* 357 (2d ed. 1895) ("at college, he was distanced in the race by men greatly his inferiors in general force of mind, but better provided with the talent for bringing their gifts to market").

[9] Leslie Stephen, note 8, at 131.

[10] *D.N.B.*, note 8, at 1054.

[11] *See* Eric Partridge, *Usage and Abusage* 174–75 (1942) (s.v. "Johnsonese").

[12] *See, e.g.*, Garner, *The Winning Brief* 3–49 (2d ed. 2004); Garner, *Legal Writing in Plain English* 5–10 (2001).

and self-editor).[13] It's a useful paradigm for thinking about writing: few writers hold these four skills in any kind of equilibrium. Yet a complete writer develops all four.

If we use this paradigm in considering Stephen's work, it seems pretty plain that he excelled as Architect and Carpenter—and mainly as Architect. He had a less well-developed Madman, and his Judge was really rather underdeveloped. Now let me defend that assessment.

As for Stephen's Madman, while he showed vision and creativity in seeing the need for codification, Sir Frederick Pollock was probably right in his assessment of Stephen: "[I]t cannot be said that he made any considerable addition to the substance of legal ideas. His mind was framed for legislation rather than for systematic interpretation and development."[14]

By all accounts, it was Stephen's zeal for organization that made him shine. That's what drove him toward codifying the law, which Stephen defined as "merely the reduction of the existing law to an orderly written system, freed from the needless technicalities, obscurities, and other defects which the experience of its administration has disclosed."[15] He was a legal cartographer: he wanted good maps. He complained that without codification, it's as if the learner "wants a general plan of a district, and you turn him loose in the forest to learn its paths by himself."[16] Or, with a different trope (a simile), he complained that "[w]orks intended for reference . . . are unavoidably crowded with details to such an extent that to get out of them any general notion of law is like looking at a landscape through a microscope."[17] He called the shape of English law "studiously repulsive."[18]

Stephen detested obscurity, especially the kind that results from a morass of cluttering detail. It was a turn of mind evident throughout his career. As early as 1856, Stephen wrote that what England needed was a code: "the old law books and reports must be distilled into a portable and intelligible form, so that the nation at large may have some conception of its rights and obligations, and the lawyers some chance of understanding their profession."[19] In the 1860s, when first in India, he said that

---

[13] Betty S. Flowers, *Madman, Architect, Carpenter, Judge: Roles and the Writing Process*, 44 Proceedings of the Conference of College Teachers of English 7–10 (1979).

[14] Sir Frederick Pollock, "Stephen, Sir James Fitzjames," in *Encyclopaedia Britannica* vol. 25, 883, 885 (11th ed. 1911). *Cf.* A.V. Dicey, *Law and Public Opinion in England* 206 n.1 (1905; 2d ed. 1914; repr. 1962) (in which Dicey, Stephen's cousin, says that Stephen "hardly claimed to be . . . a reformer of the law").

[15] Stephen, *A History of the Criminal Law of England* vol. 3, 350 (1883).

[16] Leslie Stephen, note 8, at 377.

[17] Stephen, *A General View of the Criminal Law of England* v (1863).

[18] Stephen, *Codification in India and England*, 18 Fortnightly Rev. 644 (Dec. 1872).

[19] Stephen, "Law Reform," *Saturday Rev.* 252 (2 Feb. 1856) (as quoted in John Hostettler, *Politics and Law in the Life of Sir James Fitzjames Stephen* 156–57 (1995)).

"[t]o compare the Indian Penal Code [Macaulay's work] with English law is like comparing cosmos with chaos. Any intelligent person . . . could get a very distinct and correct notion of Indian Criminal Law [from it] . . . . I appeal to you to imagine the state of mind of a man who should try to read straight through the very best of English books on the subject . . . ."[20] In that same decade, he wrote: "It surely ought to be possible to explain the principles [of criminal law] . . . in a manner both intelligible and interesting."[21] In the 1870s, in his *Digest of the Law of Evidence*, he issued a similar complaint: "The enormous mass of detail and illustration which [most legal treatises] contain, and the habit into which their writers naturally fall, of introducing into them everything which has any sort of connection, however remote, with the main subject, make these books useless for purposes of study."[22]

Hence, despite the widespread lawyer's "prejudice which exists against all attempts to state the law simply,"[23] Stephen cultivated the art of boiling down.[24] In fact, "boiling down" has aptly been called "Stephen's professional leitmotiv."[25] This was primarily an architectural enterprise: taking a huge, unwieldy array of cases and reducing their principles to a manageable system laid out in an easy-to-follow format. He yearned for "a body of law for the government of the country so expressed that it may be readily understood and administered . . . without extrinsic help from English law-libraries."[26]

And if Stephen was primarily an Architect, it's easy to see why he so disdained the gangly, ill-organized writings of Jeremy Bentham, whose work Stephen called "original chaos" that needed to be "cleaned, washed, and translated into French."[27]

Stephen was also an extraordinary Carpenter, producing great amounts of work during short periods. Sir Courtenay Ilbert called him a "Cyclopean builder," adding that he "hurled together high blocks of rough hewn law."[28] The digests of evidence and criminal law were produced in

---

[20] Stephen, note 18, at 654.

[21] Stephen, note 17, at vi.

[22] *Ev. Dig.*, note 1, at vi–vii.

[23] *Id.* at xix.

[24] Leslie Stephen was perhaps quoting a letter from his brother when, in the biography, he used quotation marks in reference to the *Digest of the Law of Evidence*: "Here was another case of 'boiling down' . . . . He undoubtedly boiled his materials down to a small size." Leslie Stephen, note 8, at 377–78.

[25] K.J.M. Smith, *James Fitzjames Stephen: Portrait of a Victorian Rationalist* 53 (1988).

[26] Stephen as quoted in Sir Courtenay Ilbert, *Legislative Methods and Forms* 149 (1901).

[27] Stephen as quoted in Abigail Smith, *James Fitzjames Stephen: The Last Great Codifier*, 139 New L.J. 954, 954 (1989).

[28] Courtenay Ilbert, *Sir James Stephen as a Legislator*, 10 Law Q. Rev. 224 (1894).

three short years (1875–1877).[29] Though at times he professed to suffer from sluggishness,[30] he never suffered seriously from writer's block.[31]

It was as Judge—or self-critic—that Stephen was most deficient as a drafter. That has been the historical consensus. In the year of Stephen's death, Courtenay Ilbert, his friend, frankly said that Stephen undeniably "left behind him some hasty work in the Indian Statute Book, some defective courses of masonry which his successors had to remove and replace."[32] Seven years later, in 1901, Ilbert called Stephen's "workmanship . . . deficient in accuracy and finish."[33] That same year, Lord Bryce commented: "His capacity for the work of drafting was deemed not equal to his fondness for it. He did not shine either in fineness of discrimination or in delicacy of expression."[34] Leon Radzinowicz has commented that Bryce's "criticism was justified."[35]

Although as a drafter I'm probably looking at points different from those of Stephen's earlier critics, in general I agree. But before I point out some of Stephen's shortcomings as a drafter, it's only fair to observe four ways in which his drafting was brilliant.

First, Stephen cut out most of the verbosity that plagued his sources. He wrote reasonable sentences. In the *Digest of the Law of Evidence*, his average sentence length was 35.5 words; in the *Digest of the Criminal Law*, his average sentence length was 22 words.[36] Anyone who has spent much time looking at 19th-century statute books would know that nothing like those averages would hold for most of them—and that this is a primary source of their obscurity.[37] Stephen explained his approach in the *Digest of the Criminal Law*: "Where the language of a statute appeared

[29] Leslie Stephen, note 8, at 377.

[30] *D.N.B.* note 8, at 1052.

[31] A.W.B. Simpson has aptly referred to Stephen's "unremitting literary achievements" *Biographical Dictionary of the Common Law* 488 (1984).

[32] Ilbert, note 28, at 224.

[33] Ilbert, note 26, at 162. *See also D.N.B.*, note 8, at 1054 (noting that Stephen's work was "marred in some ways by want of finish"). *Contra* Smith, note 25, at 53 (referring to Stephen's "impressive accuracy and clarity").

[34] James Bryce, *Studies in History and Jurisprudence* vol. 1, 129 (1901).

[35] Leon Radzinowicz, *Sir James Fitzjames Stephen 1829–1894 and His Contribution to the Development of Criminal Law* 14 (1957).

[36] By way of comparison, in the current edition of *American Jurisprudence*, the average sentence length for the evidence section is 31 words, and for criminal law 38. In the current edition of *Corpus Juris Secundum* the average sentence length for the evidence section is 34 words, and for criminal law 35.

[37] On the general importance of average sentence length in producing readable prose, *see* Rudolf Flesch, *How to Write in Plain English: A Book for Lawyers and Consumers* 20–27 (1979); Robert Gunning, *The Technique of Clear Writing* 32–34 (1952).

needlessly verbose for common purposes, the leading word or an equivalent is preserved in the text, and the words omitted are inserted in a
foot-note for reference if necessary."[38]

Second, in the *Digest of the Criminal Law*, Stephen took every statutory *shall* and replaced it with *must*.[39] Perhaps he was aware of George
Coode's warnings in 1842 about the many ambiguities of *shall*.[40] More
than a century after Stephen labored to eliminate *shall*, the battle continues in American drafting circles: the Standing Committee of Rules of
Practice and Procedure voted in 1993 to eliminate *shall* from all amendments to federal rules, and now we have two sets of rules—appellate and
criminal—that have been stripped of the chameleon-hued word, in favor
of *must*.[41] But in rulemaking committees, arguments still frequently emerge
because so many judges and lawyers remain badly ill-informed about the
troubles with *shall*. So it's a mild shock to the modern drafter to see, without further explanation, the bland statement in Stephen's *Digest*: "Where
'shall' is used as an imperative [in a statute] 'must' is substituted."[42]

By the way, the *Digest of the Law of Evidence* similarly avoids *shall*, but
generally not by using *must*. Instead, Stephen there usually states his rules
as policies, as by stating: "A declaration is deemed to be relevant if the
declarant had peculiar means of knowing the matter stated, if he had no
interest to misrepresent it, and if it was opposed to his pecuniary or pro-
prietary interest."[43] To the modern drafter, the repetitious use of the verb
deem is a fault: it would be better simply to say that "a declaration is relevant if. . . ." But all in all, it's simply a joy to see a 19th-century code
shorn of the word *shall*.

Third, Stephen wisely sticks to the present tense, perhaps once again
taking a lesson from Coode's 1842 treatise on legislative drafting. In the
preface to the *Digest of the Criminal Law*, Stephen writes: "The future and
past future [known more commonly as the "future perfect"] are uniformly

---

[38] *Crim. Dig.*, note 2, at 2.

[39] *Id.*

[40] *See* George Coode, *On Legislative Expression* (1842); *see also* Garner, *A Dictionary of Modern Legal Usage* 830–31 (2d ed. 1995) (paraphrasing and updating Coode); *id.* at 939–42; Garner, *Legal Writing in Plain English* § 35, at 105–07. Soon the Federal Rules of Civil Procedure may be purged of all *shalls*: in February 2005, the Standing Committee issued for public comment a massive redraft of the rules by recasting them according to the best modern principles of drafting. *See* Edward H. Cooper, *Restyling the Civil Rules: Clarity Without Change*, 79 Notre Dame L. Rev. 1761 (2004).

[41] *See* Garner, *Guidelines for Drafting and Editing Court Rules* § 4.2, at 29–30 (1996); reproduced at 169 F.R.D. 176, 212–13 (1997).

[42] *Crim. Dig.*, note 2, at 2.

[43] *Ev. Dig.*, note 1, at art. 28, at 36.

altered to the present tense."[44] As Coode had explained some 35 years before, "the law is regarded, while it remains in force, as *constantly speaking*."[45] Hence the wise drafter uses the present tense for all facts and conditions required to be concurrent with the operation of the legal action, and the present perfect tense to express all facts and conditions required as being precedent to a legal action. Stephen generally follows these guidelines—whereas 20th- and 21st-century drafters mostly know nothing about the guidelines and show an astonishing degree of ineptitude with tenses.

Fourth, Stephen was exceptionally forward-thinking in his use of visual devices. In his *Digest of the Criminal Law*, he uses what we would call a flowchart to illustrate the steps in analyzing homicide;[46] a tabular representation for purposes of analyzing intentional violence;[47] and an alphabetical guide of indictable offenses, once again in tabular form.[48]

But despite the brilliancies, the drafting does have blemishes. They illustrate the fallibility of Stephen's Judge in our writing-process paradigm. Somehow, in the *Digest of the Criminal Law*, Stephen let at least one *shall* creep into the text—and not even in a mandatory sense: "No person who takes any oath or engagement . . . shall be justified or excused thereby, unless . . . ."[49] Elsewhere, he introduces inconsistencies by avoiding his preferred *must* and using instead the verbose formula *It is the legal duty* . . . .[50] He would have been wiser to stick to a single method of expressing duties: the serviceable *must*.

The texts are plagued by other minute inconsistencies. In some places, he uses the serial comma; in others, he doesn't. In some places, he writes *every person* at the outset of a rule; in others, he writes *every one*; in still others, he writes *whoever*. In some places, he introduces a condition with *if*; in others, he uses *where*. Generally, he wisely sticks to the singular (*every meeting*); in places, though, he uses an ill-advised plural (*all assemblies*).

Stephen's numbering system is underdeveloped, so that he has many subparagraphs that are simply indented but unnumbered—making large parts of his digests essentially uncitable without some cumbersome description.

Also, he oddly sets out provisos—those caveats introduced with some variation of *provided that*—in separate capitalized sentences.[51] Coode had

---

[44] *Crim. Dig.*, note 2, at 2.
[45] Garner, *A Dictionary of Modern Legal Usage*, note 40, at 831 (paraphrasing Coode).
[46] *Crim. Dig.*, note 2, at 406.
[47] *Id.* at 410.
[48] *Id.* at 433–56.
[49] Art. 90, at 65.
[50] *See, e.g.*, arts. 236–239.
[51] *Crim. Dig.*, note 2, at art. 19(a) (par. 2); art. 95 (par. 2); art. 223, at 170; 260, at 200; 274, at 211; 282, at 219; 302, at 238.

warned against using provisos, but this seems to be a stylistic point on which Stephen didn't heed Coode's advice. The solution, of course, isn't to use a semicolon before *provided that*, the way so many modern drafters do, thereby grossly driving up the average sentence length. Instead, the best modern drafters would simply replace *provided that* with a capitalized *but* to introduce an exception expressed in a follow-on sentence. The United States Constitution contains eight such exceptions introduced by a capitalized *but*. In at least one place—in yet another stylistic inconsistency—Stephen uses a capitalized *but* where one would expect to find *provided that*.[52]

There are other weaknesses in the drafting. Apart from provisos, Stephen engages in a fair amount of legalese, especially the *here-* and *there-* words: *hereto, therefor, therein, thereof,* and *thereon.* He uses *the said child* for *the child*.[53] Although he often uses *such* in the sound nonlegalistic way,[54] he also engages in the legalistic *such*[55] that has been so much criticized.[56] He repeatedly mispunctuates *ten years' penal servitude* by omitting the apostrophe.[57] And his digests contain too many typographical errors,[58] including, in one place, the drafter's worst nightmare: a dropped *not*.[59]

---

[52] *Crim. Dig.*, note 2, art. 28, at 21.

[53] *Crim. Dig.*, note 2, art. 256, at 194.

[54] *See, e.g., Crim. Dig.*, note 2, art. 335, at 271 ("such a contract").

[55] *Crim. Dig.*, note 2, art. 284, at 221 ("such child").

[56] For example, Sir Frederick Pollock, while editor of the Law Reports, wrote to Justice Oliver Wendell Holmes: "As to *such*, this is the kind of attorney's clerk's slang I have tried to choke off: 'The plaintiff was the tenant of a house in X street. Such street was admitted to be a new street within etc., etc.' They think it looks more professional. And so it has crept even into judgments." *Holmes–Pollock Letters* vol. 2, 251 (Mark D. Howe ed., 1941). *See also,* among many others, H.W. Fowler, *A Dictionary of Modern English Usage* 581–82 (1926) (calling this "the illiterate *such*"); Elmer A. Driedger, *The Composition of Legislation* 88 (1957); David Mellinkoff, *The Language of the Law* 430–31 (1963); Theodore M. Bernstein, *The Careful Writer* 432 (1965) (calling it "legalistic"); Reed Dickerson, *The Fundamentals of Legal Drafting* 131 (1965); Michèle M. Asprey, *Plain Language for Lawyers* 124 (1991).

[57] *See, e.g., Crim. Dig.*, note 2, art. 259, at 198; art. 263–64, at 204; art. 274, at 211; art. 279. Even 19th-century grammarians required the possessive apostrophe. *See, e.g.,* Goold Brown, *The Grammar of English Grammars* 514 (10th ed. 1851) (calling the apostrophe-less construction "manifestly bad English").

[58] *See, e.g., Crim. Dig.*, note 2, art. 293, at 192; p. 176n.; p. 243.

[59] *Ev. Dig.*, note 1, art. 11, at 15 ("When there is a question whether a person said or did something, the fact that he said or did something of the same sort on a different occasion may be proved if it shows the existence on the occasion in question of any intention, knowledge, good or bad faith, malice, or other state of mind or of any state of body or bodily feeling, the existence of which is in issue or is or is deemed to be relevant to the issue; but such facts or words may [not] be proved merely in order to show that the person so acting or speaking was likely on the occasion in question to act in a similar manner."). This typographical error is fixed in the American edition: Stephen, *Ev. Dig.*, note 2, art. 11, at 28 (George Chase ed., Am. ed. 1892).

On a less minute scale, I might also point to some of Stephen's own maladroit drafting that is less than clear. Consider article 236 of the *Digest of the Criminal Law*, with its roundabout wordings and confusing pronouns:

> It is the legal duty of a person who is unable to provide for any person necessaries which he is legally bound to provide for him to make application to the proper authorities for parochial relief in cases in which such authorities are legally bound to furnish such relief.

Essentially, that means simply this:

> A person who is bound to provide necessaries to another but cannot do so must apply to the proper authorities for parochial relief if it is available.

Lest anyone think that the weaknesses I've pointed out—especially the small inconsistencies in wording—are niggling details, I hasten to observe that the drafter's job is to forestall arguments based on those inconsistencies. Stephen himself recognized this. In 1879, he referred to "the confusion engendered by the employment of different styles."[60] He acknowledged it in one of his last judicial opinions, in 1891. In *Re Castioni*, he wrote that precision

> is essential to everyone who has ever had, as I have had on many occasions, to draft Acts of Parliament, which, although they may be easy to understand, people continually try to misunderstand, and in which therefore it is not enough to attain to a degree of precision which a person reading in good faith can understand; but it is necessary to attain if possible to a degree of precision which a person reading in bad faith cannot misunderstand. It is all the better if he cannot pretend to misunderstand it.[61]

Stephen the Lexicographer

Throughout his work, Stephen showed a concern for words and their meanings. He was a kind of semanticist. Even in his early work on criminal law, in 1863, he was sensitive about the phrase *criminal law* itself and argued that it is not entirely apt:

> "Penal" would be a better phrase than "criminal" law, as it points out with greater emphasis the specific mark by which the province of law

---

[60] Stephen, "The Criminal Code," in *The Nineteenth Century* 136, 142 (Jan. 1880).

[61] *Re Castioni* [1891] 1 Q.B. 149, 167 (*per* Stephen, J.). Cf. Stephen's less seasoned comment of 1879: "The critic [of a statute] is trying to detect faults. The judge is trying to do justice. The one, in other words, is intent on showing that this or that expression is incomplete, or capable of being misunderstood. The other is trying in good faith to ascertain the real meaning of the words before him." Stephen, note 60, at 141.

to which it applies is distinguished from other provinces; for the distinction arises not from the nature of the acts contemplated, but from the manner in which they are treated.[62]

To the modern lawyer, familiar with the more modern writers on criminal law, Stephen's words sound as if they could be those of Glanville Williams: Stephen once said that to ask concerning any occurrence, " 'Is this a crime or is it a tort?' is . . . no wiser than it would be to ask concerning a man, 'Is he a father or a son?' For he may well be both."[63] Many writers of legal texts are not so linguistically attuned.

One more example. In the *Digest of the Law of Evidence*, Stephen sorted out an ambiguity that still plagues legal writers:

> The arrangement of the book . . . is based upon the distinction between relevancy and proof, that is, between the question What facts may be proved? and the question How must a fact be proved assuming that proof of it may be given? The neglect of this distinction, which is concealed by the ambiguity of the word *evidence* (a word which sometimes means testimony and at other times relevancy) has thrown the whole subject into confusion, and has made what is really plain enough appear almost incomprehensible.[64]

While later writers on evidence have argued that Stephen claimed too much with his principle of relevance—William Twining has said that his "efforts failed"[65]—the lexical point about the word *evidence* remains valid.

As a writer of digests and codes, Stephen defined terms assiduously—and generally pretty carefully. A reader of the digest is sometimes struck by seeming anomalies, though. Why is it a maiming to strike out a person's tooth, or castrate a man, but it isn't a maiming to cut off someone's nose?[66] That seems curious. But Stephen's definition of *maim*, which undoubtedly codifies a good deal of caselaw on the subject, sorts out why that is so:

> A maim is bodily harm whereby a man is deprived of the use of any member of his body or of any sense which he can use in fighting, or

---

[62] Stephen, note 17, at 6.

[63] J.W. Cecil, *Outlines of Criminal Law* 543 (16th ed. 1952) (quoting Stephen). Cf. the linguistic insight in Stephen's adverbial observation that "[t]he mental element of most crimes is marked by one of the words 'maliciously,' 'fraudulently,' 'negligently,' or 'knowingly.' " *R. v. Tolson*, 23 Q.B. 168.

[64] *Ev. Dig.*, note 1, at ix.

[65] William Twining, *Theories of Evidence: Bentham and Wigmore* 4 (1985).

[66] *Crim. Dig.*, note 2, at art. 227 (illustration), at 165. Under modern law, disfigurement such as cutting off a person's nose does amount to a maim. *See* Rollin M. Perkins & Ronald M. Boyce, *Criminal Law* 241 (3d ed. 1982).

by the loss of which he is generally and permanently weakened, but a bodily injury is not a maim merely because it is a disfigurement.[67]

You might wonder whether losing a nose doesn't "generally and permanently weaken" someone, but you can also see why Stephen held that it wouldn't.

As a legal lexicographer, I've found dozens of terms for which Stephen gives good definitions or insightful discussions. Among the ones from the *Digest of the Criminal Law* are these:

affray	night
barrator	perjury
bridewell	piracy
carnal knowledge	public body
champerty	rape
criminal prisoner	riot
defamatory	rout
embezzlement	seditious conspiracy
fair comment	seditious intention
false pretenses	sodomy
fining	subjection to police supervision
forgery	trade description
judicial proceeding	treating
maintenance	undue influence
making a false document	unlawful assembly
malice	whipping
material	wrong

Elsewhere, he gave a superb exposition of the dual meaning of *common law*, recording two senses: (1) "those parts of the known and ascertained law which are to be found in decided cases and in works of authoritative writers like Coke or Hale, but which have never been reduced to the form of a statute"; and (2) "the qualified power [that] judges possess of making new law, under the fiction of declaring existing law in cases unprovided for by existing statutes or other authorities."[68] So brilliant is that second sense that I intend to add it as a fifth sense to the ninth edition of *Black's Law Dictionary*—and (of course) to credit Stephen. (Yes, Stephen recorded but two senses of *common law*—and missed three others.[69])

---

[67] *Id.* (main text).

[68] Stephen, note 60, at 152.

[69] *See Black's Law Dictionary* 293–94 (8th ed. 2004).

A few of Stephen's definitions betray the fact that he was no professional lexicographer. For example, he defines the verb *break* as if it were a noun, and he uses the gerund *breaking* in the definition itself.[70] And he makes a similar mistake with *misappropriate*.[71]

On the whole, though, his definitions are sound, and taken together they provide the modern researcher with a reliable source for knowing how certain legal terms were understood during the last half of the 19th century—just as Johnson is the most reliable general guide to 18th-century meanings.

Conclusion

It's appropriate that we're holding this conference in April. It was an important month for Stephen. It was 128 years ago this month that he wrote in a letter that he had "just completed the hardest work he had ever done"—namely, the *Digest of the Criminal Law*.[72] And it was 14 years later—114 years ago this month—that Stephen resigned from the bench because of his failing mental powers.[73]

It's also appropriate that this conference is considering Stephen's work from so many angles. Stephen was famous for looking at things from various points of view. A well-known anecdote about Justice Stephen illustrates the point. A debtor before the Queen's Bench was trying to escape liability by blaming his wife for the expenditure. Stephen is reported to have blurted out characteristically: "That is a very old excuse. I often felt that Adam—I mean—that is—well! I have always wished to hear Eve's account of the transaction."[74]

A personal note: This conference has prompted me to consider the fascinating intersections that occur in life. The organizer of this conference, Christopher Ricks, was my teacher in Oxford in the summer of 1979.

---

[70] *Crim. Dig.*, note 2, at 282. For criticisms of modern legal lexicographers who have made similar blunders, see Garner, *Legal Lexicography: A View from the Front Lines*, 6 Green Bag 151, 156–57 (2003); Garner, "The Missing Common-Law Words," in *The State of the Language* 235, 245 n.21 (Christopher Ricks & Leonard Michaels eds., 1990) (reprinted here in Chapter Six).

[71] *Crim. Dig.*, note 70, at 310.

[72] Leslie Stephen, note 8, at 377.

[73] *D.N.B.* vol. 18, note 8, at 1053.

[74] Stephen, J. (as quoted in Marshall Brown, *Wit and Humor of Bench and Bar* 332 (1899)).

In the summer of 1981, two months before I was to enter law school, I was back in Oxford and arranged a lunch with Christopher on July 16 at a place called the Nosebag. Afterward, I told him that I wanted to find a used-book store that I'd been to two years before, not far from the Opium Den restaurant, and he told me how to get to Waterfield's bookseller. When we parted, I walked there, and outside I found a cart full of books discounted to £1. There was Stephen's *Digest of the Law of Evidence*—the 1881 edition that I'm holding right now—and I bought it. Inside is my signature from 1981, exactly a century from the publication date. Twenty-two years later, I learned for the first time that Christopher had an abiding interest in Stephen, that he wanted to know whether I knew anything about Stephen and his digests, and—when I said that I did—that he'd like me to speak about the digests at this conference. It's an extraordinary set of coincidences. All I can say is, Thank you, Christopher, for pointing the way to Waterfield's that day—and for pointing the way so often in my life since that day.

JUSTICE ANTONIN SCALIA

CHAPTER FIVE

English Grammar and Usage

Tending to Your Snootitude

OVER BREAKFAST ONE DAY, Justice Antonin Scalia declared that he cares a great deal about language—about words and their proper use. "There's a word for people like me. An essayist in *Harper's* coined it."

He couldn't remember the word. So I ventured to help him: "Is it *SNOOT*?"

"That's it!"

The *Harper's* essay was by the renowned novelist David Foster Wallace. It's been reprinted in an expanded form in a new anthology of Wallace's work, *Consider the Lobster* (2005). Here's what Wallace says about SNOOTs:

> SNOOT (*n*) (*highly colloquial*) is this reviewer's nuclear family's nickname à clef for a really extreme usage fanatic, the sort of person whose idea of Sunday fun is to hunt for mistakes in the very prose of Safire's column ["On Language," in *The New York Times*]. This reviewer's family is roughly 70 percent SNOOT, which term itself derives from an acronym, with the big historical family joke being that whether S.N.O.O.T. stood for "Sprachgefühl Necessitates Our Ongoing Tendance" or "Syntax Nudniks of Our Time" depended on whether or not you were one.[1]

Granting that "SNOOTs are just about the last remaining kind of truly elitist nerd," he further defines the breed as people who know what *dysphemism* means and don't mind letting you know.

Adapted from *Student Lawyer* (Nov. 2006).
[1] David Foster Wallace, "Authority and American Usage," in *Consider the Lobster* 65, 69 n.5 (2005).

As you might imagine, Justice Scalia isn't the only SNOOT on the U.S. Supreme Court. I'd venture to say that more than half the justices are SNOOTs. Justice Ruth Bader Ginsburg is certainly one: she is fastidious about the words in her opinions. And so is Chief Justice John Roberts, who is famously persnickety about restrictive *thats* and nonrestrictive *whiches*.

Is snootitude a good thing? Surely it is—if it's good to observe distinctions, to be aware of nuances, to be linguistically surefooted, to know what you're doing when handling words. Who could argue against it? That would be advocating slovenliness.

Of course, some people think they're SNOOTs when they're not—just as some people think they're good poker players, bowlers, golfers, or pianists even when the facts shout otherwise.

The distinguishing characteristic is that SNOOTs know their English usage—and they own books with *usage* in the title. According to June Casagrande, author of *Grammar Snobs Are Great Big Meanies* (2006), usage guides are "one of the biggest secrets of the language-savvy . . . . These books are the one secret those grammar fat cats don't want you to know because anyone who has one on his desk can handle almost any language situation." Despite her title, by the way, Casagrande is a true SNOOT.

So SNOOTs know usage, and non-SNOOTs don't.

Are you a SNOOT? Let's find out. Take the following quiz, being careful not to peek at the answers until you're finished. If you find out that you're a member of the SNOOT club, congratulations: it's a big part of being a good writer, though it's not everything. If you're not a member of the club, don't fret too much. Do some studying and reapply!

1. If someone's name is Betty Flowers and she's married, are she and her family (a) the Flowers, or (b) the Flowerses?

2. Was the signing of the armistice that ended World War I (a) an historic, or (b) a historic event?

3. Is it better to go (a) till 4:00 p.m., or (b) 'til 4:00 p.m.?

4. When speaking of various funds, granted you can use the collective term *money*. But if you're going to use a plural form—as is permissible—is it better to write (a) moneys, or (b) monies?

5. If you're quitting a job, do you give (a) two weeks notice, or (b) two weeks' notice?

6. If you're zeroing in on a problem, are you (a) homing in, or (b) honing in?

7. If two people both call someone else a friend, do they have (a) a mutual friend, or (b) a friend in common?

8. Is it better form to write (a) high-school friend, common-law rule, and collective-bargaining agreement, or (b) high school friend, common law rule, and collective bargaining agreement?

9. Which is the better spelling: (a) adviser, or (b) advisor?

10. Which statement is more nearly correct? (a) Good writers don't begin sentences with conjunctions such as *and* or *but*. (b) Good writers typically begin a fair percentage of their sentences with conjunctions.

Answer Key

AUS = Copperud, *American Usage and Style* (1980)

CMS = *The Chicago Manual of Style* (15th ed. 2003)

DDM = Bernstein, *Dos, Don'ts, and Maybes of English Usage* (1977)

DMLU = Garner, *A Dictionary of Modern Legal Usage* (2d ed. 1995)

GMAU = *Garner's Modern American Usage* (2d ed. 2003)

KE = Amis, *The King's English* (1997)

MEU = Fowler, *A Dictionary of Modern English Usage* (Ernest Gowers ed., 2d ed. 1965)

MTH = Bernstein, *Miss Thistlebottom's Hobgoblins* (1971)

Redbook = Garner, *The Redbook: A Manual on Legal Style* (2d ed. 2006)

UA = Partridge, *Usage and Abusage* (rev. ed. 1973)

1. (b) A proper name that ends in a sibilant forms the plural by adding "es": "Such plurals are often erroneously formed by adding an apostrophe, which indicates possession." *AUS* at 294. See also *CMS* at 279–80; *DMLU* at 670; *GMAU* at 617; *Redbook* at 107.

2. (b) The choice is a simple one: "If you pronounce 'historic' as *istoric* or 'hotel' as *otel*, then you'd better say *an historic* and *an hotel*. But the rest of us will say *a historic* and *a hotel*." *DDM* at 16. See also *AUS* at 1; *CMS* at 197; *DMLU* at 3; *GMAU* at 1; *MEU* at 1; *Redbook* at 212.

3. (a) *Till* is not a contraction of *until*, though both date from the 14th century: "While the subject of *until* is before the house, let it be said that *till* is a perfectly good word meaning the same thing. Therefore, the contraction *'til* is superfluous and unrecognized in good usage." *MTH* at 83. See also *AUS* at 383; *CMS* at 230; *DDM* at 229; *DMLU* at 882; *GMAU* at 790; *KE* at 229; *MEU* at 639.

4. (a) Dictionaries record both plurals, but: "*Monies* is only as logical as the obsolete plural *attornies*." *DMLU* at 571. See also *CMS* at 150; *GMAU* at 529; *UA* at 188.

5. (b) The possessive form is idiomatic but often mishandled: "This usage was dealt a real setback in 2002 with the release of the hit movie *Two Weeks Notice* [read *Two Weeks' Notice*], starring Hugh Grant and Sandra Bullock. It might have been a bigger hit if the good-usage crowd hadn't boycotted the movie on principle." *GMAU* at 626. See also *CMS* at 284; *DDM* at 171; *DMLU* at 674; *MEU* at 467; *MTH* at 105; *Redbook* at 144–45.

6. (a) Sharp thinkers know that *hone* doesn't fit: "In the 19th century, the metaphor referred to what homing pigeons do; by the early 20th century, it referred also to what aircraft and missiles do." *GMAU* at 410. See also *CMS* at 217–18; *Redbook* at 244.

7. (b) The distinction is not commonly understood: "*Mutual* is a well-known trap. The essence of its meaning is that it involves the relation x is or does to y as y to x, and not the relation x is or does to z as y to z. From this it follows that *our mutual friend Jones* (meaning Jones who is your friend as well as mine), and all similar phrases are misuses of *mutual*. In such places, *common* is the right word, and the use of *mutual* betrays ignorance of its meaning." *MEU* at 377. See also *GMAU* at 535; *KE* at 145; *Redbook* at 256.

8. (a) Don't trip up your readers: "While some phrasal adjectives may be clear to the writer and to most readers, the absence of hyphens will always cause some readers to misstep midway through the sentence. The better practice is to hyphenate." *Redbook* at 38–41. See also *AUS* at 188; *CMS* at 171; *DMLU* at 657–58; *GMAU* at 604–07; *MEU* at 256–57.

9. (a) Psychics tend to prefer *advisor*. But: "The *-er* spelling is sanctioned over the *-or* spelling in the dictionaries." *DMLU* at 33. See also *GMAU* at 25; *Redbook* at 118.

10. (b) Used well, these words are invaluable sentence-starters: "And the idea that *and* must not begin a sentence . . . is an empty superstition. The same goes for *but*. Indeed either word can give unimprovably early warning of the sort of thing that is to follow." *KE* at 13–14. See also *CMS* at 193–94; *DMLU* at 55, 123–24, 856; *GMAU* at 44, 118–19; *MEU* at 29.

ॐ ॐ ॐ

The Word on the Street

THE REPUBLICAN PLATFORM OF 1936 accused President Franklin D. Roosevelt of "flaunting" the United States Supreme Court with his court-packing plan. After the platform was published, a minor debate ensued— not about the rightness of Roosevelt's position (that was the major debate), but about whether the Republicans had misused *flaunt* ("to show off ostentatiously") for *flout* ("to contravene, disregard, or treat with contempt"). The struggle to keep these words separate continues to this day.

That's useful information for lawyers and judges, who, after all, may rightly be classed as professional writers. Since we write in a formal context, we ought to be judged by the highest standards; and for our writing to meet these standards, it must reflect a knowledgeable use of the language. If we choose to be relaxed or colloquial in a given piece of writing, that's one thing. But if we blur distinctions out of ignorance that they exist, it's quite another.

Most of us develop our vocabularies haphazardly, picking up a word here in reading and there in someone else's speech. So we often gain only indistinct notions about what certain words mean. Unfortunately, English words often suggest meanings quite different from their actual meanings, and writers are frequently thrown off. Occasionally, what began as an error—say, the use of *ingenuity* as the noun corresponding to *ingenious* rather than to *ingenuous*—must be accepted as standard.

As debates over English usage are waged by those who care about the language and its uses and abuses, words gradually build up reputations. *Flaunt*, for example, is well known for its mischievous encroachment on the domain of *flout*.

Similar pairs of words abound in the language. *Fortuitous* properly means "occurring merely by chance," though it is increasingly misused as if it were another word for *fortunate*. Properly, a disaster may be just as fortuitous as a windfall. *Enormity* is the victim of a similar blunder; it has to do with wickedness, not with size (literal or figurative). One speaks of the enormity of Hitler's crimes. *Enormousness* is the word to convey the notion of vastness. A simple tip to remember is that words so differentiated by their suffixes seldom have identical meanings.

Even words not readily confused with their siblings can cause trouble. Who has not heard *fulsome* used as if it meant "quite full"? The state appellate judge who recently referred to the United States Supreme

Adapted from *ABA Journal* (Dec. 1988).

Court's "fulsome" requirements for a public figure to prove defamation did not intend to defame the Supreme Court. But he should have known that *fulsome* means "offensive to normal tastes and sensibilities"—that the word expresses revulsion. Referring to an interviewee's "fulsome credentials" is insulting, not laudatory.

These points of usage are for the most part old and settled. Most of the troublesome words in our language have gained notoriety, so it is easy for the legal writer to become familiar with these words and handle them accordingly.

Bad Raps

Of course, ill repute is sometimes ill-deserved. The split infinitive is no abomination—one need merely know when to properly use it. Prepositions are not bad words to end sentences with. And it often serves the writer well to begin a sentence with *and* or *but*. Undeserved reputations sometimes persist despite the concerted efforts of authorities on English usage to eradicate them.

Professional writers are obliged to know these things. Entirely too many lawyers do not know them, apparently forgetting that ours is fundamentally a profession of writers. Our success or failure depends in large part on how adept we are at getting ideas across in writing, and doing it convincingly.

Just as fine carpenters must keep their tools sharp and well oiled, lawyers must cultivate their knowledge of the English language and its niceties. The language gives us an unparalleled word-hoard with which to work. English words have a rich literary history, and over the centuries have developed nuances that can never be entirely mastered. Yet we must try.

As a living language, English is constantly evolving because of how people like you and me use it. Whether or not we can say that the confusion of *flaunt* with *flout*, or of *enormity* with *enormousness*, causes the language to deteriorate, we know beyond question that there are better and worse uses of language in any given context. To the extent that we align ourselves with the better uses of language—by opposing what is slipshod and by striving for aptness, accuracy, concision, and even elegance—we ensure a sounder legacy for those who will follow us. In the meantime, we safeguard our own reputations; for the ill repute of a misused word often rubs off fulsomely on its user.

ک‌ ک‌ ک‌

Testing Your Command
of Grammar and Usage

IN MY WRITING SEMINARS FOR LAWYERS, I often ask them whether they feel confident they know what the passive voice is. Typically at least 98% will say they do. Then I'll offer them a pop quiz consisting of only two sentences and ask them whether there's a passive-voice verb in either one.

Guess what happens. About 80% flunk. They will have assumed that the passive voice consists of any *be*-verb (especially *is, are, was,* or *were*). Only about 20% of them will know the two essential elements of passive voice: a *be*-verb and a past participle (e.g., *was dismissed* or *were filed*).

Once when I gave this quiz at a law firm in New York, several foreign lawyers were present—people who grew up in France, Italy, and Chile. They were astounded by their American colleagues' grammatical ignorance. One French lawyer, who breezed through the quiz, assured me that every third-grader in France knows what the passive voice is. Hyperbole, perhaps, but it's no exaggeration to say that every legal writer should know what it is. As a writer or editor, how can you correct what you're ignorant of?

Learning grammar may seem like an exercise in pedantry. Who cares if you can tell whether *which* or *that* is the better pronoun in a particular sentence? Who cares if you can distinguish the present-perfect tense from the pluperfect, or the nominative case from the objective case?

My answer is fourfold. (1) Many if not most people grow up speaking a form of regional or social dialect. If you raise your comfort level with grammar, you'll have more confidence that your speaking and writing won't betray you among your more literate peers. (2) Many people who are confident that they know grammatical rules are dead wrong: they've been fed misinformation about English grammar, and their writing suffers. (3) Once you have a true command of language, you can focus more on what you're trying to say than on how you're going to say it, so the substance of your message will be more satisfying. (4) Whether we know it or not—whether we like it or not—people judge us by how we wield words; when you manage your words skillfully, you have far greater opportunities in law and in any other professional realm. That's the reality.

I concede that some drudgery is involved in learning grammar, especially if you carry bad memories of it from high school. But it isn't

---

Adapted from *Student Lawyer* (Feb. 2002 & Jan. 2005).

nearly as bad as many fear, especially when you're convinced that it's truly useful to know. And in my experience, it's best when self-taught, partly because it's hard to find a good course on the subject. My favorite book for the grammatical novice is Norman Lewis's *30 Days to Better English* (perennially in print). At under $10, it's a bargain.

Although good editing depends on much more than just detecting and avoiding errors, it certainly does require those things. Otherwise, your credibility plummets. And of all the errors that plague legal writing, incorrect word choices and grammatical blunders must rank pretty high.

Words are the only tools that lawyers have. Just as a skilled carpenter wouldn't drive a nail with a screwdriver, skilled legal writers don't use *fortuitous* when they mean *fortunate*, or *infer* when they mean *imply*. Well-chosen words are one mark of a stylist. In fact, Jonathan Swift defined style as "the right words in the right places." But putting the right words into the right places can be a tremendous challenge, even for the law-review editor.

Of course, we're all prone to verbal slips. The only antidote is constant vigilance. For most people, that's unrealistic in their daily use of language. As one English professor, T.W.H. Holland, said nearly 40 years ago, "I doubt if the lifelong vagueness of most people about their words could either possibly or usefully be cured." Here, though, we're talking not about "most people," but about lawyers (or aspiring lawyers). And we're talking not about speech, but about the written word—which invokes a higher standard of care.

Consider some word-choice errors in law reviews. In each passage quoted below, a law-review author (unnamed) and editorial board (named) allowed the wrong word to surface in print. Embarrassing, you say? Perhaps. Yet the intent is not to humiliate; it's to point up how easily these embarrassments can happen. To err is human, but so is to learn from those errors.

In taking this little quiz, you'll be testing yourself against law-review editors on one of their bad days. Just choose (a) or (b) within each bracketed phrasing. Finish the quiz before peeking (or is that *peaking*, or perhaps *piquing*?) at the answers:

1. "Aside from [(a) reining, or (b) reigning] in the public's informational rights, the government's secrecy has other significant consequences." (*California Law Review*)

2. "By [(a) flouting, or (b) flaunting] international law at home, the United States risks undermining its own authority to demand implementation of international law abroad." (*Cornell International Law Journal*)

3. "Indeterminacy in patent-law cases is expected to increase because it is expected that the Federal Circuit's caseload will [(a) unrelentingly, or (b) unrelentlessly] rise." (*UCLA Journal of Law and Technology*)

4. "It is this necessity that . . . [(a) thrusted, or (b) thrust] the state into partnership with the private sector." (*University of Pennsylvania Journal of Constitutional Law*)

5. "Mrs. Haley argued that the agreement between [(a) she, or (b) her] and the Piggs was void on several grounds." (*St. Louis University Law Journal*)

6. "Much of the increase [(a) inures, or (b) inheres] to the benefit of attorneys." (*Georgetown Journal of Legal Ethics*)

7. "Six additional soldiers were tried, convicted, and [(a) hanged, or (b) hung] for murder and mutiny before their appeal could be heard." (*William & Mary Bill of Rights Journal*)

8. "Tennessee's rationale for continuing the discriminatory practice was [(a) therefor, or (b) therefore] 'unfounded.'" (*Cumberland Law Review*)

9. "Today America is in the [(a) throes, or (b) throws] of an identity crisis with respect to consumer credit." (*Florida Law Review*)

10. "Updated in November 2000, *Bounds of Advocacy* provides guidance to lawyers practicing family law. [(a) Its, or (b) It's] purpose is to assist family lawyers when dealing with moral and ethical problems." (*Arizona Law Review*)

11. "While Rule 9(b) and the Reform Act, of necessity, tend to lengthen a [(a) well-plead, or (b) well-pleaded] complaint, they do not give license to violate Rule 8." (*U.C. Davis Law Review*)

12. "[(a) Regrettably, or (b) Regretfully], most interrogation training manuals . . . give no thought to how the methods they advocate communicate psychologically coercive messages and sometimes lead the innocent to confess." (*North Carolina Law Review*)

13. "[B]y taking the opportunity for his own, the corporate fiduciary will . . . be placed in a position [(a) inimicable, or (b) inimical] to his duties to the corporation." (*Seton Hall Law Review*)

14. "[C]ourts are not permitted to 'rehabilitate' the response of a [(a) perspective, or (b) prospective] juror at all, but only to clarify it." (*Georgia Law Review*)

15. "[P]erhaps some thought it wiser not to foreclose [(a) precipitously, or (b) precipitately] any future possibility of invoking federal jurisdiction to enforce Article I, Section 10's explicit prohibitions against such abuses." (*Yale Law Journal*)

16. "[S]tatic [towns were] those whose population had either remained [(a) stationery, or (b) stationary] or increased at a rate below the state average." (*New England Law Review*)

17. "[S]urely this is a [(a) venial, or (b) venal] sin. Who among us (especially as beginning scholars) has not used a straw person or two to motivate our analysis?" (*Wisconsin Law Review*)

18. "[T]he United States found itself receiving [(a) flak, or (b) flack] from several countries for more than just its failure to submit an offer." (*Tulane Maritime Law Journal*)

19. "[T]he Eleventh Circuit Court of Appeals found that flying the Confederate flag above the Alabama [(a) capitol, or (b) capital] building was neither a 'badge of servitude' . . . nor a violation of the Equal Protection Clause." (*Temple Law Review*)

20. "[T]he costs may be greater and [(a) less, or (b) fewer] people may benefit." (*Florida State University Law Review*)

21. "[T]he federal government sought to acquire vast [(a) tracts, or (b) tracks] of land through donation from its owners or the States concerned." (*Golden Gate University Law Review*)

22. "[T]he issue of what variables can be included in valuation will [(a) doubtlessly, or (b) doubtless] continue to be relevant." (*Columbia Law Review*)

23. "[T]o go any further—to expand the scope of takings liability to the point of presenting governments with a [(a) Hobbesian, or (b) Hobson's] choice—would interfere profoundly with those governments' ability to promote the public welfare." (*Harvard Environmental Law Review*)

24. "Then the law allowed compensation for Israeli 'residents' [(a) whose, or (b) who's] property was in the Custodian of Absentees' Property." (*Vanderbilt Journal of Transnational Law*)

25. "Well, [(a) alright, or (b) all right], the point is difficult to fathom even for many people who are trained in philosophy." (*University of Chicago Law Review*)

Scoring Guide

22–25 correct: Superb. 13–17 correct: Fair.
18–21 correct: Good.   1–12 correct: Poor.

Abbreviations in Key

CMS = *The Chicago Manual of Style* (15th ed. 2003)
DMLU = Garner, *A Dictionary of Modern Legal Usage* (2d ed. 1995)
Redbook = Garner, *The Redbook: A Manual on Legal Style* (2d ed. 2006)
TLR Manual = *Texas Law Review Manual on Style, Usage, and Editing* (9th ed. 2002)

Key to Correct Answers

1. *Reining* (a). *DMLU* at 748; *Redbook* at 266.
2. *Flouting* (a). *CMS* at 215; *DMLU* at 362; *Redbook* at 241.
3. *Unrelentingly* (a). See any general dictionary.
4. *Thrust* (b). See any general dictionary.
5. *Her* (b). *CMS* at 160; *DMLU* at 592; *Redbook* at 153.
6. *Inures* (a). *DMLU* at 446, 466; *Redbook* at 251, 297.
7. *Hanged* (a). *CMS* at 217; *DMLU* at 397; *Redbook* at 244.
8. *Therefore* (b). *CMS* at 230; *DMLU* at 878–79; *Redbook* at 274.
9. *Throes* (a). See any general dictionary.
10. *Its* (a). *CMS* at 220; *DMLU* at 475; *Redbook* at 111, 251.
11. *Well-pleaded* (b). *CMS* at 226; *DMLU* at 667; *Redbook* at 262; *TLR Manual* at 67.
12. *Regrettably* (a). *CMS* at 227; *DMLU* at 748; *Redbook* at 266.
13. *Inimical* (b). *DMLU* at 447; any general dictionary.
14. *Prospective* (b). See any general dictionary.
15. *Precipitously* (a). *CMS* at 226; *DMLU* at 681; *Redbook* at 263.
16. *Stationary* (b). *CMS* at 229; *DMLU* at 828; *Redbook* at 271.
17. *Venial* (a). *CMS* at 231; *DMLU* at 908–09; *Redbook* at 276.
18. *Flak* (a). *DMLU* at 361; any general dictionary.
19. *Capitol* (a). *CMS* at 204; *DMLU* at 130; *Redbook* at 222.
20. *Fewer* (b). *CMS* at 221; *DMLU* at 356; *Redbook* at 235; *TLR Manual* at 65.
21. *Tracts* (a). *DMLU* at 886–87; any general dictionary.
22. *Doubtless* (b). *CMS* at 211; *DMLU* at 295–96; *Redbook* at 235.
23. *Hobson's* (b). *DMLU* at 404; *Redbook* at 234.
24. *Whose* (a). *CMS* at 232; *DMLU* at 934; *Redbook* at 11, 278.
25. *All right* (b). *CMS* at 199; *DMLU* at 45.

ঽঽ ঽঽ ঽঽ

Our Blundering Law Reviews

"SOME QUITE INTELLIGENT PEOPLE have been lured into thinking that a concern for words is out of date." So wrote an anonymous employee of the Royal Bank of Canada in an excellent little 1972 book, *The Communication of Ideas*. And the law reviews—undoubtedly edited by intelligent people—show evidence today of being rather inattentive to words and their meanings.

Confusingly similar words abound in the English language. The common homophones—sound-alike words such as *they're* and *their* and *there*— don't cause much trouble for most people with a college education. They know which word they want.

But even educated folks can blunder with many English words— especially those that sound quite similar to others with dissimilar meanings. That's why English teachers have long encouraged their students to read attentively and acquire the dictionary habit: when you find a word that isn't familiar—or one you haven't seen in a while—don't guess at its meaning. Look it up. Register it in your mind. And make this a habit. Otherwise, you jeopardize your credibility with listeners and readers.

For lawyers, of course, words are particularly important. We're professional workers in words. They're our stock-in-trade. So it's (not *its*— the possessive form) worth pausing to assess (not *access*) one's command of the English vocabulary.

What follows is a survey of verbal gaffes in law reviews, presented in the form of a multiple-choice quiz. In each sentence listed below, the law review printed the incorrect choice or spelling of a word. So test yourself against the law-review editors and see how you fare. Just choose (a) or (b) within each bracketed phrasing. Finish the quiz before peeking (not *peaking* or *piquing*!) at the answers:

1. "False-statement crimes include perjury, which must be proven with at least two witnesses, or with one witness and strong corroborative evidence; false declaration, which does not require witnesses; [(a) subornation, or (b) subordination] of perjury; and the general false-statements statute." (*Columbia Law Review*)

2. "On one occasion, Malcolm even [(a) denounced, or (b) renounced] his citizenship: 'No, I'm not an American.'" (*Texas Review of Law and Politics*)

Adapted from *Student Lawyer* (Mar. 2006).

3. "In the past, farms escaped regulation under the CAA because of [(a) de minimis, or (b) de minimus] emissions exceptions." (*California Law Review*)

4. "According to the Court, the rights of the imams must be interpreted in context of modern constitutional protections, and not ancient [(a) deep-seeded, or (b) deep-seated] beliefs." (*Case Western Reserve Journal of International Law*)

5. "After the year of the fire, 1910, the Forest Service took every step possible to suppress fires, and every fire, large or small, was [(a) quelched, or (b) quelled]." (*Journal of Land, Resources, and Environmental Law*)

6. "The highly [(a) renowned, or (b) reknowned] Southern District of New York accepted the Ninth Circuit's determination." (*Rutgers Law Review*)

7. "The 'make work pay' agenda also, however, had a positive side as a rhetorical [(a) slight, or (b) sleight] of hand designed to channel demands to reduce the welfare rolls into support for providing other means-tested benefits to low-wage workers." (*New York University Law Review*)

8. "[The case valued] worthless stolen airline tickets by the face value written on them by the [(a) thiefs, or (b) thieves]." (*American Criminal Law Review*)

9. "Referring to these qualifiers, a self-described drafter of the Bybee Interrogation Memorandum later defended the memorandum [(a) thus, or (b) thusly]: . . . ." (*University of Pennsylvania Law Review*)

10. "The six leading makers of spreadsheet software were sued in 1990 with a patent that didn't use the word 'spreadsheet' anywhere, [(a) doubtlessly, or (b) doubtless] because the patent was so old that at the time it was written, the word 'spreadsheet' still referred to a leaf of ledger paper." (*Stanford Journal of Law, Business & Finance*)

11. "One need look no further than the area in and around Penn Station at rush hour to find an example of a massive, [(a) unwieldy, or (b) unwieldly] crowd that is vulnerable to attack in significantly similar ways." (*George Washington Law Review*)

12. "Sixty-one percent of those who download music claimed that they [(a) could care less, or (b) couldn't care less] if the music is copyrighted." (*Cornell Law Review*)

13. "Schlesinger describes the shanties and tarpaper towns that [(a) sprang, or (b) sprung] up, some of which were 'squalid beyond belief' with the smell of decay and surrender." (*Vermont Law Review*)

14. "Defendant had abandoned his expectation of privacy in his ship after the ship [(a) sunk, or (b) sank], defendant abandoned the ship, and thereafter made no efforts to secure or retrieve the sunken vessel." (*Wayne Law Review*)

15. "The situation of the transnational migrant has been aggravated by a paranoia that [(a) hordes, or (b) hoards] of asylum-seekers are threatening to enter the country." (*Harvard Human Rights Journal*)

16. "Malvo is expected to be tried yet again in Virginia for another homicide committed there, and he may be [(a) extradited, or (b) extradicted] to another state for even more juvenile death-penalty trials." (*American Journal of Criminal Law*)

17. "The costs [(a) born, or (b) borne] by individuals who inflict nonlegal sanctions are balanced by certain benefits of which there are three distinct types." (*Harvard Journal on Legislation*)

18. "Players are urged by their coaches to play with reckless [(a) abandon, or (b) abandonment] of self-protective instincts and with controlled rage." (*Stanford Law & Policy Review*)

19. "The Sixth Circuit Court of Appeals reversed because the District Court [(a) erred, or (b) errored] by only focusing on the dual-spring design when evaluating MDI's trade dress." (*Santa Clara Law Review*)

20. "It is [(a) fortuitous, or (b) fortunate] that a closed captioned system was developed for use in movie theaters; otherwise, deaf people today would still be waiting for their full and equal enjoyment in the simple luxury of going to the movies." (*John Marshall Journal of Computer and Information Law*)

21. "[(a) Everyday, or (b) Every day] when I skim through the paper it's the same." (*Valparaiso University Law Review*)

22. "The 'objective verifiable evidence' requirement [(a) contraverts, or (b) controverts] notions of fundamental justice because it denies certain plaintiffs an opportunity to be heard." (*Stanford Law & Policy Review*)

23. Parenthetical with case citation: "Hotel maintenance had failed to warn guest of dangerous condition of standing transparent

water that resulted when a toilet had [(a) overflown, or (b) over-flowed]." (*University of West Los Angeles Law Review*)

24. "The contest between [(a) he, or (b) him] and Snyder was, on both sides, an appeal to public opinion." (*Southern California Law Review*)

25. "On December 4, 2000, Booth met with Dr. Parent, an [(a) opthalmologist, or (b) ophthalmologist] that informed Booth that he should not have had Lasik surgery." (*Indiana Law Review*)

Scoring Guide

22–25 correct: Superb.   13–17 correct: Fair.
18–21 correct: Good.   1–12 correct: Poor.

Key to Correct Answers

Most current desktop dictionaries would guide you on these words and phrases. But for detailed guidance on matters of word choice, the sources cited below provide guidance:

CMS = *The Chicago Manual of Style* (15th ed. 2003)
DMLU = Garner, *A Dictionary of Modern Legal Usage* (2d ed. 1995)
GMAU = *Garner's Modern American Usage* (2d ed. 2003)
Redbook = Garner, *The Redbook: A Manual on Legal Style* (2d ed. 2006)

 1. *Subornation* (a). *DMLU* at 845.
 2. *Renounced* (b). *CMS* at 210; *GMAU* at 237.
 3. *De minimis* (a). *DMLU* at 263–64.
 4. *Deep-seated* (b). *GMAU* at 227.
 5. *Quelled* (b). *GMAU* at 664.
 6. *Renowned* (a). *DMLU* at 756; *GMAU* at 688; *Redbook* at 305.
 7. *Sleight* (b). *GMAU* at 730.
 8. *Thieves* (b). *GMAU* at 788.
 9. *Thus* (a). *CMS* at 230; *DMLU* at 881–82; *GMAU* at 789–90.
10. *Doubtless* (b). *CMS* at 211; *DMLU* at 295–96; *Redbook* at 235.
11. *Unwieldy* (a). *DMLU* at 904; *GMAU* at 808.
12. *Couldn't care less* (b). *CMS* at 209; *GMAU* at 204.
13. *Sprang* (a). *GMAU* at 745.
14. *Sank* (b). *DMLU* at 810; *GMAU* at 726.
15. *Hordes* (a). *GMAU* at 408; *Redbook* at 244.
16. *Extradited* (a). *GMAU* at 334.
17. *Borne* (b). *CMS* at 203; *DMLU* at 114; *Redbook* at 222.
18. *Abandon* (a). *GMAU* at 1–2.
19. *Erred* (a). *DMLU* at 325; *GMAU* at 310.
20. *Fortunate* (b). *CMS* at 216; *DMLU* at 372–73; *GMAU* at 365.

21. *Every day* (b). *CMS* at 214; *DMLU* at 332; *GMAU* at 320.
22. *Controverts* (b). *CMS* at 209; *DMLU* at 220; *Redbook* at 229.
23. *Overflowed* (b). *DMLU* at 630; *GMAU* at 583.
24. *Him* (b). *CMS* § 5.47, at 159; *GMAU* at 642–43.
25. *Ophthalmologist* (b). *DMLU* at 620; *GMAU* at 576; *Redbook* at 258.

❧ ❧ ❧

Gauging Your Editing Skills

AS WRITERS, WE ALL MAKE MISTAKES—sometimes embarrassing ones. Even our prestigious law reviews occasionally err, despite their teams of editors to scour galleys and proofs for even the slightest lapses.

If you want to edit well—either your own writing or someone else's—you need a healthy awareness of your own fallibility in grammar, usage, and proofreading. You'll take more and better precautions, and you'll achieve more credibility with your readers.

It's not enough to hope that readers will figure out what you mean. You must earn their trust—something that is hardly possible without some serious study and practice in handling the written word. Words are tricky: confusingly similar words can have quite unrelated meanings; others with very different looks can have allied meanings.

As Richard Grant White, a 19th-century scholar, put it: "The most important part of our every-day English has not to do with grammar, or with spelling, or with pronunciation. It has to do with the right use of words as to their meaning and their logical connection; and this may be learned by study and by care at almost any time of life."[1]

What follows are 25 brief passages from law reviews (mostly from the year 2000 or later). Each passage presents a usage problem that the editors never noticed. In short, they printed a mistake. In itself, the mistake may seem trifling. But errors in form tend to go alongside errors in content. No publication can ignore such a threat to its credibility.

Take this quiz and see how you stack up against law-review boards around the country—on one of their bad days. I've arranged the errors more or less in order of seriousness, from the most egregious to the least. The first few might well be easier for you than the last few. For reliable results, finish the entire quiz before checking the answers.

1. "The process provides a measure of individual accountability [(a) irregardless, or (b) regardless] of the end result." (*Columbia Law Review*)

2. "[E]vil inflicted on the offender can be a source of satisfaction for the victim and society as a whole, because the offense itself [(a) illicited, or (b) elicited] feelings of rage and displeasure." (*Ohio State Law Journal*)

Adapted from *Student Lawyer* (Jan. 2003).
[1] Richard Grant White, *Every-Day English* xxiii (1880).

3. "Critics cite his failure to acknowledge the validity of the EPA as an independent agency as an important difference between [(a) him, or (b) he] and Nixon." (*William & Mary Environmental Law and Policy Review*)

4. "President Mkapa of Tanzania has published a report disclosing the assets and income amassed by [(a) he, or (b) him] and his wife, and how those assets were acquired." (*Indiana Journal of Global Legal Studies*)

5. "This is a [(a) principal, or (b) principle] reason the socially inclusive Masons fared better in the early Republic than did the more selective Democratic–Republican societies." (*Washington Law Review*)

6. "One group of Iowa citizens is seriously [(a) effected, or (b) affected] by the increasing number of deer—Iowa's agricultural producers." (*Drake Journal of Agricultural Law*)

7. "The district court in *Davidson*, like many other courts faced with a case of some novelty which incorporates several [(a) discrete, or (b) discreet] areas of the law, claimed to be deciding the case on state grounds." (*Northern Kentucky Law Review*)

8. "As a young man, Mr. Cohen was a [(a) voracious, or (b) vociferous] reader and a bibliophile." (*Law Library Journal*)

9. "The First Department upheld the plaintiffs' claims for breach of contract, fraud, violations of New York General Business Law, and [(a) tortious, or (b) tortuous] interference with contract." (*Syracuse Law Review*)

10. "[T]his argument [is weakened] when it is applied to those child sexual battery cases where one witness's testimony is only [(a) collaborated, or (b) corroborated] by one other's." (*University of Miami Law Review*)

11. "The IJ found a Zaire applicant's testimony to be [(a) incredulous, or (b) incredible], inconsistent and contradictory." (*William Mitchell Law Review*)

12. "The newest justices, Ireland and Bridge, appeared [(a) reluctant, or (b) reticent] to use concurrences." (*Seattle University Law Review*)

13. "The concerted and sometimes conflicting efforts of feminists, transsexual persons, [and others] . . . have put increasing pressure on the conceptual and coercive [(a) apparatuses, or (b) apparati] of gender in the new millennium." (*California Law Review*)

14. "The numerous studies revealed that between 33% and 65% are [(a) adverse, or (b) averse] to receiving spam." (*Brooklyn Journal of International Law*)

15. "[I]nternational human rights should be treated as more than a series of [(a) laudable, or (b) laudatory] goals." (*Berkeley Journal of International Law*)

16. "The holding in *James* [(a) mitigates, or (b) militates] against these long-term effects by discouraging underpleading in tort suits." (*Missouri Law Review*)

17. "Authorization to enact regulations can be conferred by either of two [(a) alternate, or (b) alternative] methods." (*American Journal of Comparative Law*)

18. "Over the last two decades, the legal profession has undergone a profound change in public image. [(a) Regrettably, or (b) Regretfully], this change has been for the worse." (*UCLA Entertainment Law Review*)

19. "The courts provide the primary restraint on prosecutorial misconduct. Courts [(a) therefor, or (b) therefore] must be equipped with the tools to identify, record, and remedy the injection of prejudice by the prosecutor into criminal proceedings." (*Michigan Journal of Race and Law*)

20. "In *State Street Bank*, the Federal Circuit [(a) uncategorically, or (b) categorically] and unceremoniously eliminated the former business method exception to patentability." (*Rutgers Computer and Technology Law Journal*)

21. "[T]here are sound reasons of local and interstate policy why a state should [(a) forbear, or (b) forebear] from attempting to exercise all possible constitutional power to regulate out-of-state lawyers." (*Hofstra Law Review*)

22. "[T]he Homeless Persons' Survival Act . . . offered emergency relief initiatives, long-term solutions, and [(a) preventive, or (b) preventative] measures." (*Arizona State Law Review*)

23. "The dissent noted the [(a) corollary, or (b) correlation] between the type and number of the accessory uses and the type and number of the main uses permitted in an area." (*Widener Journal of Public Law*)

24. "When her mother died, Justice Kennard used her $5,000 inheritance to gain [(a) admission, or (b) admittance] into Pasadena

City College, where she went on to earn a scholarship that enabled her to attend the University of Southern California." (*Albany Law Review*)

25. "Were the essays less suited to one another, not discussing each and every one might be a [(a) venial, or (b) venal] sin." (*Loyola Journal of Public Interest Law*)

Scoring Guide

22–25 correct: Superb.   13–17 correct: Fair.
18–21 correct: Good.   1–12 correct: Poor.

Abbreviations in Key

DMLU = Garner, *A Dictionary of Modern Legal Usage* (2d ed. 1995)
Redbook = Garner, *The Redbook: A Manual on Legal Style* (2d ed. 2006)
TLR Manual = *Texas Law Review Manual on Style, Usage, and Editing* (9th ed. 2002)

Key to Correct Answers

1. *Regardless* (b). *Redbook* at 266; *DMLU* at 469.
2. *Elicited* (b). *Redbook* at 236; *DMLU* at 416.
3. *Him* (a). *Redbook* at 153; *DMLU* at 592.
4. *Him* (b). *Redbook* at 153; *DMLU* at 592.
5. *Principal* (a). *Redbook* at 263; *DMLU* at 691–92; *TLR Manual* at 67–68.
6. *Affected* (b). *Redbook* at 215; *DMLU* at 34; *TLR Manual* at 56–57.
7. *Discrete* (a). *Redbook* at 234; *DMLU* at 281–82.
8. *Voracious* (a). See any general dictionary.
9. *Tortious* (a). *Redbook* at 274; *DMLU* at 885–86.
10. *Corroborated* (b). *Redbook* at 225; *DMLU* at 227.
11. *Incredible* (b). *Redbook* at 230; *DMLU* at 435.
12. *Reluctant* (a). *Redbook* at 269; *DMLU* at 767.
13. *Apparatuses* (a). *DMLU* at 66.
14. *Averse* (b). *Redbook* at 214; *DMLU* at 33.
15. *Laudable* (a). *Redbook* at 252; *DMLU* at 502.
16. *Militates* (b). *Redbook* at 256; *DMLU* at 569.
17. *Alternative* (b). *Redbook* at 216; *DMLU* at 47; *TLR Manual* at 57.
18. *Regrettably* (a). *Redbook* at 266; *DMLU* at 748.
19. *Therefore* (b). *Redbook* at 274; *DMLU* at 878–79.

20. *Categorically* (b). *DMLU* at 896.
21. *Forbear* (a). *Redbook* at 241; *DMLU* at 365.
22. *Preventive* (a). *Redbook* at 263; *DMLU* at 690.
23. *Correlation* (b). See any general dictionary.
24. *Admission* (a). *Redbook* at 214; *DMLU* at 29.
25. *Venial* (a). *Redbook* at 276; *DMLU* at 908–09.

ૐ ૐ ૐ

Boo-Boos in Our Law Reviews

IN 1953, A UNIVERSITY OF MICHIGAN EDITOR named Eugene S. McCartney wrote a book called *Recurrent Maladies in Scholarly Writing.* In his preface, he noted that he'd developed a means of coping with mediocre manuscripts: "Early in my editorial career I began to assume that each new manuscript was poorly prepared, so that whatever surprise was in store for me was a pleasing one."[1]

Nowadays, many editors seem to have found a different way of coping: let the standards sink. Every year brings more news items and letter-to-the-editor lamentations suggesting that editorial standards have tumbled.

While our English lexicon grows more complex by the year, serious reading seems to be a waning pastime even for otherwise educated people. So it shouldn't come as a shock to learn that elementary blunders in grammar and word choice worm their way into even our best law reviews.

Here is yet another collection of bungled sentences from law reviews. In each example, the writers and editors (probably both) chose the wrong word.

1. "[T]he Supreme Court rejected an equal protection attack on Maryland's policy of capping family grants [(a) irregardless, or (b) regardless] of the size of the family." (*Michigan Law Review*)

2. "Mrs. Haley argued that the agreement between [(a) she, or (b) her] and the Piggs was void on several grounds." (*St. Louis University Law Journal*)

3. "[T]he United States Supreme Court granted certiorari solely on the question of whether moratoria of [(a) these type, or (b) this type] constituted a per se taking under its holding in *Lucas.*" (*University of Arkansas at Little Rock Law Review*)

4. "The court discussed the elements that must be proven to prevail on a claim of [(a) tortuous, or (b) tortious] interference with prospective business relations." (*Southern Methodist University Law Review*)

Adapted from *Student Lawyer* (Jan. 2004).

[1] Eugene S. McCartney, *Recurrent Maladies in Scholarly Writing* viii (1953).

5. "Then the law allowed compensation for Israeli 'residents' [(a) who's, or (b) whose] property was in the Custodian of Absentees' Property." (*Vanderbilt Journal of Transnational Law*)

6. "This type of regulation expressly or by clear [(a) inference, or (b) implication] identifies the forbidden effect and applies only when the effect is known to exist." (*Willamette Law Review*)

7. "[T]he . . . legislation provid[es] that aliens who donate to groups certified as terrorist organizations are subject to [(a) deportation, or (b) deportment]." (*Temple Law Review*)

8. "[T]he Californian [was] the ship that, according to some accounts, was closest to the Titanic when it [(a) sunk, or (b) sank]." (*Fordham Law Review*)

9. "[T]he FBI arrested Stewart and her codefendants on charges of [(a) perpetuating, or (b) perpetrating] fraud on the federal government." (*Maryland Law Review*)

10. "In sum, a substantial number of functional arguments [(a) militate, or (b) mitigate] against formalism in the arena of patent law." (*Columbia Law Review*)

11. "The health care industry has been targeted as an industry [(a) rife, or (b) ripe] with fraud." (*George Washington Law Review*)

12. "It is also true that even politicians do not always vote the party line, and judges do so even less often, especially if they have not agreed to [(a) tow, or (b) toe] that line if a case came before them." (*Indiana Law Review*)

13. "[I]t was necessary to show whether all of the infected patients had the same strain of the bacterium and, if so, to trace that strain to [(a) whoever, or (b) whomever] was responsible for the cases." (*University of Illinois Journal of Law, Technology & Policy*)

14. "At this point [(a) restaurateurs, or (b) restauranteurs] might object, 'Why not tax expensive clothes?'" (*Virginia Law Review*)

15. "His jurisprudence shows us how nicely much of the modern mainstream American legal thought [(a) jives, or (b) jibes] with the attitude that might makes right and that the law does not care if the devil takes the hindmost." (*Michigan Law Review*)

16. "Jacobus tenBroek summarized the proceedings [(a) thus, or (b) thusly]: 'Witness after witness spoke of beatings and woundings . . . .'" (*Yale Law and Policy Review*)

17. "Male co-workers frequently made graphic sexual comments in front of Robinson, referring to this [(a) plenitude, or (b) plenitude] of pornography." (*University of Pennsylvania Law Review*)

18. "One [(a) criterion, or (b) criteria] states: 'National action . . . shall be taken only where . . . .'" (*Oregon Law Review*)

19. "The driver may not have [(a) drank, or (b) drunk] enough alcohol to be detectable." (*Journal of Law and Policy*)

20. "The form of trial by ordeal commonly implemented in Liberia is by applying heated metal to the suspect's body to [(a) illicit, or (b) elicit] the truth." (*New York Law School Journal of Human Rights*)

21. "The U.S. overhauled many of its extradition treaties in the 1970s due to two [(a) principle, or (b) principal] reasons." (*Brooklyn Law Review*)

22. "The [(a) correlation, or (b) corollary] between the two might be mere coincidence, as no court has explicitly mentioned or endorsed the use of the regulations in drawing a line for de minimis analysis." (*University of Chicago Law Review*)

23. "The mother refused to disclose, however, whether she had taken medication that could have [(a) affected, or (b) effected] her children or whether any of them had learning disabilities." (*Cardozo Women's Law Journal*)

24. "This change was motivated by the rise in D&O insurance [(a) premia, or (b) premiums] in the 1980s." (*Northwestern University Law Review*)

25. "This reading is [(a) incredible, or (b) incredulous], overbroad, and unnecessary. It is [(a) incredible, or (b) incredulous] because this reading interprets the cases to grossly deviate from its prior facially race-neutral state action jurisprudence." (*Baylor Law Review*)

Scoring Guide

22–25 correct: Superb.   13–17 correct: Fair.
18–21 correct: Good.   1–12 correct: Poor.

Abbreviations in Key

CMS = *The Chicago Manual of Style* (15th ed. 2003)
DMLU = Garner, *A Dictionary of Modern Legal Usage* (2d ed. 1995)

Redbook = Garner, *The Redbook: A Manual on Legal Style* (2d ed. 2006)
TLR Manual = *Texas Law Review Manual on Style, Usage, and Editing* (9th ed. 2002)

Key to Correct Answers

1. *Regardless* (b). *CMS* at 220; *DMLU* at 469; *Redbook* at 266.
2. *Her* (b). *CMS* at 158–59; *DMLU* at 592; *Redbook* at 153.
3. *This type* (b). *DMLU* at 880; *Redbook* at 148.
4. *Tortious* (b). *CMS* at 230; *DMLU* at 885–86; *Redbook* at 274.
5. *Whose* (b). *CMS* at 232; *DMLU* at 934; *Redbook* at 111, 278.
6. *Implication* (b). *CMS* at 218, 219; *DMLU* at 443; *Redbook* at 201; *TLR Manual* at 64.
7. *Deportation* (a). *DMLU* at 266–67; *Redbook* at 232.
8. *Sank* (b). *DMLU* at 266–67; any general dictionary.
9. *Perpetrating* (b). *CMS* at 225; *DMLU* at 653.
10. *Militate* (a). *CMS* at 222; *DMLU* at 569; *Redbook* at 256. Notice that *the arena of* could be deleted—and should be.
11. *Rife* (a). See any general dictionary.
12. *Toe* (b). See any general dictionary.
13. *Whoever* (a). *CMS* at 232; *DMLU* at 933; *Redbook* at 191; *TLR Manual* at 73. Notice that *all of* could be reduced to *all* (see *CMS* at 199; *DMLU* at 43).
14. *Restaurateurs* (a). *DMLU* at 765; *Redbook* at 120.
15. *Jibes* (b). *CMS* at 216; *DMLU* at 385; *Redbook* at 243.
16. *Thus* (a). *CMS* at 230; *DMLU* at 881–82; *Redbook* at 274.
17. *Plenitude* (a). *DMLU* at 668; any general dictionary.
18. *Criterion* (a). *CMS* at 209; *DMLU* at 238; *Redbook* at 108.
19. *Drunk* (b). *CMS* at 212; any general dictionary.
20. *Elicit* (b). *CMS* at 213; *DMLU* at 416; *Redbook* at 236.
21. *Principal* (b). *DMLU* at 691–92; *Redbook* at 263; *TLR Manual* at 67–68. For a discussion of *due to* as used in this sentence, see *CMS* at 212; *DMLU* at 299; *Redbook* at 236; *TLR Manual* at 61.
22. *Correlation* (a). *CMS* at 209; any general dictionary.
23. *Affected* (a). *CMS* at 198; *DMLU* at 34, 305; *Redbook* at 215; *TLR Manual* at 56–57.
24. *Premiums* (b). *DMLU* at 685; *Redbook* at 107.
25. *Incredible* (a) in both places. *CMS* at 219; *DMLU* at 435; *Redbook* at 230.

ನ್ ನ್ ನ್

Words, Words, Words—and Race

IN 1999, THE ENTIRE NATION had a little lesson in how upsetting language can be—even if it's innocent. On January 15, David Howard, a white aide to Mayor Anthony Williams of Washington, D.C., sparked a scandal by using the word *niggardly* in front of some black colleagues. He lost his job over it. Fortunately, he got it back.

What is the lesson from this episode? Some people think it's how ridiculous the PC-police have become in foisting off political correctness. This malarkey should be roundly derided, the thinking goes: we should educate more people about words like *niggardly* and then use them appropriately.

Surely that's the wrong lesson. The real lessons are . . . well, I'll get to them. But first, three vignettes.

The first dates from 1989. That was when I learned that *niggardly* can be a problem. I was teaching at a law school, and two African-American law students came to my office to complain about one of my colleagues, who had accused the Supreme Court of giving a "niggardly interpretation" to a particular statute. They were convinced that he had been blatantly racist, and they came to me as the resident word expert. I quickly explained that *niggardly* derives from an Old Norse word (*hnøgger*) meaning "miser" and that it has nothing to do with the *n*-word. Though still smarting, they dropped their idea about lodging a grievance.

The second vignette dates from 1994. I was in New York lecturing a group of lawyers about persuasive brief-writing. Some briefs, I said, are like a fully lit room: you can see clearly what the writer is trying to say. Others are like a darkened room: you're groping in the dark for the writer's point. I referred twice to good briefs as "light briefs" and bad briefs as "dark briefs." At the break, several lawyers corralled me to say that I should think of a better metaphor. The light–dark distinction sounded racist.

The third incident took place in 1998. Again the subject was brief-writing, this time in Houston. I was talking about the preference that strong writers have for *before* over *prior to* and for *after* over *subsequent to*. "As a general principle," I said, "prefer the Anglo-Saxon term over the Latin. It's typically more powerful and down-to-earth." During the break, two Hispanic lawyers asked me to clarify why I thought Anglos

---

Adapted from *Student Lawyer* (Apr. 2000).

were better than Latinos. I explained that I was talking about two languages: Old English vs. Latin. The reference has nothing to do with race.

Anyone who speaks in public very often, as I do, learns how audiences react to all sorts of things. You learn the Murphy's Law of language: if a sentence can be misunderstood, it will be. So you adjust to prevent misunderstandings. I never use *niggardly*, I've abandoned the light–dark distinction, and I never contrast Latin with Anglo-Saxon (I say "Old English" instead). It's a matter of preventing miscues and needless headaches, both for my listeners and for me.

I can't imagine saying we should *call a spade a spade*, even though that ancient phrase has nothing to do with the racial epithet (which the *Oxford English Dictionary* dates back only to 1928). If I used it, I wouldn't be given the time to explain the etymology. And if I didn't explain the etymology, I'd have erected a barrier between me and some of my listeners.

I asked a black friend of mine—a 40-year-old man with a high-school education—whether he has ever heard the phrase *calling a spade a spade*. He said that he had. He and others had complained about it for years. To my surprise, he said that he has long assumed that anyone who uses the phrase is a bigot.

Is that a view worth considering? Maureen Dowd apparently thinks not. In a *New York Times* op-ed piece[1] she suggested that considering views like those of my friend would be "siding with ignorance" or "succumbing to PC poisoning."

But I say it's just smart. The racial divisions in this country are deeply etched. Some 90% of African-Americans still believe that O.J. Simpson is a victim of mad prosecutors. And 90% of whites believe that he beat the system. There probably won't ever be much movement toward reconciliation of those views. Among other things, they reflect the mistrust that exists among racial groups in our society.

So what are the lessons to be drawn from the *niggardly* contretemps? I think there are four.

1. Words or phrases that sound just like racial epithets will be misunderstood. If you care about your credibility with more than just the intelligentsia, you'd better avoid them. (Perhaps even the intelligentsia will increasingly think ill of people who use them.)

2. Words that associate blackness with badness are equally insensitive. Think before using them.

3. For word-lovers, the death of words can be a sad thing, but they're just words. If they needlessly foment serious trouble among people, they might as well die.

---

[1] Maureen Dowd, *Liberties: Niggardly City*, N.Y. Times, 31 Jan. 1999, § 4, at 17.

4. It won't be easy to draw lines between offensive and inoffensive words. Will it be all right to talk about *niggling details?* I hope so. What about *chicanery?* Surely it will. We need to be reasonable even as we draw new lines about what's reasonable.

In January and February of 1999, I was quoted in dozens of newspapers in support of Mayor Williams's view that *niggardly* is insensitive. Two of the dictionaries I've written discuss the misunderstandings to which the word gives rise. Does this mean that I approved of David Howard's losing his job? No. By all accounts, he wasn't being mean-spirited: he had learned the word years before when studying for the SAT. As soon as he sensed discomfort in his listeners, he hastened to apologize. So Mayor Williams was right to restore Howard to his old position.

David Howard did what my tenured law-school colleague had done a decade before—he used the word innocently. And surely it's the intent that matters most. But from now on, people won't have that explanation: it will be difficult if not impossible to claim innocence. The Howard–Williams brouhaha has put everyone on notice.

❧ ❧ ❧

Transcending Dialect

YEARS AGO I SERVED ON the hiring committee of a major law firm. As the junior member, I was fascinated at how the committee worked. The main focus, of course, was always on the candidate's record and writing. But there was always an undercurrent of other considerations: one candidate shoved food onto his fork with his fingers; another talked with food in her mouth and was otherwise unpleasant during a meal; still another didn't seem to know how to use pronouns, whether in memos or in speech.

Whether it was table manners or linguistic gaffes, the lapses could disqualify candidates. Though I was known even in those days as a grammar guru, I was more restrained in condemning grammatical lapses than several of my colleagues. Again and again, I heard my senior colleagues—the hiring partners—reject potential candidates because they couldn't imagine one day introducing them as colleagues. Their language was too unrefined.

Like it or not, people judge us all the time—especially by our manners and our language (both spoken and written). And with language, the judgments can be particularly hasty because a person's use of language is the most readily available means of assessing that person's knowledge, cultivation, and possibly even intelligence. Much of this assessment is unconscious.

Now, this may seem unfair. If someone didn't grow up speaking standard American English, how can the business world—or the legal world—discriminate against that person? The answer is that law has traditionally been considered a learned profession—more specifically, a literary profession. So a lawyer's education must entail immersion in the standards of standard English. As the linguist Charles Carpenter Fries once observed, "anyone who cannot use the language habits in which the major affairs of the country are conducted, the language habits of the socially acceptable of most of our communities, would have a serious handicap."[1] That remains true today.

But most people grow up using some degree of dialect—that is, a variety of language peculiar to a region or a social class. Think of the localisms that you grew up with, whether you had an urban or a rural

---

Adapted from *Student Lawyer* (Nov. 2002).
[1] Charles Carpenter Fries, *American English Grammar* 14 (1940).

upbringing. Apart from particular expressions, there are several salient characteristics of dialect: mistakes with verb tenses, subject–verb disagreement, misused pronouns, adjectives used as adverbs, double negatives, and stigmatized pronunciations.

In certain situations, of course, a modest amount of dialect may actually help you. If you're facing a jury in Wyoming or New Jersey or wherever, you may benefit from having the jury conclude that you're one of them. But in most of your professional dealings, it won't help at all. In fact, it will hurt you. So, ideally, you'll be bidialectal: able to engage in both refined discourse and street talk. You'll know when to use which type.

In the following examples, you'll recognize some of the speech markers that occur in various dialects within the United States. Many of them aren't strictly limited by geography. Although you might think at first that you'd never use any of these forms in a professional setting— and you might be tempted to scoff at them—look closely at them all. You're likely to find some that, in an unguarded moment, you might use. The purpose of the lists isn't to disparage those who speak or write using the dialectal forms; rather, it's simply to help you recognize forms that aren't suitable for most professional settings.

Mistakes with Verb Tenses

- DIALECT: I haven't drank my coffee this morning. STANDARD: I haven't drunk my coffee this morning.
- DIALECT: My torts professor drug us through *Palsgraf* in 20 minutes. STANDARD: My torts professor dragged us through *Palsgraf* in 20 minutes.
- DIALECT: If I would of known I could represent rock stars, I would of studied intellectual property instead. STANDARD: If I had known I could represent rock stars, I would have studied intellectual property instead.

Subject–Verb Disagreement

- DIALECT: They was there because they was going home together. STANDARD: They were there because they were going home together.
- DIALECT: Jane and I wasn't even there. STANDARD: Jane and I weren't even there.
- DIALECT: Neither one of us were ready. STANDARD: Neither one of us was ready.

Misused Pronouns

- DIALECT: Me and John are going now. STANDARD: John and I are going now.
- DIALECT: Give the books to either Joan or I. STANDARD: Give the books to either Joan or me.
- DIALECT: Please keep this between you and I. STANDARD: Please keep this between you and me.

Using Adjectives as Adverbs

- DIALECT: I did good on that exam. STANDARD: I did well on that exam.
- DIALECT: She talks real intelligent. STANDARD: She talks intelligently.
- DIALECT: I'm doing wonderful, thank you. STANDARD: I'm doing wonderfully, thank you.

Multiple Negation

- DIALECT: He didn't do nothing wrong. STANDARD: He didn't do anything wrong.
- DIALECT: I couldn't hardly read that case! STANDARD: I could hardly read that case!
- DIALECT: It don't make no difference. STANDARD: It doesn't make any difference.

Word Choice

- DIALECT: Where is the library at? STANDARD: Where is the library?
- DIALECT: This here dictionary is too heavy. STANDARD: This dictionary is too heavy.
- DIALECT: Since we're fixin' to go, we better eat up. STANDARD: Since we're getting ready to go, we'd better finish eating.

Pronunciations

	STANDARD	DIALECT
asked	/askt/	/ast/ or /akst/
can't	/kant/	/kaynt/ or /kent/
car	/kahr/	/kah/
Detroit	/di-TROIT/	/DEE-troit/
entire	/en-TIRE/	/IN-TIRE/

	STANDARD	DIALECT
I	/eye/	/ah/
there	/thehr/	/thahr/
these	/theez/	/deez/
umbrella	/um-BREL-uh/	/UM-brel-uh/
wash	/wahsh/	/wahrsh/
window	/WIN-doh/	/WIN-dər/
wrestling	/RES-ling/	/RAS-lin/
yellow	/YEL-oh/	/YEL-ər/

You could doubtless add to this list. (*Doubtlessly*, by the way, is a "double adverb" that isn't considered good English; *doubtless* is the adverb.) Again, the point isn't to ridicule people who use dialect. Not at all. It's simply to stress that we should be aware of all aspects of language, including dialect, and to consider what level of discourse is most appropriate in a given situation.

This is an important point. No knowledgeable teacher would ever make students ashamed of their native dialect. But it's certainly important to let students know that if they wish to compete successfully in business or in the professions, standard English is a prerequisite.

After all, if you use words inappropriately in a job interview or letter of application, you can't assume that the interviewer or recipient won't give no never-mind.

ﺘ ﺘ ﺘ

Nonsexist Language and Credibility

GENDER-NEUTRAL LANGUAGE isn't about political correctness; it's about credibility. Regardless of how you may feel about the old convention that the masculine *he* includes the feminine *she*—whether you detest or you like it—you'll need to handle the English language with some care to have credibility with a wide range of readers.

This isn't an easy task. On the one hand, readers like William Safire will think you're crazy if you write *he/she*, *s/he*, or *(s)he*. They'll know you're crazy if you write—as one book author has—the onomatopoeic symbol *s/he/it*. On the other hand, readers like Susan Estrich will think you're a troglodyte if you use *he* to refer to readers generally—as if the feminine were the unstated exception swept into the masculine rule of our language.

Is there no way to win over your readers, then?

Yes, there is. It takes some skill and a lot of effort. With those two things, you'll be able to produce a style that never induces readers to consider your personal biases. If your point is that you *want* to induce this reaction, then you're writing off part of your readership—something you may willingly do unless you have a client whose money and perhaps even freedom are on the line. If you're trying to persuade someone on a point unrelated to sexist language, then the issue shouldn't even arise.

Perhaps every reader of this essay already has opinions on the issue of sexist language. Whatever you may think, here are four points to ponder.

First, remember that readers come first—and there are many types. Don't stereotype your readers. Never assume that women are the only ones who care about sexism, or even that most women feel the same way about it. Though I'm a man, I happen to be distracted by sexist language. I'm not impressed with a book whose opening words are "For the lawyer more than for most men . . ."[1]—especially when warnings about sexist language appear fore and aft.[2]

And Chief Judge Judith S. Kaye, of the highest tribunal in the State of New York, is not alone when she declares: "I believe that gendered writing . . . will one day be immediately recognized as archaic and ludicrous."[3]

Adapted from *Student Lawyer* (Apr. 2001).

[1] Henry Weihofen, *Legal Writing Style* 1 (2d ed. 1980).

[2] *Id.* at vii, 19.

[3] Chief Judge Judith S. Kaye, *A Brief for Gender-Neutral Brief-Writing*, N.Y.L.J., 21 Mar. 1991, at 2.

Second, pronouns aren't the only pitfall. One insidious type of sexism is the disparate ways of referring to men and women. Some will give prominent men their titles (*Secretary of State Colin Powell*) and then refer to prominent women in less exalted terms (*Condoleezza Rice* or *Ms. Rice* instead of *National Security Adviser Condoleezza Rice*). Or they'll give a male writer just the last name (*Llewellyn*) while repeatedly giving the full name of a woman (*Soia Mentschikoff*) or a sex-specific honorific (*Ms. Mentschikoff*), or even just her first name (*Soia*). Some will call these imagined slights. But the disparities, even if unconscious, are hard to dismiss.

Third, keep your sense of what is good English. Remember the importance of tone—how you sound. Although it might be okay to use *he or she* once every few pages, you don't want to begin doing it at every turn. (Try pluralizing.) Write so that your prose is natural, *speakable*. The whole idea is to avoid having readers think about your words when you're trying to get them to focus on what you're saying.

Fourth, monitor what's happening to the language. It's changing. A living language always does that—sometimes for better, sometimes for worse. In the end, most losses end up being gains as well.

And the English language is steadily moving toward a solution of the age-old pronoun problem in English: like it or not, *they* is becoming a word of indeterminate number. It can be plural here (*they were*) and singular there (*everyone found their way*). Some bemoan this development. I once did. But it's inevitable: the genius of the language is finally solving a problem that has plagued it for centuries.

The language has taken big strides in this change just over the past 18 years. In 1983, here's what two linguistic scholars said: "Today, for many educated people, the use of sex-indefinite *they* is an unforgivable sin. On numerous occasions, one of the authors of this book has been admonished that advocating *they* would assure the failure of any guidelines for non-sexist usage."[4] Though it may still be an "unforgivable sin" in some quarters, those quarters are fast dwindling.

In my 1998 book *A Dictionary of Modern American Usage*, I quoted several American and British writers using *someone . . . they* and *anyone . . . they* and concluded: "Speakers of American English resist this development more than speakers of British English, in which the indeterminate *they* is already more or less standard. That it sets many literate Americans' teeth on edge is an unfortunate setback to what promises to be the ultimate solution to the problem."

---

[4] Francine Frank & Frank Anshen, *Language and the Sexes* 88 (1983).

 è&. è&. è&.

Word-Karma

YOU DON'T BELIEVE IN REINCARNATION? It exists, certainly, as a linguistic phenomenon: Words die and are reborn.

For example, I once heard the president of the State Bar of Texas, Jim Parsons, refer to "a grievable complaint." Ever on the alert for strange law words, I twitched when I heard the word *grievable*.

According to the *Oxford English Dictionary*, the word was first used in the 14th century and last used in the 15th. Naturally, upon discovering this, I deduced (what else?) that Mr. Parsons must recently have been reading the Middle English poets, in particular John Gower, who introduced the word more than 600 years ago, in 1390.

What I couldn't figure out was this: Why would Mr. Parsons spend his time with Gower instead of Chaucer, a far more durable poet? "The Parson's Tale" would surely be the appropriate place to start reading *The Canterbury Tales*.

Soon I discovered that Mr. Parsons is not alone in liking this ancient word. From about 1970 on, American legal writers have increasingly used *grievable* to mean "of or constituting a grievance." Lexis and Westlaw searches yielded more than 1,100 examples of grievable disputes, offenses, and complaints.

We'll probably never know whether the word was an unconscious reinvention or a medievalist's revival of a long-lost word. Whatever the truth of its modern origin, the word probably has good prospects for survival in its second life. After all, the world is rife these days with grievable events.

Adapted from *Dallas Bar Headnotes* (21 Jan. 1989).

ટ⬤ ટ⬤ ટ⬤

Preface to
A Dictionary of Modern American Usage

NOT LONG AGO, while I was standing at a rental-car counter in Austin, a young clerk told me that a free upgrade to a Cadillac might be available. She would have to see whether any Cadillacs were on the lot just then.

Two minutes passed as she typed, got on the telephone, twirled her hair around her index finger, and then typed some more. Finally, I said, "Can I get the upgrade?"

"You mean, 'May I get the upgrade,'" she responded.

I thought I had imagined it. "What?"

"You said, '*Can* I get the upgrade.' What you mean is, '*May* I get the upgrade.'"

As it happens, I had been working on the manuscript for this book only minutes before, so I couldn't help thinking how surreal the experience was. I felt a twinge of indignation on the one hand—the kind that almost anyone feels when corrected. But I also thought that her remark was charming in a way. She was doing her best to uphold good English.

But she was wrong, and I gently told her so: "I'm not asking for your permission. I want to know whether you have a Cadillac on the lot. I want to know whether it's physically possible for me to drive one of them. So: '*Can* I get the upgrade.'"

"Oh, I guess you're right," she said with resignation.

Experiences like that one give me hope: they show that some people still care about what happens to our language, however misplaced their concern might occasionally be.

The State of the Language

Do I contend that the language is decaying? That it was once in a pristine state and has been sliding ever since? That the glory days are over?

No, I don't. In many ways, writing today is better than ever. Our best journalists today are as talented a group as has ever worked in the language.

But a great deal of mediocre writing appears in print nowadays, and both written and oral assaults on the language do seem to come at high velocities. The speed comes from mass communications. Turn on the TV

From *A Dictionary of Modern American Usage* (1998).

and listen to commentators on football, tennis, or golf, and you'll be treated to the heights of inarticulacy. Then imagine all the millions of viewers whose linguistic perceptions are affected by this blather.

There are good, clarifying forces at work on the language. There are also bad, obscuring forces at work. One language, many realities.

The reality I care about most is that some people still want to use the language well. They want to write effectively; they want to speak effectively. They want their language to be graceful at times and powerful at times. They want to understand how to use words well, how to manipulate sentences, and how to move about in the language without seeming to flail. They want good grammar, but they want more: they want rhetoric in the traditional sense. That is, they want to use language deftly so that it's fit for their purposes.

This book is for them.

First Principles

Before going any further, I should explain my approach. That's an unusual thing for the author of a usage dictionary to do—unprecedented, as far as I know. But a guide to good writing is only as good as the principles on which it's based. And users should naturally be interested in those principles. So, in the interests of full disclosure, here are the ten critical points that, after years of working on usage problems, I've settled on:

1. **Purpose.** The purpose of a usage dictionary is to help writers, editors, and speakers use the language effectively: to help them sound grammatical but relaxed, refined but natural, correct but unpedantic.

2. **Realism.** To guide users helpfully, recommendations on usage must be genuinely plausible. They must recognize the language as it currently stands, encourage reasonable approaches to editorial problems, and avoid refighting battles that were long ago lost.

3. **Linguistic Simplicity.** If the same idea can be expressed in a simple way or in a complex way, the simple way is better—and, paradoxically, it will typically lead readers to conclude that the writer is smarter.

4. **Readers' Reactions.** Generally, writing is good if readers find it easy to follow; writing is bad if readers find it hard to follow.

5. **Tightness.** Omitting needless words is important. As long as it's accurate, the briefest way of phrasing an idea is usually best because the brevity enhances speed, clarity, and impact.

6. **Word-Judging.** A word or phrase is somewhat undesirable if it has any one of the following characteristics, and is worse if it has two or more:

   (a) it sounds newfangled;
   (b) it defies logic;
   (c) it threatens to displace an established expression (but hasn't yet done so);
   (d) it originated in a misunderstanding of a word or its etymology;
   (e) it blurs a useful distinction.

7. **Differentiation.** If related words—especially those differing only in the suffix—begin to take on different senses, it's wise to encourage the latent distinctions when they're first emerging and then to follow them once they're established.

8. **Needless Variants.** Having two or more variant forms of a word is undesirable unless each one signals a distinct meaning.

9. **Conservatism.** If two constructions are current, and one of them has been widely condemned by authorities whose values are in line with those outlined in #6, the other construction is better.

10. **Actual Usage.** In the end, the actual usage of educated speakers and writers is the overarching criterion for correctness. But while actual usage can trump the other factors, it isn't the only consideration.

Reasonable though these points may seem to the professional writer or editor, they're likely to induce hissy fits among modern linguists, for whom #10 is the only valid concern (and only after deleting the word *educated*). The problem for professional writers and editors is that they can't wait idly to see what direction the language takes. Writers and editors, in fact, influence that direction: they must make decisions.

And a good usage dictionary should help in those decisions. H.W. Fowler's groundbreaking *Dictionary of Modern English Usage* did that in 1926 and for generations after; Theodore M. Bernstein's book *The Careful Writer* did it in 1965; and Wilson Follett's *Modern American Usage* did it in 1966. That has traditionally been the job of the usage dictionary: to help writers and editors solve editorial predicaments.

The State of the Genre

Somewhere along the line, though, usage dictionaries got hijacked by the descriptive linguists, who observe language scientifically. For the pure descriptivist, it's impermissible to say that one form of language is any better than another: as long as a native speaker says it, it's okay—and anyone who takes a contrary stand is a dunderhead. That has become something of a dogma among professional linguists.

Essentially, descriptivists and prescriptivists are approaching different problems. Descriptivists want to record language as it's actually used, and they perform a useful function—though their audience is generally limited to those willing to pore through vast tomes of dry-as-dust research. Prescriptivists—not all of them, perhaps, but enlightened ones—want to figure out the most effective uses of language, both grammatically and rhetorically. Their editorial advice should accord with the predominant practices of the best writers and editors.

For the pure descriptivist, it's silly to say that *infer* shouldn't be "misused" for *imply*. Presumably, it's also silly to say that *Hobson's choice* is the correct phrase and that *Hobbesian choice* is an ignorant error, because much evidence can be found for the latter. Likewise, we shouldn't prohibit any other example of what is here called word-swapping. The extreme view is that even spell-checkers are a bad force because they ensure uniformity and stifle linguistic experimentation in spelling.[1]

Although there's little new to be said about this debate, this book does something quite new: it gathers reams of current linguistic evidence to show the many confusions into which writers fall. And they're constantly falling into them. As Joseph Epstein, the longtime editor of *The American Scholar*, has observed, "The English language is one vast San Andreas fault, where things are slipping and sliding every moment."[2] English usage is so challenging that even experienced writers need guidance now and then.

Quotations and Citations

This book contains thousands of quotations from published sources. Most are from newspapers, but many are from books and scholarly journals. These quotations came to my hand in various ways.

First, they came from my own reading. For many years, I've traveled a good deal, and whenever I go somewhere I make a point of reading and marking at least one local newspaper, usually more. When I return, I enter those sentences into my database.

---

[1] *See* Sidney Landau, *Of Lexicography, Computers, and Norms,* 64 Am. Speech 162, 163 (1989) ("I detest even the idea of spelling-correction programs. If they do not serve any heuristic purpose, they are pernicious by artificially limiting the range of spelling choices . . . . We thus artificially limit language change . . . and push all our students toward a common center of officially endorsed usages.").

[2] Joseph Epstein, *Mr. Fowler, He Live,* Weekly Standard, 20 Jan. 1997, at 29.

Second, I have dozens of allies—members of the H.W. Fowler Society, an informal organization I founded—who send me clippings from newspapers. These Fowlerians, who are spread throughout the English-speaking world, have contributed enormously to the book with hundreds of examples.

Third, I've supplemented entries with examples gleaned from two online databases: Nexis and Westlaw. For two decades, they have provided full-text searchability for millions of published documents—a luxury that earlier lexicographers never enjoyed.

But before delving further into online sources, I should address a question that many readers will wonder about. Should I really name names? Should I give full citations in the way that I do? Won't it mortify a journalist to find some badly written sentence frozen in a reference book for all the world to see?

Well, I hope it isn't mortifying, and for me it's nothing new. I used the technique in the second edition of my *Dictionary of Modern Legal Usage* (1995). The citations appear for three reasons. First, they show that the examples are real, not fabricated. Second, they show the great variety of evidence on which the judgments in this book are based. And third, they're lexicographically noteworthy: they reflect how the language is being used in our culture in our time.

I have tried to be dispassionate in choosing examples. More of them come from my favorite newspaper, *The New York Times*, than from any other source: nearly 400 of the some 5,600 illustrative quotations. But a glance at the text will show that they're from all over the country. And a small number—less than 5%—are even British.

Why should British quotations be included, given that this is a dictionary of *American* usage? Most often, the reason is that it seems useful to record differences and similarities between British and American English. It's sometimes surprising to learn that a given error occurs much more frequently in British English (as with *harp back* for *hark back*).

Yet the book is American, both in its scope and in its point of view. During the mid-20th century, the English language's center of gravity shifted from England to the United States. And with that shift comes a certain responsibility on the part of those who speak and write American English.

Lexicographic Methods

It's fair to say that the guidance given here is based on a greater corpus of current published writings than any usage guide ever before published. For contemporary usage, the files of our greatest dictionary makers pale in comparison with the full-text search capabilities now provided by Nexis and Westlaw. Thus, the prescriptive approach here is leavened by a thorough canvassing of actual usage in modern edited prose.

When I say, then, that *ethicist* is 400 times more common than *ethician*, I have searched vast databases of newspapers and journals to arrive at this round figure. As for those particular terms, the Nexis databases (as of December 1997) contain 10,138 published documents in which *ethicist* appears, but only 25 documents in which *ethician* appears. (The ratio in Westlaw's "allnews" database is 7,400 to 6.) So much for the dictionaries that give the main listing under *ethician*. They're out of step: the compilers might have 5 or 10 citation slips in their files, but that's a paltry number when compared with mountains of evidence that the searching of reliable databases can unearth.

And when I say that *self-deprecating* (traditionally viewed as incorrect) is 50 times more common than *self-depreciating* (traditionally viewed as correct), I have searched those same databases to give this conservative figure. From 1980 to 1997, *self-deprecating* appeared in 16,040 Nexis sources, and *self-depreciating* in only 353. (The ratio in Westlaw is 9,860 to 159.) So much for the usage books that continue to recommend *self-depreciating*: that battle is lost.

In this respect—the consideration of voluminous linguistic evidence to back up judgment calls—this book represents a radical departure from most other usage dictionaries.

Value Judgments

As you might already suspect, I don't shy away from making judgments. I can't imagine that most readers would want me to. Linguists don't like it, of course, because judgment involves subjectivity. It isn't scientific. But rhetoric and usage, in the view of most professional writers, aren't scientific endeavors. You don't want dispassionate descriptions; you want sound guidance. And that requires judgment.

Essentially, the ideal usage commentator needs to be both a scholar and a critic. The poet Robert Bridges knew that, when it comes to language, value judgments are crucial:

> Scientific philologists will often argue that phonetic decay is a natural process, which has always been at work, and has actually produced the very forms of speech that we value most highly; and that it is therefore a squeamish pedantry to quarrel with it at any particular stage, or to wish to interfere with it, or even to speak of decay or corruption of language, for that these very terms beg the question, and are only the particular prejudice of particular persons at a particular time. But this

scientific reasoning is aesthetic nonsense. It is absurd to pretend that no results of natural laws should be disapproved of because it is possible to show that they obey the same laws as the processes of which we approve. The filthiest things in nature are as natural as the loveliest; and in art also the worst is as natural as the best: while the good needs not only effort but sympathetic intelligence to attain and preserve it. It is an aesthetic and not a scientific question.[3]

At the same time, though, aesthetic judgments aren't enough. Bridges overstated the case: when we analyze language, scientific concerns should certainly enter the equation. But he was right, in this little-known passage, to skewer the doctrine on which descriptivism is largely based:

> [I]t is no fancy to see a beauty in human speech, and to prefer one [form of] language to another on account of such beauty, and to distinguish the qualities that make the beauty. Learning that forbids such an attitude is contemptible.[4]

Yet this willingness to judge should be tempered by scholarship. H.W. Fowler best embodied the qualities of the scholar-critic. He was a lexicographer, true, but he was also a literary critic. He wasn't exclusively one or the other. His interests were those of the professional editor more than those of the professional linguist. He shared that quality with Theodore Bernstein and Wilson Follett, but he knew more about linguistics than either of those writers. That knowledge was something he had in common with Bergen Evans, but he had better literary and editorial judgment than Evans, and he was confident in exercising that judgment. No one else has quite matched Fowler's blend of interests and talents: though not infallible, he was the most formidable prescriptive grammarian of the 20th century.

The touchstone for commenting on usage, then, is a mixture of scholarship and criticism. Whether I've reached it or not, that has been my goal.

An Autobiographical Note

What possesses someone to write a dictionary of usage? People frequently ask me that question about my *Dictionary of Modern Legal Usage*. I'll try to give an answer.

---

[3] Robert Bridges, *A Tract on the Present State of English Pronunciation* 15–16 (1913).
[4] *Id.* at 16.

I realized early—at the age of 15—that my primary intellectual interest was the use of the English language. The interest might be partly genetic. My grandfather, Frank Garner of Amarillo, had more than a passing interest in language. This was magnified three or four times in my father, Gary T. Garner of Canyon, a true language aficionado. And then, as my father tells it, his interest seemed to be magnified a hundred-fold in me. It became an all-consuming passion.

This passion has taken various forms at different times in my life. At 15 it consisted primarily in building my vocabulary. Then I discovered general semantics—the works of S.I. Hayakawa, Wendell Johnson, Stuart Chase, and Alfred Korzybski. Because I grew up in a university town—small though it was—these and other books were readily accessible. I read everything I could find on the subject.

Then, on a wintry evening while visiting New Mexico at the age of 16, I discovered Eric Partridge's *Usage and Abusage*. I was enthralled. Never had I held a more exciting book. I spent hours reading his advice on the effective use of words and his essays on everything from John-sonese to précis writing. He kept mentioning another author, by the name of Fowler, so when I got back to Texas I sought out Fowler's *Modern English Usage*. And that book turned out to be even better.

Suffice it to say that by the time I was 18, I had committed to memory most of Fowler, Partridge, and their successors: the Evanses, Bernstein, Follett, and Copperud. I knew where they differed, and I came to form opinions about whose positions were soundest on all sorts of questions. I knew the work of those writers then better than I do today.

Yet my linguistic influences weren't just in books. Dr. Pat Sullivan of the English Department at West Texas A&M encouraged me from a very early age; from him I learned both transformational and traditional grammar. And my brother's godfather, Professor Alan M.F. Gunn of the English Department at Texas Tech University, nurtured my literary interests during his twice-yearly visits with our family.

College presented a wealth of opportunities. While at the University of Texas, I studied the history of the English language (in the English Department) and the Latin and Greek element in English (in the Classics Department), as well as Latin and French. Though I never mastered Old English, I acquired a passing knowledge of the Middle English of Chaucer and Gower. Two summers at Oxford University—where I studied Chaucer and T.S. Eliot—deepened my appreciation of how language and literature intersect. It was at Oxford that I first got to know Robert W. Burchfield, the editor of the *Supplement to the Oxford English Dictionary* (then underway), and Christopher Ricks, one of the great modern literary critics.

While at Texas and Oxford, I attended many lectures by noted linguists (who, not being positive influences, shouldn't be named). The second most bothersome thing, in my view at the time, was that they were dogmatically descriptive in their approach. The most bothersome thing was that they didn't write well: their offerings were dreary gruel. If you doubt this, go pick up any journal of linguistics. Ask yourself whether the articles are well written. If you haven't looked at one in a while, you'll be shocked.

At any rate, I gravitated away from the Linguistics Department and toward English and Classics. I ended up writing a thesis on the Latin influences in Shakespeare's language, excerpts from which made their way into learned journals. My mentors were John W. Velz, a Shakespearean of the first rank, and Thomas Cable, whose history of the English language (with Albert Baugh) is a classic.

Velz made many suggestions about what to publish, and where. As a 22-year-old budding scholar, I was thrilled to have an article published alongside one by Velz himself in an issue of *Shakespeare Studies*. Unfortunately, that very article of mine contains a linguistic gaffe that has found its way into the pages of this book (cited in the entry for *bequest*).

In any event, by the time I was an undergraduate—emboldened by Professor Velz's assurances that my work was worthy of publication—I knew that I would one day write a book in my favorite genre: a dictionary of usage.

This one is my second. The first, *Modern Legal Usage*, I wrote between 1981 and 1986; the first edition was published by Oxford University Press in 1987. In 1991, Oxford asked me to undertake this book, and I finished it at the beginning of 1998.

It is the product of a warped sense of fun: the idea that there's nothing more delightful than passing the hours chasing down linguistic problems in dictionaries and other reference books.

You know my approach. You know my influences. Discount the advice as you think advisable. No usage critic is infallible—certainly not I. But be assured that I have tried to know the literature in the field, to examine great quantities of linguistic evidence, and to use my best judgment as a professional writer and editor.

෫ 𝅷 ෫ 𝅷 ෫ 𝅷

A Texan Fowler?
Answering the Critics of *Modern American Usage*

*Modern-day linguists who insist on a "nonjudgmental" approach
to language like to belittle Fowler. They are fools.*

—Erich Eichman, Wall Street Journal *(7 Jan. 2000)*

ALTHOUGH IT OFTEN SURPRISES BRITONS to learn this, H.W. Fowler is all but worshiped by many American writers and editors. In the American press in the 1980s and 1990s, he was called "immortal" (*Fortune*), "urbane" (*Boston Globe*), and even "saintly" (*L.A. Times*). Meanwhile, his 1926 *Dictionary of Modern English Usage* has been called "classic" (*New York Times*) and "indispensable" (*Christian Science Monitor*)—"one of the great works in and of the language" (*L.A. Times*).

Given that I generally agree with those assessments of Fowler, you can only imagine how pleasing it was to see the opening words of Tom McArthur's review of my *Dictionary of Modern American Usage* (*DMAU*).[1] He said: "Henry Watson Fowler, it would appear, is alive and well and living in Texas."[2] When I've quoted that line to friends, they have congratulated me at having a noted linguist draw this comparison. I had met my goal of writing a modern usage guide with Fowlerian convictions.

But McArthur didn't intend much, if any, praise in his comment.

Good sport that he is, though, McArthur has generously invited me to respond to his review—as well as that of Richard W. Bailey.[3] I welcome the opportunity to say something about my approach to lexicography and my views on how best to deal with practical questions of English usage.

First, I should say that I respect the work of Tom McArthur and Richard Bailey. Two of McArthur's books—*The Oxford Companion to the English Language* (1992) and *Worlds of Reference* (1986)—have been of significant scholarly value to me. And I have long admired Richard Bailey's work at the University of Michigan, especially *Early Modern English* (1978)

Adapted from *English Today* (Oct. 2000).

[1] *A Dictionary of Modern American Usage* (N.Y. & Oxford: Oxford Univ. Press, 1998). The publisher named the second edition of 2003 *Garner's Modern American Usage* (often referred to as *GMAU*).

[2] . . . *That Is Forever Fowler*, 15 English Today 59 (1999).

[3] *A Dictionary of Modern American Usage*, 20 Dictionaries 151 (1999).

and *Images of English* (1996). In fact, I once considered pursuing graduate
work under Bailey's direction. For various reasons this didn't work out,
and I decided to pursue law.

Now to the ripostes.

Answering Tom McArthur

- *I am intrigued by the title of this work. The contrast between the
  "English" in Fowler's original and the "American" in Garner's new
  contribution seems to be both a handy promotional ploy and a straw
  in the wind for World English. Is it intended to make a contrast
  between language in America and language in England? Or is it—
  despite the uncanny resemblances between Garner and Fowler—an
  assertion of differentness that is essentially the same as Mencken's in
  1919 . . . or indeed Noah Webster's in 1828?*

The Fowlerian echo is purposeful—not as a promotional ploy, but as
an informative disclosure. I'm not against the notion of a World English.
It's just that I'm writing from an American perspective. So to some
degree I'm also echoing Webster and Mencken: I'm interested in the
peculiarly American strain of English. Like it or not, it has become the
center of linguistic gravity.

- *The suggestion . . . is that a steady hand on the tiller will always be
  needed, but must the providers of such hands be forever self-selected?*

What's the point here? Is McArthur arguing for an English Academy? Would he really want an appointed committee? An elected one?

Usage critics are no more self-selected than novelists or biographers
or drama critics. Publishers decide to back certain authors because of
professional credentials, publishing history, and the like. The marketplace
then determines the extent to which a writer supplies a useful and enjoyable product. Buyers of usage dictionaries—a quite specialized genre that
only fairly serious writers know about—are typically both knowledgeable and demanding.

The "steady hand on the tiller" simply means, to me, that those who
want to write and speak effectively will welcome reliable guidance. Which
means they will consult and even browse the work of critics who, having made a serious study of usage and style, write books on the subject.
Some of these critics gain favor (H.W. Fowler, Theodore Bernstein,[4]

---

[4] *The Careful Writer* (1965).

Wilson Follett[5]), while others pass into relative obscurity (H.W. Horwill,[6] Clarence Stratton,[7] Margaret Nicholson[8]).

- *There are many general usage articles . . . . There is . . . nothing of a general nature on usage.*

Those sentences appear in consecutive paragraphs. McArthur's self-contradiction answers itself. If any further answer is needed, please see the section in *DMAU* entitled "First Principles" in the preface or the entry under "Word-Swapping." Or try "Class Distinctions," "Plain Language," and "Sexism." Or any other of the 167 essay entries listed on pp. xix–xxiii.

- *It's almost as if fifty years of the twentieth century never happened.*

McArthur's statement might mean a couple of things. Many would read it as implying that the scholarship in *DMAU* is half a century out of date. This is tendentious nonsense. Of the some 5,500 source quotations in the book, more than 95% appeared during the 1990s. *DMAU* is more up-to-date in its coverage of usage than any other guide now on the market.

The true purpose of McArthur's statement seems to be to anachronize the linguistic sensibility that went into the making of *DMAU*. This Fowlerian sensibility is one that Sir Ernest Gowers summed up in 1957: "first the careful choice of precise words, second the avoidance of all affectations, third the orderly and coherent arrangement of words, fourth the strict observance of what is for the time being established idiom, and fifth the systematization of spelling and pronunciation."[9] Why is it so surprising that a serious student of language might have these convictions today?

I know about many of Fowler's shortcomings. Otto Jespersen bloodied Fowler's nose on the question of "fused participles,"[10] and Randolph Quirk has pointed out other deficiencies. In *DMAU*, I point out that Fowler's entry on *exception proves the rule* is incomprehensible.

---

[5] *Modern American Usage: A Guide* (1966).

[6] *A Dictionary of Modern American Usage* (1935).

[7] *Guide to Correct English* (1949).

[8] *A Dictionary of American-English Usage* (1957).

[9] Ernest Gowers, "H. W. Fowler: The Man and His Teaching," Presidential Address to the English Association, July 1957, at 14.

[10] Otto Jespersen, *On Some Disputed Points in English Grammar*, 2 S.P.E. Tracts 805, 811–12 (1926).

But on the whole, Fowler's work—as the first of the modern dictionaries of usage—remains brilliant. Much of what he said in 1926 still stands up.

- *Unlikely sets of polysyllables unfortunately abound in sets that seek needless disambiguation, such as* **redeemable/redemptible** *and* **restitutionary/restitutional/restitutive/restitutory.** *Redemptible? Restitutionary? Maybe these do exist in tomes that Garner, a writer on law, necessarily knows but no general dictionary contains or needs to contain.*

Consider the adjectives corresponding to *restitution*. It's true that lawyers use two of these terms more than anyone else, but nonlawyer lexicographers have dealt with them incorrectly. *Webster's Third* records only *restitutive* and *restitutory*—two terms that lawyers never use. *Webster's Third* doesn't record *restitutionary* or *restitutional*—two terms that lawyers do use with some frequency. So I tried to set matters straight in a brief entry that reads, in full:

> **restitutionary; restitutional; restitutive; restitutory.** Unabridged dictionaries generally record only *restitutive* and *restitutory*. But in law—where the subject of restitution is most common—the standard term is *restitutionary*. All other forms can properly be regarded as NEEDLESS VARIANTS.

My hope was twofold: (1) to help writers who might misguidedly follow *Webster's Third*, and (2) to help everybody who cares about lexicography (especially future lexicographers) get it right.

Although several of my thousands of entries deal with legal matters, many others deal with other specialties. Medical writers occasionally pause over the correct forms in *mucous membrane* and *mucus ball*. Should I have omitted points like these as being too technical? Likewise, in pointing out that the knitting term *purl* is sometimes mistakenly written *pearl*, it didn't occur to me to omit the term as being too specialized. Knitters purl, lawyers seek restitution, and doctors deal with mucous membranes and mucus balls. And writers who report these activities occasionally err.

- *I can live with my ambivalence about this book.*

I'm happy enough about McArthur's ambivalence. I might have expected worse. But then I got worse from Richard Bailey, to whom I now turn.

Answering Richard Bailey

- *Surely this entry [on the misuse of* **wasteband** *for* **waistband**] *is ill-chosen. With only five known examples [that Bailey was able to find], is* **wasteband** *a problem to be assailed?*

Perhaps Bailey suffers from having sparser databases than I had at my disposal. I've found 34 misuses of *wasteband* for *waistband*. Several have appeared since *DMAU* went to press in July 1998:

- "A man with a gun in his pants *wasteband* [read *waistband*] walked up to the truck driver and demanded money, police said." Domingo Ramirez, Jr., "Oklahoma Truck Driver Is Robbed in Colleyville," *Ft. Worth Star-Telegram*, 13 Aug. 1998, at 4.
- "Price, 51, carries a .38-caliber revolver in the *wasteband* [read *waistband*] of her pants . . . ." "The Gun Vote: A Tale of Two States," *St. Louis Post-Dispatch*, 28 Feb. 1999, at A5.
- "One of the men showed her a handgun tucked into his *wasteband* [read *waistband*], she told police." Shane Anthony, "Law and Order," *St. Louis Post-Dispatch*, 27 July 1999, at 2.
- "[T]he robber simply walked in, demanded money and lifted his shirt to show a gun tucked into his *wasteband* [read *waistband*]." C.J. Schexnayder, *Riverside Press-Enterprise*, 23 Dec. 1999, at B1.

Those writers, I think, could have benefited from the guidance offered in *DMAU*.

- *No usage writer, before Garner, has considered a warning about the "gross error" of spelling* **waistband** *as* **wasteband**, *probably because none of them ever noticed that anyone had done so.*

Bailey is right about this. Scores of entries—perhaps hundreds—appear in *DMAU* on wording issues never before discussed in a dictionary of usage. I had considered this, and still consider it, a point of pride. I wanted to get away from the tired approach of discussing only the same old canon of usage points that every guide discusses. Too many of these books suffer from inbreeding. It was time for someone to look at what's happening to the language today.

If many years from now scholars have occasion to say something about the confusion of *wasteband* for *waistband*, I hope they'll say, "Garner was the first to note this point—in 1998." Maybe they'll add: "Oddly, a Michigan professor attacked Garner for pointing out the confusion over the words."

- *This entry [still on* **waistband**], *like many others, affirms the idea that modern usage is debased and that the ignorant foist errors on the innocent and the young.*

Well, that's one of many truths about the language. Some usage is debased. And the ignorant do pass on errors. These things have long been so. I've documented how the word *adieu* gets confounded with *ado*, *cannon* with *canon*, *flak* with *flack*, *flows* with *floes*, *gambit* with *gamut*, and on through the alphabet. When published writers in Philadelphia, Boston, Washington, and Portland write *wreckless* instead of *reckless*—a blunder committed more than 900 times in recent years in journals and newspapers—don't we have a case of debased usage? Given that no earlier writers seem to have addressed the point, isn't there something useful in citing the blunders?

Even if Bailey thinks not, it's surprising that he won't even concede that there's some lexicographic value in documenting these usages. Meanwhile, his own practice is to avoid these blunders.

Why should linguists believe—as many certainly seem to—that language, of all human activities, is uniquely incapable of being misused or abused? Why should language alone be immune to ignorant or careless handling? It's hard to imagine professionals in any other field of human endeavor making an analogous argument.

- *Garner discovered that the "usage dictionaries got hijacked by the descriptive linguists" . . . . So who are these hijackers? . . . In fact these "modern linguists" are fictitious characters, or at least unrepresented among authors of usage guides. Garner has created a linguist made of straw and enjoys an energetic bout of kicking the straw out of him.*

Perhaps I erred in not naming names. It does surprise me that Bailey doesn't even recognize the principal object of my kicks: E. Ward Gilman, editor of *Webster's Dictionary of English Usage* (*WDEU*). This is an anti-usage-dictionary usage dictionary. Although the book performs a useful service in collecting what earlier commentators said about all the usual issues, *WDEU* treats Fowler and all other predecessors as linguistic dimwits.

When boiled down to their essence, the entries in *WDEU* read predictably as follows: "Usage critics have long assailed this particular usage. But our files at Merriam-Webster show that it is current, so you're justified in using it if you want to." Or else: "Usage critics have long assailed the supposed confusion between these two similar words. But our files at Merriam-Webster suggest that the two have never actually been confused. This shows how wrongheaded the old usage guides were."

WDEU took the latter approach in dismissing critics who had warned against muddling (1) *perpetuate* and *perpetrate*, and (2) *perquisite* and *prerequisite*. Because the Merriam-Webster files apparently don't document any writers who confound these words, *WDEU* suggests that the earlier usage critics were simply making up a problem that didn't really exist in the language. To refute this implication, *DMAU* cites examples of the confusion chapter and verse—four examples of each error occurring from 1992 to 1997, in sources such as *The New York Times*, *The Washington Post*, and *The Baltimore Sun*.

A slackly permissive book, *WDEU* consistently denigrates the judgments made by Fowler, Bernstein, Follett, and many others. Here, for example, is what *WDEU* says in the entry for *at the present time*:

> Bernstein discourages the use of this phrase in place of *now*. It is difficult to see why. We have no evidence that [the phrase *at the present time*] is likely to preempt more than its share of the language, and what virtue there is in trying to limit the number of choices a writer has in expressing an idea is unclear to us. (p. 143)

And here is what *WDEU* says about *inasmuch as*:

> This phrase is disparaged by several commentators (such as Follett . . .) in terms only slightly varied from those of Fowler. Fowler calls it "pompous," and later critics apply such labels as "formal" and "stilted." As [some critics] point out, *since*, *as*, and *because* are simpler. But if you want a longer expression, there is nothing wrong with *inasmuch as*; the objections are trifling. (p. 534)

And so it goes throughout: who cares if you use two words where one will do, or twenty words where eight will do.

Of course, the English language has countless opportunities for wordiness. If you want to be a good writer, you must learn to prune your language. Follett said it well back in 1966:

> Wherever we can make 25 words do the work of 50, we halve the area in which looseness and disorganization can flourish, and by reducing the span of attention required we increase the force of the thought. To make our words count for as much as possible is surely the simplest as well as the hardest secret of style. (p. 14)

Voltaire, George Campbell, E.B. White, William Zinsser, and countless other rhetoricians have said words to the same effect. But *WDEU* will have none of it. Its editors say that we shouldn't discriminate between wordy and concise choices in the language.

- *He idolizes Fowler, but even Fowler had to be cleansed of descriptivist tendencies before being presented to Garner's readers: "He was a lexicographer, true, but he was also a literary critic." Readers of this journal might think that lexicography is a worthy calling that need not be redeemed by literary criticism.*

Of course lexicography is a worthy calling. Even apart from *DMAU*, I'm a lexicographer—as editor in chief of *Black's Law Dictionary* (since the 7th edition of 1999). And in that work, I'm descriptivist. Some law professors wish I'd exclude certain senses of words that they believe to be, though common, "doctrinally incorrect." That's balderdash. If lawyers and judges use a term in a given way, I duly record it. That's my job.

But lexicographic experience alone wouldn't qualify me or anyone else to write a good dictionary of usage. It's a different kind of dictionary— one that entails an element of literary criticism. A sustained study of literature, writing, and editing—as well as practical experience in those disciplines—is an added requirement for the usage critic. This point eludes Bailey and anyone else who believes that any competent lexicographer could write a sound dictionary of usage. As F.W. Bateson put it some years ago: "[T]he professional linguist has very little to contribute to style considered as the *best* words in the *best* order."[11]

- *Readers who hasten to these entries [the split infinitive and preposition at the end of a sentence] in Garner's book, seeking quick certainty, will be distressed to find callow descriptivism where they might have hoped for robust denunciation.*

This statement shows how misunderstood the prescriptive approach is. Just as Fowler approved many split infinitives and sentence-ending prepositions back in 1926,[12] any knowledgeable critic would do so today. Whether my rulings are "callow descriptivism" I leave it for readers to decide. In writing the entries, I intended robust prescriptive endorsements:

- "Although few armchair grammarians seem to know it, some split infinitives are regarded as perfectly proper" (p. 616). Supporting snippets from Sterling Leonard, George Curme, Joseph Lee, and Norman Lewis follow—then examples.
- "The spurious rule about not ending sentences with prepositions is a remnant of Latin grammar, in which a preposition was the one word that a writer could not end a sentence with. But Latin grammar should never straitjacket English grammar" (p. 519). This

---

[11] F.W. Bateson, *The Scholar-Critic* 100 (1972).

[12] H.W. Fowler, *A Dictionary of Modern English Usage* 457–59, 558–61 (1926).

introduces a full-page entry on the subject, showing that it is fallacious to blame 18th-century grammarians for the superstition.

Bailey presumably hoped for "robust denunciations" so that he could denounce them. I foiled him.

- *All of his examples come from the writings of journalists and lawyers, neither profession noted for unflagging elegance. And he . . . offers . . . only the mistakes and the awkwardness of writers . . . . Page after page, Garner shows you how others have done wrong.*

I don't know of any profession noted for "unflagging elegance." And although most of my examples come from journalism, it's characteristically hyperbolic of Bailey to say that all of them do. On pages 2–3 alone, I give extended examples from journals on psychology, accounting, and linguistics.

Yes, I do mostly show where others have gone wrong. I'm convinced that this approach has great value in a usage dictionary. In *The King's English* (1906), the Fowler brothers greatly popularized the tradition of emphasizing the "negative virtues" of writing by pointing out writerly lapses. That's essentially what good dictionaries of usage have done ever since. The nature of the genre is mostly to collect and comment on offenses against idiom, grammar, punctuation, and style.

- *H.W. Fowler remains interesting because his prejudices are outrageous, his judgments sensitive, and his prose engaging. Garner, unfortunately, lacks all three of these qualities.*

This, of course, is something that's useless to try to rebut. Although I hope I'm free of outrageous prejudices, I do aspire to sensitive judgments and engaging prose. But notice how Bailey puts it: he doesn't seem to see these qualities as matters of degree. Either you have them or you don't.

In any event, scores of readers and reviewers have disagreed with Bailey. Among the reviewers, Bailey stands alone on this point. Here's a fair sampling of what others have said:

- "The prose in this work is readable, interesting, witty, and lively. It will be very helpful for modern writers who desire to write correctly but unpretentiously. This resource is highly recommended."—*Booklist*
- "Bryan Garner's *Dictionary of Modern American Usage* has displaced a host of other recent guides. But fans of Fowler and Partridge won't be disappointed. The thicket of examples, drawn mostly

from newspapers (including this one), is pierced by a labyrinth of well-developed and stylish essays on larger issues."—*Providence Journal-Bulletin*

- "*A Dictionary of Modern American Usage* contains the most succinct and sensible advice on American usage to come down the pike in a long while. Garner's dictionary is a must for anyone who endeavors to use words wisely and well."—*San Diego Union-Tribune*
- "This is a thorough tour of the language—a major reference work—offering humane instruction in diction, idiom, sentence structure, and much else."—*Wall Street Journal*

- *Garner is a Texan y'all-speaker . . . . [He was] an undergraduate at the University of Texas at Austin . . . . Curiously, for an undergraduate at the University of Texas, Garner seems not to have discovered James Sledd . . . . Garner has tried to make Fowler modern, but . . . [a] Texan shouldn't . . . have tried . . . . Garner might return, in his imagination, to those thrilling days of yesteryear at the University of Texas . . . .*

Maybe what we're seeing here is the type of "outrageous prejudice" that Bailey considers so endearing. I'm reminded of a map that has been reproduced in a recent linguistic study.[13] When asked to draw a linguistic map of the United States, a Michigander circled Michigan as the home of "normal" speakers. He also circled Texas and wrote in the middle "Hillbillies"—a fascinating reflection of linguistic prejudices. Apparently even linguists are susceptible to them. It's striking how a professed egalitarian like Bailey can so transparently betray his deep (and deeply misplaced) snobbery.

Conclusion

In his review, Bailey does make one irrefutable point: in my entry on "vogue words," I engaged in what I call "inelegant variation." (Fowler's term *elegant variation* doesn't work anymore because people don't realize that the term actually refers to pseudo-elegance. Many otherwise competent stylists now refer to "elegant variation" as if it were a good thing.) In my entry, I refer first to *vogue words*, and then I refer later in the paragraph to *modish diction*. Fowler would have been most unhappy with that phrasing, and I was embarrassed that anyone could make this point against me.

---

[13] Dennis R. Preston, "They Speak Really Bad English Down South and in New York City," in *Language Myths* 143 (Laurie Bauer & Peter Trudgill eds., 1998).

But that's the lot of the usage critic. As I wrote in the preface to my first usage dictionary back in 1987:

> Undertaking to write a dictionary of this kind is a precarious task. For by setting oneself up as an arbiter of usage, one also sets one's prose before the magnifying glasses of readers, who are certain to find blemishes of one sort or another. Such was H.W. Fowler's fate in his *Dictionary of Modern English Usage* (1926), a work that has served me as both exemplar and caution.[14]

On *modish diction*, I am duly chastened.

A final thought. Why can't descriptive and prescriptive approaches coexist peacefully? In *DMAU*, I essentially use descriptive methods (lots of fact-gathering) for prescriptive ends (rulings that, given where the language stands today, guide writers toward effective choices). I am both descriptive and prescriptive, and yet the "pure descriptivists" (it's an apt term) are so besotted with what is misleadingly called a "nonjudgmental" approach that they demonize anyone who doesn't share it.

This wasn't always so. In the 1950s, descriptivists had cooler heads. One of them—G.L. Brook, a major historian of the English language—came close to conceding the value of informed prescriptivism. In 1958, he wrote: "There are welcome signs of a desire to base linguistic preferences upon a sound knowledge of the history and nature of language, and the last few decades have seen the publication of a large number of prescriptive books on language by authors who possess such knowledge."[15] Not a hint of resentment there.

But things have changed. And Bailey suggests an answer to why descriptivists can't abide prescriptivists: "There is a great thirst abroad in the land for [prescriptivism], and the millions will slake their thirst with Garner's book, since it is a 'major selection' of the Book-of-the-Month Club . . . ." Here is our answer: good prescriptivist books sell because people find them useful and enjoyable; good descriptivist books typically have a professional readership that is extremely limited. As long as this is so, a truce seems unlikely.

---

[14] *A Dictionary of Modern Legal Usage* xiii (1987).
[15] G.L. Brook, *A History of the English Language* 209 (1958).

 za za za

Making Peace in the Language Wars

"This battle between linguistic radicals and linguistic conservatives continues unabated."

—Robert W. Burchfield

SHORTLY AFTER the first edition of my *Dictionary of Modern American Usage* appeared in 1998, a British reviewer—the noted linguist Tom McArthur— remarked about it: "Henry Watson Fowler, it would appear, is alive and well and living in Texas."[1] This might have seemed like the highest praise possible. After all, Fowler is lionized in American editorial circles. But McArthur meant no praise in his comment. Fowler, you see, was a prescriptivist: he issued judgments about linguistic choices.[2] McArthur, like almost every other linguist, is a descriptivist: he mostly disclaims making judgments about linguistic choices.[3] And the describers and the prescribers (if I may call them that) haven't been on speaking terms for a very long time.

The Wars

Prescribers seek to guide users of a language—including native speakers—on how to handle words as effectively as possible. Describers seek to discover the facts of how native speakers actually use their language. An outsider might think that these are complementary goals. In fact, though, insiders typically view them as incompatible. And the battles have been unpleasant, despite being mostly invisible (or irrelevant) outside academic linguistic circles. Hence David Foster Wallace's apt query: "Did you know that probing the seamy underbelly of U.S. lexicography reveals ideological strife and controversy and intrigue and nastiness and fervor on a nearly hanging-chad scale?"[4]

Adapted from *Garner's Modern American Usage* (2d ed. 2003).

[1] *. . . That Is Forever Fowler*, 15 English Today 59 (1999).

[2] *See* H.W. Fowler & F.G. Fowler, *The King's English* (1906); H.W. Fowler, *A Dictionary of Modern English Usage* (1926). For a solid biography of H.W. Fowler, see Jenny McMorris, *The Warden of English* (2001).

[3] *See* "Descriptive and Prescriptive Grammar," in *The Oxford Companion to the English Language* 286 (Tom McArthur ed., 1992) ("A *descriptive grammar* is an account of a language that seeks to describe how it is used objectively, accurately, systematically, and comprehensively.").

[4] David Foster Wallace, *Tense Present: Democracy, English, and the Wars over Usage*, Harper's Mag., Apr. 2001, at 39, 40.

Prescribers like to lambaste their adversaries for their amoral permissiveness:

- **1952:** "Some of the vigilantes who used to waylay your themes to flog each dangling participle and lynch every run-on sentence now seem to be looking for a chance to lay the language on your doorstep like a foundling and run like hell before you can catch them and ask them how to rear the brat. They're convinced that it's healthy, that it will grow up very well-adjusted provided it's never spanked or threatened or fussed over. They're perfectly willing to furnish you with its past history, and even help you keep records on its day-to-day development, but they'll only tell you what it has done, not what it should or should not do. The English grammar textbook of the future may approach its subject in the same spirit in which the Kinsey report tackled sex."[5]

- **1965:** "The ideal philologist regards the 'misuse' of language as a psychiatrist regards murder: just one more phenomenon of human behaviour."[6]

- **1967:** "The linguisticists . . . are urgently, even fanatically, storming the classroom in order to persuade the old-fashioned grammar teacher that she, too, should be dispassionate in her attitude toward language so that the attitude of linguisticism can prevail: let her just accept the view that there are merely 'different' levels of usage—*not* 'good' and 'bad,' 'acceptable' and 'unacceptable'—and all will be well."[7]

- **2000:** "Modern-day linguists who insist on a 'nonjudgmental' approach to language like to belittle Fowler. They are fools."[8]

Describers, meanwhile, like to denounce prescribers as priggish, often ignorant, authoritarians prepared to fight to the death over nonissues such as split infinitives and terminal prepositions:

- **1960:** "Should one say 'None of them is ready' or 'None of them are ready'?

---

[5] Louis B. Salomon, *Whose Good English?* 38 Am. Ass'n Univ. Profs. Bull. 441, 442 (Fall 1952) (as quoted in *The Ordeal of American English* 160, 161 (C. Merton Babcock ed., 1961)).

[6] Gary Jennings, *Personalities of Language* 8 (1965).

[7] Bertrand Evans, "Grammar and Writing," in *A Linguistics Reader* 111, 112 (Graham Wilson ed., 1967).

[8] Erich Eichman, *Taste—De Gustibus: A Golden Age of Words About Words*, Wall St. J., 7 Jan. 2000, at W11.

"The prescriptive grammarians are emphatic that it should be singular. The Latinists point out that *nemo*, the Latin equivalent, is singular. The logicians triumphantly point out that *none* can't be more than one and hence can't be plural.

"The linguist knows that he hears 'None of them are ready' every day, from people of all social positions, geographical areas, and degrees of education."[9]

- **1970:** "Those who fancy themselves preservers of standards in language, most of whom would hotly deny the appellation 'purist,' believe quite sincerely that their stand is highly traditional and regard as dangerous subversives those scholars who devote themselves to the objective description of their first-hand observations. Many who righteously maintain that split infinitives and terminal prepositions are cardinal sins regard themselves as forward-looking men of liberal temperament . . . ."[10]

- **1982:** "The eighteenth-century grammars, and more importantly the views of language and class which underpinned them, continue to terrorize English speech."[11]

- **1999:** "There is hardly any other area in life in which people so badly informed can actually be proud of their ignorance while still proclaiming themselves to be guardians of truth and saviors of others from error."[12]

At least one describer, Edward Finegan, has conceded that "linguists have not afforded the guardians [i.e., prescribers] a fair hearing," adding that "this imbalance is exacerbated by the bad press the guardians have in turn inflicted on linguists, a bad press that has bruised the credibility of the linguistics profession."[13] Indeed, the Linguistic Society of America long ago conceded what remains true today: "a fair portion of highly educated laymen see in linguistics the great enemy of all they hold dear."[14]

In short, there's long been bad blood between the two camps. It continues to this day. Even when contemporary describers propose a rapprochement, it typically consists simply in having prescribers concede

---

[9] Bergen Evans, *Grammar for Today*, 205 Atlantic Monthly 80, 81 (Mar. 1960) (as quoted in *The Ordeal of American English* 157, 158 (C. Merton Babcock ed., 1961)).

[10] Thomas Pyles & John Algeo, *English: An Introduction to Language* 29 (1970).

[11] Colin MacCabe, *The Listener*, 12 Aug. 1982, at 13–14.

[12] Ronald Wardhaugh, *Proper English: Myths and Misunderstandings About Language* 172 (1999).

[13] Edward Finegan, "On the Linguistic Forms of Prestige," in *The Legacy of Language: A Tribute to Charlton Laird* 146, 148 (Phillip C. Boardman ed., 1987).

[14] Linguistic Society of America, *Report of the Commission on the Humanities* 156 (1964).

the error of their ways. For example, in their new *Cambridge Grammar of the English Language* (2002), Rodney Huddleston and Geoffrey K. Pullum airily note that "although descriptive grammars and prescriptive usage manuals differ in the range of topics they treat, there is no reason in principle why they should not agree on what they say about the topics they both treat."[15] That might seem like a promising statement, but in fact it's disingenuous—rather like a warring spouse who quarrelsomely proposes a "reconciliation" by insisting that all the fault lies with the other side. For in the very next sentence, we find our two conciliators claiming that prescribers (1) overrely on personal taste; (2) confuse informality with ungrammaticality; and (3) appeal to "certain invalid arguments"[16] (unspecified). That's it. In their view, it's all the fault of prescribers.

But the fault lies at least equally at the feet of the describers, many of whom (1) insist that their methods are the only valid ones; (2) disclaim any interest in promoting the careful use of language, often denouncing anyone who seeks to do so; and (3) believe that native speakers of English can't make a mistake and that usage guides are therefore superfluous.

You may think that's just hyperbole. Sadly, it isn't. True enough, there may not be such a thing as a "pure describer," since every commentator has at least some predilections about usage, however covert. But many describers also dogmatically oppose value judgments about language. That in itself is a value judgment—and a very odd one, in the eyes of ordinary people. Here's a sampling of what "pure describers" have said in the literature:

Lakoff: "For change that comes spontaneously from below, or within, our policy should be, Let your language alone, and leave its speakers alone!"[17]

McWhorter: "*Descriptive* grammar . . . has nothing to do with the rather surreal notion of telling people what they *should* say. The other grammar, which is about counterintuitive, party-pooping bizarrerie, . . . is called *prescriptive* grammar and is neither taught to nor discussed by linguists, except as the persistent little scourge that seems to have gotten hold of the Anglophone world."[18]

Trudgill: "Language change cannot be halted. Nor should the worriers feel obliged to try to halt it. Languages are self-regulating systems which can be left to take care of themselves."[19]

---

[15] *Cambridge Grammar of the English Language* 6 (2002).

[16] *Id.* at 6–7.

[17] Robin Tolmach Lakoff, *Talking Power: The Politics of Language* 298 (1990).

[18] John McWhorter, *The Word on the Street: Fact and Fable About American English* 62 (1998).

[19] Peter Trudgill, "The Meanings of Words Should Not Be Allowed to Vary or Change," in *Language Myths* 8 (Laurie Bauer & Peter Trudgill eds., 1999).

These writers see language as if it were merely a series of events to be duly recorded. They don't see it—or don't want to see it—as the product of human conduct and human decision, or its use as a skill that can either be left rudimentary or be honed.

Meanwhile, describers themselves write exclusively in standard English. If it's really a matter of complete indifference to them, why don't they occasionally *flout* (or should that be *flaunt?*) the rules of grammar and usage? Their writing could *militate* (or is it *mitigate?*) in favor of linguistic mutations if they would allow themselves to be *unconscious* (*unconscionable?*) in their *use* (*usage?*) of words, as they seemingly want everyone else to be. But they don't do this. They write by all the rules that they tell everyone else not to worry about. Despite their protestations, their own words show that correctness is valued in the real world.

Why should linguists believe—as many certainly do—that language, of all human tools, is uniquely incapable of being misused or abused? Why should language alone be immune to ignorant or careless handling? It's hard to imagine professionals in any other field of human endeavor making an analogous argument.

One surprising aspect of descriptivist doctrine is that it's essentially anti-education: teaching people about good usage, the argument goes, interferes with the natural, unconscious forces of language, so leave speakers alone. This doctrine relieves English teachers of the responsibility to teach standard English. And it dooms us all to the dialect of the households in which we've grown up. One result is rigidified social strata. After all, you're unlikely to gain any responsible position—such as that of a linguistics professor—if you can't speak and write standard English. So much for egalitarianism.

I'm mostly in the prescriptive camp (although, as I'll explain in a moment, I'm a kind of descriptive prescriber). The prescriptive camp explicitly values linguistic decisions and informed standards of correctness. It's a Fowlerian sensibility that Sir Ernest Gowers summed up as having five bases: "first the careful choice of precise words, second the avoidance of all affectations, third the orderly and coherent arrangement of words, fourth the strict observance of what is for the time being established idiom, and fifth the systematization of spelling and pronunciation."[20] Gowers and I are hardly alone among Fowler's successors:

---

[20] Ernest Gowers, "H.W. Fowler: The Man and His Teaching," Presidential Address to the English Association, July 1957, at 14.

Pei: "Don't be afraid to exercise your power of choice. If you prefer 'telephone' to 'phone,' or 'greatly' to 'very much,' don't be afraid to use them. It's your language as much as anyone else's. At the same time, try to have a good reason for your choice, because language is one of the finest products of man's intelligence, and should be intelligently employed and intelligently changed."[21]

Safire: "Some of the interest in the world of words comes from people who like to put less-educated people down—Language Snobs, who give good usage a bad name. Others enjoy letting off steam in a form of mock-anger, treating their peeves as pets. But most of the interest, I think, comes from a search for standards and values. We resent fogginess; we resist manipulation by spokesmen who use loaded words and catch phrases; we wonder if, in language, we can find a few of the old moorings. We are not groping for the bygone, we are reaching for a firm foothold in fundamentals."[22]

Marenbon: "It is far easier to destroy a standard language than to create one. A standard language requires a body of speakers who have been trained to distinguish correct constructions from incorrect ones, usual forms from those which are unusual and carry with them special implications. Such training is neither short nor easy; and it is unrealistic to expect that English teachers can give it to their pupils if, along with teaching standard English (as one form of the language, appropriate for certain occasions), they are expected to encourage speech and writing in dialect and to attend to the multiplicity of other tasks with which modern educationalists have burdened them. By devaluing standard English, the new orthodoxy is destroying it."[23]

Prescribers want to evaluate linguistic change as it occurs. They endorse the changes they consider fortunate and resist the ones they consider unfortunate—often with little success in the long run.

Explaining the Rift

The opposing views aren't easily reconciled. Prescribers like established forms in grammar and word choice. They encourage precision and discourage letting one word usurp another's meaning (*infer–imply, lay–lie,*

---

[21] Mario Pei, *All About Language* 9 (1954).
[22] William Safire, *On Language* xv (1980).
[23] John Marenbon, *Proper English*? 252–53 (Tony Crowley ed., 1991).

like–as). They dislike the indiscriminate use of two forms, especially
opposed forms, for one meaning (*categorically–uncategorically*, *couldn't care
less–could care less*, *regardless–irregardless*). They value consistency and historical continuity (preferring *home in* over *hone in*, *just deserts* over *just
desserts*, and *slough off* over *sluff off*).

Describers, meanwhile, remind us that linguistic change is a fact of
life—and conclude that it's therefore not worth opposing. As one has
asked: "If language is going to keep changing anyway—and it is—what
is the use of posting the little rules and making people uncomfortable
only to see them eventually blown away by the wind?"[24] Another
prominent describer has even seemed to tout mass heedlessness: "The
inert ignorance of the uneducated about their language . . . indeed has
had a profound and on the whole a progressive effect on language, man-
ifesting itself in an almost miraculously intricate and regular operation of
known laws of linguistic behavior."[25] Perhaps because that view involves
a value judgment (ignorance is progressive), some describers disclaim it
in favor of a value-neutral and all but valueless position, such as this:
"The most sensible view about any language is that it changes. It neither
regresses nor progresses."[26]

In one of the most mind-blowing descriptivist passages ever penned,
Donald J. Lloyd talked about linguistic change by allusively adopting a
notoriously invidious view of rape: "There is no point in tiresome carping about usage; the best thing is to relax and enjoy it."[27]

Yet not all describers endorse fatalistic or optimistic views of change.
Dwight L. Bolinger, a describer with impeccable credentials, has staked a
position that most prescribers would find satisfactory: "If rules are to be
broken, it is better done from knowledge than from ignorance, even

[24] John McWhorter, *The Word on the Street* 85 (1998). *But see* Peter Farb, *Word Play* 84
(1974) ("One justification sometimes heard for freedom in breaking the rules of the language game is that languages change with time anyway. But that argument is beside the
point. Even though the rules may change tomorrow, they are still binding while they are
in force today.").

[25] John S. Kenyon, "Ignorance Builds Language" (1938), in *A Language Reader for Writers* 175, 176 (James R. Gaskin & Jack Suberman eds., 1966).

[26] Ronald Wardhaugh, *Proper English: Myths and Misunderstandings About Language* 42
(1999).

[27] Donald J. Lloyd, "Snobs, Slobs and the English Language," in *A Linguistics Reader* 99,
102 (Graham Wilson ed., 1967).

when ignorance ultimately decides the issue."[28] Another, the Oxford professor Jean Aitchison, concedes that "language change . . . may, in certain circumstances, be socially undesirable."[29]

One major difference between the prescriber and the describer, and their views toward change, has to do with the relative immediacy of linguistic perspective. The prescriber cares about how language is used here and now. The describer views language more distantly, observing that linguistic change is inevitable. After all, Latin evolved into French, Italian, and other Romance languages—and the French, Italians, and others haven't been adversely affected by linguistic evolution. This is like a geographer's arguing that seismic disruptions along the San Andreas Fault hardly matter in the larger scheme of things, since continents and seas will come and go: in the history of the earth, an earthquake in Los Angeles doesn't amount geographically to a blip on the big screen. But of course earthquakes do matter to the people who experience them. And how language is used today—here and now—does matter to people who speak it, hear it, write it, and read it. Invoking the inevitability of linguistic drift doesn't help someone who is unsure about how to say *irrevocable*, what preposition to use after *oblivious*, or whether the verb after *a number of people* should be singular or plural. The linguistic choice that a speaker or writer makes will affect how others react. Linguists may take the long view, but good usage depends on the here and now.

Because usage constantly evolves, so must judgments about usage. Much of what Theodore Bernstein, an eminent *New York Times* editor, said in 1965 about the careful writer[30] endures to this day; some of it doesn't. That's the way usage is. The test of good usage has little to do with what endures, although good usage is fairly stable and tends to endure. It has more to do with what works for today's readership, distracting as few readers as possible. It's a test of credibility among contemporaries. Good usage reflects how a careful writer of today approaches linguistic questions.

---

[28] Dwight L. Bolinger, *Language: The Loaded Weapon* 55 (1980). *Cf.* Louis Foley, *Beneath the Crust of Words* 83 (1928) ("Ignorance has had considerable effect in the development of language. Many changes which have been made in the forms, uses, and meanings of words would certainly not have occurred if the language had been used only by those who knew it thoroughly.").

[29] Jean Aitchison, *Language Change: Progress or Decay?* 260 (3d ed. 2001).

[30] *See* Theodore M. Bernstein, *The Careful Writer* (1965).

One common tack of describers is to question all the assumptions about what is meant by "careful writers,"[31] "the best writers,"[32] or "respected people"[33]—the abstractions that prescribers postulate for establishing a standard of good usage. When it's impossible to identify exactly who these people are, describers claim victory by concluding that no such standard exists.[34]

But this idea that "careful writers" (etc.) are unidentifiable is a fallacious position for two reasons.

First, we say that usage is judged good not because the *best writers* employ it, but because it helps writers use words successfully.[35] Likewise, we say that apples are healthful not because wise people eat them, but because of their observable effects on the human body. The fact that we eat apples doesn't make them "good food."

Second, the *careful writer* may exist for the language in the same sense as the *reasonable person* exists for law, or (in other fields) the *average voter* or the *typical consumer*: it's a pragmatic construct that allows for assessing and predicting behavior. The careful writer is essentially good usage anthropomorphized. It's irrelevant that you can't point to a particular person as a "careful writer," just as it's irrelevant to the law that no one is on every occasion a "reasonable person." This doesn't mean that a real

---

[31] William Strunk Jr. & E.B. White, *The Elements of Style* 59 (3d ed. 1979) ("The careful writer, watchful for small conveniences, goes *which*-hunting, removes the defining *which*es, and by so doing improves his work."); Maxine Hairston, *Successful Writing* 118 (2d ed. 1986) ("Although the verb *to be* in all its forms (*is, am, was, were, will be, have been,* and so on) remains the central verb in our language, careful writers use it sparingly.").

[32] Strunk & White, *The Elements of Style* 72 ("It is no sign of weakness or defeat that your manuscript ends up in need of major surgery. This is a common occurrence in all writing, and among the best writers."); Thomas R. Lounsbury, *The Standard of Usage in English* vi (1908) ("The best, and indeed the only proper, usage is the usage of the best."); John F. Genung, *Outlines of Rhetoric* 9 (1893) ("A most valuable habit to cultivate . . . is the habit of observing words, especially as seen in the pages of the best writers; of tracing fine shades of meaning, and noting how suggestive, or felicitous, or accurately chosen they are. It is by keeping their sense for words alert and refined that good writers constantly enlarge and enrich their vocabulary."); Brainerd Kellogg, *A Text-Book on Rhetoric* 17 (1881) ("Rhetoric . . . has only *usage* as authority for what it teaches—the usage of the best writers and speakers. And this is variable, changing from generation to generation.").

[33] Bergen Evans & Cornelia Evans, *A Dictionary of Contemporary American Usage* v (1957) ("Respectable English . . . means the kind of English that is used by the most respected people, the sort of English that will make readers or listeners regard you as an educated person.").

[34] For a splendid example of this specious approach, *see* John Algeo, "What Makes Good English Good?" in *The Legacy of Language: A Tribute to Charlton Laird* 122–23 (Phillip C. Boardman ed., 1987).

[35] I owe this argument to I.A. Richards, *The Philosophy of Rhetoric* 52 (1936).

standard doesn't exist. Even Richard W. Bailey of Michigan, a thorough-going describer, acknowledges that the linguistic standard exists: "Linguists who pretend that there is no consensus about the elite forms of English confuse their egalitarian ideals with the social reality that surrounds them."[36]

Still another difference between the camps is that describers want comprehensive descriptions of languages, while prescribers unapologetically treat only a selective set of linguistic problems. Describers have been known to criticize prescribers for this selectivity: "The normative tradition focuses on just a few dots in the vast and complex universe of the English language."[37] Because describers are "scientists" who seek to record and catalogue all the observable linguistic phenomena they can, they will go into great detail about matters that have minimal interest to everyone else—for example, why in English we don't say *House brick built is.* Prescribers, by contrast, who write for a wide audience, deal mostly with issues that can taunt even seasoned writers—to take examples from just one small span of entries from this book, the difference between *hearty* and *hardy*; whether the correct form is *harebrained* or *hairbrained*; or whether the predominant phrase is *hark back, harken back,* or *hearken back* (perhaps *harp back*?). So prescribers tend to assume that their readers already have some competence with the language.

Yet another major difference has to do with the use of evidence. Describers have always tried to amass linguistic evidence—the more the better. Prescribers are often content to issue their opinions ex cathedra. In fact, inadequate consideration of linguistic evidence has traditionally been the prescribers' greatest vulnerability. But the better prescribers, such as H. W. Fowler and Eric Partridge, have closely considered the facts underpinning their judgments. In this book, I've taken the descriptivist tack of citing voluminous evidence—perhaps more than some readers might think necessary. But those readers should consider how useful it is to see the contextual use of words, not in made-up examples but in published passages.[38]

---

[36] Richard W. Bailey, "Whose Usage? Fred Newton Scott and the Standard of Speech," in *Centennial Usage Studies* 1 (Greta D. Little & Michael Montgomery eds., 1994).

[37] Sidney Greenbaum, *Current Usage and the Experimenter*, 51 Am. Speech 163, 163 (1976).

[38] *Cf.* Samuel Johnson, Preface, *A Dictionary of the English Language* (1755) ("Authorities will sometimes seem to have been accumulated without necessity or use, and perhaps some will be found, which might, without loss, have been omitted. But a work of this kind is not hastily to be charged with superfluities: those quotations, which to careless or unskillful perusers appear only to repeat the same sense, will often exhibit, to a more accurate examiner, diversities of signification, or, at least, afford different shades of the same meaning.").

While prescribers view language as involving a multitude of decisions, describers often discuss language as if its use were all a matter of instinct. "To a linguist or psycholinguist," writes Steven Pinker of MIT, "language is like the song of the humpback whale."[39] He tenaciously pursues this odd comparison, ridiculing prescribers as if they were essentially the same as naturalists claiming that "chickadees' nests are incorrectly constructed, pandas hold bamboo in the wrong paw, the song of the humpback whale contains several well-known errors, and monkeys' cries have been in a state of chaos and degeneration for hundreds of years."[40] He caps it off with this: "Isn't the song of the humpback whale whatever the humpback whale decides to sing?"[41]

The analogy is deeply fallacious in all sorts of ways. First, although the capacity for language may indeed be instinctive—and Pinker makes a good case for this in his book—the specifics of any given language (for example, why we call one object a *hat* and another a *table*) aren't instinctive at all. Words are arbitrary symbols that are learned, and there are lots of nuances. Second, human beings must make myriad decisions when forming sentences and paragraphs, whereas other animals aren't known to make the same kinds of decisions in following their instincts. Third, Pinker's line of reasoning would eliminate any means for judging the effectiveness of human expression. Yet we all know—and Pinker knows very well—that some human beings communicate more effectively than others.

So much for the describers' misplaced scientism: it can lead to astounding instances of muddled thought.

Reconciling the Camps

A greater sense of balance and impartiality—of where the truth lies—could end the age-old debate between describers and prescribers, if only both sides would acknowledge certain principles. More about these in a moment.

First, I should declare that I am a prescriber who uses descriptivist methods—in effect, a descriptive prescriber. I don't doubt the value of descriptive linguistics—up to the point at which describers dogmatically refuse to acknowledge the value of prescriptivism. Each side in this age-old debate should acknowledge the value of the other.

---

[39] Steven Pinker, *The Language Instinct* 370 (1994).
[40] *Id.*
[41] *Id.*

Before stating three principles that might allow for this reconciliation, I should draw attention to the danger of acknowledging my prescriptive tendencies. I may be playing into describers' hands by adopting this inflammatory label. Maybe I should instead take a lesson from D.J. Enright: "Many people without the benefit (as they see it) of a decent education still *want* to know how to use words. And since prescriptivism is the only brake we have on the accelerating spread of chaos, let's find some other name for it, one less reminiscent of the National Health Service."[42] Yet no new label readily suggests itself. Besides, changing the label probably won't change the reality.

Now to the fundamental principles.

1. Linguistically, both speech and writing matter.

When modern linguists focus exclusively on speech, they're overreacting to their predecessors' preoccupation with writing. Describers have a bias toward studying speech; prescribers have a bias toward studying writing.

Both are important. In any language, speech precedes writing. It accounts for the overwhelming majority of linguistic events. Yet writing is a form of language worth studying in its own right. For some reason, though, many linguists refuse to recognize this. As Roy Harris, the Oxford linguist, put it some years ago: "One of the sophistries of modern linguistics is to treat scriptism, which has probably dominated the concept of a language in literate societies for at least several millennia, as some kind of theoretical heresy."[43]

Writing endures and therefore helps stabilize the language. Universal literacy helps temper linguistic entropy. As more and more people become literate, the written and spoken forms of language influence each other—even while remaining distinct.

For the readers of this essay, a stable language is doubtless a desirable thing. Without some stability, the English language wouldn't be worth much as a lingua franca. Samuel Johnson rejected the idea of embalming the language,[44] and no one seriously wants to halt all change in a living language. "It is not a question of banning all linguistic changes," as F.L. Lucas put it. "Since language cannot stand still, the main thing for the public interest is that alterations in vocabulary and idiom should not become too rapid, reckless, and wanton . . . ."[45]

---

[42] D.J. Enright, *Fields of Vision* 224 (1990).
[43] Roy Harris, *The Language Makers* 7 (1980).
[44] See the Preface to his *Dictionary of the English Language* (1755).
[45] F.L. Lucas, *Style* 43 (1955; repr. 1962).

The study of writing—like the very fact that writing exists—serves as a conservative, moderating influence. Our literary heritage has helped form our culture. The means by which we record words on paper has an enormous influence on readers and on the culture as a whole.

One aspect of the writing-vs.-speech distinction is what linguists call "register": a user's style of language according to the subject, the audience, and the occasion. No one writes a job-application letter in the same style as a love letter; and no one speaks to an interviewer in the same way as to a pet. Most of us have five basic registers: (1) intimate, for conversations between family members and close friends; (2) casual, for everyday conversations; (3) consultative, for communicating with colleagues and strangers in conducting everyday business; (4) formal, for published essays and serious lectures; and (5) frozen, for religious and legal rituals.[46] Those who study oral communication (describers) incline toward 1–2 (occasionally 3); those who study written communication (prescribers) incline toward 3–4 (occasionally 2, sometimes 5). If describers and prescribers alike were more overt about the registers they're dealing with, many of their squabbles might wither away.

2. Writing well is a hard-won skill that involves learning conventions.

To educate people about the conventions of writing is good for them. Why? Because writing well requires disciplined thinking. Learning to write is a part of anyone's education.

What are the conventions that aspiring writers need to learn? Among other things, those who write expository prose must learn cognitive skills—how to:

- Summarize complicated matter.
- Maintain a cohesive train of thought.
- Support ideas with adequate evidence.

To communicate the material, the writer must also learn mechanical skills—how to:

- Vary sentence structure.
- Vary sentence length.
- Vary paragraph length.
- Connect ideas from sentence to sentence, and paragraph to paragraph.

---

[46] *See generally* Martin Joos, *The Five Clocks* (1962).

Finally, to make certain that the communication is clear to the reader and free of distractions, the writer must learn stylistic skills—how to:

- Adopt a relaxed, natural tone.
- Omit unnecessary words.
- Observe recognized grammatical niceties (subject–verb agreement, parallel constructions, logically placed modifiers, and so on).
- Distinguish between similar words that are easily confused, such as *affect* and *effect*, *principle* and *principal*, and the like.

Only the last three, for some reason, seem to trouble most describers, who overstate their objections. They like to caricature prescribers as insisting on such fripperies as *It's I* and *none is*, and as prohibiting all split infinitives, all prepositions as sentence-enders, and all conjunctions as sentence-starters.[47] The truth is that informed prescribers didn't take any of those positions at any time in the 20th century—and certainly not in the 21st. In fact, prescribers have been just as severe as describers in ridiculing such superstitions.[48]

Back to the main point: writing is a learned activity, no different in that regard from hitting a golf ball or playing the piano. Yes, some people naturally do it better than others. But apart from a few atypical autodidacts (who exist in all disciplines), there's no practical way to learn to write, hit a golf ball, or play the piano without guidance on many points, large and small. And everyone, even the autodidact, requires considerable effort and practice in learning the norms. The norms are important even to those who ultimately break them to good effect.

3. It's possible to formulate practical advice on grammar and usage.

Although 18th- and 19th-century grammarians' work was too often corrupted by whimsy and guesswork, their basic instincts were sound: we can indeed help writers on critical questions of grammar and usage.

---

[47] *See* the quotations accompanying notes 9, 10; *see also* Steven Pinker, *The Language Instinct* 373–74 (1994) ("Most of the hobgoblins of contemporary prescriptive grammar (don't split infinitives, don't end a sentence with a preposition) can be traced back to . . . eighteenth-century fads").

[48] *See, e.g.,* H.W. Fowler, *A Dictionary of Modern English Usage* 586–87 (1926) (s.v. "Superstitions"); Eric Partridge, *Usage and Abusage* 159–60 [*it is me*], 204–05 [*none*], 296 [split infinitive], 245 [terminal preposition] (1940); Wilson Follett, *Modern American Usage: A Guide* 227 [*none*], 313 [split infinitive], 64 [*and, but*] (1966); Theodore M. Bernstein, *Miss Thistlebottom's Hobgoblins: The Careful Writer's Guide to the Taboos, Bugbears, and Outmoded Rules of English Usage* (1971) (*passim*).

Usage and style operate differently in writing and in speech. In oral communication, inflection and body language and interaction help convey meaning. And a speaker can perceive cues that invite immediate clarifications. But in writing, these aids to communication are absent: you rely exclusively on marks on a page (words and punctuation). A writer rarely gets a second chance to communicate effectively, so clear writing requires much more forethought. It's no wonder that publishers have produced thousands of books designed to teach people how to improve their writing.

Authorities on the written word echo each other in stressing how difficult good writing is: "Writing is hard work. A clear sentence is no accident. Very few sentences come out right the first time, or even the third time. Remember this in moments of despair. If you find that writing is hard, it's because it *is* hard."[49] Writers must learn to have a point, to deliver it efficiently, to cut the extra words that inevitably appear in any first draft, and to maintain a clean narrative line, among many other skills. These things trouble even professionals.

Prescriptive usage guides deal with many of the small points that writers grapple with. These manuals are pedagogical books intended to be browsed in as much as consulted. In this book, for example, many entries deal with emerging confusions in diction that threaten to spread: *disburse* for *disperse, expatriot* for *expatriate, fruit melody* for *fruit medley, heart-rendering* for *heart-rending, marshal arts* for *martial arts, presumptious* for *presumptuous, reign in* for *rein in.* Other entries deal with plural forms that, for now, most careful writers want to maintain in plural senses, such as *criteria, paparazzi*, and *phenomena.* Still other entries urge wider acceptance of disputed usages such as the singular *media.*

The focus is on the particular: these are the words and phrases that writers and editors must make considered choices about daily. There aren't just a few dozen trouble spots in the language, or even a few hundred. There are several thousand of them. Given the critical acumen of many readers, for a writer to remain unconscious of these pitfalls and write whatever sounds close enough will inevitably lead to a loss of credibility. Vague intelligibility isn't the touchstone; precision is.

As a field of study, usage doesn't hold much interest for modern linguists, who are drifting more and more toward quantitative psychol-

---

[49] William Zinsser, *On Writing Well* 12 (6th ed. 1998). *Cf.* Alexei Tolstoy, "Advice to the Young Writer" (1939), in Maxim Gorky, Vladimir Mayakovsky, Alexei Tolstoy, and Konstantin Fedin, *On the Art and Craft of Writing* 231, 231–32 (Alex Miller trans., 1972) ("Nobody has ever found that writing comes easy, that it 'flowed' from the pen. Writing is always difficult, and the more difficult it is, the better it turns out in the end.").

ogy and theory. Their leading theorist, Noam Chomsky of MIT, has acknowledged, with no apparent regret, the pedagogical irrelevance of modern linguistics: "I am, frankly, rather skeptical about the significance, for the teaching of languages, of such insights and understanding as have been attained in linguistics and psychology."[50] An equally august prescriptivist, F.W. Bateson of Oxford, said just a few years later: "The professional linguist has very little to contribute to style considered as the *best* words in the *best* order."[51] If you want to learn how to use the English language skillfully and gracefully, books on linguistics won't help you at all.

Yet people *want* normative rules of language. Linguistic relativism, though valuable on some levels, has its limitations. True, it's probably helpful for students to hear insights such as this from Charlton Laird: "Nothing in language is essentially vulgar or genteel, barbarous or elegant, right or wrong, except as the users of the language want to feel that the locutions have those qualities."[52] But of course most writers believe that words and phrases can have right and wrong qualities. In a given social setting, those widely shared views matter enormously. And Laird—a sensible describer—recognized this:

> We must have standards. After all, who makes the language? You and I and everybody make the language. And what does this hydra-headed language-manufacturer want in his product? Obviously, he wants a number of things; he wants flexibility and versatility, but he also wants standards. He may not know just what standards he wants, nor how rigidly he wants them applied, but he does want them in spelling, in punctuation, in diction, in usage, in all aspects of language, and on the whole he relies on people of our sort [English teachers] to inform him which are the best standards and what he should do about them. We had better be prepared to tell him, and to know what we are talking about when we do so.[53]

Despite the describers' decades-old campaign to convince us that no uses of language are inherently better than others, literate people continue to yearn for guidance on linguistic questions. With great acuity

---

[50] Noam Chomsky, "Linguistic Theory," in *Northeast Conference on the Teaching of Foreign Languages* 43 (1966) (as quoted in J.B. Pride, *The Social Meaning of Language* 80 (1971)). *Cf.* Linguistic Society of America, *Report of the Commission on the Humanities* 155–56 (1964) ("The impact which the recent advances in linguistics have upon the general public [is] essentially zero.").

[51] F.W. Bateson, *The Scholar-Critic* 100 (1972).

[52] Charlton Laird, *And Gladly Teche* 47 (1970).

[53] *Id.* at 47–48.

half a century ago, an English teacher—Louis Salomon—characterized what remains the current state of affairs:

> The public may not care whether English teachers eat or not, but if there is any sentiment in favor of feeding them I'm willing to bet that the idea is to keep them alive as English teachers, that is, as a kind of traffic cop to tell the average person when to stop and when to move on, where he may park and where he may not. If English teachers don't want to be traffic cops—if they just want to stand on the corner and count the cars that try to beat the red light—then they might as well turn in their badges. Because sooner or later the taxpayers will (a) begin to wonder why the accident rate keeps going up, and (b) discover that a machine with an electric eye can do the counting more cheaply and more efficiently.[54]

Yet several linguists assert, essentially, that there is no right and wrong in language. Consider what one well-known linguist, Robert A. Hall Jr., famously said: "There is no such thing as good and bad (or correct and incorrect, grammatical and ungrammatical, right and wrong) in language . . . . A dictionary or grammar is not as good an authority for your speech as the way you yourself speak."[55] Some of the better theorists in the mid-20th century rejected this extremism. Here, for example, is how Max Black responded:

> This extreme position . . . involves a confusion between investigating rules (or standards, norms) and prescribing or laying down such rules. Let us grant that a linguist, qua theoretical and dispassionate scientist, is not in the business of telling people how to talk; it by no means follows that the speakers he is studying are free from rules which ought to be recorded in any faithful and accurate report of their practices. A student of law is not a legislator; but it would be a gross fallacy to argue that therefore there can be no right or wrong in legal matters.[56]

One might have thought that this no-right-and-no-wrong fallacy had long since been laid to rest. But it's very much with us, at least in academia. Through the latter half of the 20th century and still today, there has been an academic assault on linguistic standards. Today the remark "That's not good English" would likely be met with the rejoin-

---

[54] Louis B. Salomon, *Whose Good English?* 38 Am. Ass'n Univ. Profs. Bull. 441, 448 (Fall 1952) (as quoted in *The Ordeal of American English* 160, 163 (C. Merton Babcock ed., 1961)).

[55] Robert A. Hall Jr., *Leave Your Language Alone!* 6 (1950).

[56] Max Black, *The Labyrinth of Language* 70 (1968).

der, "Says who?" This is because people are increasingly hearing the dogma that no use of language is better than any other.

Today the teaching of standard English is being labeled discriminatory. An essay published in 1998 by a University of Michigan linguist, James Milroy, says this: "In an age when discrimination in terms of race, color, religion, or gender is not publicly acceptable, the last bastion of overt social discrimination will continue to be a person's use of language."[57]

In other words, the spirit of the day demands that you not think critically—or at least not think ill—of anyone else's use of language. If you believe in good grammar and linguistic sensitivity, *you're* the problem. And there is a large, powerful contingent in higher education today—larger and more powerful than ever before—trying to eradicate any thoughts about good and bad grammar, correct and incorrect word choices, effective and ineffective style.

Terms of the Truce

Prescribers should be free to advocate a realistic level of linguistic tidiness—without being molested for it—even as the describers are free to describe the mess all around them. If the prescribers have moderate success, then the describers should simply describe those successes. Education entailing normative values has always been a part of literate society. Why should it suddenly stop merely because describers see this kind of education as meddling with natural forces?

Meanwhile, prescribers need to be realistic. They can't expect perfection or permanence, and they must bow to universal usage. But when an expression is in transition—when only part of the population has adopted a new usage that seems genuinely undesirable—prescribers should be allowed, within reason, to stigmatize it. There's no reason to tolerate *wreckless driving* in place of *reckless driving*. Or *wasteband* in place of *waistband*. Or *corollary* when misused for *correlation*. Multiply these things by 10,000, and you have an idea of what we're dealing with. There are legitimate objections to the slippage based not just on widespread confusion but also on imprecision of thought, on the spread of linguistic uncertainty, on the etymological disembodiment of words, and on decaying standards generally.

---

[57] James Milroy, "Children Can't Speak or Write Properly Any More," in *Language Myths* 64–65 (Laurie Bauer & Peter Trudgill eds., 1998).

As Roy Harris has remarked: "There is no reason why prescriptive linguistics should not be 'scientific,' just as there is no reason why prescriptive medicine should not be."[58] Harris went even further, denouncing the antiprescriptive doctrine as resulting from naiveté:

> Twentieth-century linguists, anxious to claim "scientific" status for their new synchronic discipline, were glad enough to retain the old nineteenth-century whipping-boy of prescriptivism, in order thereby to distinguish their own concerns as "descriptive," not "prescriptive." When the history of twentieth-century linguistics comes to be written, a naive, unquestioning faith in the validity of this distinction will doubtless be seen as one of the main factors in the academic sociology of the subject.[59]

Elsewhere Harris has referred to "the anti-prescriptivist witch-hunt in modern linguistics."[60]

Other linguists have explained the blind spot that misleads so many of their colleagues. In 1959, C.A. Ferguson suggested that linguists too often take a blinkered look at the language, ignoring its social import: "[Describers] in their understandable zeal to describe the internal structure of the language they are studying often fail to provide even the most elementary data about the sociocultural setting in which the language functions."[61]

Maybe this, in turn, is because linguistic investigations tend to be highly theoretical—and divorced from most people's immediate interests in language. Barbara Wallraff, an *Atlantic* editor who is a prescriber with acute judgment, puts it in a self-deprecating[62] way: "I am not an academic linguist or an etymologist. Linguistics and what I do stand in something like the relation between anthropology and cooking ethnic food, or between the history of art and art restoration."[63] Other analogies might be equally apt, such as musicologists vis-à-vis musicians, or sociologists vis-à-vis ethicists.

---

[58] Roy Harris, *The Language Makers* 151 (1980).

[59] *Id.* at 151–52.

[60] Roy Harris, *The Language Machine* 128 (1987).

[61] C.A. Ferguson, "Principles of Teaching Languages with Diglossia," in *Monograph Series on Languages and Linguistics* 437 (1959).

[62] I use this phrase advisedly. See pp. 198–99 of my *Dictionary of Modern American Usage* (1998).

[63] Barbara Wallraff, *Word Court* 2 (2000).

To my knowledge, anthropologists don't denounce ethnic food, and art historians don't denounce art restorers—especially not when the cooks and the artisans know a thing or two about the material they're dealing with. Musicologists don't censure musicians who teach others how to produce a vibrato. Sociologists don't look askance at ethicists who aim to guide human behavior. Those who study language could learn something from these other fields—something about balance, civility, and peaceful coexistence.

JUSTICE ROBERT H. JACKSON • ALBERT EINSTEIN • BERTRAND RUSSELL

Legal Language

Preface to the First Edition of
A Dictionary of Modern Legal Usage

IN 1921, AN ARTICLE in the *American Bar Association Journal* called for a book on "writing legal English."[1] The author of that article, Urban A. Lavery, pointed out that lawyers rarely consult a book on grammar or composition even once to the hundreds of times they consult lawbooks; and yet, as he observed, when convincing argument is to the fore, or clearness of expression is desired, the elements of good writing are often more important than piled-up citations of cases.[2] Since Lavery proclaimed his judgment, many books on "writing legal English" have been published, but none with the broad scope or easy accessibility that might allow readers to resolve at a glance the many grammatical and stylistic questions that arise in legal writing. Filling that gap is the goal of this book.

Anglo-American law has a language of its own, consisting in a vocabulary with an unusually large number of foreign phrases, archaic words and expressions, terms of art, and argot words. Its formal style reflects the dignity and solemnity with which the profession views its mission. These distinctive qualities of legal language—evident alike in the speech and the writing of lawyers—are well enough documented. What has remained uncollected and unscrutinized in any systematic way is the vast body of legal usage.

From *A Dictionary of Modern Legal Usage* (1987).
[1] Lavery, *The Language of the Law*, 7 ABA J. 277 (1921).
[2] *Id.* at 280.

For a specialist language, the language of law remains remarkably variable, largely because it has been incompletely recorded and mapped. In this respect it is analogous to English before 18th-century grammarians attempted to reduce its variability and make logical its many quiddities. This is not to say, of course, that the language of the law has the malleable capacity of Elizabethan English, which, in the hands of a creative genius like Shakespeare, could be supremely expressive and evocative. Quite the opposite. Stare decisis remains at the core of our system of law—so much so that the continual search for precedents often discourages legal writers from straying beyond precisely how things have been said before. As a result, many locutions have become fossilized in legal language over generations. And the inheritors of that language cannot always distinguish mere form from necessary substance, to the extent that form and substance are ever separable.

Legal traditionalists may be justified in not wanting to throw over too readily what has long served well. Yet tradition alone is not sufficient reason for retaining outmoded forms of language. Modern legal writers must strike a difficult balance in the quest to simplify legal English. They should not cling perversely to archaic language, which becomes less comprehensible year by year, for its own sake. Nor should they seek to jettison every word or phrase that bears the stamp of legal tradition.

As for students of law, they learn the technical language that they will need—the quirks of legal jargon, the peculiar idiomatic expressions, the grammatical idiosyncrasies, the neologisms that cannot be found even in the most current unabridged dictionaries—largely by osmosis. These linguistic matters are, for the most part, seldom discussed by lawyers or law professors; rather, they are part of the spoken and written legal discourse that neophyte lawyers absorb every day and learn to use unconsciously. This casualness in acquiring the language frequently leads to variable and contradictory linguistic habits that need explicating, codifying, and, in some instances, taming.

Granted these basic facts of legal language—the course of its growth, the challenge of its use, the pattern of its acquisition—this book aims at serving three primary functions. First, it helps lawyers chart their way through the bogs of legal language. In the past, anyone wanting such a guide has had to make do with general writing manuals. Though this dictionary lays no claim to comprehensiveness, it offers the legal writer guidance on hundreds of specific points of usage. The advice it gives is generally on the conservative side of usage and grammar, for the simple reason that lawyers generally write in a relatively formal context. Lapses from what has come to be accepted as correct irritate and distract the educated reader, and this makes the writing less persuasive. Yet the conservative approach exemplified in these pages aspires to be an *informed* conservatism, one that neither battles hopelessly against linguistic faits accomplis nor remains blind to the inevitable growth and change that occur in language.

Second, the dictionary addresses a great many usage problems that do not ordinarily arise in the writing of persons untrained in the law, and therefore that are not addressed in standard writing guides. Certainly it covers territory common to general guides, as inevitably it must. But one of its chief uses should be in pointing out divergences between legal and lay usage, many of which have previously gone unrecorded. To this end, the dictionary serves lawyers and nonlawyers alike, for it can help both groups bridge the linguistic gulf that separates them, to the degree that is possible. The greater effort here needs to be made by lawyers, who in recent years have become increasingly aware of the importance of using legal language that is simple and direct. Indeed, simplicity and directness, two of the touchstones of good writing, are advocated throughout this dictionary in an effort to tag and to discard legalese and highfalutin jargon.

Third, this work may serve, to some extent, as an instrument of reform. Where lawyers and judges use terms imprecisely or ambiguously (or, indeed, incorrectly), this dictionary often presents standards that will enhance rather than destroy valuable nuances. If ever a prescriptive approach to language is justified, it is in law, where linguistic precision is often of paramount concern, and where ambiguity and vagueness (except when purposeful) are intolerable. Within its compass, the dictionary thus seeks to preserve the rich differentiation in our legal vocabulary, to set out some of the important grammatical usages and traditional idioms, and to oppose slipshod usages that blur well-developed distinctions. Of course, no work of this kind can be a panacea for the problems that occur in legal writing. But such a work can realistically seek to make legal writers sensitive to the aesthetic possibilities of their prose, to goad them into thinking more acutely about what works in a given context, and what does not.

Modern Legal Usage is arranged so that the legal writer, unsure of or puzzled by a particular word or point of grammar, can consult a specific entry addressing the problem at hand. Virtually all the sentences quoted to illustrate legal usage, including linguistic pitfalls, originated in judicial opinions. A few come from statutes, fewer still from lawyers' briefs and other sources. The authors of the quoted specimens generally remain anonymous because ordinarily it's unimportant *who* made a particular mistake. Attention should be focused on the mistake itself, and how to remedy it. Where stare decisis is the ruling principle, citations are necessary;

in a dictionary of usage they are not, except of course when documenting usages that are lexicographically noteworthy. Whenever specimens do
receive attribution, the importance of that fact lies in documenting the
source, not in giving context to the quoted matter; hence subsequent
histories of cases cited are not given.

Undertaking to write a dictionary of this kind is a precarious task. For
by setting oneself up as an arbiter of usage, one also sets one's prose
before the magnifying glasses of readers, who are certain to find blemishes of one sort or another. Such was H.W. Fowler's fate in his *Dictionary of Modern English Usage* (1926), a work that has served me as both
exemplar and caution. For whatever may be amiss or at fault in this dictionary, I readily acknowledge full responsibility in advance.

❧ ❧ ❧

Plain Language

A. Generally. Albert Einstein once said that his goal in stating an idea was to make it as simple as possible but no simpler. If lawyers everywhere adopted this goal, the world would probably change in dramatic ways.

But there is little reason for hope when so many legal writers appear to believe that to seem competent or smart, their ideas must be stated in the most complex manner possible. Of course, this problem plagues many fields of intellectual endeavor, as the philosopher Bertrand Russell noted:

> I am allowed to use plain English because everybody knows that I could use mathematical logic if I chose. Take the statement: "Some people marry their deceased wives' sisters." I can express this in language [that] only becomes intelligible after years of study, and this gives me freedom. I suggest to young professors that their first work should be written in a jargon only to be understood by the erudite few. With that behind them, they can ever after say what they have to say in a language "understood of the people." In these days, when our very lives are at the mercy of the professors, I cannot but think that they would deserve our gratitude if they adopted my advice.[1]

But the professors have not heeded Russell's advice. Since Russell wrote that essay in the mid-1950s, things have gotten much worse in fields such as biology, linguistics, literary criticism, political science, psychology, and sociology. And they have gotten worse in law.

Consider the following statutory provision, a 272-word tangle that is as difficult to fathom as any algebraic theorem:

> 57AF(11) Where, but for this sub-section, this section would, by virtue of the preceding provisions of this section, have in relation to a relevant year of income as if, for the reference in sub-section (3) to $18,000 there were substituted a reference to another amount, being an amount that consists of a number of whole dollars and a number of cents (in this sub-section referred to as the "relevant number of cents")—
> (a) in the case where the relevant number of cents is less than 50—the other amount shall be reduced by the relevant number of cents;
> (b) in any case—the other amount shall be increased by the amount by which the relevant number of cents is less than $1.

From *A Dictionary of Modern Legal Usage* (2d ed. 1995).

[1] Bertrand Russell, "How I Write," in *The Basic Writings of Bertrand Russell* 63, 65 (Robert E. Egner & Lester E. Denonn eds., 1961).

(12) where, but for sub-section (5), this section would, by virtue of the preceding provisions of this section, have effect in relation to a relevant year of income as if, for the reference in sub-section (3) to $18,000, there were substituted a reference to another amount, being an amount that consists of a number of whole dollars and a number of cents (in this sub-section referred to as the "relevant number of cents") then, for the purposes of the application of paragraph 4(b)—

(a) in a case where the relevant number of cents is less than 50—the other amount shall be reduced by the relevant number of cents; or

(b) in any case—the other amount shall be increased by the amount by which the relevant number of cents is less than $1.[2]

That is the type of drafting that prompts an oft-repeated criticism: "So unintelligible is the phraseology of some statutes that suggestions have been made that draftsmen, like the Delphic Oracle, sometimes aim deliberately at obscurity . . . ."[3]

With some hard work, the all-but-inscrutable passage above can be transformed into a straightforward version of only 63 words:

If either of the following amounts is not in whole dollars, the amount must be rounded up or down to the nearest dollar (or rounded up if the amount ends with 50 cents):

(a) the amount of the motor-vehicle-depreciation limit; or

(b) the amount that would have been the motor-vehicle-depreciation limit if the amount had equaled or exceeded $18,000.[4]

Few would doubt that the original statute is unplain and that the revision is comparatively plain. True, the revision requires the reader to understand what a "motor-vehicle-depreciation limit" is, but some things can be stated only so simply.

When it comes to the legislative jungle of the tax code, as Justice Robert H. Jackson once wrote, "It can never be made simple, but we can try to avoid making it needlessly complex."[5]

Still, some might protest that, after all, the law is a learned profession. Some seem to find an insult in the suggestion that lawyers should avoid complex verbiage. They want to express themselves in more sophisticated ways than nonprofessionals do.

---

[2] Income Tax Assessment Act [Australia] § 57AF(11), (12) (as quoted in David St. L. Kelly, "Plain English in Legislation," in *Essays on Legislative Drafting* 57, 58 (David St. L. Kelly ed., 1988)).

[3] Carleton K. Allen, *Law in the Making* 486 (7th ed. 1964).

[4] Revision based on that of Gavin Peck (quoted in Kelly, note 2, at 59).

[5] *Dobson v. C.I.R.*, 320 U.S. 489, 495 (1943).

Their objection needs a serious answer because it presents the most serious impediment to the plain-language movement. There are essentially four answers.

First, those who write in a difficult, prolix style risk being unclear not only to other readers but also to themselves. When you write obscurely, you're less likely to be thinking clearly. And you're less likely to appreciate the problems that are buried under such involuted prose. For the private practitioner, this could increase the possibility of malpractice.

Second, obscure writing wastes readers' time—a great deal of it, when the sum is totaled. An Australian study conducted in the 1980s found that lawyers and judges take twice as long deciphering legalistically worded statutes as they do plain-language revisions.[6]

Third, simplifying is a higher intellectual attainment than complexifying. Writing simply and directly is hard work, but a learned profession ought not to shrink from the challenge. In fact, the hallmark of all the greatest legal stylists is precisely that they take difficult ideas and express them as simply as possible. No nonprofessional could do it, and most lawyers can't do it. Only extraordinary minds are capable of the task. Still, every lawyer—brilliant or not—can aim at the mark.

Fourth, the very idea of professionalism demands that we not conspire against nonlawyers by adopting a style that feels impenetrable. Unless lawyers do the right thing and reform from within, outside forces may well cause a revolution that will marginalize the legal profession.

B. Definitions. "Plain language," generally speaking, is "the idiomatic and grammatical use of language that most effectively presents ideas to the reader."[7] Some have tried to reduce "plain language" to a mathematical formula, but any such attempt is doomed to failure. And that is no indictment of the idea: "[I]t is no criticism that Plain English cannot be precisely, mathematically defined. Neither can 'reasonable doubt' or 'good cause.' Like so many legal terms, it is inherently and appropriately vague."[8]

The fundamental principle is that anything translatable into simpler words in the same language is bad style. That may sound like a facile oversimplification that fails when put into practice—but it isn't and it doesn't.

C. An Old Idea. Of course, legal discourse has long been ridiculed for its incomprehensibility. Jonathan Swift skewered legalese when he

---

[6] Law Reform Comm'n of Victoria, *Plain English & the Law* 61–62 (1987).

[7] Garner, *The Elements of Legal Style* 7 (1991).

[8] Joseph Kimble, *Plain English: A Charter for Clear Writing*, 9 Thomas M. Cooley L. Rev. 1, 14 (1992).

wrote of a society of lawyers who spoke in "a peculiar cant and jargon of their own, that no other mortal can understand."[9]

What is less well known than the ridicule is that good legal writers have long advocated a plain-language style. In the mid-19th century, for example, the leading authority on legislative drafting said that most legal documents can be written in "the common popular structure of plain English."[10] A generation later, an English lawyer explained that good drafting "says in the plainest language, with the simplest, fewest, and fittest words, precisely what it means."[11] Other writers could be cited, decade by decade, up to the present day. In short, there is nothing new about the idea.

D. Plain-Language Principles. "No lawyer can now safely navigate," writes a well-known law professor, "without knowing the problems of legalese and the principles of plain English."[12] Experienced editors have arrived at these plain-language principles through induction—through carrying out the principles again and again. Once you have revised hundreds of legal documents for the purposes of clarifying and simplifying, you can fairly accurately predict what problems the next document might hold in store.

Of these principles, perhaps the most important is to reject the myth that legalese is precise. Traditionally, lawyers have aimed for a type of "precision" that results in cumbersome writing, with many long sentences collapsing under the weight of obscure qualifications. That "precision" is often illusory for two reasons: (1) ambiguity routinely lurks within traditional, legalistic language; and (2) when words proliferate, ambiguities tend to as well.

Of course, where clarity and precision are truly at loggerheads, precision must usually prevail. But the instances of actual conflict are much rarer than lawyers often suppose. Precision is not sacrificed when the drafter uses technical words where necessary and avoids jargon that serves no substantive purpose. As one commentator puts it, "[W]hat is often called 'legal phraseology' is no more than inept writing or the unnecessary use of obscure or entangled phrases."[13]

---

[9] *Gulliver's Travels* 154 (1726; repr. 1952).

[10] George Coode, *On Legislative Expression* xxx (1842).

[11] J.G. Mackay, *Introduction to an Essay on the Art of Legal Composition Commonly Called Drafting*, 3 Law Q. Rev. 326, 326 (1887).

[12] Robert W. Benson, *The End of Legalese*, 13 N.Y.U. Rev. Law & Soc. Change 519, 573 (1984–1985).

[13] Samuel A. Goldberg, "Hints on Draftsmanship," in *Drafting Contracts and Commercial Instruments* 7, 8 (Research & Documentation Corp. ed., 1971).

As a rule, whether one is drafting legislation, contracts, or other documents, clarity is just as important as precision. In fact, clarity helps ensure precision because the drafter with an obscure style finds it less easy to warrant what the draft itself says.

The main work of the legislative drafter is "to state the law in a form clearer and more convenient than that in which it has hitherto existed, and that is a task for experts . . . ."[14] Of course, some influences leading to complexity cannot be overcome; among these are the difficulty of the subject matter itself and the fact that a final draft may reflect a compromise between different points of view. But with hard work, other obscurantist influences—the ones that are linguistically based—can be overcome: long-windedness, needless jargon, and inconsistent style resulting from collaborative efforts.

The chief guidelines are as follows:

1. Achieve a reasonable average sentence length. Strive for an average sentence length of 20 words—and in any event, ensure that you are below 30 words. Doing this involves following a maxim that, unfortunately, makes some legal drafters unnecessarily nervous: "[I]f you want to make a statement with a great many qualifications, put some of the qualifications in separate sentences."[15]

2. Prefer short words to long ones, simple to fancy. Minimize jargon and technical terms so that you achieve a straightforward style that even nonlawyers can understand. This means rejecting legalisms such as *pursuant to* (under, in accordance with), *prior to* (before), *subsequent to* (after), *vel non* (or not, or the lack of it).

3. Avoid double and triple negatives. No reader wants to wrestle with a sentence like this one: "The investments need not be revalued at intervals of not more than two years if the trustee and the beneficiaries do not disagree." [Read: *If the trustee and beneficiaries agree, the investments need not be revalued every two years.*]

4. Prefer the active voice. *Notice must be given* compares poorly with *The tenant must give notice* because (a) the first version does not spell out who must give notice, and (b) readers take in a sentence more easily if it meets their expectation of a subject–verb–object structure.

5. Keep related words together—especially subject and verb, verb and object.

---

[14] J.L. Brierly, *The Law of Nations* 80 (5th ed. 1955).
[15] Bertrand Russell, "How I Write," in *The Basic Writings of Bertrand Russell* 63, 65 (Robert E. Egner & Lester E. Denonn eds., 1961).

6. Break up the text with headings. Headings and subheadings sign-post the structure of a document, allowing readers to find their way around the document quickly and easily.
7. Use parallel structures for enumerations.
8. Avoid excessive cross-references. They can create linguistic mazes. The problem is that readers are asked to hold in mind several different provisions simultaneously.
9. Avoid overdefining. Although definitions are sometimes helpful, legal drafters grossly overuse them. Whenever you send the reader elsewhere in a legal document to understand what you're saying in a given provision, you impede understanding. And many drafters "pass the buck" in this way repeatedly for a single term, by using cross-references in definitions.
10. Use recitals and purpose clauses. In contracts, recitals help the reader understand what the drafter hopes to accomplish; in legis-lation, purpose clauses serve this function. Except in the simplest drafting projects, such as straightforward buy–sell agreements, you should generally presume that these orienting devices are necessary. And even simple documents should have descriptive titles (not *Agreement*, but *Agreement Restricting Stock Transfers*).

Finally, to gauge how effectively the principles are carried out, plain-language advocates recommend that certain documents be tested on typical readers. For documents that go out by the thousands and hun-dreds of thousands (like government forms) and for major legislation, time spent in testing at the front end can save enormous amounts of time and money in the long run.

E. Efforts to Use Plain Language. Since the 1970s, most Amer-ican states have passed some type of plain-language legislation, and several federal statutes exist as well.[16] Statutes of this type have not caused the problems that skeptics once warned of—unworkable standards, fatal ambiguities, decline in the quality of drafting. In fact, an empirical study would probably confirm precisely the opposite effects.

In addition to plain-language legislation, lawyers in many English-speaking jurisdictions have formed commissions and committees to pro-mote plain language. In the U.S., for example, the State Bar of Michigan formed such a committee in 1979, and the State Bar of Texas formed one in 1990; other state bar associations have begun to follow suit. In Aus-tralia, the Centre for Plain Legal Language has done much to promote the

---

[16] *See* Joseph Kimble, *Plain English: A Charter for Clear Writing*, 9 Thomas M. Cooley L. Rev. 1, 31–35 (1992).

movement. In British Columbia, the Plain Language Institute thrived for a time and produced much good literature before being disbanded in 1993 for lack of governmental funding; other Canadian groups soon took up the slack. In England, the Plain English Campaign—a grassroots consumer organization—has enjoyed considerable success. England is also the home of Clarity, an international organization that promotes plain language in law. All these efforts have depended primarily on the determination of specific individuals.

Their opponents—the naysayers—have had an increasingly difficult time as more and more excellent work is published in the field of plain language. For example, in 1994 Martin Cutts, an English writing consultant, redesigned and rewrote an act of Parliament: the Timeshare Act 1992. In doing so, he convincingly showed what immense improvements are possible in legislative drafting if only the official drafters approached their task with a greater command of plain-language principles.[17] The enduring problem—here as elsewhere—is whether reform can take place while the old guard remains in place.[18]

In some places, though, official and semiofficial bodies are changing standard forms. For example, the English Law Society's 1990 and 1992 editions of the Standard Conditions of Sale use "language that is as direct as the subject-matter allows, sentences that are relatively short and jargon-free, and a layout that is clear."[19] Similarly, in 1992 the Law Society of New South Wales issued a "plainer" form of contract for the sale of land—"plainer" than its predecessor, though not yet quite "plain."[20] In the early 1990s, the Real Estate Forms Committee of the State Bar of Texas issued plain-language forms for deeds, deeds of trust, leases, and other forms. These are but a few examples.

F. The Trouble with the Word *Plain*. It is unfortunate that the set phrases *plain language* and *plain English* contain the word *plain*. For that word, to many speakers of English, suggests the idea of "drab and ugly." But plain language is not drab: it is powerful and often beautiful. It is the language of the King James Version of the Bible, and it has a long literary tradition in the so-called Attic style of writing.[21]

---

[17] *See* Martin Cutts, *Lucid Law* (1994).

[18] For a challenging but partly tongue-in-cheek approach to a legislative mandate for plain language, see David C. Elliott, *A Model Plain-Language Act*, 3 Scribes J. Legal Writing 51 (1992).

[19] Peter Butt, *Plain Language and Conveyancing*, Conveyancer & Prop. Law., July–Aug. 1993, at 256, 258.

[20] *Id.*

[21] *See* Garner, *The Elements of Legal Style* 7–15 (1991).

Despite the unfortunate associations that the word *plain* carries, it has become established and is without a serious competitor. As a result, plain-language advocates must continually explain what they mean by "plain" language—or else critics and doubters will misunderstand it.

G. Prospects. We can point to significant progress in this area, but it remains sporadic. In the end, E.B. White may have been prescient: "I honestly worry about lawyers. They never write plain English themselves, and when you give them a bit of plain English to read, they say, 'Don't worry, it doesn't mean anything.'"[22]

There are those who say that "lawyers spend half their time trying to understand what other lawyers wrote; and the other half of their days writing things that other lawyers spend half their time trying to understand."[23] That cynical view holds true only when poor writing becomes pervasive; and, alas, there is some truth in it today.

Beyond the mere inconveniences of obscurity, however, people actually suffer from it. Not least among the sufferers are judges who must try to make sense out of nonsense. But the vexation that judges feel pales in comparison with the economic and emotional suffering that clients often experience.

It is hardly an overstatement to say that plain-language reform is among the most important issues confronting the legal profession. And until this reform occurs, the profession will continue to have a badly tarnished image—no matter how many other altruistic endeavors it carries out. If we want the respect of the public, we must learn to communicate simply and directly.

H. A Plain-Language Library. Those wishing to consult further sources in the field may find the following books helpful:

- Mark Adler, *Clarity for Lawyers: The Use of Plain English in Legal Writing* (1990).

- Robert D. Eagleson, *Writing in Plain English* (1990).

- Carl Felsenfeld & Alan Siegel, *Writing Contracts in Plain English* (1981).

- Rudolf Flesch, *The Art of Plain Talk* (1951; repr. 1978).

- Rudolf Flesch, *The Art of Readable Writing* (1949).

---

[22] E.B. White (as quoted in Thomas L. Shaffer, *The Planning and Drafting of Wills and Trusts* 149 (2d ed. 1979)).
[23] Samuel A. Goldberg, "Hints on Draftsmanship," in *Drafting Contracts and Commercial Instruments* 7, 10 (Research & Documentation Corp. ed., 1971).

- Rudolf Flesch, *How to Write Plain English: A Book for Lawyers and Consumers* (1979).

- Ernest Gowers, *The Complete Plain Words* (Sidney Greenbaum & Janet Whitcut eds., 3d ed. 1986).

- Robert Gunning, *The Technique of Clear Writing* (rev. ed. 1968).

- *How Plain English Works for Business: Twelve Case Studies* (U.S. Dep't of Commerce, Office of Consumer Affairs, 1984).

- Richard Lauchman, *Plain Style: Techniques for Simple, Concise, Emphatic Business Writing* (1993).

- *Plain English and the Law* (Law Reform Commission of Australia, Report No. 9, 1990).

- *Plain Language: Principles and Practice* (Erwin R. Steinberg ed., 1991).

- *The Plain English Story* (Plain English Campaign, rev. ed. 1993).

- Richard Wincor, *Contracts in Plain English* (1976).

- Richard Wydick, *Plain English for Lawyers* (3d ed. 1994).

ﭗ ﭗ ﭗ

Legalese

IRONICALLY, MANY DICTIONARIES label *legalese* a "colloquialism." Actually, legalese denotes what is perhaps the least colloquial of all forms of English writing: the complicated language of legal documents. The *OED* traces *legalese*—the word, not the thing—back to the second decade of the 20th century, with this example: "He signed his name at the foot of a bald formal agreement, written in the most incomprehensible *legalese*."[1]

Though the name for it is fairly new, legalese itself has, throughout the history of Anglo-American law, been a scourge of the profession. Thomas Jefferson railed against statutes "which, from their verbosity, their endless tautologies, their involutions of case within case, and parenthesis within parenthesis, and their multiplied efforts at certainty, by *said*s and *aforesaid*s, by *or*s and *and*s, to make them more plain, are really rendered more perplexed and incomprehensible, not only to common readers, but to the lawyers themselves."[2]

The same is true of all types of legal writing, not just statutes or even just drafting. Perhaps the epitome of legalese is this 19th-century example, describing a collision:

> The declaration stated, that the plaintiff theretofore, and at the time of the committing of the grievance thereinafter mentioned, to wit, on, etc., was lawfully possessed of a certain donkey, which said donkey of the plaintiff was then lawfully in a certain highway, and the defendant was then possessed of a certain waggon and certain horses drawing the same, which said waggon and horses of the defendant were then under the care, government, and direction of a certain then servant of the defendant, in and along the said highway; nevertheless the defendant, by his said servant, so carelessly, negligently, unskilfully, and improperly governed and directed his said waggon and horses, that by through the carelessness, negligence, unskilfulness, and improper conduct of the defendant, by his said servant, the said waggon and horses of the defendant then ran and struck with great violence against the said donkey of the plaintiff, and thereby then wounded, crushed, and killed the same, etc.[3]

But even in the 20th century, collisions have sounded much the same in legalese, as this example shows: "On information and belief, Defendants

---

From *A Dictionary of Modern Legal Usage* (2d ed. 1995).

[1] C.J.C. Hyne, *Firemen Hot* 189 (1914).

[2] *The Writings of Thomas Jefferson* vol. 2, 65 (Andrew Adgate Lipscomb ed. 1903).

[3] *Davies v. Mann* [1842] 10 M.&W. 546, 152 Eng. Rep. 588.

Newton and Kautz, immediately prior to operating their vehicles on the aforesaid Route 315, had attended a party sponsored by defendant Roach Incorporated on Powell Road in Powell, Ohio; said Defendants left the party at approximately the same time; said Defendants Newton and Kautz were racing their automobiles pursuant to an agreement reached at said party shortly prior to the aforesaid collision . . . ."[4]

Legalese is often highly compressed—e.g.: "The question here is whether service of citation was proper in the face of a writ of error attack on a default judgment." And it flaunts legal ceremony, which arguably has a place in some documents: "In testimony whereof, I have hereunto subscribed my name and affixed my seal, this 24th day of June, in the year of our Lord, one thousand nine hundred and eighty five."

We have enough examples, however, of what not to do. The nauseating effect of the passage from *Davies v. Mann*, and other passages throughout this work, should purge readers of any attraction to legalese.

---

[4] Pleading quoted in *Baird v. Roach, Inc.*, 462 N.E.2d 1229, 1231 (Ohio App. 1983).

ह\ ह\ ह\

Reworking Your Vocabulary

MASTERING THE LANGUAGE of the law proves a particularly daunting
challenge for all law students. Bad enough that you're daily bombarded
by lots of arcane words and phrases such as *res judicata* and *ancillary proceeding*. But you also keep running into ordinary English words that seem
to have acquired foreign meanings.

For example, when you first read, in some casebook, that a contract
isn't supported by "consideration," you sense a disconnect. Your parents
may have asked you throughout your childhood to show consideration
for others. Your teachers have referred to a book you were discussing as
the book "now under consideration." But this "consideration" surely isn't
kindness, and it surely isn't examination, either.

So with fingers crossed, you open your big *Black's Law Dictionary*, in
hopes of nailing it down. Sure enough, it's there. It means "something of
value (such as an act, a forbearance, or a return promise) received by a
promisor from a promisee." But what on earth is *forbearance*? So you turn
next to that entry and read: "the act of refraining from enforcing a right,
obligation, or debt."

While you're starting to understand *consideration*, you're still feeling
overwhelmed. You're probably not accustomed to thinking about so
many types of human behavior (acts, refraining from acts, and return
promises) under one abstract heading. But there's no simpler way of
defining an abstract word like *consideration*. Lawyers, you see, think about
the world a little differently from nonlawyers: they've categorized types
of human behavior in ways that don't occur to most people.

As you read on in the casebook, you see that the contract you're
reading about has been "avoided." You may figure that someone has
"gotten around" or "escaped from" contractual obligations, but you discover later that you had missed the essential meaning. *Avoid*, in this context, means "to make void" or "nullify." It has nothing to do with the
ordinary meaning of the word.

Some meanings you'll pick up gradually, by context and osmosis,
just from reading a lot of law. But it's dangerous to rely on intuition.
Eventually, law students discover the importance of cultivating the habit
of regularly consulting a good dictionary. Below are some common

Adapted from *Student Lawyer* (Dec. 2001).

English words that students must relearn in law school. A student who understands them is well on the way to reading law accurately.

alibi. *Common meaning:* any excuse to avoid blame for something. *In law:* the specific defense of proving that the defendant was somewhere else when the crime was committed.

appropriation. *Common meaning:* money allocated for a certain purpose, esp. by a legislature. *In law:* (1) the taking away of private property, esp. by a court; (2) the tort of making commercial use of another person's name or likeness; or (3) in some states, the acquiring of water rights.

assault. *Common meaning:* a physical attack. *In law:* at common law (but not under modern penal statutes) the act of putting someone in reasonable fear of a physical attack or offensive touching.

assignment. *Common meaning:* a task or appointment to a position. *In law:* the transfer of one person's legal interest in property to another person <assignment of account>, or an appellant's charge that the trial court made a mistake <assignment of error>.

attachment. *Common meaning:* one thing stuck to another thing, or affection for another person. *In law:* seizure of property to secure or satisfy a money judgment <attachment of wages>.

bargain. *Common meaning:* something bought at a discounted price; a good buy. *In law:* an agreement between two people for the exchange of promises or performances <benefit of the bargain>.

bona fide. *Common meaning:* genuine; real. *In law:* done in good faith <bona fide effort at mediation>.

consortium. *Common meaning:* a collection of companies working together toward a common goal. *In law:* a family member's companionship, love, help, and (of a spouse) capacity for sexual relations, the loss of which may give rise to a claim in tort.

constructive. *Common meaning:* positive; promoting further development. *In law:* irrebuttably established by operation of law <constructive knowledge>; established by a legal fiction to craft a remedy <constructive trust>.

contribution. *Common meaning:* a donation. *In law:* (1) the right of a tortfeasor who has paid more than a proportionate share of a judgment to recover the excess from other liable defendants; or (2) the right of a cotenant who has paid more than a proportionate share for upkeep to recover from other cotenants.

conversion. *Common meaning:* the changing from one form into another, or adopting a new religion. *In law:* the act of treating the property of another as one's own, as by possessing it or disposing of it.

depose. *Common meaning:* to dethrone a monarch. *In law:* to take someone's testimony in a sworn deposition; to testify.

determine. *Common meaning:* to decide something. *In law:* to end (terminate) something, usually an interest in property <cease and determine>.

devise. *Common meaning:* to think up a scheme for doing something. *In law:* to pass on property to someone through a will; or, as a noun, the property itself, the provision in the will, or the will itself.

disability. *Common meaning:* a debilitating physical condition. *In law:* a legal incapacity, such as being a minor and therefore unable to contract.

distress. *Common meaning:* anguish. *In law:* the seizure of property to secure a debt; the property seized; a court order for such a seizure <distress sale>.

foreign. *Common meaning:* of another country. *In law:* (in addition to the common meaning) of another jurisdiction, esp. another state <a judgment from a foreign court>.

garnish. *Common meaning:* something added to a plate of food to add color, ornamentation, or flavor. *In law:* to attach property being held by a third party (such as wages held by an employer) to pay the owner's debt (such as child support).

impeachment. *Common meaning:* a formal charge against a government official, esp. a president or judge (but not, as many believe, the removal from office). *In law:* a challenge to the truthfulness of a witness or the reliability of documentary evidence.

impertinent. *Common meaning:* rude. *In law:* irrelevant, esp. said of matter contained in a pleading that does not pertain to any issue material to the cause of action.

infant. *Common meaning:* a baby. *In law:* as easily, a strapping 17-year-old fullback; a minor (under 18 in most jurisdictions), with the legal disability of infancy.

information. *Common meaning:* knowledge. *In law:* a criminal charging instrument filed by a prosecutor without the need of a grand-jury indictment, often used for misdemeanors but also used by many states for felonies.

notorious. *Common meaning:* infamous; widely known for some evil or misdeed. *In law:* of common knowledge, so that anyone with an adverse interest is deemed to have been on notice <open and notorious>.

permissive. *Common meaning:* tolerant of behavior that others might object to. *In law:* permissible, esp. of claims that may or may not be joined in a suit as the party wishes.

positive. *Common meaning:* certain. *In law:* formally enacted or established by an act and not an omission <positive law>.

prefer. *Common meaning:* to favor one thing over another. *In law:* to bring (a charge) against a criminal defendant, or to present a case to a grand jury <prefer charges>.

preference. *Common meaning:* the tendency to favor one thing over another. *In law:* a transfer of money or property to a creditor by an insolvent person or company before filing for bankruptcy, to the detriment of other creditors.

prejudice. *Common meaning:* to evoke a bias, esp. one based on emotions. *In law:* to put one at a legal disadvantage; to impair a legal right or claim <disallowing this evidence will unfairly prejudice our case>.

prescription. *Common meaning:* an instructed course of action, esp. a regimen of medicine. *In law:* a rule or set of rules; also, the gain or loss of title by long-term open and notorious possession or by prolonged nonuse <easement by prescription>.

recital. *Common meaning:* an artistic performance, esp. by music or dance students; repetition of poetry or prose, esp. to an audience. *In law:* a statement in a contract or deed, identifying the parties and summarizing the facts surrounding the transaction (once introduced by "whereas" and "therefore," but that usage is fading).

service. *Common meaning:* assistance; rite; repair. *In law:* the formal delivery to someone of a legal paper such as a pleading, a summons, or a writ <service of process>.

set aside. *Common meaning:* to put to one side; to earmark for some purpose. *In law:* to overturn a conviction or to vacate a judgment or court order <the appellate court set aside the money judgment and remanded the case for relitigation on that issue>.

style. *Common meaning:* fashion, flair, manner, rhetoric. *In law:* a case name <the complete style of the case is *Vanna White v. Samsung Electronics America, Inc.*>.

ৰ৯ ৰ৯ ৰ৯

Steeling Yourself Against Legalese

THE JURY IS STILL OUT on Christopher Columbus Langdell (1826–1906), the Harvard law professor who invented the casebook method of instruction. For it he has been both revered and derided. One of his chief critics was Yale law professor Grant Gilmore, who wrote that Langdell "was an essentially stupid man who, early in his life, hit on" the casebook method, an idea that was "absurd," "mischievous," and "deeply rooted in error."[1] Others disagree. But regardless of what anyone thinks about Langdell's casebook method, it's undeniably responsible for helping perpetuate what judges everywhere detest—legalese.

By *legalese*, mind you, I don't mean terms of art, such as *allocution*, *habeas corpus*, *indemnity*, and *tortious interference with a contract*. No, I mean highfalutin, self-parodying legal jargon, such as *hereinbefore stated*, *instant case*, *pursuant to*, and *said claims* or *such claims* (meaning "these claims").

There have been lots of studies over the years on how legalese costs clients money, impairs persuasiveness, and undercuts a writer's reputation. A new book on the subject, by Professor Joseph Kimble, is called *Lifting the Fog of Legalese* (2005), and the incisive essays in it are enough to make any legal writer swear off legalese forever.

Yet generation after generation, law students strive to learn it— partly because they don't entirely believe all the warnings about it, partly because they won't feel like lawyers until they've mastered it, and partly because Christopher Columbus Langdell set things up so that law students would always be reading old cases with fossilized language.

Having written a great deal about legalese over the years, I decided recently to ask some judges and respected lawyers all around the country what they think. The results are illuminating.

First I asked Theodore B. Olson, former Solicitor General of the United States and one of the finest writers you'll ever encounter. My question: "What do you think of legalese?" His answer: "Legalese is jargon. All professions have it. All professions use it as a substitute for thinking, and they all use it in a way that makes them appear to be superior. Actually, they appear to be buffoons for using it. The legal profession may be the worst of all professions in using jargon. It's not necessary to communicate that way. You're really not communicating, and you're

---

Adapted from *Student Lawyer* (May 2006).
[1] Grant Gilmore, *The Ages of American Law* 42 (1977).

really not thinking. I do a lot of television, and I do a lot of articulating of positions on behalf of clients. One of the reasons I'm asked to do that is that I understand that the people on the other side of that camera don't want you to speak like a lawyer. That's a pejorative term: talking like a lawyer is, to most people, talking in terms that sound boorish, condescending, and unintelligible. And lawyers need to be able to speak to people and forget the jargon and forget the legalese because you can communicate the same thoughts without being swept up in the technicalities of a particular legal issue. They want to know what you're talking about. What do you mean? If you can't express that, you shouldn't waste people's time."

Then I interviewed a renowned Los Angeles litigator, James P. Clark, who is also an excellent writer. I asked him, "What does it tell you about a lawyer who uses a lot of legalese—'such' instead of 'the,' 'said' instead of 'the,' and so on?" Clark replied: "A couple of things, both negative. One, I think that use of jargon is a crutch. I think it's a way of avoiding working harder—if you will, a way of avoiding putting yourself in the position of the reader. And I also think it shows an unfortunate lack of creativity. If you're not creative in your writing, I'm afraid you might not be creative in your thinking, and the best lawyers are the most creative ones."

I turned next to judges. When I asked Judge Stephen Williams of the D.C. Circuit about legalese such as *Comes now the plaintiff,* he scoffed at the idea that any lawyer would write something so absurd in his court.

Wanting to know whether other judges felt that way, I asked Judge Deanell Tacha, Chief Judge of the United States Court of Appeals for the Tenth Circuit. Here's what she said: "I despise legalese, and I know I'm not alone. I dislike all the old-fashioned terms. In my chambers, for example, we use a process called 'cold reading' of opinions, where one of the law clerks is assigned to be not the lawyer in the case, but the litigant in the case, and read the draft opinion to see whether it's expressed in plain English. Even if the litigant wouldn't understand what the legal principles involved were, would he or she understand what happened and why? That's where we get rid of the legalese."

Then I asked another federal appellate judge, Morris S. Arnold of the Eighth Circuit. He declared without reserve: "I hate legalese. It's to be avoided at all costs. There's much too much of it. There's too much jargon."

I went to yet another court, the Fifth Circuit, and asked Judge Thomas M. Reavley. He called legalese "a substitute for good writing, for thinking, for editing, and for focus." When asked what it says about the writer who uses legalese, Judge Reavley answered: "Either they're pretending to be what they're not or maybe they think they can impress you with legalese. But they don't help their cause."

I wondered whether these views might be peculiar to appellate judges. So I asked some eminent trial judges. First I asked Judge William R. Wilson Jr. of Little Rock. He put it plainly: "There's a tremendous amount of legalese that hangs on, and it's always to the detriment of the writer." Then I asked Judge Barbara M.G. Lynn of Dallas, and she answered pointedly: "Legalese consists of empty words that don't have any persuasive character. Speaking plain English is just so much more persuasive than loading your brief up with the *wherefores* and the *henceforths*. They're just archaic and don't really have any persuasive quality. It should all be about persuasion, and I think lawyers get lost in their jargon in brief-writing and in other aspects of advocacy."

With all these answers expressing a bias against legalese, it occurred to me that I'd been speaking mostly with federal litigators and federal judges. So I went to one of the most respected state judges in the country, Justice Nathan Hecht of the Supreme Court of Texas. Without hesitation, he said that there are several things wrong with legalese: "It's obscuring. But mostly it says about the people who use it unnecessarily that they don't know how to say what they're saying in a way that makes sense to anyone else. They're covering up their own lack of understanding about the issue by using words or phrases that distract, that don't convey a clear meaning. And these days—I suppose there may have been a time when legalese was more accepted—but these days, our society does not look well upon speakers and writers who resort to insider language, insider phrases, to explain themselves. So unless the Latin phrase has a particular meaning in a case, or some special historical significance, it's better to use plain English."

Eloquent denunciations, all. Perhaps you believe them.

But law students will pore over their casebooks, as Langdell hoped they would, and they'll see this: "Pursuant to section so-and-so, the instant claim does not pass statutory muster. As hereinbefore stated, it is well settled in this jurisdiction that . . . ." And subconsciously, they'll probably come to believe that expressing ideas that way is the essence of what it means to be a lawyer.

So the cycle repeats itself.

The novice legal writer yearns to acquire legalese. But the expert yearns to eliminate it. Strive to become an expert.

ða ða ða

Terms of Art

TERMS OF ART ARE WORDS having specific, precise meanings in a given specialty. Having its origins in Lord Coke's *vocabula artis*, the phrase *term of art* is common in law because the legal field has developed many technical words whose meanings are locked tight (e.g., *bailment, replevin*). It has also developed more than its share of jargon—would-be terms of art whose meanings are often unhinged.

How can one say "unhinged"? Take *per stirpes*, a phrase that many lawyers cite as a quintessential term of art. Yet, as a leading expert in the field of wills and estates has remarked, "*per stirpes* is a textbook example of legalese that seductively suggests certainty but actually can produce ambiguity and litigation."[1] The phrase creates a problem in this scenario: Mary's will bequeaths property "to my descendants *per stirpes*." She has two children—John, who has two children, and Bob, who has four. The complication arises when both of Mary's children die before she does. Some courts would say that the shares are divided between John and Bob, others that the shares must be divided at the level of John's and Bob's children. And in many states, the issue has never been decided and would therefore have to be litigated.[2]

Jargon, then, creates more than just aesthetic problems, though some writers lament those most prominently: "the unnecessary or inartistic employment of more or less technical terms in the drafting of legal documents is by no means rare . . . ."[3] Expert drafters, who know that clear, simple drafting is less subject to misinterpretation than legalistic drafting, recommend avoiding jargon precisely because it invites substantive problems.

On the other hand, "Not to use a technical word, even if it is a long one, in its proper place, would be an affectation as noticeable as the overfrequent use of such words where they are not needed."[4] Lawyers need not invent homegrown ways of saying *res ipsa loquitur*.

From *A Dictionary of Modern Legal Usage* (2d ed. 1995).

[1] Stanley M. Johanson, *In Defense of Plain Language*, 3 Scribes J. Legal Writing 37, 37 (1992).

[2] *Id.* at 38.

[3] *Lancaster Malleable Castings Co. v. Dunie*, 73 A.2d 417, 418 (Pa. 1950).

[4] E.L. Piesse, *The Elements of Drafting* 46 (J.K. Aitken ed., 7th ed. 1987).

One secret of good legal writing is to distinguish rigorously between terms of art and mere jargon. It is elementary to know that *and his heirs* and *elegit* have historically been terms of art; yet only the first is a living term of art, the second having become archaic (and therefore useful primarily in historical contexts).

Is *res gestae* a term of art? Or *scire facias* and *fieri facias*? Many such questions are debatable: but the debate is important, for we must attempt to winnow the useful law words from the verbal baggage amid which so many of them are buried.

ﬁ ﬁ ﬁ

Doublets, Triplets, and Synonym-Strings

AMPLIFICATION BY SYNONYM has long been a part of the English language, and especially a part of the language of the law. In the English Renaissance, this habit was a common figure of speech called *synonymia*. It is often supposed that the purpose of these paired or strung-along synonyms was etymological, that is, that writers in the Middle Ages and Renaissance would pair a French or Latinate term with an Anglo-Saxon approximation as a gloss on the foreign word. Thus we have, as survivals in legal language, *acknowledge and confess* (Old English and Old French), *act and deed* (Latin and Old English), and *goods and chattels* (Old English and Old French).

The philologist George Philip Krapp argued against this explanation. He saw the purpose of this mannerism as "rhetorical or oratorical rather than etymological."[1] He pointed out that such doubling occurred abundantly in Old English, when no substantial foreign element existed in the language, and that it often occurs in later writings without regard for etymology. Although Krapp was undoubtedly correct to emphasize the rhetorical importance of doubling, he was wrong to assume that the figure did not take on a utilitarian significance as well in Middle and early Modern English. The purpose of doubling was dual: to give rhetorical weight and balance to the phrase, and to maximize the understanding of readers or listeners.

Still another explanation has emerged for the particular fondness that lawyers have for this stylistic quirk. It is a cynical one: "This multiplication of useless expressions probably owed its origin to the want of knowledge of the true meaning and due application of each word, and a consequent apprehension, that if one word alone were used, a wrong one might be adopted and the right one omitted; and to this something must be added for carelessness and the general disposition of the profession to seek safety in verbosity rather than in discrimination of language."[2]

The phrases most obviously inspired by rhetorical concerns are alliterative. Rhetoricians call them reduplicative phrases—e.g.: *aid and abet*; *have and hold*; *part and parcel*; *trials and tribulations*; *rest, residue, and remainder*; *laid and levied*; *mind and memory*. Many others, in addition to conveying no nuance in meaning, have no aesthetically redeeming qualities, but

---

From *A Dictionary of Modern Legal Usage* (2d ed. 1995).

[1] George P. Krapp, *Modern English: Its Growth and Present Use* 251 (1909).

[2] Charles Davidson, *Precedents and Forms in Conveyancing* vol. 1, 67 (3d ed. 1860).

even informed opinions on a point of this kind are likely to diverge. Following are two lists, the first containing common doublets in legal writing, the second containing some of the common triplets. Any number of variations, as by inversion (or, with triplets, by reordering), are possible.

Doublets

able and willing
act and deed
agree and covenant
agreed and declared
aid and abet
aid and comfort
all and singular
all and sundry
amount or quantum
annoy or molest
annulled and set aside
answerable and accountable
any and all
appropriate and proper
attached and annexed
authorize and direct
authorize and empower
betting or wagering
bills and notes
bind and obligate
by and between
by and through
by and under
by and with
canceled and set aside
cease and come to an end
cease and determine
chargeable and accountable
covenant and agree
custom and usage
deed and assurance
deem and consider
definite and certain
demises and leases
deposes and says

desire and require
do and perform
dominion and authority
due and owing
due and payable
each and all
each and every
ends and objects
escape and evade
exact and specific
execute and perform
false and untrue
final and conclusive
finish and complete
fit and proper
for and in behalf of
force and effect
fraud and deceit
free and clear
from and after
full and complete
full faith and credit
good and effectual
goods and chattels
have and hold
indemnify and hold harmless
keep and maintain
kind and character
kind and nature
known and described as
laid and levied
leave and license
legal and valid
liens and encumbrances
made and signed

maintenance and upkeep
make and enter into (a contract)
make and execute
means and includes
messuage and dwelling-house
mind and memory
name and style
new and novel
nominate and appoint
null and of no effect
null and void
object and purpose
order and direct
other and further (relief)
over and above
pains and penalties
pardon and forgive
part and parcel
peace and quiet
perform and discharge
power and authority
premeditation and malice
    aforethought
repair and make good
restrain and enjoin
reverts to and falls back upon
save and except

seised and possessed (of)
separate and apart
separate and distinct
set aside and vacate
shall and will
shun and avoid
similar and like
sole and exclusive
son and heir
successors and assigns
supersede and displace
surmise and conjecture
terms and conditions
then and in that event
title and interest
total and entire
touch and concern
true and correct
truth and veracity
type and kind
uncontroverted and uncontradicted
understood and agreed
unless and until
uphold and support
used and applied
various and sundry
will and testament

Triplets and Longer Strings

cancel, annul, and set aside
form, manner, and method
general, vague, and indefinite
give, devise, and bequeath
grant, bargain, sell, and convey
grant, demise, and let
hold, possess, and enjoy
lands, tenements, and hereditaments
make, publish, and declare
name, constitute, and appoint
ordered, adjudged, and decreed
pay, satisfy, and discharge

possession, custody, and control
promise, agree, and covenant
ready, willing, and able
remise, release, and forever discharge
remise, release, and forever quitclaim
repair, uphold, and maintain
rest, residue, and remainder
right, title, and interest
signed, sealed, and delivered
situate, lying, and being in
vague, nonspecific, and indefinite
way, shape, or form

One commentator recommends avoiding virtually all coupled synonyms.[3] At least one writer has taken issue with this recommendation on grounds that doublets are a prosodic feature of English and many other languages. He fallaciously argues that superfluities seldom create unclarity: "Since coupled synonyms are by definition redundant, they do not increase the density of ideas contained within a sentence; therefore, they rarely endanger its clarity. Since coupled synonyms add beauty to writing without sacrificing clarity, I see nothing sinful in their moderate use."[4]

The primary problem with such arguments, on either side of the issue, is that they fail to identify the types of writing in which doublets may appear or should not appear. In drafting documents to be interpreted, for example, the legal effects of this stylistic mannerism must be considered. *Stroud's Judicial Dictionary* (4th ed. 1971), under *contiguous*, q.v., states that *contiguous* is "as nearly as possible" synonymous with *adjoining*, but points to a case in which the phrase *adjoining or contiguous* was read by the court as if it were *adjoining or near to*, "so as to give *contiguous* a cognate, but not identical, meaning with *adjoining*." If the drafter of that phrase meant *contiguous* when writing *contiguous*, then coupling it with *adjoining* caused trouble. The problem stems, of course, from the fundamental canon of construing legal documents that states that every word is to be given meaning and nothing is to be read as mere surplusage. In drafting, then, doublets may be given unforeseen meanings by clever interpreters. This danger, however, is more likely to appear with less common doublets and triplets: no judge would interpret *rest, residue, and remainder* as referring to three discrete things.

A second context to be considered is ritual language, as in *the truth, the whole truth, and nothing but the truth*, a resounding phrase that conveys the gravity and majesty of the oath being taken. *Last will and testament*, q.v., may also properly be placed under the heading of ritual language, which is always directed to a lay rather than to a legal audience, the purpose being as much emotive as it is informational.

A third context in which doubling occurs is that of legal commentary and judicial opinions. Here the coupling of synonyms can rarely be said to "add beauty," as the writer quoted above suggested; rather, it is almost always a blemish. For in this context, legal style most nearly approximates literary style, and amplification by synonym has been out of rhetorical fashion for hundreds of years. Although one might well title a client's will *Last Will and Testament*, if one were to write an opinion con-

---

[3] *See* David Mellinkoff, *Legal Writing: Sense and Nonsense* 189–90 (1982); *The Language of the Law* 349–62 (1963).

[4] Robert P. Charrow, Book Review, 30 U.C.L.A. L. Rev. 1094, 1102 (1983).

struing that document, it would be better to begin, "In this appeal we are called on to construe the disposition of realty in *John Doe's will*" rather than *John Doe's last will and testament*.

Yet one might well write *vague and indefinite* in patent practice, in which that doublet is generally considered a term of art describing a patent application that lacks particularity and distinctness.[5] The inclusion of both words is widely thought to add a nuance. That is the test in ordinary legal prose: Is a shade of meaning supplied by the second or third synonym, or is it just so much deadwood?

---

[5] *See* Louis B. Applebaum et al., *Glossary of United States Patent Practice* 126 (1969).

 za za za

A Grammatical Grotesquerie
in Texas Practice

ONE OF THE FIRST POINTS of law that a Texas practitioner learns is the
peculiar wording of the traditional general denial in a defendant's answer.
When I first came across it several years ago, I tried to make it parse:
"Defendant generally denies each and every, all and singular, the allegations contained in the plaintiff's original petition." If you break down
the adjectives into individual modifiers, only one works grammatically:

> "Defendant generally denies each the allegations."
> "Defendant generally denies every the allegations."
> "Defendant generally denies all the allegations."
> "Defendant generally denies singular the allegations."

The third version, with *all*, makes perfect sense. The other versions look
like howlers collected from a beginners' course in English as a second
language.

Before filing my first answer, I found myself rewording the traditional
form so as to minimize the offense against the language: "Defendant generally denies each and every one of the allegations, all and singular, in the
plaintiff's original petition." The *singular* still did not quite work, but it
was part of a hoary legal doublet, *all and singular*, which is roughly the
inverted equivalent of *each and every*. With the exception of *singular*, then,
the sentence now parsed and said the same thing as the old ungrammatical form. To be sure, it was still unbecomingly couched in redundant
legalese, but it appeared presentable.

The question nagged at me: How did this unidiomatic curiosity—*each
and every, all and singular, the allegations*—become encysted in Texas practice?
Why do so many Texas litigators remain wedded to it, when it makes
so little sense? I did not expect to be able to uncover the origin of the
odd phrase. It seemed likely that Chief Justice John Fortescue's famous
15th-century statement supplied the answer to the enigma: "We have several set forms which are held as law, and so held and used for good reason, though we cannot at present remember that reason."[1] That, of course,
explains much of why we lawyers do what we do in the way we do it.

Adapted from *Dallas Bar Headnotes* (18 July 1988).
[1] Y.B. 36 Hen.VI pl. 21 (pp. 25–26) (translated in Holdsworth, *A History of English Law*
vol. 3, 626 (3d ed. 1923)).

Perhaps Judge Stayton's formbook, once widely used in Texas, had popularized the phrase. A look at it revealed a simplified but still redundant and unidiomatic form: "Defendant denies all and singular the allegations contained in plaintiff's original petition."[2]

A more up-to-date formbook recommends an admirably simplified wording: "defendant generally denies the allegations in plaintiff's original petition."[3] So much for those who believe that a departure from traditional legalese is fraught with peril. Messrs. Elliott and Edgar are to be commended for their streamlined wording, which will withstand either judicial or grammatical challenge.

More to the point, Messrs. Elliott and Edgar cite the 1847 rule, promulgated by the Supreme Court of Texas, that gave rise to the old anomalous wording. It appeared in the first volume of the Texas Reports, published in that year.[4] Rule 12 of the Supreme Court Rules stated as follows:

> Now comes the defendant and denies each and every, all and singular the allegations in plaintiff's petition contained, and demands strict proof thereof.[5]

The anonymous drafter of that rule, perhaps a justice of the Supreme Court, perpetrated a syntactic blunder that would be repeated (with minor variations) in Texas pleadings for more than a century and a half. To my knowledge, no one celebrated its sesquicentennial.

There is virtue in the plain-language movement in law. As lawyers, we ought to give some thought to our writing, rather than thoughtlessly parroting our predecessors. For those who would like to consult guides to plain language, I recommend two serviceable books: Richard C. Wydick's *Plain English for Lawyers* (1979) and Irwin Alterman's *Plain and Accurate Style in Court Papers* (1987). Texas lawyers might consider following the lead of the Michigan bar, which has established a plain-language committee for the purpose of goading lawyers to avoid legalese.

[Note: The author was the founding chair of the Plain Language Committee of the State Bar of Texas. It was established in 1990 and persisted through 1995—and carried out worthwhile projects each and every, all and singular, those years.]

---

[2] R.W. Stayton, *Stayton Texas Forms* vol. 9, § 4749, at 31 (1961).

[3] F.W. Elliott & J.H. Edgar Jr., *West's Texas Forms* vol. 9, § 5.41, at 303 (1978).

[4] The rule quoted appears only in the 1847 printing of the Texas Reports, not in the 1881 reprint that most firms and libraries have. Sue Johnson, Carrington Coleman's omnicompetent librarian, was unable to confirm the existence in Dallas of an original volume containing the rules promulgated by the Supreme Court in 1847.

[5] 1 Tex. 855 (1847).

ε❧ ε❧ ε❧

Going Hence Without Day

IN APRIL AND MAY OF 1982, Judge Jerry Buchmeyer's "Et Cetera" column in the *Dallas Bar Headnotes* brimmed with speculations about the origin and meaning of *going hence without day*. The phrase traditionally ends the prayer of the general denial in Texas: "Wherefore, premises considered, defendant prays that the plaintiff take nothing, and that this defendant go hence with his costs without day." (Rather than "traditionally ends the prayer," I would have liked to write "formerly ended with a prayer"—but we still encounter this bit of legalese.)

Lyman Hughes of Carrington Coleman wrote that he had always explained to associates that *going hence without day* originated in "a typographical error that has been perpetuated through the use of formbooks and the common practice of associates' adopting without change the phraseology used in the last pleading prepared by the partner to whom the associate reports." The true phrase, wrote Hughes, was *go hence without delay*. (One of my students inquired about the phrase, thinking that it might have been a typographical error for *go hence without pay*. Nice try.)

Stephen Maris of Fulbright & Jaworski whimsically speculated that "Day, you see, is a small gnome-like creature with unruly orange hair and a somewhat frog-like body that, from times Medieval, has lurked about the basement of the Dallas County Courthouse." Day, then, was obviously something that, whenever you happened to be going hence, you would want to go hence without. Maris's theory seemed plausible, but he ignored the question, "Whence came this Day?"

Bryan J. McGinnis of Beaumont claimed to have witnessed the birth of the phrase. He and his colleagues, he wrote, had set out to draft an elegant answer, with perfectly balanced phrasing. They had written *each and every, all and singular*, those dulcet tones in the first sentence of the denial.[1] When they wrote *with costs*, a sage colleague, T. Fortesque Clemmons, decided to balance that phrase by adding *without day*. McGinnis did not know what his learned colleague meant by the phrase, but rested assured that, "Clemmons being as brilliant as he is, I am certain that whatever the reason is, it is a brilliant one."[2]

Adapted from *Dallas Bar Headnotes* (16 Oct. 1989).

[1] *See* Garner, *A Grammatical Grotesquerie in Texas Practice*, Dallas B. Headnotes, 18 July 1988, at 12 (reprinted as the previous essay in this chapter).

[2] The letter is reprinted in F.W. Elliott & J.H. Edgar Jr., *West's Texas Forms* vol. 9F, § 5.41, at 383–85 (1989).

Perhaps it was T. Fortesque's 15th-century forebear, Chief Justice John Fortescue, who set the precedent for McGinnis's reasoning: "we have several set forms which are held as law, and so held and used for good reason, though we cannot at present remember that reason."[3] What Fortescue said in 1458 applies with undiminished force today: many lawyers still ask that their clients be allowed to *go hence without day*, though unsure just what the request means.

In Texas, the phrase goes back to the mid-19th century.[4] But where did the Texas originator—perhaps the same grammatical bungler who wrote *each and every, all and singular, the allegations*—find the phrase? Why did he think that defendants ought to go hence without day?

He may have adapted the phrase from a treatise such as Henry John Stephen's *Pleading in Civil Actions*, which recommends the following prayer: "The said defendant prays that the suit may remain or be respited without day until, etc."[5] Doesn't the Texas version (*going hence*) sound much better than *being respited without day*? (And who today would know just what to put in place of *etc.*? Doesn't that mean *with costs*?)

Actually, the hoary legal phrase is even hoarier than you might have thought. It comes from what Chief Justice Matthew Hale called "the golden age of pleading"[6] before 1500. In medieval times, lawyers spoke a mongrel dialect called Law French, in which the phrase of dismissal was *aller sans jour*, literally "to go without day." The phrase denoted an adjournment taken with no date set for resumption of the proceedings.

At common law, sometime after Law French increasingly fell into disuse, a longer Latin phrase appeared in orders of dismissal: *eat inde sine die*, that is, "that he may go hence without day." The defendant was free to go; he would not have what he did not want—his day in court. This form of order was used in England until 1733, when use of the English language became compulsory.[7]

Yet the English translation of the phrase, *without day*, cropped up well before 1733. In the 1701 edition of John Cowell's *Interpreter*, we learn that "[t]o be dismissed without *Day*, is to be finally discharged the Court." (Sic—Cowell apparently did not maintain a proper respect for the preposition *by*.) Dismissed cases were said to be *put without day*.

Though we have an answer to our question about the origin of *go hence without day*, another question lingers: Why should defendants pray

---

[3] Y.B. 36 Hen. VI pl. 21 (pp. 25–26) (translated in Holdsworth, *A History of English Law* vol. 3, 626 (3d ed. 1923)).

[4] *See* Elliott & Edgar, *West's Texas Forms* vol. 9F, § 5.41 at 383–85.

[5] H.J. Stephen, *A Treatise on the Principles of Pleading in Civil Actions* 394 (5th ed. 1845).

[6] *See* M. Hastings, *The Court of Common Pleas in Fifteenth Century England* 186 (1947).

[7] *See* W. A. Jowitt, *The Dictionary of English Law* 692 (1959).

merely to *go hence without day*, when they might ask for so much more? The alternate form of dismissal in medieval times was *aller a dieu*, which we might render "to go hence with God." The French *adieu*, brought into English in the 1300s, literally means "I commend you to God!"

We can't be certain, but perhaps our legal ancestors, when they finally came to use English, wisely decided that asking to go hence with God ought to be left to a different kind of prayer.

ਦੇ ਦੇ ਦੇ

The Lawyer's *imply*

THE PHRASE *by implication* signifies "by what is implied, though not formally expressed, by natural inference."[1] Anglo-American judges, who continually evaluate facts, often use the phrase, along with its various cognates. Judges (by implication) draw "natural inferences" and thereby decide that something or other was, in the circumstances, "implied." Through the process of hypallage—a semantic shift by which the attributes of the true subject are transferred to another subject—the word *imply* has come to be used in reference to what the judges do, as opposed to the circumstances. This specialized use of *imply* runs counter to popular lay use and is not adequately treated in English-language dictionaries. The usage is unrecorded in all dictionaries of which I am aware, apart from my own *Dictionary of Modern Legal Usage.*[2]

Specifically, the word *imply* often means "(of a court) to impute or impose on equitable or legal grounds." An *implied* contract is not just one implied from the facts of the case, but implied by the court, i.e., imposed by the judge or judges as a result of their inferences.

In using *imply* in this way, courts are said to find a doctrinally posited fact (a condition, restriction, remedy, right of action, or the like) that controls a judicial decision. Thus:

> [I]t would be more literally accurate to acknowledge that . . . the court *implies* the conditions from reasons of equity.[3]

> This court cannot, upon some supposed hardship, defeat an estate by *implying* a condition which the grantor has not expressed, nor in the least intimated by the language of his conveyance.[4]

> The difficulty with the arguments seeking to *imply* Mary Silva's survival of Joseph as a condition is that they would result in holding that because it is expressed that Joseph must survive until the period of distribution to take an inheritable interest, a similar contingency should be *implied* as to Mary.[5]

Adapted from *Centennial Usage Studies* (Greta D. Little & Michael Montgomery eds., 1994).

[1] *Oxford English Dictionary* (2d ed. 1995) (*OED2*).

[2] The definition was later included in the 7th (1999) and 8th (2004) editions of *Black's Law Dictionary*.

[3] *Susswein v. Pennsylvania Steel Co.*, 184 F. 102, 106 (C.C.S.D.N.Y. 1910).

[4] *Brown v. State*, 5 Colo. 496, 504 (1881).

[5] *In re Estate of Ferry*, 361 P.2d 900, 904 (Cal. 1961) (in bank).

Judicial willingness to *imply* new remedies in areas governed by federal law has been expressed in a number of ways.[6]

> [I]n my view, the Members of Congress merely assumed that the federal courts would follow the ancient maxim "ubi jus, ibi remedium" and *imply* a private right of action.[7]

When put in the passive voice, this use of *imply* may be especially confusing because the person who does the implying is left unclear. The user of any unabridged English-language dictionary either would find it hard to divine precisely what *imply* means or would deduce an incorrect meaning:

> [T]he remaining provisions of the Insurance Law would lack substance if no private right of action were *implied*.[8]

Here the passive voice masks the subject. The writer apparently means to say that a court would allow such a cause of action: Thus the court would *imply* a right of action, i.e., impose it on equitable or legal grounds.

This special legal sense is most keenly demonstrated when *imply* is coupled with *impute*, as here:

> When deciding the shares, we look to their [the husband's and the wife's] respective contributions and we see what trust is to be *implied* or *imputed* to them.[9]

Often one could actually read *impute* in place of *imply* and have the same sense (read *impute to* for *imply on*):

> Under special circumstances the Court may *imply* knowledge *on* the speaker, such as the inventor of a machine, "who must be fully informed as to [the machine's] good and bad qualities."[10]

In some contexts, *imply* seems to take on a slightly different sense, "to read into (a document)," as here:

> [O]ne has merely to look at what is clearly said. There is no room for any intendment . . . . Nothing is to be read in, nothing is to be *implied*. One can only look fairly at the language used.[11]

But such uses comport with the general sense here outlined, since "reading in" provisions has the same effect as "imputing" them.

---

[6] *S.E.C. v. Texas Gulf Sulphur Co.*, 312 F.Supp. 77, 91 (S.D.N.Y. 1970).

[7] *California v. Sierra Club*, 451 U.S. 287, 300 (1981) (Stevens, J., concurring).

[8] *Corcoran v. Frank B. Hall & Co.*, 545 N.Y.S.2d 278, 284 (App. Div. 1989).

[9] *Cracknell v. Cracknell* [1971] 3 All E.R. 552, 554.

[10] *Brickell v. Collins*, 262 S.E.2d 387, 390 (N.C. App. 1980).

[11] *Cape Brandy Syndicate v. I.R.C.* [1921] 1 K.B. 64, 71.

The lawyer's *imply* has directly encroached on the word *infer*. Whereas nonlawyers frequently use *infer* for *imply*, lawyers and judges conflate the two in the opposite direction, by using *imply* for *infer*. In analyzing the facts of a case, judges will *imply* one fact from certain others. (*From* is a telling preposition.) Nonlawyers believe they must be *inferring* an additional fact from those already known; if contractual terms are *implied*, they must surely be implied by the words or circumstances of the contract and not by the judges.

Perhaps using this reasoning, some legal writers have recoiled from *imply* and have resorted instead to *infer*:

> Apart from the difficulty of *inferring* a contract where none has been made, no agreement between husband and wife for future separation can be recognised.[12]

> When a party voluntarily accepts a valuable service or benefit, having option to accept or reject it, the Court may *infer* a promise to pay.[13]

In the following sentence, in which the court writes *imply or infer from*, the word *imply* adds nothing, unless *by the circumstances* (i.e., *implicit in the circumstances*) is to be understood, and *or* is to be read as *and*:

> Rather, the crucial question is when can a waiver of rights be *implied or inferred from* the actions and words of the person interrogated.[14]

In the following sentences, *infer* might have served better than *imply*. One would be tempted to call these misuses, were not some specimens so ancient:

> [T]here is nothing averred from which the court can *imply* that those conditions were performed.[15]

> The requirements of the rule are met if such an intention may be clearly *implied* from the language, the purposes of the agreement, and all the surrounding facts and circumstances.[16]

Note that the facts here posited (performance of a condition, intention) are of a lower level of abstraction than those in the examples given at the outset of this essay. Using *imply* with low-level abstractions, as opposed to doctrinally posited facts, is comparatively uncommon in modern legal usage.

---

[12] *Pettitt v. Pettitt* [1970] A.C. 777, 811 (H.L.).
[13] *Lewis v. Holy Spirit Assn.*, 589 F.Supp. 10, 13 (D. Mass. 1983).
[14] *McDonald v. Lucas*, 677 F.2d 518, 520 (5th Cir. 1982).
[15] *Cutting v. Myers*, 6 F. Cas. 1081, 1082 (C.C.D. Pa. 1818) (No. 3520).
[16] *Salamy v. New York Central Syst.*, 146 N.Y.S.2d 814, 817 (App. Div. 1955).

Adding still more color to this chameleon-hued word in legal contexts is the ordinary nonlegal sense:

> We do not mean to *imply* that where joint ownership is set up in conformity with the statutory provisions, a court of equity is thereby foreclosed from looking behind the form of the transaction and determining questions of real and beneficial interest as between the parties.[17]

> There is nothing in the former decision that would *imply* that the "sole discretion" vested in and exercised by the trustees in this case is beyond court review.[18]

Similarly, the nonlegal confusion between the words inhabits the legal realm:

> Exclusion from venires focuses on the inherent attributes of the excluded group and *infers* [read *implies*] its inferiority . . . .[19]

It is not wholly surprising that the legal uses of *imply* have not found a place in English-language dictionaries. Common in American and British law alike, the uses here outlined have not yet spread from legal to nonlegal contexts—and may never do so. Moreover, because lexicographic reading programs seldom glean citations from legal texts, lexicographers often overlook linguistic innovation in law. Any attempt to marshal such a voluminous specialized vocabulary, whatever the scale of the effort, will fail to uncover every new item. But we certainly ought to direct more lexicographic energy into a field as important as law, which affects myriad aspects of everyone's life.

---

[17] *Frey v. Wubbena*, 185 N.E.2d 850, 855 (Ill. 1962).

[18] *In re Ferall's Estate*, 258 P.2d 1009, 1013 (Cal. 1953) (in bank).

[19] *United States v. Leslie*, 759 F.2d 381, 392 (5th Cir. 1985) (en banc) (Garwood, J., dissenting).

ea ea ea

Novelties in Lawyer Talk

DON'T LET ANYONE persuade you otherwise: *conclusory* is a perfectly good, useful English word. Lawyers have recently debated a great deal about the word, in the wake of a *New York Times* article noting that most English dictionaries omit it.[1] That, however, is the fault of the dictionary-makers, not of the litigators who find the word so apt.

When we think of innovation in law, linguistic innovation hardly comes to mind. After all, it is commonly thought, the legal vocabulary was petrified years ago in phrases such as *voir dire, cestui que trust*, and *trespass vi et armis*. Yet just as the law grows luxuriantly beyond what lawyers of a century ago might have envisioned, many of our legal words and phrases have sprung forth only recently. You might be surprised to learn that such everyday phrases as *blind trust, decriminalize, freedom of information, living will, public-interest lawyer*, and *victimless* have been with us only a very short time.

Many such innovations in the law have remained unrecorded and undefined. *Conclusory* is perhaps the prime example. Like many other legal neologisms, it is not recorded in any general English-language dictionary in its current legal sense. That mystifies, since the word crops up in most lengthy discussions of testimonial evidence. The word has been used for more than 60 years, originally in the New York courts and more recently throughout the United States, in the sense "expressing a mere conclusion of fact without stating the specific facts upon which the conclusion is based." For example, "He shot the dog" is conclusory, whereas "I saw him shoot the dog" is not.

When Judge Walter Urbigkit of the Wyoming Supreme Court felt the need to use *conclusory* in 1987, he justified his word choice in a footnote:

> After painstaking deliberation, we have decided that we like the word *conclusory*, and we are distressed by its omission from the English language. We now proclaim that henceforth *conclusory* is appropriately used in the opinions of this court. Furthermore, its usage is welcomed in briefs submitted for this court's review. Webster's, take heed.[2]

Adapted from *The Appellate Advocate* (Summer 1989).
[1] *A Proper Word in Court*, N.Y. Times, 13 Aug. 1987, at A21. Since the first publication of this essay in 1989, most American dictionaries have added *conclusory*.
[2] *Greenwood v. Wierdsma*, 741 P.2d 1079, 1086 n.3 (Wyo. 1987).

Fifty-four years earlier, a New York court had employed the word with considerably less fanfare: "[The] recitals add nothing to the facts, except invective of a conclusory sort."[3] I have found no earlier specimen in the modern legal sense. But many have followed: the word has been used in more than 21,000 state and federal cases.

* * *

In April 1988, several months after my *Dictionary of Modern Legal Usage* (*DMLU*) had been published, I received a letter from the Honorable Robert E. Keeton, the distinguished federal trial judge in Boston. Commenting on *DMLU*, he said, "I was . . . delighted until I saw that you have embraced *conclusory*. I wish I could persuade you to reconsider this one." Judge Keeton continued:

> There was no need for such a neologism as *conclusory*. As you have noted, both Oxford English and American dictionaries demonstrate that *conclusional* is a word of ancient and respected lineage. We never did and do not now need *conclusory*, which also is objectionable because it inevitably carries the misleading nuance of meaning a statement that is officially decisive ("conclusive," as you have noted) rather than the ordinarily intended meaning of a statement that is merely an allegation . . . . I have been fighting an almost lonely battle to convert at least my law clerks (who generally have pretended to be enthusiastic converts), if not other judges, lawyers, and professors. Unless you reconsider, I will have lost the battle for preserving *conclusional*.

To my good fortune, Judge Keeton sent a copy of his letter to Professor Charles Alan Wright, who, like all great appellate advocates, shares Judge Keeton's fascination with language.

Professor Wright responded to Judge Keeton with characteristic sagacity. He pointed out that his Westlaw search called up some 21,613 opinions in which *conclusory* appears, whereas *conclusional* appeared in fewer than 1,000 opinions. Wright said:

> I would certainly be the last to suggest that questions of English usage can be determined wholly by counting. I think it is the duty of those of us who are educated and who care about the English language to fight against all seeming odds to hold back the night so eagerly awaited by the ignorant armies of many camps. You and Bryan and I stand as

---

[3] *Ringler v. Jetter*, 201 N.Y.S. 523, 524 (App. Div. 1923).

one in our suspicion of neologisms, but we should not reject them when, as with *conclusory*, they fill a demonstrable void.

I, too, of course, responded to Judge Keeton. Here is a part of what I wrote:

> *Conclusional* is really a revival, a word with no record of continual use in English. The *Oxford English Dictionary* cites two uses, one from the 15th and one from the 17th century. I have been able to document no earlier use in law than from the 1940s, whereas *conclusory* is somewhat older in American legal writing. *Conclusory* is certainly far more widespread . . . . Although, as the *OED* notes, *conclusory* was once used as a synonym of *conclusive*, I don't think any modern legal reader understands the word in that sense.

The debate was a fascinating one that brought up a recurrent issue for advocates. What do you do when a word you want to use cannot be found in the dictionary? "Recurrent," I say, because of the many examples to be found in modern legal writing of "nonwords," if you take as your authority the available unabridged dictionaries. Among these are *asylee, certworthy* (used by Supreme Court practitioners), *communitize, depecage* (a choice-of-law principle), *discriminatee, enbancworthy* (invented by Fifth Circuit judges), *litigational, pretextual, quashal, recusement* (a variant of *recusal*), *restitutionary, substitutionary*, and *veniremember* (a nonsexist variant of *venireman*). The list could go on and on.

Professor Wright and I had not heard the last about *conclusory*. In 1989, the redoubtable Judge Keeton wrote again, this time referring to *City of Richmond v. J.A. Croson, Inc.*, in which Justice O'Connor states: "The District Court also relied on the highly conclusionary statement of a proponent of the Plan that there was racial discrimination in the construction industry 'in the area, and the State, and around the nation.'"[4] Judge Keeton concluded: "All hail the power of the Supreme Court to speak to modern legal usage as well as to the law of the land!"

These are not fighting words, exactly, but they led Professor Wright to respond: "I fear that in this instance our masters have been the recipients of miserable advice—perhaps from a district judge in Boston—and, as Bernie Ward told us, 'we must read their judgments shorn of the miserable advice.' They should heed your wise counsel on legislative facts, 73 MINN. L. REV. 1, and ignore your unsound views on English usage."

---

[4] 488 U.S. 469, 500 (1989).

There we have the last word on the law of usage in federal courts. My own response was far more prolix; I quote it at length because I can give no better analysis of the question:

> Professor Wright has already shown that *conclusory* has "taken the field"— that it far outstrips *conclusional* in frequency of use . . . . Even so, I would not say that frequency is entirely determinative (I almost said *conclusive*). I can imagine three possible objections to *conclusory*. The first might be that it is a neologism. The second might be that its use blurs a well-developed distinction. And the third might be that the word is badly formed.
>
> None of these objections is sound. We have developed a new meaning—"expressing a mere factual inference without stating the underlying facts upon which the inference is based"—for which we need a word. The word is to be based on *conclusion*. Surely we cannot object to a neologism in such a circumstance.
>
> Now, leaving aside *conclusive*, *conclusible*, and *concludent*, we find in the *OED* only two adjectives that correspond to the noun *conclusion*. The first (alphabetically and chronologically) is *conclusional*, which is documented in only two sources, from 1471 and 1695, in the sense "of or pertaining to the conclusion; final." It does not appear (in the *OED*'s sense) to be a live word. The other is *conclusory*, documented in three 19th-century sources, meaning "relating to or tending to a conclusion; conclusive." This word was also stillborn, apparently, because the *OED* Supplement does not bring it into the 20th century.
>
> The idea of "tending to a conclusion" is very near the definition we have newly developed, but *conclusion* has two different senses, "termination" and "inference," and the 19th-century examples of *conclusory* in the *OED* relate to the former rather than to the latter.
>
> Let us move to the second possible objection: that in giving *conclusory* this new sense, we are blurring a well-developed distinction. Since neither word came into the 20th century with a widely recognized meaning, this objection hardly seems worth lodging. If anything, *conclusory* was merely a needless variant of *conclusive*, and we would want to encourage any possible differentiation.
>
> Our third possible objection is morphology, or word-formation. Of the three variants—*conclusory*, *conclusional*, and *conclusionary*—only the first is formed on the word-stem *conclus-*. Just as we prefer *litigatory* to *litigational*, or *restitutive* to *restitutionary* or *restitutional*, we ought to prefer *conclusory* . . . . I note that the Latin verb *concludo* is of the same type as the verb *illudo* (which gives us *illusory*). Even so, neither *conclusionalis* nor *conclusorius* was known to Cicero, nor, probably, to medieval Latinists.
>
> Then we look to the history of the variants in legal usage, and find that *conclusory* has been used with increasing frequency since 1923 in our special sense. *Conclusional* (1947) and *conclusionary* (1945) are relative latecomers.

Moreover, *conclusionary* is not countenanced by any dictionary I know of. Why hail Justice O'Connor's use of the phrase, then? Continued use of the variants only perpetuates the confusion of legal writers. "It is a source not of strength," wrote Fowler, "but of weakness, that there should be two names for the same thing [by-forms differing merely in suffix or in some minor point], because the reasonable assumption is that two words mean two things, and confusion results when they do not." H.W. Fowler, *Modern English Usage* 373 (1926).

*   *   *

We can learn a lesson from all this. The language of the law has remained largely untraversed by lexicographers. It therefore contains many inconsistencies—no natural consensus, for example, on whether to use *conclusory*, *conclusionary*, or *conclusional*. It contains surprises of other kinds. New words constantly arise, such as *antisuit*[5] (a Texanism) and *double-breasting*.[6] Frequently, words thought to be new are found to be much older in law than anyone suspected.

Adversarial is a good example. At one time, *adversary* was the standard adjective used in legal contexts. But *adversarial* had overtaken *adversary* in legal writing by the late 1970s. As to origins, the *Second Barnhart Dictionary of New English* (1980) labels *adversarial* "British" and dates the word from 1967. Other recent dictionaries follow suit. But the word appeared almost half a century before in a judicial opinion from California: "[N]o adversarial interest between parties is intrinsically involved."[7] The word had a considerable history in American law before finding its way to Great Britain.

Monitoring the entry of words into the legal lexicon is a fascinating pastime, now made far easier by our ability to conduct computer searches. I recently came across the phrase *chicanerous litigant* in Wright and Miller's *Federal Practice and Procedure*.[8] Not recognizing the adjective *chicanerous*—though its sense was clear—I consulted the *Oxford English Dictionary* (to

---

[5] *E.g.*, "Where the two courts involved are a state and federal court, special attention should be given to such an *antisuit* injunction." *Blanchard v. Commonwealth Oil Co.*, 294 F.2d 834, 839 (5th Cir. 1961); "Appellant advances the argument that since the appellee husband violated the *anti-suit* injunctions issued in the Connecticut court . . . he may not now be protected by Texas law." *Nowell v. Nowell*, 408 S.W.2d 550, 555 (Tex. Civ. App.—Dallas 1966).

[6] *Double-breasting* is said to occur when "the owner splits its employees between two companies, one that is party to a labor agreement and one that is non-union." *Virginia Sprinkler Co. v. Local Union 669*, 868 F.2d 116, 118 (4th Cir. 1989).

[7] *McWilliams v. Hopkins*, 11 F.2d 793, 795 (S.D. Cal. 1926).

[8] § 1283, at 372 (1969).

no avail) and then *Webster's Third New International Dictionary* (again to no avail). A computer search turned up several judicial uses, one from 1969 ("vexatious, oppressive, chicanerous") and another from 1975 ("chicanerous actions").

When I brought the word to the attention of Professor Wright, the senior author of that great treatise, he replied: "You have commented on a word in the Treatise that I did not know was there. I certainly had at least constructive knowledge, since I read every word that goes into the Treatise . . . . Professor Arthur R. Miller of the Harvard Law School carries the laboring oar on Civil Rule 8. He must be the one who decided that if there is no adjective as *chicanerous*, there ought to be." Noting that the articles cited in his Treatise do not make use of *chicanerous*, Professor Wright concluded that the adjective "sprang full-blown from the mighty Miller mind."

With only a smattering of published uses to its credit, *chicanerous* has hardly proved as useful as many other neologisms. But it may be on its less glorious way, for all of us to use when the need arises. After all, we have no other adjective to match the noun *chicanery*; and, sad to say, there is enough chicanery afoot calling out for description.

Have you noticed, by the way, the common ingredient in most of the neologisms we have just examined? It is an ingredient of probably nine of every ten legal neologisms: differentiation by suffix. We tend to couple new word-endings (*-al, -ment, -ory, -ous*) with existing roots. Prefixes come into play far less often.

Sensing the need for additional words in our language, then filling that need by innovating them, is anything but chicanerous. Of course, the English language is well stocked as it is, with more than half a million words to its credit. Even so, we occasionally come upon gaps in our available vocabulary, and it behooves us all when some mighty mind like Arthur Miller introduces a truly useful word. That phenomenon seems to occur in legal language with great frequency nowadays. As always, however, a word invented merely for the sake of novelty—and not out of some felt need—is but a tawdry bauble.

HENRY CAMPBELL BLACK • JOHN BOUVIER

CHAPTER SEVEN

Legal Lexicography

The *Oxford Law Dictionary*:
A Historical Dictionary
for English-Speaking Jurisdictions

In 1988, the University of Texas and Oxford University Press joined forces to establish the Texas/Oxford Center for Legal Lexicography as a joint venture. I was named visiting associate professor of law, director of the Center, and editor in chief of the Oxford Law Dictionary—*which would have been the first and only historical law dictionary ever created. Despite considerable fundraising success for the project, neither joint venturer was willing to risk having to fund any shortfall. So both the Center and the* Dictionary *project were scuttled in 1990. From that debacle, LawProse was born. This piece and the following one were written when work on the dictionary project was at its height.*

—B.A.G.

NOT UNMINDFUL OF Learned Hand's famous admonition—"It is one of the surest indexes of a mature and developed jurisprudence not to make a fortress out of the dictionary"[1]—the University of Texas School of Law and Oxford University Press have joined to undertake the first-ever historical law dictionary. Not a fortress, perhaps, but a comprehensive tool for those who need to know the historical and modern meanings of legal words and phrases throughout the English-speaking world.

Adapted from *The Law Librarian* (Aug. 1989).
[1] *Cabell v. Markham*, 148 F.2d 737, 739 (2d Cir. 1945).

For the first time, the entirety of the legal vocabulary will be mar-
shaled and defined so as to trace its historical development from the 16th
century to the present day. (Etymologies, of course, will go back considerably further.) The scope of the *Oxford Law Dictionary* (or *OLD*) will
include the terminology of all English-speaking jurisdictions, though the
primary emphasis will be American and English. Even so, the reading
program will cover legal writings from Scotland, Ireland, Australia, New
Zealand, South Africa, Zimbabwe, India, and several other countries.

The dictionary takes as its model the *Oxford English Dictionary*. Oxford
University Press, which will publish the *OLD*, has given permission to
use the law-related definitions of the second edition of the *Oxford English Dictionary* as the starting point for the *OLD*. While the great mother-
dictionary provides the methodology and scholarly standards on which
the work will proceed, the *OLD* will be a work of original scholarship
rather than an updating or slight revision of the legal entries in the
OED. Even the definitions deriving in part from the *OED* will be written anew to account for legal nuances. Ultimately, no more than 10% of
the final work—in the form of parts of definitions, etymologies, and
illustrative quotations—will derive from the *OED*.

Using the resources of the renowned Tarlton Law Library at the University of Texas, as well as other libraries, the staff of the newly formed
Texas/Oxford Center for Legal Lexicography, with the help of volunteer
readers, will seek to trace all legal words and phrases as far back as possible. The work is to begin in the fall of 1989.

Far fuller than any existing law dictionary, the *OLD* will be a multivolume work comprising nearly six million words in more than 25,000
entries. Most of the 250 words in each entry will be devoted to illustrative quotations that show how the legal words and phrases being defined
have been used during the past five centuries.

Legal scholars have long seen the need for such a work. When the
Oxford English Dictionary was completed some 60 years ago, an American
legal historian commented: "Perhaps in some distant future there may be
written a legal dictionary. The *OED* is a magnificent beginning, . . . but
the responsibility rests mainly with lawyers. Less learned professions . . .
have already furnished themselves with historical dictionaries . . . . When
shall we get a real law dictionary on historical principles?"[2] Much earlier, when work on the *Oxford English Dictionary* had just begun, a
learned English lawyer lamented that "we have no such thing as a law
Dictionary worthy of the name."[3] More recently, it has been said, "I

---

[2] Theodore F.T. Plucknett, *Words*, 14 Cornell L.Q. 263, 273 (1929).
[3] M.O. Chalmers, *Wanted—A Law Dictionary*, 8 Law Q. Rev. 283, 283 (1892).

think that the complete law dictionary on historical principles, in the path of the *OED*, will remain a scholar's dream."[4]

As a result of our lack of such a work—and despite the plethora of short legal glossaries—much of the legal lexicon has remained unrecorded. Until the appearance of my *Dictionary of Modern Legal Usage* (Oxford 1987), many 19th-century and 20th-century legal neologisms found no place in existing dictionaries, legal or nonlegal. Examples include *ancillarity, asylee, benefitee, certworthy, condemnee, conveyee, discriminatee, enbancworthy, enjoinable, litigational, non-refoulement, pretextual, quashal, recusement,* and *veniremember.* (You can see what we American lawyers are doing to the language.) These are only a few of what surely amounts to hundreds of ghost-words in law.

More important than tracking down all these neologisms, however, is setting forth the changes in meaning that particular legal terms have undergone. The work should usefully guide judges, lawyers, and legal scholars concerned with the interpretation of historical materials, whether statutes or judicial decisions. Up to now, we have had to work more or less in the dark on such legal-linguistic questions.

The primary users of the *OLD* will be those whose need for enlightenment on such questions is most immediate and most frequent—that is, those engaged in the practice, interpretation, study, administration, and enforcement of the law. Outside the legal profession, the *OLD* will be useful to students, scholars, and professionals in the humanities and social sciences.

The *OLD* will be unique. No law dictionary has yet been compiled on modern lexicographical principles. Many existing law dictionaries are poorly written, function more as encyclopedias than as dictionaries, lack comprehensive treatment, and provide little if any guidance on the development of legal language (apart from occasionally labeling words and phrases vaguely as deriving from "old English law").

The effort to marshal the legal vocabulary will be two-pronged. First, the in-house and outside reading programs will involve much the same type of scholarly endeavor as went into the *Oxford English Dictionary* (1878–1928) and Burchfield's *Supplement* (1957–1986). Members of the *OLD* staff and volunteer readers will systematically read and excerpt historical legal texts, so that the Center for Legal Lexicography may build a storehouse of lexical items, in the form of illustrative quotations, from which to construct the *OLD*.

---

[4] David Mellinkoff, *The Myth of Precision and the Law Dictionary,* 31 U.C.L.A. L. Rev. 423, 440 (1983).

Second, and equally important, the *OLD* will be the first major dictionary project to make extensive use of computer databases to conduct word-searches for collecting illustrative quotations. The Texas/Oxford Center for Legal Lexicography will have its own dedicated computer-research terminals, and the Center's staff will use these to ascertain the earliest known judicial uses of given law words. These searches will also supplement the *OLD* files with representative uses of terms so as to fill chronological gaps, and to broaden the geographic base for illustrative quotations.

It may be instructive to give an example of the benefits to be reaped from using computer research as an adjunct to the reading programs. *The Second Barnhart Dictionary of New English* (1980), in guiding users to emerging vocabulary that has not yet been recorded in general English-language dictionaries, shows 1976 as the earliest known use of the phrase *joint custody*, and quotes an example from that year in *The New York Times*. This may accurately tag the point at which the phrase came to appear in contexts not specifically legal. But a computer search calls up 60 law cases in which the phrase was used before 1960, the earliest being the 1887 New York case of *Pickett v. Bartlett*.[5] In the modern sense of the word—that of divorced parents agreeing to joint custody of a child—the earliest instance occurs in *Delaney v. Mt. St. Joseph's Academy*,[6] a New York case decided in 1921.

This instance of antedating the use of a term illustrates two important points. First, it is one of numberless examples that show how poorly the language of the law has been mapped both in law dictionaries and in general English-language dictionaries. Second, it shows how valuable computer research can be to the lexicographer. Computers will not replace human research in original sources because so much material needs to be covered that is not in the computer databases, but they certainly give a fairer view of lexical development in law by virtue of their comprehensive inclusion of judicial opinions. The technology to be used in the *OLD* project serves merely as the handmaid of traditional scholarship.

The idea underlying the project, though it has never been realized, is venerable. As Lord Bowen wrote toward the end of the 19th century, "The only reasonable and the only satisfactory way of dealing with English [or American] law is to bring to bear upon it the historical method. Mere legal terminology may seem a dead thing. Mix history with it, and it clothes itself with life."[7]

---

[5] 14 N.E. 301, 302 (N.Y. 1887).

[6] 189 N.Y.S. 775 (App. Div. 1921).

[7] Quoted in Van Vechten Veeder, *The Judicial Characteristics of the Late Lord Bowen*, 10 Harv. L. Rev. 351, 365 (1897).

A contemporary of Lord Bowen's, James Bradley Thayer, the Harvard law professor, made an allied point when he observed, "As our law develops it becomes more and more important to give definiteness to its phraseology; discriminations multiply, new situations and complications of fact arise, and the old outfit of ideas, discriminations, and phrases has to be carefully revised . . . . If terms in common legal use are used exactly, it is well to know it; if they are used inexactly, it is well to know that, and to remark just how they are used."[8]

Lord Bowen emphasized the need to apply the historical method in the study of legal terminology, and his insight applies *a fortiori* to legal lexicography. Professor Thayer noted that the meanings of legal terms periodically change; he tacitly raises the issue of marking the points in history when those semantic changes occur, and of analyzing law words into their most specific senses. The *OLD* will be the first law dictionary to meet the precision demanded by these scholars.

In addition to applying the historical method to legal lexicography, the *OLD* will refine the lemmatization (or choice of headwords) for a law dictionary by including all lexical items that make up the legal idiom. So terms like *law review* and *asylee* would find definition, along with rarer legal terms such as *multital* and *paucital* (both coined by Wesley Newcomb Hohfeld), although none of these is included as a headword in either a legal or a nonspecialist dictionary. Selecting headwords, then, will depend on a term's being a part of, or unique to, the legal idiom.

The method of composing entries will be much the same as for the *Oxford English Dictionary*. The headword will be followed by its pronunciation, part of speech, and etymology. The definitions of each word will then be ordered logically and chronologically, from the earliest known use to the most recent. Because the *OLD* is a specialized dictionary, its definitions will almost uniformly be written afresh to account for historical legal nuances and broken down into minute senses that reflect those nuances. Illustrative quotations will appear in support of and below each definition.

The project has no precedent in the history of Anglo-American legal scholarship. It promises to contribute significantly to our understanding of our legal heritage, and thereby to enhance not only future works of legal scholarship, but also the continuing administration of justice in English-speaking societies. In the words of Sir James A.H. Murray, the first editor of the *Oxford English Dictionary*, "Good work, once done and in print, becomes an eternal inheritance which will remain of value for generations to come."

---

[8] *Preliminary Treatise on Evidence* 190 (1898).

ès ès ès

The Missing Common-Law Words

OF THE COMMON-LAW WIFE, Lord Denning once wrote that "no such woman was known to the common law."[1] Nor *by* the common law, one might add, for lawyers often personify the law. The common-law wife is certainly well known to Anglo-American lawyers, although the circumstances surrounding the creation of her status vary from jurisdiction to jurisdiction.[2] Notably, the term *common-law husband* occasionally appears but is little known in comparison with its spouse.

That is but one of numberless curiosities in Anglo-American legal language, which has reached a stage in its development similar in some ways to that of the English language in the 17th century. The assertion may seem an odd one in this day, when legal writers increasingly attempt in their prose to approximate good idiomatic English. Yet it remains that the legal vocabulary has been imperfectly recorded at best, even in law dictionaries. The legal lexicographer of the late 20th century finds something akin to what Samuel Johnson found when he undertook his great *Dictionary*: a speech copious without order, and energetic without rules; perplexities to be disentangled, and confusion to be regulated; choices to be made out of boundless variety. One may hope that this has been a "time of rudeness antecedent to perfection," which Johnson, in the famous preface to his *Dictionary of the English Language* (1755), optimistically attributed to every language. None has yet approached that postulated state of perfection, and legal writers do not even dream of it.

The imperfections in legal language are easily pointed out. What is one to make of a learned profession whose most exalted members, the judges, elevate malapropisms to the level of near-standard idioms? A historical misnomer like *common-law wife* is at worst a venial blunder, at best a convenient neologism. Not so certain other developments, such as the confusion of *testamentary* with *testimonial*. The one has to do with wills, the other with testimony; the first syllable in each of the words is identical in form and etymology, but there the similarities end. Nevertheless, American judges have had difficulty keeping the words straight. Upon first seeing the phrase *documentary and testamentary evidence*, one might

---

From *The State of the Language* (1990).
[1] *Davis v. Johnson* [1979] A.C. 264, 270.
[2] *See A Dictionary of Modern Legal Usage* (1987), s.v. "common-law marriage."

call it an unfortunate anomaly. With only a little research, however, one finds many examples in published judicial opinions.[3]

The misusage would not occur outside a legal context, and might go unnoticed by a layman anyway. Bungles of this kind seem to be on the rise. Now that Latin is a forgotten as well as a dead language, once-established legal phrases such as *corpus delicti* have been transmogrified into erroneous forms. The macabre solecism that often appears today is *corpus delecti*, which is not merely a clever attempt at necrophiliac humor.[4] Similarly, *lex loci delicti*, which refers to "the law of the jurisdiction in which a wrong was committed," has become *lex loci delecti*.[5] The reader with training in Latin might suppose that to be "the law of the jurisdiction where delight occurred." *Delictual*, meaning "tortious," has not yet become *delectual*—a good thing, too, since some readers might further confuse that with *delectable*. Cicero, that great lawyer, would weep at what has become of his language in the hands of modern lawyers.

These are "learned bloopers," so to speak. Judges also partake of the more amusing type of malapropism, the howler that any educated reader recognizes. Thus a federal appellate judge writes, "To overturn the judge's denial of the motion to recuse would be an effrontery to his character." Other legal writers emulate Mrs. Malaprop and Mistress Quickly more closely still; a writer for a law journal states, "The main impotence for recruiting someone who has published is to ensure that he is used to long hours." And then there is the lawyer who requested judgment on his client's "meretricious" claim, noting that several witnesses had vouched for the client's "voracity."

---

[3] For instance, the United States Court of Appeals for the Eighth Circuit has written: "Bankrupts then offered documentary and testamentary evidence to rebut the Government's proof." *Solari Furs v. United States*, 436 F.2d 683, 685 (8th Cir. 1971). Nary a testator nor a beneficiary appears in that case; the writer meant to say *testimonial evidence*. Following is another example: "In the present case the subpoena *duces tecum* called only for non-testamentary [read *nontestimonial*] evidence to which was added an oral option." *United States v. Santucci*, 674 F.2d 624, 628 (7th Cir. 1982). Why *nontestimonial*, even, in place of *documentary*?

[4] A search of the American state-court decisions on Westlaw, the online database, conducted on 31 Oct. 1988 turned up 260 cases in which the spelling *corpus delecti* appears. For example, "The confession may be used to establish the *corpus delecti*." *Wooldridge v. State*, 653 S.W.2d 811, 816 (Tex. Crim. App. 1983).

[5] "At one time Arkansas courts followed the traditional approach of the First Restatement, termed *lex loci delecti* (law of the place of injury)." Carmen L. Arick, Student Author, *Multistate Torts*, 10 U. Ark. Little Rock L.J. 511, 516 (1987–1988) (repeatedly spelling the phrase incorrectly). "Most of the numerous inadequacies inherent in *lex loci delecti* also exist in the other traditional *lex loci* rules." *Duncan v. Cessna Aircraft Co.*, 665 S.W.2d 414, 421 (Tex. 1984).

Of course, lexicographers need not account for such freaks of usage, unless, like the misuse of *testamentary*, these begin to gain currency. (*Webster's Third*, after all, notes without comment that *flaunt* is sometimes used for *flout*.) What lexicographers should account for, all would agree, is the growth of the English vocabulary. It is a never-ending task.

Although any dictionary is obsolete to some extent by the time it appears in print, modern lexicographers strive to record linguistic innovations as soon as these prove to be something more than *hapax legomena*. It is a delicate balance, staying current while not giving sway to overnight fads. Delicate though that balance is, currency is what our dictionary-makers seem to pride themselves on most highly. In his preface to the second edition of *The Random House Dictionary of the English Language* (1987), Stuart Berg Flexner writes, "The twin explosions of knowledge and vocabulary from many sources have increased in magnitude during these past twenty-one years." The result, he says, is an expanded English vocabulary,

> not only from such obvious fields as science and technology and new forms and styles in the arts, fashion, and leisure activities, but also from history itself and from such social and cultural movements as concern with the environment, the women's movement, and a new awareness of and respect for ethnic diversity.[6]

When the controversial *Webster's Third* appeared in 1961, its editor, Philip B. Gove, explained in his preface that "the scientific and technical vocabulary has been considerably expanded to keep pace with progress especially in physical science (as in electronics, nuclear physics, statistics, and soil science), in technology (as in rocketry, communications, automation, and synthetics), in medicine, and in the experimental phases of natural science."[7] Similarly, the redoubtable Robert Burchfield stated, in his preface to the second volume of the *OED Supplement*, "The rapid expansion of work in all the sciences has been fully taken into account: anyone interested in the history of scientific words will find much of permanent value in the pages that follow. The terms of the printing industry and the names of plants and animals have continued to yield lexical material of considerable interest."[8] The printing industry—he would be interested in that, wouldn't he?

---

[6] Stuart Berg Flexner, Preface, *The Random House Dictionary of the English Language* vii (2d ed. 1987).

[7] Philip B. Gove, *Webster's Third New International Dictionary* 4a (1961).

[8] Robert W. Burchfield, *A Supplement to the Oxford English Dictionary* vol. 2, viii (1976).

Amid all this talk of the explosive growth of the English vocabulary, hardly a word is to be found about the language of the law. The reason is not, as one might suppose, that linguistic innovation is rare in law. On the contrary, neologisms abound in modern legal writing, though both writer and reader are often unaware that certain commonplace law words have yet to find a home in English dictionaries. Why is it, for example, that a word like *conclusory*, in its modern legal sense, so long remained unaccounted for in all the major English-language dictionaries, though it has been used by lawyers since at least 1923? (More about this word in a moment.)

The answer lies in ignorance of legal language, coupled with a strong (however understandable) aversion to it. The pervasive misconception among laymen is that legal language is stranded somewhere between Chaucer and Shakespeare; that legal terminology consists in centuries-old words and phrases that lawyers dare not stray from. Vallins gave voice to this myth when he wrote, in *Good English*:

> The "standard" language, or current usage, has within it or, as it were, around it, all kinds of special languages which have their own constructions, modes of expression, syntax, idiom. Legal language is perhaps the best example. They, like the main standardised language, have their natural changes, though these changes are usually very slow, and sometimes (as in legal language) scarcely exist at all.[9]

Lexical changes occur in legal language far more than "scarcely at all," despite what our best dictionaries would suggest.[10] In truth, legal terminology is a curious mixture of the old and the new; what is new merely tends to be ignored amid all the archaic words.

Lexicographers fail to discover legal neologisms in part because legal writing both intimidates and bores them. They therefore tend to omit it from their research. One sympathizes with the lexicographers here, for who could think of a fate worse than having to read page after page of

---

[9] G.H. Vallins, *Good English: How to Write It* 2–3 (1952). Cf. Bonamy Dobrée's misconceived statement that law and science are "realms in which prose seems to have remained static [from 1934 to 1964]" (*Modern Prose Style* vii [2d ed. 1964]). Even apart from vocabulary development, Dobrée's statement was incorrect; to give an elementary example, in discursive legal prose, as opposed to drafting, syntax came to be less tortuous (on the whole) during this period.

[10] Legal scholars have long been aware of terminological changes in law, as this turn-of-the-century statement demonstrates: "As our law develops it becomes more and more important to give definiteness to its phraseology; discriminations multiply, new situations and complications of fact arise, and the old outfit of ideas, discriminations, and phrases has to be carefully revised." James Bradley Thayer, *Preliminary Treatise on Evidence at the Common Law* 190 (1898).

legalese?[11] Even so, the oversight is a serious one, given the number of meritorious (some might say meretricious) headwords that are excluded purely because the lexicographer has no clue about their frequency in law, or perhaps even about their existence. Besides, readers would find that legalese is gradually fading away; it is not all that difficult nowadays for an educated layman to read, for example, the opinions of the United States Supreme Court.

A less plausible explanation for these oversights we may reject out of hand. Lexicographers do not view legal English as being largely outside their purview, since they include *per stirpes, remittitur, replevin,* and thousands of other purely legal terms in our general unabridged dictionaries.[12] Vallins's reference to a standard language having specialized language all around it calls to mind the famous statement from the preface to the *Oxford English Dictionary*: "the circle of the English language has a well-defined centre but no discernible circumference." The lexicographer, it is true, "must draw the line somewhere . . . , well knowing that the line which he draws will not satisfy all his critics."[13]

Well, here is one critic dissatisfied with the treatment accorded to legal language in our modern dictionaries, both legal and general. The circle as drawn is no circle at all: it is a pie with a piece missing. To illustrate the reasons for my dissatisfaction, I have collected a number of 20th-century neologisms that, despite their indisputable currency in law, remain nonwords in the pages of our most highly touted reference works.

---

[11] Presumably, also, the outside readers who volunteer to do systematic reading for a work like the *OED* do not ordinarily clamor for the law reports or law reviews.

In the preface to volume 3 of the *OED Supplement*, Burchfield acknowledged that "changes of emphasis or detail here and there" reflected "the research interests of scholars in various subjects, and the vicissitudes of the OED Department and of my own life" (p. v). Similarly, Frederick Mish, the editorial director at Merriam-Webster, has referred to the "strong influence of the editors' interests" on the selection of materials read for Merriam-Webster dictionaries. *See* John Willinsky, *Cutting English on the Bias: Five Lexicographers in Pursuit of the New*, 63 Am. Speech 44 (1988).

[12] Of one of the major American dictionary publishers, a scholar has (generously) written: "Though the Merriam Company admits the possibility of sometimes inadequate reading programs (as in mathematics, as noted in the preface to *6,000 Words*, p. 17a), secretarial errors, and/or debatable editorial judgment, their data are generally reliable because of the company's long-time integrity and huge continuing files . . . . While Merriam's bases for inclusion or noninclusion are a bit shadowy, their long experience precludes capricious decisions." Garland Cannon, *Viability: The Death of Recent New Items in English*, 38 Word 155, 157 (1987).

[13] Preface to the *Oxford English Dictionary* (1933).

Conclusory is perhaps the prime example. The word is included in the *OED* really as nothing but a needless variant of *conclusive*, and is illustrated by three 19th-century quotations. One finds no hint in the *OED* of the modern legal sense. *Webster's Second* lists it as "rare" for *conclusive*, and *Webster's Third* leaves it out altogether. The first edition of the *Random House* omitted it; the second edition revived it as a main entry, presumably because its editors began to run across the word in legal contexts, but they misdefined it by following the *OED* and giving *conclusive* as its synonym. Most law dictionaries are equally unavailing; the word appears in no law dictionary other than my own *Dictionary of Modern Legal Usage*, which defines the word as "expressing a mere conclusion of fact without stating the specific facts upon which the conclusion is based." Thus a border-patrol agent's statement, "He is an illegal alien," is conclusory, whereas "I saw him swim across the Rio Grande, and when I questioned him, he admitted that he had crossed the border illegally" is not.

An accurate dictionary entry for the word (modeled after *OED* entries) might appear as follows, the modern legal sense being sense (2):

> **conclusory** (kŏn-**klū**-sŏ-rē), *adj.* [f. L. *conclus-* ppl. stem + *-ory:* on L. type *conclūsōri-us] 1. Relating or tending to a conclusion; conclusive. *Rare.*
>
> **[1846] 1876** Contemp. Rev. XXVIII. 128
> This conciliatory and conclusory chapter.
>
> 2. *U.S.* Expressing a mere conclusion of fact or a factual inference without stating the underlying facts on which the conclusion or inference is based.
>
> **1923** *Ringler v. Jetter*, 201 N.Y.S. 525, 525 (App. Div.) The motion [is] granted, to the extent of directing the service of an amended complaint, omitting paragraphs 16, 17, and 30, and all conclusory matter of the nature pointed out herein. **1931** *Sprung v. Zalowitz*, 250 N.Y.S. 352, 354 (App. Div.) The description of the threats is conclusory in character. No facts are set out to support this conclusion. **1940** *People v. Hines*, 29 N.E.2d 483, 487 (N.Y.) Facts in detail supporting conclusory statements herein are available in the record. **1954** *Mietlinski v. Hickman*, 136 N.Y.S.2d 321, 325 (App. Div.) A conclusory statement by a layman on such a question is not entitled to substantial weight as an admission. **1985** *Oregon Dept. of Fish & Wildlife v. Klamath Indian Tribe*, 473 U.S. 753, 787 (Marshall, J., dissenting) Ultimately, this produces a largely insensitive and conclusory historical inquiry that ignores how events almost certainly appeared to the Tribe. **1987** *Senate of Puerto Rico v. U.S. Dept. of Justice*, 823 F.2d 574, 585 (D.C. Cir.) [I]t is enough to observe that

where no factual support is provided for an *essential* element of the claimed privilege or shield, the label "conclusory" is surely apt. **1988** *United States v. Chaudhry*, 850 F.2d 851, 857 (1st Cir.) [D]efendant relies on the bare, conclusory, and entirely self-serving assertion that such "selective recording [constituted] a violation of his right to due process, confrontation, and a fair trial."

A computer search of American judicial opinions, conducted in April 1988, revealed more than 21,000 cases in which *conclusory* appears.[14] It has been used for more than 60 years in state and federal courts, including the United States Supreme Court. Yet when a justice on the Wyoming Supreme Court felt the need to use the word in 1987, he was troubled by its omission from our collegiate dictionaries: "After painstaking deliberation," he wrote for the court, "we have decided that we like the word *conclusory*, and we are distressed by its omission from the English language. [As if omission from a dictionary equaled omission from the language!] We now proclaim that henceforth *conclusory* is appropriately used in the opinions of this court . . . . Webster's, take heed."[15]

The justice's reaction to the omission is laudable, and unusual. The more frequent reaction is for the dictionary-user to conclude, with exaggerated deference to the dictionary-maker, that the use of such a word is incorrect. Thus in the 1880s, a bill was thrown out of the British Parliament because one of the words used in it was not in "the dictionary"—a reference, naturally, to Johnson's work.[16] Several judges have actually tried to wage a minor battle against *conclusory* on grounds that it has no support in the dictionaries. Hence the lexicographers' oversight has led to confusion among legal writers, who often derive their views about right and wrong in language from dictionaries. (Few modern lexicographers, of course, labor on the assumption that their work will be relied on in this way.)

When *The New York Times* printed a story on *Modern Legal Usage* shortly after its publication in late 1987, the article suggested that I was "more accommodating" than "lawyer purists and nearly all dictionaries," which were said to "resist" *conclusory*.[17] The statement may be entirely

---

[14] On 25 April 1988, Charles Alan Wright wrote, in a letter to Judge Robert E. Keeton of Boston: "As of this morning the Allfeds database [of Westlaw] shows 12,248 documents in which *conclusory* appears, and the Allstates database has 9,365. This is 389 new federal instances and 681 new state instances in the last eight months."

[15] *Greenwood v. Wierdsma*, 741 P.2d 1079, 1086 n.3 (Wyo. 1987).

[16] *See* H. Whitehall, "The English Language," in *Webster's New World Dictionary* xxxii (1962).

[17] Laura Mansnerus, *Lawyer Talk? You Can Look It Up*, N.Y. Times, 11 Dec. 1987, at 18.

correct about the lawyer purists, but it is quite wrong about the lexicographers, who have simply overlooked much of the linguistic innovation in law.

Among the more than 30 legal neologisms that were first documented in *Modern Legal Usage* are *ancillarity, asylee, benefitee, certworthy, condemnee, conveyee, discriminatee, enbancworthy, enjoinable, litigational, nonrefoulement, pretextual, quashal, recusement,* and *veniremember.* To be sure, some of these words are more apt than others, but they have all gained currency in law. Like many other words that receive no mention in our unabridged dictionaries, they are used daily by American judges and lawyers. Would not the editors of, say, the second edition of the *Random House* have seized the opportunity to document these words, if only they had known of their existence and the extent of their use? And would not the users of that dictionary be better served if the words had been documented and defined?

Quashal, the noun corresponding to the verb *to quash,* is a striking example of a legal word that has been neglected in conventional English lexicography. The word dates back to the 1880s, when the Florida Supreme Court seems to have invented it: "Yet the judgment might . . . have been put there *nunc pro tunc* . . . with the effect of removing the ground of quashal."[18] Today this lexicographic ghost-word appears frequently (and usefully) in legal contexts.

Because the language of the law has remained largely untraversed by our best lexicographers since the days of Noah Webster (himself a lawyer), abundant inconsistencies have grown up within it. In the absence of authoritative dictionaries to settle questions about standard usages, competing neologisms—often, indeed usually, with no differentiation in sense—have cropped up. The opinions of the United States Supreme Court, for example, contain not just *conclusory,* but *conclusionary* and *conclusional* as well.[19] These two variants sprang up in federal-court opinions in the 1940s; since then, they have been largely ousted by *conclusory* (whose sense they share), though some legal writers persist in using them.

One might proliferate examples of the "choices to be made out of boundless variety." Restitution being a common subject in law, we find

---

[18] *Adams v. Higgins,* 1 So. 321, 324 (Fla. 1887). The reporter for the Texas Supreme Court soon adopted the word: "*Held,* that the court of appeals affirmed the quashal of the distress proceedings." *Brown v. Collins,* 14 S.W. 173, 173 (Tex. 1890) (case summary).

[19] *Conclusional* is a revival, not a neologism. The *OED* records uses from 1471 and 1695 (in the sense "final"), but nothing more recent. The Supreme Court used the word in 1954: "These conclusional allegations add nothing." *United States v. Employing Plasterers Assn.,* 347 U.S. 186, 192 (1954). Many other examples appear in American judicial opinions, though *conclusory* outnumbers *conclusional* by a ratio of about ten to one.

any number of examples of *restitutionary* and *restitutional* in law reports, although our unabridged dictionaries give only *restitutive* and *restitutory*. (These last two are little known to American lawyers.) Although our lexicographers keenly picked up *recusal*, a neologism dating from 1950, they are apparently unaware that, in some jurisdictions, *recusement* and *recusation* prevail.[20] The new *Random House* omits both of these. Though its battle for supremacy has certainly been lost to *injunctive*, the adjective *injunctional* might deserve a quick nod with more than 180 uses to its credit. What is the neutral adjective—that is, not *litigious*—corresponding to *litigation*? Even our most authoritative unabridged dictionaries do not tell us whether to use *litigational*, *litigatory*, or *litigation* itself. Most law dictionaries supply no help on these questions.[21]

Sadly for the lawyer—indeed, for anyone in need of legal-linguistic guidance—English-language dictionary-makers have been far more keen on recording novelties in the vocabulary of scientists and doctors than those in the vocabulary of lawyers, even though the legal word-hoard has been growing at a surprising rate. That is one of the many reasons why the law needs its own unabridged historical dictionary, to be for lawyers what the *OED* is for everyone else. Then lexicographers would no longer "resist" new legal words out of ignorance that they even exist.

Nor would we be mistakenly led to believe that a word like *adversarial* was first used in 1967, or thereabouts. That is what *Webster's Ninth New Collegiate Dictionary*, published in 1983, indicates is "the date of the earliest recorded use in English, as far as it could be determined."[22] A simple computer search of legal databases would have yielded this American

---

[20] The second edition of *Random House*, in accordance with its practice of dating the entry of words into the English language, gives 1955–1960 as the spread of years within which *recusal* first appeared; the *OED* gives 1958 as the earliest known date of the use of the word. Yet the word appeared at least eight years earlier, in an opinion of the Alabama Supreme Court: "On the 13th of April, Judge Longshore filed an order of *recusal* accompanied by an order vacating his former order." *Methvin v. Haynes*, 46 So.2d 815, 817 (Ala. 1950).

[21] Pre-1999 editions of *Black's* actually defined *litigious* as if it were a noun: "Litigious. That which is the subject of a lawsuit or action; that which is contested in a court of law. In another sense, 'litigious' signifies fond of litigation; prone to engage in suits." *Black's Law Dictionary* 841 (5th ed. 1979).

[22] *Webster's Ninth New Collegiate Dictionary* 17 (1983). *The Second Barnhart Dictionary of New English* (1980) also gives 1967 as the date of the earliest known use of the word, and erroneously suggests that the word is of British origin.

example from 1926: "No adversarial interest between parties is intrinsically involved."[23] That same computer search would have provided other specimens in law cases from 1949, 1952, and 1954.[24]

The ability to conduct computer searches has vastly improved our ability to monitor the entry of words into the legal lexicon.[25] Recently, for example, I came across the phrase *chicanerous litigant* in the celebrated treatise on federal practice by Professors Charles Alan Wright and Arthur Miller.[26] Not recognizing the adjective *chicanerous*, though its sense was clear, I turned to the second edition of the *Oxford English Dictionary* (to no avail), and then to *Webster's Third* (again to no avail). A computer search called up several uses of the word in published judicial opinions, the earliest dating from 1969.[27] Who would argue against the merits of having an adjective that corresponds to the noun *chicanery* (or *chicane*)? One wonders, however, whether we'll have to wait half a century before we can verify the word's existence in English-language dictionaries.

When it comes to neologisms, common-law English is, after all, not so very different from the common-law wife. Both live in the shadows, having attained a status of minimal respectability, even though they deserve better. Yet a large segment of the population continues to think that anything unsanctioned by the legislative codes is illicit. (Most people consult dictionaries precisely as if they were legislative codes.) How else can one explain why *common-law wife* is often loosely applied to a concubine or mistress?[28]

In venturing upon the *Oxford Law Dictionary*, of which I have assumed the chief editorship, the University of Texas School of Law and

---

[23] *McWilliams v. Hopkins*, 11 F.2d 793, 795 (S.D. Cal. 1926).

[24] For example: "This clearly shows an adversarial element which appears to have been absent in the Rainger case." *Brooks v. United States*, 84 F.Supp. 622, 629 (S.D. Cal. 1949). *See also Sanitary Farm Dairies v. Gammel*, 195 F.2d 106, 115 (8th Cir. 1952), and *Your Food Stores of Santa Fe, Inc. v. AFL*, 124 F.Supp. 697, 700–01 (D.N.M. 1954).

[25] *See* Fred R. Shapiro, *Legal Data Bases and Historical Lexicography*, 3 Legal Refs. Servs. Q. 85 (1983).

[26] "[I]t was believed that a pleading containing inconsistent allegations indicated falsehood on its face and was a sign of a chicanerous litigant seeking to subvert the judicial process." Charles Alan Wright & Arthur R. Miller, *Federal Practice and Procedure* vol. 5, § 1283, at 725 (3d ed. 1998).

[27] *See United States v. Jefferson*, 257 A.2d 225, 226 (D.C. 1969). *See also State v. Kay*, 350 A.2d 336, 337 (N.H. 1975) ("such unfair, deceptive, and chicanerous actions as the defendant is charged with committing").

[28] *See* David M. Walker, *Oxford Companion to Law* (1980), s.v. "common-law marriage."

Oxford University Press have done much to address the problem. If legal lexicography has been in a shambles over the past century, this historical law dictionary, following in the path of the *OED*, should go a long way toward rectifying the numerous lexical oversights in law. The fruits of the *Oxford Law Dictionary* should be of value to general English lexicographers. Among the least consequential advantages is that judges will no longer feel compelled to write, out of defensiveness about using a common legal word, "Webster's, take heed!"

Of greater consequence will be the ability of judges, lawyers, and scholars to determine what the old words meant, not what the new ones mean. For the first time, we will be able to determine how certain words were used and understood at specific points in the evolution of Anglo-American jurisprudence. Thus, what did *jurisdiction* generally mean in legal texts contemporaneous with the American Constitution? The *Oxford Law Dictionary* promises to rekindle the interpretative debate between those who hold to the original intention of constitutional and statutory framer and those who would give constitutional and statutory words their modern acceptations. The *Oxford Law Dictionary* will supply not just the missing common-law words, but the missing common-law meanings as well.

For the inauspicious end that befell the project, see the prefatory note to the preceding essay, on page 335.

ஐ ஐ ஐ

Preface to the First Pocket Edition
of *Black's Law Dictionary*

EVERY SUBJECT HAS its seminal reference book—the one that becomes a household word. When you think of world records, you think of *Guinness*; of encyclopedias, *Britannica*; of anatomy, *Gray's*; of music dictionaries, *Grove's*; of English-language dictionaries, *Webster* (in the U.S.) and *Oxford* (in the U.K.).

And whenever somebody thinks of law dictionaries, *Black's* seems inevitably to come to mind. Henry Campbell Black (1860–1927) first published his magnum opus in 1891, and his achievement might easily be taken for granted today. He entered a crowded field, for there were many law dictionaries then in print—several more major ones, in fact, than there are today. But who today, apart from the specialist, remembers the names of Anderson, Burrill, English, Kinney, Lawson, Rapalje, Sweet, Wharton, or even the better-known Bouvier?

What happened is that Henry Campbell Black's dictionary took the field and became incontestably supreme, partly because of his comprehensiveness, partly because of his academic standing, and partly because he had the good fortune of publishing his work with West Publishing Company.

Black's Law Dictionary has evolved over its six unabridged editions. And this pocket edition continues that evolution. Indeed, because it was compiled on modern lexicographic principles, the book you're holding is something of a radical leap forward in the evolutionary line.

Lexicographic Methods and Features

Little is known about exactly how Black and his contemporaries worked, but one thing is certain to anyone who has spent any time examining 19th-century and early-20th-century law dictionaries: a great deal of the "work" was accomplished through wholesale borrowing from other dictionaries. To cite but one example, in Bouvier (1839), Anderson (1890), Black (1891), Kinney (1893), Shumaker & Longsdorf (1901), and several other law dictionaries of the period, the phrase *disorderly house* is defined in the following word-for-word sequence: a "house the inmates of which

From *Black's Law Dictionary* (1st pocket ed. 1996).

behave so badly as to become a nuisance to the neighborhood." Hundreds of other definitions are virtually verbatim from book to book.

Although this practice of heavy borrowing is suspect today, it may be wrong to judge these early lexicographers by modern standards. They might have copied for various reasons. First, even nonspecialist lexicographers of the time commonly borrowed from each other; that is, apart from a few notable exceptions such as Samuel Johnson (1709–1784), Noah Webster (1758–1843), and James A.H. Murray (1837–1915—the first editor of the *Oxford English Dictionary*), a high percentage of entries in early English-language dictionaries were directly traceable to even earlier dictionaries. Second, dictionary editors in the legal field were trained as common-law lawyers, under the Anglo-American system of precedent. As a result, they might have thought that accuracy precluded a reconsideration of their predecessors' words—especially if the earlier dictionary-maker cited caselaw in support of a definition. And third, notions of plagiarism were much less well defined than they are today (and, in any event, have always been looser in lexicography than elsewhere).

But the result of all this is that, as the legal language has grown, law dictionaries have generally strayed further and further afield from actual legal usage. Instead of monitoring legal language for new entries—words that emerge in a given practice area, legal slang that crops up in a certain context, words that take on meanings different from their traditional ones—compilers of law dictionaries have tended to look too much at their forerunners.

This book, however, represents a stem-to-stern (very stern) reconsideration of legal terms—an entirely fresh edition of *Black's Law Dictionary* compiled on modern lexicographic methods. This means that my colleagues and I have done several things:

- Attempted a thorough marshaling of the language of the law from original sources. Many terms make their debut in this edition.
- Examined the writings of specialist scholars rather than looking only at judicial decisions.
- Considered entries entirely anew rather than merely accepting what previous editions have said. We have often checked Westlaw and other sources when trying to decide which of two competing forms now predominates in legal usage.
- Imposed analytical rigor on entries by avoiding duplicative definitions and by cataloguing and numbering senses.
- Shown pronunciations that reflect how American lawyers actually say the words and phrases—not how English lawyers used to say them (and not how Latin teachers would have us say them).

- Recorded cognate forms—for example, the verb and adjective corresponding to a given noun.
- Ensured that specialized vocabularies are included—from bankruptcy to securities law, from legal realism to critical legal studies.

As a result, this book represents a balanced and up-to-date treatment of legal terms—even within the strict confines of a pocket dictionary.

≥ ≥ ≥

Preface to the Seventh Edition
of *Black's Law Dictionary*

WHEN HENRY CAMPBELL BLACK published the first edition of *Black's Law Dictionary* back in 1891, the *Oxford English Dictionary* had not yet been completed. Nor was the *OED* finished when Black prepared his second edition in 1910. By today's standards, the "gentle art of lexicography,"[1] as it has been called, was yet to experience the tremendous dictionary-making developments that the 20th century had in store, the highlights being the *OED* (1928), *Webster's Second* (1934), *Webster's Third* (1961), and the second edition of the *OED* (1989). Largely through the influence of these major works, dictionaries today are much better than they used to be.

Legal scholarship has also made tremendous strides—even in describing pre-19th-century law. The great legal historians Pollock, Maitland, and Holdsworth had not yet produced their monumental works when Black put out the first edition. Our understanding of Roman law is better today than it was a century ago. Our understanding of feudal law is much better. Meanwhile, our precedent-based system still has not entirely escaped the influence of Roman and feudal law.

At the same time, modern law hurtles headlong into decade after decade of new statutes, new doctrines, and new tripartite tests. The world—as well as the law that tries to govern it—is changing at a dizzying pace. If you want evidence of this change, look inside for the hundreds of new entries such as *cyberstalking, jurimetrics, parental kidnapping, quid pro quo sexual harassment, reproductive rights,* and *viatical settlement.*

Given all these developments—both in lexicography and in law—it is hardly surprising that, by the end of the 20th century, *Black's Law Dictionary* had come to need a major overhaul. This edition is the result of that effort.

New Features in the Seventh Edition

Significant strides have been made both in modernizing this edition and in improving its historical depth. The editors' goal was to make it at

---

From *Black's Law Dictionary* (7th ed. 1999).

[1] Eric Partridge, *The Gentle Art of Lexicography, as Pursued and Experienced by an Addict* (1963).

once the most scholarly and the most practical edition ever published. More than 4,500 entries in the book are entirely new. (Some of the new entries are surprising: previous editions had omitted some commonplace terms such as *act of Congress*, *circuit judge*, *motion for summary judgment*, *senatorial courtesy*, and *sidebar comment*.) Of the remaining 20,000 entries, all have been thoroughly revised: sharpened and tightened.

Aside from the thousands of new entries and subentries, the differences between earlier editions and this one are many. The headwords show whether a term should be uppercase or lowercase, roman or italic. The pronunciation symbols are easy to understand. For the first time ever, etymologies systematically appear. Senses of words are analytically broken down and given numbers—as never before. Definitions are clearer than ever (though the battle for clarity, when the subject is feudal law, can never be completely won). Bullets now appear within definitions to help differentiate definitional information (before the bullet) from encyclopedic information (after the bullet). More than 2,000 newly added quotations from some 400 important works of Anglo-American legal scholarship appear throughout the text to help convey the nuances of the legal vocabulary. (More about these in a moment.) The 2,200 legal maxims, mostly Latin, are conveniently collected in an appendix, instead of cluttering the main lexicon. In addition, my colleagues and I have:

- Attempted a thorough marshaling of the language of the law from original sources.
- Examined the writings of specialist scholars rather than looking only at judicial decisions.
- Considered entries entirely anew rather than merely accepting what previous editions have said. We have often checked Westlaw and other sources when trying to decide which of two competing forms now predominates in legal usage.
- Imposed analytical rigor on entries by avoiding duplicative definitions and by cataloguing and numbering senses.
- Ensured that specialized vocabularies are included—from bankruptcy to securities law, from legal realism to critical legal studies.

This modern approach to legal lexicography is only a beginning. To its great credit, the West Group has now made the editing of *Black's Law Dictionary*, in its various editions, an ongoing project. This means that *Black's*, like all major dictionaries outside the law, will be a continuing work in progress. As the law continues its rapid evolution, *Black's Law Dictionary* will keep apace.

The Inclusion of Scholarly Quotations

In a novel feature, more than 2,000 quotations from scholarly works appear throughout the text to help round out the treatment of various terms. In selecting these quotations, my colleagues and I have sought a blend of characteristics: temporal and geographic range, aptness, and insight. Some scholars show great astuteness in discussing terminology—particularly Blackstone (English law), Glanville Williams (criminal law and jurisprudence), Rollin Perkins (criminal law), and Charles Alan Wright (federal procedure). Although Blackstone and Wright are well known to American lawyers, Williams and Perkins are not: their work deserves more widespread attention.

In the List of Works Cited (Appendix H) appear the 400-plus lawbooks cited in these pages. We have tried to locate the best scholarly discussions of legal terminology and to give snippets of them. In future editions, we intend to continue this practice, and we encourage readers to submit published quotations for this purpose.

The Challenge of Legal Lexicography

Law dictionaries have a centuries-old tradition of apologizing in advance for errors and omissions. Some of the apologies are moving—especially to one who understands the arduousness of lexicography—and a few border on the humorous:

> **1607:** "[I]f I have either omitted any hard word within my circuit, or set it downe not expounded, I give you good leave to impute the one to my negligence, the other to mine ignorance: and so commend these my paines to your best profit, and you unto God."[2]

> **1670:** "If I have sometimes committed a *Jeofaile*, or hunted Counter in any explication or Etymology, in so large a field of words, and stor'd with such variety of Game, it will be no wonder, and, I hope, will draw no censure upon me from the Ingenuous . . . . [I]f I leave some words with a *Quaere* . . . to be resolved or corrected by the more learned; it is but what Cowell frequently, and Spelman has sometimes done."[3]

> **1732:** "[W]here there is such great Variety of Learning and abundant Quantity of Nice Matter, with the utmost Care, there must be some Faults and Failings to be Pardon'd by the Reader."[4]

---

[2] John Cowell, *The Interpreter* 5 (1607).
[3] Thomas Blount, *Nomo-Lexicon: A Law-Dictionary* [n.p.] (1670).
[4] Giles Jacob, *A New Law-Dictionary* 4 (2d ed. 1732).

1839: "To those who are aware of the difficulties of the task, the author deems it unnecessary to make any apology for the imperfections which may be found in the work. His object has been to be useful; if that has been accomplished in any degree, he will be amply rewarded for his labour; and he relies upon the generous liberality of the members of the profession to overlook the errors which may have been committed in his endeavours to serve them."[5]

1848: "It is not without very considerable diffidence, that this Lexicon is submitted to the indulgence of the Profession and the Public, for no man can be more conscious of the difficulties besetting such a subject—of the many requisites of the task—and above all, of the great discrepancy usually exhibited between what a book *ought to be*, and what it *is*—than the Author of the present undertaking."[6]

1859: "[T]he work is now submitted to the examination of the profession. That its execution has fallen far short of its design, is already but too apparent to the author's own observation. Of the defects that may be discovered in its pages, some seem to be inseparable from the task of first compiling any matter of the kind from sources so numerous, and scattered over so wide a field."[7]

1874: "[W]ithout craving the indulgence of the public, whose servant he is, and to whom, therefore, if he serve up anything he should in all conscience serve up a proper dish, [the Author] is reluctant to acknowledge that an unaccustomed feeling of diffidence has once or twice assailed him, lest his work should not prove so absolutely faultless or so generally useful as it has been his wish to make it."[8]

In the first edition of this book (1891), Henry Campbell Black broke the tradition, boldly asserting the exhaustiveness of his work:

"The dictionary now offered to the profession is the result of the author's endeavor to prepare a concise and yet comprehensive book of definitions of the terms, phrases, and maxims used in American and English law and necessary to be understood by the working lawyer and judge, as well as those important to the student of legal history or comparative jurisprudence . . . . Of the most esteemed law dictionaries now in use, each will be found to contain a very considerable number of words not defined in any other. None is quite comprehensive in itself. The author has made it his aim to include *all* these terms and phrases here, together with some not elsewhere defined."[9]

---

[5] John Bouvier, *A Law Dictionary* viii (1839).
[6] J.J.S. Wharton, *The Legal Lexicon, or Dictionary of Jurisprudence* iii (1st Am. ed. 1848).
[7] Alexander M. Burrill, *A Law Dictionary and Glossary* xv (1859).
[8] Archibald Brown, *A New Law Dictionary* vi (1874).
[9] Henry Campbell Black, *A Dictionary of Law* iii (1891).

There is no lack of confidence expressed anywhere in his preface.

Yet in putting forth this seventh edition, I confess that my feelings incline more to those of Black's predecessors than to those of Black himself.

A Lot of Help from Our Friends

Diffidence, though, can lead to safeguards. And so it has in this work. I engaged several distinguished scholars who thoroughly vetted the entire manuscript:

- Tony Honoré, former holder of the Regius Chair in Civil Law at Oxford University, and author of many important books, including *Causation in the Law* (with H.L.A. Hart).

- Joseph F. Spaniol Jr., former Clerk of the Supreme Court of the United States, whose wide-ranging experience includes decades of service in federal rulemaking as a consultant to the Standing Committee on Rules of Practice and Procedure.

- David M. Walker, former holder of the Regius Chair in Civil Law at Glasgow University, perhaps the most prolific legal writer in the British Isles, and author of the renowned *Oxford Companion to Law* (1980).

Additionally, in about a third of the manuscript, we had the help of Hans W. Baade, holder of the Hugh Lamar Stone Chair in Civil Law at the University of Texas. He is a comparativist of the first rank whose expertise ranges from domestic relations to international transactions to conflict of laws.

On the editorial side, several of my colleagues at LawProse, Inc. played crucial roles. David W. Schultz, a seasoned editor who joined the *Black's* team in 1995, was invaluable in producing both the pocket edition (which appeared in 1996) and this unabridged edition. His editorial judgments have improved every page. Lance A. Cooper, an aspiring legal historian, joined the team in 1997, working skillfully on thousands of entries for more than 18 months. Elizabeth C. Powell arrived in 1998, bringing with her a keen intellect, ten years of lawyerly experience, and an amazing capacity for hard work. All three—Schultz, Cooper, and Powell—are splendid lawyers who, not so long ago, never imagined they would one day be legal lexicographers. Yet they learned dictionary-making as the best lexicographers do: on the job. And they've become quite accomplished.

When it came to pronunciations, though, I knew we needed someone already expert in the art. This dictionary presents extraordinary

challenges to a pronunciation editor, being full of Latin and French as
well as Law Latin (the impure Latin of Renaissance lawyers) and Law
French (the Norman French of medieval lawyers). Fortunately, Charles
Harrington Elster of San Diego, an orthoepist with several excellent
books to his credit, was willing to take on the task. He wisely guided us
through the confusing mazes of Anglo-Latin, the only type of Latin with
a continuous tradition in Anglo-American law. Even if some of the pronunciations strike you at first as odd, you can be sure that there is sound
authority for them.

On translating Greek, Latin, and French, we had the benefit of many
scholars' expertise. Professors Honoré and Walker supplied many of our
etymologies. So did Edward Carawan and Alison Parker, both of whom
hold Ph.D.s in Classics; they examined all the maxims listed in Appendix
A and supplied new translations and annotations for them.

As the manuscript deadline approached, I asked 30 judges, lawyers,
and academics—mostly practicing lawyers—to read and comment on a
batch of 150 pages of manuscript each. All of them generously agreed. I
am enormously grateful to each of these learned lawyers:

Paul H. Anderson	James K. Logan
Beverly Ray Burlingame	Margaret I. Lyle
Jordan B. Cherrick	Kent N. Mastores
Charles Dewey Cole Jr.	Lann G. McIntyre
Dana Fabe	Paul G. McNamara
Stephen F. Fink	John W. McReynolds
Neal Goldfarb	Wayne Moore
C. Kenneth Grosse	James L. Nelson
Harris L. Hartz	R. Eric Nielsen
Molly H. Hatchell	George C. Pratt
Lynn N. Hughes	Carol Marie Stapleton
Susan L. Karamanian	Scott Patrick Stolley
Joseph Kimble	Randall M. Tietjen
Edward J. Kionka	Carla L. Wheeler
Harriet Lansing	Richard C. Wydick
Clyde D. Leland	

What I hadn't fully reckoned, when sending out batches of manuscript,
was how challenging it would be to integrate more than 4,500 pages of
lightly to heavily edited text. Evaluating and entering the edits into our
database took three full-time lawyers the better part of six weeks. Fortunately, Beverly Ray Burlingame of Dallas, an immensely talented editor
and prodigiously hard worker, took time off from her busy law practice
to help complete the project. She made huge contributions during the
final stage.

But hers was not the only extraordinary act of voluntarism. During the final months, Michael L. Atchley of Dallas, upon learning of our deadline, began sending us draft entries for several hundred terms that were missing from the sixth edition. His broad legal knowledge, as well as his natural aptitude for lexicography, showed in all his work. Then he generously read and commented on large stacks of manuscript.

Several lawyers made important contributions beyond those I've already described. Ann Taylor Schwing of Sacramento painstakingly culled through the 90 volumes of *Words and Phrases* for possible inclusions, and she read large portions of the manuscript. Elizabeth Sturdivant Kerr of Fort Worth contributed drafts of many entries for the letters E, H, and T, and she read much of the manuscript. Michelle D. Monse of Dallas contributed drafts of many L entries. Stephen W. Kotara of Dallas contributed to the letters F and G. Meanwhile, Terrence W. Kirk of Austin submitted many helpful drafts of criminal-law definitions.

As the work progressed, I occasionally ran queries by scholars in various legal specialties, and they all responded helpfully. Many thanks to J.H. Baker, Peter Butt, Robert W. Hamilton, Herbert J. Hammond, Geoffrey C. Hazard Jr., Gideon Kanner, Robert E. Keeton, John S. Lowe, Neil MacCormick, Joseph W. McKnight, Sir Robert Megarry, Richard A. Posner, William C. Powers Jr., Thomas M. Reavley, Christoph Schreuer, and Charles Alan Wright. In a specialized review, Marc I. Steinberg commented on the business-law terms throughout the book.

Several universities provided significant assistance. While working on the project, I was an adjunct professor at Southern Methodist University School of Law. Meanwhile, I had stints as a visiting scholar at the University of Glasgow (July 1996), under the sponsorship of Professor David M. Walker; at the University of Cambridge (July 1997), under the sponsorship of Vice-Chancellor Emeritus Sir David Williams; and at the University of Salzburg (July 1998), under the sponsorship of Professors Wolfram Karl and Christoph Schreuer. I used the libraries at each of those universities to good advantage. I also made good use of the renowned Tarlton Law Library at the University of Texas (thanks to Professor Roy M. Mersky and his colleagues). And the entire *Black's* team constantly used the Underwood Law Library at Southern Methodist University (thanks to Professor Gail Daly and her colleagues). Also, I was able to carry out some research at the Langdell Law Library at Harvard University. To all of these libraries and their staffs, I am grateful for the cordial help they unfailingly gave.

Professor Mersky helped in another notable way: he and several of his colleagues—Beth Youngdale, Marlyn Robinson, and Monika Szakasits—generously verified the accuracy of our List of Works Cited (Appendix H).

Five research assistants—extraordinarily talented law students at Southern Methodist University School of Law—verified citations throughout the book. The editors are much indebted to Daniel Alexander, Julie Buffington, Nicole Schauf Gambrell, Peggy Glenn-Summitt, and Kenneth E. Shore. I especially thank Julie Buffington for organizing this team and ensuring the timely completion of a complex task.

Karen Magnuson of Portland, Oregon, who has worked on several of my other books, courageously proofread the entire 3,500-page single-spaced manuscript as we worked through the final draft. Her talents as a proofreader are, in my experience, unmatched.

Many others contributed to the book in various ways: the late Alexander Black of Rochester began a reading program to gather illustrative quotations for our files; Thomas G. Fleming of Rochester continued that program for most of its duration; Caroline B. Garner of Dallas located historical legal terms in early dictionaries; E.N. Genovese of San Diego helped supply some foreign pronunciations; Tanya Glenn of Dallas typed the initial list of maxims; Michael Greenwald of Philadelphia helped on terms relating to the American Law Institute; and Tinh T. Nguyen of Dallas, with unusual enthusiasm, carried out the tedious but necessary task of checking cross-references and alphabetization.

At the West Group, David J. Oliveiri, Doug Powell, John Perovich, and Brendan Bauer had the imagination and the forcefulness to make the book a reality. Their logistical support, not to mention their moral support, helped everyone involved in the project. In the production department, Kathy Walters worked wonders to produce the book within a tight deadline.

Tremendous amounts of talent and toil have gone into the making of this book. Yet the worries of early lexicographers have a haunting ring: this work might not prove as absolutely faultless as it has been my wish to make it. If that turns out to be so, as it inevitably will, I can only hope that readers will recognize the genuine merits residing in these pages.

ð ð ð

Preface to *A Handbook of Family Law Terms*

OF ALL LEGAL FIELDS, family law—known also as *domestic-relations law* or simply as *domestic relations*—is the one that affects most people's lives most directly. It is also probably the field that traditional legal lexicography has most neglected over the years. The terminology is varied and vast, and it often differs from state to state.

So this book, the fourth in the line of glossaries known as the Black's Law Dictionary Series, is perhaps the most ambitious one in the series. Far from being a mere culling of family-law terms from the seventh edition of *Black's Law Dictionary*, this work reflects a painstaking review of recent family-law literature.

Although many points of family law are traceable back more than two millennia to Roman law, many others are quite recent. Family law is a fast-changing field. This is perhaps most dramatically illustrated in the fact that it is now possible—thanks to modern technology and developing legal theories of parenthood—for a child to have as many as 16 parents:

- biological mother;
- biological father;
- gestational mother;
- intentional mother;
- intentional father;
- foster mother;
- foster father;
- adoptive mother;
- adoptive father;
- de facto mother;
- de facto father;
- stepmother;
- stepfather;
- psychological mother;
- psychological father;
- legal father (the husband of whoever is found to be the mother).

How could a single child have all these parents? It would be an improbable saga reminiscent of a Charles Dickens or Victor Hugo novel, but it's

---

From *A Handbook of Family Law Terms* (2001).

hardly impossible given today's technology and legal doctrines. An infertile couple decides to have a child (Leslie), so the doctors take sperm from a man (the biological father) and an egg from a woman (the biological mother), and they implant the fertilized egg into a woman (the gestational mother); the infertile couple are the intentional parents who raise Leslie. These parents die, and Leslie is put into the care of two foster parents until she is taken into the home of her adoptive parents. These adoptive parents divorce, and both begin living with significant others who support Leslie emotionally and financially; these unmarried significant others become the de facto mother and the de facto father. The adoptive parents leave their significant others and separately remarry the persons who become Leslie's two stepparents. Both of Leslie's adoptive parents begin suffering from a debilitating mental disease, and a woman who is a family friend bonds with Leslie and becomes her psychological mother; the same happens with a male family friend, who becomes her psychological father. Leslie's biological mother then sues for custody, and the court decides in her favor over the stepparents and the psychological parents; the biological mother's husband (married even when she donated the egg several years before) is declared by the court to be Leslie's legal father.

As all this suggests, traditional notions of what constitutes a family have yielded to newer theories—even to the extent that "family law" now resolves disputes involving unmarried cohabitants and those who participate in novel means of reproduction. As one commentator eloquently says, it's cutting-edge and it's controversial:

> Family law is now central to many of the most difficult, and emotional, of social issues: Should same-sex couples be able to marry? Should couples who live together without marriage be entitled to benefits that have traditionally been available only to "family members"? Should a law degree be considered marital property to be "divided" at divorce? Who is the mother of a child born to one woman with genetic material from another? Should a lesbian "co-parent" be able to adopt her partner's child? Absent an adoption, should she have an entitlement to visitation when her relationship with the child's mother ends?[1]

From a moral point of view, some people lament the modern trends as indicators of contemporary decadence. Others cheer them as harbingers of more expansive and liberating ways of dealing with clanship in modern society. Still others would view the question in a neutral way: the modern view of family relationships has simply had to evolve in a society in which most children born today aren't reared in a traditional household of two parents of the opposite sex who are married to each other indefinitely. Modern life isn't so tidy—and maybe life never was.

---

[1] Harry D. Krause et al., *Family Law: Cases, Comments, and Questions* 8–9 (4th ed. 1998).

Our vocabulary reflects the realities of a changing world. Sadly, many terms in these pages deal with abuse (e.g., *secondary abuse*), neglect (e.g., *developmental neglect*), delinquency (e.g., *blended sentence*), miscellaneous other crimes (e.g., *impairing the morals of a minor*), and broken promises (e.g., *deadbeat dad*). Meanwhile, old categories such as *bastard* and *illegitimate child* don't work very well in a society in which one-third of all children are born outside marriage.[2]

The terminology with which we describe family law is a fascinating mixture of the old and the new. Aunts and uncles are pretty much what they used to be, but now we have all kinds of newish words and phrases, from *advance directive* to *family leave* to *parental-consent statute* to *wrongful adoption*.

When you add in legislative neologisms, not to mention names of various federal and uniform statutes, there's enough to keep lexicographers quite busy for nearly a year.

That's what it took to prepare this book, and I had some extraordinary help in preparing it. Cynde L. Horne, a talented lawyer with years of experience in family practice, researched and drafted hundreds of entries and edited the entire manuscript. David W. Schultz researched and drafted dozens of entries. Tiger Jackson painstakingly checked all cross-references and proofread the entire manuscript; she also contributed many draft entries. Once again, as with my other books in recent years, Karen L. Magnuson proofread the manuscript three times and, as always, improved it at each stage.

This book was complicated enough that I decided to engage several specialists to read the manuscript: two academics, a judge, and a practitioner. Professor Lucy McGough of Louisiana State University read and commented extensively on the manuscript in two batches. So did Judge Janice M. Rosa of the New York Family Court in Buffalo. Their erudition has improved every page.

After incorporating Professor McGough's and Judge Rosa's suggestions, I asked Professor Joseph W. McKnight of Southern Methodist University and Dawn Fowler, a Dallas practitioner, to read through the manuscript. They both had many valuable suggestions even at that late stage, and I was fortunate that they were willing to devote the time necessary for a close review on short notice.

For all this excellent help from so many quarters, I am grateful. My hope is that the book will prove useful not only to family-law judges and practitioners everywhere, but also to anyone who needs a better understanding of this important legal field.

---

[2] Tamar Lewin, *Is Social Stability Subverted If You Answer 'I Don't'?* N.Y. Times, 4 Nov. 2000, at A21 (contrasting the current figure of 1 in 3 children born out of wedlock to the 1960 figure of 1 in 20).

❧ ❧ ❧

Preface to Rastell's *Exposition of Certain Difficult and Obscure Wordes* (1579)

JOHN RASTELL (1470?–1536), a printer and barrister of Lincoln's Inn, wrote and then published the first edition of this book in 1527. Originally, it was in Law Latin and Law French. In the second edition of 1530, a parallel English translation was added—perhaps by Rastell's son William (1508?–1565), who had been studying law at Oxford and would soon become a barrister himself. This seventh edition reflects the joint efforts of father and son. A reviser named Paget (a barrister of the Middle Temple) may also have contributed to the work, although it is unclear whether his unacknowledged contributions appeared in this posthumous 1579 edition or in one of the three editions printed in the 1590s.[1]

The Rastells' work is notable in several ways. First, it is a lexicographic landmark because it antedates by 11 years the first general English dictionary, written by Sir Thomas Elyot.[2] Second, for its time it was a sophisticated piece of lexicography that would provide definitions for legal terms in other dictionaries for generations to come.[3] Third, the side-by-side translations marked a typographic innovation for dictionary-makers; apart from the typefaces, the columns look surprisingly modern more than 400 years later. Fourth, the dictionary had an extraordinary life through 29 editions that spanned a period of 292 years (the final American edition having appeared in 1819)—a longevity that few if any other lawbooks can rival.

This seventh edition, the last one printed by Richard Tottell of London, incorporated several new features. For the first time, Kentish customs (e.g., *gavelkind*) and various antiquarian civil-law terms appeared. The civil-law additions seem to have been borrowed from the 15th-century legal wordbook entitled *Expositiones vocabulorum*. And with this edition the book took on a new title: *An Exposition of Certain Difficult and Obscure Wordes, and Termes of the Lawes of This Realme.* Earlier editions had all used

---

Reprinted (with this introduction) by the Lawbook Exchange in 2004.

[1] *See* John D. Cowley, *A Bibliography of Abridgments, Digests, Dictionaries, and Indexes of English Law to the Year 1800* lxxxiii (1932).

[2] Sir Thomas Elyot, *The English Dictionarie* (1538).

[3] *See* De Witt T. Starnes & Gertrude E. Noyes, *The English Dictionary from Cawdrey to Johnson 1604–1755* 35, 40, 49–50 (1946) (noting that John Bullokar (1616), Thomas Blount (1656), Edward Phillips (1658), and Henry Cockeram (1670) borrowed heavily from Rastell—and through the 18th century still other writers borrowed from them).

expositions (or the Latinate *expositiones*) in the plural. For example, the sixth edition of 1575 had been called *The Expositions of the Termes of the Lawes of England*. It was not until the 16th edition of 1624 that the book became known by the now-familiar title: *Les Termes de la Ley*.

Pre-1600 editions of this book are rare. Modern researchers are fortunate that the Lawbook Exchange has made the 1579 edition so broadly available in this handsome reprint.

ૐ ૐ ૐ

Introduction to Cunningham's
New and Complete Law-Dictionary
(3d ed. 1783)

TIMOTHY CUNNINGHAM (1718?–1789), the compiler of this book, was
sanguine about lexicography: "Nothing can contribute more to the
knowledge of any art or science, than a Dictionary of it, compiled with
attention and care, and digested with skill and method . . ." (preface). His
efforts produced the most copious of 18th-century law dictionaries—an
attempt to restate the whole of the law and to arrange it alphabetically.
Hence his subtitle: "General Abridgment of the Law."

In calling his work an "abridgment," Cunningham was following a
tradition begun in the 15th century of trying to restate the whole of
English law in a single text, but all within an alphabetical arrangement.
Only one other writer, Giles Jacob (1686–1744), had ever taken this
approach. The result (for both Cunningham and Jacob) was more of an
encyclopedia than a dictionary in the modern sense.

Seizing the Opportunity

The modern reader might wonder what led Cunningham, a barrister, to
compile this tome. The record is sketchy, but three motivations seem
clear enough. First, Cunningham had already shown a propensity to
write. When the first edition of the dictionary appeared in 1764–1765,
he had already written three books: *A New Treatise on the Law Concerning
Tithes* (3d ed. 1748); *The Practice of a Justice of the Peace* (1762); and *The
History of the Customs, Aids, Subsidies, National Debts, and Taxes of England*
(3d ed. 1764). Second, he was undoubtedly aware of the great fame and
success that Samuel Johnson's magisterial *Dictionary of the English Language* had brought to Johnson just nine years before—in 1775.[1] And
third, he was acutely conscious of what was surely the most successful
reference book of the 18th century: Giles Jacob's *New Law Dictionary*,
first published in 1729 and already in an eighth edition by 1762.

Twenty years after Jacob's death (in 1744), Cunningham wanted to
supplant his work. He said so in his original preface of March 1764.

Reprinted (with this introduction) by the Lawbook Exchange in 2003.

[1] *See generally* James H. Sledd & Gwin J. Kolb, *Dr. Johnson's Dictionary: Essays in the Biography of a Book* (1955).

As reprinted verbatim in this third edition, Cunningham suggested that readers would find his book superior to that of his rivals (his only real rival being Jacob): "Nothing more need be said in favour of the utility of the work proposed: it remains only to see, in what amount it will be executed, and in what respect it will be more useful than, or preferable to, the other performances of a similar nature that have been published" (preface).

What Cunningham didn't realize, apparently, is that readers—even lawyer–readers—inevitably prefer one manageable volume (like Jacob's) over two bulky ones (like Cunningham's). This bulk, more than any other fact, probably accounts for why Cunningham's law dictionary was at an end after his third edition of 1783 was published. It wouldn't be reprinted for another 220 years (until this very reprinting by the Lawbook Exchange). One can understand the 20th-century commentator who wrote, partly in reference to Cunningham, that "[t]he law-dictionary had now grown beyond the bounds of reason and was suffering from the same complaint as the abridgments of the seventeenth and early eighteenth centuries; in both cases too much matter was included without arrangement."[2]

Jacob's more compact dictionary proved more durable. It went into a tenth edition in 1782, was later enlarged in 1797 by Thomas Edlyne Tomlins in an 11th edition, and finally evolved into Tomlins's own 19th-century dictionaries, the last of which appeared in 1834. Cunningham's prediction that users would find his dictionary "more useful than, or preferable to, the other performances"—i.e., competing works—wasn't borne out.

The Lexicographer as Copyist

But what of the scholarly merits of the book? Notably, Cunningham's early employment was as a copyist.[3] This shows throughout, although it would take a lifetime's work for a modern researcher to track down all the sources. Consider the entry here for *agreement*. It runs to more than eight long columns (compared to three in the 1772 edition of Jacob [the ninth edition]). Paragraph after paragraph consists of quotations from statutes and other sources. In fact, almost every paragraph in Jacob's 1772 dictionary appears also in Cunningham's 1783 edition, with little variation.

---

[2] John D. Cowley, *A Bibliography of Abridgments, Digests, Dictionaries, and Indexes of English Law to the Year 1800* xcii (1932).

[3] *See Dictionary of National Bibliography* vol. 5, 318 (1917).

Beginning in the second full paragraph in the fourth full column on *agreement* ("The common law required . . ."), 12 full paragraphs of text are reproduced verbatim, with the same citations at the end of each paragraph.

So the question is, Who copied whom? In this instance (though hardly in all), Cunningham fares well: the relevant passage under *agreement* is missing from the 1762 eighth edition of Jacob, but it is present in the 1764–1765 first edition of Cunningham. It appears that the two revisers of Jacob's ninth edition—Owen Ruffhead and J. Morgan—"greatly enlarged" Jacob (as their preface states) by copying from Cunningham (as their preface doesn't state). All quite fascinating.

But there's more. In the 12 paragraphs I've cited—apart from Cunningham's seemingly erroneous interpolation of a second "Section 4" of the statute quoted under *agreement*—the typesetting (ignoring column breaks) is identical in the competitors' books. The line breaks are at the same spots line after line. This suggests that the typesetters may have played a significant role in bulking up 18th-century lawbooks: if the plates of movable type were set in a form that could be reused, the typesetters may have been in a position to help one compiler by incorporating material from another compiler's work.

One other point supports this inference. Many of the people for whom the printers worked were the same for both Jacob in 1772 and Cunningham in 1783: J. and F. Rivington; S. Crowder; T. Longman; W. Flexney; and G. Robinson. They're all mentioned on both title pages. Overlapping interests in the publishing business may well account for the uncanny sameness of the typesetting.

As a literary form, lexicography was still inchoate. It wasn't until the bloody dictionary battles of the early 19th century—especially from 1830 to 1864 in the United States, with publisher-fueled battles raging between Noah Webster and Joseph Worcester[4]—that competitors grew wary of the wholesale copying of one another's work.

Some Notable Entries

Many items in this book will prove interesting to professional and amateur historians alike. The entry for *infant* provides insight into how the law regarded children, their capabilities, their rights, and their responsibilities. Some of the law is similar to 21st-century legal norms. The entry

---

[4] *See* Sidney I. Landau, *Dictionaries: The Art and Craft of Lexicography* 72–74 (2d ed. 2001).

includes a lengthy account of a toddler's grotesque killing committed by a 10-year-old boy, who was eventually convicted of murder and sentenced to death. The exposition of the case, as well as its outcome, is well worth reading, especially now that the topic of capital punishment for minors has become fodder for headlines.

Other entries reveal a world unrelated to ours. *Free-bench* referred to a widow's dower estate in copyhold. Cunningham's entry describes how, if the widow forfeited her estate through a forbidden act, she could recover the land by entering the court riding backwards on a black ram, and then, while holding the ram's tail in her hand, reciting these words:

> Here I am
> Riding on a black ram
> Like a whore I am
> And for my *crincrum crancrum*
> Have left my *bincum bancum*
> And for my tail's game
> Have done this worldly shame.
> Therefore I pray you, Mr. Steward, let me have my land again.

In these lines—and between them—we get a glimpse of how the law treated women.

Some of the long, encyclopedic entries here also make for fascinating reading. They are essentially the Nutshells of their time, summaries of the law and its permutations distilled into a handful of pages. Even a nonexpert in law could gain some understanding of a subject—or at least appreciate how a seemingly simple matter can really be quite complex. For example, in a little more than nine pages, the entry for *fraud* not only defines the term but also explains what kinds of acts are considered fraudulent, addresses fraudulent conveyances to defeat creditors and purchasers, and describes the penalties for fraud—all under appropriate headings. This coverage is much more thorough than the entry in Jacob's dictionary, which defines the term and presents a digest-format list of fraudulent acts and situations with no headings for the reader's guidance.

Cunningham's Zenith

Although this third edition represents Cunningham's final work on the book—and is therefore the most authoritative edition—it isn't dramatically different from the first edition of 1764–1765. The third-edition title page declares that entries have been "corrected, augmented, and improved," and the statutes have been updated to July 1783. Although many entries show citations to statutes enacted during the reign of George III, one wonders whether the work's comparative lack of endurance resulted partly from the rather insignificant changes made between editions.

Timothy Cunningham might well have been inspired by the groundbreaking work of Samuel Johnson, but there is one way in which Johnson wasn't his model at all. Johnson famously defined *lexicographer* as "a writer of dictionaries."[5] But that's not really what Cunningham was. He seems to have written comparatively little. He was mostly a compiler.

Taken as a compilation, and not as a work of original scholarship, Cunningham's work still has great historical interest to American lawyers and judges. It was, along with Jacob's tenth edition, one of only two law dictionaries published within a decade of the American Revolution. For the strict constructionist who wants contemporaneous definitions of the words and phrases used in the Constitution and early American statutes, this book provides a wealth of material.

The United States Supreme Court has already cited Cunningham's dictionary in six cases (twice as many as Jacob's).[6] Now that the Lawbook Exchange is making the book more freely available, courts at all levels will probably cite it more frequently. Not many 18th-century works of nonfiction have enjoyed such longevity.

---

[5] More famously still, Johnson's subdefinition for *lexicographer* reads: "a harmless drudge, that busies himself in tracing the original, and detailing the signification of words."

[6] *Atwater v. City of Lago Vista*, 532 U.S. 318, 332 (2001); *United States v. Hubbell*, 530 U.S. 27, 38 (2000); *Helling v. McKinney*, 509 U.S. 25, 38 (1993); *Browning-Ferris Indust. of Vt., Inc. v. Kelco Disposal, Inc.*, 492 U.S. 257, 265 n.6 (1989); *Doe v. United States*, 487 U.S. 201, 220 n.2 (1988); *Joseph Burstyn, Inc. v. Wilson*, 343 U.S. 495, 537 (1952).

ه ه ه

Introduction to Burn's
New Law Dictionary (1792)

WHY THE *Dictionary of National Biography* characterizes this 1792 two-volume dictionary as "a posthumous work of little value" is hard to fathom.

Richard Burn (1709–1785) was, according to the *DNB*, a "legal writer and topographer." He wrote books on justices of the peace (29 editions), on ecclesiastical law (nine editions), and on poor laws (apparently only one edition), among others. He was the editor of the 9th, 10th, and 11th editions of Blackstone's *Commentaries on the Laws of England*. By all accounts, this dictionary was "probably designed as a sort of appendix to [his] other works, calculated to explain concisely such professional terms as occurred in them."[1]

In fact, the bibliographer J.G. Marvin doubted whether Richard Burn ever intended the book to be published at all.[2] John Burn (1744–1802), the author's son, had the book published both in London and in Dublin seven years after his father's death.

John Burn insisted that it was "an *original work*, not copying (as is too often done) from other books of the kind; in some of which the servility of transcribing, from one work to another, is but too obvious." Yet a random comparison of entries with those of the 1782 tenth edition of Giles Jacob's *Law Dictionary* shows too great a similarity of wording to be a mere coincidence. Still, it's fair to say that Richard Burn showed a greater freedom in paraphrasing and simplifying than many of his fellow lexicographers—as is evident both in his definitions and in his supporting citations.

Then again, maybe Richard Burn never intended to be a lexicographer at all. Although the book may have been a kind of appendix, as Marvin suggested, dictionaries don't get compiled accidentally. Any manuscript of this magnitude must have been purposeful. It would be interesting to know just how much was Richard's work and how much was John's.

In any event, the book appeared during the formative years of American law, and it is a valuable reference for those who want to see how certain legal terms were understood in the 18th century.

Reprinted (with this preface) by the Lawbook Exchange in 2003.

[1] J.G. Marvin, *Legal Bibliography* 163 (1847).

[2] *Id.*

ন্ধ ন্ধ ন্ধ

Introduction to Williams's
Law Dictionary (1816)

IN SOME WAYS, the career of the barrister and legal lexicographer Thomas Walter Williams (1763–1833) finds parallels in the career of Henry Campbell Black (1860–1927). Like Black, Williams "was not much known as a pleader, his repute chiefly resting on his writings."[1] And both men published copiously. Williams abstracted many acts of Parliament and wrote several books, among them *A Compendious Digest of the Statute Law* (2 vols., 1787, and later editions); *Original Precedents and Conveyances* (4 vols., 1788–1792); *The Whole Law Relative to the Duty and Office of a Justice of the Peace* (3 vols., 1793–1795); *An Abridgment of Cases Argued and Determined During the Reign of George III* (5 vols., 1798–1803);[2] *The Practice of the Commissioners, Assessors, and Other Officers Under the Acts Relating to the Assessed Taxes* (1804); and *The Farmer's Lawyer* (1819).[3]

The main difference between the two authors is that Black came to be celebrated for his *Dictionary of Law*, whereas Williams has remained relatively obscure despite his lexicographic endeavors. The *Dictionary of National Biography* (1917) reports that he published *A General Dictionary of the Law* in 1812, followed by the present work in 1816. Today both volumes are rare, and copies are extraordinarily difficult to obtain in the antiquarian-book trade.

In his dictionary, Williams's stated purpose was to "combine . . . within a moderate compass, an exposition of all the known Terms, and general Principles of Law and Equity." In his note "To the Public," he mentions having minutely examined all the "Interpreters of the Law" as well as the "larger Law Dictionaries." He concludes with the claim that his dictionary "contains an accurate exposition of a very great variety of words, terms, and rules, not to be found in any other Dictionary on the same subject now extant."

Reprinted (with this introduction) by the Lawbook Exchange in 2006.

[1] *Dictionary of National Biography* vol. 21, 457 (1917) (*DNB*).

[2] In 1932, Cowley referred to Williams's abridgment of cases argued as one of "[t]wo minor common law abridgments [that] appeared before the close of the [18th] century." John D. Cowley, *A Bibliography of Abridgments, Digests, Dictionaries, and Indexes of English Law to the Year 1800* lxv–lxvi (1932).

[3] *DNB* vol. 21, 457.

Certainly his coverage has a greater scope than any contemporaneous one-volume law dictionary of similar size. In Williams, the letter *A* contains 492 headwords, an impressive number. In Giles Jacob's abridged dictionary of 1743, there are 317 headwords under *A*. And in Thomas Potts's *Compendious Law Dictionary* (1803)—surely the closest competitor to Williams—there are 246.

A comparison with Potts's dictionary shows that Williams does include many more terms, and they're treated more informatively. There are many notes on terms' derivation, history, statutes, related principles, and more. Also, the language is more modern, and even today Williams is markedly easier to understand than Potts. Potts tends to be terse, even cryptic at times; Williams is explanatory, tending toward verbosity.

Of course, many definitions in these earlier dictionaries are precisely the same—word for word. In addition to the work of Potts and any of various editions of Jacob, Williams may have drawn on John Cowell's *Interpreter* (1607, 1684, 1708, 1727, or maybe another edition), John Rastell's *Termes de la Ley* (1624, 1636, 1685, 1721, or maybe another edition), Timothy Cunningham's *New and Complete Law-Dictionary* (editions of 1764, 1771, and 1783), Richard Burn's *New Law Dictionary* (2 vols., 1792), and perhaps even *The Student's Law-Dictionary* (1740). The wordings of many entries are remarkably alike. What Williams did was blend encyclopedic comprehensiveness with a greater degree of readability.

This dictionary marks an important stage toward the evolution of the modern law dictionary: it is half dictionary, half encyclopedia. Much if not most of the text is copied from earlier sources—the usual practice in those days—but Williams has often modernized the language to make it more accessible.

Williams may have been ahead of his time in producing a handy quarto edition of a law dictionary. Apart from various editions of *Termes de la Ley*, huge folios, such as those by Jacob and Cunningham, seem to have been the order of the day. It wasn't until precisely a century after Williams—with the publication of James A. Ballentine's *Law Dictionary*[4]—that short, small law dictionaries gained popularity. In some sense, Williams's work might be considered a predecessor of Steven H. Gifis's small *Law Dictionary* (1975) or my own pocket edition of *Black's Law Dictionary* (1995, 2002). It wasn't until there was a large body of law students that people really needed a portable reference of this kind.

---

[4] San Francisco: Bancroft-Whitney Co., 1916.

ટ**&** ટ**&** ટ**&**

Introduction to Bouvier's
Law Dictionary (1857)

JOHN BOUVIER WAS BORN IN 1787 in Condognan, France, and moved
with his family at age 15 to Philadelphia. At 21, he became a printer; at
25, a newspaper publisher; and at 29, a lawyer. In 1839, 21 years after he
was first admitted to the bar in Uniontown and while he was serving as
an associate justice of the Philadelphia Court of Criminal Sessions, his
Law Dictionary first appeared. This was his major contribution to American law.

The book went through three editions during Bouvier's lifetime.
After his death in 1851, his papers were mined to produce an important
fourth edition, which appeared in 1852. This is a reprint of the seventh
edition, published in 1857. Because all the mid-19th-century editions
are quite rare, I have not been able to compare the fourth to the seventh. But to a working lexicographer, four points about the book are
clear:

- After the first edition of 1839, Bouvier's dictionary grew more
  and more encyclopedic, and encyclopedia-style entries accounted
  for the greater part of its growth over the years.
- John Bouvier was the legal counterpart to Noah Webster: each
  developed an American dictionary because of perceived inadequacies in British dictionaries.
- Like Webster, Bouvier was boldly original: he disdained predecessors' dictionaries, which he called "servile copies, without the
  slightest alteration."
- Bouvier had a panoramic view of legal lexicography, surpassing all
  forerunners in the coverage of civil law, international law, business
  law, admiralty, and jurisprudence.

Bouvier took lexicography quite seriously. Unlike so many other
writers of law dictionaries, he was no dilettante. He assiduously took notes
as terms came to his attention, and he promptly prepared draft entries.
For inevitable imperfections that got into print, he thought it unnecessary to apologize "to those who were aware of the difficulties of the
task." Yet probably no contemporary of Bouvier and few lawyers who
have lived since could appreciate the difficulty of his task.

Reprinted (with this introduction) by the Lawbook Exchange in 2004.

Maybe his literary executors (possibly his widow and daughter?) understood the difficulties involved in legal lexicography. The post-humous preface to the fourth edition, reproduced in this edition at page vi, says that two lawyers reviewed the manuscript "in order that it might be purged, as far as possible, from all errors of every description." This type of close vetting by independent reviewers is essential to first-rate lexicography.

There were two great lexicographers of 19th-century Anglo-American law: John Bouvier (1787–1851) and Henry Campbell Black (1860–1927). Bouvier's dictionary held sway in America long after his death—for nearly 100 years. The availability of this reprinted 1857 edition will be a boon to legal researchers everywhere.

JUSTICE BENJAMIN N. CARDOZO • WILLIAM L. PROSSER

Writing in Law School

Some Truths About Legal Writing

WHAT'S THE MOST IMPORTANT SUBJECT you'll study in law school? While some might try to make the case for contracts or torts or procedure—the teachers of those subjects will train you to think like a lawyer—the answer is surely legal writing. Unlike most other subjects, it involves a skill that you'll need to continue developing long after leaving law school.

Writing is one of the two great skills that will advance your career in law. (The other is people skills.) If you can write well, you must necessarily do other things well: analyze cogently, organize logically, distill accurately, argue persuasively, cite knowledgeably, punctuate skillfully, and phrase smoothly, among other things. Becoming proficient at all these things is no small feat.

Evaluating Yourself

So how well do you write? Some students enter law school thinking they're already good writers. Others consider themselves mediocre. Still others consider themselves poor.

Before deciding where the truth lies, let's recognize that wherever you are on the scale of proficiency, your skills will inevitably (one hopes temporarily) nosedive in law school—especially during the first year.

Adapted from *Student Lawyer* (Sept. 2002).

Whenever you enter an entirely new field, particularly a technical field
with a jargon and logic all its own, your writing skills will decline until
you become comfortable with the subject matter. It's inescapable. Studies
amply support this commonsense observation. That's why, in my view, it
makes little or no sense to concentrate on legal writing during the first
year of law school: it should be the special province of the second and
third years.

But that's another argument—one that could shake up legal academia.

Let's return to the question, How well do you write? If you think
you're quite good because you had an English or journalism major as an
undergraduate, or because you wrote a master's thesis or Ph.D. dissertation, or because you have published short stories, or because various
people have said that you have talent as a writer, it's probably a delusion.
Sorry, but it's true. Consider the words of Gorham Munson, who was an
accomplished writer and teacher of writing: "[P]rofessional writers, discounting inspiration, discounting even marked talent, say that nobody
can be called a writer until he has written a million words, the equivalent of ten good-sized books."[1] That's a lot of practice—and few law
students have had that much. For that matter, few law professors have
had it.

If you think you're a mediocre or poor writer, on the other hand,
you may underestimate your skills. But it's a healthy turn of mind if you
see considerable room for improvement. Assuming that you recognize
the value of good writing, you'll do more to hone your skills if you
combat any sense of self-satisfaction. You'll see yourself as never having
mastered the skill, but instead as always needing to learn more. That's the
way of the true writer.

By the way, don't ever believe that writers are born (not made). It
isn't true, any more than the idea that golfers or violinists or cooks are
born. The fact is that even those with talent—Tiger Woods or Itzhak
Perlman or Martha Stewart—have worked extraordinarily hard to develop
their technique. It's no different for writers.

Psychological Warfare

If you seriously embark on a lifelong quest to master writing skills,
you'll fight three major psychological battles, both with yourself and
with others. The harder battles will be internal.

---

[1] Gorham Munson, *The Written Word* 35 (rev. ed. 1962).

The first struggle will be to avoid insulating yourself from criticism. Writers tend to guard themselves against it and then to reject it if they can't help hearing it. The healthier attitude is to seek out criticism and learn from it—and to continue seeking it. You'll never surpass the need for a good edit. And the more you welcome frank criticism from readers of all types, the more you'll learn to anticipate their reactions while you write. But if your ego is so delicate that you resent learning that readers often find you confusing or verbose or boring, your writing will probably never improve.

Second, you must struggle to achieve simplicity—and learn to achieve it without oversimplifying. That's a tall order in an intellectually challenging discipline like the law. And it's especially tall when you think of the overwhelming attraction that legalese presents to the average mind. With *pursuant to* and *assuming arguendo* and *hereinafter* and *inter alia*, you have ready-made shortcuts for feeling lawyerly. They're like secret handshakes. They seem to make you a member of the club. Without them, you'll feel like your pre-law-school self at a time when you may really want to feel a difference. Never mind that they typify low-grade legal writing.

Third, you may feel as if your professional advancement demands that you adopt a legalistic style. Although I won't deny that at some early point in your career you may have a benighted boss who insists on your using legalese, the idea that this is good professional practice is naive. A humongous lie. To the contrary, you'll open up all sorts of doors for yourself if you can become a first-rate legal writer—a down-to-earth, sensible stylist with a command of the ideas you're writing about. If you write well, you'll be a better litigator, a better transactional lawyer, a better judge, a better legal (or nonlegal) journalist, a better whatever you want to be with your law degree.

Meanwhile, of course, there are many obstacles. Perhaps the first is getting the experience of having written a million words. So practice every chance you get, and think hard every time you put words to paper, even if you're jotting a thank-you note. That's what it means to be a writer.

 る♦ る♦ る♦

Taking a Lesson from Tiger Woods

WHAT YOU LEARN IN first-year torts, contracts, criminal law, or civil procedure—no matter where you're going to law school—is fairly predictable. You may be required to learn largely through the Socratic method, or you may have professors who use more of a lecture format. Yet the knowledge that you're acquiring, including the techniques for analyzing legal problems, is fairly consistent. This is because most first-year courses represent mature fields of study that have been well tilled since the 1870s.

Not so legal writing. It's still a fairly embryonic field of study. In fact, it wasn't really incorporated into the academy until the 1970s. Of course, this was a significant advance in legal studies, and the field has steadily progressed in the intervening decades. But its relative newness means there is great variability in what gets taught in legal-writing courses.

What does this mean to you? Take an elementary example: issue statements. In your legal-writing course, you may be asked to write:

- one-sentence issue statements beginning with *Whether* (traditional but retrograde);
- one-sentence issue statements beginning with *Can, Is, Does,* or some other interrogative word (slightly better);
- one-sentence issue statements in a straitjacketed *Under–does–when* format (a smidgen better but unchronological and usually difficult to comprehend); or
- multisentence issue statements, in chronological order, with an upper word limit of 75 words (the so-called deep issue, which, when done well, is comprehensible to lawyers and nonlawyers alike).

These are very different approaches. And the approach you'll take will depend directly on what course materials your instructor uses.

There are other examples of variability. In one legal-writing class, students will learn a stiff, hyperformal style of writing; in another, they'll learn a relaxed but polished style that allows them to sound like themselves. In one class, they'll learn never to begin a sentence with *And, But,* or *So* (and start using *Moreover, However,* and *Consequently* instead);

Adapted from *Student Lawyer* (Oct. 2001).

in another, they'll learn that robust writers have always used *And*, *But*, and *So* as sentence-starters (usually in about 10% of their sentences!). In one class, they'll learn to cite lots of cases and be graded almost exclusively on citation form; in another class, they'll learn to cite cases selectively and to develop arguments based on those cases (while, one hopes, being graded partly on citation form). In some classes, they'll learn research to the exclusion of writing.

This raises a fundamental point. Why teach writing at all? Shouldn't we assume that by the time students get to law school, they know how to write?

No. We can't assume this and probably never could. Back in 1954, William Prosser was complaining in the *Journal of Legal Education* that his students in torts couldn't write.[1] Even those who enter law school as strong writers—with, say, years of journalism under their belts—will find that their skills deteriorate when they're thrown into the brave new world of legal studies.

Even if that weren't so, we'd still need courses in legal writing. If Tiger Woods still needs golf lessons (he gets them constantly), don't ever assume that you're beyond the need for help yourself.

Three bits of advice:

First, learn what approach your legal-writing instructor prefers, and deliver that. Make the grade. But keep an eye on new techniques that effective legal writers are using. You'll need them as a law clerk and later as a lawyer.

Second, start collecting books on legal language and legal writing, so that you'll be conversant with these topics. Below are some good candidates. Dip into them whenever you can, over the winter vacation or spring break.

- David Mellinkoff, *The Language of the Law* (1963) (a wonderful history of lawyers' language).

- Ronald L. Goldfarb and James C. Raymond, *Clear Understandings: A Guide to Legal Writing* (1982) (a fine guide with ten commandments for legal writers).

- Tom Goldstein & Jethro K. Lieberman, *The Lawyer's Guide to Writing Well* (1989) (with an excellent chapter on the writing process).

- Richard C. Wydick, *Plain English for Lawyers* (4th ed. 1998) (the classic guide to simplicity in legal writing).

---

[1] William L. Prosser, *English as She Is Wrote*, 7 J. Legal Educ. 155, 162 (1954).

- Bryan A. Garner, *Legal Writing in Plain English* (2001) (a primer with many tips on persuasive writing and contractual drafting).

- Bryan A. Garner, *The Elements of Legal Style* (2d ed. 2002) (a Strunk-and-White-inspired guide for legal writers).

Whenever you're in a discussion about language or writing, take some time to check out what the authorities say. Learn to support your position.

Third, if your law school has a well-regarded advanced course in legal drafting, take it. Every lawyer needs to know the practicalities of drafting contracts and should know something even about legislative and regulatory drafting. Only about half the law schools offer such a course; if yours is one of them, count yourself lucky and take it.

ذِ‏   ذِ‏   ذِ‏

How Serious Is Your School About Writing?

THERE'S A DIRTY, NOT-SO-LITTLE and not-so-secret secret in legal academia today: most law schools, though they profess the importance of good writing, treat their own legal-writing programs pretty shabbily. Students and alumni suffer as a result, and so do the poor souls who must teach in those programs.

Since I've happily never been part of a first-year legal-writing program myself, I have no personal ax to grind here. But having taught CLE courses and upper-level law-school courses for most of the past two decades, I've been close enough to the front lines to offer some informed observations.

To help you see how your own school measures up, let me pose five questions that seem to me crucial ones to ask:

1. Does legal writing have parity with torts and contracts and civil procedure?

To answer that, you need to ask yourself two subquestions.

First, is legal writing a graded subject? A few years ago it often wasn't. And so naturally students didn't take the course as seriously as their other ones. Neither did the deans and faculty who put the courses on a pass–fail basis. Now things have improved: at most schools, legal writing is a graded course.

Second, who teaches your legal-writing classes? Are they full-time teachers? Local practitioners? Third-year law students? In one way or another, most schools teach legal writing on the cheap. The cheapest way, by far, is to staff the legal-writing program mostly with third-year law students, and then give them credit hours for their service. (This essentially costs the school nothing. Yet the thought of doing this with any other course would be considered scandalous.) If you're taught by a local practitioner—often junior lawyers who have their own harried work schedules to contend with—you'll rarely get the kind of editing that will prove genuinely eye-opening. And in either case—third-year students or local practitioners—you'll find that the teacher's writing expertise is quite hit-or-miss. Some will know relatively little about the subject: they

---

Adapted from *Student Lawyer* (Oct. 2000).

won't have invested much effort in the course, apart from adopting someone else's course plan and pretending hard that it's their own.

Ideally, you'll get a full-time professional—someone who has made a
personal investment in the field of legal writing and who has a real
grounding in the literature on the subject. This brings us to the next
question.

2. Are those who teach legal writing on a par with those who teach other courses?

Are they truly professors? It's not enough that they, like other faculty
members, are called "professors." There's an informal tendency to call anyone who teaches at a law school "Professor." To answer the question intelligently, you'll have to find out their formal academic title: full professor,
associate professor, or assistant professor. Check your school's catalogue
or law review. Chances are that you'll see none of these titles attached
to your legal-writing teacher. What you'll probably see is "lecturer" or
"instructor," both of which are low-status titles. That tells you something.

"No, it doesn't," some faculties will contend. "You see, we don't use
the same hiring standards for legal-writing teachers as we do for professorial positions. We hardly expect them to have sterling academic records,
federal clerkships, and the like, so how could they be genuine professors,
with the promise of tenure?"

To which one could reply, "Why entrust something as crucial as legal
writing to teachers who don't measure up to the standards expected of
other law-school teachers?"

Here, the party-line response is this: "Legal writing is just a skill. It's
not as intellectually demanding as torts and contracts and civil procedure. People of great intellectual aptitude simply don't gravitate toward
the field. After all, it's just *writing*."

To which the next riposte is "Just writing? You don't take writing
seriously, do you?" And the salary scale proves it. How in the world
could we expect people of great intellectual aptitude to gravitate toward
a field when the salaries are often half what the beginning tenure-track
people make? At one law school I know of, the full legal-writing teachers (talented, motivated, and conscientious) make less than the professors'
secretaries.

Legal writing isn't "the stepchild of legal education," as it's sometimes called. It isn't even the foster child. It's more like an abused child.

At the moment, it seems pure folly to think there might someday be
a law school with a Chair in Legal Writing.

3. Have you seen the writing of your legal-writing teachers?

You probably haven't. Why? Because they generally aren't expected to publish. And besides, they don't have the time, given all the papers they have to mark.

Mary Kay Kane publishes on civil procedure, and all the students at Hastings know it. Monroe Freedman publishes on legal ethics, and all the students at Hofstra know it. The same is true of Robert Berring (legal research) at Berkeley. Robert Hamilton (corporations) at Texas. Yale Kamisar (criminal law) at Michigan. Lucy McGough (family law) at Louisiana State. You choose the school, you'll find professors whose work the students have read.

But in legal writing, this is the exception. For the reasons, look back at the discussion under question #2.

Consider the absurdity of this situation, though. In a music school, if you're going to hire a professor of flute—someone who teaches flute performance—the first requisite for the entire pool of candidates is that they be virtuoso players. You can't teach flute credibly if you can't play it well. By the same token, you can't teach writing without knowing how to write well.

Yet most faculties pay little attention to how well their writing instructors write. It doesn't come into play much in hiring, in promotion, or in contract renewals. Not surprisingly, then, some legal-writing teachers are comparable to a choral instructor who can't carry a tune. I hope you've managed to escape them.

4. How well funded is the legal-writing program? Does it receive the same kind of funding as a clinic? How good are the resources? Is there a center for legal writing, with a library and a small staff to help you with writing issues?

Only a handful of schools would fare well with this question. If you're at one of them, congratulations.

5. Did you have more confidence in your writing after the first year of law school than when you entered, or did you have less? And do you get any further instruction after the first year?

Most of my upper-division law students—I have 100 each semester—will confess, in our first class meeting, that they've lost confidence in their writing skills since entering law school. They say that the first year has left them seriously confused—about the differences between legal writing and other types of writing, about what's expected of them in legal memos and briefs, about how to succeed as a legal writer, and so on.

That's too bad. You see, a good teacher will almost always instill greater levels of confidence in a student. That's the essence of teaching: establishing realistic standards and then showing students exactly how to achieve them. Students shouldn't be left floundering with vague advice such as, "Just think clearly and write down your thoughts cogently. That's all you have to do to succeed." For the neophyte struggling with a new academic discipline, such advice will seem a joke.

Final Grades

So how does your school stack up? Is it one of the exceptional schools where legal writing is counted a core discipline? Or is it a school in which legal writing has little more than secretarial status? Or is it somewhere in between?

Many legal-writing teachers are agitating for reform. They already have, in fact, made some modest gains—for example, eliminating the two-year cap for teachers of legal writing. The big gains will come, though, only when dissatisfied students and alumni insist that the schools change their benighted ways.

ზა ზა ზა

Why Students Should Support LRW Classes

AT MOST LAW SCHOOLS in this country, a grave injustice is going on. The professors who work hardest with their students, week by week, have the lowest status. They're badly overworked and grossly underpaid. They often have little or no job security and aren't even considered members of the "regular" faculty. They teach legal research and writing, known on many campuses as LRW.

With some effective student activism, you could help set things aright. But why should you care about this issue? The answer is that LRW is central to your development and success as a lawyer. And without your efforts, inertia is likely to control the outcome.

Consider the benefits of your LRW class. They're unique for many 1Ls. In your substantive classes you may interact with the professors only on occasion. And you'll probably receive no feedback about your work until final grades are posted. Even then you usually won't find a critique on the exam, just marks and numbers.

By contrast, most LRW classes offer direct feedback and one-on-one critiques. That's the main focus of the course. And the feedback goes far beyond research skills and writing style. It goes to thought processes such as problem-solving, research strategies, and selecting and constructing arguments. You learn how to reason as well as how to communicate.

Research and writing remain third-class citizens among the legal disciplines, and efforts by LRW professionals to boost law schools' commitment to teaching the subject usually fail. Some schools even cap the length of time LRW instructors and directors can be employed before being forced to move aside for someone else—someone who will take the job for less money and who typically brings less teaching talent and experience.

The status of today's LRW programs also gives law schools an appearance of sex discrimination. Women make up about 10% of law-school deans but 70% of the legal-writing faculty. It's a "pink ghetto," in the words of a 1996 report issued by the ABA Commission on Women in the Profession.

Adapted from *Student Lawyer* (Mar. 2003).

In a 1988 *Pennsylvania Law Review* article, Richard Chused put it this way: "The lower pay and prestige of the contract legal writing slots, together with the low rate of hiring for traditional teaching positions, creates an impression that some schools 'track' women into lower status legal writing jobs rather than into the classroom or clinical work, pay them less than they are worth, and then let them go."

A law school undoubtedly saves money by stinting on LRW programs. But you, the student, lose. No matter what other courses are offered, no matter what courses you take, if you can't reason out a problem, research it, and effectively explain the problem and its solution in writing, you haven't been adequately prepared for your career in law.

Using your advocacy skills, you can help in two ways.

First, if you've had a great LRW professor, let the dean and others in the administration know about it. If your experience is typical, you'll probably realize that you've obtained more practical knowledge in LRW than in any other course in your first year of law school—perhaps in your entire law-school career. You've probably learned how to find cases, how to read them, how to digest them, how to construct a legal argument, and how to write memos and briefs. These are among the most tangible skills you'll need for getting and keeping a legal job. If you've learned them well, then praise your teachers whenever the opportunity arises.

Second, and more ambitiously, do what a good lawyer does: Master the facts. Become informed about the policies at your school. Ask questions. You'll probably find all of these to be pertinent:

- Ask why LRW isn't given as many credits as other courses and why it isn't graded in the same way as other courses, considering that it's a required course. It's probably the only required skills course, and certainly the only one that teaches students what they'll be doing for the rest of their careers.
- Ask why instruction in research and writing is so undervalued when (1) law professors get promoted for their own research and writing, and (2) law-review experience is so highly prized for developing students' research, writing, and editing skills.
- Ask why LRW teachers have low-status titles and bad offices.
- Ask why LRW teachers aren't allowed to teach other courses when they're among the best teachers on the faculty.
- Ask why most LRW teachers are young women in low-status positions and receiving relatively low pay. If the course isn't taught by full-time faculty, ask why no other required course is taught by adjuncts or upper-division students.

- Ask why the law school doesn't seek financial support to upgrade the LRW program from the very law firms that seek students based on evidence of their research and writing skills. Note that investments in LRW would give the school a huge advantage in the marketplace over competing schools.

And read up on the subject. Have a look at Jan Levine & Kathryn M. Stanchi, *Women, Writing & Wages*, 7 Wm. & Mary J. of Women & the Law 551 (2001); Richard K. Neumann Jr., *Women in Legal Education*, 50 J. Legal Educ. 313 (2000); and Jan Levine, *Legal Research and Writing: What Law Schools Are Doing, and Who Is Doing the Teaching*, 7 Scribes J. Legal Writing 51 (1998–2000).

It was in 1990 that I decided to begin teaching legal writing full time. That's where my passion lies. When I informed the dean at the law school where I was then teaching, he replied unforgettably: "Bryan, the people who teach legal writing are making less money than your secretary. And besides, if that's your subject, you'll never be taken seriously by your colleagues."

Things have changed a bit for LRW teachers since then—but just a bit. Things won't change much more without some serious agitation. Do what you can.

After all, you're about to embark on a career of legal research and writing.

 è✦ è✦ è✦

The Art of Briefing Cases

YEARS AGO, IN THE *Journal of Legal Education* (1973), Professor Peter W. Gross sounded an alarm: "Beware: The case method of instruction often accustoms students to lazy and analytically ineffective reading of judicial opinions."[1] Though this seems counterintuitive—judicial opinions, after all, are the very essence of the case method—he had it exactly right: few students are proficient readers of cases.

For an ambitious law student, becoming one is an opportunity to stand out from the crowd. I'm not talking about anything as heady as buying and reading I.A. Richards's classic book *How to Read a Page* or Ezra Pound's *ABC of Reading*. No, save those for spring break sometime—and read them only if you have a literary bent. Instead, I mean nothing more ambitious than taking the time to carefully brief every case you read.

Perhaps because of the widespread availability of commercial outlines containing "canned cases," case-briefing is a skill too many law students think they can neglect. That's naive because you won't *really* grasp cases until you've briefed them. And the technique will benefit you well beyond law school.

If you acquire the technique, you'll be among the few who do—and you'll have a real edge in law.

Properly done, a case brief will summarize, succinctly and clearly, four things: the relevant facts, the precise legal issue or issues presented, the court's holding, and the court's reasoning. All these things you will express in your own words, with a close paraphrase and minimal quotations. That's the only way to *own* the material. You'll come to know the law as you couldn't possibly do if you were simply highlighting your casebook and jotting marginal notes.

Although briefing methods vary, all case briefs include the style of the case (be sure to use correct citation form) and the four essential elements listed in the previous paragraph. Other points you might include are the rule of law, the procedural posture of the case, notes on concurring or dissenting opinions, and your own additional comments.

Adapted from *Student Lawyer* (Nov. 2004).

[1] Peter W. Gross, *On Law School Training in Analytic Skill*, 25 J. Legal Educ. 261, 272 (1973).

The most important task in preparing a case brief is to study exactly how the court applied a legal rule to the facts of the case. To do that, you must break down the opinion into its components and focus on each in turn—especially on what guided the court to choose a particular legal principle over another. You'll find that the case brief will help you discuss the case in class and analyze how changes in the facts would affect the holding.

But assiduously producing case briefs isn't enough. As you master the technique, you'll need to work hard to avoid some common faults. Let me tell you how to avoid them. Here are five *don'ts*.

First, don't read the opinion as if it were a textbook. A case brief requires you to think critically—to focus on the opinion's logical structure, to understand the court's thought processes, and to determine what led to the decision. Read skeptically. Look for weak logic in the analysis. Also, compare the facts, issue, and reasoning to those in other cases with a very different outcome. If you credulously accept a court's statements as gospel, you'll probably produce an inadequate case brief.

Second, don't confuse dicta with law. Dicta are statements that aren't a necessary part of the court's reasoning or holding. (*Dicta*, by the way, is a plural word; the singular is *dictum*.) A judge may, for any number of reasons, good or bad, expound on irrelevant facts, hypothetical variations of the facts, or a theory of law that was not applied. Dicta have no authority, though they may offer insight into how the court might decide other cases.

Third, don't write without mulling over the case thoroughly. As Justice Benjamin Cardozo once observed: "Cases do not unfold their principles for the asking. They yield up their kernels slowly and painfully." (The worse the writing, the slower and more painful the kernels are yielded up.) To extract the essential elements of the court's opinion, you must read all of it and think hard about it. The relevant facts aren't always clear, especially on a first reading. Underlying policy or social considerations may turn out to play more of a role in the outcome than a statute or a common-law principle, yet they may be hard to identify from the text of the opinion. And a court's opinion is not necessarily unassailable merely because it has been published as citable authority. In reaching its decision, the court may have made certain assumptions and not recorded them. The court may have distorted precedent or ignored some facts. There may even be logical fallacies in the court's reasoning.

Fourth, don't include too much detail. As a rule, if your case brief is more than one single-spaced typewritten page, including any critical notes and observations you make, it's probably too detailed. Reexamine the facts and the issue. Eliminate trivial details in the facts, such as exact dates or irrelevant personal information about the parties. If they have no bearing on the court's reasoning or decision, skip them. State the issue in no more than 75 words—preferably in separate sentences. (There's no rule requiring you to cram the issue into one sentence. In fact, doing so is folly.) If your first draft has woven dicta into the reasoning, delete them; if the dicta are useful for some other purpose, save them for your observations. If there is a significant concurrence or dissent, capsulize the key points of difference in two or three sentences. A very long and complex case may require more than a page to brief, but three pages will almost never be necessary.

Fifth, don't try shortcuts. To save time, some students buy "canned briefs." Your professors have probably warned you not to, and you should take their advice to heart. These so-called study aids are actually harmful because it's the *skill* of case-briefing that you need, not somebody else's predigested work product.

You'll find—if you haven't found already—that accurate case-briefing goes to the very core of what professors mean when they refer to "thinking like a lawyer."

A Model Case Brief

Lentini v. California Center for the Arts
370 F.3d 837 (9th Cir. 2004)

Facts: Lentini took her service dog to several concert-hall performances. The dog yipped during intermission on two occasions, at different concerts, when people got too close to Lentini's wheelchair. No patrons complained about the dog, and the dog remained silent during all the performances. (Meanwhile, the humans who made sounds during the performances were never admonished, much less excluded.) The hall's managers did not tell Lentini that the dog was a problem. But the hall's director told the staff not to admit Lentini again. When Lentini returned for another performance and was told that the dog would not be admitted, she entered with the dog anyway. She left after police were called and the hall's manager demanded her arrest.

Issue: The Americans with Disabilities Act (ADA) requires that public places allow service animals access to the premises. An exception is made if the accommodation is unreasonable or unnecessary, or if it would fundamentally alter the nature of the services provided. Lentini's dog yipped only during intermissions to warn Lentini that people were near her wheelchair. Did the dog's behavior warrant permanent exclusion?

Holding: No. Allowing the dog into the concert hall was reasonable and necessary. The dog's behavior did not disrupt the performance.

Reasoning: Lentini showed that she needed the dog's support. The dog did not make more noise than a coughing human reasonably would. When it did yip, it did so only to alert Lentini to a possible danger. The dog's yips produced no complaints from patrons, and the dog never made a sound while performers were on stage, so it did not fundamentally alter the services provided at the concert hall.

DAVID L. BAZELON

CHAPTER NINE

Writing in Practice

The Perpetual Struggle for Clarity

Notwithstanding anything to the contrary contained in any
other document (or any part thereof) . . . .

THERE'S AN AGE-OLD CYCLE of bad writing in law. You can help break it. The first part of the cycle, the starting point, is familiar enough: writing well isn't easy. Most people who graduate from college don't write well, though many think they do. Most of our future doctors, accountants, and businesspeople—even professors—aren't accomplished writers. So why should it be any different for lawyers?

The second part of the cycle is insidious: When you plunge lots of mediocre writers into a complex field that's rife with moldy jargon, the unhappy results are predictable enough. But it's even worse: make them read reams upon reams of tedious, hyperformal, creaky prose. Acculturate them to pomposity. What do you suppose you'll get?

You'll get your average legal writer: verbose, stuffy, obtuse, and frequently ungrammatical.

In the last part of the cycle, each generation of lawyers trains the next to follow its ingrained habits. Meanwhile, generation after generation, lawyers get ridiculed for their pompous writing.

It doesn't have to be this way—for you or anybody else. Even if you're entering law as a fairly weak writer, you can help break the cycle.

Adapted from *Student Lawyer* (Oct. 1999).

It won't be easy, of course. Few worthwhile things in life come easily. Yet once you become a skillful writer—especially a skillful writer on legal subjects—your rewards will be great.

Before we talk about rewards, however, let's ponder the hurdles you'll be overcoming. There are several.

First, though it's possible for just about anyone to learn to write effectively, it takes hard work. Good style is something you must strive to attain. In that way it's like skillful golfing: There are comparatively few 5-handicappers in the world, and those who attain that level of skill don't get there by birthright. They work at it. So remember: Writing is like golf—you can improve, but you'll have to dedicate yourself to it. The easier path is to be a duffer.

If you want to become a first-rate writer, you'll be undertaking a big commitment.

Second, since you're in law, you're swimming in a sea of bad examples. We learn our trade by poring over reams of linguistic dreck—jargon-filled, pretentious, flatulent lawbooks that seem designed to dim any flair for language. Once you get on the job, you'll be reading poor prose almost exclusively. It's wordy and high-flown—oddly antique-sounding. And part of you may well come to believe that you must sound that way to be truly lawyer-like.

You'll have to inoculate yourself against legalese.

Third, the world is complex, and so is our law. You may well come to believe that good legal writing is necessarily complex, too. You may even be tempted to make your writing more complex than necessary just to impress. Part of you will want to do this: You'll feel the impulse to shun simplicity.

You'll have to learn to treasure simplicity—while always resisting oversimplification. Of your undertakings thus far, this will be the most difficult of all. It requires mental independence and confidence.

This brings us to the fourth and final point. You'll have to be psychologically mature. It's a prerequisite. After all, law school is a life-changing experience. When you're through with it, you'll be a different person—very likely a better one. Ultimately, you'll have to answer a question that your parents started helping you answer before you understood a single word: What kind of person am I? And every time you write, you'll be answering some related questions: What kind of person am I—on paper? What do I sound like?

Again, if you wish to write well, you'll have to resist sounding like a machine. Or an old-fashioned pontificator. You'll have to learn to sound like the best version of yourself. You might even find yourself by learning to write well.

But the rewards are more tangible than that. They're by-products of good writing. Because legal employers prize writing ability as highly as any other skill, you'll find several immediate advantages:

- You'll be more likely to get the kind of job you want.
- You'll be more likely to be promoted quickly.
- You'll have greater opportunities for career mobility, with a broad spectrum of possibilities.

If you can write—really write—people will infer certain other things about you. The most important of these is that you're a clear thinker.

But you'll surely encounter some obstacles along the way. Maybe an employer will tell you that you're being too clear in your writing—that you should learn to obfuscate better. Maybe an employer will disapprove of your departing from some mind-numbing convention (such as doubling up words and numerals) that ill-informed legal writers adhere to. Maybe an employer will tell you to leave court papers vague so that the specific arguments can be fashioned orally before the judge—a seat-of-the-pants approach. So how do you deal with it?

The answer is twofold. First, do what you must in the short run. Don't butt heads with someone who refuses to engage in an intelligent discussion about style. If such a person happens to be your supervisor, simply learn what you can from working with that person. (The lessons might have more to do with the human psyche than with good writing.) Second, don't lose your critical sensibility; instead, cultivate it. Monitor your own reactions as a reader. Think independently about why you consider some pieces of writing good, and others bad.

In the end, you might decide to write in a bold, clear, powerful way. It will be a struggle for you—in combatting both the natural human tendency to write poorly and the unnatural pressure from colleagues to write poorly. But you'll have struck a blow for yourself and for the law. You'll be championing clarity, cogency, truth, and beauty. The law could certainly stand to have those qualities in greater abundance.

ès ès ès

Why IRAC Is Good for Exams but Bad in Practice

"Remember that IRAC is your mantra," say Professors Thomas E. Baker and David Epstein in a spoken-word CD entitled "All the Things You Need to Hear About Succeeding in Law School." They're talking about writing law-school exams, and they're exactly right. For filling out bluebooks, the IRAC formula is terrific.

For almost every other kind of legal writing, though, it's terrible. Let's see why.

The IRAC formula (issue–rule–application–conclusion) envisions a time-pressured exam answer in which you might write:

> Did Father Prynne's actions give rise to vicarious liability for the Church? [Issue.] The rule is that only an employee acting within the scope and course of the employment can give rise to vicarious liability on the part of the employer. [Rule.] Here, although Father Prynne was on his way to the Church, he had stopped at the grocery store to buy food for the weekend. So he was not within the "course and scope." [Application.] A court would probably hold that there is no vicarious liability. [Conclusion.]

In a single exam answer, you might go through that type of IRAC discussion eight to ten times, since most professors include a phantasmagoria of facts and often put a premium on "issue-spotting." The idea is to find the copious subissues half-buried by a given factual scenario. Learning to do this is an essential part of your law-school education. You're being trained in critical thinking.

But what's rewarded in law-school exams tends *not* to be rewarded in real-life writing. So the coveted IRAC mantra—deservedly touted for these nerve-racking finals—will produce mediocre to worse results in memo-writing and brief-writing. Why? Because if you were to write a one-issue memo using the IRAC organization, you wouldn't reach the conclusion—the answer to the issue—until the end. So the memo itself becomes "all middle." That is, it deprives the busy reader of an up-front summary—precisely what you yourself would demand if you were a supervisory attorney.

Adapted from *Student Lawyer* (May 2005).

Knowing this, some legal-writing professors recommend another strategy for the writing you do after law school. They call it CREAC, which stands for conclusion–rule–elaboration–application (of the rule to the facts)–conclusion (restated). Although you'd probably be penalized for that organizational strategy on most law exams, it's actually superior to IRAC for other types of writing. But it, too, has a serious shortcoming: Because it doesn't really pose an issue, it presents a conclusion to an unknown problem.

An advocate using CREAC with the vicarious-liability issue might argue in this way:

> Father Prynne has done nothing that would give rise to vicarious liability on the part of the Church. [Conclusion.] Under California law, only an employee acting within the scope and course of the employment may give rise to vicarious liability for the employer. [Rule.] The courts have validated this rule in the context of Church employees. For example, in *Jenkins* a friar stopped at a gas station to pick up snacks for his drive home and negligently hit and scraped the side of another car. The court immunized the Church because the friar was acting outside the scope and course of his employment. [Elaboration.] Here, Father Prynne acted for himself: he stopped at a grocery store to buy food for the weekend, and he allegedly broke a spigot in the lot. [Application.] Because he was acting for himself and had no churchly duties at the time, his actions cannot be imputed to the Church. [Conclusion restated.]

When you expand this type of argument over several pages, the CREAC format outperforms the IRAC format. But without a clear issue, the conclusion may feel ungrounded and untestable.

Another big problem with these formulas is that they don't tell you where to put a full recital of the facts. IRAC can suffice for an exam because the facts are stipulated: the professor has provided them right in the exam question. Typically, you get an involved factual scenario and then a series of short questions to discuss. So a full presentation of facts doesn't have to fit in anywhere. Your facts are literally a given.

But for just about every reader other than an exam-grader, the facts are anything but a given. When you're in law practice, for example, you need to set out the facts if only to memorialize how you understood them when you wrote the memo, opinion letter, or brief. And the "application" of the law to the facts would make no sense to someone who doesn't already know the facts.

So, then, should you lead off with your factual scenario? No, that's a bad strategy as well, for what busy reader wants to have to winnow the important from the unimportant?

What you need for your opener, then, is a succinct summary or overview: a couple of paragraphs that distill the issues, the answers, and the reasons for those answers—all the main conclusions that you're reaching. (Remember that readers need to understand an issue before seeing a conclusion.) State all this information so plainly that any smart high-school senior would understand. If you can do that, you'll ensure that you really know what you're writing about—and that your reader knows that you know.

Don't assume, though, that you need to state each issue in a single sentence. Allot yourself several, weaving in all the most important facts. But keep each issue to 75 or fewer words. Then give your answer to it just below it, and couple that answer with a nutshell explanation of the reason for the answer. Hence this issue for a memo:

Issue

At 7 a.m. one Friday last May, Father Prynne stopped at a grocery store to buy some weekend food for himself. He allegedly ran his car over a spigot and broke it. The landowner has now sued the Church as well as Father Prynne. Is the Church vicariously liable for Father Prynne's actions?

Brief Answer

Father Prynne has done nothing to trigger vicarious liability on the part of the Church. Under California law, only an employee acting within the scope and course of the employment may make the employer vicariously liable. Father Prynne was acting for himself, not the Church, more than two hours before his duties began at 9:30 a.m. Therefore, the Church should not be liable for his alleged negligence.

If you can master the art of summarizing complex information both accurately and succinctly, and if you learn always to begin with your summaries, you'll be rewarded again and again in the long term. In the short term, though, on law-school exams, you'll want to master IRAC. Just remember that it's not a good way to write much of anything else.

Although the mnemonic acronyms may help beginners, you'll soon transcend the need for them, especially as you key on your reader's needs. Set out issues and answers as plainly as possible right at the start. Don't keep your reader in the dark.

ટ⊶ ટ⊶ ટ⊶

Ten Tips for Writing
at Your Law Firm

AS A SUMMER CLERK, intern, or new associate at a law firm, you'll be judged primarily on two things: your interpersonal skills and your writing. Although the requirements of your writing assignments will vary depending on your organization, your supervisor, and your clients, here are ten points you can be certain about:

1. Be sure you understand the client's problem. When given an assignment, ask plenty of questions. Read the relevant documents and take good notes. Learn all you can about the client's situation. If you're asked to write a memo but aren't told anything about the client's actual problem, ask what it is. There's almost no way to write a good research memo in the abstract. As you're reading cases and examining statutes, you'll be in a much better position to apply your findings to the problem at hand if you know at least some of the specifics.

2. Don't rely exclusively on computer research. Combine book research with computer research. Don't overlook such obvious resources as *Corpus Juris Secundum* and *American Jurisprudence.* The new eighth edition of *Black's Law Dictionary* may help you get into West's key-number system. Look at indexes, digests, hornbooks, and treatises to round out your understanding of the subject.

3. Never turn in a preliminary version of a work in progress. A common shortcoming of green researchers, especially when a project is slightly overdue, is to turn in an interim draft in hopes of getting preliminary feedback. That can be ruinous. What busy supervisor wants to read serial drafts? And you shouldn't turn in tentative work—it's better to be a little late than wrong. That goes for turning in projects to impatient clients as well.

4. Summarize your conclusions up front. Whether you're writing a research memo, an opinion letter, or a brief, you'll need an up-front summary. That typically consists of three things: the questions, the answers to those questions, and the reasons for the answers. If you're drafting a motion, try to state on page one why your client should win—

Adapted from *Student Lawyer* (Mar. 2005).

and put it in a way that your mom or dad could understand. That's your biggest challenge.

If you're writing a research memo, put the question, the answer, and the reason up front. Don't delay the conclusion until the end, as unthinking writers do, naively assuming that the reader will slog all the way through the memo. And never open with a full-blown statement of facts—despite what you may have learned elsewhere. Why? Because facts are useless to a reader who doesn't yet understand what the issue is.

5. Make your summary understandable to outsiders. It's not enough to summarize. You must summarize in a way that every conceivable reader—not just the assigning lawyer—can understand. So don't write your issue this way: "Whether Goliad can take a tax deduction on the rent-free space granted to Davidoff under I.R.C. § 170(f)(3)?" That's incomprehensible to most readers because it's too abstract, and it assumes insider knowledge. Also, it doesn't show any mastery of the problem.

You'd be better off setting up the problem in separate sentences totaling no more than 75 words: "Goliad Enterprises Inc., a for-profit corporation, has granted the Davidoff Foundation, a tax-exempt charity, the use of office space in Goliad's building free of charge. Will the Internal Revenue Service allow Goliad to claim a charitable deduction on its income-tax return for the value of its rent-free lease to Davidoff?"

Then you put the brief answer: "No. Section 170(f)(3) of the Internal Revenue Code disallows charitable deductions for grants of partial interests in property such as leases."

If you're a summer associate aiming for a full-time offer, you'll look much smarter for considering your secondary as well as your primary audience. Hiring decisions are made partly by committees that review writing samples—and those committees have no knowledge of the original assignment.

6. Don't be too tentative in your conclusions, but don't be too cocksure, either. Law-school exams encourage students to give the one-hand–other-hand approach: It could be this or it could be that. In law practice, this approach can look wishy-washy. What's wanted is your best thought about how a court will come down on an issue.

Let's say your firm represents clients in two cases involving similar issues. One case is in the Northern District of Florida, the other in the Southern District. You've been asked to write about whether the cases in different districts can be consolidated.

As it happens, the answer is actually clear-cut: no. The Federal Rules require both actions to be before a single judge for the cases to be consolidated. One of the cases will have to be transferred before they are consolidated. So you should say just that. "Probably not" just makes you sound spineless when the rest of your memo shows that the conclusion is pretty clear.

But always second-guess yourself before concluding "yes" or "no." Why might it be otherwise? If it might be otherwise, explain why. If your answer is "probably," say what facts might make the decision go the other way. You can do all this as part of a short, tidy summary.

7. Strike the right professional tone—natural but not chatty. Some law students, when told to avoid legalese, end up being blithely informal and flouting the norms of standard English, especially in their e-mail messages. For example, they write "u" instead of "you" and "cd" instead of "could." And they use emoticons ;-). Even if you find yourself working for a firm where some people do these things, exercise restraint. Use conventional punctuation and capitalization in your e-mail messages. Your colleagues won't think any less of you, and your supervisors will appreciate your professionalism.

8. Master the approved citation form. Your firm may well cover this in orientation. If not, you'll need to find out what the standards are for citing authority. In California, lawyers follow the *California Style Manual* (4th ed. 2000). In New York, they should (but frequently don't) follow the *New York Law Reports Style Manual* (2002). In Texas, every knowledgeable practitioner follows the *Texas Rules of Form* (10th ed. 2003). Other states have their own guides. Even if you're not inclined to care much about these things, you'd better learn to obsess over them. Otherwise, you'll look unschooled.

9. Cut every unnecessary sentence; then go back through and cut every unnecessary word. Verbosity will make your writing feel cluttered and underthought. Never pad, and learn to delete every extra word. For example, *general consensus of opinion* is doubly redundant: a consensus relates only to opinions, and a consensus is by its very nature general. You can replace the phrase *a number of* with *several* or *many*. And the phrase *in order to* typically has two words too many—*to* can do the work alone. So instead of *in order to determine damages*, write *to determine damages*.

Judge David Bazelon of the United States Court of Appeals for the District of Columbia was a stickler for super-tight prose. Once, when his student clerk, Eugene Gelernter (now a New York litigator), brought him a draft opinion, the great judge said: "Nice draft, Gene. Now go back and read it again. Take out every sentence you don't need. Then go back and take out every word you don't need. Then, when you're done with that, go back and do it all again." We should all have such a mentor.

10. Proofread one more time than you think necessary. If you ever find yourself getting sick of looking at your work product and start to do something rash such as turn it in at that moment, pull yourself up short. Give it a good dramatic reading. Out loud. You'll find some slips and rough patches—and you'll be glad you did. Better that you find the problems than that your readers do.

⅋ ⅋ ⅋

Demand Letters That Get Results

ONCE YOU HAVE your law license—or maybe even before, as a summer intern—you'll have to write something for which most fledgling lawyers feel ill-prepared: a demand letter, by which you explain your client's legal position in a dispute and request that the recipient take some action, or else risk being sued. It's often your initial contact with your client's adversary or potential adversary.

Gauge Your Reader

A demand letter should aim to goad a party to capitulate—that is, to do whatever is demanded. So it needs to feel reasonable and realistic, but it also needs to carry the threat of litigation and its attendant costs and headaches if the adversary isn't reasonable and realistic in turn. As a writer, you must try to get inside the recipient's head to understand what approach is most likely to succeed.

Sometimes, a demand letter gets sent only to comply with a statutory prerequisite for filing suit. Say the demanding party hopes to recover double or even treble damages. To do this, the demander may have to attach the letter to the initial pleading (usually either a complaint or a petition). At this point, there may be no real possibility of resolving the dispute before legal proceedings begin. But the demanding party must send a letter that adequately alleges harm, requests a remedy, and allows a reasonable period for a resolution.

In thinking through the specific goals of your demand, you'll want to do four things.

First, consider the problem strategically. Discuss with your client exactly what you hope to accomplish with the demand letter. But don't lead your client to expect such a favorable (and relatively inexpensive) outcome. (For that matter, never project an overoptimistic attitude about what you might accomplish.) Instead, help the client understand just what it might take to resolve the dispute satisfactorily short of litigation: the return of property, a payment of money, the acknowledgment of a right, or whatever it might be. This should amount to something less than what you would ask for in court—so that the adversary will have an incentive to settle early.

Adapted from *Student Lawyer* (Apr. 2002).

Second, strike the right tone and the right level of specificity. One legitimate purpose of a demand letter is to intimidate. Be sure that the recipient understands (1) your client's point of view, (2) what your client wants, (3) the deadline for complying (e.g., "by 4:00 p.m. (CST) on Wednesday, March 24"), and (4) that you understand the recipient's position and find it either wholly or partly unmeritorious. (You seek satisfaction only to the extent that the adversary's position lacks merit.) Adopt a formal tone.

Third, know who should best receive the letter. If you're writing to a company or association, consider closely to whom the letter should be addressed. If your client has been dealing unsuccessfully with a midlevel manager, perhaps your letter should be directed to someone more senior— maybe the owner or the president, but perhaps instead a vice president who handles legal claims. You may need to call the company to learn the name of a person with authority to handle your demand. Get the full name (with the correct spelling) and title.

Fourth, ensure that your letter reaches its intended recipient. How? Send the original by registered or certified mail (whichever is customary within your jurisdiction) and a copy by regular U.S. mail. If you know both a home address and a work address, consider sending copies by both methods to both addresses (four letters in all). Your seriousness will not be lightly questioned.

Avoid the Common Faults

Demand letters often fail on several counts. They may exaggerate and be needlessly inflammatory, achieving just the opposite of the desired result. They may contain incorrect allegations of facts. (Before writing, you must elicit reliable information from your client, preferably using documents to establish names and dates.) They may misstate the law. They may be vague about what the client wants in resolving the matter without litigation. They may get bogged down in minutiae. Any one of these common pitfalls might lead the recipient to question your seriousness or even your competence.

Two final caveats: (1) Never, never send a demand letter to someone who has already retained counsel in the matter, for then the demand must go to the lawyer, not to the adversary. (2) Never seek civil restitution by threatening criminal punishment. This is unethical and typically illegal. The Model Code of Professional Responsibility prohibits a lawyer from threatening to present "criminal charges solely to obtain an advantage in a civil matter."[1]

---

[1] DR 7-105(A).

Study Effective Demand Letters

As you establish your practice, ask senior colleagues to share with you some model demand letters. If you're allowed to, photocopy the best ones and start a file of them. Most jurisdictions have some characteristic variations here and there. In Georgia, for example, demands typically end with the sentence, "Govern yourself accordingly." Whether you make such phrases habitual in your own demands is for your supervisor (if you have one) to decide in the short run, and for you to decide in the long run.

But before you can decide, you must know what good demand letters look like. What you're looking for is a delicate balance: pithy treatment yet with adequate detail; a threatening tone yet with a sensible suggestion for resolving the dispute; formal distance yet with the sense that a forceful, persistent human being (not an automaton) has written the letter. The successful demand letter requires adequate preparation, a plausible air of self-assurance, and a command of tone.

Two Examples

In the first letter, a lawyer has written to a publisher in a borderline situation: an academic author appears to have misappropriated the title of another professor's work, with the false implication that the new work is a continuation of the old. Nothing has been published yet, and the letter seeks to ensure that no real misappropriation will take place. In the second letter, the wrong is more clear-cut and the demand is considerably more forceful.

David X. Sterling
Attorney-at-Law
Sterling Plaza, 5949 Sherry Lane
Suite 1400
Dallas, Texas 75225-8008

Telephone (214) 212-8888
Fax (214) 212-7777

5 December 2006

Ms. Phyllis Torping
Editor, Marginalia Publishing Inc.
717 Avenue of the Americas
New York, NY 10028

Sent by Certified and Regular Mail

Dear Ms. Torping:

I represent Professor Daniel Martin Schimmelman, with whom you have exchanged letters about Bertrand Katt's annotated bibliography of articles on the English Renaissance. As you know, Professor Schimmelman's book *The English Renaissance (1475–1525): An Annotated Bibliography* (1985) is an important work of scholarship that has become standard in the field. Now Mr. Katt seeks to appropriate this title by calling his own book *The English Renaissance (1525–1575): An Annotated Bibliography*.

Before we even get into the law, you should concede that this matter has been handled poorly by Mr. Katt (who didn't bother to check with the author of the seminal work he sought to update) and by Marginalia (which apparently did the same back in 1996). At the very least, this breach of academic courtesy is one that I'm sure Mr. Katt would not care to have come to light within the field.

More than that, though, Professor Schimmelman has been legally harmed. First, the fact that Mr. Katt and Marginalia have made it possible for *Books in Print* to record that Mr. Katt's book already exists seriously limits the marketing possibilities for Professor Schimmelman's own updating of his work. Second, this misrepresentation in the marketplace—apparently an attempt to forestall competition—suggests to reasonable observers that Mr. Katt's book is somehow an "official" updating of Professor Schimmelman's work. Third, it suggests that Professor Schimmelman himself isn't engaged in that work or perhaps is no longer capable of doing the work. And all this is seriously exacerbated by the fact that Mr. Katt has used the same title in *Books in Print*—regardless of what you now intend to call the book.

Given the harm to Professor Schimmelman's reputation, your actionable conduct could easily lead to a substantial award of damages, possibly including an assignment of all profits from the sale of Mr. Katt's book, a published apology, and attorney's fees. I therefore make immediate demand upon you to:

- ensure that Mr. Katt's book in no way infringes my client's rights;
- ensure that, if you do publish a noninfringing work, you include a full acknowledgment of Professor Schimmelman's seminal work dealing with 1475–1525, which was the germ of Mr. Katt's idea;
- upon publication, send two copies to Professor Schimmelman and two to me so that we can evaluate for ourselves whether any infringement has occurred; and
- take immediate corrective action with *Books in Print* and any other source that may have disseminated your misrepresentations about the existence and title of Mr. Katt's work.

These are reasonable demands. If I do not hear from you by December 15, my client and I will assess what legal recourse we should take against Marginalia and Mr. Katt.

Very truly yours,

David X. Sterling

Copy to Mr. Bertrand Katt (by certified and regular mail)

Potsdam, Herald & Schiffering
Attorneys-at-Law
419 Crystal Avenue, Suite 500
Detroit, Michigan 48801

Telephone (517) 212-8888
Fax (517) 212-7777

29 January 2007

Dr. Francis B. Bolling
Medical Associates of Dearborn
32345 Dearborn Parkway, #745
Dearborn, MI 48954

By Hand Delivery, Certified Mail, and Registered Mail

Dear Dr. Bolling:

Our firm represents the Michigan Commercial Bank, N.A., where you have several accounts. I am writing to demand immediate repayment of the $350,000 erroneously posted to your savings account.

On November 15, 2006, through clerical error at the Bank, a deposit of $350,000 was wrongly credited to your account #5214-1829-93. At the time, you had a little more than $12,000 in that account. Two weeks later, the Bank mailed out account statements, and then on December 4, you withdrew $362,519 and closed the account.

The Bank discovered the error in mid-December 2006 and has tried repeatedly to work with you to correct it. Specifically, Vice President Laura S. Diller spoke with you on the morning of December 18, asking for only the return of $350,000, without interest. You told her that you intend to keep the money—to which you have no legal entitlement.

Unless you deliver cash or a cashier's check (made payable to the Bank) in the amount of $350,000 to my office by 3:00 p.m. on Friday, February 9, 2007, we will promptly institute civil proceedings against you, seeking damages significantly in excess of $350,000, including interest, attorney's fees, and possibly punitive damages.

Very truly yours,

Bertrand R. Frankelshouse

ào ào ào

The Importance of Other Eyes

IN 1987, SHORTLY AFTER my first book on legal writing was published by Oxford University Press, I learned a valuable lesson. I had handwritten seven draft letters and given them to my law-firm secretary to type. In that batch were some letters of great importance both to me and to my clients. When I got the letters back, I revised them slightly and asked my eagle-eyed secretary to make the changes and then proofread them herself.

During a break from a deposition, she handed me the final versions on firm letterhead. I asked whether she'd closely proofread them all. Yes, she said, she had. Good: I signed them and asked her to be sure they went out in the morning mail.

A few days later, I was thumbing through my "read file"—the set of all my correspondence kept in chronological order. When I came to one of the really important letters, I paused to read it again. My eyes stopped on this sentence: "Please understand that client considers its position untenable and expects you to reasonable accommodations." Two important words had been dropped: *our* (before *client*) and *make* (before *reasonable*).

I was furious. And my secretary soon became aware of this: "I signed those letters, and I take the ultimate responsibility for them. But I did ask you to proofread them closely. Didn't you do that?"

"Yes, I did."

"Well, didn't you see these typos? Two words are missing from the crucial sentence!"

"Yes, I saw that. I thought it was really weird, so I compared it to your handwritten version, and I made sure that what I had typed was just the same as what you wrote."

"Still, it's wrong," I said.

"Well," she responded, "I showed it to Gloria"—the secretary in the adjoining workstation—"and she thought it was weird, too. But she reminded me that you wrote that dictionary about legal writing and said you undoubtedly know what you're doing and probably had a good reason for doing it that way."

Never again, I vowed, would staffers blindly trust what I've written. Instead, I want them to scrutinize every sentence. If the average reader doesn't understand what I've written, it almost surely needs revision.

Adapted from *Student Lawyer* (May 2007).

And so I've developed a culture in my workplace—a culture designed to improve everyone's work product.

Specifically, here's what I do. When I finish a business letter (these days I type my own), I'll hand it to two or three colleagues—perhaps to the two lawyers who work at LawProse (Tiger and Jeff) and to an intern (say, Tim)—and ask them to proofread it for me. But I don't stop there. I insist that each reader find two suggested improvements before giving it back to me. No one is allowed to say, "It looks all right to me; I didn't find anything."

Any critical reader should be able to make two good suggestions. By requiring them, I invariably get them—and the work product is much better for the effort.

As in the old days of handwritten drafts, I still have a habit of occasionally skipping over important words. Then, in my own proofing, I somehow supply the missing word in my imagination, so that I don't see this sort of hard-to-detect typo. But my new method of never allowing myself to send out a business letter without having others vet it has lessened my error rate dramatically.

This habit has also affected LawProse culture in important ways. First, nothing I write is considered sacrosanct. Second, my colleagues think more critically and edit more actively. Third, they know that their suggestions are taken seriously, and so they take their editing seriously. Fourth, they understand why I don't give *them* the authority to send letters or faxes on LawProse letterhead until two others (including one lawyer) have proofed the document. Fifth, everyone recognizes what a crucial element letters are to the success of the business.

Over the years, I've learned that employees feel empowered when I listen to them. If I write *susceptible of*, and my secretary thinks it should be *susceptible to*, I don't respond by saying, "The two phrases mean different things, and if you'd just consult my *Dictionary of Modern Legal Usage*, you'd know this." Instead, I find another way of phrasing the idea—one that won't result in any raised eyebrows from anyone, no matter how well-read or ill-read. I certainly won't condemn an employee for a poor suggestion. And I try hard to accept at least one edit from each of my colleagues—often two.

There's no good reason why every practicing lawyer can't capitalize on this approach. No *good* reason.

But there is a reason why it won't work for thin-skinned, overproud types: they can't tolerate criticism from any quarter. They're there to *teach* their subordinates, not to *learn* from them. They think they've paid their dues and are therefore above criticism. Others bear the blame for their mistakes. You know the type.

Let's see how the method suggested here works in practice. One of my clients has been billed by a hospital for a charge four years after submitting the "final" bill—and two years after the statute of frauds expired. A collection agency is now dunning my client. I draft a demand letter to the hospital.

After giving it to three colleagues, I receive these suggestions:

Jeff: You mention a "late charge," apparently meaning "a late-submitted charge." But most people interpret that phrase as an extra charge for being late. So I'd replace "late charge" with "old charge." Also, you might add this sentence at the end of the next-to-last paragraph: "We've tried diligently to work this matter out, but your office has been negligent in handling this charge every step of the way." (Much of the rest of the letter had itemized that negligence.)

Tiger: You might add this at the end of the first paragraph: "Quite probably the charge was written off years ago. Why has it been revived—much less sent to a collection agency?" In the third paragraph, instead of "Your office has bungled this matter rather seriously," consider making it "Your office has seriously bungled this matter."

Tim: In the first paragraph, you've written: "our client paid her part of the bills." Why not say "promptly paid"? The file shows that she paid three days after the bill was mailed. Instead of "Your office never sent the detailed charges," how about "Even now your office still hasn't sent the detailed charges"? That increases the impact.

All good suggestions. After incorporating these ideas, I have a stronger letter.

Remember that every document you send out reflects on both you and your office—on the degree of care you take and on your level of competence and professionalism. When you look at it that way, it's hard not to recognize that we all need all the help we can get.

ॐ ॐ ॐ

Planning an In-House Writing Workshop?

As PROFESSOR WILLIAM PROSSER once observed, the law is one of the principal literary professions. So you'd think that lawyers, being professional writers, would hone their craft as tirelessly as professional golfers or concert violinists. And you'd think that law schools would devote considerable resources to teaching their students to write well.

But neither lawyers nor law schools do these things. In fact, recent studies confirm what critics have long said: when it comes to writing, the legal profession gets flunking grades. A study in Vancouver, British Columbia, found that consumers believe that, of all professionals, lawyers are the worst communicators. An Australian study has shown that lawyers and judges, when asked a series of questions about the law, took twice as long to answer them when working with actual statutes than with plain-language versions. A consumer survey by the State Bar of California showed that Californians consider the simplification of legal documents more significant than *any other issue* confronting lawyers; even so, bar leaders everywhere tend to see it as a relatively unimportant issue. And finally, research by the American Bar Foundation showed that young lawyers today consider writing a critical skill yet complain that their law schools slight it.

The law schools don't or can't help much because of their current budgeting priorities. Teaching writing, after all, is extremely labor-intensive, hence costly.

So if the partners in a law firm find themselves lamenting the state of writing within the firm, what can they do? Increasingly, they're turning to in-house writing workshops.

My own experience in running such workshops for firms, courts, and house counsel began in 1991, when I formed LawProse, Inc. My colleagues and I dedicated ourselves to combining all the best elements from CLE programs we had attended over the years. But we also soon learned a great deal from our own teaching, and these lessons have shaped our philosophy.

The LawProse Philosophy

The LawProse faculty—in addition to me, we have two well-known English professors with business-consulting experience, John R. Trimble and Betty S. Flowers—spent many hours planning our offerings before we ever announced our enterprise. Out of these discussions, several shared

Adapted from *Lawyer Hiring and Training Report* (Spring 1993).

convictions emerged. To this day, they give our workshops a coherent philosophy.

First, we believe that the best legal style is simple and direct. Without simplicity and directness, lawyers themselves are liable to get mired in the obscurity of their reasoning. Their readers certainly won't be able to sort out the meaning. That's why mature writers, when editing their own work, tend to strip out their complex expressions. George Bernard Shaw once wisely said that the chief aim of the novice writer is to acquire the literary language, while the chief aim of the adept writer is to eliminate it. The analogous point holds true for lawyers: the chief aim of the novice lawyer is to acquire the legal language, while the chief aim of the adept lawyer is, wherever possible, to eliminate it.

Second, we are convinced that any writer can learn a simpler, more direct style, but it takes real work. It's the same with writing as it is with any other skill. You no more "drift into" being a good writer than you "drift into" being a scratch-handicap golfer or an accomplished violinist.

Third, we believe that achieving a better writing style involves rejecting many archaic conventions that have evolved over the years. To immunize themselves against the prevailing legal habits, writers must learn to:

- Handle citations so that they don't impede readability.
- Weave quotations deftly into the text.
- Distinguish between terms of art and needless jargon.
- Edit their own and others' writing knowledgeably.
- Exploit the many resources of typographical design—typefaces, margins, white space, hanging indents, and the like—to improve their documents' readability.
- Cut the word count in a first draft by about 25%.
- Connect sentences and paragraphs so that the argument feels seamless.

Fourth, the LawProse faculty is committed to helping legal writers achieve and then maintain credibility. We teach lawyers both to reason well and to become more accomplished wordsmiths. We believe that writing must be approached holistically: while the organization must be sound and the argument compelling, the mechanics must be sound, too. All these things can be covered in a writing workshop.

Finally, we believe that empathy for the reader is one hallmark of effective legal writers. To put it negatively, good writers fear misleading, distracting, or boring anyone. Why? Because they intuitively grasp two truths for which my colleague John Trimble has coined these maxims:

- Readers are impatient to get the goods.
- They resent having to work any harder than necessary to get them.

Those maxims hold true for every judge I've talked with about writing—
and I'd be surprised if they didn't hold true for you.

Attitudinal Baggage

Many lawyers attending a writing workshop are apt to bring with them
at least a few self-defeating assumptions and attitudes. Among the most
common are these:

1. *Style doesn't matter.* Many lawyers view style as merely ornamen-
   tal. They believe that the law and the facts are what counts. "Oh,
   I'm no stylist—I just get the facts and the law down on the
   page." This attitude often begins with a flawed premise about
   just what "style" is. It's not mere adornment. It's how one pack-
   ages one's ideas—in fact, it's their very embodiment. Everyone
   has a style, not just the "stylist." There are good styles and bad
   styles. Good ones deliver the ideas efficiently and accessibly, without distraction. So if you care about getting your ideas across that
   way—if, in short, you care about your reader, not to mention
   your own credibility—you'll surely concede that style matters.

2. *Legalese is precise—we shouldn't tamper with it.* What do you mean
   by *legalese*? If you confine the word (as almost no one does) to
   unsimplifiable terms of art such as *res judicata* and *special appearance*, then the position is defensible. But if you mean the legal
   profession's characteristic style—stuffy, pedantic, archaic, overparticularized in some spots and waffly in others—then the statement is false. Legalese is, ironically, riddled with ambiguities,
   vaguenesses, and other types of imprecision. For example, *herein*
   begs the question. In this document? In this section? In this sub-
   section? The word *same* isn't as clear as *it* or *them* because you
   can't tell whether the antecedent is singular or plural. The use of
   an ambiguous *same* in Article II of the United States Constitution necessitated a constitutional amendment on the question of
   presidential succession.[1] Examples could be multiplied.

3. *To be accepted in the legal community, you have to "talk the talk."*
   Actually, the legal community provides considerable evidence to
   the contrary. Some of the very best legal writers of the past half-
   century—Charles Alan Wright, Grant Gilmore, Glanville Williams, Thomas Gibbs Gee, and Lord Denning, among others—
   write in a style virtually free of jargon.

---

[1] *See Garner's Modern American Usage* 704 (2d. ed. 2003).

4. *To challenge something I've written is to challenge my intellect.* Here's an attitudinal hurdle all of us must clear. We tend to associate our intellect so closely with our written product that we instinctively resist being edited. Yet seasoned writers and editors know that *everyone* can use a good edit. Until you've had an experienced editor tinker with your writing, you may never know just how much it can be improved.

5. *Writing is a wretched subject to hear about—I remember yawning through English with Miss Fidditch.* Well, it needn't be boring. In fact, it can be both entertaining and hugely enlightening, especially when the faculty approaches the subject not as schoolmarms but as savvy legal editors. If they address legal reasoning, the use of caselaw, and effective argumentation in a fresh and eye-opening way, the participants will also welcome pragmatic discussions of punctuation, common grammatical errors, and the like.

6. *All this might be nice in an ideal world, but I don't have the time to revise.* An ivory-tower approach will fail, and deservedly. That's why a workshop must address how lawyers can become more efficient as writers and editors. Without attention to the writing process itself—for example, how to pace a writing project, how to develop an outlining technique that facilitates writing, how to dictate effectively—the instruction can seem interesting but impractical.

Teaching Style

We've tried to cultivate a teaching style that works in almost any professional setting. It is authoritative but not dogmatic, and it's thoroughly up-to-date. For example, we use a wealth of modern examples to dispel some common superstitions: that it's wrong to begin a sentence with *and* or *but*; that you should never split an infinitive; that it's wrong to end a sentence with a preposition; that you should never say *I* or *me* in business correspondence; and the like. And we briefly explain the history of these superstitions and why, for all their wrongheadedness, they've remained entrenched.

Though we incorporate many lessons from modern linguistics, we minimize grammatical arcana—for example, references to fused participles, the pluperfect tense, irregular verbs, etc. We even avoid talk of *nominalizations* (a current buzzword) by using a simpler, more descriptive term: *buried verbs*. Most lawyers resist arguments that they should abandon legalese when the instructors themselves mouth their own linguistic jargon.

Ideally, a workshop is interactive, so the LawProse faculty encourages audience participation. Though we move briskly, we happily pause for questions and brief discussions.

Finally, a writing workshop can be either a teacher-and-pupil exercise or a leader-and-colleague exercise. At LawProse, we take the latter approach, recognizing that everyone in the room is a professional and should have ideas worth hearing. We're there partly to draw on the group's collective wisdom.

Content and Materials

The most successful workshops blend large, rhetorical points with smaller, technical ones. Believe it or not, many lawyers want to hear about the current status of the serial comma, about the proper use of semicolons, about how and when to use bulleted lists, and about commonly confused words in legal writing.

But these technical questions are best addressed during discussions of the larger issues that every writer wrestles with: how to reduce clutter; how to organize memos, briefs, and legal instruments effectively; how to improve clarity; how to smooth the flow between paragraphs; how to frame a legal issue concisely yet intelligibly; how to manage tone; how to format documents for greater readability; and how best to approach the various stages of the writing process. The LawProse faculty abhors needless complexity and abstractness, so we discuss these issues with copious examples—both exemplary and cautionary.

Finally, although workshops can be effective even when using only generic examples of legal prose, the best ones integrate passages from the participants' own writing samples. Otherwise, the participants are apt to shrug and say, "Well, that's all fine. But your examples are from an insurance-defense practice, and in this firm we're oil-and-gas lawyers." At LawProse, we try to allot time to discuss, and improve, an anonymous passage or two by participants. Our aim is to show the value of artful editing.

Logistical Needs

Workshops should be tailored to a firm's needs and wants. The questions here are several: Is the firm litigation-oriented or does it do primarily transactional work? Within a larger firm, which sections will be represented? Is the firm willing to invest in a seminar for 20—including partners as well as associates—or does it want to invite (perhaps even require) everyone to come? Does the firm want a more in-depth program of up to three days, including individual tutorials, or does it want a one-day workshop addressed to everyone simultaneously? If it's a three-day program, will it be three consecutive days or three consecutive Fridays or Saturdays?

We've done variations on all those programs. The best, we're convinced, are the more in-depth ones that combine large-group sessions with small breakout sessions and individual tutorials. In three consecutive days, for example, we'll cover 250 pages of materials contained in two workbooks loaded with exercises and explanations that will outlive the seminar.

And we offer a fourth day on "Advanced Legal Drafting," which stands apart from our other offerings because it addresses many problems specific to contracts, statutes, rules, and the like.

Anything beyond those four days would probably best be devoted to individualized instruction, which most lawyers find enormously beneficial.

Beyond the makeup and length of the program, the planners within the firm ought to give some thought to:

- Briefing the LawProse faculty beforehand on the most common writing problems that junior colleagues struggle with.
- Arranging the workshop room to allow us to move about freely and interact with all the participants.
- Having a respected partner introduce the program and emphasize the firm's commitment to good writing.
- Having several partners enroll in the program alongside their juniors.

Real-World Lessons

While imparting lessons on writing, any CLE teacher is likely to learn a few lessons as well. Here are ten that we've learned at LawProse:

1. The better writers tend to be the most enthusiastic participants. The less able writers—the more insecure ones—are most likely to report scheduling conflicts, to have no writing sample available, or to fault the entire enterprise.
2. Firms of equal size can vary a lot in their writing standards. On balance, firms that talk more about professionalism produce better writing than firms that talk more about profitability.
3. The more involved the partners are in a writing program, the more seriously the associates will take it.

4. Particular bad habits tend to pervade each firm. In one firm, seemingly everyone will be addicted to *under the auspices of* and other stock phrases; in another firm, the brief-writers will revel in *ad hominem* attacks; in still another firm, the writing will drown in 19th-century formalisms. A firm's predominant writing problems are impossible to know until you see the writing samples.

5. For two reasons, the faculty must cover a great deal of territory fast. First, lawyers are quick studies, so they get bored quickly. Second, the firm's greatest investment is not in the faculty's fee, but in the time that their lawyers spend in the workshop— cumulatively, say, $5,000 or $10,000 *an hour.* So every minute ought to be spent usefully.

6. Despite the stereotypes, most lawyers are willing to dispense with legalese. In fact, deep down, they really want to, but they need major encouragement, mostly in the form of demonstrations of how much more intelligent their own prose seems without it.

7. Within a law firm, it's helpful for the lawyers to share a common vocabulary with which to discuss writing problems. Once everyone knows what a "buried verb" is, for example, the firm will save editing time while producing better documents.

8. A good workshop cannot transform a mediocre writer into a Robert H. Jackson, but it can ratchet everyone up a notch or two. And if it ignites an interest that may have lain dormant, the long-term progress for even a mediocre writer can be extraordinary.

9. The faculty must be conversant with legal subjects. If they aren't, they will always develop a credibility problem with at least some participants.

10. The workshop must be interactive. The faculty should assume that they are not just teaching lots of new things but *reminding* participants of things they perhaps once knew but haven't applied consistently.

Once you've had an in-house program, you ought to find yourself grimacing less often over colleagues' briefs and letters. In fact, you'll probably find yourself saving some time as everyone begins identifying issues and positions more lucidly at the outset of memos and briefs. Contracts will become more accessible and stylistically consistent. And people will enjoy working in a culture that prizes good writing.

JUSTICE RUTH BADER GINSBURG

Judicial Writing

The Art of Judicial Writing

Understand the Main Goals
of a Judicial Opinion

(a) *Purposes.* Judicial opinions serve three major functions: (1) to help the writing judge think through the problems raised by the case; (2) to justify the outcome to parties and counsel, especially to the losing litigant and losing counsel; and (3) to serve as a source of precedent. There are other purposes as well: to persuade colleagues on the court to join in the ruling, to alert the legislature to inadequacies in statutory law, and to publish the law and ensure its acceptance in society generally.

(b) *An extraordinary challenge.* Opinion-writing is an especially hard job, different from ordinary discursive or persuasive writing. The decision must generally be consistent with previous judicial decisions and must at the same time conform to the judge's notions of justice. Often, and especially in difficult cases, the doctrine of stare decisis plays tug-of-war with conscientious fairness. The dilemma is especially acute because some of the most complex problems of society and of individual human lives must be reduced to the simplest of dichotomies: yea or nay. Not all the uncertainties can be plumbed by the judge

---

From *The Redbook: A Manual on Legal Style* (2d ed. 2006).

writing the opinion; the task is to justify the court's determination sensibly and clearly, while not ignoring whatever merits there may be on the losing side.

Write for as Broad an Audience as Possible

(a) *Many possible readers.* In various polls, state and federal judges have cited all sorts of different readers that they envision when writing judicial opinions. Among these are judicial colleagues; the bar; future judges; the legislature; the losing litigant; the losing lawyer; law students; newspaper readers; oneself; a higher court; advertisers (e.g., in a prospective opponent's campaign); and the general intelligent reader.

(b) *"Ordinary reader" as a useful fiction.* Some of the most effective judicial writers have a person of average intelligence and average education in mind as their reader. Many judges acknowledge that people other than lawyers or law students might actually read their opinions. In his Supreme Court confirmation hearings, Justice Stephen Breyer said that as an appellate judge, he wanted his opinions to be understandable to a high-school student. This approach helps law serve the sense of fairness and decency in society by making judicial decision-making as accessible as possible to all members of society. The judge who writes plainly, clearly, and straightforwardly helps instill confidence in our legal system and respect for the judiciary.

Develop a Good Protocol for Working on Opinions

(a) *Working habits.* Although judges take various approaches to working on opinions, all start by sorting out the issues in the case. Some judges read through the briefs sequentially—in the order in which the parties filed them. Others read the briefs in reverse order (reply brief first) on the theory that the reply brief will have the most focused discussion of the complaining party's issues. If there is a "best practice" among appellate judges—a prevailing norm among the best writers on the appellate bench—it is reading in this order: (1) the trial court's opinion; (2) the appellant's reply brief; (3) the appellee's brief; and (4) the appellant's main brief. It is certainly acceptable to switch #2 and #4. Many judges sketch out each party's contentions, together with the opposing party's answers to those points. This practice helps the judge develop a good understanding of the dispositive points. Some judges do all this in a routine way. Others claim to have no set pattern for approaching cases. But a good routine fosters efficiency. And by no means does it result in predictable, cookie-cutter opinions. It simply suggests a level of discipline that professional writers in any field should have.

(b) *Deficiencies in law-clerk style.* Again, judges' practices vary with law clerks. A few judges draft all their own opinions from scratch and use their law clerks to amplify and verify the research. Others delegate opinion-drafting to their clerks—sometimes with detailed directions about how to write the opinion, but sometimes with little more direction than which party wins. The law clerk then drafts the opinion for the judge, and perhaps others in chambers, to edit. The rise of clerk-drafted opinions in recent years has brought these attendant problems: (1) a law-review style in judicial writing, with excessive citation of authority; (2) a certain immature grandiloquence as fledgling lawyers reach for the rhetorical heights they imagine to be appropriate to judicial writing; and (3) a structurally diffident approach in which every point is considered ad nauseam, including all the facts in detail, because the writer is not confident about what really matters and what doesn't. Unless the judge has a heavy editorial hand—and a sure-footed way to train new clerks shortly after they arrive—the judge's style will probably be infected to some degree with such flaws. The greater the judge's involvement, of course, the better.

(c) *Advice to law clerks.* If you clerk for a judge who expects you to draft opinions, your role is to give the opinion the judge's voice, not your own. Do your best to learn your judge's style. Study the judge's tone—especially at its best. You'll be trying to create the best opinion that the judge would write given the time to do so. Once the judge accepts a draft opinion, it is the judge's—not yours. If the judge has a heavy editorial hand and seems not to accept the draft that you've prepared, learn from the experience. Study what changes were made, and figure out why. Even if the judge has a light editorial hand—or accepts the draft as you prepared it—remember that it's still the judge's opinion, not yours.

Understand the Paramount Importance of Style

(a) *Pure vs. impure.* A "pure" opinion style has an up-front summary: it gives the outcome as part of the opener. An "impure" style delays the outcome to the end; it has been called a mystery-novel approach. Most American judges prefer the pure style, but not all. Two of the most influential writers on the American bench—Richard A. Posner and Frank H. Easterbrook, both of the U.S. Court of Appeals for the Seventh Circuit—prefer the impure style. Whichever approach one takes, the essential ingredient is logic. With the pure style, the challenges are (1) to state the problem clearly (preferably in separate sentences—not one long convoluted sentence that begins *This case presents the question whether . . .*), (2) to capsulize the reasoning, and (3) to state the result. Few openers are more embarrassing than one that says, essentially, *This is a torts case. We affirm.* Although that's a gross non sequitur, it's fairly common. Instead, the opener should be truly informative and comprehensible, like this:

> In May 2005, Andrew McNair pleaded guilty to burglary in order to receive deferred adjudication, but he now regrets that decision because he has been charged with violating the terms of his plea agreement and may face harsher punishment. We must decide whether McNair can now change his initial plea to avoid the harsher punishment. Because Ohio criminal procedure prohibits a defendant from withdrawing a guilty plea after being sentenced, we hold that he cannot.

(b) *Only the necessary facts.* Three points. First, there is a balance to be struck with facts. Enough of them need to be included for the reader to understand what gave rise to the legal problem. But don't simply summarize all the facts in the record, as many lawyers do in their briefs. Rarely can a lawyer's statement of the facts be adapted into a judge's. The only exception occurs when the advocate has done a magisterial job of laying out all the pertinent facts fairly and without argumentation. Some judicial writers set out all the facts as a starting point. This overinclusiveness tends to make the opinion muddy, exceedingly dull, and so detailed as to become readily distinguishable from other cases. Second, overspecificity in facts is deathly. Precise dates, in particular, can be distracting. If you say *On January 4, 2006, X happened*—as writers so often do—you're suggesting that there is something significant about the date, as if it matters that it wasn't the 3rd or the 5th of January. The best practice is to include specifics (such as *5 grams of heroin* or *48 hours after the deadline*) only when they matter. Don't crowd the reader's mind with details. Third, it's important to remember how opinions are typically found and used—electronically, with a mere screenful of an opinion to be read at once. In other words, most opinions today are not read linearly. So the best practice is to give a bare-bones statement of facts toward the outset (after a good summary paragraph) and then to incorporate some of the factual discussion as it bears on the legal analysis. If all the facts are set out before the analysis and never again mentioned—or only glancingly—the opinion becomes much harder for researchers to use. Key facts, the ones that make a difference in the outcome, can and should be introduced during the analysis of the relevant point.

(c) *Mandate.* As a practical matter, judges must learn to worry about the clarity of their orders. Is the court reversing? Reversing and remanding—and, if so, remanding for what purpose? What is the trial court to do? Is the court affirming in part and reversing in part? Precisely which parts? Among the vaguest mandates are *So ordered* and *Ordered accordingly*—especially if the opinion itself has been unclear. And even with a more specific direction in the mandate, the judicial writer should word it fastidiously. For example, writing *The trial court is affirmed* is careless because the appellate court cannot act on the trial court—only on its judgment. In the most careful judicial usage, an appellate court may affirm, reverse, or modify a judgment or order; it may agree with, approve, or disapprove an opinion or decision; and it remands cases and actions. For more guidance on drafting mandates, see Bryan A. Garner, *A Dictionary of Modern Legal Usage* 482–83 (2d ed. 1995).

Avoid the Common Shortcomings of Opinions

(a) *Verbosity.* In 1940, the ABA president, Charles A. Beardsley, campaigned for shorter judicial opinions and plain language in the law. Long opinions, he said, waste time in four ways. First, they waste the writer's time. Second, they waste the time of the other judges on the court. Third, they waste the time of the editorial staff at legal publishers, which prepare headnotes and digests. Finally, they waste the time of every American lawyer who ever needs to consult the opinions. The cumulative effect of this waste, Beardsley said, is immeasurable. Yet judicial opinions have gotten longer and longer since Beardsley's day. The best judicial writers know that shorter is better. As Judge Alex Kozinski of the Ninth Circuit routinely tells his clerks about opinions, "Everything you put in that doesn't help, hurts." His analogy: A fifth leg wouldn't help a gazelle move more swiftly and gracefully.

(b) *Wigmore's six complaints.* In his great treatise on evidence, the scholar John Wigmore noted six recurrent shortcomings in American judicial opinions. They are still telling points. (1) Judges cite authority without enough discrimination. He said that modern judges need to be well grounded in legal history and legal literature. (2) Judges often show unfamiliarity with controlling precedents. This problem, Wigmore believed, has three causes: the brief tenure of most appellate judges; the crush of work; and the lack of a body of capable appellate advocates to help judges reach the highest standards. The problem might also be traced to unnecessarily complex law. But the problem is surely less pronounced today than it was in Wigmore's day, especially because of the widespread use of electronic research. (3) Judges often tend to treat judicial questions mechanically. Too much of our law, Wigmore said, is "dead bark." Reasons can be lost from sight. (4) Judges often misconceive the doctrine of precedent. Wigmore complained of the constant "loose resort to the law of other states," which he said makes the doctrine "optional," since decisions of other states are not precedents. (5) Judicial writers often overwrite—they consider far too many points in dicta. This habit, wrote Wigmore, "tends to remove the decision from the really vital issues of each case and to transform the opinion into a list of rulings on academic assertions." (6) Too many judges think of opinions as being single-judge opinions as opposed to a full-court or a full-panel opinion. As Wigmore put it: "All the law of every opinion should be affirmed by the whole court."

(c) *Tone.* The tone of a judicial opinion should be judicial: controlled, calm, assured, and dignified—yet it can also be relaxed and idiomatic. It needn't be stuffy, and it shouldn't be. A good opinion is, as much as possible, in plain English. In a dissent, the tone shouldn't be sarcastic and unpleasant. It's especially unwise for judges to use textual footnotes to spar with each other.

Develop a Sensible Approach to Concurrences

(a) *Origin of concurrences.* A concurring opinion is really a vestige of the old seriatim-style opinion common in the American federal courts in the 1790s. It means that an individual appellate judge is having his or her say separately from the rest of the court.

(b) *Reasons for proliferation.* Court-watchers have offered any number of reasons for the growth of concurrences and dissents in American law. Some believe that they reflect our increasingly complex and ideologically charged legal atmosphere. Others say that they are the practical outcome of a divided court. On the federal level, Chief Justice William H. Rehnquist attributed the rise of separate opinions to the sharp jump in the percentage of cases in which a constitutional issue is involved.

(c) *A cynical view of Frankfurter.* Justice Felix Frankfurter was known as the "concurringest" of the Supreme Court justices when he served. In the 1955–1956 term, when 94 opinions were handed down, there were 21 concurrences—two-thirds by Frankfurter. Noting that Frankfurter's concurrences have almost never been cited by anyone since, one commentator has said that Frankfurter might just as well have folded his concurrences into paper airplanes and thrown them out a Supreme Court window.

(d) *Concur with caution.* The "opinion of the court"—a development originally instituted by Chief Justice John Marshall of the Supreme Court—should be viewed as an important ideal in American law. A concurring opinion can reduce a majority opinion to a plurality, thereby making its authority questionable. For the sake of clarity and desirable simplicity, judges would do well to write concurring opinions as seldom as possible. And when they do, it would be advisable to explicitly join the main opinion so that a clear ruling remains.

Develop a Sensible Approach to Dissents

(a) *Dissents generally.* Over a century ago, one scholar compared the dissenter to a kid who makes faces at a tougher kid across the street. Chief Justice Charles Evans Hughes, in his 1928 book on the Supreme Court, described the idea with more dignity—and surely with more accuracy: "A dissent in a court of last resort is an appeal to the brooding spirit of the law, to the intelligence of a future day, when a later decision may possibly correct the error into which the dissenting judge believes the court to have been betrayed."

(b) *Purposes.* Dissents have five main purposes: (1) to set forth the argument that did not convince a majority of the court, but did convince a minority; (2) to attract the attention of a higher court; (3) to avoid stretching out a compromise opinion that, in the end, reads unclearly; (4) to speak to future judges; and (5) on courts of last resort—mostly on the Supreme Court of the United States—to complete the picture of a justice's philosophy of constitutional jurisprudence and to mark the road map of constitutional history.

(c) *The old view.* Through the mid-20th century, many legal scholars argued that dissents had no place in our system of justice because they are unnecessary and divisive. The view was that dissents should not be filed unless it was reasonably certain that a public gain, as distinguished from a private one, would result. Chief Justice John Marshall's approach typified the judicial practice of his day: in 35 years on the U.S. Supreme Court, he dissented only nine times. Today, our views of dissenting opinions are generally much more tolerant, though we still hear laments that unanimity on the Supreme Court is no more common than it is in our appellate courts. Some modern scholars believe that Justice Oliver Wendell Holmes, the "Great Dissenter," made dissents fashionable. Whether that is true or not, few judicial writers today carry off their dissents with anything approaching his level of articulateness and panache.

(d) *The voice of a dissenter.* Dissenting judges are not constrained by the voice or language of precedent. While majority opinions try to interpret the law objectively, dissents can be more passionate. As Justice J. William Brennan Jr. has said, dissents often "seek to sow seeds for future harvest." These tend to be separate opinions that have the ring of rhetoric, and they can, in Brennan's words, "straddle the worlds of literature and law." The judge's word choice, tone, and structure of presentation are crucial. Avoid clichés such as "I vigorously dissent." If you're going to dissent, be vigorous about it; but don't call yourself vigorous.

Study Effective Judicial Writing

(a) *Widely admired judicial writers.* What follows is something of a pantheon of federal judicial writers whose work may be studied to good effect: Justice Robert H. Jackson (1892–1954) of the U.S. Supreme Court; Judge Richard S. Arnold (1936–2004) of the Eighth Circuit; Judge Henry J. Friendly (1903–1986) of the Second Circuit; Judge Thomas Gibbs Gee (1925–1994) of the Fifth Circuit; Judge Learned Hand (1872–1961) of the Second Circuit; Judge Spottswood W. Robinson (1916–1998) of the D.C. Circuit; Judge Alvin B. Rubin (1920–1992) of the Fifth Circuit; and Judge John Minor Wisdom (1905–1999) of the Fifth Circuit. Among the living judges whose work might be carefully studied are:

- Chief Justice John G. Roberts of the U.S. Supreme Court.
- Justice Antonin Scalia of the U.S. Supreme Court.
- Justice Ruth Bader Ginsburg of the U.S. Supreme Court.

- Justice Stephen G. Breyer of the U.S. Supreme Court.
- Chief Judge Michael Boudin of the First Circuit.
- Judge Frank H. Easterbrook of the Seventh Circuit.
- Judge Robert H. Henry of the Tenth Circuit.
- Judge Alex Kozinski of the Ninth Circuit.
- Judge Richard A. Posner of the Seventh Circuit.

(b) *Books on judging.* Among the very best books on the art of judg-
    ing are Erwin N. Griswold, *The Judicial Process* (1973); Robert E.
    Keeton, *Keeton on Judging in the American Legal System* (1999); Karl
    N. Llewellyn, *The Common Law Tradition: Deciding Appeals* (1960);
    David Pannick, *Judges* (1987); and *Judicial Decision-Making* (Glendon
    Schubert ed., 1963). Also useful—and highly amusing—are R.E.
    Megarry's three books: *Miscellany-at-Law: A Diversion for Lawyers and
    Others* (1956); *A Second Miscellany-at-Law: A Further Diversion for
    Lawyers and Others* (1973); and *A New Miscellany-at-Law: Yet Another
    Diversion for Lawyers and Others* (Bryan A. Garner ed., 2005).

(c) *Guidance on judicial writing.* The following publications will prove
    helpful: Bryan A. Garner, "Opinions, Style of," in *The Oxford Com-
    panion to the Supreme Court of the United States* (2d ed. 2005); Joyce J.
    George, *Judicial Opinion Writing Handbook* (4th ed. 2000); Walker
    Gibson, *Literary Minds and Judicial Style*, 36 N.Y.U. L. Rev. 915
    (1961); Joseph Kimble, *The Straight Skinny on Better Judicial Opinions*,
    9 Scribes J. Legal Writing 2 (2003–2004); Robert A. Leflar, *Quality
    in Judicial Opinions*, 3 Pace L. Rev. 579 (1983); Glen Leggett, *Judicial
    Writing: An Observation by a Teacher of Writing*, 58 Law Lib. J. 114
    (1965); George R. Smith, *A Primer of Opinion Writing for Four New
    Judges*, 21 Ark. L. Rev. 197 (1967); Patricia Wald, *The Rhetoric of Results
    and the Results of Rhetoric*, 62 U. Chi. L. Rev. 1371 (1995); Irving
    Younger, *On Judicial Opinions Considered as One of the Fine Arts*, 51
    U. Colo. L. Rev. 341 (1980).

(d) *Example.* The following opinion, using the "pure" style, has been
    rewritten as a model. For an interesting contrast, see the original
    opinion, which appeared as *Israel v. Allen*, 577 P.2d 762 (Colo. 1978).

Supreme Court of Colorado, En Banc

**Martin Richard ISRAEL and Tammy Lee Bannon Israel,
Plaintiffs–Appellees**

v.

**Norman C. ALLEN, County Clerk and Recorder of Jefferson County,
Defendant–Appellant**

No. 27823

April 24, 1978

PRINGLE, Chief Justice.

Summary

Martin and Tammy Israel, who are siblings only by adoption, were denied a marriage license because the Colorado Uniform Marriage Act[1] prohibits marriage between adoptive siblings. The trial court declared the prohibition unconstitutional because it found that marriage is a fundamental right, and subject to equal protection. We find that the prohibition is unconstitutional because it does not meet minimum rationality requirements. On that basis, we affirm the judgment.

When Martin Met Tammy

Before they married in 1972, Raymond Israel and Sylvia Bannon each had a child from a previous relationship. Raymond Israel legally adopted his wife's daughter, Tammy. She thus became his son Martin's adoptive sister.

Martin Israel and Tammy Bannon Israel applied for a marriage license. Their application was denied because the Colorado Uniform Marriage Act specifically prohibits "marriage between an ancestor and a descendant or between a brother and sister, whether the relationship is by the half or the whole blood *or by adoption*; . . . ."[2]

---

[1] C.R.S. § 14-2-101, et seq. (1973).
[2] C.R.S. § 14-2-110(1)(b) (1973) (emphasis added).

The couple sought declaratory relief. The trial court decided that marriage is a fundamental right, and applied an equal-protection standard of review, which requires a compelling state interest to support barring a marriage between a brother and sister related only by adoption. Finding no such interest, the court held that the prohibition was unconstitutional. The court severed the words "or by adoption" from the statute.

Why the Act Is Unconstitutional

The basic test of constitutionality is the minimum rationality standard or rational-basis test. A law or a provision in a law must have some reasonable relationship to a legitimate state interest, and it must serve to further that interest. If it doesn't, then we must find the law unconstitutional.[3]

The only argument offered to support the prohibition is that the state has an interest in preserving family harmony and that prohibiting the marriage between this adoptive brother and sister furthers this interest. But the proposed marriage does not threaten the Israel family's harmony. Raymond Israel and Sylvia Bannon are in favor of the marriage. Also, Bishop Evans of the Roman Catholic Archdiocese of Denver finds no religious bar to the marriage.

There are other reasons for a state to forbid marriages between a brother and sister, but they do not apply when the man and woman are related only by adoption.

Society objects to marriages between blood relatives because they are considered more likely to produce children with serious genetic defects. This does not apply to people related only by marriage.[4] Like marriage, adoption into a family does not change blood relationships. So while there is a rational basis to prohibit siblings of the full or half blood from marrying, it doesn't logically extend to brothers and sisters related only by adoption.

Colorado law recognizes that adoptive siblings are different from siblings related by blood. In some statutes, the legislature makes adopted and natural children equal, such as in matters of inheritance and parental duties. But the legislature exempts adoptive siblings from other statutes that affect families. For example, the criminal-incest statute does not forbid sexual relationships between an adopted brother and sister.[5] If such a relationship is not forbidden outside of marriage, it is illogical to forbid it within.

---

[3] *Stevenson v. Indus. Comm'n*, 545 P.2d 712, 716 (Colo. 1976). *See also Dandridge v. Williams*, 397 U.S. 471, 484–487 (1970).

[4] *See* 1 Vernier, *American Family Laws* 183 (1971) (comparing English, ecclesiastical, and American law regarding marriage between people related only by affinity).

[5] C.R.S. § 18-6-301 (1973).

We hold that the portion of the statute forbidding marriage between a brother and sister related only by adoption is unconstitutional because there is no rational basis for the prohibition.

Severability of the Provision

Language in a statute may be declared unconstitutional and severed if the severance has no effect on the remaining provisions.[6] The prohibition against marriage between a brother and sister related by blood is independent of the words "or by adoption,"[7] so the rest of the statute is still effective. The trial court did not err in holding that this statute was severable and striking the unconstitutional provision.

Disposition

Although the trial court held that the statute infringed a fundamental right, and the rational-basis test usually applies only when no fundamental right is implicated, we have found that prohibiting marriage between a brother and sister related only by adoption does not satisfy minimum rationality requirements. So we need not decide whether marriage is a fundamental right in Colorado.

Affirmed.

---

[6] *Shroyer v. Sokol*, 550 P.2d 309, 311 (Colo. 1976).
[7] *See* C.R.S. § 14-2-110(1)(b) (1973).

ಕ್ಕಿ ಕ್ಕಿ ಕ್ಕಿ

The Style of U.S. Supreme Court Opinions

A CLOISTERED BRANCH of government, the Supreme Court communicates with the rest of the nation primarily through written opinions. Whether they come to us through newspaper synopses, straight from the papers of the *United States Reports*, or from some intermediate source, it is almost exclusively by these opinions that we know the Court. If the opinions explaining the Court's decisions make sense to us, then all is well; if they confuse or strike us as false or unjust, then our sense of the fairness of our society is weakened. The words of the Court, then, must be well chosen—its use of language skillful and clear—or else we all, to one degree or another, suffer. To preserve our faith in it, the Court must write well.

Period-Styles. The form of Supreme Court opinions has changed greatly over the past 200 years. There is no evident apex or nadir, but it is possible to generalize about what Karl Llewellyn called "period-styles." In the first half of the 19th century, the "grand style" was common in American courts, as exemplified by Chief Justice John Marshall and Justice Joseph Story, and on state appellate courts by John Bannister Gibson of Pennsylvania and Lemuel Shaw of Massachusetts. Judges spoke as the "mouthpieces of divinity" in polished, spartan opinions. The quality of judicial writing declined after 1850, when the "formal style," stressing logic and precedent, emerged. Opinions became much less readable: turgid, obscure, jargonistic, repetitious, and full of string citations and careless English. At the turn of the 20th century, Justice Oliver Wendell Holmes's brilliant writing shone brightly amid this dreary gray. Perhaps as a result of his influence, the better Supreme Court opinions in the 20th century have become, rhetorically speaking, increasingly powerful and persuasive. But the grand style has been dead since 1900, and the formal style, although mostly moribund since the rise of legal realism, lives on in the form of newly elaborated constitutional doctrines with layered sets of "tests" and "prongs" and "standards" and "hurdles."

This broadly conceived evolution of Supreme Court opinions is explainable partly on pragmatic grounds. In Marshall's day, the Court had more time to perfect its work product than in Chief Justice Melville Fuller's day, when dockets had become more and more crowded and

---

From *The Oxford Companion to the Supreme Court of the United States* (2d ed. 2005).

judges more and more rushed. Further, the judges of 1900, according to some commentators, were not as well educated as those of 1800, and therefore less likely to have a command of the language. By the latter half of the 20th century, the justices had been cast more in the role of editors than of authors of their opinions; increasingly, law clerks have been delegated the task of putting into words what the justices have decided and why—hence the pervasive "law-review style" so often decried by Court observers.

From a literary perspective, the gems in the *United States Reports* are well hidden. That exalted set of books has been called "a great literary wasteland."[1] A collection of first-rate writings might be gleaned from its more than 500 volumes, but it would account for less than half a percent of the whole. Likewise, from a substantive legal perspective the opinions may be said to be wanting. Few of the Court's opinions genuinely illuminate the area of law with which they deal.

Whatever its inadequacies, the Supreme Court opinion is one of the most powerful tools of law and of rhetoric in American life. The practice of issuing written opinions has added immensely to the power and prestige of the Court. Justice William Brennan spoke in 1979 of the "fundamental . . . interdependence of the Court and the press," for it is through the press that the majority of Americans—probably the majority even of lawyers—learn what they know of the Court's activities. More important, though, is the role of opinion-writing in coming to a just resolution of any given case. Chief Justice Charles Evans Hughes said that "there is no better precaution against judicial mistakes than the setting out accurately and adequately [of] the material facts as well as the points to be decided."[2] As anyone who has set out to write a judicial opinion knows well, the writing hones the thinking and sometimes exposes weaknesses in a tentative determination that was ill-conceived. As judges often say, "Some opinions just won't write."

Reduction to Writing. Nothing in the federal Constitution, of course, requires that opinions be reduced to writing. In fact, during the Court's first decade, most were not; during the 1790s, the Court reduced its opinions to writing in only the most important cases. Justice James Iredell's draft opinion in *Chisholm v. Georgia* (1793) is the earliest known manuscript and just about the only one of that decade. We do not know just how much of the early reporting is the product of justices and how much is the handiwork of the unofficial reporter, Alexander James Dallas, who reported only 60 cases in the first 16 terms after 1790.

---

[1] John P. Frank, *Marble Palace: The Supreme Court in American Life* 130 (1958).
[2] Charles Evans Hughes, *The Supreme Court of the United States* 64 (1928).

William Cranch, the first official reporter (appointed in 1801), expressed relief at "the practice which the court had adopted of reducing their opinions to writing in all cases of difficulty or importance." By Cranch's time, written opinions had become the rule, but it was not until 1834 that an order required all opinions to be filed with the clerk.

Opinion of the Court. The justices' own great uncertainty in the early 19th century was not whether to reduce opinions to writing, but whether to deliver seriatim opinions. During the 1790s, the justices delivered opinions in turn, after the manner of the King's Bench, except that the justices spoke in inverse order of seniority. For example, in *Ware v. Hylton*, the most important case of 1796, Justice Samuel Chase delivered a long opinion and then every other justice gave his separate opinion.

This practice changed abruptly when Marshall became chief justice in 1801. Marshall instituted what we now know as the "opinion of the Court," that is, an opinion attributed to a single justice but speaking for the entire Court or a majority of its members. In Marshall's day, almost all the opinions were attributed to Marshall himself, although some of these were written by his colleagues. By means of the univocal opinion, Marshall was able to increase not only his own authority as chief justice but also the Court's authority within the American polity.

President Thomas Jefferson, in well-known correspondence, protested against judicial opinions that were "huddled up in a conclave, perhaps by a majority of one, delivered as if unanimous, and with the silent acquiescence of lazy or timid associates, by a crafty chief judge, who sophisticates the law to his mind by the turn of his own reasoning."[3] Jefferson wanted a rule requiring judges to announce their opinions seriatim and thus to take their positions publicly. Although he urged his own appointee Justice William Johnson, known as the "First Dissenter," to write separately so as to attack Marshall's dominance, Johnson did so only sporadically. Had he done so more frequently, Johnson might have weakened his influence on the Marshall Court.

From Marshall's time until the death of Chief Justice Hughes—for well over a century—the Court spoke generally in single opinions, with occasional concurrences and dissents in matters of great importance. In his 35-year tenure on the Court, Marshall dissented only nine times, less often in a long career than most of today's justices dissent in a single year. From Chief Justice Harlan Fiske Stone's time (1941–1946) to the present day, both concurring and dissenting opinions have been

---

[3] Letter to Thomas Ritchie, 25 Dec. 1820, in *Works of Thomas Jefferson* vol. 12, 177–78 (1905).

commonplace. Some commentators have called the modern fragmentation a return to seriatim opinions.

Scholars who follow the Court seem to agree—without dissent—that the proliferation of separate opinions is an undesirable trend. John P. Frank writes that "no single thing has more depreciated the standing of the institution since the time of Hughes than the impression that it is overtalkative."[4] Other Court-watchers agree that separate opinions have become excessive.

Proliferation of Dissents. At its best, a dissent in the high court is, as Chief Justice Hughes termed it, "an appeal to the brooding spirit of the law, to the intelligence of a future day, when a later decision may possibly correct the error into which the dissenting judge believes the court to have been betrayed."[5] That description applies nicely to what Justice Holmes and Justice Louis D. Brandeis did in giving dignity to dissenting opinions; indeed, Holmes was known as "the Great Dissenter" and was paid the honor of having an anthology of his dissents published. But as often as not, nowadays, dissents express disagreements over matters once considered too inconsequential to merit a separate opinion, and in Justice Lewis F. Powell's words, they are not "a model of temperate discourse." Thus, popularizers of the Court's activities are prone to speak of personal enmities on the Court, basing their inferences on nothing more than the language used in this or that justice's separate opinion.

Whereas the rhetoric of separate opinions may have become less restrained than yesteryear merely because of the gradual change of mores, the frequency of such opinions probably reflects something deeper than a mere loss of restraint. Justice William H. Rehnquist attributed the rise of concurrences and dissents to the sharp jump in recent years in the percentage of cases in which a constitutional claim is raised and, more to the point, in which a constitutional claim is sustained. Constitutional adjudication may well invite more separate opinions than does adjudication in other areas of law.

Justice Brennan's philosophy of dissenting illustrates just how different the modern view is from Chief Justice Hughes's. In an essay entitled "In Defense of Dissents," Brennan noted a justice's duty to dissent when in disagreement with the majority. As he wrote in the *Hastings Law Journal*, "Each justice must be an active participant, and, when necessary,

---

[4] Frank, note 1, at 129.

[5] Hughes, note 2, at 68.

must write separately to record his or her thinking. Writing, then, is not an egoistic art—it is duty. Saying, 'listen to me, see it my way, change your mind,' is not self-indulgence—it is very hard work that we cannot shirk."[6]

Jefferson might relish this near-return to his ideal, but it robs the Court's opinions of the oracular quality they once had. Multiplicity of opinions may also impair the work of the Court. Frank studied the separate opinions of Justice Felix Frankfurter—the "concurringest" member of the Court during his time—and showed that they were almost never cited by anyone. So the conclusion that Frankfurter "consumed a large portion of his energy and talent in essays which, for all practical purposes, might as well have been written on paper airplanes and thrown out a Supreme Court window."[7]

Law Clerks and Verbosity. The crush of work at the Court is undoubtedly the single greatest influence on the style of modern opinions. Justice Harry Blackmun was perhaps being delicate when he used the future tense to forecast a "breaking point" at which "one's work becomes second-rate."[8] Opinion-writing is the most time-consuming of the justices' work. Today, justices average more than 25 signed opinions apiece each year.

Traditionally, opinion-writing has been viewed as that aspect of the justices' work in which law clerks are least competent to help. Yet federal judges at all levels are being transformed from writers into editors of their law clerks' work; the process is all but complete at the Supreme Court. The transformation is a recent one. Chief Justice Fred Vinson was anomalous in "writing with his hands in his pockets," telling his clerks generally what he wanted and then criticizing drafts and suggesting revisions. In the 1990s, the anomaly would be to find a justice regularly writing his or her own opinions.

Ghostwriting does not present the problem most often raised by those unfamiliar with the practice; it does not empower inexperienced law clerks to participate in the decision-making. It does, however, gravely affect the deliverances of the Court. They are longer and more diffuse, loaded with footnotes, impersonal in tone, and unimaginative in presentation. Drafted by clerks who are former law-review editors, the opinions partake of most of the negative traits of law-review articles. As the

---

[6] William J. Brennan Jr., *In Defense of Dissents*, 37 Hastings L.J. 427, 427 (1986).

[7] Frank, note 1, at 126.

[8] In response to a question by the Commission on Revision of the Federal Court System, Structure and Internal Procedure: Recommendations for Change, 67 F.R.D. 195, 404 (1975).

number of clerks almost doubled between 1969 and 1979 (to a total of 32), so these qualities associated with their work on opinions also increased.

Very likely, the clerks increase verbosity rather than productivity. In 1889, the Court produced 265 signed opinions with no help from law clerks. (Granted, this period did not mark the high point of the Court's judging or of its literary style.) In 1973, when each associate justice had three clerks and the chief justice had four, the Court produced only about 130 signed opinions, but their length vastly outstripped the length of the 19th-century opinions. Indeed, just in the 50 years from 1936 to 1986, the average opinion doubled in length. In the flurry of concern over the length of the Court's opinions, Joseph W. Little half-mockingly suggested a constitutional amendment limiting opinions to five pages. That would be a far cry indeed from the 243 pages—50,000 words, all told—in which the Court expressed its nine separate opinions in *Furman v. Georgia* (1972).[9] The effect of such editorial competition can only be to drive the reader to the opinion's summary preface and away from the text.

Not alone have law clerks been blamed for the Court's blossoming wordiness. Some commentators have cited the increasingly complex and ideologically heated issues generated by our ever-growing administrative state and our heightened notions of personal rights. As Justice William O. Douglas once observed, "the decision-making process is not getting any easier." Others maintain that the issues are no more difficult than in Justice Holmes's day, that it is patronizing to suggest that they are, and that the real problems are instinctive verbosity and lack of time to hew the clerks' work down to proper size.

The modern style of judging is no doubt also responsible. It was not just Holmes's habit of standing at a drafting table that helped him achieve brevity—"Nothing conduces to brevity like the caving in of the knees," he once said. It was also his elliptical treatment of legal issues, a treatment that most judges and scholars today would find unacceptable. In one of his most famous sententious formulations, in *Buck v. Bell*—"Three generations of imbeciles are enough"[10]—Holmes justified a vote that he might not have been able to sustain if he had had to detail his eugenic reasoning. Judges in the latter half of the 20th century value an explicitness and a painstaking process of working through every step of the reasoning. Holmes would have been impatient with all that.

As a result of the prevailing legal ethos, we have lost much that is subtle and suggestive, and we have gained longer opinions and bulkier volumes. But not all that bulk is justified by a modern yearning for

---

[9] *Furman v. Georgia*, 408 U.S. 238 (1972).
[10] *Buck v. Bell*, 274 U.S. 200, 207 (1927).

greater specificity. Generally, it is no trick at all to do what law professors regularly do in producing their casebooks: excise large chunks of the Court's opinions to expose the factual and analytical discussions that are of true importance in deciding a given case.

The exceptions often delight readers. In the shortest opinion in recent memory, Justice John Paul Stevens—the only justice who, in the 1990s, wrote his own first drafts of opinions—dispensed with *McLaughlin v. United States*[11] in five short paragraphs. The opinion harks back to the pithy style of Holmes.

Evaluating the Justices. In the history of the Supreme Court, Marshall, Holmes, and Robert H. Jackson are at the first rank of judicial stylists. Marshall's grand style, of course, is distinctly rooted in the 19th century: orotund, divine-sounding, inerrantly lawgiving. Holmes and Jackson, as 20th-century judges, are more nearly our contemporaries. Whereas other modern judges have usually made adventurous ideas dull, Holmes and Jackson could make the very dullest case a literary adventure.

Holmes habitually used rhetorical devices such as alliteration, metaphor, and periodic sentences to emphasize his points. His antitheses are legion. For example: "If a business is unsuccessful it means that the public does not care enough for it to make it pay. If it is successful the public pays its expense and something more."[12] The literary critic Edmund Wilson went so far as to call Holmes's style "perfect."

Legal commentators have not been quite so kind to Holmes's style. Judge Richard A. Posner suggests that the power of Holmes's famous dissent in *Lochner v. New York*[13] derives more from rhetorical devices than from close reasoning.[14] Judge Abner Mikva says that a purely Holmesian approach is now untenable, inasmuch as Holmes was "not above shaping or neglecting certain facts to preserve the force of a narrow analysis."[15] Professor Jan Deutsch finds Holmes's persuasive power in sketching the selective vignette, not by detailing the "murky and confusing truth of how things are, but by confirming our felt certainties about how we know they should be."[16]

These criticisms say as much about the critics as they do about Holmes. Holmes was no doubt conscious of his omissions: "The eternal

---

[11] *McLaughlin v. United States*, 476 U.S. 16 (1986).

[12] *Arizona Copper Co. v. Hammer*, 250 U.S. 400, 433 (1919).

[13] *Lochner v. New York*, 198 U.S. 45, 74–76 (1905).

[14] Richard A. Posner, *Law and Literature: A Relation Reargued*, 72 Va. L. Rev. 1351, 1379–85 (1986).

[15] Abner J. Mikva, *For Whom Judges Write*, 61 S. Cal. L. Rev. 1357, 1363 (1988).

[16] Jan G. Deutsch, *The Reality of Law in America: An Invitation to Dialogue* 103 (1988).

effort of art, even the writing of legal decisions, is to omit all but the essentials."[17] If Holmes had written so as to remedy the vices that his critics perceive, he would have introduced many others, including prolixity. The considerable virtues in his almost laconic style may necessarily have entailed a few vices.

Nor has Jackson been without detractors. But when it came to phrasing a thought aphoristically, memorably, pungently, Jackson was without equal. Like Holmes, Jackson was masterly with antithesis: "Very many are the interests which the state may protect against the practice of an occupation, very few are those it may assume to protect against the practice of propagandizing by speech or press."[18] His wordplay was never merely playful; it was usually telling: "We can afford no liberties with liberty itself."[19] His famous example of chiasmus expressed an insight about the Court incomparably well: "We are not final because we are infallible, but we are infallible only because we are final."[20] Justice Frankfurter wrote of Jackson that his writing "mirrored the man in him" more completely than any other "who ever sat on the Supreme Court," and that Jackson belonged to "the naturalistic school [of opinion-writers]. He wrote as he talked, and he talked as he felt."[21]

But talented writers on the Court have been rare. Justice Douglas was the only justice in the history of the Court who inarguably could have made his living as a professional writer on nonlegal subjects. The Court has had more justices of the ilk of Justice James Moore Wayne, whose style was criticized around 1850 as being "overloaded with words; scarcely any of his sentences convey a distinct idea; and some of them are quite beyond the pale of criticism."[22] That description fits much of what Justices George Shiras and Samuel Blatchford or Chief Justice Edward D. White wrote, as well as the early opinions of Justice Harold M. Burton or the work of any number of others. In his later years, Chief Justice Warren Burger received more criticism than his colleagues for incoherent footnotes and artless opinions.

Among the highly regarded judicial writers are Holmes, Jackson, and Douglas, but also Justices Louis Brandeis, Benjamin Cardozo, Frankfurter, and Hugo Black. Brandeis had great rhetorical skill and brought to the bench his penchant for the "Brandeis brief," which took tirelessly thor-

[17] Letter from Oliver Wendell Holmes to Felix Frankfurter (19 Dec. 1915).
[18] *Thomas v. Collins*, 328 U.S. 516, 545 (1945).
[19] *United States v. Spector*, 343 U.S. 169, 180 (1952).
[20] *Brown v. Allen*, 344 U.S. 443, 540 (1953).
[21] Felix Frankfurter, *Mr. Justice Jackson*, 68 Haw. L. Rev. 937, 939 (1955).
[22] *Opinions of the Judges of the Supreme Court of the United States*, 16 S.Q. Rev. 501 (Jan. 1850).

ough account of sociological as well as case-specific facts. Holmes is said to have remarked of Brandeis, "He believed in footnotes, and I didn't."

Cardozo would take a page to say what Holmes could say in a sentence, and on occasion his quest for exalted eloquence made his writing vacuous. In *Welch v. Helvering*, involving the question whether a person who paid his employer's debts could take a tax deduction, Justice Cardozo said: "Life in all its fullness must supply the answer to the riddle."[23] As Dean Erwin Griswold once pointed out, these are nice words, but essentially meaningless. On the whole, Cardozo's writing as a state judge—as a common-law judge—ranks more highly than his writing on the Supreme Court.

Frankfurter is a special case. English was his second language; his feel for words has been compared to Vladimir Nabokov's. That comparison is extravagant, however, unless it merely stresses Frankfurter's fascination with ornate words, such as *adumbrate, excogitate, quixotism,* and *sub silentio.* Frankfurter often lapsed into "abstractitis": "The problems that are the respective preoccupations of anthropology, economics, law, psychology, sociology and related areas of scholarship are merely departmentalized dealing, by way of manageable division of analysis, with interpenetrating aspects of holistic perplexities."[24]

Both Black and Douglas had bold, no-nonsense styles. Their broad strokes of the pen to resolve constitutional uncertainties met with scorn from law professors. Both Black and Douglas might have been called technically deficient, result-oriented, and unscholarly, but part of the reason is that they were the only justices of their time whose opinions displayed a concern that nonlawyers might ever read the reports.

On the Court today, Justices Antonin Scalia and Ruth Bader Ginsburg are among the strongest writers. Their opinions delight in metaphor; they are piquant, witty, and sometimes biting. From all that one gathers, though, these qualities emerge when the justices have the time to edit and rewrite the work of their clerks. What is more usual are the tendencies that all the modern justices' opinions show: a plodding, pedantic style that unnecessarily emphasizes minor points and does not stop when the job is done.

Unfortunately, the Court's opinions rarely receive the literary scrutiny that might gradually lead to better opinions. Perhaps this failure on the part of academics, lawyers, and judges is due to the mistaken notion that the writing is merely incidental to the judging, not the greater part of its essence.

---

[23] *Welch v. Helvering*, 290 U.S. 111, 115 (1933).
[24] *Sweezy v. New Hampshire*, 354 U.S. 234, 261 (1957).

ȝ✿ ȝ✿ ȝ✿

Clearing the Cobwebs
from Judicial Opinions

"[A]ny interruption in the flow of language is a source of difficulty
and of irritation to the reader . . . ."

—Adams Sherman Hill[1]

I PROPOSE THAT JUDGES, in their opinions, put citations in footnotes
and generally abstain from using substantive footnotes.[2] And I propose
that courts adopt a rule that brief-writers may single-space footnotes if
they contain only citations (or parentheticals coupled with citations) but
must double-space all footnotes that contain sentences. These simple proposals, if widely adopted, would promote better writing within the legal
profession by encouraging legal writers to:

- Use shorter sentences.
- Compose paragraphs that are more coherent and forceful.
- Lead their readers to focus on ideas, not numbers.
- Lay bare poor writing and poor thinking.
- Discuss the controlling caselaw more thoroughly.
- Use string citations with impunity.

Before going any further, I must point out that I'm not a proponent
of footnotes generally. For a decade I edited the only U.S. law journal
that prohibits footnotes—well, substantive footnotes.[3] So please don't
judge my proposal based on your feelings about footnotes generally. I
dislike them as much as anyone reading this essay. But there's a world of
difference between reference notes and so-called "talking" footnotes. I'm
championing notes largely for bibliographic details such as volume and
page numbers.

Adapted from *Court Review* (Summer 2001).

[1] *Our English* 56 (1888).

[2] You shouldn't be looking at this. Nothing important will appear in footnotes. Please
just read past the superscripts and concentrate on the content. Oh, and by the way, you
won't ever have to put your eyes on fast-forward to zip past citations—except, of course,
when I'm quoting some outlandish passage with citational vortexes. Now please look
back up.

[3] *See generally* Scribes J. Legal Writing (1990–2000).

Advantage #1:
Enhanced Readability
Through Shorter Sentences

Footnoting citations allows writers both to vary and to reduce their sentence length. Currently, any really short, punchy sentence that is sandwiched between citations is apt to get lost, so why risk it? Even first-rate writers will be hard-pressed to keep their average sentence length to manageable proportions. Consider the following example from a judicial writer of indisputably high standing—Judge Richard A. Posner. The average sentence length (excluding so-called citation sentences) is 50 words:

> The district court dismissed the suit as barred by the Tax Injunction Act, 28 U.S.C. § 1341, which withdraws from the federal courts jurisdiction to "enjoin, suspend or restrain the assessment, levy or collection" of state taxes (including local taxes, *Platteville Area Apartment Ass'n v. City of Platteville*, 179 F.3d 574, 582 (7th Cir. 1999); *Hager v. City of West Peoria*, 84 F.3d 865, 868 n. 1 (7th Cir. 1996); *Folio v. City of Clarksburg*, 134 F.3d 1211, 1214 (4th Cir. 1998)) unless the taxpayer lacks an adequate state remedy. See *In re Stoecker*, 179 F.3d 546, 549 (7th Cir. 1999), *aff'd.* under the name *Raleigh v. Illinois Dept. of Revenue*, 530 U.S. 15 (2000). The Act is a gesture of comity toward the states; recognizing the centrality of tax collection to the operation of government, the Act prevents taxpayers from running to federal court to stymie the collection of state taxes. E.g., *RTC Commercial Assets Trust 1995 NP3-1 v. Phoenix Bond & Indemnity Co.*, 169 F.3d 448, 453 (7th Cir. 1999). The Act's goal could not be achieved if the statutory language were read literally, as barring only injunctions, and so it's been stretched to cover declaratory judgments, *California v. Grace Brethren Church*, 457 U.S. 393, 408–13 (1982), and, what is as necessary to prevent the Act from being completely undone, suits for refund of state taxes. *Marvin F. Poer & Co. v. Counties of Alameda*, 725 F.2d 1234 (9th Cir. 1984); *Cities Service Gas Co. v. Oklahoma Tax Commn.*, 656 F.2d 584, 586 (10th Cir. 1981); *United Gas Pipe Line Co. v. Whitman*, 595 F.2d 323 (5th Cir. 1979). It is an open question whether the Act covers damages suits under 42 U.S.C. § 1983 as well, see *Fair Assessment in Real Estate Ass'n v. McNary*, 454 U.S. 100, 107 (1981), which would be another method of making an end run around the statutory prohibition. The Supreme Court held in the *Fair Assessment* case that such a suit was in any event barred by the principle of comity, operating independently of the Tax Injunction Act. The Court declined to rule on whether that principle "would also bar a claim under § 1983 which requires no scrutiny whatever of state tax assessment practices, such as a facial attack on tax laws colorably claimed to be discriminatory as to race." *Id.* at 107 n. 4.[4]

---

[4] *Wright v. Pappas*, 256 F.3d 635, 636–37 (7th Cir. 2001).

Once the citations are gone, it's fairly easy to reduce that average to just 22 words, while summarizing the information contained in citations:

The district court dismissed the suit as barred by the Tax Injunction Act,[1] which withdraws from the federal courts jurisdiction to "enjoin, suspend or restrain the assessment, levy or collection" of state taxes. We have held that this includes local taxes.[2] But there's an exception: the federal court may have jurisdiction if the taxpayer lacks an adequate state remedy.[3] The Act is a gesture of comity toward the states. Recognizing the centrality of collecting taxes for governmental operations, the Act prevents taxpayers from running to federal court to stymie state tax collection.[4] The Act's goal could not be achieved if the statutory language were read literally, as barring only injunctions. So the Supreme Court has stretched it to cover declaratory judgments.[5] Further, to prevent the Act from being completely undone, the Fifth, Tenth, and Ninth Circuits have stretched it to cover suits for refund of state taxes.[6] It remains an open question whether the Act covers damage suits under 42 U.S.C. § 1983 as well,[7] which would be another method of making an end run around the statutory prohibition. The Supreme Court held in the *Fair Assessment* case that such a suit was in any event barred by the principle of comity, operating independently of the Tax Injunction Act. The Court declined to rule on whether that principle would also bar a § 1983 claim that "requires no scrutiny whatever of state tax assessment practices, such as a facial attack on tax laws colorably claimed to be discriminatory as to race."[8]

[1] 28 U.S.C. § 1341.

[2] *Platteville Area Apartment Assn. v. City of Platteville*, 179 F.3d 574, 582 (7th Cir. 1999); *Hager v. City of West Peoria*, 84 F.3d 865, 868 n. 1 (7th Cir. 1996); *Folio v. City of Clarksburg*, 134 F.3d 1211, 1214 (4th Cir. 1998).

[3] *See In re Stoecker*, 179 F.3d 546, 549 (7th Cir. 1999), *aff'd.* under the name *Raleigh v. Illinois Dept. of Revenue*, 530 U.S. 15 (2000).

[4] *E.g., RTC Commercial Assets Trust 1995 NP3-1 v. Phoenix Bond & Indem. Co.*, 169 F.3d 448, 453 (7th Cir. 1999).

[5] *California v. Grace Brethren Church*, 457 U.S. 393, 408–13 (1982).

[6] *Marvin F. Poer & Co. v. Counties of Alameda*, 725 F.2d 1234 (9th Cir. 1984); *Cities Service Gas Co. v. Oklahoma Tax Commn.*, 656 F.2d 584, 586 (10th Cir. 1981); *United Gas Pipe Line Co. v. Whitman*, 595 F.2d 323 (5th Cir. 1979).

[7] *See Fair Assessment in Real Estate Assn. v. McNary*, 454 U.S. 100, 107 (1981).

[8] *Id.* at 107 n. 4.

Also, when case names and numbers aren't splashed across the page, it's not just average sentence length that improves. It's average paragraph length, too.[5]

---

[5] *See* Garner, *Legal Writing in Plain English* § 26, at 72 (2001).

Advantage #2:
More Coherent and Forceful Paragraphs

Subordinating citations allows greater variety in sentence structure, since it provides more opportunities for using phrases and dependent clauses. To the professional writer, this is no small matter. Variety adds interest. And the sentences can connect smoothly, resulting in paragraphs that are well-composed exposition rather than an assemblage of disjointed sentences. Consider this fairly clotted example:

> In a manner consistent with this hierarchy of political entities, the Arizona Constitution in Article 13, Section 1, gives the legislature plenary power over the "methods and procedures for [municipal] incorporation." *State ex rel. Pickrell v. Downey*, 102 Ariz. 360, 363, 364–65, 430 P.2d 122, 125, 126–27 (1967); *see Territory v. Town of Jerome*, 7 Ariz. 320, 326, 64 P. 417, 418 (1901) (state has absolute power to "create, enlarge and restrict municipal franchises"). Thus, those persons seeking municipal incorporation are "mere supplicants, with no rights beyond those which the legislature [sees] fit to give them." *Burton v. City of Tucson*, 88 Ariz. 320, 326, 356 P.2d 413, 417 (1960), citing *Hunter*, 207 U.S. 161, 28 S.Ct. 40, 52 L.Ed. 151. Furthermore, the "legislature may delegate to a subordinate body" discretion over the procedures for municipal incorporation. *Pickrell*, 102 Ariz. at 363, 430 P.2d at 125; *see City of Tucson v. Garrett*, 77 Ariz. 73, 267 P.2d 717 (1954) (legislature may delegate to municipality total discretion whether to grant or deny annexation); *Skinner v. City of Phoenix*, 54 Ariz. 316, 320–21, 95 P.2d 424, 426 (1939) (legislature free to delegate this power to existing cities and towns "upon such terms as [it] may think proper"); *see also Holt*, 439 U.S. at 70–71, 74, 99 S.Ct. 383 (State has "extraordinarily wide latitude . . . in creating various types of political subdivisions and conferring authority upon them."). With that understanding, we consider the voting-rights doctrine of the Equal Protection Clause.[6]

Stripping out the citations makes plain just how clunky and laborious the prose is:

> In a manner consistent with this hierarchy of political entities, the Arizona Constitution in Article 13, Section 1, gives the legislature plenary power over the "methods and procedures for [municipal] incorporation." Thus, those persons seeking municipal incorporation are "mere supplicants, with no rights beyond those which the legislature [sees] fit to give them." Furthermore, the "legislature may delegate to a subordinate body" discretion over the procedures for municipal incorporation. With that understanding, we consider the voting-rights doctrine of the Equal Protection Clause.

---

[6] *City of Tucson v. Pima County*, 19 P.3d 650, 657 (Ariz. App. Div. 1 2001).

Now it's possible to improve the sentence structure and flow, while restoring the parenthetical material that contributes to the reasoning:

Consistently with this hierarchy of political entities, the Arizona Constitution[1] gives the legislature plenary power over the "methods and procedures for [municipal] incorporation,"[2] including the power to "create, enlarge and restrict municipal franchises."[3] Those seeking municipal incorporation are "mere supplicants, with no rights beyond those which the legislature [sees] fit to give them."[4] And since the legislature "may delegate to a subordinate body" discretion over procedures for municipal incorporation,[5] it may also give municipalities total discretion to grant or deny annexations.[6] It is within this context that we consider the voting-rights doctrine of the Equal Protection Clause.

[1] Ariz. Const. Art. 13, § 1.
[2] *State ex rel. Pickrell v. Downey*, 102 Ariz. 360, 363, 364–65, 430 P.2d 122, 125, 126–27 (1967).
[3] *Territory v. Town of Jerome*, 7 Ariz. 320, 326, 64 P. 417, 418 (1901).
[4] *Burton v. City of Tucson*, 88 Ariz. 320, 326, 356 P.2d 413, 417 (1960), citing *Hunter*, 207 U.S. 161, 28 S.Ct. 40, 52 L.Ed. 151.
[5] *Pickrell*, 102 Ariz. at 363, 430 P.2d at 125.
[6] *See City of Tucson v. Garrett*, 77 Ariz. 73, 267 P.2d 717 (1954); *Skinner v. City of Phoenix*, 54 Ariz. 316, 320–21, 95 P.2d 424, 426 (1939); *Holt*, 439 U.S. at 70–71, 74, 99 S.Ct. 383.

With citations up in the text—the traditional format—writers have an unfortunate choice. They can put citations consistently at the ends of their sentences, typically leading to a monotonous sentence structure, or they can embed their citations within sentences, in support of subordinate clauses. This latter choice is quite common, as in this example from the Nebraska Supreme Court:

The warrantless search exceptions recognized by this court include: (1) searches undertaken with consent or with probable cause, *see State v. Lara*, 258 Neb. 996, 607 N.W.2d 487 (2000), and *In re Interest of Andre W.*, 256 Neb. 362, 590 N.W.2d 827 (1999); (2) searches under exigent circumstances, *see State v. Silvers*, 255 Neb. 702, 587 N.W.2d 325 (1998); (3) inventory searches, *see State v. Newman*, 250 Neb. 226, 548 N.W.2d 739 (1996); (4) searches of evidence in plain view, *see State v. Buckman*, 259 Neb. 924, 613 N.W.2d 463 (2000); and (5) searches incident to a valid arrest, *see State v. Ray*, 260 Neb. 868, 620 N.W.2d 83 (2000), and *State v. Roach, supra.*[7]

[7] *State v. Roberts*, 623 N.W.2d 298, 305 (Neb. 2001).

Such listing becomes transparent once the citations are removed, and there's no question how good the caselaw is or what court it issued from:

> The warrantless search exceptions recognized by this court include: (1) searches undertaken with consent or with probable cause,[1] (2) searches under exigent circumstances,[2] (3) inventory searches,[3] (4) searches of evidence in plain view,[4] and (5) searches incident to a valid arrest.[5]
>
> [1] *See State v. Lara*, 258 Neb. 996, 607 N.W.2d 487 (2000), and *In re Interest of Andre W.*, 256 Neb. 362, 590 N.W.2d 827 (1999).
> [2] *See State v. Silvers*, 255 Neb. 702, 587 N.W.2d 325 (1998).
> [3] *See State v. Newman*, 250 Neb. 226, 548 N.W.2d 739 (1996).
> [4] *See State v. Buckman*, 259 Neb. 924, 613 N.W.2d 463 (2000).
> [5] *See State v. Ray*, 260 Neb. 868, 620 N.W.2d 83 (2000), and *State v. Roach*, 234 Neb. 620, 452 N.W.2d 262 (1990).

This need for listing in a visually appealing way is ubiquitous within the legal profession. But with citations festooned throughout, the lists lose their accessibility and power.

Advantage #3: Ideas Control, Not Numbers

When cases are cited in text, invariably the most prominent characters on the page are the numbers, which can equally numb the brain. Once more, consider an integer- and italic-laden example from a recent opinion by Judge Posner:

> A law that grants preferential treatment on the basis of race or ethnicity does not deny the equal protection of the laws if it is (1) a remedy for (2) intentional discrimination committed by (3) the public entity that is according the preferential treatment (unless, as is not argued here, the entity has been given responsibility by the state for enforcing state or local laws against private discrimination, *City of Richmond v. J.A. Croson Co.*, 488 U.S. 469, 491–92 (1989) (plurality opinion)) and (4) discriminates no more than is necessary to accomplish the remedial purpose. *E.g., Shaw v. Hunt*, 517 U.S. 899, 909–10 (1996); *Adarand Constructors, Inc. v. Pena*, 515 U.S. 200, 224, 235, 237–38 (1995); *Wygant v. Jackson Board of Education*, 476 U.S. 267, 277 (1987) (plurality opinion); *Chicago Firefighters Local 2 v. City of Chicago*, 249 F.3d 649, 654–55 (7th Cir. 2001); *Billish v. City of Chicago*, 989 F.2d 890, 893 (7th Cir. 1993) (en banc); *Associated General Contractors of Ohio, Inc. v. Drabik*, 214 F.3d 730, 735 (6th Cir. 2000). Whether nonremedial justifications for "reverse discrimination" by a public body are ever possible is unsettled. *Hill v. Ross*, 183 F.3d 586, 588 (7th Cir. 1999); *McNamara v. City of Chicago*, 138 F.3d

1219, 1222 (7th Cir. 1998); *Brewer v. West Irondequoit Central School Dist.*, 212 F.3d 738, 747–49 (2d Cir. 2000); *Wessmann v. Gittens*, 160 F.3d 790, 795 (1st Cir. 1998). This court upheld such a justification in *Wittmer v. Peters*, 87 F.3d 916 (7th Cir. 1996), but the Fifth Circuit has stated flatly that "nonremedial state interests will never justify racial classifications." *Hopwood v. Texas*, 78 F.3d 931, 942 (5th Cir. 1996). The Supreme Court will have to decide the question eventually (maybe it will do so next term in the *Slater* case, cited below, in which certiorari has been granted), but it is of no moment here, because the County has not advanced any nonremedial justification for the minority set-aside program.[8]

It's hard even for lawyers, much less nonlawyers, to concentrate on ideas presented in this fashion. A revision that strips out the numbers can be every bit as respectful of precedent as the original, but far more readable. And notice that the sentence structure gets cleaned up a little, too, so the numbered items are now grammatically parallel:

A law that grants preferential treatment on the basis of race or ethnicity doesn't necessarily deny the equal protection of the laws. It is constitutional if three conditions are satisfied: (1) the preferential treatment is a remedy for intentional discrimination, (2) a public entity is responsible for according the preference,[1] and (3) the preference discriminates no more than is necessary to accomplish the remedial purpose.[2] Whether nonremedial justifications for "reverse discrimination" by a public body are ever possible is unsettled in this and other circuits.[3] We upheld such a justification in *Wittmer v. Peters*;[4] the Fifth Circuit, meanwhile, stated flatly in *Hopwood v. Texas* that "nonremedial state interests will never justify racial classifications."[5] The Supreme Court will have to decide the question eventually. Maybe it will do so next term in the *Slater* case,[6] in which certiorari has been granted. But that is of no moment here because the County has not advanced any nonremedial justification for the minority set-aside program.

  [1] *But see City of Richmond v. J.A. Croson Co.*, 488 U.S. 469, 491–92 (1989) (plurality opinion) (stating an exception to this second element when, as is not argued here, the entity has been given responsibility by the state for enforcing state or local laws against private discrimination).
  [2] *E.g., Shaw v. Hunt*, 517 U.S. 899, 909–10 (1996); *Adarand Constructors, Inc. v. Pena*, 515 U.S. 200, 224, 235, 237–38 (1995); *Wygant v. Jackson Board of Education*, 476 U.S. 267, 277 (1987) (plurality opinion); *Chicago Firefighters Local 2 v. City of Chicago*, 249 F.3d 649, 654–55 (7th Cir. 2001); *Billish v. City of Chicago*, 989 F.2d 890, 893 (7th Cir. 1993) (en banc); *Associated General Contractors of Ohio, Inc. v. Drabik*, 214 F.3d 730, 735 (6th Cir. 2000).

---

  [8] *Builders Assn. of Greater Chicago v. County of Cook*, 256 F.3d 642, 643–44 (7th Cir. 2001).

[3] *Hill v. Ross*, 183 F.3d 586, 588 (7th Cir. 1999); *McNamara v. City of Chicago*, 138 F.3d 1219, 1222 (7th Cir. 1998); *Brewer v. West Irondequoit Central School Dist.*, 212 F.3d 738, 747–49 (2d Cir. 2000); *Wessmann v. Gittens*, 160 F.3d 790, 795 (1st Cir. 1998).

[4] *Wittmer v. Peters*, 87 F.3d 916 (7th Cir. 1996).

[5] *Hopwood v. Texas*, 78 F.3d 931, 942 (5th Cir. 1996).

[6] *Adarand Constructors, Inc. v. Slater*, 228 F.3d 1147 (10th Cir. 2000), *cert. granted in part*, *Adarand Constructors, Inc. v. Mineta*, 121 S.Ct. 1598, 69 U.S.L.W. 3670 (U.S. 13 Apr. 2001) (No. 00-730).

Some will argue that because the numbers and italic type are more prominent than plain text, they stand out, thus helping the reader skip over the citation. Well, try to find the beginning of all three sentences in this California opinion—without backtracking:

> Such erroneous instructions also implicate Sixth Amendment principles preserving the exclusive domain of the trier of fact. (*Carella v. California, supra*, 491 U.S. at p. 265, 109 S.Ct. 2419; *People v. Kobrin, supra*, 11 Cal. 4th at p. 423 [45 Cal. Rptr. 2d 895, 903 P.2d 1027].) In *People v. Avila* (1995) 35 Cal. App. 4th 642, 651–652, 43 Cal. Rptr. 2d 853, we synthesized the federal constitutional authority on the right to instruction as to the elements of an offense as follows: "It is well established that the Sixth Amendment guarantees a criminal defendant the right to require the prosecution to prove [. . .] guilt [. . .] beyond a reasonable doubt. (*Victor v. Nebraska* (1994) 511 U.S. [1, 5] [114 S.Ct. 1239, 127 L.Ed.2d 583].) In *Sullivan v. Louisiana* (1993) 508 U.S. [275, 277] [113 S.Ct. 2078, 124 L.Ed.2d 182], the United States Supreme Court held . . . .[9]

Advantage #4:
Poor Writing and Poor Thinking
Get Laid Bare

Mid-text citations are often—not sometimes, but often—camouflage for poor writing and poor thinking. As a class, lawyers have lost the ability to write shapely paragraphs. Stripping out the bibliographic references immediately reveals threadbare ideas and underdeveloped paragraphs, as well as other problems. Consider the following passage:

> Government agents "flagrantly disregard" the terms of a warrant so that wholesale suppression is required only when (1) they effect a "widespread seizure of items that were not within the scope of the warrant," *United States v. Matias*, 836 F.2d 744, 748 (2d Cir. 1988), and (2) do not

[9] *People v. Marshall*, 99 Cal. Rptr. 2d 441, 446 (Cal. App. 2000).

act in good faith, *see Marvin v. United States*, 732 F.2d 669, 675 (8th Cir. 1984) (holding that complete suppression is inappropriate where government "agents attempted to stay within the boundaries of the warrant and . . . the extensive seizure of documents was prompted largely by practical considerations and time constraints"); *United States v. Lambert*, 771 F.2d 83, 93 (6th Cir. 1985) (similar); *United States v. Tamura*, 694 F.2d 591, 597 (9th Cir. 1982) (similar); *United States v. Heldt*, 668 F.2d 1238, 1269 (D.C. Cir. 1981) (similar); *see also United States v. Foster*, 100 F.3d 846, 852 (10th Cir. 1996) (ordering blanket suppression when "at the time he obtained the warrant, [the officer who applied for it] . . . knew that the limits of the warrant would not be honored"); *United States v. Rettig*, 589 F.2d 418, 423 (9th Cir. 1978) (similar).

The cornerstone of the blanket suppression doctrine is the enduring aversion of Anglo-American law to so-called general searches. Such searches—which have been variously described as "wide-ranging exploratory searches," *Maryland v. Garrison*, 480 U.S. 79, 84, 107 S.Ct. 1013, 94 L.Ed.2d 72 (1987), and "indiscriminate rummaging[s]," *United States v. George*, 975 F.2d 72, 75 (2d Cir. 1992)—are especially pernicious, and "have long been deemed to violate fundamental rights." *Marron v. United States*, 275 U.S. 192, 195, 48 S.Ct. 74, 72 L.Ed. 231 (1927); *see also, e.g., Go-Bart Importing Co. v. United States*, 282 U.S. 344, 357, 51 S.Ct. 153, 75 L.Ed. 374 (1931) ("Since before the creation of our government, [general] searches have been deemed obnoxious to fundamental principles of liberty. They are denounced in the constitutions or statutes of every State in the Union. The need of protection against them is attested alike by history and present conditions." (internal citation omitted)). Eliminating general searches was the basic impetus for the Fourth Amendment's Warrant Clause, *see Garrison*, 480 U.S. at 84, 107 S.Ct. 1013, and the instruments that authorized government agents to conduct such searches were much-reviled throughout the colonial period.[10]

In that example, the first sentence contains a glaring ambiguity. It literally says that government agents flagrantly disregard warrant terms so that suppression will be required. But why would they do that?

When the citations are stripped out, it becomes apparent that the first "paragraph" is only a sentence—one that doesn't make literal sense—and the final sentence has clauses that are out of order, being unchronological:

Government agents "flagrantly disregard" the terms of a warrant so that wholesale suppression is required only when (1) they effect a "widespread seizure of items that were not within the scope of the warrant," and (2) do not act in good faith.

---

[10] *United States v. Liu*, 239 F.3d 138, 140–41 (2d Cir. 2000).

The cornerstone of the blanket suppression doctrine is the enduring aversion of Anglo-American law to so-called general searches. These
searches—which have been variously described as "wide-ranging
exploratory searches" and "indiscriminate rummaging[s]"—are especially pernicious, and "have long been deemed to violate fundamental
rights." Eliminating general searches was the basic impetus for the
Fourth Amendment's Warrant Clause, and the instruments that authorized government agents to conduct such searches were much-reviled
throughout the colonial period.

With a little editing, the passage becomes more coherent:

Federal courts have held that wholesale suppression of evidence is necessary only when the government agents (1) effect a "widespread seizure of items that were not within the scope of the warrant,"[1] or (2) do
not act in good faith.[2] When the agents "flagrantly disregard" the terms
of the warrant this way, the blanket-suppression doctrine applies.

The cornerstone of this doctrine is the enduring aversion of Anglo-
American law to so-called general searches. These searches—which
have been variously described as "wide-ranging exploratory searches"[3]
and "indiscriminate rummaging[s]"[4]—are especially pernicious. In the
words of the Supreme Court, they "violate fundamental rights."[5] The
instruments that authorized government agents to conduct general
searches were much-reviled throughout the colonial period. And eliminating such searches was the basic impetus for the Fourth Amendment's Warrant Clause.[6]

[1] *United States v. Matias*, 836 F.2d 744, 748 (2d Cir. 1988).
[2] *See Marvin v. United States*, 732 F.2d 669, 675 (8th Cir. 1984) (holding that
complete suppression is inappropriate where government "agents attempted to
stay within the boundaries of the warrant and . . . the extensive seizure of documents was prompted largely by practical considerations and time constraints"); *United States v. Lambert*, 771 F.2d 83, 93 (6th Cir. 1985) (similar);
United States v. Tamura, 694 F.2d 591, 597 (9th Cir. 1982) (similar); *United States
v. Heldt*, 668 F.2d 1238, 1269 (D.C. Cir. 1981) (similar); *see also United States v.
Foster*, 100 F.3d 846, 852 (10th Cir. 1996) (ordering blanket suppression when
"at the time he obtained the warrant, [the officer who applied for it] . . . knew
that the limits of the warrant would not be honored"); *United States v. Rettig*,
589 F.2d 418, 423 (9th Cir. 1978) (similar).
[3] *Maryland v. Garrison*, 480 U.S. 79, 84, 107 S.Ct. 1013, 94 L.Ed.2d 72 (1987).
[4] *United States v. George*, 975 F.2d 72, 75 (2d Cir. 1992).
[5] *Marron v. United States*, 275 U.S. 192, 195, 48 S.Ct. 74, 72 L.Ed. 231 (1927);
see also, e.g., Go-Bart Importing Co. v. United States, 282 U.S. 344, 357, 51 S.Ct.
153, 75 L.Ed. 374 (1931) ("Since before the creation of our government, [gen-
eral] searches have been deemed obnoxious to fundamental principles of liberty. They are denounced in the constitutions or statutes of every State in the
Union. The need of protection against them is attested alike by history and
present conditions." (internal citation omitted)).
[6] *See Garrison*, 480 U.S. at 84, 107 S.Ct. 1013.

Advantage #5:
You Have to Discuss the Controlling Caselaw

Surprising as it may seem, footnoting citations ordinarily results not in the subordination or even the hiding of caselaw, but in better discussions of it. Why? Because you have to talk about the controlling precedents—how and why they apply. Too many advocates and judges are splattering their pages with citations and parentheticals but never really discussing the living past of the law. Citations have displaced reasoning.

In the following passage, from a dissent by Justice Thomas, the relevance of the cited case is unclear from the text. It is not directly discussed either here or on the earlier page referred to. One is left with the impression that the *Bose* case is a precedent concerning trial length and the appropriate standard of review:

> [T]he Court appears to discount clear error review here because the trial was "not lengthy." *Ante*, at 1458–1459. Even if considerations such as the length of the trial were relevant in deciding how to review factual findings, an assumption about which I have my doubts, these considerations would not counsel against deference in this action. The trial was not "just a few hours long," *Bose Corp. v. Consumers Union of United States, Inc.*, 466 U.S. 485, 500, 104 S.Ct. 1949, 80 L.Ed.2d 502 (1984); it lasted for three days in which the court heard the testimony of 12 witnesses. And quite apart from the total trial time, the District Court sifted through hundreds of pages of deposition testimony and expert analysis, including statistical analysis. It also should not be forgotten that one member of the panel has reviewed the iterations of District 12 since 1992. If one were to calibrate clear error review according to the trier of fact's familiarity with the case, there is simply no question that the court here gained a working knowledge of the facts of this litigation in myriad ways over a period far longer than three days.[11]

But this impression turns out to be wrong. In the original passage, Justice Thomas added a clarifying footnote in which he explained the real reason why he considered the *Bose* case bad authority:

> *Bose*, which the Court cites to support its discounting of clear error review, *ante*, at 1459, does state that "the likelihood that the appellate court will rely on the presumption [of correctness of factual findings] tends to increase when trial judges have lived with the controversy for

---

[11] *Hunt v. Cromartie*, 532 U.S. 234, 260–61 (2001) (Thomas, J., dissenting).

weeks or months instead of just a few hours." 466 U.S., at 500, 104 S.Ct. 1949. It is unclear, however, what bearing this statement of fact—that appellate courts will defer to factual findings more often when the trial was long—had on our understanding of the scope of clear error review. In *Bose*, we held that a lower court's "actual malice" finding must be reviewed *de novo, see id.*, at 514, 104 S.Ct. 1949, not that clear error review must be calibrated to the length of trial.*

* *Id.*, 532 U.S. at 261 n.2, 121 S.Ct. at 1472 n.2.

When the passage is revised to incorporate the footnote's substantive language and relegate the citations to the footnotes, the point becomes much clearer. The substantive footnote is gone, the backwash of citations is no longer splashing through the passage, and the paragraph is more closely reasoned:

[T]he Court discounts clear-error review here because the trial was "not lengthy."[1] The Court cites *Bose*[2] as support, apparently relying on its dicta that appellate courts will defer to factual findings more often when the trial was long.[3] But in *Bose*, a case that lasted "just a few hours,"[4] we held that a lower court's "actual malice" finding must be reviewed *de novo*, not that clear-error review must be calibrated to the length of trial. In fact, how the length of the trial affects our understanding of the scope of clear error remains unclear. What is clear is that this trial lasted for three days in which the Court heard the testimony of 12 witnesses. The District Court also sifted through hundreds of pages of deposition testimony and expert analyses. And one member of the panel has reviewed the iterations of District 12 since 1992. If clear-error review is to be calibrated according to the trier of fact's familiarity with the case, the Court here gained thorough knowledge of the facts in myriad ways over a period far longer than "just a few hours."

[1] *Ante*, at 1458–1459.
[2] *Bose Corp. v. Consumers Union of States, Inc.*, 466 U.S. 485, 500–501, 104 S.Ct. 1949, 80 L.Ed.2d 502 (1984).
[3] *Id.* at 514.
[4] *Id.* at 500.

If readers want more information, they can use the citation to look up the case. And if the substantive material is important enough to include in your opinion, include it in the text. There is no good reason to give citations in the text and force readers to combine the substance of a vague textual discussion with a substantive footnote. It may be easier on the writer that way, but it's harder on the reader.

Advantage #6:
String Citations Are No Longer Bothersome

Judges and advocates have never been able to agree about string citations. But if they're in footnotes, nobody should care that even five or six
cases have been cited. Until 1985 or so, we didn't have any real choice
about where to put citations: we were using typewriters. Now we've
been liberated from this technological constraint. We should liberate the
page from the numerical hiccups that appear between sentences or in
midsentence. If you have, say, five Nebraska cases on point and you want
to cite all five, fine. And if one of those cases bears further discussion, then
you can discuss it by name in the text. But citing five, or even fifteen,
cases is no problem if they're in footnotes. When they're tucked away
there, you keep your narrative line moving and your reader unimpeded.

Why Citations Have Grown So Thick

As caselaw has proliferated, so have citations. And they've gotten much
longer, too, for two reasons: (1) parallel citations are now used routinely,
and (2) parenthetical snippets now routinely get appended to citations.
In the following example, just the parentheticals are enough to create little thickets that ensnarl the reader but add little if anything to the content. Imagine this passage if there were various *cert. denied* citations to all
three Supreme Court reporters:

> [O]ur review of decisions by other courts of appeals reveals a consen-
> sus that the Speedy Trial Act requires the dismissal of only those
> charges that were made in the original complaint that triggered the
> thirty-day time period. *See United States v. Miller*, 23 F.3d 194, 199 (8th
> Cir. 1994) ("A defendant's arrest on one charge does not necessarily
> trigger the right to a speedy trial on another charge filed after his
> arrest."); *United States v. Nabors*, 901 F.2d 1351, 1355 (6th Cir. 1990)
> ("18 U.S.C. § 3162(a)(1) only requires the dismissal of the offense
> charged in the complaint . . . ."); *United States v. Giwa*, 831 F.2d 538, 541
> (5th Cir. 1987) ("The Act requires dismissal of only those charges con-
> tained in the original complaint."); *United States v. Napolitano*, 761 F.2d
> 135, 137 (2d Cir. 1985) ("The statutory language is clear: it requires
> dismissal only of 'such charge against the individual contained in such
> complaint.'"); *United States v. Heldt*, 745 F.2d 1275, 1280 (9th Cir. 1984)
> ("Charges not included in the original complaint are not covered by
> the Act . . . ."); *United States v. Pollock*, 726 F.2d 1456, 1462 (9th Cir.
> 1984) ("We hold that when the government fails to indict a defendant
> within 30 days of arrest, § 3162(a)(1) requires dismissal of only the
> offense or offenses charged in the original complaint."); *United States
> v. Brooks*, 670 F.2d 148, 151 (11th Cir. 1982) ("An arrest triggers the

running of § 3161(b) of the Speedy Trial Act only if the arrest is for the same offense for which the accused is subsequently indicted.").
Moreover, courts have rejected the application of the transactional test suggested by Oliver and point out that Congress itself considered and rejected this option. *See, e.g., United States v. Derose*, 74 F.3d 1177, 1184 (11th Cir. 1996) ("Congress considered and declined to follow the suggestion that the Speedy Trial Act's dismissal sanctions should be applied to a subsequent charge if it arose from the same criminal transaction or event as those detailed in the initial complaint or were known or reasonably should have been known at the time of filing the initial complaint."); *Napolitano*, 761 F.2d at 137 ("[T]he legislative history of the Act clearly indicates that Congress considered and rejected defendant's suggestion that the Act's dismissal sanction be applied to subsequent charges if they arise from the same criminal episode as those specified in the original complaint or were known or reasonably should have been known at the time of the complaint.").[12]

When you digest what the cases stand for and where they come from, the passage becomes much cleaner:

[O]ur review of decisions by other courts of appeals reveals a consensus that the Speedy Trial Act requires the dismissal of only those charges made in the original complaint that triggered the 30-day time period. During the past two decades, the Second,[1] Fifth,[2] Sixth,[3] Eighth,[4] Ninth,[5] and Eleventh Circuits[6] have all so held. Moreover, the Second[7] and Eleventh[8] Circuits have rejected the idea of applying the transactional test suggested by Oliver, both pointing out that Congress itself considered and rejected this option.

[1] *United States v. Napolitano*, 761 F.2d 135, 137 (2d Cir. 1985) ("The statutory language is clear: it requires dismissal only of 'such charge against the individual contained in such complaint.'").

[2] *United States v. Giwa*, 831 F.2d 538, 541 (5th Cir. 1987) ("The Act requires dismissal of only those charges contained in the original complaint.").

[3] *United States v. Nabors*, 901 F.2d 1351, 1355 (6th Cir. 1990) ("18 U.S.C. § 3162(a)(1) only requires the dismissal of the offense charged in the complaint . . . .").

[4] *United States v. Miller*, 23 F.3d 194, 199 (8th Cir. 1994) ("A defendant's arrest on one charge does not necessarily trigger the right to a speedy trial on another charge filed after his arrest.").

[5] *United States v. Pollock*, 726 F.2d 1456, 1462 (9th Cir. 1984) ("We hold that when the government fails to indict a defendant within 30 days of arrest, section 3162(a)(1) requires dismissal of only the offense or offenses charged in the original complaint.").

---

[12] *United States v. Oliver*, 238 F.3d 471, 473 (3d Cir. 2001).

You may say that the information within parentheticals is often important. I agree, though in practice anything in parentheses has been subor-
dinated already. It typically ought to be in the text. Highlight that information by weaving it in there, and then subordinate the numbers. Give
due proportion to the elements of your writing. Consider this passage:

While § 1997e(a) does not expressly define the term "prison conditions," similar language is used and explicitly defined in a different section of the PLRA, 18 U.S.C. § 3626(g)(2). This definition, by its own
terms, only applies to "this section"—*i.e.*, 18 U.S.C. § 3626. Nevertheless, the defendants urge that § 1997e(a) should be read *in pari materia*
with 18 U.S.C. § 3626, based on the interpretive canon that language
"used in one portion of a statute . . . should be deemed to have the
same meaning as the same language used elsewhere in the statute."
Mertens v. Hewitt Assocs., 508 U.S. 248, 260, 113 S.Ct. 2063, 124
L.Ed.2d 161 (1993); *see also Russo v. Trifari, Krussman & Fishel, Inc.*, 837
F.2d 40, 45 (2d Cir. 1988) ("Construing identical language in a single
statute *in pari materia* is both traditional and logical."). Other courts
have read the "prison conditions" language of § 1997e(a) *in pari materia*
with the definition provided in 18 U.S.C. § 3626(g)(2). *See, e.g., Booth*,
206 F.3d at 294; *Freeman*, 196 F.3d at 643–44; *Beeson*, 28 F.Supp.2d at
888; *Giannattasio*, 2000 WL 335242, at *11–*12. *But see Carter*, 1999
WL 14014, at *3–*4 (declining to rely upon the § 3626(g)(2) definition to interpret meaning of "prison conditions" under § 1997e(a)).
The text of § 3626(g)(2), however, is no less ambiguous than the text
of § 1997e(a) itself—indeed, judges have reached opposite conclusions
on whether § 1997e(a) encompasses excessive force and assault claims
notwithstanding their common reliance on 18 U.S.C. § 3626(g)(2) for
guidance. *Compare, e.g., Booth v. Churner*, 206 F.3d at 294–95 (opinion
of the court) (excessive force claims are encompassed within the
§ 3626(g)(2) definition); *and Beeson*, 28 F.Supp.2d at 888–89 (same),
with Booth, 206 F.3d at 301–02 (Noonan, J., concurring and dissenting)

(excessive force claims do not fall within the definition of 18 U.S.C. § 3626(g)(2) and are therefore outside the scope of § 1997e(a)); *Basker-ville*, 1998 WL 778396, at *4–*5 (same).[13]

Now look what happens when you elevate the parenthetical informa-tion and minimize the volume and page numbers:

While § 1997e(a) does not expressly define the term "prison condi-tions," the phrase is defined in a different section of the statute—but that definition explicitly applies only to "this section."[1] Yet the defen-dants urge that § 1997e(a) should be read *in pari materia* with § 3626. The United States Supreme Court has recognized the interpretive canon that language "used in one portion of a statute . . . should be deemed to have the same meaning as the same language used elsewhere in the statute."[2] Some courts have read the "prison conditions" language of § 1997e(a) *in pari materia* with the definition provided in § 3626(g)(2).[3] But whether the latter section provides a definition may not matter at all, since § 3626 is itself ambiguous. On the critical question here, even judges who rely on the definition in that section do not agree on whether § 1997e(a) encompasses excessive-force and assault claims. The Third Circuit has held that it does.[4] So has a judge sitting in the Southern District of New York.[5] On the opposite side of this question are Circuit Judge John T. Noonan[6] and yet a different district judge sit-ting in the Southern District of New York.[7]

[1] 28 U.S.C. § 3626(g)(2).

[2] *Mertens v. Hewitt Assocs.*, 508 U.S. 248, 260, 113 S.Ct. 2063, 124 L.Ed.2d 161 (1993); *see also Russo v. Trifari, Krussman & Fishel, Inc.*, 837 F.2d 40, 45 (2d Cir. 1988) ("Construing identical language in a single statute *in pari materia* is both traditional and logical.").

[3] *See, e.g.*, *Booth*, 206 F.3d at 294; *Freeman*, 196 F.3d at 643–44; *Beeson*, 28 F.Supp.2d at 888; *Giannattasio*, 2000 WL 335242, at *11–*12. *But see Carter*, 1999 WL 14014, at *3–*4 (declining to rely upon the § 3626(g)(2) definition to interpret meaning of "prison conditions" under § 1997e(a)).

[4] *Booth v. Churner*, 206 F.3d at 294–95 (opinion of the court).

[5] *Beeson*, 28 F.Supp.2d at 888–89.

[6] *Booth*, 206 F.3d at 301–02 (Noonan, J., concurring and dissenting).

[7] *Baskerville*, 1998 WL 778396, at *4–*5.

The ideas are more crisply expressed in the revised version. The para-graph is now about 40% shorter. Oh, and by the way, the average sen-tence length has dropped to just 21 words. It's hard to know what the average sentence length is in the original: if you count the citations, it's 39; if you don't, it's 30.

---

[13] *Nussle v. Willette*, 224 F.3d 95, 101–02 (2d Cir. 2000).

Refuting the Opposition

So, you may ask, are there no good arguments against my proposals? Well, there are some, but the weight of the evidence is against them.

The first counterargument, and the most serious one, is that citations tell the knowledgeable reader important things: what cases you're relying on, what courts they derive from, and how old they are. This isn't much of an argument. For any but the most basic propositions, a good writer will give this information in the text. Consider how Charles Alan Wright, the great procedural writer, used his own words to introduce authorities in his magisterial treatise *Federal Practice and Procedure*:

- "It was not until *Rhode Island v. Innis*, in 1980, that the Court had an opportunity to shed further light on what it had meant in *Miranda* by 'interrogation.' Writing for the Court, Justice Stewart agreed that the repeated references in *Miranda* to 'questioning' might suggest that . . . ."[14]

- "The second kind of prejudice, that proof of defendant's guilt of one crime may be used to convict him or her of another even though proof of that guilt would have been inadmissible at a separate trial, was considered by the Court of Appeals for the District of Columbia in *Drew v. United States*."[15]

- "The federal attitude was best expressed by Justice O'Connor, speaking for the Court in *Zafiro v. United States*. She wrote . . . ."[16]

- "In a 1964 case the Court was unanimous in speaking, through Justice Clark, of 'the erroneous holding of the Court of Appeals that criminal defendants have a constitutionally based right to a trial in their own home districts.' "[17]

Good scholarly writers have long used these techniques. Yet judges who cite in the text almost never use explanatory sentences like those.

The second major counterargument is that readers shouldn't have to look down at footnotes. I agree. I don't think that readers should be distracted by a netherworld of talking footnotes. The important stuff— including the court and the date (didn't I just say this?)—should be up

---

[14] Charles Alan Wright, *Federal Practice and Procedure* vol. 1, § 76.1, at 201 (1999) (introducing *Rhode Island v. Innis*, 446 U.S. 291 (1980)).

[15] Charles Alan Wright, *Federal Practice and Procedure* vol. 1A, § 222, at 480 (2000) (introducing *Drew v. United States*, 331 F.2d 85 (D.C. Cir. 1964)).

[16] *Id.* § 223, at 493 (introducing *Zafiro v. United States*, 506 U.S. 534, 539 (1993)).

[17] Charles Alan Wright, *Federal Practice and Procedure* vol. 2, § 301, at 297 (2000) (quoting *Platt v. Minnesota Min. & Mfg. Co.*, 376 U.S. 240, 245 (1964)).

in the body. Despite what some say, the tiny superscript isn't nearly as distracting as a 45-character citation.

The other counterarguments are hard to take seriously. Some say that footnoted citations will encourage unscrupulous writers to fudge their authorities. Some say that footnoted citations undermine the doctrine of precedent. Some say that footnoted citations will encourage greater use of substantive footnotes. And some say that footnoted citations are bad simply because they're nontraditional. Surely the best refutation of these objections is merely to state them.

When I teach my seminar called Advanced Judicial Writing—which I've conducted for courts in 19 states—I ask judges whether they think ordinary people should be able to read and understand judicial opinions. One or two judges may say no, that they write only for lawyers, but the overwhelming majority say yes, since reasonably well-educated people ought to understand why disputes come out the way they do.

Yet most judicial writers do something that would cause the average citizen to stop reading almost instantly: they interrupt their prose with lots of arcane names and numbers, which leave the ordinary reader feeling unable to track the argument itself. One more example:

> Our opinions in *Hughes Aircraft Co. v. United States*, 86 F.3d 1566, 39 USPQ2d 1065 (Fed. Cir. 1996) (*Hughes XIII*) and *Hughes Aircraft Co. v. United States*, 140 F.3d 1470, 46 USPQ2d 1285 (Fed. Cir. 1998) (*Hughes XV*) do not lead to a different result. *Hughes XIII* explicitly held that *Hughes Aircraft Co. v. United States*, 717 F.2d 1351, 219 USPQ 473 (Fed. Cir. 1983) (*Hughes VII*) was entirely consistent with our intervening en banc decision in *Pennwalt Corp. v. Durand-Wayland*, 833 F.2d 931, 4 USPQ2d 1737 (Fed. Cir. 1987). *Hughes XV* held that *Warner-Jenkinson* provides no basis to alter the decision in *Hughes VII* because the court properly applied the all-elements rule. 140 F.3d at 1475, 46 USPQ2d at 1289. In neither case was there controlling authority that in the interim had made a contrary decision of law applicable to the relevant issue.[18]

The passage becomes significantly clearer when shorn of the citations:

> Our opinions in *Hughes XIII*[1] and *Hughes XV*[2] do not lead to a different result. *Hughes XIII* explicitly held that *Hughes VII*[3] was entirely consistent with our intervening en banc decision in *Pennwalt Corp. v. Durand-Wayland*.[4] And *Hughes XV* held that *Warner-Jenkinson* provides

---

[18] *Litton Sys., Inc. v. Honeywell, Inc.*, 238 F.3d 1376, 1380 (Fed. Cir. 2001).

no basis to alter the decision in *Hughes VII* because the court properly applied the all-elements rule.[5] In neither case was there controlling authority that in the interim had made a contrary decision.

[1] *Hughes Aircraft Co. v. United States*, 86 F.3d 1566, 39 USPQ2d 1065 (Fed. Cir. 1996) (*Hughes XIII*).

[2] *Hughes Aircraft Co. v. United States*, 140 F.3d 1470, 46 USPQ2d 1285 (Fed. Cir. 1998) (*Hughes XV*).

[3] *Hughes Aircraft Co. v. United States*, 717 F.2d 1351, 219 USPQ 473 (Fed. Cir. 1983) (*Hughes VII*).

[4] *Pennwalt Corp. v. Durand-Wayland*, 833 F.2d 931, 4 USPQ2d 1737 (Fed. Cir. 1987).

[5] *Hughes XV*, 140 F.3d at 1475, 46 USPQ2d at 1289.

Conclusion

In a *New York Times* piece dealing with this issue, Judge J. Michael Luttig of the Fourth Circuit was quoted as supporting the idea that nothing could make ordinary people read court decisions: "[T]he lay public still won't read legal opinions. They're too complex, laborious, and uninteresting to the lay public."[19] If I understand the comment correctly, it represents a retrograde view—that lawyers deal with matters that surpass most people's ability to understand.

But it's not really so, and never has been. We just think our subject necessitates overhead flying. Let's face it: if you can't explain the case to a nonlawyer, the chances are that you don't understand it yourself. This is true of the advocates who come before courts and of the judges who decide their cases. And as every judge knows, it's much harder to write a clear opinion when the advocates haven't fully grasped their cases or can't demonstrate their grasp through cogent exposition.

Even one citation, such as *Spartan Mills v. Bank of Am. Ill.*, 112 F.3d 1251, 1255–56 (4th Cir.), *cert. denied*, 522 U.S. 969, 118 S.Ct. 417, 139 L.Ed.2d 319 (1997) (quoting *Pacor, Inc. v. Higgins*, 743 F.2d 984, 994 (3d Cir. 1984) (internal quotation marks omitted)), is enough to drive sensible readers away from legal writing. I urge you to do what you can to make the law more accessible to more people. You should do it for selfish reasons, too: you'll think more clearly if you do.

---

[19] William Glaberson, *Legal Citations on Trial in Innovation v. Tradition*, N.Y. Times, 8 July 2001, at 1, 16.

An Afterthought

A columnist in the *Colorado Lawyer* has opined that "if better readability is the goal, citations are not the biggest impediment," adding: "There are simple techniques to keep citations from seriously interrupting the train of thought. One of the simplest is to move most citations to the end of sentences. Also, most writers can better improve readability by concentrating on their writing techniques."[20] She quotes a judge as saying that good legal writing is "about writing in the active voice and keeping the sentences short. It's not just about where you put the cites."[21]

I respectfully disagree. I hope that the many examples in this essay show that good legal writing is not just about active voice and short sentences and such; it's also about where you put your citations. Those at the ends of sentences are better than those in midsentence, true. But they are still major impediments to clarity. If you want a clean narrative line, you must kill your clutter. You can't just wish it away.

---

[20] K.K. DuVivier, *Footnote Citations?* Colo. Law., May 2001, at 47.
[21] *Id.*

JOHN MINOR WISDOM • SPOTTSWOOD ROBINSON III • RICHARD A. POSNER

CHAPTER ELEVEN

Citations

Foreword to the *Texas Rules of Form*

CITATIONS ARE ALL ABOUT being credible and reliable. Although good citation form won't win over many readers, poor form will assuredly put off those who prize accuracy. So if you're a graduate student, you must know Turabian's *Manual for Writers of Term Papers, Theses, and Dissertations*. If you're a scholar in the humanities, you must know your *MLA Style Manual*. If you're on the editorial side of book publishing, you must know your *Chicago Manual of Style*. And if you're a Texas lawyer, you must know your *Texas Rules of Form*, more commonly known as the *Greenbook*.

Published by the *Texas Law Review*, and now in its tenth edition, the *Greenbook* authoritatively guides scholars and practitioners through the thickets of citing Texas legal authorities. If you learned the basics years ago, spend some time with this new edition: you'll be surprised (as I was) at the extent of what you've forgotten. If you're learning this stuff for the first time, try not to be intimidated by it. You may have to try hard, but it's worth the effort.

If you're writing about Texas law and hope to seem to know what you're doing, you'll need to follow the guidance here. Many readers—perfectly decent and humane people in other respects—won't give your writing a serious look if you don't.

From the *Texas Rules of Form* (10th ed. 2003).

❧ ❧ ❧

The Place for Bibliographic Numbers

SMART AND INTERESTING PEOPLE, lawyers. How astonishing, really, that
nearly everyone else finds their prose dull, slow, cumbersome, abstruse,
verbose, and pedantic. The causes of bad legal writing are both technical
and cultural. The technical ones include such things as unnecessary jargon, excessive use of passive voice, overreliance on abstract nouns, overlong sentences, overlong paragraphs, and the failure to differentiate between
useful and useless details. These problems are actually common to most
writers, not just lawyers. The cultural causes, though, are another matter.
Lawyers are both the inheritors and the bequeathers of a set of stylistic
conventions that would mar anyone's writing.

Although legal writing is the least skimmable prose known to human-
kind, those who create it commonly do something that forces readers to
skip over dozens, even hundreds, of characters in almost every paragraph.
These superfluous characters amount to useless detail that distracts the
reader from the content. Paradoxically, this habit results both in overlong
sentences and paragraphs (the extra characters bulk it up, after all) and in
underdeveloped paragraphs. I refer, of course, to citations: the volume
numbers and page numbers that clutter lawyers' prose.

Some readers of this essay are already familiar with my view on this
issue. It caused such an uproar that it provoked an above-the-fold front-
page article in *The New York Times*.[1] My view is simply this: we'd all be
better off if lawyers and judges would put bibliographic information in
footnotes—and also refrain from putting any discussion there.

When you do this, the stylistic advantages are many:

- You shorten your paragraphs.
- You find it far easier to vary your sentence structure.
- You have the freedom to write some shorter sentences, since you no
  longer need to spread out the citations with longer sentences.
- You write paragraphs that no longer invite readers to skip over
  extraneous characters.

More important to legal prose, though, are the substantive advantages.
First you find that you can develop your ideas better within those paragraphs. Second, you find that you can discuss caselaw more effectively, since
you're no longer kidding yourself that citations substitute for legal analysis.

Adapted from *Student Lawyer* (Sept. 2003).

[1] William Glaberson, *Legal Citations on Trial in Innovation v. Tradition*, N.Y. Times, 8 July
2001, § 1, at 1.

Of course, putting citations in footnotes isn't traditional except in legal scholarship—and not really even there, because legal scholars are addicted to substantive footnotes.

You may wonder why lawyers haven't seriously considered subordinating citations in all their writing. The answer is simple: until 1985 or so, we really didn't have the option because we were still using typewriters. The convention was set long ago when the Royal typewriter—take your choice of pica or elite!—represented cutting-edge technology. Now, of course, we can easily put these interruptions, like 529 U.S. 277, 289, 120 S.Ct. 1382, 1391, 146 L.Ed.2d 265, 278 (2000), in their proper place.

So would this shift in technique result in all gain and no loss? I wouldn't say that at all. But whenever we see the new convention practiced, the gain is pretty overwhelming. Imagine being able to focus on tightly reasoned analysis, while being told what authority the writer relies on, without all the numerical hiccups.

Naturally, not everyone agrees with my proposal, even though it's gaining adherents month by month. My principal detractor is a judicial heavyweight who's mostly a wonderful writer: Judge Richard A. Posner. He and I debated the point in the Summer 2001 issue of *Court Review*, a law journal for judges.[2] Judge Posner raised three main counterarguments: (1) "very few [laypersons] read judicial opinions or will do so," and the judge "need not rewrite an opinion so that it will attract a lay audience"; (2) the proposal makes nonscholarly writing (he says briefs and opinions are nonscholarly) unduly resemble scholarship; and (3) it's distracting to be expected to read past superscripts. And let it be said that he wasn't amused by my revisions of his judicial opinions. Yes, I argued by trying to show how the proposal might improve even Judge Posner's opinions.

My answers to Judge Posner's points are as follows. First, it matters—it matters a lot—whether nonlawyers can make sense of legal writing. Textual citations make legal writing all but impenetrable to the uninitiated. They contribute to mumbo jumbo. If lawyers and judges write only for and among themselves, the result bodes ill for our legal system, which is supposed to be accessible to everyone. Second, it hardly matters if lawyers' and judges' writing resembles a scholarly format, as long as the result is more readable. Third, surely it's easier to skip over a superscript than to skip over two or three lines of number-laden type—especially when you can count on nothing of any substance appearing in a footnote.

---

[2] Garner, *Clearing the Cobwebs from Judicial Opinions*, Court Rev., Summer 2001, at 4–21; Richard A. Posner, *Against Footnotes*, Court Rev., Summer 2001, at 24–25. Anyone who wants to see the Garner–Posner debate will find it at http://aja.ncsc.dni.us/courtrv/cr38-2/CR38-2Garner.pdf; [same prefix]/CR38-2Posner.pdf; [same prefix]/CR38-2GarnerAfterword.pdf.

Of course, you'll end up writing differently once you subordinate volume and page numbers. You'll often need to say, in the text, what your authority is and how old it is. For example, you won't write this: "The conflict here hinges on the meaning of *Hammond Packing Co. v. Arkansas,* 212 U.S. 322, 29 S.Ct. 370, 53 L.Ed. 530 (1909)." Instead, you'll write this: "The conflict here hinges on the meaning of *Hammond Packing Co. v. Arkansas,*[62] decided by the Supreme Court in 1909." You may think that those two sentences are essentially the same, but they're not. With the second, it's much easier for the writer to maintain a narrative line—something that lawyers aren't generally adept at.

Many judges around the country—not a majority, to be sure, but a worthy minority—have already adopted the proposal. You'll find them in Alaska, California, Delaware, Georgia, Louisiana, Michigan, Texas, Washington, and elsewhere. Some readers of this essay will someday adopt the proposal upon becoming judges.

But whether or not you ascend to the bench someday or already are a judge, you'll need to make up your own mind on this issue. What you decide will affect almost every paragraph you write.

≈ ≈ ≈

Is there a *Bluebook* rule on this? you may ask. Not really: in 1991, the *Bluebook* editors (mostly Harvard law students) issued the 15th edition, which for the first time included a practitioner section putting citations in the text. (There's a pretty horrendous example that's been in Rule B.2 ever since, up through the current 18th edition.) It was precisely the wrong message at precisely the wrong time. Given the advent of advanced word processing, *The Bluebook* should have given brief-writers a choice.

❧ ❧ ❧

The Citational Footnote

BACK IN 1984, when I was clerking for the Fifth Circuit, I noticed that
Judge John Minor Wisdom and Judge Alvin Rubin were writing some
wonderfully clean judicial opinions. They had stripped the text of all citations—not case names, but all the numbers and other bibliographic information that typically follow the case names—and put them into footnotes. As a result, those judges' opinions actually had a discernible train
of thought. They were following the lead of Judge Spottswood Robinson of the D.C. Circuit, who footnoted every citation from the date of
his confirmation to the bench in 1966.

Today, more and more judges and lawyers are themselves starting to
subordinate bibliographic references by relegating them to footnotes.
They're smart to do so, I think. But before exploring their reasons, let's
be clear what we're talking about. Two points merit attention here.

First, let's agree that our readers shouldn't have to look at footnotes
to understand our point. And they shouldn't have to glance down to see
what primary authority we're relying on, either. That ought to be up in
the text, as part of a sentence in which we discuss the authority. But the
bibliographic information ought to be out of the way. While the names
of important cases (and perhaps of the courts that decided them) should
appear in the textual discussion, cases cited for preliminary propositions
might be cited exclusively in footnotes.

Second, we're not talking about substantive footnotes. I've long
fought so-called talking footnotes,[1] and this journal, which I edited for a
decade, is probably the only law journal that all but forbids them.[2] What
we're talking about is the noxious habit of interspersing bibliographic
data throughout legal analysis—or what commonly passes for it.

Getting Inured to Thought-Interrupters

Do you remember when you first started reading law? You were probably reading a judicial opinion, and surely among the most irksome
things about the experience was encountering all the citations in the text.

Adapted from *The Scribes Journal of Legal Writing* (1998–2000).

[1] *See, e.g.*, Garner, *The Elements of Legal Style* 92–94 (2d ed. 2002); Garner, *A Dictionary
of Modern Legal Usage* 364 (2d ed. 1995); Garner, *The Winning Brief* 145, 148–49 (2d ed.
2004).

[2] *See The Scribes Journal of Legal Writing* (since 1990).

For beginning legal readers, the prose is quite jarring—as if you were driving down a highway studded with speed bumps.

These thought-interrupters were born of a technologically impoverished world. Originally, lawyers used scriveners who interspersed authorities in their notes. Then, in the 1880s, typewriters became popular, and it was all but impossible to put citations in footnotes because one could never calculate the requisite spatial proportions of text and notes on the page. That's why citations have traditionally appeared in the text. They were there in 1900, they were there in 1925, they were there in 1950, and they were still there in 1975. It became a frozen convention.

Meanwhile, of course, the number of cases being cited in legal writing erupted during the years leading up to 1975. And by the turn of the 21st century, things had gotten even worse. With computer-aided research and the proliferation of caselaw, it has become easier than ever to find several cases to support virtually every sentence. Only today I was reading a brief that cited, on average, 12 cases per page.

Over time, the pages of judicial opinions, briefs, and memos have become increasingly cluttered. Some have become unreadable. Others are readable only by those mentally and emotionally hardy enough to forge through the underbrush.

As much as citations handicap readers, though, they handicap writers even more. Whenever you put citations within and between sentences, it's hard to make consecutive sentences feel seamlessly connected. There's just too much intervening clutter. And, worse, sometimes your paragraph won't be able to get beyond a single sentence because that sentence, followed by a string citation with parentheticals, turns out to consume nearly half a page. So much for "paragraph development."

In short, it doesn't really matter whether readers can negotiate their way through eddies of citations—because, on the whole, writers can't.

Reference notes can cure the problem. Just put citations—and generally only citations—in footnotes. And make it so that no reader would ever have to look at your footnotes to know what important authorities you're relying on. If you're quoting an opinion, put right in the text the name of the court you're quoting, the year of the case, and (if necessary) the name of the case. They're all part of your story line. But as for the numbers—the volume, reporter, and page references—park that stuff out of the way.

If footnoting your citations seems like such a revolutionary idea, ask yourself why you've never seen a biography that reads like this:

> Holmes was ready for the final charge. His intellectual powers intact (Interview by Felix Frankfurter with Harold Laski, 23 Mar. 1938, at 45, unpublished manuscript on file with the author), he organized his work efficiently so that little time was wasted (3 Holmes Diary at 275,

Langdell Law Library Manuscript No. 123–44–337; Holmes letter to Isabel Curtain, 24 June 1923, Langdell Law Library Manuscript No. 123–44–599). He volunteered less often to relieve others of their caseloads (Holmes court memo, 24 July 1923, at 4, Library of Congress Rare Book Room Doc. No. 1923-AAC-Holmes-494), and he sometimes had to be reassured of his usefulness (Brandeis letter to Felix Frankfurter, 3 Mar. 1923, Brandeis Univ. Manuscript Collection Doc. No. 23-3-3-BF). His doctor gave him a clean bill of health (Mass. Archives Doc. No. 23–47899–32, at 1), told him his heart was "a good pump" (Holmes letter to Letitia Fontaine, 25 June 1923, at 2, Langdell Law Library Manuscript No. 123–44–651), and told him that very few men of Holmes's age were "as well off as he was" (*id.*)—to which Holmes drily replied that "most of them are dead" (Memo of Dr. Theobald Marmor, 26 June 1923, at 2, Morgan Library Collection, copy on file with the author). But he was pleased that the "main machinery" was "in good running order" (Holmes letter to Letitia Fontaine, 25 June 1923, at 1, Langdell Law Library Manuscript No. 123–44–651), and he frequently felt perky enough to get out of the carriage partway home from court and walk the remaining blocks with Brandeis (Brandeis letter to Clare Eustacia Bodnar, 22 July 1923, Brandeis Univ. Manuscript Collection Doc. No. 23–7–22-BCEBB).

No self-respecting historian would write that way. But brief-writers commonly do something very much like it:

Agency decisions are entitled to the greatest weight and to a presumption of validity, when the decision is viewed in the light most favorable to the agency. *Baltimore Lutheran High Sch. Ass'n v. Employment Security Admin.*, 302 Md. 649, 662–63, 490 A.2d 701, 708 (1985); *Board of Educ. of Montgomery County v. Paynter*, 303 Md. 22, 40, 491 A.2d 1186, 1195 (1985); *Nationwide Mut. Ins. Co. v. Insurance Comm'r*, 67 Md. App. 727, 737, 509 A.2d 719, 724, *cert. denied*, 307 Md. 433, 514 A.2d 1211 (1986); *Bulluck v. Pelham Wood Apartments*, 283 Md. 505, 513, 390 A.2d 1119, 1124 (1978). Thus, the reviewing court will not substitute its judgment for that of the agency when the issue is fairly debatable and the record contains substantial evidence to support the administrative decision. *Howard County v. Dorsey*, 45 Md. App. 692, 700, 416 A.2d 23, 27 (1980); *Mayor and Aldermen of City of Annapolis v. Annapolis Waterfront Co.*, 284 Md. 383, 395–96, 396 A.2d 1080, 1087–88 (1979); *Cason v. Board of County Comm'rs for Prince George's County*, 261 Md. 699, 707, 276 A.2d 661, 665 (1971); *Germenko v. County Board of Appeals of Baltimore County*, 257 Md. 706, 711, 264 A.2d 825, 828 (1970); *Bonnie View Country Club, Inc. v. Glass*, 242 Md. 46, 52, 217 A.2d 647, 651 (1966). The court may substitute its judgment only as to an error made on an issue of law. *State Election Board v. Billhimer*, 314 Md. 46, 59, 548 A.2d 819, 826 (1988), *cert. denied*, 490 U.S. 1007, 109 S.Ct. 1644, 104 L.Ed.2d 159 (1989); *Gray v. Anne Arundel Co.*, 73 Md. App. 301, 308, 533 A.2d 1325, 1329 (1987).

Overkill, for sure, but in fact it's mild compared to what writers do when coupling parentheticals with the citations.

The problem wasn't so bad 150 years ago, when few cases might appear over a span of several pages. Today, partly because caselaw has mushroomed, much legal writing has become unreadable. I'd like legal writers to stop producing so-called prose that looks like this:

> To state a claim under Rule 10b-5, a complaint must allege that the defendant falsely represented or omitted to disclose a material fact in connection with the purchase or sale of a security with the intent to deceive or defraud. *See Ernst & Ernst v. Hochfelder*, 425 U.S. 185, 96 S.Ct. 1375, 47 L.Ed.2d 668 (1976). A party's specific promise to perform a particular act in the future, while secretly intending not to perform that act or knowing that the act could not be carried out, may violate § 10(b) and Rule 10b-5 if the promise is part of the consideration for the transfer of securities. *See, e.g.*, *Luce v. Edelstein*, 802 F.2d 49, 55 (2d Cir. 1986) (citing *McGrath v. Zenith Radio Corp.*, 651 F.2d 458 (7th Cir.), *cert. denied*, 454 U.S. 835, 102 S.Ct. 136, 70 L.Ed.2d 114 (1981)); *Wilsmann v. Upjohn Co.*, 775 F.2d 713, 719 (6th Cir. 1985) (concluding that plaintiff's securities-fraud claim against acquiring corporation was in connection with defendant's purchase of plaintiff's stock where plaintiff alleged that part of consideration for sale of stock was false promise by acquiring corporation concerning future payments for stock plaintiff received in acquired corporation but holding that evidence of fraud was insufficient to support jury's verdict), *cert. denied*, 476 U.S. 1171, 106 S.Ct. 2893, 90 L.Ed.2d 980 (1986). *But see Hunt v. Robinson*, 852 F.2d 786, 787 (4th Cir. 1988) (holding that defendant's failure to tender shares in new company in return for plaintiff's employment did not state securities-fraud claim because the defendant's alleged misrepresentation concerned its tender of shares as required by the terms of the employment contract, not the actual sale of stock). The failure to perform a promise, however, does not constitute fraud if the promise was made with the good-faith expectation that it would be performed. *See Luce*, 802 F.2d at 56.

Double-spacing only aggravates the problem because consecutive sentences get further separated and paragraph breaks become more infrequent.

Even if you strip out the citations, something the careful reader will have to do anyway (by mental contortion), you end up with plodding, stiff prose:

> To state a claim under Rule 10b-5, a complaint must allege that the defendant falsely represented or omitted to disclose a material fact in connection with the purchase or sale of a security with the intent to deceive or defraud. A party's specific promise to perform a particular act in the future, while secretly intending not to perform that act or

> knowing that the act could not be carried out, may violate § 10(b) and Rule 10b-5 if the promise is part of the consideration for the transfer of securities. The failure to perform a promise, however, does not constitute fraud if the promise was made with the good-faith expectation that it would be performed.

But now that you can see what you're actually saying, you can more easily focus on style—on making the sentences speakable. So you edit the paragraph:

> To state a claim under Rule 10b-5, a complaint must allege that the defendant—intending to deceive or defraud—falsely represented or failed to disclose a material fact about the purchase or sale of a security. A party's specific promise to do something in the future, while secretly intending not to do it or knowing that it can't be done, may violate Rule 10b-5 if the promise is part of the consideration for the transfer. But not performing the promise isn't fraud if the promisor expected in good faith to be able to perform.

The revised passage isn't a work of art. But it's much closer to being one than the original is—and probably as close as most discussions of Rule 10b-5 ever could be.

Go back and look at the original passage. Look at how much more difficult it is to tease out the essential ideas. In your imagination, try double-spacing it, so that you fill up the entire page. Now imagine page after page of that . . .

Although objectors say there is no sound reason for footnoting citations, in fact there are at least ten good reasons. Some are related, but they're subtly distinct. Here's what happens when you effectively use citational footnotes:

1. You can strip down your argument and focus on what you're really saying—and how you're saying it.
2. You can write more fully developed paragraphs.
3. You can simultaneously shorten your paragraphs.
4. You can connect your sentences smoothly, with simple transitional words. (Typically, when citations interrupt sentences, writers feel pressure to repeat several words that would otherwise be redundant.)
5. You can introduce greater variety in sentence patterns, especially through subordinate clauses.
6. You have a better chance of discovering a patch of poor writing—or poor thinking—since it's no longer camouflaged by a flurry of citations. And you won't be tempted to bury important parts of your analysis in parentheticals.

7. String citations become relatively harmless. I don't favor them, but I'm not adamantly opposed to them either—not if they're tucked out of the way.

8. You'll find it necessary to discuss important cases contextually, as opposed to merely relying on bare citations to do the work for you. You'll pay more respect to important precedent by actually explicitly analyzing it instead of simply identifying it in a "citation sentence," which isn't really a sentence at all.

9. You'll give emphasis where it's due. That is, the court and the case and the holding are often what matters ("Three years ago in *Gandy*, this Court held . . ."), but the numbers never are ("925 S.W.2d 696, 698"—etc.). Numbers, when sprinkled through the main text, invariably distract.

10. The page ends up looking cleaner, more inviting, more accessible.

Many brief-writers and judges have been persuaded by these points. They've begun using citational footnotes because they see them as a quick way to improve as writers. That is indeed the case.

Over the past decade, I've conducted more than 35 judicial-writing seminars for state judges throughout the country. Although this point about footnoting citations is only the tiniest part of my teaching, you see a trend emerging nationally. In Delaware, for example, four of the five supreme court justices put all their citations in footnotes. In Alaska today, virtually all reported cases have citations in footnotes. And you see the trend elsewhere—in Georgia, Minnesota, Texas, and Washington, to cite but a few examples.

Will It Really Work?

Some legal writers feel queasy about departing from established custom. Let me respond to three common qualms.

First, many writers fear that if they don't put citations up in the text, their readers won't know what court is being cited or how recent the cases are. In fact, though, you generally won't be footnoting naked propositions of law. Instead, you'll be saying something like "Just last year, the Third Circuit held . . ." or "Section 28.007 of the Insurance Code requires . . ." so that one gets the gist of your authority without having to glance down at the bottom of the page.

Second, on a similar note, some fear that footnoting citations will undermine the importance of precedent. Yet no one ever found this to be the case with Judge John Minor Wisdom or Judge Alvin Rubin, two of the most respected Fifth Circuit judges who, from about 1983 to the end of their careers, footnoted all their citations. As Judge Wisdom, a careful stylist, put it in a 1993 article: "Citations belong in a footnote: even one full citation such as 494 U.S. 407, 110 S.Ct. 1212, 108 L.Ed.2d 347 (1990), breaks the thought; two, three, or more in one massive paragraph are an abomination."[3]

Third, many judges complain about footnotes.[4] True, other judges praise them,[5] but if you listen closely, the complaints are strong enough to give any sensible writer pause. In fact, the complaints are valid when directed at footnotes that contain substantive discussion. But most judges who hear the merits of reference notes and see good examples find themselves agreeing that textual citations are blemishes. Whenever I teach a seminar on judicial writing, a strong majority of the judges finally concur that it makes sense to put citations in footnotes. A few others, however, will still think otherwise. And if you know that's what a judge thinks, take heed of the judge's preference. Just don't let your temporary heed become your regular habit.

Until the mid-1980s, law offices and judicial chambers had no choice. Citations had to go into the text. Only professional printers had a realistic option of footnoting citations. (Before typewriters were introduced in the 1880s, of course, mid-text citations were a scribal convention.) The personal computer liberated us of this technological constraint.

Speaking of technology, what about the argument that putting citations in footnotes complicates online legal research? Even if there are some shortcomings in some media, I'm confident that they're short-term problems. For example, hypertext links to footnotes will cure the problem of having them appear inconveniently as endnotes. In any event, though, I unabashedly believe that (1) the print form must have primacy, and (2) technology will readily adapt to footnoted citations for purposes of online research. If you have complaints, lobby the companies that provide Westlaw and Lexis and the courts that post their opinions on websites.

---

[3] John Minor Wisdom, *How I Write*, Scribes J. Legal Writing 83, 86 (1993).

[4] *See, e.g.*, *In Justice Breyer's Opinion, a Footnote Has No Place*, N.Y. Times, 28 June 1995, at B18; David Margolick, *The Footnote in Judicial Opinions*, N.Y. Times, 4 Jan. 1991, at B14; Abner J. Mikva, *Goodbye to Footnotes*, 56 U. Colo. L. Rev. 647 (1985).

[5] *See, e.g.*, Edward R. Becker, *In Praise of Footnotes*, 74 Wash. U. L.Q. 1 (1996); Timothy R. Rice, *In Defense of Footnotes*, Natl. L.J., 20 June 1988, at 13.

Helping Along the Glacial Change

In every state where I've spoken to judges, a majority have said that they would prefer footnoted citations. It may take a generation or two for the new convention to gain wide acceptance, but it's coming. Gradually, legal writers will learn to put all citations in footnotes but to refrain from saying anything else in footnotes. The only frightening prospect is that, when you're putting together an opinion or brief, piling citations onto the page won't be enough: you'll actually have to have a coherent thought worth expressing.

If the citational footnote becomes the norm, it's a sure bet to revolutionize the quality, and readability, of legal prose.

Examples of Cases Using
Citational Footnotes

Anyone curious about what citational footnotes look like in context might look at any of the following cases. It's especially enlightening to compare them stylistically with other cases in the same volumes.

- *Alizadeh v. Safeway Stores, Inc.*, 802 F.2d 111 (5th Cir. 1986).
- *Alamo Rent A Car, Inc. v. Schulman*, 897 P.2d 405 (Wash. App. 1995).
- *Curry v. Curry*, 473 S.E.2d 760 (Ga. 1996).
- *Warden v. Hoar Constr. Co.*, 507 S.E.2d 428 (Ga. 1998).
- *KPMG Peat Marwick v. Harrison County Fin. Corp.*, 988 S.W.2d 746 (Tex. 1999).
- *M.P.M. Enters. v. Gilbert*, 731 A.2d 790 (Del. 1999).
- *Aleck v. Delvo Plastics, Inc.*, 972 P.2d 988 (Alaska 1999).
- *State v. Martin*, 975 P.2d 1020 (Wash. 1999) (en banc).
- *In re Nolo Press/Folk Law, Inc.*, 991 S.W.2d 768 (Tex. 1999).
- *Temple-Inland Forest Prods. Corp. v. Carter*, 993 S.W.2d 88 (Tex. 1999).
- *Williams v. Kimes*, 996 S.W.2d 43 (Mo. 1999) (en banc).
- *Fitzgerald v. Advanced Spine Fixation Sys., Inc.*, 996 S.W.2d 864 (Tex. 1999).
- *United States v. Parsee*, 178 F.3d 374 (5th Cir. 1999).
- *McGray Constr. Co. v. Office of Workers Compen. Programs*, 181 F.3d 1008 (9th Cir. 1999).
- *Minneapolis Public Housing Auth. v. Lor*, 591 N.W.2d 700 (Minn. 1999).

ào ào ào

ALWD vs. *The Bluebook*:
The Great Style Debate

FOR MOST OF THE 20TH CENTURY, a little blue book published jointly by four law reviews—at Harvard, Yale, Pennsylvania, and Columbia—reigned supreme in the field of legal citations. It was called *A Uniform System of Citation* through its first 14 editions. In 1991 its unofficial title became the official one: *The Bluebook.*

Through its many editions, the booklet evolved into a book: It became longer, more technical, and more difficult to follow. Successive editors, seemingly eager to leave their mark on the text, changed the meanings of signals such as *See, See also*, and *See, e.g.* This bred confusion and widespread dissatisfaction.

In 1989, the editors of *Chicago Law Review*, encouraged by Judge Richard Posner (a former University of Chicago law professor), mounted a challenge by publishing the *Maroonbook*.[1] It advocated clarity as its touchstone. The idea was that there's no "right" and "wrong" way to cite legal authority as long as readers can readily figure out how to look it up.

For example, users were encouraged to omit periods from all abbreviations, but nothing was mandatory. Writers were given discretion—loads of it. But most legal writers wanted sure-footed rules more than they wanted discretion, and the *Maroonbook* fizzled.

Having established a virtual monopoly in the field, the *Bluebook* editors squandered their lead in the 1990s by fabricating some seriously flawed rules, such as these:

- Whereas law reviews usually put citations in footnotes, brief-writers must insert them in the text.
- The abbreviation of a given word depends on whether it is used in a case name, a title, or a court reporter.
- Underlining appears instead of *italics* in court documents and legal memorandums (a holdover from typewriting).

The *Bluebook* editors have also tinkered with essential rules—such as those for using signals—making them inconsistent and unreliable. Mean-

---

Adapted from *Student Lawyer* (Nov. 2003).

[1] *University of Chicago Manual of Legal Citation* (1998). *See* Richard A. Posner, *Goodbye to the Bluebook*, 53 U. Chi. L. Rev. 1343, 1352 app. (1986) (original 15-page version of manual).

while, in the 1991 and 1996 editions, the book became more hypertechnical than ever—and more vulnerable to attack.

Into the breach stepped Darby Dickerson, an energetic, multitalented legal-writing professor at Stetson University. First, she wrote a detailed article about the 1996 edition of *The Bluebook* for *The Scribes Journal of Legal Writing*, critiquing the most significant changes between the 15th and 16th editions.[2] Then, with the support of the Association of Legal Writing Directors (ALWD), she wrote a guide with the avowed intent of ousting *The Bluebook*.

The *ALWD Citation Manual: A Professional System of Citation* differs from *The Bluebook* in many ways. It restates the rules of citation based on the forms actually used by practitioners and scholars. It is designed to be a teaching tool as well as a reference book. And it has eliminated many of the needless complexities and inconsistencies of *The Bluebook*.

For instance, in stark contrast to *The Bluebook*, case-citation forms don't rely on whether the case is cited in a brief, a law-review footnote, or an article's text. Only two typefaces are used for all types of citations: italic and roman. (*The Bluebook* prescribes four, depending on the application.) *ALWD* addresses topics not found in *The Bluebook*, such as local citation rules. All the examples are explained; they're not just used to illustrate. Most important, and most unlike *The Bluebook*, each new edition of *ALWD* is unlikely to change just for the sake of change (though naturally it will evolve).

Here are other ways in which the *ALWD Citation Manual* differs from *The Bluebook*:

- It abandons the use of small caps altogether (a plus).
- It adopts a permissive rather than a *Bluebook*-style mandatory rule about abbreviations in cited case names (a minus). At the same time, it also includes a much longer list of standard abbreviations than Table 6 of *The Bluebook* (a plus).
- It adopts a new abbreviation style, abandoning apostrophes in contracted abbreviations (requiring, for example, *Intl.* instead of *Int'l*). This style takes some getting used to, as it flouts some long-standing rules for contracted abbreviations (a toss-up).
- It allows full references as well as elided ones in citing page numbers—that is, either *pp. 123–125* or *pp. 123–25* is okay (a minus). *The Bluebook* specifies the latter style.
- It simplifies capitalization rules in headings by permitting caps on all prepositions, not just those longer than four letters, avoiding,

---

[2] Darby Dickerson, *Seeing Blue: Ten Notable Changes in the New* Bluebook, 6 Scribes J. Legal Writing 75 (1997).

for example, the unequal treatment of *with* and *Without*. (This contradicts most style manuals: a minus.)

- Generally, it more closely conforms legal citation of books and periodicals to academic citation forms (a big plus). For example, it moves the volume number of books and treatises to a more logical position, after the author and title.

Many observers predicted that the *ALWD Manual* would go the way of the *Maroonbook*: into oblivion. Not so. It's now in a third edition, and legal-writing programs across the country have adopted it. Of the 188 ABA-approved law schools, almost 100 now train first-year students to follow the *ALWD Manual*. That's truly extraordinary, given that the text is only three years old.

Meanwhile, law reviews still mostly follow *The Bluebook*. Only 15 or so follow the *ALWD Manual*. So a dual system may be emerging: one for legal-writing programs and another for law reviews.

What about practicing lawyers? *The Bluebook* still broadly holds the field—but in name only. Few practitioners, even those who are former law-review editors, know its intricacies. And there is much officially sanctioned local variation: Texas lawyers follow the *Greenbook*;[3] California lawyers follow the *California Style Manual*;[4] New York lawyers follow the *New York Official Reports Style Manual* (aka the *Tanbook*);[5] and so forth.

State-by-state variations aside, the *ALWD Manual* will probably continue to gradually eclipse *The Bluebook* for several reasons. First, the disagreements between the two systems are hardly visible to the untrained eye. Second, the *ALWD* rules are organized more logically and laid out much more clearly. Third, *ALWD* doesn't include the retrograde *Bluebook* rules I catalogued above. Fourth, the first crop of students trained in the *ALWD* system graduated in 2003, and more waves are coming. As they gain seniority in the profession, the change will gradually percolate up through the ranks.

Whether your school requires *The Bluebook* or the *ALWD Manual*—it almost certainly will require one or the other in the first year—get that one alone and learn it well. Then, in the second or third year, invest in the other one. I believe you'll be drawn to the *ALWD Manual* for most purposes, but you'll almost certainly need to know something about *The Bluebook* at some point early in your career. Be prepared.

---

[3] 10th ed., Texas Law Review Association, 2003.
[4] 4th ed., West Group, 2002.
[5] 15th ed., New York State Law Reports Bureau, 2002.

≥æ ≥æ ≥æ

An Uninformed System of Citation: The *Maroonbook* Blues

The University of Chicago Manual of Legal Citation. San Francisco: Bancroft-Whitney Co., Lawyers Co-operative & Mead Data Central, 1989 Pp. 63. $4.50.

Why a second manual of citation? We need a better one, but the *Maroonbook* does not fill the bill. *The Bluebook* has its imperfections—it is overlong, unclear at points, and conducive to pedantry. But its alternative does not merit serious consideration.

In citation, as in procedural matters, "[i]t is almost as important that the law should be settled permanently, as that it should be settled correctly."[1] And settled it has been these many years, as American lawyers everywhere have used *The Bluebook* as their guide. The *Maroonbook* would unsettle us all by replacing our old standards with new illusory ones, these based on individual discretion. If, for example, you need to cite a 19th-century statute, the *Maroonbook* would have you use your discretion to make it all clear; you cannot err, as long as you use your discretion sensibly (and, of course, as long as you get the page and volume numbers right).

I am reminded of the structural linguists, who insist that native speakers of English cannot make mistakes in using their language. Whatever a native speaker says is perfectly acceptable. (When backed into a corner, these linguists try to distinguish between blunders and mistakes.) Never mind that standard English is a lingua franca, we should not bother teaching it to our students because it is time-consuming, it is discouragingly hard to learn, and it is no better than any other dialect. Now we can likewise forget that *The Bluebook* has provided lawyers with a lingua franca: It is time-consuming, it is discouragingly hard to learn, and it is no better than any other system of citation.

Whatever we might say about the purported difficulty of the *Bluebook*—and I will say something about it in a moment—we cannot deny one significant advantage it has over other systems of citation that we might invent: namely, it is ubiquitously authoritative. If we are to talk about pedagogical malpractice, the charge should be leveled not against those who teach *The Bluebook*, but against legal-writing instructors who teach the seat-of-your-pants *Maroonbook*. How will law students fare

---

Adapted from *The Scribes Journal of Legal Writing* (1990).
[1] *Gilman v. Philadelphia*, 70 U.S. 713, 724 (1865).

once they hit the streets? The law school that follows Douglas Laycock's recommendation may briefly "raise student morale,"[2] but in the upper echelons the improvement will disappear shortly, once the top students learn that judges such as John Minor Wisdom and Thomas Gibbs Gee are reluctant to hire clerks whose knowledge of citing legal materials extends only to the breadth of their discretion. Morale at the bottom of the class may get a sustained boost from schadenfreude.

Laycock is right, of course, that many legal writers, including the editors of *Harvard Law Review*—and, for that matter, the editors of this journal—depart in insignificant ways from *The Bluebook*.[3] But there is a difference between, on the one hand, knowing the rules and deciding to depart from them and, on the other, never learning them at all. In Texas, legal writers follow the *Texas Rules of Form*, published by *Texas Law Review*. Popularly known as the *Greenbook*, it provides supplemental information about how to cite Texas materials. Louisiana has its own supplementary citation manual,[4] which provides another regional gloss on *The Bluebook*. Other states, and several law reviews, though they generally follow *The Bluebook*, have their own special conventions. That is to be expected. But to set up a rival system with variations on the current standard does not make good sense. If the new system gains adoption here and there, and the regional conventions remain in effect, then our "uniform" system of citation will become still further atomized.

What if the *Maroonbook* were our guide? Apart from its liberating us all with discretion, the most dramatic change is the removal of periods from abbreviations. We are told to write "Fed Secur L Rptr" and "Fed Sent Rptr" instead of "Fed. Secur. L. Rep." and "Fed. Sent. Rep." (the latter being *Bluebook* forms). The old "So. 2d" would become "S2d." Does this de-pointing bespeak a desire to eliminate all punctuation from legal writing?[5] Little else changes, except for what we may do when we follow the injunctions at various points to cite sources reasonably, unambiguously, and sensibly.

What changes there are serve the *Maroonbook* editors' belief that "consistency within a brief, opinion, or law journal is important but that uniformity across all legal materials is not."[6] Why not leave it to every legal journal, then, to devise its own system? And to every law firm, or, for that matter, to every lawyer? That is what the *Maroonbook* does, in

---

[2] Douglas Laycock, *The* Maroonbook *v. the* Bluebook: *A Comparative Review*, 1 Scribes J. Legal Writing 181, 189 (1990).

[3] *Id.* at 184.

[4] *See Louisiana Law Review Streamlined Citation Manual*, 50 La. L. Rev. 197 (1989).

[5] *See* Richard C. Wydick, *Should Lawyers Punctuate?* 1 Scribes J. Legal Writing 7 (1990).

[6] *The University of Chicago Manual of Legal Citation* (1989) (*Maroonbook*).

essence, by leaving "a fair amount of discretion to practitioners, authors, and editors."[7]

The *Maroonbook* editors are wrong to discount the importance of a uniform method of citing legal authority. In this age of automated research, in which computers save so much time and effort, the *Maroonbook* may hinder research. Say you need to find out whether *Jones v. Johnson* is still good law in the Ninth Circuit. There are several other cases by that name. You do not feel comfortable relying on Shepard's because it may not be as current as Westlaw. You therefore conduct a Westlaw search of the citation: 781 F.2d 769. Unfortunately, you had no way of knowing that Judge Smith, who wrote an opinion disapproving *Jones v. Johnson* last week, follows the *Maroonbook*, and used what in his discretion he thought to be the most sensible citation: 781 Fed. Sec. 769. The example may be far-fetched, but the potential confusion it illustrates is real.

Perhaps we are to accept the reasonable discretion of nonlawyers in citing legal materials. If so, I have been wrong to persuade the editors of the *Oxford English Dictionary* to begin using the conventional forms of legal citation when citing legal materials. Up until now, you see, they have adapted their own forms; for example, the second edition of the *OED*, in citing the first known use of the verb *surveil*, has: "1960 *Federal Suppl.* CLXXII 750/1." If I were to use such forms in one of my dictionaries, the profession might justifiably ride me out of town on a rail.

In effect, the frequent grants of discretion only increase the amount of work (not to mention the worries) of practitioners, authors, and editors. Users of the *Maroonbook* must now decide what before had been decided for them. Do I use *infra* and *supra*? *The Bluebook* tells me when to use them, but the *Maroonbook* says merely that I "need not." (It does not say that I "should not"—merely that I "need not.") What to do? I must give it some thought. Should I italicize *ex parte* and *de facto*? I consult the *Maroonbook* to discover that I "need not." Let me think on it.

That is precisely the problem with the *Maroonbook*. You must consciously consider what before had been the merest matter of form, too insignificant to require thought. If Erwin Griswold sends a first-year associate to verify the citations in a brief to the Supreme Court, should he expect that associate to use "discretion" in citing the cases? To remove all the periods except those in names and those that separate sentences? If that happened, Dean Griswold would in turn have to review the citations for an abuse of discretion. (The standard of citation review would be clear: If the *Maroonbook* gets a toehold, there may be no such thing as "clearly erroneous" in citation form.) What a waste.

---

[7] *Id.* at 7.

Speaking of waste, let us turn now to what, after all, is the crucial question in this debate: How difficult is *The Bluebook* to learn? A run-of-the-mill law student, I had mastered the essentials within my first two weeks of law school, without any special effort. The essentials are contained in the first chapter of *The Bluebook*. I spent perhaps a couple of hours reading through the book, and many more hours reading cases in which citations followed *The Bluebook*. Even if Professor Laycock is correct that first-year students now spend far too much of their time learning the *Bluebook* minutiae,[8] the *Maroonbook* would not remove their onus. Being told to cite something "reasonably" simply will not do, since law students thirst for certainty and authority. Perhaps that explains the *Maroonbook*'s four appendixes prescribing abbreviations; these come dangerously close to stifling discretion.

If we put consistency to one side, there may be an advantage to greater competition in the citation-book market, but only if the rivals are well done. The *Maroonbook*, wish as we might, is poorly done. The main text consists of 22 pages of slipshod prose. There are abrupt shifts in voice and other indicia of carelessness. (For example, one never *cites* something; one always *cites to* something.) The introduction concludes with this sentence, puzzling because of its prominent placement: "The rules leave this responsibility [adapting the rules to particular needs] to users of this manual editors [*sic*] without imposing on them the burden of conforming exactly to the rest of the legal world."[9] Apparently the *Maroonbook*, even with its short text, was published without anyone's imposing on those intrusive editors (who should not have made an appearance in the previous sentence) the burden of carefully proofreading the galleys.

There is a place for something like a *Maroonbook*—namely, an abridgment of *The Bluebook*. Alan Dworsky's *User's Guide*[10] is now the closest thing we have to an abridgment. Yes, *The Bluebook* has grown unwieldy in its effort to answer every question that arises. (It will never succeed in that effort.) It is nice to be able to refer to the full text to make an informed decision about what is standard. But *The Bluebook*'s publishers ought to consider a drastically pared-down version for ready reference—and certainly for law students to learn from. The failure to see this need in the lawbook market is what brought the *Maroonbook* into existence in the first place. Let it go the way of its precursor.[11]

---

[8] Laycock, note 2, at 183.

[9] *Maroonbook*, note 6, at 8.

[10] Alan Dworsky, *User's Guide to a Uniform System of Citation: The Cure for the* Bluebook Blues (1988).

[11] *The University of Chicago Law Review Form Book* (rev. ed. 1950).

John R. Brown • Irving L. Goldberg • Bruce M. Selya

CHAPTER TWELVE

Bizarreries

Mrs. Malaprop Makes Law Review

MALAPROPISMS ARE WORDS that are used so incorrectly that they result in unintended humor. The eponymous term derives from the character Mrs. Malaprop in Richard Brinsley Sheridan's play *The Rivals* (1775). Mrs. Malaprop loves big words but habitually uses them ignorantly to create hilarious blunders and occasionally embarrassing double entendres. In a famous simile, she refers to someone's being *as headstrong as an allegory on the banks of the Nile.* Elsewhere, she refers to the *geometry* of *contagious countries.*

What many sources don't point out is that Sheridan borrowed the device from Shakespeare, who used it quite often for comic effect, always in the mouths of lower-class characters who are unsuccessfully aping the usage of their social and intellectual betters and saying something quite different (sometimes scandalously different) from what they meant to say. For example, Elbow, the incompetent constable in *Measure for Measure*, calls a bawdy house "a respected [i.e., *suspected*] house." Several hilarious misusages in the play have the judge standing bemused as both the accused and the accuser get their meanings tangled up.

Real-life examples aren't hard to come by. One lawyer apparently mistook *meretricious* (= of or relating to a prostitute; superficially attractive but false) for *meritorious*, with embarrassing consequences: he asked a judge to rule favorably on his client's "meretricious claim." Similarly,

---

Adapted from *Student Lawyer* (Mar. 2007).

Senator Sam Ervin recalled a lawyer who, in arguing that his client had been provoked by name-calling (*epithets*), said: "I hope that in passing sentence on my client upon his conviction for assault and battery, your honor will bear in mind that he was provoked to do so by the *epitaphs* hurled at him by the witness." The phrase *hurling epitaphs* conjures up images of heaving headstones.

One hardly expects to see the wrong-word syndrome evident in reputable legal sources, but it certainly occurs. What follows is a list of the top 18 malapropisms I've found in law-review articles published in recent years. One might say that these mistakes suggest that the law reviews are having a heyday (*field day*) with malapropisms; that the errors are spreading like wildflower (*wildfire*); that this column intends to pillar (*pillory*) the sentences in which they appear; that the usages are uncategorically (*categorically*) wrong; that they should be treated unmercilessly (*unmercifully* or *mercilessly*); and that care for language provided the impotence (*impetus*) for the collection.

1. "Counsel for the hiring party would no doubt cast the web site designer as an uncreative lackey who is at the *beckon call* [read *beck and call*] of the hiring party." Rinaldo Del Gallo III, *Who Owns the Web Site?* 16 John Marshall J. Computer & Info. L. 857, 875 (1998).

2. "Oftentimes, the first goal of a legal system is negative—to *advert* [read *avert*] the social disasters done in the name of the common good." Susan Block-Lieb, *The Logic and Limits of Contract Bankruptcy*, U. Ill. L. Rev. 503, 520 n.67 (2001), quoting Richard A. Epstein, *Principles for a Free Society* at 4 (1998).

3. "[A]ny balance in a CESA must be distributed to the beneficiary upon *obtaining* [read *attaining*] age 30." Richard O. Jacobs & Tye J. Klooster, *Asset Protection Tools for Florida Professionals*, 4 Fla. St. U. Bus. Rev. 1, 128 (2004–2005).

4. "The reasons for the delay in action can be *contributed* [read *attributed*] to possible concerns with local enforcement of federal immigration laws." April McKenzie, *A Nation of Immigrants or a Nation of Suspects?* 55 Ala. L. Rev. 1149, 1156 (2004).

5. "According to one account, this language was added at the *bequest* [read *behest*] of Chief Justice Burger, who feared that judges might otherwise be required to hire female law clerks." Laura T. Kessler, *The Attachment Gap*, 34 U. Mich. J.L. Reform 371, 409 (2001).

6. "Yet this suggestion is undone in *climatic* [read *climactic*] scenes that ultimately reassure the viewer that the whole truth has been revealed." Austin Sarat, *The Cultural Life of Capital Punishment*, 11 Yale J.L. & Humanities 153, 166 (1999).

7. "Few in or in contact with the NAACP seemed to doubt how widespread or *deep-seeded* [read *deep-seated*] these practices were in the 1940s South." Risa L. Goluboff, *"We Live's in a Free House Such as It Is,"* 151 U. Pa. L. Rev. 1977, 2005 (2003).

8. "First as a trial lawyer and then as a trial judge, I personally found the *Swain* rule offensive and an *effrontery* [read *affront*] to my dignity, much like *Plessy v. Ferguson*." Hon. James H. Coleman Jr., *The Evolution of Race in the Jury Selection Process*, 48 Rutgers L. Rev. 1105, 1127 (1996).

9. "For all *intensive purposes* [read *intents and purposes*], the district court acknowledged that illegal immigrant children are inevitably members of American society, regardless of their legal status." Halle I. Butler, *Educated in the Classroom or on the Streets*, 58 Ohio St. L.J. 1473, 1491 n.120 (1997).

10. "Such criticism has run the *gambit* [read *gamut*] between labeling the Court's current approach as a 'poor criterion' for governing the Confrontation Clause to labeling the current approach as one which would 'constitutionalize the hearsay rule.'" Jerome C. Latimer, *Confrontation After Crawford*, 36 Seton Hall L. Rev. 327, 336 (2006).

11. "Is it possible to *breach* [read *bridge*] the gap, to reduce the uncertainty and to affirm precisely what is the 'law' resulting from 'war'?" Dr. Pierre d'Argent, *Which Law Through Which War?* 52 Buff. L. Rev. 635, 640 (2004).

12. "In making the case of irreparable harm, the plaintiffs in *Stahl* set forth one *heart-rendering* [read *heart-rending*] story after another." Susan A. Schneider, *Shared Appreciation Agreements*, 7 Drake J. Agric. L. 107, 119 n.74 (2002).

13. "But to go any further—to expand the scope of takings liability to the point of presenting governments with a *Hobbesian* [read *Hobson's*] choice—would interfere profoundly with those governments' ability to promote the public welfare." Mark E. Sabath, *The Perils of the Property Rights Initiative*, 28 Harv. Envtl. L. Rev. 249, 279 (2004).

14. "[Igor] Primoratz explains that evil inflicted on the offender can be a source of satisfaction for the victim and society as a whole, because the offense itself *illicited* [read *elicited*] feelings of rage and displeasure." Doug Janicik, *Allowing Victims' Families to View Executions*, 61 Ohio St. L.J. 935, 963 n.135 (2000).

15. "While Section 530 can provide an island of relief, these are very dangerous, *shark-invested* [read *shark-infested*] waters that can prove disastrous." David Williams II, *A Warning on Employee Status*, 5 Bus. L. Today 48, 52 (1995).

16. "[C]itizens increasingly recognize the personal responsibilities and obligations *inhering* [read *inuring*] to them as critical participants in the ongoing struggle to ensure that the 'air, water, earth, and food be of a sufficiently high standard that individuals and communities can live healthy, fulfilling, and dignified lives.'" Scott LaFranchi, *Surveying the Precautionary Principle's Ongoing Global Development*, 32 B.C. Envtl. Affairs L. Rev. 679, 718 (2005).

17. "The fact that alternative channels exist for cable programming, however, does not *mute* [read *moot*] the point that the must-carry rules strip away a certain amount of editorial control from the cable operator and cable subscriber." Nancy J. Whitmore, *The Evolution of the Intermediate Scrutiny Standard*, 8 Comm. L. & Policy 25, 88 (2003).

18. "One prominent example of the need for environmental agencies to *make due* [read *make do*] with less money is the refusal of Congress and the President to reauthorize the corporate tax mechanisms." Robert L. Glickman, *From Cooperative to Inoperative Federalism*, 41 Wake Forest L. Rev. 719, 775 (2006).

To learn more about these and other malapropisms, and to read other examples, see *Garner's Modern American Usage* (2d ed. 2004).

ॐ ॐ ॐ

On Pun Control

PUNS CAN ADD ZEST to writing if artfully used. H.W. Fowler and
Theodore M. Bernstein have dispelled the notion that puns are the lowest form of wit. Bad puns, of course, create a bad impression in either
speech or writing. But the well-wrought pun often serves to reinforce
the point one is making. A good pun should give the sentence added
meaning in both (or all) its senses, and it should not be so obvious that
anyone would think of it. Obviousness undermines that important element of surprise.

Puns seem increasingly popular in American legal prose. Some are
good and some are not. Those found in titles to law-review articles are
often delightfully clever. For example, the title of an article by Robert P.
Mosteller, *Simplifying Subpoena Law: Taking the Fifth Amendment Seriously*,[1]
plays effectively on two English idioms, *to take the Fifth Amendment* and *to
take (something) seriously*. Both senses fit the purpose of the article, hence
the aptness of the pun.

A student note in 1987 was entitled *Designer Genes That Don't Fit:
A Tort Regime for Commercial Releases of Genetic Engineering Products*.[2] The
pun on *designer jeans* conveys the faddishness, or at least the currency, of
genetic engineering. The strict regime offered, the title implies, will
make genetic engineering "fit" into modern society, just as a good diet is
a virtual necessity for one who wants to wear designer jeans. In short,
the pun works on two levels, though the comparison made by the pun
is quite far-fetched.

Indeed, the editors of *Harvard Law Review* appear to have become
fascinated with paronomasia (the rhetorical name for punning), perhaps
in an effort to counteract "law-reviewese." Wrenching a legal cliché into
an entirely fresh and literal application, one student titled his note *Facial
Discrimination: Extending Handicap Law to Employment Discrimination on the
Basis of Physical Appearance*.[3] What a piquant and illuminating use of the
phrase *facial discrimination*!

A more strained but nevertheless clever pun occurred to the federal appellate judge who wrote, "Ticonic's cloth cannot be cut to fit

---

Adapted from *Dallas Bar Headnotes* (21 Nov. 1988).
[1] 73 Va. L. Rev. 1 (1987).
[2] 100 Harv. L. Rev. 1086 (1987).
[3] 100 Harv. L. Rev. 2035 (1987).

Interfirst's suit."[4] Here *suit* carries the double sense, on the one hand, of completing the tailoring metaphor (cutting cloth for a suit) and, on the other hand, of denoting the lawsuit at issue.

Yet another aesthetically pleasing pun is this subtle one from the pen of Justice Felix Frankfurter: "The liability rests on the inroad that the automobile has made on the decision of *Pennoyer v. Neff*, as it has on so many aspects of our social scene."[5] Ordinarily, of course, *inroad* is an abstract word, but Justice Frankfurter's placement of *automobile* next to it gives the word a new and unexpected concrete sense; again, the pun is felicitous.

Probably half the puns one sees in modern legal writing are the empty kind of wordplay in which one of the senses is inapt or, worse yet, gibberish. E.g., "The bells do not toll the statute of limitations while one ferrets out the facts."[6] The pun here is *toll*, which on the obvious level (*bells . . . toll*) means, nonsensically, "to ring"; the legal sense of *toll*, the one that gives meaning to the sentence, is "to abate." The pun in no way contributes to the sense. In fact, it is more likely to confuse than to enlighten.

Here is another ill-wrought specimen: "The official cannot hide behind a claim that the particular factual predicate in question has never appeared in a reported opinion; if the application of settled principles would inexorably lead to a conclusion of unconstitutionality, a prison official may not take solace in ostrichism."[7] *Ostrichism* here apparently means "the practice of hiding one's head in the sand" (foreshadowed earlier in the sentence in the phrase "hide behind a claim"). The pun is on *ostracism* (= exclusion from association with another or others), but this near-homophone has nothing to do with the meaning of the sentence. Hence the writer has gone out of his way to create a punning neologism whose suggestiveness bewilders, rather than charms, the reader.

As Charles Lamb observed, "A pun is not bound by the laws which limit nicer wit. It is a pistol let off at the ear; not a feather to tickle the intellect."[8] Even so, in punning one is best advised not to abandon the intellect, for then one becomes a nuisance to the reader. Lamb also cautioned that puns sometimes show "much less wit than rudeness. We must," he wrote, "take in the totality of time, place, and person."[9]

---

[4] *Interfirst Bank Abilene v. F.D.I.C.*, 777 F.2d 1092, 1097 (5th Cir. 1985) [discussing *Ticonic National Bank v. Sprague*, 303 U.S. 406 (1938)].

[5] *Olberding v. Illinois C. R.R.*, 346 U.S. 338, 341 (1953).

[6] *Prather v. Neva Paperbacks, Inc.*, 446 F.2d 338, 341 (5th Cir. 1971).

[7] *Little v. Walker*, 552 F.2d 193, 197 (7th Cir. 1977).

[8] Charles Lamb, "Popular Fallacies: That the Worst Puns Are the Best," in *The Last Essays of Elia* 307, 307 (1833; repr. 1915).

[9] *Id.* at 308.

🐦 🐦 🐦

Cruel and Unusual English

WHEN, SOME YEARS AGO, a Dr. Louis Prickman wrote William F. Buckley, saying that the latter showed "abominable taste and insensitivity" in his novels, many of us laughed at Buckley's retort, which read in full: "Dear Doc: Please call me Bill. Can I call you by your nickname?" Of course, the doctor seemed to invite the response, and his name may have been fair game for Buckley. In a related vein, John Simon's remark in a movie review that the name Ursula Andress had always seemed to him to be a spoonerism showed a charming cleverness.

Wordplay of this kind, however, is hardly appropriate in judicial opinions. After all, litigants do not heap unsolicited abuse on the courts they seek to persuade, nor are they public performers who expect critics to review their work. Everyone but the occasional pro se oddball approaches the courts with polite deference. How must litigants feel, then, when they find a judge playing the jester with their names and occupations, or caricaturing their actions?

Several federal judges have succumbed to the temptation. The prime offender, perhaps, is Judge Bruce Selya, of the United States Court of Appeals for the First Circuit. Three years ago, for example, when Brad Foote Gear Works appealed an adverse judgment to the First Circuit, Judge Selya drew the opinion. Behind the company name, one assumes, is a person named Brad Foote, who probably had to put up with sophomoric jokes about his name throughout his adolescence. Judge Selya allowed Mr. Foote to revisit those years. In *Matthewson Corp. v. Allied Marine Industries, Inc.*,[1] the judge wrote that "Foote's stance . . . sidesteps the established principle"; that "Foote stumbled";[2] that "Foote's position does not toe the mark;"[3] that "the appellant, confronted with what seemed a substantial exposure, put its best foot forward";[4] and that the trial court had properly disallowed "the appellant to slip free of the laces. The shoe, fitting, must be worn."[5]

It is one thing, no doubt, to engage in wordplay by saying that a party believed "his property rights to have been incinerated by the creation of

Adapted from *Dallas Bar Headnotes* (20 Feb. 1989).
[1] 827 F.2d 850, 853 (1st Cir. 1987).
[2] *Id*. at 854.
[3] *Id*. at 856.
[4] *Id*. at 857.
[5] *Id*.

a fire lane."[6] That is harmless, really (though of questionable literary merit as a metaphor). It is another thing to call a litigant pharisaical because of arguments advanced by the litigant's attorney: "Like the Pharisees, [Curran] seems obsessively concerned with the symbols of piety at the expense of adequate concern for the spirit."[7] In still another case, Judge Selya characterized a party, "the defense—with eyes wide open—[of having] swaggered venturesomely into a jungle of its own cultivation," and of "buccaneering."[8]

Caricatures of that kind, however, are nothing in comparison to a judge's poking fun at a litigant's métier or name (as with Foote), even if that litigant is a large corporation. An egregious example of occupational abuse occurs in Judge Selya's opinion in *Arriaga-Zayas v. International Ladies' Garment Union*.[9] The opinion begins: "In plaintiffs' judgment, Splendorform International, Inc., a lingerie manufacturer, made a slip when it laid off some ninety sewing machine operators . . . ."[10] (Who laughs at this pun? Surely not the workers who lost their jobs.)

In that same opinion, Judge Selya disclaims setting out the entire factual background, stating that the court "need not re-stitch that fabric in any great detail."[11] Other clothing metaphors abound in the opinion, the "sheer" sequence of four events, for example, not having been "conclusively buttoned down."[12]

The metaphors gradually become more suggestive: "Plaintiffs' own filings place them snugly within the tightest of corsets."[13] These plaintiffs "claimed then to have lifted the petticoat of 'pretensions' and to have glimpsed the perfidy which underlay it."[14] (What metaphor is this, that implicitly equates the female pudenda with perfidy?) Of these plaintiffs, Judge Selya concludes: "By neglecting to file a complaint for well over a year . . . , they are undone." Nakedness characterizes both sides of the dispute, however: the defendants' "challenged conduct . . . had been laid bare to plaintiffs' view . . . ."[15]

Although, in Judge Selya's words, the plaintiffs contended that the International Ladies' Garment Workers' Union had "played pantywaist,"

---

[6] *Golemis v. Kirby*, 632 F.Supp. 159, 161 (D.R.I. 1985) (*per* Selya, J.).

[7] *Curran v. Dept. of Justice*, 813 F.2d 473, 476 (1st Cir. 1987).

[8] *Chappee v. Vose*, 843 F.2d 25, 31 (1st Cir. 1988).

[9] 835 F.2d 11 (1st Cir. 1987).

[10] *Id.* at 12.

[11] *Id.*

[12] *Id.* at 13.

[13] *Id.*

[14] *Id.*

[15] *Id.* at 15.

the "law required considerably more bustle than was displayed" by the plaintiffs.[16] Judge Selya concludes: "Whatever slips [Ha!] may have been made in the course of the company reorganization, none was made by the court below."[17] Thus the union, whose workers supplied most of the grist for the puns and extended metaphors, won in the court of appeals. Who, then, might be left to complain about all that playfulness in the First Circuit's opinion?

No one, perhaps, except a hypersensitive rhetorician. Then again, what are those union members, or indeed the management of Splendor-form, to think of the federal judiciary when they read the opinion? How seriously has the court taken the appeal? From a lawyer's point of view, one wonders whether the other judges on the panel felt perfectly comfortable in joining in the opinion. Did they decide that not offend-ing Judge Selya by objecting to his style was more important than spar-ing the litigants any anger or embarrassment they might feel over the issuance of such an opinion? Or did Judge Selya's colleagues relish the verbal wit as much as the inventor did?

When the Boston Edison Company, an electric utility, appealed a money judgment, Judge Selya wrote that the appeal "sheds considerably more heat than light."[18] Yet he characterized Edison as "light[ing] up the sky with a barrage of postulates,"[19] which leads one to wonder how hot it must have been, if indeed the heat was far greater than the light. Edi-son's major argument had "blown a fuse," and "most of the remaining surges [in its argument were] of low voltage."[20] As Judge Selya explained it, "This means, of course, that the lights go out for Edison's appeal."[21] What happened to the heat?

The delight in wordplay—an admirable quality when tempered by a sense of context and decorum—so pervades Judge Selya's opinions that the reader may find puns where none was intended. The opinion in *Neron v. Tierney*[22] addresses whether a man convicted of gross sexual mis-conduct might be entitled to a new trial after he showed that one of the female jurors had dated his son Robert for more than a year. Judge Selya characterized this juror as "Robert's inamorata" and "Robert's erstwhile infatuate," and noted that she and Robert "saw each other once or twice

[16] *Id.*
[17] *Id.*
[18] *RCI N.E. Servs. Div. v. Boston Edison Co.*, 822 F.2d 199, 200 (1st Cir. 1987).
[19] *Id.* at 204.
[20] *Id.*
[21] *Id.* at 205.
[22] 841 F.2d 1197 (1st Cir. 1988).

weekly, usually at her apartment. Robert never said why the relationship petered out."[23] Have I just imagined a pun in that last sentence?

As in the example just cited, Judge Selya's linguistic playfulness sometimes becomes more callous than flippant. In *Chase v. Quick*,[24] a pro se prisoner—not an oddball, from all that appears—sued prison officials over inadequate and unsanitary food service in a certain Rhode Island prison. One of his complaints read: "The Muslim meals are not to consist of pork but my tray and other Muslims have received pork."[25]

In affirming the dismissal of Mr. Chase's lawsuit, Judge Selya had a field day. "The action," he wrote, "provides scant food for judicial thought."[26] Mr. Chase "grieves . . . of a full menu of lingering commensal suspicions."[27] The First Amendment claims "cannot be swallowed whole."[28] In opining that the Constitution does not require "that institutional cuisine be presented in a manner which Guide Michelin would applaud," Judge Selya concludes that the prisoners "are receiving their just desserts."[29] One blushes to read that "Chase's complaint is not judicially digestible."[30] Only Judge Selya could feign indigestion in denying Mr. Chase a hearing.

All this is to suggest that judges often seem to distance themselves too much from the parties whose rights they adjudicate. Judges are not, after all, cartoonists, in whom it is a virtue to make humorous caricatures. It is surely dangerous for a judge to make abstractions of litigants to the extent that he feels free to pun on their names, belittle their occupations, and basically provide fun for himself at their expense. George Rose Smith, formerly of the Arkansas Supreme Court, once sagely wrote that "for a judge to take advantage of his criticism-insulated, retaliation-proof position to display his wit is contemptible, like hitting a man when he's down."[31]

Benjamin Cardozo warned against such practices half a century ago, though the judicial humor he envisioned was of a much milder kind.

---

[23] *Id.* at 1203.
[24] 596 F.Supp. 33 (D.R.I. 1984).
[25] *Id.* at 33.
[26] *Id.* at 34.
[27] *Id.*
[28] *Id.*
[29] *Id.* at 35.
[30] *Id.*
[31] George Rose Smith, *A Primer of Opinion Writing for Four New Judges*, 21 Ark. L. Rev. 197, 210 (1967).

In his classic essay "Law and Literature," Cardozo recalled the story of a man who wanted to consult the writings of the 18th-century French naturalist Buffon. This inquisitive man startled the bookstore clerks by asking, rather pompously, "Have you the books of the celebrated Buffoon?" "One of the difficulties about the humorous [judicial] opinion," wrote Cardozo, "is exposure to the risk of passing from the class of Buffons where we all like to dwell and entering the class of the celebrated Buffoons."[32]

---

[32] 52 Harv. L. Rev. 471, 483 (1939).

ਟ੍ਰਾ ਟ੍ਰਾ ਟ੍ਰਾ

More on Peccant Punning

ROBERT W. COLEMAN and Collyn A. Peddie have taken me to task for my critical view of Judge Bruce Selya's brand of judicial humor. Judge Selya, you will remember, is the First Circuit judge whose opinions often contain wordplay that jabs at litigants. So in one case, the International Ladies' Garment Workers' Union "played pantywaist" and didn't display enough "bustle," and the company sued by the Union made a number of "slips." In another case, Foote "stumbled," "failed to toe the mark," and so on.

Believing my aversion to punning on litigants' names and occupations to be misplaced, Mr. Coleman writes that the examples I "garnered" show that my sense of humor is more like that of a resident of the City of Bryan than of Austin. He further notes that "Bryan's song" could have "bagged" judges within the Fifth Circuit.

Ms. Peddie—whose name cries out for the type of wordplay that Judge Selya indulges in (though, under the circumstances, I will refrain)—leaps to the defense of Judge John R. Brown and Judge Irving Goldberg, apparently believing that my essay was a veiled criticism of them. It was not.

To my knowledge, Judge Brown and Judge Goldberg do not use humor at the expense of litigants. That is the detestable practice I harpooned: punning on litigants' names (to their disadvantage) and belittling their occupations. As the examples quoted by Ms. Peddie attest, Judge Brown and Judge Goldberg leaven their opinions with a humor that hurts no one, and charms many.

"Garner's view that humor has no place in judicial opinions," as Ms. Peddie (in her manner) characterizes it, is not my view at all. Let me quote from a book that Mr. Coleman cites, *A Dictionary of Modern Legal Usage*: "Lest we assume . . . that judicial writing should be cheerless and sobersided, it is worth noting Cardozo's tempered judgment: 'In all this I would not convey the thought that an opinion is the worse for being lightened by a smile.'"[1]

In striking the right tone, judicial opinions should probably be neither uproarious nor dry as dust. The subject of the suit, as opposed to the litigants' names or occupations, usually determines the opportunity for

---

Adapted from *Dallas Bar Headnotes* (18 Sept. 1989).
[1] Garner, *A Dictionary of Modern Legal Usage* 393 (1987).

injecting humor. My own favorite example of judicial lightness is Judge Gee's masterly opinion in *Macpherson v. Texas Department of Water Resources*.[2] For an opinion exhibiting civilized humor, I have not seen its equal.

Questions of taste in judicial opinions are unlikely to go away. Nor are they new. Justice Oliver Wendell Holmes himself butted heads with an old sobersides on the Supreme Court who objected to Holmes's writing that amplifications of a statute would "stop rat holes" in it. Holmes recalled his answer in a letter to Sir Frederick Pollock: "I said our reports were dull because we had the notion that judicial dignity required solemn fluffy speech, as, when I grew up, everybody wore black frock coats and black cravats."[3]

No one wants a return to the dismal tone of 19th-century judicial opinions. But are we entirely ready to make judicial opinions the platform for a Don Rickles?

---

[2] 734 F.2d 1103 (5th Cir. 1984).
[3] *Holmes–Pollock Letters* vol. 2, 132 (M. Howe ed., 1941).

Lapsus Memoriae

OF THE MANY EXCELLENT CARTOONS that have appeared in *The New Yorker* over the years, one of my favorites shows two American stonecutters etching a Latin phrase (*Omne vivum ex . . .*) into a stone edifice. Just having finished the Latin preposition *ex*, one laborer says to the other, "Does 'ex' take the ablative or the dative?" The cartoon pokes fun at our persistent fondness for Latin inscriptions (though most of us cannot read them), and ironically suggests that the stonecutters have composed the inscription extemporaneously (or *ex tempore*, if you prefer the Latin phrase showing that *ex* takes the ablative).

Not so long ago, one straight-faced lawyer might have posed the question to another. Nothing unusual. But today it would be extraordinary.

After many centuries, Latin has finally lost its stranglehold on legal writing. Today, only isolated words and phrases remain scattered throughout the law. Only rarely do modern legal writers use Latinisms that have not been thoroughly naturalized. Even within the 20th century, the change was dramatic. Most lawyers today would blush to write *contradictio in adjecto* rather than *contradiction in terms*, as Benjamin Cardozo did in 1926.[1]

We ought to take pride in our simplified expressions of today. "The cases are comparatively few," Baron du Parcq once cautioned, "in which much light is obtained by the liberal use of Latin phrases. . . . Nobody can derive any assistance from the phrase *novus actus interveniens* until it is translated into English."[2] What lawyer today would disagree?

Yet our widespread gains in simplicity have not been without considerable losses in knowledge. Our lamentable handling of the Latin survivors in our language provides embarrassing illustration of the decline and fall of the Romans' language. Today lawyers often mistreat Latinate words and phrases by mangling roots, mistaking parts of speech, and confounding plurals.

Some of the most amusing examples of linguistic retching involve mistaken root-senses that create double entendres. Two especially delectable ones are *corpus delecti* and *lex loci delecti*. (The proper form in these phrases, of course, is *delicti*, not *delecti*.) I have it on high authority that

---

Adapted from *Dallas Bar Headnotes* (15 May 1989).
[1] *See Kerr S.S. Co. v. Radio Corp. of Am.* 157 N.E. 140, 142 (N.Y. App. Div. 1926).
[2] *Ingram v. United Auto. Servs. Ltd.* [1943] 1 K.B. 612, 2 All E.R. 71.

corpus delecti does not have its origins in the lingo of necrophiliacs. As to the other phrase, we have no choice-of-law principle governed by "the law of the place where delight occurred"—my best attempt at a translation. Many of us seem to have forgotten that a *delict* is a tort, that *actio ex delicto* is the old-fashioned phrase for *action in tort*. Amazingly, a search on Westlaw reveals more than 300 judicial opinions containing one of the erroneous phrases using *delecti*, many from Texas opinions of the past two decades. To stem the tide of error, we ought perhaps to sponsor legislation making the use of *delecti* delictual.

Another linguistic gaffe: *sui generis* (= one of a kind) mistakenly used for *sui juris* (= of full age and capacity). Thus we have a judge writing that, unless the court has subject-matter jurisdiction, "a guardian ad litem [may not] maintain a suit in court on behalf of persons not *sui generis*."[3] Most of us think that everyone is *sui generis*. Besides, if the court has jurisdiction, even clones ought to be able to represent themselves without the aid of a guardian ad litem.

Last year, a federal appellate judge wrote an opinion in which he referred to "the compendious record in this long-running suit"; elsewhere in the opinion, the judge mentioned the "girth of the record."[4] An acquaintance with Latin, of course, would have told this judge that a *compendium* is a shortcut or abridgment, and that *compendious* means "succinct," not "voluminous." Lesson: Before using words having the root *compend-*, be sure you comprehend.

When it comes to parts of speech, many lawyers show less care than those stonecutters in the cartoon, by failing to distinguish the ablative from the nominative case. (Put aside the dative for now.) English has no ablative case. In Latin, the ablative makes the word or phrase adverbial: note the difference between *intent to revoke* and *with intent to revoke*. This is the very difference between *animus revocandi* and *animo revocandi*. Although these and similar *animus*-phrases have ready English equivalents, they are frequently used and misused in the American law of wills. It is bad enough to use them, but it is unforgivable to misuse them, as by writing *the animo revocandi*.

Latin plurals present yet another problem for the modern lawyer. In Latin, *syllabus* differs from *ignoramus* because the former is a noun, the latter a verb (meaning "we do not know," and originally the phrase for a grand jury's endorsement of a no bill). Those who know enough Latin to say *syllabi* sometimes lapse into *ignorami*, as if the English word derived

---

[3] *See Morsman v. C.I.R.*, 90 F.2d 18, 25 (8th Cir. 1937).

[4] *HMG Prop. Investors, Inc. v. Parque Indus. Rio Canas, Inc.*, 847 F.2d 908, 919–20 (1st Cir. 1988).

from a Latin noun ending in -*us*. (*Ignorami*, you might say, is the plural preferred by ignoramuses.) *Mandami*, too, is (sadly) not unknown, though *mandamus* is likewise a verb in Latin (literally, "we command").

The opposite error—noun taken for verb—led to *cestuis que trustent*, which has been called a "hopelessly wrong" plural of *cestui que trust*, because the basic phrase is a noun, not a verb.[5] But mistakes often take root and propagate. Of the erroneous plural, Sir Robert Megarry once regretfully acknowledged that "the Law Reports have ascribed this deplorable version to one of His Majesty's judges."[6] The safer course is to write *beneficiaries* rather than *cestuis que trust* (the correct plural form).

But who can expect that from the would-be Latinists in our ranks who write *fora* and, far less defensibly, *insurance premia*? You get the distinct impression that some of these legal writers might say *octopi* if they saw more than one octopus.[7] The trick here is that *octopus* is Greek, not Latin—hence *octopodes*. Unless your context is Greek, however, you are best advised to use *octopuses*.

Legal phrases such as *sua sponte*, literally "on its own motion," can cause trouble when writers use them to modify nouns with which they do not agree in number. To say *The court, sua sponte, enjoined the picketing* works grammatically, but not, strictly, this: *The judges, sua sponte, enjoined the picketing*. Many legal writers accept this use of the phrase; but the best solution, when possible, is to stick to English (*on its own motion* or *on their own motion*). Still, even though established phrases such as *amicus curiae*, or, in the plural, *amici curiae*, continue to create problems, lawyers and judges are unlikely to adopt the journalists' alternatives, such as *friend of the court*, merely because a few of their colleagues cannot get the Latin right.

One only wonders what the great Roman lawyers, such as Cicero and Gaius, would make of our modern tendency to butcher the language they bequeathed to us. And what, for that matter, are we modern lawyers to make of the tendency? On the one hand, we ought to rejoice at our liberation from Latin maxims, which have so often displaced real thought about legal problems. On the other hand, we should combat the further corruption of the Latin words and phrases that we continue to find useful. If they must be corrupted, let someone else be charged with the responsibility, not our learned profession. Else might we not have to change our profession's descriptive adjective?

Sic transit gloria Latinitatis!

---

[5] *See* Note, 26 L.Q. Rev. 196 (1910).
[6] *Miscellany-at-Law* 33 (1955).
[7] *See, e.g.*, *Snow v. Reid*, 619 F.Supp. 579, 585 (S.D.N.Y. 1985) ("squid and octopi").

ॐ ॐ ॐ

Testamentary Depositions and Other Curiosities

WHEN I CLERKED for the Fifth Circuit a few years ago, the clerks had the rather enjoyable duty of reading all the Court's slip opinions on the day they were issued. Sometimes, the judges and their clerks receive the slip opinions a day or two before their issuance. Occasionally, a judge not on the panel considering the case, or his or her clerk, will run across something in an opinion that merits being brought to the attention of the writing judge, so that adjustments may be considered before the opinion appears in the official reports.

I remember reading the slips one day and coming upon the following sentence: "Appellee filed a motion to remand the contractual indemnity claim to allow procurement of documentary and testamentary evidence." Something about that final phrase struck me as quite odd. Then it came to me: this was not a case involving a will or even a decedent. The reference was to evidence found in documents and testimony, but the adjective came out *testamentary* rather than *testimonial*. (The word *testamentary*, of course, means "of or relating to a will.") The word *documentary* threw off the writer, who tried to make the second adjective in the phrase parallel to the first; hence he wrote *documentary and testamentary evidence.*

You would be surprised how often this blunder occurs. Since discovering it in that slip opinion, I have found a number of examples from across the country. An Eighth Circuit opinion states: "Bankrupts then offered documentary and *testamentary* [read *testimonial*] evidence to rebut the Government's proof."[1] Perhaps not wanting to create a split in the circuits, the Seventh Circuit followed suit in 1982: "In the present case the subpoena duces tecum called only for *nontestamentary* [read *nontestimonial*] evidence to which was added an oral option as to where the response could be made."[2] One might argue, I suppose, that it would have been wasteful to write *nontestimonial evidence*, thereby provoking the Supreme Court to have to take up the issue to remedy the adjectival discrepancy in the opinions of the circuit courts. But it would have been

---

Adapted from *Dallas Bar Headnotes* (16 May 1988).
[1] *Solari Furs v. United States*, 436 F.2d 683, 685 (8th Cir. 1971).
[2] *United States v. Santucci*, 674 F.2d 624, 628 (7th Cir. 1982).

right, after all, and the Seventh Circuit probably could have counted on an affirmance. (Why *nontestimonial*, even—would not *documentary* have served the Seventh Circuit's purposes?)

I am sorry to say that I have lost the citation to the Fifth Circuit case I referred to at the time, nor do I know what happened once the writing judge's clerk was politely informed that *testimonial* was probably the word called for in the context.[3] Whether the language was modified before appearing in the Federal Reporter 2d, I cannot say. If it was changed, though, the resulting split in the circuits might yet prompt the Supreme Court to rule on this important point of federal jurisprudence!

* * *

While we're on the subject of *testamentary* and its disposition, has anyone else noticed the encroachment of the newfangled word *testorial*? It does not appear in the *Oxford English Dictionary*, in *Black's Law Dictionary*, or in any other unabridged dictionary. We are accustomed to reading of *testamentary intentions*, but a few legal writers have begun to refer to *testorial intentions*. Thus the Oklahoma Supreme Court: "[T]he *testorial* intention will control."[4] And the revered D.C. Circuit: "The construction properly to be placed on the survivorship language is, of course, a product of *testorial* intention."[5]

One wonders whether *testorial* is meant to correspond with the noun *testator*, since *testamentary* corresponds etymologically with *testament*. Even so, it seems that *testatorial* would be the better form for such a word. Does anyone have a clue to its origin?

---

[3] *Weathersby v. Conoco Oil Co.*, 752 F.2d 953, 958 (5th Cir. 1984) (using *testamentary* instead of *testimonial*).

[4] *In re Estate of Hixon*, 715 P.2d 1087, 1090 (Okla. 1985).

[5] *In re Estate of Kerr*, 433 F.2d 479, 484 (D.C. Cir. 1969).

ॐ ॐ ॐ

Insane Committees

THE WORD *committee*, in the sense "a person who is civilly committed, usually to a psychiatric hospital," is a splendid example of how lawyers take an ordinary English word and give it an alien sense and pronunciation (*com-i-tee*). The usage invites double takes from lawyers as well as nonlawyers: "The civil commitment hearing does not address whether the committee has engaged in conduct that constitutes the elements of a crime; rather, that hearing focuses on whether the committee is mentally ill and dangerous . . . ."[1]

Of course, those who have had the privilege of serving on more than a few committees (in the usual sense) may see this usage as a logical extension of meaning.

Some writers have used the spelling *commitee* to differentiate the legal from the ordinary use of the word. That spelling, however, violates spelling principles and merely suggests that the writer possesses neither an ear for the language nor a computer with a spell-checker.

Confusingly, *committee* has still another legal sense—formerly common in British English—referring not to the psychiatric patient but to the guardian for the patient: "[T]he 'committee' of a person of unsound mind was a single person to whom the care of such person was entrusted by the court, the stress being on the last syllable. Committees are no longer appointed."[2]

If everyone agreed to abstain from using *committee* in the two confusing senses here discussed, the language of the law would be a little better off.

Adapted from *The Scribes Journal of Legal Writing* (1992).

[1] *Benham v. Edwards*, 678 F.2d 511, 538 (5th Cir. 1982), *vacated sub nom. Ledbetter v. Benham*, 463 U.S. 1222 (1983); *see Allen v. Illinois*, 478 U.S. 364, 381 (1986) (referring to the civil committee's right to silence); *Hickey v. Morris*, 722 F.2d 543, 547 (9th Cir. 1983) (referring to the "differences between insanity acquittees and civil committees").

[2] Glanville Williams, *Learning the Law* 64 (11th ed. 1982).

ᘺ   ᘺ   ᘺ

Alliteritis

ELSEWHERE I HAVE DISCUSSED effective and ineffective alliteration in legal writing, as well as the clink of unconscious alliteration.[1] What I had never before seen until the late 1980s is the conscious use of alliteration that seems callously flippant. Could that *possibly* have been what the writer intended? Surely not.

In *Boatright v. State*,[2] the Georgia Court of Appeals reviewed a trial involving aggravated sexual abuse of eight- and nine-year-old children. After a sober opinion affirming the defendant's conviction, Presiding Judge Deen wrote a separate concurrence. Rather than characterizing the concurrence or drawing conclusions for the reader, I set it out in full:

> While I concur fully with the majority opinion, additional comments are appropriate.
>
> The crimes of aggravated child molestation and enticing a child for indecent purposes, under the facts of this case, include infliction of both mental and physical pain and abuse of the two young children. A micro, modicum, or major part of motivational manipulation of the molestation modus, relating to the mental aspects, is the obvious operandi of obsession with the obscene magazines and other material evident in this case. Introduced into evidence and before the jury were books included in the lengthy transcript amounting to almost a thousand pages. These massive magazine materials include close-up pornographic photographs with stimulating and sensuous sexually suggestive titles, which will not be here enumerated.
>
> The production and providing of pornographic photography promoting permissiveness and perversion pointing to mental pain and abuse is no less pertinent than physical abuse portions and ingredients of the aggravated child molestation charges and enticing a child for indecent purposes, as perpetrated against the eight- and nine-year-old children in this case.[3]

Adapted from *The Scribes Journal of Legal Writing* (1991).

[1] Garner, *The Elements of Legal Style* 76–77, 168 (2d ed. 2002); Garner, *A Dictionary of Modern Legal Usage* 44 (2d ed. 1995).

[2] 385 S.E.2d 298 (Ga. App. 1989).

[3] *Id.* at 305 (Deen, P.J., concurring).

ᴈ ᴈ ᴈ

Sesquipedality

SESQUIPEDALITY IS THE USE OF big words, literally those that are "a foot and a half" long. Although the English language has an unmatched wealth of words available for its users, most of its resources go untapped. The *OED* contains more than 600,000 words, yet even highly educated people have only about 10% of that number in their working vocabularies.[1]

This discrepancy gives rise to a tension between two ideals. On the one hand, vocabulary-builders have long maintained that a rich personal word-stock is your key to success:

- "A rich vocabulary is the most common and invaluable possession of the leaders in every profession, in every commercial enterprise, and in every department of active living. . . . Vocabulary is so intimately tied up with success that from now on we might as well talk of the two as though they were one and the same thing."[2]
- "You are likelier to succeed (both in school and after) if you have the words you need at your command. You can, by using this book diligently, attain not only a *larger* vocabulary but, even more, an *improved* vocabulary."[3]
- "It has been stated on the basis of a study of student academic mortality at one large university that the lack of an adequate vocabulary is the most important single factor contributing to failure in college."[4]

On the other hand, writing guides are full of advice to shun big words:

- "There is a tendency, almost an instinct in the American, to use and prefer high-sounding words. The American, as such, likes to be unsimple and grandiloquent when it comes to his manner of expression."[5]

Adapted from *Garner's Modern American Usage* (2d ed. 2003).

[1] David Crystal, *The Cambridge Encyclopedia of the English Language* 123 (1995); Tom McArthur, *The Oxford Companion to the English Language* 1091–92 (1992).

[2] Wilfred Funk, *The Way to Vocabulary Power and Culture* 1 (1946).

[3] Arthur Waldhorn & Arthur Zeiger, *Word Mastery Made Simple* 8 (1957).

[4] Donald M. Ayers, *English Words from Latin and Greek Elements* xiv (rev. Thomas D. Worthen, 2d. ed. 1986) (citing G. Rexford Davis, *Vocabulary Building* 1 (1951)).

[5] Richard Burton, *Why Do You Talk Like That?* 124 (1929).

- "It is a habit, amounting almost to mania, among inexperienced and ignorant writers to shun simple words. They rack their brains and wear out their dictionaries searching for high-sounding words and phrases to express ideas that can be conveyed in simple terms."[6]
- "Those who run to long words are mainly the unskillful and tasteless; they confuse pomposity with dignity, flaccidity with ease, and bulk with force."[7]
- "The more you surrender to the temptation to use big words . . . the further you are apt to stray from your true feelings and the more you will tend to write in a style designed to impress rather than to serve the reader."[8]

Which of these two views is correct? It's entirely possible to resolve the seeming paradox and to hold that they're both essentially right. Build your vocabulary to make yourself a better reader; choose simple words whenever possible to make yourself a better writer.

The last part of that antithesis is hard for some wordsmiths to accept. And it needs tempering, because hard words have a legitimate literary tradition. English has inherited two strains of literary expression, both deriving ultimately from ancient Greek rhetoric. On the one hand is the plain style now in vogue, characterized by unadorned vocabulary, directness, unelaborate syntax, and earthiness. (This style is known to scholars as Atticism.) On the other hand we have the grand style, which exemplifies floridity, allusiveness, formal and sometimes abstruse diction, and rhetorical ornament. Proponents of this verbally richer style (called Asiaticism) proudly claim that the nuances available in the "oriental profusion" of English synonyms make the language an ideal putty for the skilled writer to mold and shape precisely. The Asiaticist sees the opulence of our language as providing apt terms for virtually every conceivable context.

Still, using the abundant resources of English is widely, if not wisely, discouraged. This attitude is as old as modern English. During the 16th century, when our language had just begun to take its modern form, learned Englishmen who enriched their lexically impoverished tongue with Latin and Greek loanwords were vilified as "smelling of inkhorn" or as "inkhornists." Thus one of the more notable borrowing neologists

---

[6] Edward Frank Allen, *How to Write and Speak Effective English* 57 (1938).

[7] H.W. Fowler, *A Dictionary of Modern English Usage* 342 (Ernest Gowers ed., 2d. ed. 1965).

[8] John R. Trimble, *Writing with Style* 80 (1975).

of the Renaissance, Sir Thomas Elyot, author of *The Governour*, wrote in 1531: "Divers men, rather scornying my benefite ['beneficence,' i.e., adding to the English word-stock] than receyving it thankfully, doo shew them selves offended (as they say) with my straunge termes."[9] The "straunge termes" this redoubtable inkhornist gave us include *accommodate*, *education*, *frugality*, *irritate*, *metamorphosis*, *persist*, and *ruminate*, He sought not to parade his formidable erudition, but rather "to augment our Englyshe tongue, wherby men shulde as well expresse more abundantly the thynge that they conceyved in theirs hartis (wherefore language was ordeyned) having wordes apte for the purpose."[10] In retrospect, of course, the efforts of Elyot and others like him were not in vain because they enriched the language.

The question, though, remains: to what extent is it advisable to use big words? The Fowler brothers generally thought it inadvisable: "Prefer the familiar word to the far-fetched."[11] But *prefer* raises an important question: How strong is this preference to be? Sheridan Baker elaborates the idea more fully, and quite sensibly:

> "What we need is a mixed diction," said Aristotle, and his point remains true 24 centuries and several languages later. The aim of style, he says, is to be clear but distinguished. For clarity, we need common, current words; but, used alone, these are commonplace, and as ephemeral as everyday talk. For distinction, we need words not heard every minute, unusual words, large words, foreign words, metaphors; but, used alone, these become bogs, vapors, or at worst, gibberish. What we need is a diction that weds the popular with the dignified, the clear current with the sedgy margins of language and thought.[12]

Intermingling Saxon words with Latin ones gives language variety, texture, euphony, and vitality. The best writers match substance with form. They use language precisely, evocatively, even daringly. So we shouldn't assume that Hemingwayan spartanism is the only desirable mode, unless we're ready to indict T.S. Eliot, H.L. Mencken, Vladimir Nabokov, Edmund Wilson, John Updike, and many another masterly writer.

Having established a reputable pedigree for the judicious employment of unfamiliar words, we can approach a standard for discriminating between useful and relatively useless abstrusities. Consider words as analogues to mathematical fractions, both being symbols for material

---

[9] Sir Thomas Elyot, *The Dictionarie* [n.p.] (1538).
[10] H.W. Fowler & F.G. Fowler, *The King's English* 12 (1906).
[11] *The King's English* 14 (3d ed. 1931).
[12] Sheridan Baker, *The Practical Stylist* 133 (8th ed. 1998).

or conceptual referents: Would a self-respecting mathematician use $^{12}/_{48}$ instead of $^1/_4$ just to seem more erudite? Certainly not. Likewise a writer or speaker generally should not say *obtund* when the verbs *dull* and *blunt* come more readily to mind. Nor would one say *saponaceous* for *soapy*, *dyslogistic* for *uncomplimentary*, or *macrobian* (or *longevous*) for *long-lived*.

Of course, it's impossible to set down absolute rules about which words are and are not useful. Still, it's almost always degenerate to avoid the obvious by clothing it in befogged terminology, as one might by writing *arenaceous* or *sabulous* for *sandy*, *immund* for *dirty*, *nates* for *buttocks*, or *venenate* for the verb *poison*. In the words of Coleridge, "Whatever is translatable in other and simpler words of the same language, without loss of sense or dignity, is bad."[13]

But what about the mathematician who arrives at $^{15}/_{16}$? Is it really best to round off the fraction to 1? Maybe in some contexts, but not in all—certainly not in the professional context. Likewise with the writer who, when describing an asthenic person, should not balk at using *asthenic* rather than the vaguer *weak*, because the former evokes the distinct image of muscular atrophy, which the latter lacks. And why engage in circumlocutions when a single word neatly suffices?

One could make similar arguments for thousands of other English words. *Coterie* and *galere* have almost identical meanings—something like "a group of people united for a common interest or purpose"—but no everyday word exists for this notion. The same is true of *cathexis*, *eirenicon*, *gravamen*, *obelize*, *oriflamme*, *protreptic*, or any of numberless other examples. Samuel Johnson came closest to rationalizing his sesquipedalian penchant when he wrote: "It is natural to depart from familiarity of language upon occasions not familiar. Whatever elevates the sentiments will consequently raise the expression; whatever fills us with hope or terror, will produce some perturbation of images and some figurative distortions of phrase."[14]

Certainly you might have occasion to use abstruse vocabulary for reasons other than stylistic dignity or the lack of a simpler term. Three stand out. First, it's often desirable to avoid the apt but voguish word. To select one of several examples, in the days when *aggravate* was first coming to be widely used for "irritate, annoy," the fastidious speaker or writer could either combat the word's debasement and use it correctly or seek refuge in *exacerbate*. As a result, *exacerbate* is no longer an unusual word. (And of course, *make worse* is always an available standby.)

---

[13] Samuel Taylor Coleridge, *Biographia Literaria* 253 (1817).

[14] Samuel Johnson, *The Rambler* (vol. 2), in *The Works of Samuel Johnson*, L.L.D. vol. 3, 149 (1825).

Second, big words can often have a humorous effect, though the fun is limited to those who can understand them. Such jocular phrases as *campanologist's tintinnabulation* (= bellringer's knell), *alliaceous halitosis* (= garlic breath), *pernoctative nepotation* (= riotous carousing through the night), and *bromidrotic fug* (= sweaty stench) can be delightfully amusing.

A third reason for waxing lexiphanic is to soften one's scurrility—to abstract it so that one's audience does not immediately visualize an unpleasant image. For example, R. Emmett Tyrell, the political analyst, once used *fecalbuccal* to describe certain politicians. He couldn't—and wouldn't—have said that if he'd been forced to simplify.

In the end, there seem to be three legitimate stances for the writer. The first is that if you truly want to communicate with a wide readership, you have to build your core of small, familiar words. The second is that if one of your purposes is to edify, use challenging words while allowing the context to reveal their meanings, as in the following examples:

- **umbrelliferous**: "His arms were like pipes, and had a way of branching from his shoulders at sharp angles so that the umbrella-bearing, or *umbrelliferous*, limb, for example, shot up on a steeply ascending vertical before articulating crisply at the elbow into a true vertical."[15]

- **enucleate** [A psychiatrist is talking to a woman in love with a madman.] "Appearances to the contrary, Edgar Stark is a deeply disturbed individual." "I know this, Jack." "I wonder if you do. Do you know what he did to that woman after he killed her?" She said nothing. "He decapitated her. Then he *enucleated* her. He cut her head off, and then he took her eyes out."[16]

- **synaesthesia**: "The *synaesthesia* (mixing of senses) of 'visible sob' might seem too rich to apply to a golf ball, if it didn't occupy the climactic position in the description."[17]

The third stance is that if you know you're writing for a specific audience with a prodigious, specialized vocabulary—whether one particular reader or the intelligentsia generally—then use hard words that are truly unsimplifiable. But question your motives: Are you doing it to express yourself well, or are you just showing off?

---

[15] Patrick McGrath, *Blood and Water and Other Tales* 68 (1988).
[16] *Id.* at 72.
[17] David Lodge, *The Art of Fiction* 148 (1992).

Whatever your motive, if you want to learn hard words, there is no shortage of books on the subject. These are among the best:

- Robert H. Hill, *A Dictionary of Difficult Words* (1st Am. ed. 1971).

- Russell Rocke, *The Grandiloquent Dictionary* (1972).

- I. Moyer Hunsberger, *The Quintessential Dictionary* (1978).

- J.N. Hook, *The Grand Panjandrum: And 1,999 Other Rare, Useful, and Delightful Words and Expressions* (1980).

- George S. Saussy, *The Oxter English Dictionary: Uncommon Words Used by Uncommonly Good Writers* (1984).

- Paul Hellweg, *The Insomniac's Dictionary: The Last Word on the Odd Word* (1986).

- *Dictionary of Uncommon Words* (Laurence Urdang ed., 1991).

- Norman W. Schur, *2000 Most Challenging and Obscure Words* (1994).

- David Grambs, *The Endangered English Dictionary: Bodacious Words Your Dictionary Forgot* (1994).

- Josefa Heifetz Byrne, *Mrs. Byrne's Dictionary of Unusual, Obscure, and Preposterous Words* (2d ed. 1994).

- Charles Harrington Elster, *There's a Word for It: A Grandiloquent Guide to Life* (1996).

- Eugene Ehrlich, *The Highly Selective Dictionary for the Extraordinarily Literate* (1997).

- Erin McKean, *Weird and Wonderful Words* (2002).

ἐ֍ ἐ֍ ἐ֍

Smelling of the Inkhorn

ANY SERIOUS PERSCRUTATION of juridical sesquipedality must include more than a decurtate perlustration of the pronouncements of Judge Bruce Selya. Far from an exiguity or hypoplasia of the recherché, we find that his lexical armamentarium—inconcinnate in the view of some readers, perhaps perficient in the view of others—necessitates using a dictionary as an internuncio. Without circumambaging, let me vaticinate that his scumbled wordings may cause you to: (1) repastinate; (2) fall into paralogism—perhaps even depart the encincture of compos-mentis; or (3) suffer from dyspepsia, with a furculum lodged in your tracheal membrane. To avoid this last consequent, don't read the opinions postcibally.

Readers who fully understood that paragraph must be among the top vocabularians in the nation—deserving a place alongside Judge Selya himself, who has used most of those words in his opinions.

What are we to make of big words? What are we to make of their users? I once defended the use of unfamiliar words on grounds that they are sometimes the only ones available to convey one's precise meaning.[1] But in recent years I have retreated from that position because an approximate meaning is usually much better than a wholesale failure to communicate.

That reasoning has never appealed to William F. Buckley, probably our best-known dabbler in difficult diction. Long ago, Buckley assailed what he called the "phony democratic bias against the use of unusual words."[2] He was defending one of his favorite words, *energumen*, meaning "one possessed by an evil spirit; a fanatic." You can easily guess the political bias of those whom Buckley brands energumens.

For all but energumens of the single syllable, hard words very occasionally—to the appropriate audience—prove irresistible. I think of *smellfungus*, meaning "a captious critic," or *ultracrepidarian*, meaning "one who pontificates about matters of which he or she knows nothing." We need such words if only because the meanings are so exquisite.[3]

Adapted from *The Scribes Journal of Legal Writing* (1991).

[1] Garner, *Learned Length and Thund'ring Sound: A Word-Lover's Panegyric*, 10 Verbatim 1 (Winter 1984).

[2] William F. Buckley, "The Hysteria About Words," in *The Jeweler's Eye* 284 (1969) (essay first printed in 1963).

[3] For another example, see the discussion of *mumpsimus* in *The Wright–Garner–Maugans Correspondence on Complimentary Closes*, 2 Scribes J. Legal Writing 83, 97–98 (1991), or in Chapter Twelve here.

William Safire recently laid down a sensible rule. In answer to the question, "Should you ever use a word that you know most of your audience will not know?" he said:

> Fly over everybody's head only when your purpose is to teach or to tease . . . .
>
>   ·   ·   ·
>
> Overhead flying is . . . allowed, in my view, when the writer or speaker is dealing with an elite audience that will appreciate arcana and consider unfamiliar words and obscure allusions to be delicious inside stuff, caviar for the general . . . .
> I would not, however, use big words to a mass audience when my primary aim is to persuade rather than to educate. Lay off *sclerotic*, fellas, lest frustrated viewers become choleric.[4]

You might try applying Safire's test to Judge Selya's use of big words. Conclusions may differ. For myself, I'm grateful for the opportunity to add to my vocabulary, though I'll probably never want to use any of the words that follow. If I practiced in the First Circuit, of course, I'd consider it a professional obligation to learn them, so frequently do they appear in Judge Selya's opinions.

Here, then, are 30 of the more difficult words that Judge Selya has used. The definitions are based on those of the *Oxford English Dictionary*.

1. **armamentarium**: a doctor's equipment; an array. "The cost-of-living provision was a part of this armamentarium . . . ."[5]

2. **decurtate**: curtailed; shortened. "A decurtate recital of certain crucial facts is, however, useful . . . ."[6]

3. **encincture**: an enclosure or encirclement. "[I]t is presently unclear to what extent (if at all) the framing of answers would invade the encincture of the Hague Convention . . . ."[7]

4. **eschatocol**: the concluding part of a protocol. "The matter before us is in a sense an eschatocol to an earlier, more complex piece of work."[8]

---

[4] William Safire, *Take My Word for It* viii–ix (1986).
[5] *Sierra Club v. Secretary of the Army*, 820 F.2d 513, 523 (1st Cir. 1987).
[6] *United States v. Puerto Rico*, 721 F.2d 832, 833 (1st Cir. 1985).
[7] *Boreri v. Fiat S.P.A.*, 763 F.2d 17, 24 (1st Cir. 1985).
[8] *United States v. Reveron Martinez*, 836 F.2d 684, 685 (1st Cir. 1988).

5. ***exiguous***: scanty; meager. "Faced with such an exiguous record, the trial judge concluded that the juror did not remember either Lucy or Paul Neron from what were (at most) casual encounters with them."[9]

6. ***furculum***: a wishbone, or forked process or part. "The last furculum of the petitioner's challenge is not so facilely to be dismissed."[10] "We hold, therefore, that on the most salient furculum of the *Cohen* paradigm, the appellant has fallen several leagues short of making out the requisite showing of urgency."[11]

7. ***hypoplasia***: underdevelopment of an organ or other bodily part. "Such hypoplasia inhibits the careful evaluation needed in order to resolve the central inquiry which lies at the core of Fiat's entreaty."[12]

8. ***imbrication***: an overlapping. "Given the imbrication between appellant's claim and those earlier advanced by his co-defendants, the doctrine of *stare decisis* bars relitigation of that issue."[13]

9. ***imprecation***: a curse. "The Sierra Club would have us extend this principle to the EAJA .... The imprecation asks too much."[14] (Not since the 17th century has *imprecation* been current in the sense in which Judge Selya uses it, i.e., "an entreaty or petition.")

10. ***impuissant***: powerless; feeble. "[W]e judge appellant's contentions to be not only factually inaccurate, but legally impuissant as well."[15]

11. ***inconcinnate***: unsuitable; awkward. (Archaic) "When Erasmus mused that '[a] common shipwreck is a source of consolation to all,' he quite likely did not foresee inconcinnate free-for-alls among self-styled salvors."[16]

12. ***internuncio***: a messenger between two parties; a go-between. "The third admitted that he was merely an internuncio; he did not know what decisions might or might not be made on such a subject."[17]

[9] *Neron v. Tierney*, 841 F.2d 1197, 1203 (1st Cir. 1988).
[10] *Puleio v. Vose*, 830 F.2d 1197, 1204 (1st Cir. 1987).
[11] *Boreri*, 763 F.2d at 25.
[12] *Id.*
[13] *Reveron Martinez*, 836 F.2d at 687.
[14] *Sierra Club*, 820 F.2d at 524.
[15] *United States v. Chaudhry*, 850 F.2d 851, 853 (1st Cir. 1988).
[16] *Martha's Vineyard Scuba H.Q. v. Unidentified, Wrecked & Abandoned Steam Vessel*, 833 F.2d 1059, 1061 (1st Cir. 1987) (alteration in original).
[17] *Moores v. Greenberg*, 834 F.2d 1105, 1114 (1st Cir. 1987).

13. **neoteric**: modern; recent. "[T]he request leapfrogs the district court, which has never been accorded an opportunity to consider the plaintiff's neoteric theory."[18]

14. **ossature**: the skeletal framework. "The ossature of the workplace is fleshed out by job description forms . . . ."[19]

15. **paralogical**: illogical; unreasonable. "To suggest that early foot *ipso facto* carries the 'substantial justification' day . . . would be paralogical."[20]

16. **paralogism**: a piece of false reasoning. "[S]uch paralogism would disserve common sense as well."[21]

17. **perficient**: effective; actual. (Archaic) "Congress must not have believed that the perficient enforcement of state standards required, ipso facto, a non-federal forum."[22]

18. **perfrication**: thorough rubbing. (Archaic) "The test consisted of rubbing Real's hands and fingernails with filter paper and, after this perfrication . . . , applying certain chemicals . . . to the filter paper."[23]

19. **perlustration**: a thorough survey. "Putting the novel issue presented for our consideration in proper perspective necessitates . . . perlustration of the proceedings below . . . ."[24]

20. **perscrutation**: thoroughgoing scrutiny. "The court summarily dismissed *Habeas II* on initial perscrutation . . . ."[25]

21. **postcibal**: occurring after a meal. "Hunger, food-poisoning, postcibal illness and the like are apparently not the problem . . . ."[26]

---

[18] *Northeast Fed. Credit Union v. Neves*, 837 F.2d 531, 534–35 (1st Cir. 1988).

[19] *Vazquez Rios v. Hernandez Colon*, 819 F.2d 319, 321 (1st Cir. 1987).

[20] *Sierra Club*, 820 F.2d at 519.

[21] *Golemis v. Kirby*, 632 F.Supp. 159, 164 (D.R.I. 1985).

[22] *Puerto Rico*, 721 F.2d at 838.

[23] *Real v. Hogan*, 828 F.2d 58, 60 (1st Cir. 1987).

[24] *Puerto Rico*, 721 F.2d at 834.

[25] *Lefkowitz v. Fair*, 816 F.2d 17, 19 (1st Cir. 1987); *see United States v. Mejia-Lozano*, 829 F.2d 268, 271 (1st Cir. 1987) ("four issues for our perscrutation"); *Puleio*, 830 F.2d at 1203 ("perscrutation of the full record"); *Moores*, 834 F.2d at 1108 ("careful perscrutation of the record"); *Chaudhry*, 850 F.2d at 856 ("close perscrutation of the record"); *Mele v. Fitchburg Dist. Ct.*, 850 F.2d 817 (1st Cir. 1988). ("closer perscrutation of the ALOFAR").

[26] *Chase v. Quick*, 596 F.Supp. 33, 34 (D.R.I. 1984).

22. **prescind**: to withdraw the attention from. "The petitioner's argument prescinds in the first instance from *Tinder* . . . ."[27] "[H]e presented it to the jurors as an accomplished fact, a fact prescinding from the collaborative 'check[ing of] the record.' "[28]

23. **pruritis**: itching. "The plaintiffs' pruritis cannot be scratched [Why not *perfricated*?] by the federal judiciary . . . ."[29]

24. **repastinate**: to dig again. "We see no need to repastinate that familiar soil."[30]

25. **resupination**: a turning upside down. (Obsolete) "[B]y some thaumaturgical feat of resupination, NEFCU seeks magically to transmogrify itself from a neutral into a belligerent."[31]

26. **scumble**: to render (as a painting) less brilliant by spreading a thin coat of opaque color over the surface. "On this scumbled record, it remains entirely possible that the substantive question which Fiat urges us to reach may not, in the long run, require appellate resolution . . . ."[32]

27. **struthious**: resembling an ostrich. "[T]he law is not so struthious as to require courts to ignore the obvious."[33]

28. **trichotomous**: divided into three parts or categories. "Their appeal is trichotomous . . . ."[34]

29. **vaticinate**: to prophesy; to foretell. "[S]ince no Maine court of record has spoken to certain of the issues before us, it becomes our duty to vaticinate how the state's highest tribunal would resolve matters."[35] "[S]o many 'ifs' dot the landscape that such a prediction can only be woven of the gossamer strands of vaticination, conjecture, surmise, and speculation."[36]

---

[27] *Lefkowitz*, 816 F.2d at 21.

[28] *United States v. Argentine*, 814 F.2d 783, 787 (1st Cir. 1987) (second alteration in original).

[29] *Duffy v. Quattrocchi*, 576 F.Supp. 336, 342 (D.R.I. 1983).

[30] *Chappee v. Vose*, 843 F.2d 25, 26 n.1 (1st Cir. 1988).

[31] *Northeast Fed. Credit Union*, 837 F.2d at 534.

[32] *Boreri*, 763 F.2d at 24.

[33] *Onujiogu v. United States*, 817 F.2d 3, 5 (1st Cir. 1987).

[34] *Sierra Club*, 820 F.2d at 515.

[35] *Moores*, 834 F.2d at 1107.

[36] *Boreri*, 763 F.2d at 24.

30. **zoetic**: living; vital. "The dispute remained zoetic as to the $13,750 of EHA–B funds, more or less, which had been rerouted to Franklin, Greenfield, and Franklin County . . . ."[37] "Ochoa . . . maintains . . . that its claims for prospective relief are nevertheless zoetic."[38]

You never can tell how readers will react to unusual words. The editors of the *Texas Lawyer* not so long ago came upon the word *burglarious* in a judicial opinion and, in the "Inadmissible" column on the second page, reported the word as a "novelty" and "invention." Of course, the word is listed in all the unabridged dictionaries and in the better collegiate dictionaries. Blackstone used it more than 200 years ago. In calling this fact to the attention of the newspaper's editor, I jokingly suggested that the news item "was itself inadmissible, though probably infelonious."

At first, I thought I had coined a word, but an entry in the *Oxford English Dictionary* shows that George Eliot used the phrase *infelonious murder* in 1876. That's an oxymoron: Murder is by definition a felony.

But I have digressed. There are more English words than most of us have ever dreamt of; to get an inkling of just how many more, I suggest either browsing the *Oxford English Dictionary* or scanning a few of Judge Selya's opinions.

---

[37] *Massachusetts Dept. of Educ. v. United States Dept. of Educ.*, 837 F.2d 536, 540 (1st Cir. 1987).

[38] *Ochoa Realty Corp. v. Faria*, 815 F.2d 812, 816 (1st Cir. 1987).

ʾ❧ ʾ❧ ʾ❧

One Bite

One bite at the apple; one bite at the cherry. The first is the usual American idiom today, the latter the invariable British idiom. Each one denotes the idea that a litigant gets but one chance to take advantage of certain opportunities or rights. American courts sometimes use *cherry* in place of *apple*, but the latter fruit vastly predominates. The American version is that rare set phrase that is not so well set, variations on the phrase being more common than the main phrase itself—e.g.: "[U]nless a litigant gets a real *bite at the apple* of discord he should not be foreclosed from another attempt."[1] "Because 'one fair opportunity to litigate an issue is enough,' . . . we generally will not allow a *second bite at a single apple*."[2] "The interest of finality requires that parties generally get only *one bite at the Rule 59(e) apple* for the purpose of tolling the time for bringing an appeal."[3]

Some British lawyers insist that their idiom—*one bite at the cherry*—makes more sense because the cherry is a fruit that, by its nature, is eaten in only one bite: it makes little sense to think of multiple bites at a cherry.

But it was not logic that seems to have led American lawyers to speak of apples. Up to the late 1940s, American lawyers, like their British counterparts, regularly said *one bite at the cherry*: dozens of examples appear in the law reports. But by the 1920s, *cherry* had assumed another sense in American English, namely "hymen" or "virgin." The *OED* quotes an American book from the 1970s explaining that " '[t]o take or eat a cherry' means to deflower a virgin."

So *one bite at the cherry* may well be the only legal idiom that has changed because its users felt embarrassment over a newfound double entendre.

From *A Dictionary of Modern Legal Usage* (2d ed. 1995).

[1] *Angel v. Bullington*, 330 U.S. 183, 207 (1947) (Rutledge, J., dissenting).

[2] *A.J. Canfield Co. v. Vess Beverages, Inc.*, 859 F.2d 36, 37 (7th Cir. 1988) (citation omitted).

[3] *Charles L.M. v. Northeast Indep. Sch. Dist.*, 884 F.2d 869, 871 (5th Cir. 1989).

᪥ ᪥ ᪥

Pronunciation's Scofflaws

HOW MANY ENGLISH-LANGUAGE law dictionaries do you suppose there are? Whenever I ask even the most knowledgeable law librarians, their wildest guesses rarely exceed 50. In fact, if we construe *law* broadly, we have more than 400. Many of these are highly specialized glossaries, such as the law dictionary for morticians or the one for genealogists. As you might expect, many of them—often those written by laymen—induce mild laughter from the lawyer who browses through them.

On this score, my favorite is Julian A. Martin's *Law Enforcement Vocabulary*, published in 1973. Mr. Martin is no layman, though; he is a lawman who holds a B.S. and an M.S. in addition to a law degree. When his book was published, he was chairman of the Department of Law Enforcement at Louisiana State University.

The purpose of the book, Mr. Martin tells us in his preface, is "to bring together . . . the words, phrases, and slang expressions which the law enforcement officer will encounter . . . ." We also learn that "pronunciations are shown phonetically . . . ."

It is on pronunciations that I want to focus, but let me first give you the flavor of *Law Enforcement Vocabulary*. In its pages, we find entries not only for *asportation*, *Magna Carta*, and *right-of-way*, but also for *ass-kisser*, *fag bar*, and *smartypants*. For those unfamiliar with the last of these, Mr. Martin defines it as "one who overly demonstrates his knowledge" (p. 214).

Similarly, we are told in the entry for *go to bed with (someone)* that the phrase means "to have sexual relations with someone." One frets at the thought that there might exist a law-enforcement officer who would have to look up the phrase to understand it. The entry for another common phrase, *rock-and-roll*, reads: "Slang: Popular music, of the hillbilly style, usually loud, with active performers, vocalists, and instrumentalists." Do you suppose the author had ever listened to any of that hillbilly-style music? Surprisingly, *rock-and-roll* is not tagged, like several other phrases, as "a hippy word."

I could go on at length about the contents of *Law Enforcement Vocabulary*, in which *misprision* comes out *misprison (of a felony)* and headwords such as *res ipsa loquitor* [sic] and *Saphist* [sic] are misspelled. Instead, though, let us concentrate on pronunciations, for here we may have the

Adapted from *Dallas Bar Headnotes* (20 Nov. 1989).

key to a linguistic mystery. Why is it that law enforcers often seem to speak a different language from the rest of us, especially on the witness stand? Not only their vocabulary, but also the sound of their words varies greatly from what most Americans are accustomed to hearing.

The answer may lie in our law enforcers' having closely studied and assimilated Mr. Martin's book. Here are some pronunciations taken verbatim from its pages. Remember Mr. Martin's instruction: "Accented syllables are italicized." (I recommend trying each one aloud.)

abeyance . . . . a *bay* ons
abrogate . . . . *ab* ree *gait*
academician . . . . . *ack* ed e dee *mish* en
addict, n. . . . . . . a *dikt* ["One who has
    developed an addiction to drugs."]
alcoholism . . . . al ko *hall* ism
alien . . . . *ail* yen
alienate . . . . *ail* ye nate
angina pectoris . . . . *an* ji na *peck* tow iss
aural . . . . *aw* ral
barricade . . . . bear a *kade*
bastard . . . . *bass* terd "bass as in ass;
                        (terd as in herd)"
Bolshevik . . . . *bowl* she vick
calendar . . . . *cow* len dar
caucasoid . . . . *kaw* ke saw id
certiorari . . . . *sir* she *rah* ree
chloroform . . . . *klow* row form
coercion . . . . ko *er* chen
confidence . . . . *kon* figh dens
                        "(figh as in high)"
confidential . . . . *kon* figh *din* shel
constitution . . . . kon sty *tue* shun
criminalist . . . . krimi na *list*
culpable . . . . *kul* pay bul
culture . . . . *kul* shur
debter . . . . de *tur*
decision . . . . dee *sizz* un
denounce . . . . dee *now* unz
desertion . . . . des *zert* shun
desperado . . . . des pay *rod* o
disqualification . dis kwol i figh *kay* shen
dynamite . . . . dee na *might*
ecstasy . . . . *ek* sto see
electronic . . . . ee *lek* tron ick
empathy . . . . *im* pay the
espionage . . . . es *pea* e nige
executioner . . . . ex e *que* sher ner

expert, n. . . . . eks *purt*
fiduciary . . . . figh *do* she ery
fluorine . . . . *flu* e reen
forcible . . . . *for* see bul
fume . . . . *few* m
genial . . . . *geen* yel
gonorrhea . . . . gon e *rear*
hallucination . . . ha loose sigh *nay* shun
hallucinogenic . . . . ha *loose* na a jin ick
heterosexuality . . het er a *sek* shoe al ity
image . . . . *em* i j
incapable . . . . in *kap* er bul
incarcerate . . . . in *kar* see rate
juror . . . . *jew* ror
legible . . . . *leg* i bul
        [but legislate is "*lej* is late"]
linear . . . . *lin* yer
magistrate . . . . maj is *trate*
mania . . . . *mane* ye
merger . . . . *mur* gur
miscarriage . . . . miss *kar* ige
molester . . . . *mo* les ter
moral . . . . *mo* ral "(mo as in bah)"
motivate . . . . *mow* tea vait
muzzle . . . . *mus* el
nautical . . . . *naw* tie coll
negligence . . . . *neg* lee jence
nonjuror . . . . non *jew* er
obligation . . . . ob ly *gay* shun
perpetrate . . . . *purr* pea trait
prohibition . . . . pro high *bi* shen
proletariat . . . . pro lee *tare* it
promulate . . . . pro *mul* gate
proof . . . . pruff
publicity . . . . pub *liz* i ti
punitive . . . . *pewn* i tiv
rampage . . . . ram *page*
ruckus . . . . ruc *kus*

rural . . . . *roor* el as in jewel
saliva . . . . sa *live* er
scruples . . . . *srew* pye less
self-discipline . . . . *dis* c plin
shrewd . . . . shrud

status quo . . . . (kwo as in two)
straight . . . . *stray* t
toxicology . . . . tok i *kol* o gee
unbalanced . . . . un *bal* enst ed
visual acuity . . . . *eh* que e ty

To test the theory, some Ph.D. student in linguistics ought to research a dissertation on whether these pronunciations have currency among law enforcers. If they were found to have currency, a second doctoral student might write a dissertation on whether the pronunciations were current before as well as after the publication of *Law Enforcement Vocabulary*. That way we would know whether the book has influenced law enforcers' pronunciation, or has merely reflected it. Whatever the outcome, we may now hope for a solution to the case of the mysterious mouthings.

ʕ͜ ʕ͜ ʕ͜

An Epistolary Essay

The Wright–Garner–Maugans Correspondence on Complimentary Closes[1]

Charles Alan Wright to Bryan A. Garner, 18 February 1988 [excerpt]

In the last couple of weeks I was looking for something else in one of my reference books and happened to note an article that said that it is incorrect to use "sincerely" as the complimentary close in a letter, and that it must be "sincerely yours." I have tried to conform to this edict but I find it so confining that I wanted to go back and see what reasons the great authority gave for this. I had thought that I had seen this in Follett, but I cannot now find it there, nor can I find it in *DMLU* [*A Dictionary of Modern Legal Usage*]. Do you have any notion where I might have seen this? Do you agree with this?

Sincerely yours,

Charles Alan Wright

Charles Alan Wright to Bryan A. Garner, 3 March 1988 [excerpt]

Did you know that *The Practical Lawyer*, the periodical for which I do reviews of mysteries under the heading "The Fictional Lawyer," also carries a very good column each month titled "The Grammatical Lawyer"? That column is currently being written for them by a Philadelphia lawyer, James Maugans. It was originated by Morton Freeman, and indeed ALI-ABA published in hardback a collection of his columns from 1976 through 1979. Freeman, *The Grammatical Lawyer* (1979).

In pulling his book off of my shelf to find the date, I see that he is the one who says I cannot close a letter with "Sincerely." I enclose a photocopy of page 326 of his book. I do not want to have my confidence in

---

Adapted from *The Scribes Journal of Legal Writing* (1991).

[1] This correspondence is printed with the permission of Charles Alan Wright, Bryan A. Garner, and James D. Maugans. Mrs. Clement F. Haynsworth, Jr., kindly granted permission to quote Judge Haynsworth's letter dated 11 May 1988.

him shaken, but I hope you will tell me on this point he is wrong. I see that you sign your letters "Yours sincerely," but, as I wrote you recently, I find it confining and stuffy to have to include the "yours" in the complimentary close.

Sincerely yours,

Charles Alan Wright

Bryan A. Garner to Charles Alan Wright, 7 March 1988 [excerpt]

I thought you had probably happened upon the suggestion that "sincerely" is an incorrect complimentary close in the Evanses' *Dictionary of Contemporary American Usage* [1957], which states: "For some reason the English are perturbed at the custom of many Americans of using the single word *sincerely* at the close of an informal letter" (p. 455). The Evanses seem to give this prejudice little credence. Having just received your letter of March 3, I learn that Morton Freeman's book was the source. He is wrong here. What he ignores, I believe, is that *yours* is understood in the complimentary close *sincerely*. If his reasoning were correct that *yours* must always be included explicitly, then other closing phrases like *cordially*, *fondly*, and the like would be incorrect. Fowler sanctions *faithfully* as a complimentary close in letters to the editor (*MEU1* at 323).

Sincerely,

Bryan

Charles Alan Wright to Bryan A. Garner, 10 March 1988 [excerpt]

[Thank you] for giving me the comforting assurance that I can sign letters "sincerely" and that "yours" can be taken for granted. I certainly had not happened upon the book by the Evanses. I do not own it and never read it. They are far too willing to tolerate every new fad. I agree with you on why Morton Freeman is in error on this point. I quite often close letters "affectionately." I think that to add "yours" would seem quite stilted, and I think the same principle applies, even if less obviously, to "sincerely." I do not have at my office the first edition of Fowler, which you cite. I keep that at home. In the office I have only the Gowers edition. I am unclear on how to interpret what is said there. The entry at 332, which I think probably corresponds with what was at 323 in the first edition, mentions "yours faithfully" three times and never sanctions "faithfully" by itself. (I have just noted that even though I think the usage stilted, Fowler says that I do have to add "yours" to "affectionately.") There is an entry at 185 in which the first item for "faithfully" says "for *yours f.* see LETTER FORMS." I did not know whether to interpret that as allowing "faithfully" by itself or not, but I no longer care what Fowler thinks now that I know what Garner thinks.

Sincerely,

Charles Alan Wright

Charles Alan Wright to Paul A. Wolkin [Director, American Law Institute], 10 March 1988 [in full]

A few weeks ago I was looking up something in Morton Freeman's valuable book *The Grammatical Lawyer.* Quite by accident my eye fell on the final entry in the book at page 326, where I am told that it is wrong to use "sincerely" by itself as a complimentary close on a letter. Naturally I have obeyed this command, but I found it quite stultifying to do so. Finally I wrote to my friend and former student Bryan Garner, the author of the splendid *Dictionary of Modern Legal Usage,* which we found you already had in your library when the Nominating Committee met there in December. Garner has released me from the bondage of Freeman. He says: [quoting letter of March 7]. I do not think that Morton Freeman was often wrong. I agree with Garner, however, that in this one point he is.

Sincerely,

Charlie

Bryan A. Garner to Charles Alan Wright, 28 March 1988 [excerpt]

Thank you also for sending your correspondence with Mr. Wolkin. I thought you might like the added comfort of knowing that the *Britannica Book of English Usage* (1980)—not exactly a heavyweight authority, but not dismissible either—gives

Sincerely (yours)

Cordially (yours)

as common complimentary closes in general correspondence (p. 561). Five sample letters (pp. 551–55) end merely with "sincerely." *Britannica* also quite rightly sanctions "respectfully" and "fondly." How is that for a lagniappe?

Sincerely,

Bryan

Judge Clement F. Haynsworth, Jr., to Charles Alan Wright, 11 May 1988 [excerpt]

Thank you also for your review of Garner's *A Dictionary of Modern Legal Usage*. I was so impressed with it I have ordered a copy for myself. Moreover, I am delighted to learn that the simple "sincerely" as the complimentary close of a letter is proper and acceptable. It saves me from having been a serious transgressor for many years.

Sincerely,

Clement

Excerpt from "The Grammatical Lawyer," in the *ALI-ABA CLE Review*, 5 August 1988 [This column appeared also in the April 1988 issue of *The Practical Lawyer*.]

"I think the complimentary close should be '*Sincerely yours*,' rather than just '*Sincerely*.'"

"You're absolutely correct. It goes back to our rule that adverbs modify adjectives, verbs, and other adverbs. They do not, however, modify nouns or pronouns.

"When you write '*Sincerely yours*' as a complimentary close, what you are writing, in effect, is 'I am sincerely yours.' In this construction, *sincerely*, an adverb answering the question *how*, modifies the predicate *am*. Without the addition of *yours*—which is a pronoun acting as a predicate nominative—to complete the thought, we are left with the incomplete sentence of 'I am sincerely.' And that doesn't make a great deal of sense. What does that mean, 'I am sincerely'? Sincerely *what*? The answer, of course, is sincerely *yours*.

"The same principle applies to 'Very truly yours,' namely, that *yours* must be included. And, of course, the same rule applies to both 'Yours sincerely,' and 'Yours truly.'"

Bryan A. Garner to Charles Alan Wright, 12 August 1988 [excerpt]

I send you the enclosed column from "The Grammatical Lawyer" because it duplicates Morton Freeman's ill-premised thoughts on complimentary closes. Do you know James Maugans (Professor Snaguam, as he calls himself)?

Best,

Bryan

Charles Alan Wright to James D. Maugans, 6 September 1988 [in full]

I regard your column, "The Grammatical Lawyer," as the best thing that appears in *The Practical Lawyer*. I have written Paul Wolkin and Mark Carroll in the past to tell them how much I have enjoyed your column. I only see the magazine when my own column on mysteries appears, but when I do get a copy of it I always turn to your column and read it with pleasure and profit.

A few weeks ago I was in England and my office sent on to me a photocopy of a letter that had come to my office in my absence. In it a fine young Dallas lawyer, Bryan Garner, who is the author of the excellent recent book *A Dictionary of Modern Legal Usage*, called my attention to a column of yours that is reprinted in *CLE Review* for August 5th. In his letter he says that he is sending it to me "because it duplicates Morton Freeman's ill-premised thoughts on complimentary closes."

As you can imagine there is a history behind Mr. Garner's recent letter. In a letter to him on March 3rd I said: [quoting previous excerpt]. In his response of March 7th he agreed with me. He said: [quoting previous excerpt].

I reported all this at the time to our distinguished editor, Paul Wolkin. I enclose a photocopy of his letter to me on the subject.

I am sad indeed to find not only that you disagree on this point but that, having given the readers of *The Practical Lawyer* so much wise guidance on English usage, you have misled them on this point.

Sincerely,

Charles Alan Wright

James D. Maugans to Charles Alan Wright, 12 September 1988 [in full]

Thank you for your letter of September 6 concerning the proper form of the complimentary close to a letter—*Sincerely* or *Sincerely yours*.

You have heard the evidence for the prosecution; but before you convict me of grammatical heresy, perhaps you will hear the evidence for the defense.

To the charge of disagreeing with Bryan Garner, I plead guilty. To the charge of misleading my readers on this point, I plead most definitely not guilty!

The primary evidence against me seems to be the appearance of the word *faithfully* in a list of suggested complimentary closes on page 323 in the first edition of *Modern English Usage*. Based on this single entry,

Mr. Garner extrapolates the omission of *yours* in this instance to apply equally to "*cordially, fondly*, and the like" and finally to *sincerely*. Thus he arrives at the conclusion that *yours* need never appear in a complimentary close because "*yours* is understood."

But Mr. Garner's evidence is only half the evidence. Indeed, a good deal less than half the evidence, if you consult the source of authority that Mr. Garner cites to support his proposition. If you examine the other entries on page 323 (copy enclosed), you will notice that *every* other entry (including *yours sincerely*) includes the word *yours* in the recommended complimentary closes. Thus it would appear that the entry *faithfully* (without *yours*) is an aberration rather than a foundation for building a general rule for the proper form of the complimentary close.

In support of my contention that *faithfully* (without *yours*) is, at best, an exception, I refer you to page 332 of the second edition of *Modern English Usage* (copy enclosed). There you will note that not only does every entry from the first edition continue the use of *yours* but also *faithfully* has now acquired a *yours*. Whether this was to correct a misprint in the first edition or was the result of a reconsideration of the point I cannot say. But regardless of the reason the entry now includes *yours*.

If the analysis I presented in my article, which I believe is quite sound, does not convince you of the correctness of my position, I hope that this appeal to authority will.

The defense rests.

Sincerely yours,

James D. Maugans

Charles Alan Wright to James D. Maugans, 14 September 1988 [in full]

Thank you for your letter of September 12th. I regret to say that neither your appeal to reason nor your appeal to authority persuaded me.

I am sending on a copy of your answer to Bryan Garner with great confidence that he will answer for himself. I cannot refrain, however, from first interposing a word of my own between you two experts.

I do not read the passage from his letter that I quoted in my letter to you of September 6th as using *MEU1* as the "primary evidence" against you. It seemed to me that he was making an argument based on reason and that he offers two reasons, both of which seem to me persuasive, why "yours" is not required.

The first, and in my judgment the more important, of these is that it is unnecessary because "yours" is understood in a complimentary close.

Certainly there are many instances in which words are understood rather than articulated and in which the rules of grammar take into account the unarticulated word. I had an extensive correspondence a year or so ago with a distinguished English mystery writer, Michael Gilbert. In his book *Flash Point*, which was recently reissued and which I reviewed for the September 1987 issue of *The Practical Lawyer*, he has a sentence in which the narrator says: "Actually he is the same age as me." Gilbert at first tried to defend his usage, but I think eventually he could not escape the force of the many authorities I mustered, including Fowler, Follett, Bernstein, *The Oxford Miniguide to English Usage*, and others for the proposition that "me" would be simply incorrect. It must be "I" with "am" understood. I agree with Bryan Garner that in a complimentary close one can have the "yours" understood or we could even understand "I am, Sir, yours" if we are old-fashioned enough to prefer that usage.

I agree also with Bryan Garner's second reason, though I would give it much less weight. If "yours" must always be used, then such expressions as "cordially" or "fondly" would be incorrect. I think that these are correct and indeed the fault lies the other way. I think the recipient of a letter signed "cordially yours" or "fondly yours" would laugh aloud at such a terribly stilted usage. I recognize that Fowler gives his blessing to "yours affectionately," and I suppose that might barely pass muster. If I were ten years older than I am, perhaps I could close a letter to a goddaughter with "yours affectionately," but I certainly would not think I could use that for anyone with whom I had a closer relationship.

It is interesting to see that in *MEU2*, perhaps because of the influence of Gowers, "faithfully" has been converted into "yours faithfully," but I do not think this undercuts Bryan Garner's argument. I thought he was referring to that as an interesting example and not as an element of his proof. Indeed when I wrote him in March, responding to the letter in which he set out the arguments for omitting "yours," I expressed some doubt about the reference to Fowler, since I also looked at *MEU2*, but I said: "I no longer care what Fowler thinks now that I know what Garner thinks."

Sincerely,

Charles Alan Wright

Bryan A. Garner to James D. Maugans, 16 September 1988 [in full]

Professor Wright has kindly—or perhaps not so kindly—suggested that I respond to your recent discussion with him about *sincerely* as a complimentary close. I am glad to give you my thoughts. As you know, in writing on this subject you stumbled onto terrain that he and I had thought we rather thoroughly traversed.

I would frame the issue rather differently from you. I see the question as being whether your ruling that *sincerely* alone is "incorrect" as a complimentary close can be sustained, not whether I have laid "a foundation for building a general rule for the proper form of a complimentary close."

What struck me in your column—apart from your erroneous labeling of *yours* as a "predicate nominative" when the case is clearly possessive*—was your implicit statement that *I am* is understood in

   Sincerely yours,

but that *yours* somehow cannot be understood in

   Sincerely, ...

Nothing is magic about *I am* that allows it to be understood, while other words like *yours* are disallowed from being understood. I have a brief discussion of the general phenomenon in *Modern Legal Usage* in the entry entitled "Understood Words."

Complimentary closes are by their very nature, and have long been, elliptically phrased. One thinks of the 19th-century writers who merely put "&c." after *I am,* for the reader to supply whatever he thought appropriate. What is one to make, for instance, of complimentary closes in letters between good friends that read merely

   Yours,

   or

   Best,?

The reader simply supplies what is missing. Even then, complimentary closes do not make literal sense: "I am yours [in whatever way]"?

I do not know which of my letters Professor Wright sent you, but I added, in a letter of 28 March 1988:

   I thought you might like the added comfort of knowing that the *Britannica Book of English Usage* (1980)—not exactly a heavyweight authority, but not dismissible either—gives

   Sincerely (yours)
   Cordially (yours)

---

* Curme terms this use of a pronoun the "predicate genitive."

as common complimentary closes in general correspondence (p. 561). Five sample letters (pp. 551–55) end merely with "sincerely." *Britannica* also quite rightly sanctions "respectfully" and "fondly." How is that for a lagniappe?

One would think enough ink has been used up on this point. I hasten to add, however, that I own probably one of the fullest collections of dictionaries of usage anywhere, and I cannot find any support for your position that *sincerely* alone is wrong, or even less good than *sincerely yours*. I would pronounce it less formal, but no less acceptable.

I hope you will reconsider what you have mistakenly told your readers, because pronouncements such as yours are likely to give rise to the types of linguistic superstitions that benefit no one.

Your "ruling" indicts many of our finest writers, including the incomparable Charles Alan Wright, who habitually closes his letters in the way that you would forbid. In looking through Edmund Wilson's collected letters, I find that in 1939 he closed two letters to Harry Levin, that great Harvard English professor, by using *sincerely* without saying whose. *See* Wilson, *Letters on Literature and Politics 1912–1972*, at 181–82 (Farrar, Straus & Giroux 1977). (Wilson's complimentary closes varied greatly.)

Another great writer and poet, Randall Jarrell, wrote a letter to Edmund Wilson on August 5, 1941, and closed with *sincerely*. See *Randall Jarrell's Letters* 49 (Houghton Mifflin 1985). Jarrell frequently used *affectionately* without *yours*. You will also find, in the *Letters of E.B. White* (Harper & Row 1976), that White often signed off with *sincerely*.

What is worse than convicting you of a simple mistake, are we to convict Wright, Wilson, Jarrell, and White of using a solecism? With best wishes,

Sincerely,

Bryan A. Garner

P.S. After finishing this letter, I found an entry on the complimentary close in a book I recently added to my library, J. Harold Janis's *Modern Business Language and Usage in Dictionary Form* (1984). Janis writes, "The particular expression chosen is determined by the nature of the letter and the tone desired" (p. 98) and gives the following list:

Formal and deferential	Respectfully yours
	Respectfully
	Very respectfully
Merely polite	Yours truly

For general correspondence	Very truly yours
	Yours very truly
For more warmth	Sincerely yours
	Yours sincerely
	Sincerely
	Very sincerely
Informal	Cordially yours
	Cordially
	Very cordially
Very informal and personal	As always
	As ever
	Fondly.

Charles Alan Wright to Bryan A. Garner, 20 September 1988 [excerpt]

My wife certainly enjoys your literary style. Almost the only time I ever hear her laugh out loud is when she is reading one of your letters. There were chuckles last night as she read a copy of your letter to Mr. Maugans . . . .

> Sincerely,
>
> Charlie

James D. Maugans to Charles Alan Wright, 26 September 1988 [in full]

Thank you for your letter of September 14, continuing our discussion on the correct form of the complimentary close.

I am sorry to hear that neither reason nor authority can convince you of the correctness of my position. I must confess that I find your arguments and authority equally unpersuasive.

Although it is true that in some instances words can be understood rather than articulated, I do not believe that this is one of those instances for the grammatical reasons I set forth in my article. (The example of the omitted *am* seems to me to be wholly inapposite. That is comparing apples and oranges.)

Since both Fowler and Gowers approve *yours affectionately*, I am certain that they would also approve *cordially yours* and *fondly yours*, although you find them "stilted" and would not use them for anyone with whom you had a close relationship. I, too, would not use either expression for anyone with whom I had a close relationship, but then neither would I use *cordially* or *fondly*, which I find equally stilted. But that's just a personal preference, not a grammatical one.

The position I advocate is supported not only by reason but also by eminent authority (Fowler, Gowers, Freeman). You may, if you choose, follow Mr. Garner. I prefer to cast my lot with the established authorities.

Sincerely yours,

James D. Maugans

Bryan A. Garner to Charles Alan Wright, 3 October 1988 [in full]

We have a word for it—*mumpsimus*—but somehow we have allowed it to become obsolete. A story from the early 16th century has it that an ignorant English priest, when corrected for saying *quod in ore mumpsimus* instead of *sumpsimus*, replied to his critic: "I will not change my old mumpsimus for your new sumpsimus."

By extension, the word came to refer to stubborn adherence to a mistaken verbal form in the face of correction, or to a person determined to perpetuate a wrong usage or word. The most recent use noted by the *OED* is from 1862.

Of course, here we have an example of the "mumpsimus invert," that is, one who, despite gentle correction to show the acceptability of a term he has wrongly obelized, persists in his ill-founded prejudice. He has cast his lot indeed!

Best wishes,

Bryan

Charles Alan Wright to Bryan A. Garner, 5 October 1988 [excerpt]

Every time I receive a letter from you my vocabulary is enriched. I never before heard the word *mumpsimus*, and sometimes I go months on end without using the verb *obelized*. Incidentally even if *OED* shows the most recent use of *mumpsimus* as 1862, Random House 2d has quite a full entry for it without any suggestion that it is obsolete.

. . . If [these letters should ever be published], that could provide a contemporary example of mumpsimus that the editors of the *OED* can include in the Second Edition that I understand is to be published next year.

Sincerely,

Charlie

James D. Maugans to Bryan A. Garner,
24 October 1988 [in full]

Thank you for your letter of September 16, dealing with the question of *sincerely* and *sincerely yours*.

Before I respond on that point, I would like to digress for a moment and address my "erroneous labeling of *yours* as a 'predicate nominative' when the case is clearly possessive." It is true that "Curme terms this use of a pronoun the 'predicate genitive,'" but Curme also says (in a slightly different context, but not so different as to invalidate the point):

> The fact that we cannot supply a noun after *yours* . . . shows plainly that the old possessive genitive in all these cases has become a substantive adjective form, or we may call it a possessive pronoun, for in fact, . . . the substantive form of an adjective is a pronoun. But it should be clearly understood that this pronoun is not the genitive of the old personal pronoun, but the *nominative* of the new pronoun, formed from the substantive form of the possessive adjective. (Vol. II at p. 527. Emphasis added.)

What he has to say two pages later, however, seems to be directly on point: "The substantive forms are also used as nouns, . . . '*Yours* truly' (at the close of a letter)." (*Id.* at 529.)

Therefore, I believe that my labeling *yours* a predicate nominative was correct.

On the question of *sincerely* or *sincerely yours*, I'm afraid that we will have to politely agree to disagree. The only hope for reconciling our differences is your statement that you would consider *sincerely* "less formal." Because the column deals with writing on a formal level, perhaps this is where our disagreement exists.

In any event, thank you for writing. I always enjoy hearing from others who share my interest in the language.

Sincerely yours,

James D. Maugans

CHARLES ALAN WRIGHT

❧ CHAPTER THIRTEEN

Tributes and Autobiographical Essays

The Wit and Wisdom of Charlie Wright: 1927–2000

On Friday, July 7, 2000, Charles Alan Wright died after a series of complications from lung surgery. It was a great loss to law and to letters—a loss noted in moving obituaries that appeared throughout the land. Unlike so many, Wright was fortunate to have had great recognition in life: well-deserved tributes and awards came his way during his last several years.

In 1997, I was fortunate to have been asked to give a talk in his honor. It was delivered on November 1, 1997, in Austin, Texas, as the Orgain Endowed Lecture for Texas Law Review. *Since Professor Wright did so much for the* Scribes Journal—*some of which is discussed in this tribute—the editors decided to dedicate this volume of the* Journal *to him, to reprint this tribute, and to have me update it with a note at the end.*

—B.A.G.

LAST SUMMER, I passed some agreeable hours in Cambridge reading Lord Devlin's memoirs, and I noticed that Devlin referred to Sir Geoffrey Butler as the godfather of his career.[1] For me, that phrase sums up the role that Charles Alan Wright has played in my life. I wouldn't have been reading Devlin, and I certainly wouldn't have been a visiting scholar at Cambridge, if it hadn't been for Wright.

Adapted from *The Scribes Journal of Legal Writing* (1998–2000).
[1] *See* Patrick Devlin, *Taken at the Flood* 47 (1996).

⠀

543

Others have written more or less objective tributes to him.[2] I've been asked instead to write a personal and subjective one. Besides, no one expects a godson—even a figurative one—to be objective.

In August 1977, I arrived at the University of Texas from Canyon, a small college town in the Panhandle. Toward the end of the first semester, I found myself thought-struck by my English professor's brief digression. Dr. James Ayres, of "Shakespeare at Winedale" fame, was telling the class that we all had a rare opportunity: Charles Alan Wright was chairing an investigation into some alleged professorial misconduct at the Pharmacy School. Ayres recommended that we all make time to see Wright in action. Ayres called him a great man.

The next day, in mid-November 1977, I found myself on an elevator with the great man—whom I instinctively recognized—and told him I was there to watch. "Fine," he said. I remember little else of that day, except that, having watched Professor Wright, I felt inspired. I was in awe of Ayres, and Ayres seemed in awe of Wright, so even his "Fine" went a long way.

In 1981, only slightly less green, I enrolled at the law school, where Wright's name is pervasive. I was disappointed to learn that I wouldn't be having Wright's class in constitutional law because he would be teaching a different section—and that wouldn't happen until the spring semester anyway. When the spring semester began, the entire first-year class was buzzing about what had happened on the first day of Wright's course. Professor Wright had walked into class and asked for someone to recite the facts in *Marbury v. Madison*. When nobody responded, he said: "I'm not asking for the law in *Marbury v. Madison*, just the facts. [Pause.] I don't need to learn the facts in *Marbury v. Madison*; I already know them. But I want to be sure that we all have a common understanding. [Pause.] Well, if nobody will recite the facts in *Marbury v. Madison*, there's nothing more to say. Please be prepared tomorrow to discuss *Martin v. Hunter's Lessee*." And he walked out.

I don't recall whether that event influenced me, but I do remember deciding not to enroll in Wright's course on federal courts. Finally, though, after two of my classmates razzed me mercilessly for that decision, I signed up for his Supreme Court seminar. Although I learned that I had been accepted, and was eagerly looking forward to it, I soon discovered that the registrar's office had made a clerical error. I wouldn't be in Wright's seminar after all. So I went through law school without ever hearing Wright lecture.

---

[2] *See, e.g.*, Douglas Laycock, *Charles Alan Wright and The University of Texas School of Law*, 32 Tex. Intl. L.J. 367 (1997).

In a strange way, though, I had developed an imaginary rapport with him. I had discovered his preface to the *Texas Law Review Manual on Style*—a brilliant little essay introducing a well-known style manual. And I had read, and reread, his tribute to Professor Bernie Ward—another remarkable essay.[3] This had led me to *The Law of Federal Courts* for pleasure reading. I admired his writing style.

And in the second conversation that took place between us—if you can call it a "conversation"—I nervously told him so. In 1983, we were again on an elevator together, riding to the fourth floor of Townes Hall, and I told him that I greatly admired his tribute to Professor Ward. His reply was to the point: "Thank you."

Two elevator rides and three words.

I supposed I might never again speak to him. This was no source of anguish or even disappointment to me, really—just a matter of fact. So the friendship that we ultimately developed, as you might gather, was all the more improbable.

My admiration for Wright's prose style, though, was deeper than I've let on. During law school, I was immersed in writing a book that few people knew about. I named it during the first week of my first year: *A Dictionary of Modern Legal Usage*. And I kept it to myself, for the most part.[4] (Once, toward the end of my first year, I told a professor that I was working on it, and he rebuked me scornfully for wasting my time.) Sometime during my second year, I decided that Professor Wright would be my intended reader. After writing each dictionary entry, I'd ask myself, "What would Charles Alan Wright make of this?" It's often a useful device to invent an imaginary critic in this way—especially when the critic is someone whose taste and judgment surpass your own.

Oxford University Press planned to publish the book in 1987, and that spring my editor asked for the names of readers who might supply short reviews for the dust jacket. I suggested two: Professor Wright and Irving Younger. A few weeks later, Oxford sent me a terrific blurb from Younger, but nothing ever came from Wright.

At the time, I was a second-year associate in a Dallas law firm, feeling overworked and underappreciated. Imagine my amazement when I received a congratulatory call from Don Mau, the law school's director of development, during the course of which he told me that Charles Alan Wright was "miffed" at me. Essentially, he said: "You asked Charlie Wright to say something for your dust jacket, and then you didn't even use it.

---

[3] *See* Charles Alan Wright, *The Wit and Wisdom of Bernie Ward*, 61 Texas L. Rev. 13 (1982).

[4] *See* Garner, *Finding the Right Words*, 67 Mich. B.J. 762 (1988).

Let me just tell you—you don't ask Charlie Wright to write something for you and then not use it." Not only did he suggest that Professor Wright was angry at me, he also told me that Wright was preparing a review of the book.

All this had me trembling, of course. When I called Oxford—still never having had any direct contact with Wright—my editor assured me that nothing had come in from Wright's office. So I suggested that she call Professor Wright to clear this up because I certainly didn't want him angry at me.

Two days later—on November 20, 1987, almost precisely a decade after first laying eyes on the man—I received a letter from Professor Wright. This letter became, for a week or so, the hottest topic of conversation among my closest friends from law school. He allayed my fears, but only after building some suspense:

November 18, 1987

Dear Mr. Garner:

When I was abroad in June the Oxford University Press sent me an advance copy of your book, *A Dictionary of Modern Legal Usage*, and asked if I would care to make some comment that could be used for publicity purposes. My secretary wrote to say that she did not know if I would be back in time or if, with the press of things when I got back, I would be able to undertake that. I certainly have a clear impression that when I came back I did send Oxford University Press something of the sort and that I sent you a copy of it, but my secretaries cannot find any trace of this in my files so perhaps I am simply dreaming about it.

In any event the Law School alumni publication, *Townes Hall Notes*, received a review copy and I have agreed to do a short review for them. I almost wish that I had not accepted their invitation, since now that I have had a chance to look more closely into the book I find so many splendid things in it that I wish I were doing a longer review than the 500 words I am allowed by *Townes Hall Notes*. I care a good deal about words and their proper usage and on every point I have looked up so far—the serial comma, the difference between "that" and "which," the spelling of "judgment" and "willful," and whether to use "a" or "an"— you and I agree. This shows what a good book you have written. What I like especially is the light touch that shows up so many places in the book. I think you have made a truly valuable contribution to legal writers and to the language, and I congratulate you on it.

I am of course calling to the attention of the editors of the *Texas Law Review* the fact that at page 542 you characterize their *Manual of Style* as among the "lightweight authorities." . . .

I do have two specific questions for which the answer would be helpful for even a much-too-short review. First, what is the price of the book? . . . Second, do you have any academic training in linguistics or lexicography or any such discipline, or does this book just show that a graduate of The University of Texas Law School can take on any task and do it splendidly?

Sincerely,

Charles Alan Wright

I must have read this letter a hundred times before responding. It's undoubtedly the most important letter I've ever received for several reasons, the most prominent of which is that it marked the beginning of my friendship with Charlie.

Of course, he didn't become "Charlie" immediately—in fact, the gestation period for that change was nine months. During those months between November 1987 and September 1988, we began corresponding voluminously, mostly on questions of language. I remember once receiving three letters in one day, plus a fax. And I would always respond immediately. On rare days when the mail brought nothing from Austin, I felt quite disappointed.

In July 1988, he sent me a five-page letter—not so unusual—in which, toward the end, he acknowledged how copious our exchanges had gotten:

> I was going to look back through our correspondence to see if we have ever exchanged views on the use of italics or similar typographical tricks as a means of emphasis. Unfortunately, though we did not begin to correspond until the end of November, the file is now 2⅛ inches thick and I do not have time to search through it. This is a point that I hope will appear in your *Elements of Legal Style* because to me it is important. I am strongly against this practice. I was taught many years ago that the way to emphasize something is to use emphatic words rather than a different type style. As you know, I do a great deal of work with other lawyers in litigation, and ordinarily have them do the first draft of briefs. I have more trouble trying to persuade them not to use italics every other sentence than with any other single point. [7 July 1988]

My wife said one day, "Why does he write all these letters to *you*?" (I must italicize to show her inflection. Sorry, Charlie.) She intuitively grasped what I had long been wondering. Why me? How does he manage these long, involved letters, given all the other things he has to do? And how many correspondents does he have?

I've since learned, of course, that his letters to me are only a drip from the faucet. And one delightful thing about his letters is the glimpse you'll often get into his working life and his personal life. Still early in our friendship—before we'd ever spoken face to face, apart from the two elevator rides—he began a letter in a way that shed some light on his copiousness:

> One of my least endearing characteristics is that I find it very hard to do only one thing at a time. My mind is capable of operating on two levels, and it seems the most efficient use of my time to do two things. This is a terrible nuisance to my secretaries. I will be dictating to them as I am working on something else at my desk, but then I will get so interested in the thing I am working on that I will forget what it was I was saying in my dictation, and will have to have them read their notes back to me to find out where I was. All of this lengthy explanation is necessary because this morning I was dictating a letter to Pat Higginbotham . . . to put in a plug for you . . . . [9 May 1988]

That last part, of course, was typical. In short order, he was going to extraordinary lengths to put in plugs for me. He drew me into correspondence with Supreme Court justices, with English judges, and with American and English academics who, among lawyers, are household names. He became not only a mentor but also an enthusiastic promoter. I've always thought that was unusual, coming from such an eminent person.

Within a few months, his letters revealed more about himself personally and about his family. One of the most heartening letters I ever received was the one in which he introduced me to Custis:

> My wife certainly enjoys your literary style. Almost the only time I ever hear her laugh out loud is when she is reading one of your letters. There were chuckles last night as she read a copy of your letter to Mr. Maugans, and I am sure there will be some tonight when I take home your letter of September 16. [20 Sept. 1988]

Once I learned that Custis reads all his correspondence every night, I started taking some account of that in my own letters. And shortly after that exchange, Custis became a researcher for me, gathering lots of lexicographic information that I find useful to this day.

But I'm getting ahead of myself. Our progression from a purely *in rem* friendship to an *in personam* friendship was a quick one. During the year or so in which we communicated only by mail, I worried about whether he would like me in person. I suppose he might have worried a little as well, though Charlie has never been racked with self-doubt. In the summer of 1988 we met at the law school, shortly before I became a faculty member. It was a brief meeting in his office, and soon after that we saw each other often as I commuted each week between Dallas and Austin.

Shortly before Charlie and I met, Ellen Dupree—a classmate of mine who had become a journalist—called me because she was at work on an article about him. Somebody had suggested that she should interview me.

In her manuscript, which unfortunately was never published, she quoted me as saying, "It was a big step when the letters went from 'Charles Alan Wright' to 'Charlie' all of a sudden, which was a couple of months ago. Naturally, I still address him as Professor Wright, and I think I always will." Soon after she finished the manuscript and sent it both to me and to Wright, he wrote me a three-page letter that ended: "I notice in Ellen's article that you are going to continue to call me 'Professor Wright.' You surely cannot do that when you join this faculty. I have had many colleagues over the years and I have always been 'Charlie' to all of them." And so, in my next letter, I forswore myself and called him "Charlie." He responded promptly:

> I am glad that you have forsworn yourself [and begun using my first name]. But now that I am "Charlie," how is it that you have become [in your signature] "Bryan A. Garner"? Am I now required to call you "Professor Garner"? [12 Sept. 1988]

I hadn't before noticed how often people sign their full name even when the salutation mentions only the recipient's first name. I've since noticed, though, that lawyers engage in this abominable practice all the time. Charlie cured me of it.

Of course, Charlie has always been a stickler for matters of propriety. Sometime after I joined the UT law faculty in September 1988—a development that, as you might suspect, Charlie was largely responsible for— I asked my secretary to send him an article. Later that morning I had a memo in response. It concluded as follows:

> Since I started writing this memorandum, there has appeared on my desk a photocopy of an article from *Verbatim* on "The 23rd Psalm and Me, or Has the Nightingale Become a Crow?" This is attached to a note that says, in its entirety: "TO: Professor Charles Alan Wright FROM: Professor Bryan A. Garner." From this I deduce that you must have sent me the article. I look forward with great interest to reading it, and am heartened to see some indication that you still recognize the existence of the Bible. I hope the note does not mean that I may no longer call you "Bryan" and am required always to address you as "Professor Bryan A. Garner." Even if I am now required to use your title in Townes Hall, may I dispense with it when I take you to Tarry House for dinner? [1 Nov. 1988]

As you might imagine, I enjoyed making him call me "Professor Garner" throughout dinner.

Soon after I established my office at the law school—and no doubt before we ever had dinner—I invited Charlie to lunch. The message I got back was that he would be in the small faculty lunchroom near his office at 12:05, and that he would be finished at 12:15. He said he'd be having a can of soup prepared by his secretaries, and that I should bring my own lunch. When I told some other colleague that day that I'd be lunching with Charlie, he expressed great surprise: "No one ever has lunch with Charlie. That is, not since Bernie Ward died." Well, I occasionally did meet Charlie for lunch, but only when we had something pressing to talk about. He would walk in at 12:05, sit down, and talk genially. At 12:15—sometimes in mid-conversation—he would stand. And before the stroke of 12:16, he was gone. He had books to write, after all.

More often than having lunch, though, we'd have dinner together. Whenever Custis was out of town and I was in town, Charlie would have me as his guest at the Tarry House, one of his clubs here in Austin. Having dinner with Charlie was very different from lunching with him: whereas lunch was largely a functional refueling, dinner was an aesthetic experience to be savored while engaging in leisurely conversation and good-natured banter. Charlie always introduced me to various members of the club—such as the late James Michener and his wife—and even introduced me to his favorite wines and his favorite aperitif: a gin martini on the rocks, very dry, with several green olives. (No one should assume that Charlie is a great influence in every way.)

This drink finds its apotheosis at one of Charlie's two clubs in Manhattan: the Century Association. When we were there a few years ago, he introduced me to the Century martini: a dry gin martini (with extra-large olives) with a small pitcher of extra gin on the side. The amazing thing is that he dines there only once a year or so, but when he walks in everybody knows who he is.

What I mean to suggest—though I haven't yet said it directly—seems to go to the core of Charlie's being. For him, life is an art form, and the good life means striving for excellence in all things. He does this in various ways: the finest scholarship, the finest tastes, the finest clothes, the finest suites in the finest hotels, the finest restaurants, the finest classes of travel, the finest in everything. Excellence is an end in itself.

Charlie allows that he doesn't always have the finest possible taste, so he relies on Custis—his *arbiter elegantiarum*, as he often calls her. And for anyone who knows her, she is just that.

He doesn't ever talk this way about fine things, of course. He simply epitomizes them. He certainly has demanded excellence of me in our dealings. I think, for example, of an exchange we had a few months after I joined the law faculty. On April 17, 1989, he asked me about a statement I had made in *A Dictionary of Modern Legal Usage*—which, by then, we both referred to as *DMLU*. I had written that the generic feminine pronoun is "commonly used by American legal publishers."[5] He wanted my evidence. I responded, but he didn't find the response satisfactory. Ten days later I found a long memo waiting for me. It began as follows:

> On April 17th I sent you a typically terse and to-the-point note inquiring to what you were referring when you said, at page 500 of *DMLU*, that *as anybody can see for herself* "is commonly used by American legal publishers." I expected that within the hour, or surely by the next morning if you were not in the building that afternoon, I would have an answer. The following day you did send me a memorandum on the subject, but you were something less than your usual didactic—or perhaps even dogmatic—self. Your response was four paragraphs long, but only one spoke to my question.

He didn't like my answer and, in an 1800-word memo, explained why. Toward the end, he wrote:

> Almost two weeks have now gone by since I first put this question to you and I am no wiser than I was then about feminine pronouns as generic or about the supposed practices of American legal publishers. But even if I am unenlightened on this subject, I have had great insight into why dictionaries take so many years to produce. To those who take the long view that "44 years is a small period in the life of a language," it is not an oxymoron to speak of "all deliberate speed." . . . Like a glacier ponderously creeping down to the sea, crushing everything in its path, the progress of a dictionary is not visible to the naked eye. [27 Apr. 1989]

I must have responded by e-mail, but my files don't contain the answer. (I'm reluctant to admit this precisely because Professor Wright might be tempted to utter, "Typical. Typical.") Later that same day, though, I received a 1200-word response suggesting that my new reply was little better. It began with a continuation of his metaphor:

> The glacier is a silly millimeter nearer the shore. Your belated response to my question about your statement at page 500 of *DMLU* has at last arrived. It shows that you and I are in significant accord on how a writer should handle this problem . . . . It does little to justify what you have said in print about "American legal publishers."

It ended with yet another fillip:

> It is now 6:10 and my secretaries have left for the day, so that I cannot get it to you immediately. We are leaving on a 6:05 plane tomorrow

---

[5] Garner, *A Dictionary of Modern Legal Usage* 500 (1st ed. 1987).

morning, but I will leave this and ask Mrs. Kieke to get it to you early tomorrow. I regret the delay. [27 Apr. 1989]

I'm sure that my next response was no better. It came on May 2. I think it took me that long to recover.

As I've mentioned, our correspondence has been abundant. Some of it has already been published in *The Scribes Journal of Legal Writing*—no fewer than 17 pages on the fascinating question whether it's acceptable to sign off a letter with the complimentary close *Sincerely*—as opposed to *Sincerely yours*.[6] That exchange, on what might mistakenly seem a trivial issue, generated a greater response than any other piece that has ever appeared in the *Scribes Journal*. Three Supreme Court justices—William Brennan, Harry Blackmun, and Sandra Day O'Connor—reacted favorably to the piece, as did Judge Ruth Bader Ginsburg (then on the D.C. Circuit).[7] And Justice Blackmun mentioned that Justice White was discussing the *Journal* in Conference sometime in March 1992.[8]

I had begun editing the *Scribes Journal* in 1989, and Charlie helped get it off to a good start by contributing to several of our first volumes. In doing this, he was breaking with his long-standing practice of not writing for law reviews. But I didn't realize what a treacherous question it was when, in October 1989, I asked him to write a short piece for the *Journal*. His memo took me aback:

October 4, 1989

TO: BRYAN A. GARNER

FROM: CHARLES ALAN WRIGHT

Via Hand Delivery

You have done enough. Have you no decency, sir, at long last? Have you left no sense of decency?[9]

Is there to be no end? First, I am asked to do a Preface for *Elements*. Then I am asked to read the manuscript of that work to see if I have any suggestions. Now I am asked to write something for a publication of which I have never heard, *Scribes Journal of Legal Writing*. Worse yet, this request is pressed upon me after I have already declined it once,

---

[6] *See An Epistolary Essay: The Wright–Garner–Maugans Correspondence on Complimentary Closes*, 2 Scribes J. Legal Writing 83 (1991).

[7] *See A Sequel to "An Epistolary Essay": More on Complimentary Closes*, 3 Scribes J. Legal Writing 95 (1992).

[8] *See id.* at 100.

[9] Joseph N. Welch, counsel for the U.S. Army, responding to Senator Joseph McCarthy on 9 June 1954, during the Army–McCarthy hearings (as quoted in *Respectfully Quoted* 223 (Suzy Platt ed., 1989)).

pointing out that to accept it would violate my long-held policy of writing no articles except tributes to dead or retiring friends.

It is true that I have told you that I am always willing to act as research assistant and Westlaw operator for your beautiful and brilliant researcher, Custis Wright. But there are only 168 hours in the week, and if I am to devote as many of these as you seem to expect to the greater glory of The University of Texas School of Law [and your projects], which of my own activities do you suggest I give up?

1. Vice presidency of the American Law Institute.
2. Coaching Legal Eagles.
3. Keeping Austin safe for classical music.
4. Outside litigation.
5. Sleep.
6. All of the above.

If you were a man of decency, you would not make this request.

If I were a man of common sense, I would refuse the request. But how can I say "No" to you? I will do a short piece, building on my exchange of letters with Judge Haynsworth, on the proper use of literary and Biblical allusions. I will leave it to you to offer one of your patented rationalizations when some indignant editor says to me: "What do you mean you can't write for me because you never write articles? You wrote one for the *Scribes Journal of Legal Writing*. Is it better than the (*Harvard Law Review, Supreme Court Historical Society Yearbook, American Bar Association Journal*, etc., etc.)?"

What can I possibly say on literary allusions that is not already better said in *DMLU*? (As you know I am less enchanted by your essay on BIBLICAL AFFECTATION.) What is the deadline? Am I correct in assuming that I should not refer to you or to *DMLU*? At a quick look I see nothing on point in Fowler, Follett, or Strunk & White.

Have you no decency, sir, at long last? Have you left no sense of decency?

I'm sure I found this quite unsettling. I certainly wasn't overjoyed that he had said he would contribute something under these circumstances, and so I replied without reference to that:

October 4, 1989

TO: CHARLES ALAN WRIGHT

FROM: BRYAN A. GARNER

By hand delivery

Alack, I have no eyes.

—Gloucester, in *King Lear*, IV.v.60.

Nor any decency, by that lack of vision. I will extenuate only by saying that I have seen you write letters and memoranda—or, more accurately, not the writing but the products themselves—that surpass in thought, complexity, and art what I would be overjoyed to include as a note in the first issue of the *Scribes Journal*. I meant no indecency with my impetrations, even if the result was indecent.

I cheerfully withdraw my request, and beg your forgiveness.

Later that afternoon came another memo from Charlie. He was serious about wanting to contribute:

October 4, 1989

TO: BRYAN A. GARNER

FROM: CHARLES ALAN WRIGHT

Via Hand Delivery

"O reason not the need!" said poor mad old Lear, and in this case I am with him.[10]

May I please have answers to the questions I put to you in the penultimate paragraph of my memorandum to you of even date?

The "hand delivery" notation on these memos means a different thing for him and for me, by the way. On his, it means that he had one of his secretaries—either Miss Bartsch or Mrs. Kieke—bring his memos to me. On mine, it means that I personally took my memos to his secretaries. I had one memo left to write on that fateful October day:

October 4, 1989
4:55 p.m.

TO: CHARLES ALAN WRIGHT

FROM: BRYAN A. GARNER

By hand delivery

In writing my previous memorandum to you, I addressed only the questions in the ultimate paragraph of yours, where you let fly the upshot. I no longer thought of the questions in the penultimate, much less the antepenultimate, paragraph.

You might develop the thought that you have already so well expressed to Judge Haynsworth, namely, how well Judge Friendly used literary allusions that, even if they were unfamiliar to the reader, nevertheless aided the reader's comprehension. That is a rare art indeed. I see

---

[10] Bernard J. Ward, in a 1971 letter to Judge J. Braxton Craven, Jr., quoted in Wright, *The Wit and Wisdom of Bernie Ward*, 61 Texas L. Rev. 13, 27 (1982).

no reason why you should be asked not to refer to *DMLU*. (But that may simply be another manifestation of my indecency.)

Seriously, though, I realize now that I have asked too much. It is one thing to be as indebted to another human being as much as I already am to you; it is quite another to presume to increase the debt beyond all reasonable limits. Please therefore ignore the penultimate paragraph of this memorandum, and thereby help me preserve my belatedly discovered sense of decency.

But he didn't ignore my request, and he has now contributed three pieces to the *Scribes Journal*.[11] I haven't imposed on him any further since 1993— at least not for the *Journal*.

In corresponding with Charlie, I often felt that his side of the letters ought to be published. He sometimes refers to what historians will one day make of our letters. As with his comment in the very first letter I received—the one saying that the soundness of my book was demonstrated by the fact that he agreed with it—I wonder whether it's a joke or a straight-faced comment. Whatever the answer is, I also earnestly hope that our letters won't be made public until the year 2020 or so. Though I'm sharing a few of the letters here, historians should have to wait awhile.

But just in case that doesn't happen, I might as well share the most embarrassing exchange I ever had with Charlie. It happened on February 14, 1989. By then, of course, Charlie and I had seen each other and dined together many times. He had even sent me a birthday card the previous November (and has always done so since). When I arrived that morning from Dallas, I had an e-mail from Charlie with only three words: "Where's my valentine?" I puzzled over this for a few minutes, and then responded: "I hadn't realized that you expected one. Happy Valentines!" This embarrassed me somewhat, but it was nothing compared to the embarrassment I felt when he sent me his next message: "Where's Custis? I've been trying to locate her and thought she might have stopped by your office." In fact I had seen her, and I told him where she could be found. But somehow I hadn't realized what he meant when he said, in a three-word message, "Where's my valentine?"

I could quote endlessly from Charlie's letters to illuminate his various qualities as a man, scholar, and mentor. What I most want to illustrate is that he is every bit as demanding as he is loyal: even as he publicly promoted

---

[11] See *An Epistolary Essay: The Wright–Garner–Maugans Correspondence on Complimentary Closes*, note 6; Charles Alan Wright, *How I Write*, 4 Scribes J. Legal Writing 87 (1993); Charles Alan Wright, *Literary Allusion in Legal Writing: The Haynsworth–Wright Letters*, 1 Scribes J. Legal Writing 1 (1990).

me, he privately goaded me. In November 1989, he sent me a copy of a letter to his friend in Houston, W. Dalton Tomlin, with whom he was collaborating on a brief. The opening line of the letter was vintage Wright: "Your memory has improved with age. (But then there was always much room for improvement.)" Essentially, it was a two-and-a-half-page letter saying that *coconspirator* should not be hyphenated. He quoted me three times in support of his view. Four days later, I sent him a *DMLU* entry that he had missed, on page 119, in which I suggested that *coconspirator* actually should be hyphenated. In response I got a one-page blast:

October 29, 1989

TO: BRYAN A. GARNER

FROM: CHARLES ALAN WRIGHT

"This ties it, *this* does." I quote of course from the late great Bernard J. Ward, 61 Texas L. Rev. at 26.

I perhaps could have found words enough on my own to express my shock and dismay that we should have on this faculty someone so careless that he does not even read his electronic mail. My vocabulary, however, is not equal to expressing my feelings when I received your note yesterday concerning *coconspirator*.

As you will have seen from the memorandum I received yesterday from Dalton Tomlin, a copy of which I have sent you, he has come to like *coconspirator* without a hyphen. I am going to advise him immediately that he must burn all copies of *DMLU* that may have accidentally crept into Vinson & Elkins . . . . You may be sure that never again will I send out memoranda singing the praises of the author of that scurrilous book or the forthcoming *The Elements of Legal Style*.

I am torn between surprise, sorrow, and anger. It is fortunate that I must not have noticed page 119 of *DMLU* or my review of it would have taken a very different tone. Your attempt there to give guarded support to the use of a hyphen is not convincing even on its own terms. This is not an instance in which "the hyphenated form is established," there is no risk that "the unhyphenated form may leave the reader to mistake the syllables," and surely no writer can believe that he is "creating a new form" when he uses the word. Thus, it does not fall under any of the three exceptions you state earlier on the page to your general rule that a hyphen should not be used with the prefix *co*. The strange justification—I will not dignify it by calling it a reason—that you offer for putting a hyphen when the prefix is attached to *conspirator* would apply to *codefendant*, yet you do not even suggest that there should be a hyphen in that word.

I cannot imagine why Oxford University Press would even think of having you prepare a new edition of Fowler. He was forward-looking enough to say that "perhaps we may write *coworker*, as Americans already do, without feeling nervous about the cow.". . . [Y]ou are better qualified to be president of the Society for the Prevention of Cruelty to Bovines than you are to revise Fowler.

My response to this—dated the same day—must have been somewhat more satisfactory than some of my others. That's largely because it arrived on the same day as the memo to which it was responding. But I know a response is good when it doesn't elicit any further reply from Professor Wright.

Dalton Tomlin and I, of course, aren't alone in receiving Charlie's letters about English usage. His collaborators get instructions anytime they send something his way. In fact, his contributions on usage are so prolific—yet so unknown—that *Texas Law Review* ought to do an entire issue called "Wright on English Usage." It would contain gems like these:

On *and/or*

"[With] horror . . . I read for the first time this morning the entry on 'and/or.' I am shocked that you could find anything to say in defense of that barbarous phrase. Actually you could not find much to say in its defense. . . . [Almost] everything you say in three-quarters of a page on the subject is critical and shows why this should never be used. You and I had occasion very early in our correspondence to exchange views on the *Texas Law Review Manual on Style*. It is certainly fallible, but on this subject it is much sounder than Garner. It does not waste three-quarters of a page on 'and/or.' Half a line is enough. The entry, in its entirety, says: 'Do not use this construction.' From the mouths of babes." [10 Mar. 1988]

"I found your comments on 'and/or' interesting, but ultimately unpersuasive. It seems to me that the only people who say this is okay in legal documents, though they would not allow it at other times, are nonlawyers who do not feel confident enough to tell us lawyers how we should write . . . . I must have written millions of words on legal matters in the last 42 years, but I never once have found any need to use the expression. I do not think that this is 'a battle that was long ago lost.' If hopes were dupes, fears may be liars. It may be, in yon smoke concealed, your friends chase e'en now the fliers and but for you possess the field." [21 Mar. 1988]

On *befriend*

"Your letter to Ted Megarry is an excellent one. I wonder if I dare even ask whether you, the great expert on usage, could perhaps have nodded in . . . your statement that you wrote the example using *perspicacious* 'long before I befriended Charlie.' To me 'befriend' carries the suggestion of taking another person under one's wing. I do not have *OED* in my office. The *Concise Oxford Dictionary* defines 'befriend' as 'help, favour.' The *Oxford American Dictionary* gives the definition 'to act as a friend to, to be kind and helpful to.' *Random House 2d* gives similar definitions and provides an example: 'to befriend the poor and the weak.' I would be the first to admit that I am poor and weak and that at least in matters of usage I need to be taken under an expert's wing, but is that the meaning you wanted to convey to Sir Robert?" [8 Nov. 1988]

On Quotations

"It is always very dangerous to say something that can be quoted against you to devastating effect because the quotation, while absolutely precise, is wildly out of context. The classic example, of course, is to ask someone if they know that it says in the Bible 'there is no God.' If you look at Psalm 14:1 (or Psalm 53:1—why did the compilers of the Old Testament not recognize that these two Psalms are essentially identical?), you will see how misleading even a precise quotation can be." [4 Apr. 1990]

On *that* and *which*

[A correspondent of mine argued that the use of *that* and *which* is "at least a question on which reasonable people can differ." Professor Wright responded:] "I do not think this is true, but even if I did I would wonder what that proved. Reasonable people can differ on whether it is more desirable to drive on the right-hand side of the road, as in this country and Europe, or on the left, as in England and many parts of the Empire. But if you rent a car when you are in England in December, I fervently pray that you will stay on the left-hand side, regardless of all the reasonable arguments you might make for the superiority of right-hand driving. I fear people would be confused if they saw you driving in the right-hand lane and this confusion could cause sad consequences. Similar confusion and sad consequences follow when writers do not observe the distinction between *that* and *which*." [8 Nov. 1988]

For anyone with access to Wright's letters—not just to me, but to all his correspondents—it would be quite possible to increase this small sampling a hundredfold. But for now, his offerings are all unpublished and scattered.

I could go on with endless digressions about Charlie. He's complex in some ways, but he has simplicity of character. I haven't even hinted at

many parts of the man: his devotion to family; his service to the Episco-
pal Church; his love of football and coaching of the Legal Eagles; his tireless work on behalf of KMFA to ensure that Austin has an endless supply of first-rate classical music; his representation of President Richard
Nixon in the Watergate-tapes cases; his work as president of the American Law Institute; his work as principal author of *Federal Practice and Procedure*, the most widely cited treatise in American law. He and I have
talked about these things, but between the two of us they're not nearly
as interesting as whether a hyphen belongs in *coconspirator.* And I have the
uneasy feeling that this question is even more interesting to him than it
is to me. Which is simply to concede that he's the greater scholar.

Indeed, he's the quintessential scholar. In a memorable law-review
article, he has defined a true scholar as someone who doesn't let answerable questions go unanswered.[12] Whenever a question comes up between
us, even over dinner—once it was which U.S. Open was the last that
Walter Hagen won—I'll receive a message the next morning letting me
know the answer. He doesn't sit idly by and say, "Well, I wonder." He
always finds the answer if it's possible to do so.

But though he's a great scholar—probably the greatest legal scholar
of our day—he's no pedant. He never gets lost in a welter of citations.
And he has warned me when he thought I was getting pedantic, as he
did back in 1990:

> I admire your pedantry in footnote 9 in citing an article, published long
> before you were born, in the University of Western Australia Law
> Review. When I was your age I used to indulge in such amiable fool-
> ishness. See Wright, *The Law of Remedies as a Social Institution*, 18 U. Det.
> L.J. 376, 378 n.3 (1955), with a nice quotation about "such anachro-
> nisms as the platypus" quoting from a speech reported in the Australian
> Law Journal. [20 Apr. 1990]

In saying that he's probably the greatest legal scholar of our day, I
don't mean to sell him short. Here's what Justice Ruth Bader Ginsburg has
said: "Like a Colossus, Charles Alan Wright stands at the summit of our
profession, and all who practice the lawyer's craft profit from his prodigious

---

[12] Charles Alan Wright, *How Many Catz Can Stand on the Head of a Pin, or Andrew Lloyd
Webber, Where Are You Now That We Need You?* 13 Nova L. Rev. 1 (1988) ("The hallmark
of a true scholar is that he or she cannot stand idle whenever an answerable question
remains unanswered. It does not matter how far removed the question may be from the
scholar's field or how important, indeed even pedantic, the question may be. Nature's
reaction to a vacuum is positively tolerant compared to the true scholar's reaction to an
unanswered question.").

production."[13] He's also quite possibly the most gifted advocate of our day. Here's what Arthur Miller says about him as an adversary: "When he argues, you get the feeling that you're up against Moses . . . . And Moses can bring down the word of God! [Wright] project[s] an almost divine status, an enormous self-assuredness backed up by an enormously imposing physical presence—his size, his voice, just who he is!"[14]

To have been a friend of this man—a close friend—is one of the greatest honors I could ever have. When I stood with him in the elevator in November 1977, he uttered one word to me, and I was awed. When he wrote to me in November 1987, saying that he liked my book, I was overawed. And now I stand before you, in November 1997, paying tribute to the man who, if I put family aside, is my very closest friend. There's a wonderful symmetry to that highly improbable sequence of events.

Of course, there are many who feel similarly about Charlie. Despite his intimidating exterior, there's not a more companionable person in the world. John P. Frank of Phoenix summed it up well in a letter he recently shared with me:

> [H]is friendships . . . have an intensity and a steadiness that most of us can't match. Bernie Ward and Ron Degnan are illustrations among the departed. Charlie and I have been linked with iron bands since about 1950, though we are rarely together. The companionship is among the warmest in my life when we are at the same place. . . . By repute, Charlie is austere in many of his dealings. But there are those of us, and I assume at Austin too, who don't have a warmer friend in the world. His capacity for affection is as great as his capacity for loyalty . . . or his capacity for formality. For his friends, at least, there is no more comfortable companion. [7 Oct. 1997]

I know there are others who feel that way, and some are assembled at this symposium.

But this tribute, unlike most, doesn't mark an end. It marks the beginning. Now that Charlie no longer has full-time teaching duties at the law school, much of his time has been freed up. He and I no longer

---

[13] Ruth Bader Ginsburg, Statement Presenting the 1989 Fellows Research Award of the American Bar Foundation 7 (4 Feb. 1989) (on file).

[14] Michael Bowden, *Arthur Miller*, Law. Wkly. USA, 28 July 1997, at B5 (naming Wright as one of the two most formidable advocates Miller has faced); *see also May It Please the Court: The Most Significant Oral Arguments Made Before the Supreme Court Since 1955*, at 321 (Peter Irons & Stephanie Guitton eds., 1993) (reproducing Wright's argument in *San Antonio Independent School District v. Rodriguez*, 411 U.S. 1 (1973), the landmark case on public-school finance).

exchange daily 1200-word memos—primarily because he knows that I don't use e-mail. (Recently he dubbed me the Last of the Luddites.) And although his secretaries tell me that his lunches have expanded from 10 to 15 minutes, that doesn't use up much time. So now that he has all this free time on his hands, I think we should expect many more volumes of *Federal Practice and Procedure* each year, and a new edition of *The Law of Federal Courts* at least every six months.

Your readers are eager for more, Charlie. And I've let the secret out.

In the modern age, it's unfashionable to think of a "great man" or a "great woman." But most people who know Charles Alan Wright in more than a passing way think of him as a great man. That in itself is an extraordinary tribute. And the people who hold that opinion are judges and lawyers of the first rank, and many others—even English professors. It says something that I can't capture in words. And together we can't capture it in our applause, but I ask you to join me in expressing gratitude and affection for this great man for what he is.

* * *

I saw Charlie three times in the last year of his life—in December, in March, and in May. Although he didn't look well, he traveled extensively, and less than a month before going into the hospital, he chaired the four-day proceedings of the American Law Institute in Washington, D.C. At the ALI's annual banquet, he introduced Lord Woolf of Barnes with great verve, and in his concluding remarks his impromptu wit was as sharp as ever.

We corresponded up until the time he went into the hospital. On June 12, he sent a letter explaining that he would have to undergo an operation to remove a fungus ball in one lung—and that he was canceling his trip to Europe scheduled for June 14. It ended stoically but not hopefully:

> It seems terribly unfair that the fungus should come just at this time. But early Saturday, as I was awake briefly in a Philadelphia hotel, the words of a hymn went through my mind. I know the words of the third and fourth verses of the hymn and I remember the tune. I know the hymn is one of those sung each year at graduation at St. Stephen's School. But I have no idea what the first or second verses are or what the name is. The words that came to me are the last half of the third verse:
>
> > Take what He gives.
> > And praise Him still
> > Through good or ill,
> > Whoever lives.

My life has been richly blessed. Many, many good things have come to
me over the years, and little that is bad. Sad as this disappointment is, I
have no right to complain about it.

As always,

Charlie

On July 7, I had just finished teaching a seminar in Kansas City
when I heard the devastating news of Charlie's death a few hours before.
I was on my way to New York City for the Scribes annual meeting. On
the way to the airport, I felt I couldn't really travel to New York. I
needed to be in Austin to see Custis. So that's where I went.

Several days later, I received a note in the mail from Nancy Kruh, a
Dallas journalist who interviewed Charlie for a 1999 article about me.
To my astonishment, she sent me a transcript of the interview. Her penul-
timate question to Charlie was whether he considered himself my mentor.

He answered: "I don't know. I can't think of anything I have taught
him, and that's what I would think of as a mentor. Perhaps I've been an
example of how to carry yourself. I've learned from him, and I do my
best to prove him wrong."

Then she asked whether he kept score. "It's like a romance," Charlie
said. "You don't keep score."

That's exactly how it was—for me and for many others who knew
the colossus we called Charlie.

≈ ≈ ≈

Charles Alan Wright:
The Legend and the Man

*This eulogy was delivered as a luncheon speech at a daylong symposium
at the University of Texas School of Law commemorating the life and work
of Professor Wright. The symposium took place in October 2000.*

THIS IS NOT GOING to be easy for me. As many of you know, I had the
opportunity to eulogize Charlie in life. Many of you were there. That
was challenging but fun—enormous fun. I had 45 minutes to talk about
some little-known sides of a man I loved deeply. To eulogize him in
death is infinitely harder—and, even after four months, hardly bearable.
But Charlie was nothing if not dignified, and he always expected me to
be dignified, so I will try here to measure up.

While we may comfort ourselves that Charlie is now in a better
place—a place he fervently believed in—it is difficult for any of us to
understand—truly understand—the loss to American law that occurred
on July 7.

Maybe I can put it into perspective by relating one of my last face-
to-face conversations with Charlie, on May 16. We were in Washington,
D.C., at an ALI reception. Charlie and Custis and I were together at a
table, and I decided to tell Charlie about a small joke I had worked into
my lecture on providing smooth transitions between paragraphs—something that very few lawyers do competently. For years I've used one of
Charlie's briefs—a 1984 Fifth Circuit brief—to illustrate how a masterly
writer provides, at the beginning of every paragraph, not just a topic
sentence but a transition from the previous paragraph. Since I do many
seminars every year out of state, I had worked in a new segment to lead
into Charlie's brief—a segment that I think this audience in particular
can appreciate. It went like this, and this is what I told Charlie and Custis
that night:

> Before we look at this example from Charles Alan Wright, let me just
> say a word about him. He's the most widely cited writer in Anglo-
> American legal history. It's fair to say that he has eclipsed Blackstone.
> His writings have been cited in more than 62,000 judicial decisions

Adapted from *Charles Alan Wright: The Man and the Scholar* (2000).

and law-review articles. Imagine that. On average, the United States Supreme Court relies on his writings about ten times a year—whether it's *The Law of Federal Courts* or the multivolume treatise, *Federal Practice and Procedure.*

And then I'd add:

You know, I was trying to remember just this morning where he teaches. Does anybody know?

Invariably, someone would speak up: "Texas." And then I'd say: "Oh, yes, Texas. Thank you for reminding us all."

Charlie guffawed when he heard this. Custis was also amused. I used it in probably 50 lectures earlier this year. The last time was in Kansas City, on that fateful day of July 7.

Like many of you—maybe all of you except for his family—I knew Charlie as a legend before I knew him as a man and as a friend. He said one word to me in November 1977, in response to something I said on an elevator; he said two words to me in 1983, in response to something I said on our second elevator ride together; and then I got a long letter from him in November 1987—a letter that would change my life, one that he wrote in response to my first book. But I've written extensively about all that in *Texas Law Review.*[1]

I've said repeatedly, and I told Charlie several times, that I'm glad I never had a class from him. I would never, I think, have developed the rapport with him that I did. That gain had a corresponding loss, though: I never felt the terror of having Professor Wright call on me in class—or even of fearing that he might.

All in all, I'm glad that I knew him only as a friend. I seemed to be one of the few people who felt comfortable ribbing him. And he ribbed *me* mercilessly—if a little formally.

I could tell countless anecdotes about Charlie, but this isn't the time or the place. Let me sum up with four big lessons I learned from Charlie. He lived by these, and he conveyed each of them in countless letters to me. The first is never to leave till tomorrow what you can do today— I think this goes a long way toward explaining his productivity. The second is never to leave an answerable question unanswered. This, I think, helps explain the depth and quality of his scholarship. The third is never to worry about things outside your control. He soothed me with this thought on many occasions, and I'm sure he lived it: I can only imagine

---

[1] Garner, *The Wit and Wisdom of Charlie Wright*, 76 Tex. L. Rev. 1587 (1998), reprinted at the beginning of this chapter.

that he approached his surgery in June with this very attitude. The fourth is never to travel unless you're going first class. He certainly lived by this maxim—and I have tried to follow suit if not quite so grandly. When we were together at the Fairmont in San Francisco in May 1999, I learned with some amusement that an African head of state was in the second largest suite because Charlie had taken the best and largest one.

A week after Charlie's death, I received a note in the mail from Nancy Kruh, a Dallas journalist who interviewed Charlie for a 1999 article about me. To my astonishment, she sent me a transcript of the interview. Her next-to-last question to Charlie was whether he considered himself my mentor.

He answered: "I don't know. I can't think of anything I have taught him, and that's what I would think of as a mentor. Perhaps I've been an example of how to carry yourself. I've learned from him, and I do my best to prove him wrong."

Then she asked whether he kept score. "It's like a romance," Charlie said. "You don't keep score."

I can only say that if proving me wrong gave Charlie any pleasure, I must have given him a great many pleasurable moments.

*   *   *

One of the sweetest sentiments I've ever heard is this one: May your rewards be on earth as well as in heaven. It's sweet because most of us don't get our rewards on earth. We get them only in heaven—if at all. And it comforts most of us to think that we might get our rewards in heaven.

Did Lon Fuller get his rewards on earth? Did Karl Llewellyn? Did H.L.A. Hart? Did Roscoe Pound get his rewards on earth? Did John Wigmore? Did Arthur Corbin or William Prosser? What about Leon Green and Page Keeton? Did Charlie's mentors, Charles E. Clark and Fred Rodell, get their rewards on earth?

I don't really know. Most people—even great people—don't.

But Charlie did. He was recognized in his lifetime with copious accolades and awards. Austin can be proud. Texas can be proud—the United States can be proud—even the English-speaking world can be proud that we recognized a great one among us. During his lifetime, he received ample thanks for all that he gave us.

And if there's a heaven, he's getting his rewards there as well.

That's a happy thought—I'll leave it at that rather than asking who's to carry on from here with his brand of scholarship. That's an unhappy thought. Let's all think happy thoughts today. Thank you very much.

ॐ ॐ ॐ

Remembering Judge Thomas Gibbs Gee

WE BOTH CARED A LOT about style. That's what we had in common. And
we both believed that the style of one's writing powerfully influences
the content.

I discovered this shared interest during my Fifth Circuit clerkship—
for Judge Thomas M. Reavley in 1984–1985—when I read every slip
opinion issued by the court. I dreaded reading the opinions of certain
judges, but I relished every word that Gee wrote. He made every word tell.

Shortly before my clerkship began, Judge Gee issued the now-famous
opinion in *Macpherson v. Texas Department of Water Resources.*[1] Because
Judge Reavley's outgoing clerks knew of my interest in writing, they
alerted me to it. The opinion shows what can happen when literary talent, profound empathy, worldly wisdom, conservative judicial views, and
lightheartedness all converge in one human being.

That's an enviable and unusual combination. And it led to an enviable and unusual style. In the hands of a lesser writer, Gwendolyn Macpherson's case would have been quite unremarkable; but Gee brought his
unusual combination of qualities to the case. In his first four paragraphs,
notice the progressive foreshadowing that prepares us for the wry hyperbole of the fifth:

> This appeal concerns whether Ms. Gwendolyn Macpherson was dis-
> missed from her position with an agency of the State of Texas for a
> wrong reason: being female. In a bench trial, the court gave judgment
> for the defendant, entering detailed findings of fact and conclusions of
> law. On the peculiar facts of the case, we conclude that one of his find-
> ings—which is supported by the record evidence—is dispositive, so
> that we need not look beyond it to affirm.
>
> The record indicates that Ms. Macpherson is a graduate geologist of
> high intelligence, independent mind and—one may infer—somewhat
> venturesome spirit. Employed by a predecessor department of the defen-
> dant agency in March 1976, she established an enviable work record,
> marred by only a single verbal reprimand for climbing a fence to exam-
> ine certain deposits on private property without obtaining the land-
> owner's permission. During her brief tenure with the state, she received
> more promotions and merit raises than any other employee in her section.
>
> In September 1977, her department was merged with two other state
> water agencies to become the present defendant agency and defendant

---

Adapted from *Review of Litigation* (Winter 1996).
[1] 734 F.2d 1103 (5th Cir. 1984).

Harvey Davis became executive director of the new entity. One may
infer from the record that in the months immediately following the
merger Davis was strained by the inevitable tensions consequent to his
new position and the effort to harmonize his amalgamated charges into
a functional entity.

In January 1978, Mr. Davis circulated a memorandum over his signature to his division directors within the agency. The memo had
actually been prepared by a staff attorney and was entitled "Outside
Requests of [sic] Staff Testimony at Administrative and Judicial Hearings." Like the title, portions of it were poorly worded. Ms. Macpherson
determined that it required grammatical and stylistic improvement. She
therefore proceeded to correct Mr. Davis's memo in searching detail,
appending both specific and general comments calculated to bring
home to the author his literary ineptitude. Her final observation fairly
gives the flavor of the whole:

> You frequently leave out articles (a, an, the) in front of nouns.
> You tend to obfuscate by using long, unwieldy phraseology. Sim-
> plify! Simplify! This will help correct your tendency to misplace
> modifiers. The content of this memo is confusing. It is obvious
> to me that when one is subpoenaed one must appear, regardless
> of the opinion of the Department. Furthermore, one must tell
> the truth when under oath.
>
> Please rewrite and resubmit.

She then anonymously mailed her revision to Mr. Davis in an enve-
lope marked "Personal," and thus it came directly to his hand.

While adhering to the ceiling of his office, revised memo in hand,
Mr. Davis determined to fire the reviser, whomever he or she might
be. As the trial court chastely put it in Finding of Fact No. 16, "The
termination decision was made prior to the discovery of the identity
of the employee who revised the memo and anonymously sent it to
Mr. Harvey Davis." After an investigation in the course of which she
readily admitted the revision and anonymous return of the memo, and
a meeting between Mr. Davis and the director of Ms. Macpherson's
division, her immediate supervisor, and the agency general counsel,
Davis reiterated his decision that the reviser, her identity now known,
should be dismissed and she was.[2]

Although the court affirmed because Davis decided to fire Macpherson before knowing her sex—much less her identity—this was no typical affirmance. Judge Gee did not do what so many judges tend to do.
He didn't exaggerate the strengths of the winning side and minimize
those of the losing side. He knew something that not enough judges seem

---

[2] *Id.* at 1104–05 (footnotes omitted).

to fully recognize: that he was no "lowly worker in words."[3] Through his adept and humane handling of language, he was "engaged in expressing in words the chaos of life . . . ."[4] He was "attempting 'a momentary stay against confusion.' "[5] He was poetic—instinctively, not artificially—within the confines of a judicial opinion.

His nobility of spirit, his very person, showed through once again in the final paragraph of this short opinion:

> In closing, we observe that although the unique facts of today's case lend themselves irresistibly to somewhat ironic treatment, we do not view lightly the small bureaucratic tragedy that the record reveals: a harried executive has lost his temper and a valuable—if somewhat pert—state employee has lost her position. On this record, however, we cannot hold the trial judge clearly erroneous in finding that it was Ms. Macpherson's pertness and not her gender that cost her the job she held. We do not sit to revise employment decisions taken hastily or for insufficient reasons, only those taken for illegal ones. And so, with all sympathy and good wishes for the future to Ms. Macpherson, we conclude that the trial court's judgment must be
> AFFIRMED.[6]

Some readers have told me that they find the last sentence out of place. To me it seems essential: it is Gee through and through.

My first conversation with Gee was about *Macpherson*. On a trip to New Orleans in September 1984, my fellow Reavley clerks suggested that we have dinner at Galatoire's—which, somehow, everyone knew as Judge Gee's favorite restaurant. And sure enough, he appeared with his clerks in tow some 30 minutes after we arrived. After dinner, I summoned the nerve to walk over and introduce myself and to say how much I'd been enjoying his opinions—especially *Macpherson*. He was unhurried, unpreoccupied, and unpretentious, and we spoke for probably three minutes as he told me that Gwendolyn Macpherson had written him to thank him for the opinion (and to correct a couple of perceived blemishes in the opinion).[7]

---

[3] Walker Gibson, *Literary Minds and Judicial Style*, 36 N.Y.U. L. Rev. 915, 930 (1961).

[4] *Id.*

[5] *Id.*

[6] *Macpherson*, 734 F.2d at 1105.

[7] Perhaps she pointed out that, in the second paragraph, *verbal* should (strictly speaking) be *oral*. *See* Garner, *A Dictionary of Modern Legal Usage* 910–11 (2d ed. 1995). And perhaps she corrected *whomever* in the fifth paragraph; it should be *whoever*. *See id.* at 932–34. Then again, perhaps she observed that (strictly speaking) *gender*, in the final paragraph, should be *sex*. *Id.* at 382.

Judge Gee had foreseen this possibility. In footnote 3 of the opinion, he said: "In anticipation of a critical review of our remarks, we have been at some pains with their style and grammar." 734 F.2d at 1105 n.3.

Incidentally, the *Macpherson* opinion—not just snippets from the case, but the full text—now graces the introductory chapter of Richard Lanham's fine book, *Revising Business Prose*.[8] In Lanham's view, Gee's writing shows "that he can both see a prose style and see through and around it."[9]

During my clerkship, I had only a few more conversations with Judge Gee, but many more with his clerks. And they told me something fascinating: Gee had a style sheet that he had his clerks follow. Gee had adapted it from Judge John Minor Wisdom's style sheet, and he called it (with typical self-depreciation) "A Few of Wisdom's Idiosyncrasies and a Few of Ignorance's."

That style sheet contained some gems that it took me years to appreciate fully. The first two style tips hold the key to the way Gee opened his judicial opinions:

> Try to state the principal question in the first sentence.

> Give the court's holding in the first paragraph, preferably in a short introductory sentence. Put the sex appeal in the first sentence and the last sentence of each opinion—or at least in the first paragraph and last paragraph of each opinion.[10]

Once you realize what Gee is doing with his judicial openers—opinion after opinion—you can see why he deserves to be considered among the greatest writers ever to sit on the federal bench.

Take any Gee opinion, even the most humdrum case, and you'll find yourself well oriented at the outset. Take even *Bhandari v. First Natl. Bank of Commerce*,[11] a complicated mess of a case:

> Appellant Jeetendra Bhandari sued appellee First National Bank of Commerce after First National declined to issue him a credit card. First National refused Bhandari credit in part because he was not a citizen of the United States. The district court held that neither 42 U.S.C. § 1981 nor the Equal Credit Opportunity Act ("ECOA") gave Bhandari a legal remedy for private alienage discrimination. The court determined, however, that First National had violated the ECOA by not telling Bhandari all its reasons for denying him credit. The court awarded damages, costs, and attorneys' fees. Bhandari appeals, contending that

---

[8] Richard A. Lanham, *Revising Business Prose* 82–86 (2d ed. 1987).

[9] *Id.* at 96.

[10] Thomas Gibbs Gee, *A Few of Wisdom's Idiosyncrasies and a Few of Ignorance's: A Judicial Style Sheet*, 1 Scribes J. Legal Writing 55, 56 (1990).

[11] 808 F.2d 1082, 1084 (5th Cir.), *superseded*, 829 F.2d 1343 (5th Cir. 1987), *vacated*, 492 U.S. 901 (1989), *reinstated*, 887 F.2d 609 (5th Cir. 1989), *cert. denied*, 494 U.S. 1061 (1990).

the district court erred in various respects. We hold that the law of this Circuit recognizes actions for private alienage discrimination under § 1981, but that alienage discrimination is not actionable under the ECOA. Accordingly, we affirm in part, reverse in part, and remand.[12]

The brilliance of that opening paragraph lies in the phrase *in various respects*. Not one judge in 100 would get to the heart of the case so quickly. Many judicial writers would put eight lengthy paragraphs in place of those three words. And the resulting opinion would be a mishmash.

As you might have gathered, my early admiration for Gee was mostly from afar. But in 1990, things changed. I was asked to become editor in chief of *The Scribes Journal of Legal Writing*, and soon after I thought of asking Judge Gee to publish his style sheet in the first issue. When I called him, he agreed immediately and said he remembered me well, even though we hadn't seen each other for five years.

Beginning in May 1990, we talked on the phone about his *Scribes Journal* piece, and our friendship grew. He told me that he would soon be leaving the bench to join Baker & Botts, and I told him that I would soon be leaving the University of Texas Law School to start a company called LawProse, Inc. He expressed an interest in LawProse and agreed to become one of our CLE instructors in legal writing. By the spring of 1991, he and I were team-teaching courses in judicial writing, along with Betty S. Flowers and John R. Trimble, both of the UT English Department.

In May 1991, I told Gee that I'd been thinking of working on a book about the decline of civility in law. He sounded fascinated by the subject, and when I suggested that we work together he enthusiastically agreed. And so began a piece not about writing style, but about style in the larger sense: style in practicing law.

Later that month, I flew to Houston to meet with Judge Gee, and we spent half a day together planning what we thought would become a book. Toward the end of the day, he told me that the damnedest thing had happened to his left hand: he had lost control of two fingers on that hand, and the doctors were trying to figure out what the problem was.

Not long after, he told me the diagnosis: Lou Gehrig's disease.

At first, the disease didn't slow him down at all. We traded chapters every few months: he would supplement my writing, and I would supplement his. And by 1993, we had filled out most of the seven chapters and had fully written the first and the last.

---

[12] *Id.*

Meanwhile, though, we had both gotten caught up in other projects: he was briefing and arguing a great many appeals, and I was flying all over the country teaching CLE courses. So the project stalled, and time passed.

I last saw Judge Gee in July 1994, when I was in Houston to deliver a lecture. As usual, he had me as his guest for a long lunch at the Houston Club. And when I met him there, I realized that I might not see him again. The disease had shriveled the strong man's hands, had bent his ramrod backbone, and had stricken his vocal cords, thus weakening his voice.

We talked a great deal about death: about his death in particular, about his mother's recent death, and about death in general.

In two weeks, my own mother would be suddenly dead. And Judge Gee's words before and after the fact consoled and fortified me.

But on that last day when we were together, he did what he had always done when I was in Houston. He insisted on driving me to the airport. This stalwart man, who could barely handle a fork and had difficulty walking, wouldn't let me take a cab. And on the way to Hobby Airport, we talked of many things: of the good and bad writers now sitting on the federal bench, of good and bad brief-writers, of litigators' habits, of law in its broadest sense, and even of the meaning of life.

And we spoke about our little project on civility. I told him of my plan to make an article from the first part of chapter 1 and all of chapter 7. He nodded and smiled. It was something like my promise to him.

ð» ð» ð»

Sir Robert Megarry, RIP

1910–2006

*This was one of two eulogies delivered at the memorial service
in the Great Hall of Lincoln's Inn on 12 March 2007.*

I'VE BEEN ASKED TO SAY a few words before reading a passage from *A New Miscellany-at-Law*, Sir Robert's final book. When I think of the man, several adjectives come to mind. Urbane. Scholarly. Witty. Tireless. Subtle. Dry. Caring. Empathetic. Painstaking. Oenophilic. Genuine. Kind.

Sir Robert Megarry was a hero to me even before I met him in 1988. It was the formidable American legal scholar Charles Alan Wright who introduced me first to Ted's books—and then to Ted himself. I always knew him as "Ted."

I quickly became a fan of his *Miscellanies-at-Law*, the first of which was published three years before I was born. Ted's sense of humor and his keen insights into legal language were immediately appealing. During my ten or so visits to England from 1988 to 2004, I saw Ted every single time. This occasionally involved significant exertions on his part. In 2000, when he was 90, he trekked over to the Grosvenor Hotel for breakfast on a visit when I wouldn't otherwise have been able to see him. In one of his final notes to me last fall, he said he well remembered our breakfast at the Grosvenor.

Then, as always, he took a great deal of interest in my daughters—talking with them almost as much as he did with me.

Every time I saw Ted, beginning in 1988, I asked about the progress on his third *Miscellany*. He always reported good progress until 2003, when he told me he'd stopped reading. I assumed that the book wouldn't be finished. In 2004, when I last saw him, he remarked once again that he'd stopped reading, but then he said he had a nearly finished manuscript on the shelf. I asked to see it, and within minutes found myself offering to help him finish the book and see it through to publication.

I thought it would be a straightforward task, but I soon realized that my involvement meant that Ted was definitely reading once again and writing copious notes disagreeing with various editorial decisions I'd made. We spent more than two months debating whether the words *boyfriend* and *girlfriend* are hyphenated or solid, among countless other points. His 1933 *Shorter Oxford* hyphenated those words and many others, and it took many citations to the current *Shorter Oxford*, *Collins*, *Chambers*, *Longman's*, and other modern British dictionaries to win the day. Of course, American authorities counted for nothing.

I quipped to my colleagues in Dallas that this was surely the only 500-page book in history that was backed up with 16,000 pages of notes between the author and the editor.

But even if I won an occasional editorial tussle like that one—we didn't hyphenate *boyfriend* or *girlfriend*—the book was Ted's through and through. I'm honored to have played a modest role in it.

It never occurred to me that we might have arbitrated our minor editorial disputes. But the *New Miscellany-at-Law* lays out an admirable procedure for doing just that. Here's the relevant passage:

> Arbitrations . . . take place in a wide variety of places and may exhibit a wide range of peculiarities. In some part of County Down in the nineteenth century a somewhat unusual form of arbitration was current. The parties agreed upon an impartial chairman, who sat at the head of a long table with the parties on either hand. Down the middle of the table a line was drawn, and grains of oats were placed along it at intervals of a few inches. A foot or so from the head of the table the line stopped, and two grains of corn were placed a few inches from the middle, one in front of each party. Then, with the chairman as umpire, a hen turkey was gently placed on the table at the far end. The turkey would then delicately peck her ladylike way all up the table until, when she reached the two grains of corn at the top, she delivered her award in favour of one party or the other by taking first the grain nearer to him.
>
> Once, however, the loser in such an arbitrament was a litigious creature who refused to accept the decision as just, and brought a civil bill in the county court against the winner. On the facts having been proved, the county court judge dismissed that action, whereupon the plaintiff exercised his right to appeal to the assize judge. This was that aged and learned equity lawyer, Lefroy C.J., who, unlike counsel for the defendant, knew little of local customs. During the cross-examination of the plaintiff, the following passage occurred.

Counsel:	"Tell me, wasn't the turkey for the defendant?" (No answer)
Counsel:	"Tell my Lord the truth, now. Wasn't the turkey for the defendant?"
Chief Justice:	"What on earth has a turkey to do with this case?"
Counsel:	"It's a local form of arbitration, my Lord."
Chief Justice:	"Do you mean to tell me that the plaintiff has brought this case in disregard of the award of an arbitrator?"
Counsel:	"That is so, my Lord."
Chief Justice:	"Disgraceful! Appeal dismissed with costs here and below."
Counsel (*sotto voce*):	"The Lord Chief Justice affirms the turkey."

We can all be thankful for the way Sir Robert Megarry enriched legal literature. And I know I'm not alone in feeling thankful that my life is so much richer for having known him.

ટ્રા ટ્રા ટ્રા

Finding the Right Words

WHEN PEOPLE LEARN that the name of my recently published book is *A Dictionary of Modern Legal Usage*,[1] they commonly ask one of three questions: How did you go about writing a dictionary? Why write a legal dictionary, when everyone knows that *Black's Law Dictionary* is a standard reference? How did you, a full-time lawyer, find the time to write a dictionary? (Or, less politely, how could a 29-year-old lawyer have written a dictionary?)

Usually the short-form answers suffice. First, I compiled the materials for the dictionary by noting down every word or phrase I encountered that had some unique application in law, that was a source of confusion to legal writers, or that could be more simply or precisely expressed. Second, as a dictionary of usage, *DMLU* (as Robert Burchfield, the editor of the *Oxford English Dictionary*, calls it) does not compete directly with *Black's*; rather than merely defining words, it shows how they are most effectively used. Third, I began when I was 22, during my first year of law school, and completed the manuscript just as I began to practice law.

Since, however, the editors of the *Michigan Bar Journal* have invited me to go somewhat beyond the simple answers, I'll do so. Let me say at the outset that, although I was quite aware and supportive of the plain-English movement in law, I had no idea that *DMLU* would touch such a nerve within the legal community. Now in its sixth month since publication last fall, the book is nearing its third (substantial) printing by Oxford and has received what I would have considered unimaginable endorsements from Charles Alan Wright, Irving Younger (rest his soul), and the *Harvard Law Review*.

Having written a thesis on Shakespearean language as an undergraduate and published a number of articles on the subject, I was as fascinated in law school by the language of Anglo-American jurisprudence as I was by its substance. When my first-year classmates at the University of Texas Law School began to notice that I carried around a passel of three-by-five index cards in my shirt pocket, and saw me continually making notes on them, they thought I had some secret system for mastering our assignments. (My friends all knew that my regular notes, like everyone else's, were on letter-size tablets.)

Adapted from *Michigan Bar Journal* (Aug. 1988).
[1] Oxford University Press, 1987.

Though I did not want to publicize that I had undertaken a dictionary of usage for lawyers and was collecting specimens, I finally did disclose what it was all about. Otherwise, I thought, several friendships might be jeopardized.

By the end of that first year, several classmates were supplying me almost daily with sentences, drawn from judicial opinions, that they found puzzling, inelegant, or simply incorrect. Indeed, as lawyers who think much about the subject of legal style know, it is hard to find a judicial opinion that is free from usages that are puzzling, inelegant, or simply incorrect. In a sense, first-year law students are more adept at spotting these than seasoned lawyers, for they have not yet become inured to (much less enamored of) the many graceless and completely superfluous legalisms.

By 1985, when I clerked for the United States Court of Appeals for the Fifth Circuit, I had collected some 10,000 index cards containing material for inclusion in my dictionary. By that time, virtually every question posed to me by other legal writers found an answer in my "manuscript." What is the difference between *consist in* and *consist of*? What is the noun corresponding to *supersede*? Why do we more and more frequently see *undocumented worker* rather than *illegal alien*? Why do courts commonly say that they are *implying* terms into contracts, when surely they must be *inferring* those terms from the underlying circumstances? How does one pronounce *cestui* in *cestui que trust*, and is there any reason for preferring that phrase over *beneficiary*? And on and on.

These and hundreds of similar questions were not answered in any legal-reference work. Even Fowler's *Modern English Usage* could provide guidance on only one of these questions—distinguishing between *consist in* and *consist of*. (Distressingly, the distinction is rarely observed by American legal writers.) *Black's Law Dictionary*, of course, being a defining dictionary rather than a dictionary of usage, does not touch on such issues, though legal writers regularly confront them. That explains why I had the audacity to undertake *DMLU* in the face of queries that I might be competing with *Black's*.

Unlike a conventional dictionary, a dictionary of usage contains, in addition to word-entries, short essay-entries on myriad stylistic and grammatical subjects. Its purpose is fundamentally different from that of a conventional dictionary; the task is not to marshal and define all legal words and phrases, but rather to guide the legal writer who comes upon a word or phrase that for some reason proves troublesome.

During my judicial clerkship, I began writing publishers, 20 in all. (One question I was frequently asked was whether the dictionary was for myself, as an aid to learning, or whether I intended to have it published. Like George Bernard Shaw, I believe that if you do not write for

publication, there is little point in writing at all.) I sent each publisher a letter explaining the work, together with a page of sample entries. In rather
short order, I received 17 rejections. An 18th response all but amounted
to a rejection: A minor legal publisher offered to take my typewritten
pages, reproduce them, bind them, and sell the resulting bundle. I began
to understand, over the course of several months, just what Saul Bellow
meant when he said, "You write a book, you invest your imagination in
it, and then you hand it over to a bunch of people who have no imagination and no understanding of their own enterprise."[2]

The exception to that aspersion, naturally, was Oxford University
Press, which I had considered from the outset to be the ideal but least
likely publisher of *DMLU*. Some eight or nine months after my initial
letter, I received offers from Oxford and from one other major publisher.
(These were the only two left!) Given Oxford's fine list of publications,
and the tradition embodied in works such as the *Oxford English Dictionary* and Fowler's seminal book, the choice was easy.

Before joining my law firm in Dallas, I took three months off to
work day and night finishing the book. The work was daunting and
exhausting, and not without moments of exasperation. I cannot say how
many times I thought of Samuel Johnson's characterization of a lexicographer as a harmless drudge. In the midst of the drudgery, though, I tried
to keep a sense of humor. Many of the witticisms that have been so
widely quoted I wrote at 3 or 4 in the morning during these months.
Thus, my entry on the noun *prophylactic*:

> To an educated layman, this word is synonymous with *condom*. Doc-
> tors use the term for anything that prevents disease. To lawyers, it
> means "anything that is designed to prevent something undesirable."
> E.g., "The Supreme Court recognized that the predeprivation notice
> and hearing were necessary *prophylactics* against a wrongful discharge."
> The example quoted does not demonstrate the keenest linguistic sen-
> sitivity: in view of the layman's understanding, it is perhaps unwise to
> use *prophylactic* in the same sentence with *discharge*.

Or my entry on *arguendo*:

> *Arguendo* is unnecessary in place of *for the sake of argument*. Although
> brevity would commend it, its obscurity to laymen is a distinct liabil-
> ity. . . . *Arguendo* is one of those Latinisms that neophyte lawyers often
> adopt as pet words to advertise their lawyerliness.

Friends who read parts of the manuscript asked whether I was not
going out on a limb by peppering the work with a wry sense of humor.

---

[2] As quoted in *Writers on Writing* 132 (Jon Winokur ed., 2d ed. 1987).

The wryness came naturally; I certainly didn't set out to be funny. How can one refrain from commenting, though, on the writer who refers to a *prophylactic* against a wrongful *discharge*?

Actually, the smiles one finds in *DMLU* are in the Fowlerian tradition. Fowler, after all, was the one who divided the English-speaking world into five categories: (1) those who neither know nor care what a split infinitive is; (2) those who do not know, but care very much; (3) those who know and condemn; (4) those who know and approve; and (5) those who know and distinguish.[3] Fowler showed that a work of scholarship need not be dry as dust, that a substantial reference work need not bore its users.

To the extent that I have gone out on a limb, it is by documenting the lapses in diction, grammar, and style of our judges. Far more than half the sentences that I quote to demonstrate some common error or pitfall derive from published judicial opinions. Many of these, in my judgment, required citation if for no other reason than to enhance the scholarly reliability of the book. Surely the appellate judges who wrote *irregardless* rather than the correct *regardless* and *thusly* rather than *thus* will not thank me for citing their opinions, when others have committed the same blunders. I could cite a thousand other examples of judges' writing errors documented in *DMLU*, including some from the United States Supreme Court.

The idea, of course, is not to mock these mistakes, but to learn from them; it is not to offer stylistic improvements as ad hominem attacks, but to guide legal writers safely through the bogs in which some of their unwary predecessors have sunk. And I include myself among the unwary predecessors; I quote (with citation) from an article in which I erred in using *bequest* as a verb in place of *bequeath*.

To the extent that I have gone out on a limb by supplying citations to particular opinions and law-review articles, my sole object was the future betterment of legal writing. Nor is that aspect of *DMLU* without precedent: Fowler created quite a stir in England in the 1920s by pointing out a great many lapses in the pages of the London *Times*, considered by many to be a guardian of the language. That he did so has put us all in his debt.

---

[3] H.W. Fowler, *A Dictionary of Modern English Usage* 558 (1926).

?? ?? ??

How I Stumbled on a Literary Treasure

I'M A RAVENOUS BOOK-COLLECTOR in the fields of language and law (as opposed to the *field* of language and law—something much narrower). For years I've concentrated on English-language dictionaries and grammars. And I've built up quite a library because, since the late 1970s, I've bought thousands of books at used-book stores. These days, I visit about 200 antiquarian bookshops each year, mostly outside my home state.

Like any book-collector, I'm always looking to unearth something great. Here in the U.S., I've had many modest discoveries that fill important niches in my library. For example, once when I was in Milwaukee, I found a rare first printing of Fowler's *Modern English Usage* (1926) for a mere $3. Because I now write dictionaries of usage for Oxford University Press—and therefore take the genre quite seriously—a find of this type keeps my adrenaline running high for weeks on end.

But my greatest discovery occurred in August 1996.

It happened on a family trip to Britain. In late July my family went with me to Glasgow, where the law school had arranged for me to be a visiting scholar. I worked every morning in an office in the historic Stair Building of Glasgow University, and each afternoon the entire family would go sightseeing. And whenever I could, I'd sneak in some book-shopping.

At one Glasgow bookshop, I bought several early-19th-century lawbooks for no more than £8 apiece. In the U.S., these would have been considerably more expensive.

Another Glaswegian bookseller offered me an antiquarian "spelling book" that appeared to be from the early 19th century. Although the frontispiece was missing, I bought it because he was asking only £7 for it. It's a book that seems to have been published in the first decade of the 19th century.

This spelling book nicely complements two acquisitions from earlier in 1996: an 1807 abridgment of Lindley Murray's *English Grammar*, and an 1821 unabridged edition of that same book.

By August 3, when we flew from Glasgow to London for a few days, I had acquired two big boxes of books, not to mention the ones that I'd

---

Adapted from *Bookman's Weekly* (13 Jan. 1997).

stuffed into my oversized briefcase. Those books are fabulous. Among them, for example, is Glanville Williams's edition of *Salmond on Jurisprudence*—a work I constantly encounter references to but had never actually seen. I got it in Stirling, Scotland, for a mere £3.

At any rate, we were in London on August 3 and decided to have dinner in Chinatown. So we took the Underground (or "Tube," as it's called) to Tottenham Court Road, and walked down to Chinatown. What I didn't realize at the time, though, is that we were stepping out into Charing Cross Road, which is famous for its used-book stores. And the moment we left the tube station, We spotted a bookshop. My daughters generously suggested that we all go in because I might find something.

As it happened, the store sold mostly remainders. But in the basement were some used books. I wasn't finding much of anything there, but on my way out, I spotted a handsome leatherbound edition of Samuel Johnson's *Dictionary of the English Language* (1755), in five volumes. It was the 1818 edition, revised by H.J. Todd.

This might be a nice addition to my library, I thought, because at the time I had only a facsimile reprint of Johnson's *Dictionary*. The price as marked was £395—very good indeed, compared to others I'd seen—but I remembered my recent pledge to my family: resolve every close question against buying a new book.

As I was about to reshelve the first volume, I found an inscription inside the front cover, in ornate handwriting: "William Murray Tuke, from Lindley Murray." That name resonated with me: Murray was the biggest name among 19th-century English grammarians. My pulse doubled as I turned the page to find a handwritten letter attached inside (imagine *sic*s throughout):

> I desire that the following books, from my Library may be given to the said Samuel Tuke, in trust for his son, William Murray Tuke, when he attains the age of fifteen years: and if he should die before that time, for his next eldest son that may attain the said age of fifteen years, or be of that age: namely,
>
> Todd's Johnson's Dictionary, Five volumes Quarto.
>
> The Edinburgh Gazetteer, in Six volumes large Octavo.
>
> Cruden's Concordance, one volume Quarto.
>
> The Holy Bible, in three volumes large Octavo; edited by Fitter.
>
> Blair's Sermons.—5 volumes Octavo.

*   *   *

I give, after the decease of my wife to our friend Hannah Richardson, from my own Library, the following Books.

Doddridge's Family Expositor 6 vols. 8vo

Orton's Exposition of the Old Testament. 6 vols. Octavo.

Bishop Horne's Commentary on the Psalms—2 vols. Octavo.

And, on my decease, I give to the said Hannah Richardson, my writing Desk, which I have made use of for many years.

Holdgate 26th of 3d month, 1825.

Lindley Murray.

While I was reading this, a man whom I took to be an American English professor started edging in front of me, handling the second volume of Johnson's *Dictionary*. I kept the first volume with me as I went to get my daughters, who understood that I was rather excited but didn't particularly share in the excitement.

Buying the books right then was out of the question, I knew, because I had already exceeded any reasonable limit in Glasgow. Still, I imagined—judging from the catalogues I'd seen—that this set might fetch $2,000 or more from a specialist bookseller in the United States.

The girls were getting hungry, and we needed to leave, but that English professor was still downstairs looking at what I was already considering "my" books. I nonchalantly reshelved volume one right in front of him, as he was now thumbing through volume four. We left, and I spent the next 36 hours hoping that the name Lindley Murray lay beyond the limits of his knowledge—and that of anyone else who might look at the set.

The next evening we had dinner at the house of my original editor at Oxford University Press, William Mitchell, and his family. They could not have been better hosts, for they confirmed what I already knew: this set of books would be well worth having, to say the least. We looked up Lindley Murray in *The Oxford Companion to English Literature* and found that Murray is referred to as the "father of English grammar."

By Sunday, August 5, it was decided that I'd buy the set the next day—if it was still there. It was, and I did. For £375. The bookshop owner wouldn't go any lower, so I persuaded him to throw in a £40 set of Alexander Schmidt's *Shakespeare Lexicon* (1874), a two-volume work I used years ago when writing about Shakespearean language.

The bookseller told me that an elderly couple had brought the multivolume dictionary into his store about six weeks before and that the bindings were very shabby. He had had them rebound in three-quarter calf (at a cost of £200, he said). They're now beautiful.

And they're in Dallas. After we arrived home, I looked up a few references to Murray. When buying the books, all I recalled was that Murray—along with Bishop Lowth—is often decried as the archconservative 18th-century grammarian who laid it down that you should never split an infinitive or end a sentence with a preposition. Soon I would discover that this characterization is wholly inaccurate: he never wrote such nonsense.

For me, the value of these books is that they are the premier 18th-century grammarian's copy of the premier 18th-century lexicographer's work. It wouldn't mean nearly as much to own any of the other books mentioned in Murray's codicil. It's the combination of Johnson and Murray that makes the set unique.

My guess is that I'll play out my book-addicted days without ever discovering a comparable treasure.

Lindley Murray's Holographic Will
Disposing of His Books

I desire that the following books,
from my Library may be given to
the said Samuel Tuke, in trust
for his son, William Murray
Tuke, when he attains the age
of fifteen years: and if he should
die before that time, for his next
eldest son that may attain the
said age of fifteen years, or be of that
age: namely,

Todd's Johnson's Dictionary,
   Five volumes Quarto.
The Edinburgh Gazetteer, in
   Six volumes large octavo.
Cruden's Concordance, one
   volume Quarto.
                                        The

The Holy Bible, in three volumes
large Octavo; edited by Titler.

Blair's Sermons ___ 5 volumes Octavo

I give, after the decease of my wife
to our friend Hannah Richardson,
from my own Library, the following Books.
Doddridge's Family Expositor 6 vols. 8vo
Orton's Exposition of the Old Testament.
6 vols. octavo ___

Bishop Horne's Commentary on the
Psalms ___ 2 vols. octavo.

And, on my decease, I give to the said
Hannah Richardson, my writing
Desk, which I have made use of
for many years.

Holdgate 26th of 3d month, 1825.

Lindley Murray.

JUDITH S. KAYE • PATRICIA M. WALD

Interviews

From *For the Defense*

Q: Why should I work on writing? It's not rewarded in our profession—and besides, either you're born with the ability or you're not.

A: Let me address the last point first: nearly anyone can become a good writer, but it takes hard work and real dedication. You must learn to marshal your thoughts, organize them, record them in a natural but polished style, and critique them rigorously. These skills probably aren't anyone's from birth.

As with any other craft—and writing *is* a craft—there's a lot of technical stuff to master: grammar, punctuation, conventions of style and usage, syntax, formatting. A lot of psychology, too. So much of writing comes down to artful strategizing, whether in opening paragraphs or in individual sentences. So you must learn to *think* the way skilled writers think.

Becoming a good writer doesn't just "happen" to you, no matter how great your talent may be. You may have athletic talent, but unless you work at it regularly you won't be a good athlete. The same is true of music—and of writing.

You say that good writing isn't rewarded? Of course it is. Writing ability routinely plays a crucial role in hiring and promotion decisions. And cases are won or lost on writing. As Judge Murry Cohen of Houston puts it, good writing is rewarded so automatically that you don't even notice it.

Adapted from *For the Defense* (Dec. 1998).

Q: But is CLE on writing really helpful? It's practice that you need, right?

A: Certainly you do need practice. Lots of it. You ought to be writing every day—if not on the job, then in a daily journal. Acquiring fluency as a writer means writing routinely.

But practice isn't enough. You need guidance—and most lawyers don't get the kind of guidance they really need if they just rely on their own instincts and on the lawyers they work with.

In a one-day CLE program, it's possible to set people on a better path than they're currently on. Many lawyers have talent as writers. But they've gotten into a stream of bad writing, and they've picked up bad habits. They need some direction, and they need some prodding. That's something that CLE can usefully provide.

You'd think that lawyers, being professional writers, would hone their craft just as assiduously as professional tennis players or concert pianists. And you'd think that law schools would devote considerable resources to teaching their students to write well. But they don't. So CLE is a critical part of the lawyer's education.

Q: I remember struggling through junior-high English with Miss Fidditch. Isn't CLE in legal writing just a tiresome rehash of grammar school?

A: No, and it needn't be boring. In fact, it can be fun—really eye-opening. The key is for the instructor to approach the subject not as a schoolmarm but as a pragmatic legal editor. If the course addresses legal reasoning, the use of caselaw, and effective argumentation in a genuinely instructive way, the participants will also welcome useful tips on grammar and punctuation. And why not? They face grammar and punctuation issues every time they write.

Q: But does style really matter? What counts are the law and the facts, right?

A: Many lawyers think that style is superfluous polish—that what counts are the law and the facts. "Oh, I'm no stylist. I just get the facts and the law down on the page." This attitude often begins with a flawed premise about just what "style" is. It's not floral adornment. It's the way you package ideas; it's their very form. Everyone has a style, not just the "stylist." There are good styles and bad styles. Good ones deliver the ideas promptly, without distraction. So if you care about getting your ideas across clearly and swiftly—if you care about your reader, not to mention your credibility as a competent wordsmith—you'll surely concede that style matters.

Q: Okay, maybe litigators have to care about their writing, but what about transactional lawyers?

A: Transactional lawyers rarely get their papers graded the way litigators do—once the contracts are signed, they're filed away—so it's easy for them to think they have little to learn about how to prepare better documents.

But that's a delusion. When Lon Fuller, the great Harvard law professor, conducted an empirical study some years ago, he found that about 25% of all contract litigation is the direct result of poor drafting. My own experience with contracts bears out Fuller's finding. Think of the economic impact of bad drafting and you'll have to conclude that transactional lawyers could be doing much better.

Most transactional drafting today is riddled with technical problems that could easily be fixed by a skilled hand. And these technical problems—such as provisos, inconsistent *shall*s, and inadvertent ambiguities—commonly result in costly litigation. Transactional lawyers have a lot to learn.

Q: If a supervisor wants and expects legalese, what's a good legal writer to do?

A: You need to please your supervisor, of course. But try to engage in a dialogue about writing. If you can back up your position with a usage book on a stylistic question—say, that *question whether* is preferable to *question as to whether* or *question of whether*, or that *collective-bargaining agreement* should be so hyphenated and not written *collective bargaining agreement*—then mention that such-and-such an authority strongly recommends the way you've expressed the idea. Gently say that you can't find any authority on the other side of the issue (the supervisor's side). Despite what many junior lawyers seem to think, most supervisors will appreciate this sort of tenacity—especially if you have some good basic skills in human relations. If you succeed at that, the entire organization might benefit.

If you have a supervisor who's inveterately unreceptive to suggestions about writing, then you can simply bite your tongue and wait till you achieve more seniority.

Empirical evidence suggests that lawyers ought to move away from legalese. In 1990, the Plain Language Committee of the State Bar of Texas formally polled all sitting district judges and appellate judges in the state, and their overwhelming preference was that lawyers should dispense with legalese. Down with "Now comes . . . ," they said. In every other state where judges have been polled, the results have been the same.

Back in the mid-1980s, a California survey showed that judges tend to assume that court papers full of legalese were prepared by lawyers with little prestige and that these lawyers had graduated low in their law-school classes. Interesting, isn't it? It suggests that legalese is the last refuge of uncritical minds.

Q: We learned in law school how precise legal language is. Isn't it risky to be tampering with words in legal documents?

A: You can achieve precision without lapsing into legalese. And ironically, most legal jargon is imprecise. For example, *per stirpes* is ambiguous and may give rise to litigation; *such property* may mean "the property I just mentioned" or "property of that kind"; *said land* is no more precise than *the land*, *that land*, or *this land*. Scholars who address these and similar legal–linguistic issues have long agreed on these points.

Q: What's the most serious mistake that new lawyers make in their writing?

A: It depends on what they're writing. Take the research memo. By far the most common mistake is not including an executive summary—a half-page statement of the question being addressed, the answer to the question, and the reasons for that answer. A busy supervising lawyer ought to be able to glean those things within 60 seconds of picking up a research memo. And an uninvolved colleague ought to be able to do the same. The writer must learn to take account of not only the primary audience, but also the secondary audience that almost any memo will ultimately have.

But few legal writers do this. Of the 800 or so research memos I review each year from law firms all over the country, only about 1% met the 60-second test. That statistic has held steady since 1995.

Not only does an executive summary help the reader, it also helps the writer ensure that the memo has a point. With many of the memos I read, I can't tell why they were written at all—apart from the obvious inference that a supervising attorney asked for something.

Q: If I were really serious about becoming a good legal writer, what would you recommend?

A: Become preoccupied with framing issues well. This, too, is a very large subject—one that I've discussed extensively elsewhere. It's by far the most important aspect of analytical and persuasive writing.

Beyond that, your dedication should move you to undertake a reading program. Read John Trimble's *Writing with Style* (2d ed. 2000) and William Strunk and E.B. White's *The Elements of Style* (4th ed. 2000). Get Theodore Bernstein's *The Careful Writer* (1965) and browse through it periodically. In the interest of being disinterested, I'll exempt my own books from the list.

Finally, ask colleagues who are good writers to edit your writing, and do so repeatedly. You can learn a lot from a good edit.

Q: What legal writers are worth emulating?

A: There are many. Charles Alan Wright's *The Law of Federal Courts* (5th ed. 1994) is, I think, one of the two greatest hornbooks ever written. The other is Grant Gilmore and Charles L. Black's *The Law of Admiralty* (2d ed. 1975). I wouldn't purport to make that judgment if I hadn't spent a great deal of time reading through most of the hornbooks now available. Those two books make for great reading.

Besides Wright and Gilmore, among my favorite legal writers are:

- Lord Denning
- Patrick Devlin
- Ronald Dworkin
- Thomas Gibbs Gee
- Ruth Bader Ginsburg
- Learned Hand
- Robert H. Jackson
- Judith S. Kaye
- Karl Llewellyn
- Robert E. Megarry
- Richard Posner
- Fred Rodell
- Antonin Scalia
- Patricia Wald
- Elizabeth Warren
- Glanville Williams

As different as their styles are, you'll find this common characteristic: they all have the ability to simplify difficult ideas without oversimplifying. That's what we all ought to strive for.

Q: You've taught judicial-writing courses for appellate judges in several states. What did you learn from that experience?

A: Principally, I learned just how privileged we are in this country to have such an extraordinary collection of people within our judiciary. My overall impression—after spending a good deal of time with judges in more than a third of the states: Alaska, California, Delaware, Florida, Georgia, Indiana, Kentucky, Michigan, Minnesota, Missouri, Nebraska, Nevada, New Jersey, New Mexico, Texas, Utah, Virginia, and Washington, as well as Washington, D.C.—is that they are conscientious, smart, quick-witted, and surprisingly humble.

On a more mundane level, I've learned just how much the judges value good writing. They are concerned about improving the brief-writing they see, and they care about improving the quality of their own opinions. As a group, they're the most receptive "students" I've ever had. And I'm not just referring to a few judges: they've consistently been this way.

Q: If judges are amenable to learning more about writing, how about lawyers?

A: In my CLE teaching, I find that there's a continuum. Generally, the most enthusiastic participants are senior partners in law firms, general counsel of corporations, and department heads in federal and state agencies. The least enthusiastic are first-year lawyers.

Several reasons come to mind. First, experience teaches you just how important good writing is. Second, some points—such as the importance of issue-framing—simply won't register as well with a novice as they will with a more seasoned writer. Third, the senior lawyer is often secure enough to admit the need for improvement. Fourth, for the junior lawyer to admit this need might imply that a recently completed law-school education wasn't quite complete—something you hardly want to think of when you're trying to pay off a huge sum in student loans.

Q: What writing convention would you most like to see changed in law?

A: I'd like to see citations stripped from the text and put into footnotes, and footnotes confined to references of this kind—that is, stripped of all talk. To appreciate the enormous difference this would make, you've got to see examples. Some opinions from the Fifth Circuit, as well as from some Delaware, Washington, and Texas courts, provide good models. If we could unclutter memos and briefs in this way, the writing would have to get better because writers would have to start focusing on what they're saying rather than on merely what they're citing. And without the citations between sentences, writers would find it easier to supply transitions as they move from sentence to sentence.

Of course, you'd still need to say in the text what decision you're talking about, what court issued it, and how old it is, but you'd eliminate all the numbers and string citations with parentheticals. The reform is urgently needed, and word processors have now made it possible.

ঌ ঌ ঌ

From *The Record*

Q: We all know your credentials as a fine lawyer. So what prompted you to shift to making legal writing your primary career?

A: Writing and language have been my passions from the time I was 15 or 16. As a teenager, I idealistically thought that law might be the perfect profession for someone committed to excellence in the written and spoken word, so I planned to become a lawyer. Then, as an undergraduate, when I began writing scholarly articles on Shakespearean linguistics, my mentors in the English department at the University of Texas were urging me to pursue a Ph.D. in English. I thought hard about it but stuck to my original plan and entered law school at Texas right after getting my B.A.

During my first week of law school, I began writing *A Dictionary of Modern Legal Usage*, and I worked on it steadily as a law student. When Oxford decided to publish it a few years later, all sorts of doors opened for me.

Meanwhile, I was on the regular law-firm track that so many other law graduates take, and my goal as a practicing lawyer was to make partner at my firm. But when the books began to blossom, I realized that I might be able to do something very different and, for me, much more meaningful.

Q: Have you always been a strong writer?

A: Relative to my peers, yes. But there have certainly been times, in high school and as an undergraduate, when I overestimated my writing skills. It took some English professors to mark up my papers thoroughly to show that I wasn't being as clear and cogent as I thought I'd been. Meanwhile, though, in my spare time I'd pretty much memorized H.W. Fowler's *Modern English Usage*, Wilson Follett's *Modern American Usage*, and Bergen Evans and Cornelia Evans's *Dictionary of Contemporary American Usage*.[1] So, in terms of grammatical knowledge, I was unusually advanced

---

Adapted from *The Record* (Florida Bar, Winter 2005) (interviewed by Dorothy F. Easley).
[1] H.W. Fowler, *Modern English Usage* (Ernest Gowers ed., 2d ed. 1965); Wilson Follett, *Modern American Usage* (1966); Bergen Evans & Cornelia Evans, *Dictionary of Contemporary American Usage* (1957).

as an undergraduate. Two of my English professors openly said I should be teaching their classes.

Q: Do you still practice law?

A: Yes, but it's an unusual sort of law practice. For the past decade, I've been hired by courts to help rewrite their rules and jury instructions. At the federal level, this resulted in the publication of my booklet *Guidelines for Drafting and Editing Court Rules* (1996). I also work on two or three major briefs each year.

Q: Today, do you consider yourself an appellate lawyer or a writer, or both?

A: In about equal measure, I'm a lawyer, a lexicographer, an author, a grammarian, and a teacher. Last week when I came back from England, I filled in the immigration form by putting "teacher/writer." But I suppose I should have added "lawyer."

Q: Do you think the IRAC [issue–rule–application–conclusion] method of argument is the most effective method in an appellate brief?

A: It never has been, except for filling up bluebooks in law-school exams. Actually, the way I teach issue-framing, the issue itself consists of rule–application–conclusion followed by a question mark. Part of the problem with "IRAC" is that it postulates a highly superficial issue statement.

One of my more original contributions to the field of written advocacy is to urge the use of the multisentence issue statement of no more than 75 words, written in the form of a syllogism with a concrete minor premise and ending with a question mark. I call it the "deep issue," and the advantage is that anyone can pick it up, read it, and understand it. Even nonlawyers.

The deep issue promotes clear thinking. We really must get away from this IRAC nonsense, except when it comes to law-school exams.

Q: Do great lawyers still outline their appellate briefs?

A: Yes, and always before they begin writing in earnest.

Q: What are the critical methods to good appellate brief-writing?

A: Take time to think hard about what you want to say and why. Plan your beginning, middle, and end. Write swiftly, without stopping to edit. Revise, and enlist as many good editors as you can.

Q: Is it practical in appellate briefs to put case citations in footnotes, as you advocate, rather than in the body of the brief?

A: It's a lightning-rod issue. The answer is that of course it's practical, and many lawyers that I consider really good writers do it routinely. The key is to say in the text what the authority is, and to discuss the cases contextually so that no one ever has to glance down at the bottom of the page to know what case you're talking about or what court decided it. I'm strongly against anything but reference notes. I don't want people looking down at footnotes to get the context. I want the authority up, but the volume numbers and page numbers down.

Q: Do most appellate courts favor it?

A: Well, judges around the country have begun doing it in their judicial opinions. For example, look at the reports for decisions in Alaska, Delaware, Ohio, and Texas. Every time I take a vote, having explained my position fully, most judges in judicial-writing seminars vote to begin doing it.

Q: Why is the change necessary?

A: It allows you to remedy the nonparagraphs that are endemic in our profession—string citations followed by parentheticals. It also lets you shorten your average sentence length; vary your sentence patterns; write good, meaty paragraphs; write shorter paragraphs when you need them for variety; avoid the unsightliness of volume numbers and page numbers pockmarking the text; check your citations for accuracy more readily; and maintain a cleaner narrative line in the prose. So the advantages are huge.

One last note of caution: don't say anything substantive in a footnote except in a life-threatening circumstance.

Q: What tips do you have for minimizing harmful facts in appellate briefs?

A: Don't let your opponent bring them up for the first time. Get them out on the table in the middle of your argument, not at the beginning or end, and show why they shouldn't affect the result.

Q: What tips do you have for organizing briefs into their most readable form?

A: Organize around deep issues. These are the points of decision for the court expressed in a way that your nonlawyer relatives would understand.

Figure out how many of those points there are and what they are, then order them logically from strongest to weakest. Narrow them down to three or four points if possible. Scrap the truly weak points. Then write good point headings corresponding to the issues you're going to include. That gives you a good outline and a working table of contents.

Q: What is the average number of revisions you'd expect an appellate brief to go through?

A: I can't imagine filing a brief without at least 3; I've done as many as 65. But it all depends on how we're counting. If each little change that you save on the computer counts as another "version" of the document, then it could go into hundreds. For major revisions in which several team members are involved, I imagine 3 could be adequate.

Q: I've heard of Justice Thurgood Marshall's famous ten-page briefs, before he became a Supreme Court Justice. Can a 10- or 15-page brief in 14-point font sufficiently cover one complex legal issue?

A: In the hands of a skillful thinker who also knows how to write, I think it typically can. But advocates often mistakenly want to fill all the available space.

Q: What jurists do you think are outstanding writers today?

A: Judge Frank Easterbrook has extraordinary flair with the written word. So does Judge Alex Kozinski. Although I admire Justice Antonin Scalia's rhetorical deftness, no one on the Supreme Court today is as masterly as Justice Robert H. Jackson was in the mid-20th century.

Q: Have you seen work of certain appellate lawyers that you think was especially outstanding?

A: Yes. Anyone who's looked at my books will see that I favorably quote from the work of Beverly Ray Burlingame of Dallas (clean, tightly reasoned arguments); Steven Hirsch of San Francisco (great introductions); Steven Shapiro of Chicago (great introductions); and, of course, Theodore Olson of Washington, D.C. (terrific overall). There are certainly others whose work I admire—for example, Terence G. Connor of Miami; Mike Hatchell of Tyler, Texas; Evan Tager of Washington, D.C.; and Steven Wallach of New York City. I'm fortunate to see the work each year of some superb advocates.

Q: Are law schools today doing a better job of producing lawyers who can write?

A: Yes, but . . . oh, there's so much to say here, and it would overwhelm the rest of this interview. The law schools are better than they used to be. But we must remember that almost all highly effective writers are to a great degree self-taught. So it's not as if your schooling marks an end with this type of skill.

Q: How far have we come in legal writing in the last ten years?

A: I see improvements, but they're glacial.

Q: What more is needed to improve writing in law?

A: In law schools, hiring for legal-writing positions needs to be on a par with hiring for torts or contracts professors; there need to be chairs and professorships in the subject to attract the best minds. In practice, lawyers as a whole need to view themselves as professional workers in words. They need to study the literature on effective writing and speaking—the old-fashioned arts of rhetoric—to hone their skills.

They also need to be less self-satisfied, and to realize that no matter how adept they think they already are, they've barely scratched the surface. There's an enormous body of knowledge that they need to master, and few have come close. It's partly a matter of not letting your previous schooling get in the way of your ongoing education.

Q: What do you recommend lawyers read in their free time to improve their writing?

A: Start with reading John Trimble's book, then Sheridan Baker's, then perhaps my *Elements* book. Round out the first year of reading with William Zinsser's work.[2] Seriously, I recommend that lawyers read at least one book each quarter on language and writing.

---

[2] The published works are: John R. Trimble, *Writing with Style* (2d ed. 2000); Sheridan Baker, *The Practical Stylist* (8th ed. 1998); Garner, *The Elements of Legal Style* (2d ed. 2002); William Zinsser, *On Writing Well* (6th ed. 1998).

Q: What projects are you spending most of your professional time on these days?

A: I've just finished the big new eighth edition of the unabridged *Black's Law Dictionary*,[3] as well as *The Rules of Golf in Plain English*.[4] Now that I have 14 or so books in print, my workdays are often a matter of trying to keep these books up to date. So at any given time I'm working on improvements to future editions of one book or another. And then, of course, I'm teaching seminars for lawyers and judges week after week.

Q: What are some of your upcoming projects?

A: I'll soon be starting a new slate of seminars, mostly on the West Coast. You can find out the locations by checking lawprose.org.[5]

Conclusion

A California state appellate court underscored the vital nature of high-quality appellate brief-writing this way:

> The appellate practitioner who takes trial level points and authorities and, without reconsideration or additional research, merely shovels them into an appellate brief, is producing a substandard product. Rather than being a rehash of trial level points and authorities, the appellate brief offers counsel probably their best opportunity to craft work of original, professional, and, on occasion, literary value.[6]

Anyone familiar with the works of Bryan Garner knows that he is revolutionizing appellate brief-writing to help the appellate community do just that.

---

[3] *Black's Law Dictionary* (West, July 2004).

[4] Jeffrey S. Kuhn & Bryan A. Garner, *The Rules of Golf in Plain English* (Univ. Chicago Press, May 2004).

[5] Anyone wanting more information can reach Bryan Garner through LawProse, Inc., at www.lawprose.org.

[6] *In re Marriage of Shaban*, 105 Cal. Rptr. 2d 863 (Ct. App. 4th Dist. 2001).

 è** è** è**

From *Copy Editor*

Q: You state in the preface to *A Dictionary of Modern American Usage*, the first edition of your recently revised usage manual, that H.W. Fowler "was the most formidable prescriptive grammarian of the 20th century." What would you say to editors and writers who appreciate Fowler's prescriptive approach but find his "formidable" tone a little off-putting?

A: Well, Fowler's tone reflects both his personality and the times in which he wrote. He was British; he was old-fashioned. But sometimes, in surprising ways, he could be disarmingly informal. It may be impossible that he would strike us as anything but a little donnish in his tone, being an early-20th-century British writer. But if you take him for who he was and what he was, you'll find things to like in his tone.

Q: You find that the words of wisdom make up for any distance there might be between him and the rest of the world?

A: I guess I'm just willing to discount the occasional creakiness that I see in his prose, so grateful am I for his wit and wisdom.

Q: How would you compare your tone with his?

A: I'm less formal, I'm more unbuttoned—I'm a lighter read, I think. But I believe I'm probably just as confident in the positions I take on usage questions. It takes some time to cultivate a style in which you're really comfortable with how you come across on the page. But ultimately, that's what any good writer is looking for—a natural style that reflects oneself.

Q: The new edition of your book is called *Garner's Modern American Usage*. The title change signals an uptick in authority, doesn't it? How does it feel to be an established expert in language?

A: It was Oxford University Press's idea to change the title in this way. The debate within the press was whether it should happen on this edition or on the third edition, as it did with *Fowler's Modern English Usage*. I guess the idea was that it was time, and I was flattered by the decision.

Adapted from *Copy Editor* (Jan. 2004).

Q: In the essay "Making Peace in the Language Wars," which appears in the new edition of your usage dictionary, you discuss at some length the ongoing tension between the descriptivist and prescriptivist language camps. Could you sum that up in a couple of sentences?

A: Actually, I attempted to do just that at the end of the book in the select glossary, where I sought to be very evenhanded and fair toward both camps. I define *descriptivism* as "[a]n approach to language study that forswears value judgments in deciding what is 'correct' or 'incorrect,' effective or ineffective, and instead describes how people use the language without ever disapproving of the forms they use." *Prescriptivism* I define this way: "An approach to language study that embraces the role of value judgments in deciding what is linguistically effective or ineffective, better or worse, and therefore guides people toward mastering a standard language." That's a fair summary, and yet there's so much more underlying those definitions. Many people who haven't kept up with the debate between prescriptivists and descriptivists would be surprised at the rancor between the two camps.

Q: Did you write this essay mainly to inform nonacademic readers of the debate? Or did you really hope to persuade describers and prescribers to tolerate each other and even work cooperatively?

A: Mostly the latter. That essay is a serious effort to advance the debate. And I think there are glimmers of hope among the descriptivists. I could point to some descriptivists—I'm thinking of Edward Finegan in particular—who seem to be fair-minded in talking about what prescriptivists do. I really want descriptivists to study more closely what prescriptivists do and to stop constructing straw men to tear down. It is an amazingly nonscholarly, nonobjective approach that many descriptivists take, so I name names in the essay and show some of the absurd positions they adopt. And the idea is to promote a greater degree of responsibility among scholars and among linguistics students, whether you're going to call them linguists or language critics.

Q: One obvious reason for language rules, it seems to me, is clarity. If someone uses the word *flaunt* instead of *flout* but means "treat with contempt" rather than "show off," listeners may well be confused. Why would anyone object to imposing rules that prevent misunderstanding?

A: Well, that's just the point. It's hard to believe that anyone *would* oppose promoting clarity, and yet the dogma that so many linguists have adopted—

that it's wrong to impose or encourage any kind of distinction at all, as opposed to seeing the language as a self-regulating system—will lead people into astounding instances of betraying common sense.

Q: You note in "Making Peace . . ." that prescribers are sometimes charged with overreliance on personal taste. How much does taste figure into your work? And is it necessarily a bad thing?

A: I think taste is critical. Certainly in any language commentator or rhetorician, you want taste, but it must be tempered by knowing what people actually do with their language—by empirical evidence. One advantage that I have over somebody like Fowler is that I have the luxury of much greater empirical resources at my disposal and a much better library. So it has allowed me to do all sorts of empirical work to test or support my judgments.

Q: A self-described "descriptive prescriber," you provide lots of usage examples from published work to support your judgments about language. How often do the examples you dig up trump the principles you begin with? In other words, how often do you change your mind while you're conducting research?

A: That happens quite often, especially in chasing down tangents. Most of the usage items that I have listed in the entry on "differentiation," for example, I discovered upon looking at dozens and then hundreds of examples; and in places, I had to override my initial judgments. When I'd get into the databases and begin doing some comparative research, I'd often find points of differentiation that had emerged in practice and that I hadn't seen before. Some of these points I'd never heard of before. They needed to be recorded.

Q: Can you offer an example?

A: *Conversant in* and *conversant with*. Or *heritable* and *inheritable*. Or *reparable* and *repairable*. The uses of a tricky word like *timpani*. Many of these are just really arcane byways of the language, but in a usage book, they all add up to something significant.

Q: At what point is a language rule deservedly (or at least justifiably) abandoned?

A: If it's a valid rule or distinction, I don't think you want to be among the first to let go of it. I don't think you want to be the very last person to jettison it, either. So if I were to try to quantify this, I'd feel comfortable being one of the last 3% to 5% giving up a distinction. For example, *hopefully*: it's a word that I don't even use, and I probably will not use it for the rest of my life. I'm sure that at least 98% of the instances of *hopefully* are in what has traditionally been the disapproved sense, but I'm not going to use that word. I consider it a skunked term; some people will object to it. I'm willing to be, as I say, one of the final 3% to 5% who say "ər," for example, instead of "er" [for *err*]; who say "**flak**-sid" instead of "**flas**-id" [for *flaccid*]. And I will try to promote the idea that the traditional pronunciation or usage is the better one and get the numbers up above 5% if I can. Ultimately, I'm afraid, "er" and "**flas**-id" are going to win out. But I'm not giving up on those yet.

Q: Can you name some rules you were glad to see go?

A: I'm generally unhappy to see any valid rule or convention fall by the wayside. But I'm quite happy to spread the word about superstitions. Never end a sentence with a preposition, never split an infinitive, never begin a sentence with a conjunction—these ideas are just outright shibboleths that no informed prescriptivist has adhered to over the last century. And yet, when people think of prescriptivism, they're often thinking of these superstitions and false notions about grammar and usage. So of course I want very much to spread the word that these are mistaken ideas about writing.

Q: It's weird, but I've found that many authors don't want to be told that it's okay to split an infinitive. When you say it is, they think you must be wrong.

A: That's an extraordinary one. It appeared in grammar books only from about 1840 to about 1900. It's fairly rare that you'll find a post-1900 book defending the idea that you shouldn't split an infinitive. So it was in written texts only for a comparatively short time, and yet that idea still has a stranglehold on the popular mind.

Q: Who started the rumor?

A: I've traced it back to a fairly minor grammarian in the 1840s. I have not been able to find an earlier instance than, I think, 1843. I don't have it here at my fingertips. I wrote about this in a letter published in *Harper's* in the fall of 2001.

Q: Are there any rules that you wish were still in play?

A: I wish people were more fastidious in the use of *Jr.* and *Sr.* with names. I'm sorry to see the old rule, by which *Jr.* disappears upon the death of the father, falling into disuse. I won't go into it here because it's actually a very lengthy entry in *GMAU*, but I'd like to see that one restored. There are others, I'm sure. I'm not happy about the position I've had to take on *self-deprecating* versus *self-depreciating*, but I'm a realist.

Q: Your manual takes a very different stance from that of *Merriam-Webster's Dictionary of English Usage*. What do you think of that book?

A: I once described it in an essay as the "anti-usage-dictionary" usage dictionary. Some people have looked at that book and my book and said that the conclusions aren't so very different. In some cases, the judgments may end up being quite similar, but the way we get there is really quite different—and so is the whole view of language. What I respect about *Merriam-Webster's Dictionary of English Usage* is the exhaustive research in the grammatical literature on each point that it discusses. What I don't like about the book is the tone that it takes toward earlier commentators such as Fowler and Theodore Bernstein. It's a highly condescending tone that tends to suggest that all these earlier writers were know-nothings who didn't have the advantage of the Merriam-Webster files. And *Merriam-Webster's* entries often suggest that if the editors can find examples of a given usage, then it must ipso facto be correct. Of course, that's only the beginning of the question, as far as I'm concerned.

Q: Does the book go as far as to distinguish between "correct" and "incorrect"?

A: It wouldn't use those words. It'd probably say something like "appropriate." Another thing: I happen to believe that a usage book should give us the upshot of the analysis up front and then the fuller justification in the body of the entry, as in a well-written essay. But every one of those entries begins with a summary of the literature to date and only gradually winds up to the point, which is often quite predictable. So I tend to view the entries in the *Merriam-Webster's* book as badly written essays.

Q: How did you decide what to cover in the chapter on grammar and usage that you contributed to the 15th edition of *The Chicago Manual of Style*? Wasn't it difficult just to hit the highlights when you'd been writing an almost 900-page book on the same subject?

A: *GMAU* is probably 80% usage and 20% grammar, and the grammar in that book is alphabetically arranged—making it easy to find what you need, in some ways, but a little bit tricky in others. When I sat down to write the chapter for *The Chicago Manual*, I decided to write about each part of speech exhaustively and systematically. And I found myself getting into all sorts of grammatical points that I had never written about before. It was a very useful, educational exercise for me, but to write about grammar in the way that a grammarian would—as opposed to a usage writer—required a much more thoroughgoing approach. Because you're not slicing it up alphabetically and dealing *only* with the problem points in the language, you end up having to be more comprehensive. So I tried to write a "restatement" of English grammar. Now, some will fault me for restating points that native speakers don't have any trouble with; but the challenge for me was to deal with English grammar systematically and not assume that users of the manual already knew all sorts of things. So it is one of the longer chapters in the book. I decided to put the most important usage points in the glossary at the end and to deal with the prepositional problems that come up all the time in terms of idiom. It ended up being a chapter that really does not duplicate much of my other work.

Q: When I taught composition at West Virginia University about ten years ago, the program director told us teaching assistants that most people speak better than they write. Do you agree with that assessment?

A: In one sense, yes; in one sense, no. In the first part of the answer, I can say that people who sit down to write often freeze up and adopt a hyperformal, alien-sounding, stuffy style, because they have picked up somewhere along the way that that's what writing is all about. This may have come from bad schooling in junior high school, in which the teaching of writing is often a negative experience—and maybe some of these writers never got beyond having lots of ink spilled on their papers and disapproval of anything that seemed natural in their style. Those very same writers, if you talk to them, will speak quite naturally; but when they write, they start using lots of genteelisms and formalisms. On the other hand, I don't think that speech is any better than writing in terms of usage. We seem to have a proliferation, now, of malapropisms. We're gradually returning to the days of being an oral culture. There seem to be more and more people who go through their daily lives without having to read—by taking in their news from television, by doing all sorts of things other than reading. And even people of a literary type probably do less reading than in yesteryear. I think it's interesting that Lindley Murray's grammar books of the early 19th century (from 1795 until 1850) sold something like 30 million to 40 million copies. Today, it's astounding to think that any book could sell that well. Even Stephen King would be envious of that kind of record. It's just that we have so many more demands on our time and so many other ways of taking in information—but the upshot of all this is that people seem to be confusing words never before confused. And that's why it's so important to keep usage books up to date. All kinds of new problems are constantly arising in the language that never used to be there. I really like recording usage problems for the first time. Hundreds of entries in *GMAU* are about entirely new sorts of linguistic issues. They're not the same old hackneyed usage points that every little guide discusses.

Q: What are some of the craziest malapropisms you've come across?

A: One error that's not really a malapropism is the growing misuse of *as such* in place of *therefore*. I think I was the first to deal with that. Also, *wreckless* driving—that's a good one. I quoted *The Philadelphia Inquirer* twice with that one in the first edition, but I updated the examples in the second. Using *gambit* for *gamut*: "running the gambit." There are thousands of them. *Heart-rendering* instead of *heart-rending*. Words like *uncategorically* and *unmercilessly*, for *categorically* and *unmercifully*. *Flamingo* dancers. The *entomology* of words. The asteroid was *hurdling* toward the earth. I didn't include things that are so rare that there are only one or two examples of them. I tried to find ones that are fairly common. Any two words that sound vaguely alike will ultimately be misused for each other.

Q: When I taught, I had a student write an essay about Bette E. Davis.

A: There's a great 19th-century book—written by Caroline LeRow around 1890—collecting bloopers from student papers. It's called *English as She Is Taught*. Mark Twain wrote a preface to it in a later edition.

Q: Since you've been researching language for decades and weighing heaps of evidence largely from journalistic publications, you may be in a better position than anyone to evaluate the state of mainstream American usage. In what ways is it getting worse? What improvements have you noticed over the years?

A: Malapropisms are spreading, and more and more people seem to be going through life rather uncritical of language—they're not critical listeners and not self-critical users. On the other hand, you see improvements as well. One big improvement in writing over the last century is that the average sentence length has gotten much shorter. You don't see the kinds of involuted sentences giving rise to grammatical problems today that Fowler made his stock-in-trade. That's probably a good thing, by and large.

Q: In light of your discoveries about language, and about the politics of language, what big-picture advice can you give copy-editors?

A: I'd say three things: First, do everything you can to educate yourself about the language. I'd recommend reading one book per quarter on language or rhetoric. You don't have to do as I do and read two or three a week—I'm trying to be realistic about this. Second, keep making distinctions. Don't think that you're the only one who cares about linguistic distinctions, because you're not. You may be the only one in your immediate surroundings who seems to care, but there are many of us out there. Third, understand that copyediting involves people skills as well as technical skills. A big part of what you're trying to do is sell good edits, so you have to be realistic in your working life about what points you can push and what points you can't. And be willing to back up what you say, but do it in a charming, nonthreatening way.

Lon L. Fuller • Roscoe Pound • Grant Gilmore

CHAPTER FIFTEEN

Book Recommendations

A Lifetime Reading Program

BECAUSE WRITING IS fully as complex an activity as the practice of law, even great teachers do not great writers make. Ernest Hemingway spoke all too truly when he said that writing is a lifelong apprenticeship. This is both a curse and a blessing. It's a curse because we're left always in a state of trying to measure up to our ever-higher self-expectations. It's a blessing because writing well is a challenge that never grows old. We're always learning and always building on what we've learned. If life is a journey, so is writing. In any event, we writers must accept a difficult truth: we are essentially self-taught.

But what exactly does that mean?

We teach ourselves, first, by imitation. We learn from all the best writers we read. We observe how these pros, themselves great teachers-by-example, handle the language. We copy their manners and effects to see how they achieve both an attractive "voice" and a companionable relationship with us, their reader. We study their paragraphing style, their sentence structures, their spelling, their punctuation, their openers and closers, their transitions between sentences and paragraphs, their verbs and adverbs, their style of wit, their allusions, and so on.

We teach ourselves, second, by avoidance. We also learn from all the inept writers we read. We observe how they mishandle the language, how they misdirect or bore or exhaust us, and how they fail to achieve a voice worth listening to—and we try hard to avoid doing those same things.

Adapted from *Student Lawyer* (Sept. 2005).

We teach ourselves, third, by self-study. We scrutinize our own writing. We learn by obsessively revising it, phrase by phrase, draft after draft. We try to make it ever more simple and direct, ever more intelligent, ever more varied, and ever more tightly organized. In other words, we try to make it ever more as if it came from our favorite writer.

And last, we teach ourselves by avidly reading the self-help literature—the published advice of acknowledged writing experts. Many of them are great teachers that we can meet and learn from only through their books: books on style, grammar, usage, rhetoric, reader psychology, and the many other facets of language.

For a reading regimen, I suggest two kinds of texts: those that illustrate good writing and those that explain how to produce it. Having spent the better part of 20 years reading books about effective writing—on average about two a week—I think it's reasonable to expect lawyers, as professional writers, to read one such book per quarter. The problem is finding the right ones. As Mark Twain once quipped, nine out of ten books on how to write well are badly written.

So a select list can be a valuable time-saver. What follows are 12 books that will help you no matter how adroit (or maladroit) you may be right now with the written word. Consider them suggestions for the first three years of your lifetime reading program. I think you'll find them both engaging and exceedingly worthwhile. But if you disagree once you've gotten a dozen pages into the book, don't despair. Just pick up another book for that quarter. I'm wagering that you won't have to.

Among the books on writing, I've interspersed a few examples of superb prose stylists writing about legal subjects. Rounding out each year of the reading program, they're notable because their bright style stands out amid the dreary gray style that typifies legal writing.

1. John R. Trimble, *Writing with Style* (2d ed. 2000): This may be the single best book for getting started as a serious writer. It's unintimidating and conversational—and full of common sense about writing. Trimble will become your friend and guide, and he'll make sense of some things that have probably puzzled you—such as why you may have always thought that people who preach about careful language are dowdy stuffed shirts. Once you learn Trimble's techniques, you'll understand that the stuffed shirts aren't really writing well at all.

2. S.I. Hayakawa & Alan R. Hayakawa, *Language in Thought and Action* (5th ed. 1991): This book will change the way you think about language. It'll go a long way toward inoculating you against propaganda and educating you about how advertisers work. It'll

explain why it's so important to avoid abstractions if you want to think clearly. And it'll keep you from falling into the many verbal snares that we're all susceptible to, such as confusing words with the things they represent. As Hayakawa says, the map is not the territory.

3. Rudolf Flesch, *How to Write Plain English: A Book for Lawyers and Consumers* (1979): Flesch, an innovator of readability tests and the author of several classics on producing readable writing, shows here how to apply his techniques to legal prose. For several years he was an FTC consultant charged with putting the agency's regulations into plain English. He fortifies his points with incomparably good before-and-after examples.

4. Grant Gilmore, *The Ages of American Law* (1977): What a fast-moving, bright writing style Gilmore had. In 111 pages, he imparts extraordinary insights into American law and its development. Here's a typical Gilmore passage, on the casebook method of legal instruction that C.C. Langdell invented: "Langdell seems to have been an essentially stupid man who, early in his life, hit on one great idea to which, thereafter, he clung with all the tenacity of genius. However absurd, however mischievous, however deeply rooted in error it may have been, Langdell's idea shaped our legal thinking for fifty years." Don't skip the endnotes: they're as good as the text.

5. William Strunk & E.B. White, *The Elements of Style* (4th ed. 2000): It's just a primer, of course, and too short to serve as a real reference book, but what's there is pure diamond. You'll be inspired by the wisdom that springs from its pages. After you've read it, which will take at most four hours, plan on revisiting this book at least once a year.

6. Sheridan Baker, *The Practical Stylist* (8th ed. 1998): This book, by a leading modern rhetorician, has perhaps the finest discussion I've ever read on how to structure an essay. The opening 30 pages alone are well worth your time and investment. But there's much else to learn here, such as the smart entries on commonly misused words.

7. Aristotle, *Rhetoric* (350 B.C.): Parts of this book will be heavy going, especially its anatomy of different types of syllogisms, but you'll benefit from reading it carefully. Aristotle is brilliant on techniques of argumentation. You'll be astounded at how fresh his insights seem.

8. Charles Alan Wright, *The Law of Federal Courts* (5th ed. 1994): Here you'll see a beautiful legal mind at work. In 1963, it was the first book to sum up its subject in one crisp volume; it catapulted Wright to the pinnacle of the profession. The fifth edition was the last one that's pure Wright. Observe his control of tone and the confidence with which he assesses the cases he discusses. If a hornbook can be a page-turner, this is it.

9. William Zinsser, *On Writing Well* (6th ed. 1998): This book is very much in the Trimble mode, and it's well done. Zinsser will tell you why *But* is the single most powerful word for beginning an English sentence. He'll tell you that fighting verbosity is like fighting weeds: you're never finished. And he'll tell you that if you want to write well as part of a large organization, you must do everything you can to avoid sounding like an automaton.

10. Bryan A. Garner, *The Elements of Legal Style* (2d ed. 2002): Inspired by the Strunk and White classic, this book shows how to write specifically about legal subjects. And it goes into more depth, with enlightening examples from judicial opinions, briefs, law reviews, and legal texts. It includes a unique chapter on the rhetorical figures used by legal writers, plus an appendix provides you with a collection of some of the most important statements ever made about prose style.

11. David Mellinkoff, *The Language of the Law* (1963): This seminal book helped spawn the plain-language movement in law. With admirable clarity, Mellinkoff shows that there's no good reason why lawyers should use legalese—and many reasons why they shouldn't. You'll be edified about legal terminology as you never thought you could be.

12. Lon Fuller, *Anatomy of the Law* (1977): Like Wright and Gilmore, Fuller proves that great legal minds write about complex legal subjects in a simple, direct way. (Mediocre minds, on the other hand, move toward muddlement.) Lon Fuller, one of Harvard Law School's premier thinkers, explains our legal system and our legal techniques as few others have been able to. Enjoy both his thought and his expression. They're well worth emulating.

A parting word: Even if you were to heed all the advice in these books or to try to mimic their style, you'd still end up with your own style. We all begin by imitating things we like. But ultimately, if we're serious in our efforts, we fashion a style of our own.

ả ả ả

Sources for Answering Questions
of Grammar and Usage

WHAT MAKES A LAWYER A LAWYER? The answer certainly isn't that the lawyer knows all the law in a given jurisdiction. That's impossible. What makes a lawyer a lawyer is knowing, when a legal question arises, how to go about finding the answer—if there is one. Lawyers don't purport to give off-the-cuff answers without hitting the books. Anyone who does that probably won't remain a lawyer very long.

But if lawyers know about hitting the books on legal questions, what happens when a language question arises? Somebody asks whether it's acceptable (or even desirable) to start a sentence with *And* or *But*, whether it's wrong to end a sentence with a preposition, or some other grammatical or stylistic question. Where should the adverb go in relation to a verb phrase—inside or outside? Is splitting an infinitive always forbidden? Does *data* take a singular or a plural verb? What's the preferred plural of *forum*? Unfortunately, many lawyers aren't so fastidious about finding answers to these questions. They're likely to feel satisfied with a seat-of-the-pants approach. Yet even educated guesses about what the experts say are likely to be wrong.

Every practicing lawyer is, by the very nature of the job, a professional writer. That's why lawyers, of all people, need to know how to find the answers to questions of grammar and usage. Although most journalists generally know where to look, most lawyers are at a loss. Many might look at a book called *English Grammar*, but most books bearing that title don't answer the questions. Others would look at a primer such as Strunk and White's *Elements of Style* (a superb weekend read), and still others would turn to the *AP Stylebook* or some other style manual. But on the finer points of grammar and usage, they'd come up empty.

The vast majority, though, wouldn't even crack a book: they'd give off-the-cuff answers based on half-remembered things that middle-school teachers told them. If they did this with legal questions, it would be prima facie legal malpractice. In writing, it's literary malpractice.

Adapted from *Student Lawyer* (Feb. 2000).

To avoid it, you'll need to own some dictionaries of usage. Very simply, they are guides to grammar, usage, and style arranged in alphabetical order—according to well-known terms of grammar and usage. So if you want to know whether you can justifiably begin a sentence with *And*, look under that word; with *But*, look there; on split infinitives, see "SPLIT INFINITIVES"; on the placement of adverbs, see "ADVERBS"; on ending sentences with prepositions, see "PREPOSITIONS."

If you're at all serious about writing, you'll need to own some usage guides. They'll arm you with knowledge when language questions arise.

Now, before I tell you about various dictionaries of usage, a disclaimer is in order: I've written two of them. That's not really surprising, given that the dictionary of usage has long been my favorite literary genre. I'm not saying that you should go out and buy my books: you can have a good usage library without them. Have a look at what's available and judge for yourself.

Although hundreds of usage guides have appeared over the years, the following are five that I think you'll find most helpful. They appear in chronological order:

- H.W. Fowler, *A Dictionary of Modern English Usage* (Ernest Gowers ed., 2d ed. 1965). More than anybody else, H.W. Fowler invented the modern dictionary of usage. The first edition appeared in 1926. Although he was largely unconcerned with American English—and had a peculiarly British style—he still has many useful things to say to modern writers. Among the classic entries are "battered ornaments," "inversion," "polysyllabic humour," and "superstitions." The last of these is about the most common misconceptions of what it means to write well.

- Theodore M. Bernstein, *The Careful Writer* (1965). For many years, Bernstein was an editor at *The New York Times*, and this book— one of several he wrote—represents the culmination of his wisdom on writing and editing. With a light, wry, oh-so-sensible touch, Bernstein provides guidance on such issues as "absolute constructions," "one idea to a sentence," "puns," and "rhetorical figures and faults." His brilliant introduction, entitled "Careful—and Correct," should be required reading for all writers, especially lawyers.

- Bryan A. Garner, *A Dictionary of Modern Legal Usage* (2d ed. 1995). This was the first dictionary of usage targeting legal writers. It discusses hundreds of usage problems that arise in law but not elsewhere. Among the entries worth consulting are "doublets, triplets, and synonym-strings," "plain language," "sexism," and "words of authority." There's even an entry called "lawyers, derogatory names for."

- Wilson Follett, *Modern American Usage: A Guide* (Erik Wensberg ed., 2d ed. 1998). The book is a quite conservative guide to good usage. It has excellent essays on why grammar matters, on journalese, and on the sound of prose. Follett was the first usage critic to take issue with the modern use of "hopefully" (to mean "I hope"). Originally published in 1966, this book was nicely updated by Erik Wensberg in 1998.

- Bryan A. Garner, *Garner's Modern American Usage* (2d ed. 2003). This fully modern usage guide quotes thousands of recent examples from newspapers, magazines, and books—with full citations. The most frequently cited grammatical bunglers are writers for *The New York Times*. Although the book treats the traditional usage problems and has, for example, a full discussion of how every punctuation mark is used, it contains hundreds of entries on word-choice problems that older books omit.

No single usage guide, you'll discover, has the final word. Part of the fun is learning to judge for yourself, item by item, the value of one writer's guidance as compared to another's. And as you browse through these manuals (that's inevitable), you'll learn all sorts of things that you never dreamed (or is it *dreamt*?) of.

If you consider yourself weak in grammar and usage, browsing through dictionaries of usage is probably the easiest—and most enjoyable—way to brush up. You don't have to study the subject systematically: just read a little bit each day, for a few minutes a day. Try a usage guide as idle-time reading for a few weeks, and you'll be on your way. That's the way it has worked for many excellent writers and editors. You could join their ranks.

A Usage-Guide Sampler

Here are some typical examples of entries you'll find in various dictionaries of usage.

H.W. Fowler, *A Dictionary of Modern English Usage* 264 (2d ed. 1965).

if and when. Any writer who uses this formula lays himself open to entirely reasonable suspicions on the part of his readers. There is the suspicion that he is a mere parrot, who cannot say part of what he has often heard without saying the rest also. There is the suspicion that he likes verbiage for its own sake. There is the suspicion that he is a timid swordsman who thinks he will be safer with a second sword in his left hand. There is the suspicion that he has merely been too lazy to make up his mind between *if* and *when*. Only when the reader is sure enough of his author to know that in his writing none of these probabilities can be true does he turn to the extreme improbability that here at last is a sentence in which *if and when* is really better than *if* or *when* by itself.

Theodore Bernstein, *The Careful Writer* 73–74 (1965).

between you and I. Just as one swallow doesn't make a drunkard, so an isolated instance or so of bad grammar culled from even the most gifted writers does not constitute a valid authentication for that particular misusage. Thus, it is idle to pretend that *between you and I* must be a legitimate construction because Shakespeare used it in *The Merchant of Venice*, or because it can be found elsewhere, lonely and loose. The greatest writer may have committed a grammatical offense because he was preoccupied, or because he was negligent, or because he had in mind a reason that is obscure to his readers now, or merely because he had a bellyache .... [The phrasing] is grammatically indefensible. *Between* is a preposition and it is followed by the objective case: *me*. To say *between you and I* is a needless, pointless, and ignorant exception to a good rule.

Bryan A. Garner, *A Dictionary of Modern Legal Usage* **162 (2d ed. 1995).**

Clichés. Why is it that, in legal prose, common sense always *dictates* certain actions? That precedents are never to be *lightly overruled*? That to look at something a second time is invariably to *revisit* it? Why are trial judges whom the appellate courts agree with always *learned,* but never wise or perspicacious or erudite? Why is any significant evidentiary hearing always termed *full-blown*? Too often in legal writing, parties *strenuously object*; judges write *vigorous dissents*; legal principles are never settled but that they are *well-settled*; trial judges always have *sound discretion* rather than mere discretion; exceptions are never created— instead they are *carved out* . . . .

Clichés should generally be used sparingly in any writing, but especially in legal writing. Yet we are beset with hackneyed phrases inappositely employed in legal briefs and judicial opinions. To begin with, good writers have sensitized themselves to what a cliché is. Acquiring this sensitivity requires some literary taste, but mostly a background that includes wide reading. One need not read very many American judicial opinions to find, e.g., that *We do not write on a clean slate* is a commonplace often repeated.

Wilson Follett, *Modern American Usage: A Guide* **164 (2d ed. 1998).**

irregardless. This is *regardless* changed by mistake to resemble *irrespective*, its cousin in meaning. *Regardless* says *without regard, unmindful*, and is usually followed by *of*, as in *Regardless of drops of rain, they continued to climb*. By adding the negative prefix *ir-*, the careless produce the meaning *not being without regard*. This notable nonsense is just what *regardless* does not mean.

ào ào ào

Is Law a Literary Profession?

IF YOU ENTERED LAW SCHOOL with the idealistic view that law is a literary profession—in fact, that a career in law depends on using words well and wisely—you're not alone. Two of the greatest legal writers of the 20th century back you up. William Prosser, the most famous exponent of the law of torts, viewed law as "one of the principal literary professions." Indeed, warming to his theme, he said, "One might hazard the supposition that the average lawyer in the course of a lifetime does more writing than a novelist." Charles Alan Wright, our premier authority on federal practice and procedure, took a similar view: "The only tool of the lawyer is words," he said. "Whether we are trying a case, writing a brief, drafting a contract, or negotiating with an adversary, words are the only things we have to work with."

But however true these views are, or should be, you may find that your own experience won't entirely square with them. In all sorts of ways, law as ordinarily practiced isn't a literary profession at all. I can point to two large chunks of evidence.

First, much of the writing to be found in lawbooks seems as if it belongs in a morgue. That style died years ago. Small wonder that one leading scholar has called that exalted set of books, *United States Reports*, a "great literary wasteland." And most of the judicial opinions in law-school casebooks, especially opinions issued between 1880 and 1930, are so ill-written that it's often hard to wrest any ideas from the wretched language in which they're expressed.

Second, modern lawyers aren't, on the whole, an especially literary group. In fact, many don't even go in for books—and those who do typically stay away from legal subjects. As Gregory Talbot, owner of the Lawbook Exchange of Clark, N.J., puts it: "Because many lawyers aren't having fun in day-to-day practice, the idea that they'd continue reading in the legal discipline when they get home doesn't appeal to them. The mundane legal reading that they must do keeps them from looking into the literature of law." But then there's his even more sobering afterthought: "A lot of lawyers just aren't readers at all. It's a frightening thought." Indeed.

Because lawbooks have been stereotyped as involving boring recitations of facts and subtle procedural points, the wealth of first-rate legal literature often gets overlooked. That's worse than unfortunate because

---

Adapted from *Student Lawyer* (Sept. 2005).

many lawyers will never see—or learn from—the inspired legal writing that exists.

Let's assume, though, that you want a true liberal education in the law—that you want a grounding in law that will serve you well no matter what your specialty might end up being. Here are about a dozen books that you might profitably read and relish. You'll find all of them in the law library. Make time to read at least a few chapters each week. They'll entice and enlighten you, and they'll broaden your legal education enormously.

1. Benjamin Cardozo, *The Nature of the Judicial Process* (1921). Cardozo, a great judge both in New York and on the U.S. Supreme Court, gave us what is probably the wisest exposition of judging ever written. He begins this way: "The work of deciding cases goes on every day in hundreds of courts throughout the land. Any judge, one might suppose, would find it easy to describe the process which he had followed a thousand times or more. Nothing could be further from the truth."

2. Roscoe Pound, *An Introduction to the Philosophy of Law* (rev. ed. 1955). Long the revered dean of Harvard Law School, Pound explains in this classic text of only 168 pages all the major trends in traditional legal philosophy. If you're more interested in history than philosophy, try one of Pound's other classics, *The Formative Era of American Law* (1938).

3. Oliver Wendell Holmes, *Collected Legal Papers* (1920). The great thing about this classic collection is that Holmes's major speeches, such as "The Path of the Law" (1897), are here, as well as extremely brief papers and addresses. You can dip into everything from "The Use of Law Schools" to "Legal Interpretation" to "Natural Law." Holmes's words resonate as clearly today as they did when written.

4. Learned Hand, *The Spirit of Liberty* (3d ed. 1960). This book is a collection of 41 papers by a beautiful legal mind. Some are eulogies of important judges (Justices Holmes, Brandeis, and Cardozo), some are commencement addresses and other orations, and some are essays of undeniable importance: "Morals in Public Life," "A Plea for the Open Mind," and "The Spirit of Liberty."

5. Max Radin, *The Law and You* (1948). In 153 brisk pages, Max Radin—an immensely learned law professor who specialized in everything from Roman law to business law to legal lexicography—gives a thumbnail sketch of ten major areas of law and how they affect everyone in society. Of all the books on the model of

"everybody's guide to the law," this is the most readable—and the one written by the most learned author.

6. Lon Fuller, *Anatomy of the Law* (1968). Fuller, a Harvard law professor and extraordinarily lucid stylist, did the same thing for legal philosophy that Radin did for law in general. If you've assumed that philosophy is dull or esoteric, this book will change your mind—and expand it.

7. R.E. Megarry, *A Miscellany-at-Law* (1955); *A Second Miscellany-at-Law* (1973); *A New Miscellany-at-Law* (2005). Have you ever wondered whether it's contempt to throw a dead cat at a judge? Whether "oomphies" can be trademarked? What's the legal status of stolen dung? Legal humor isn't limited to derogatory jokes, and it isn't always intentional. These books, by an enormously erudite barrister and later judge, are treasure troves of wit and oddities from judicial opinions, treatises, and statutes spanning more than six centuries.

8. Glanville Williams, *Learning the Law* (any edition). Perhaps the most highly respected English law professor of the latter half of the 20th century, Glanville Williams wrote this book to prepare entering law students to think about their studies, their profession, and their path in the law. Although America has produced similar books, none comes close to equaling this first-rate analysis.

9. Charles E. Wyzanski, *Whereas—A Judge's Premises* (1965). Judge Wyzanski, of the federal district court in Boston, was a first-rate thinker and writer. This book is a collection of his enlightening essays on judges, the compass of the law, the bar generally, and values in modern society.

10. Grant Gilmore, *The Death of Contract* (1974). Gilmore, another of the great 20th-century legal thinkers, opens with a grabber: "We are told that Contract . . . is dead. And so it is. Indeed the point is hardly worth arguing anymore. The leaders of the Contract is Dead movement go on to say that Contract, being dead, is no longer a fit or worthwhile subject for study." In 103 sprightly pages, Gilmore shows how contract law is being absorbed into tort law.

In sum, while many lawyers see themselves as mere pushers of words, the legal writers just cited remind us that, at its best, law is one of the highest of all literary callings. And if you look hard enough, you'll find that amid all the mind-numbing drivel that fills up lawbooks, there is also a heritage in legal literature that rivals the best of literary traditions.

SAMUEL JOHNSON

CHAPTER SIXTEEN

Book Reviews

There It Is in Writing, Fairly Drawn[1]

Reed Dickerson, *The Fundamentals of Legal Drafting* (2d ed., Boston: Little, Brown & Co. 1986). Pp. xxix, 393.

TOO OFTEN WHEN WE SPEAK of legal writing, we conceive of it as being a single genre, though drafting a contract differs as much from writing an appellate brief as a how-to article differs from an essay. If discursive legal prose—the kind we use in persuading courts—is a form of literary art, then the drafting of legislation and of legal instruments is a craft, and certainly an important one. Though some might argue that the Code Napoleon or Article 9 of the UCC is an exalted work, the fact remains that the medium of setting out rights, obligations, powers, and privileges simply does not lend itself to artistic expression.

The special skills essential to the craft seldom receive the attention they merit. Reed Dickerson has championed those skills for more than a quarter-century, and has straightforwardly addressed most of the recurring issues that crop up in legal draftsmanship. Now in its second edition, *The Fundamentals of Legal Drafting* is the most authoritative American guide to the subject.

Yet for all its strengths, I find Dickerson's book somewhat inferior to its major Australian counterpart, E.L. Piesse's *Elements of Drafting*.[2]

Adapted from *ABA Journal* (Feb. 1989).

[1] "The Taming of the Shrew," III.i.70, in *The Riverside Shakespeare* (G. Blakemore Evans ed., 1974).

[2] E.L. Piesse, *Elements of Drafting* (5th ed. 1976).

Consider one signal difference between the two works: the extent to which drafting is candidly acknowledged to be primarily a matter of technique. Dickerson is reluctant to concede this. He devotes his second chapter to "Drafting and Substantive Policy," and in his final chapter sets out the "substantive" and then the "formal" benefits of good drafting. Piesse, meanwhile, forthrightly states at the very outset: "This book on *Elements of Drafting* treats of expression more than of substance." Surely we can accept that statement at face value without minimizing the benefits of well-honed drafting. My guess is that many shortsighted academicians would therefore say that legal drafting is not a field worthy of study. Dickerson was probably reacting self-consciously to them.

Indeed, Dickerson's emphasis on substantive aspects of drafting—which seem to me self-explanatory—reflects an understandable defensiveness. "[M]any lawyers have tended to . . . downgrade important aspects of drafting," he says, and have "treat[ed] legal drafting as if it were a mere literary exercise." Although Dickerson rightly observes that drafting involves far more than searching for the accurate and felicitous phrase, he spends too much time explaining why that is so. Is it really necessary, for example, to drag into the discussion the Sapir–Whorf theory of how a given language influences the thought patterns of native speakers?

Fortunately, this new edition covers much more material than its predecessor. Dickerson has added fresh chapters on "Verbal Sexism," "Amendments; Redesignation," and "Computers and Other Scientific Aids." In his chapter on sexism, Dickerson states that "[v]erbal sexism includes language that is conducive to treating women unfairly," and perceptively observes, "The problem is to determine not only what is currently and significantly sexist but the extent to which removal is, under the circumstances, the wisest alternative or even feasible." Though he includes a section on the suffix *-man*, and briefly refers to the possibility of writing *drafter* rather than *draftsman*, Dickerson curiously does not explain his preference for *draftsman*, the form he uses throughout.

In that same chapter, Dickerson addresses the pronominal problem—the fact that the English language has no common-sex singular pronoun other than *his*—with clarity and common sense. He refers to seven different ways to avoid what some perceive to be a sexist male pronoun, and lucidly points out the merits and demerits of each. Dickerson rightly states, for example, that avoiding male pronouns by "repeating the nouns adds a degree of awkwardness that legal utterances hardly need, and it thus helps frustrate current efforts to alleviate a writing malaise that remains a continuing embarrassment to the legal profession."

If only the revisers of the Federal Rules of Evidence had consulted this work before perpetrating their handiwork in the revision! They have adopted throughout the very awkwardness that Dickerson aptly criticizes, repeatedly replacing simple pronouns with whole phrases. Here, for example, is the newly bowdlerized Rule 608: "The giving of testimony, whether by an accused or by any other witness, does not operate as a waiver of [his] *the accused's or the witness'* privilege against self-incrimination . . . ." The aggregate effect is that the rules are now even more taxing to plod through. Perhaps the gains to society are great if we eliminate the generic *he* and *his*, but the replacements should be unobtrusive.

One of the most common pitfalls of drafting—using the future rather than the present tense to describe future actions—receives scant attention from Dickerson. In one page he purports to cover the subject, giving three correct examples (without showing the pitfalls) and paraphrasing Coode's 1843 treatise as follows: "When it is necessary to express a time relationship, the draftsman should recite facts concurrent with the operation of the instrument as present facts, and facts precedent to its operation as past facts." Yet few readers will grasp the problem that this abstract statement addresses.

Piesse, by contrast, devotes nine pages to the subject of tenses in drafting. He discusses it so concretely and thoroughly that the reader cannot fail to understand the problems attendant to using the word *shall* as a modal auxiliary. One preferably writes, in a conditional sentence, *If the purchaser fails to pay any installment,* not *If the purchaser shall fail* . . . . The latter wording, though it creates all manner of problems with tense, is distressingly common in modern American drafting. If Dickerson's influential book were as thorough as it might be on technical points of this kind, Congress and other legislative bodies might not so pervasively flout sound conventions of drafting.[3]

One may point to other imperfections. What reader is likely to slog through the three-page block quotation at 93–96, which is followed by the statement, "Similar boilerplate regulations were issued . . ."? We also might expect Dickerson to attend more closely to his words: not to confuse *simile* with *metaphor*,[4] or to misspell *idiosyncrasy* as if it were a form of government,[5] or to call two closely related senses of the word *shall* "homonyms."[6] And we might expect him to punctuate better than

---

[3] Example: "It *shall be* [read *is*] unlawful for any person to obtain or use a report . . . ." 28 U.S.C. app. I, § 305(c)(1) (1986) (enacted in 1978). Specimens of poor drafting abound in our state and federal statutes; the root cause appears to be the lack of law-school training in the subject.

[4] Dickerson at 85.

[5] *Id.* at 74, 242.

[6] *Id.* at 34.

this: "Without more documentation, we may surmise that for other private instruments amendments are only occasionally a problem."[7] Surprisingly, Dickerson's style feels flat and repetitive throughout. In just the first 11 pages, for example, he permits himself "a wholesome concern for legal drafting,"[8] "a wholesome point of view,"[9] and "a wholesome attitude of service."[10] The effect is unwholesome.

Nonetheless, *The Fundamentals of Legal Drafting* remains a valuable reference as newly embodied in this second edition. Dickerson is at his best in explaining the architectonics of drafting. His specific suggestions on rewording legalese are still illuminating. And his explanations of the types of ambiguity that so often ensnare legal writers are superb.

In the newly added Appendix F, a previously published essay entitled "On Teaching Legal Writing, Particularly Legal Drafting,"[11] Dickerson points out the root causes of our languishing legal-writing programs in law schools:

1. We have trivialized legal writing by calling it a "skill," when expository writing, of which legal drafting is one kind, is a basic discipline, perhaps the most basic of all disciplines. . . .
2. We have demeaned legal writing by treating it as mainly a matter of language . . . . [Well, so what? Language is our sole arsenal, and therefore of indisputable importance. Sadly, law schools often fail to recognize this fact. —B.G.]
3. We have further demeaned legal writing by trying to crowd too much into single, elementary courses.
4. The growing practice of importing English teachers . . . into law schools tends to confuse the need for special instruction in forensic legal writing, or in legal drafting, with the need for remedial general writing.
5. Misreading the need to join form with substance, we have needlessly diluted writing courses by requiring the student to do the kind of time-consuming legal research traditional to courses on law-library research, term papers, or law-review assignments.[12]

Alas, how many law schools have taken note of this acute diagnosis?

---

[7] *Id.* at 241.
[8] *Id.* at xxii.
[9] *Id.* at 10.
[10] *Id.* at 11.
[11] *Id.* at 353–63.
[12] *Id.* at 353–54.

ข้ ข้ ข้

Harmless Drudgery?

Johnson on the English Language. The Yale Edition of the Works of Samuel Johnson, vol. 18. Edited by Gwin J. Kolb and Robert DeMaria Jr. (New Haven: Yale University Press 2005). Pp. xlviii, 506.

SAMUEL JOHNSON: "Sir, your book is both good and original. But the part that is good is not original, and the part that is original is not good." F.W. Bateson: "I have chosen this particular example not because of the grossness of its inaccuracies but because of the general inadequacy it exhibits to meet scholarly requirements."

In the Yale Edition of the Works of Samuel Johnson, the work that constitutes Johnson's greatest legacy to the English-speaking world—his *Dictionary of the English Language*—isn't included. Imagine, if you will, the collected works of Shakespeare minus *Hamlet*; of Voltaire minus *Candide*; of Flaubert minus *Madame Bovary*; of Mark Twain minus *The Adventures of Huckleberry Finn*. Inconceivable, you think. When you collect an author's works, surely you don't omit the magnum opus.

But one cannot really fault the editors for shying away from Johnson's huge *Dictionary* of 1755. As they say, "The body of the *Dictionary* falls outside the scope of the Yale Edition because of its vast size."

Instead, the scholars who prepared the volume entitled *Johnson on the English Language*—Gwin J. Kolb and Robert DeMaria Jr.—present an annotated version of all of Johnson's writings incident to the *Dictionary*: the original proposal for the great work (1747); forematter from the work itself (1755), namely, the preface, the history of the English language, and the grammar of the English language; a preface to Johnson's abridgment (1756); an advertisement to the fourth folio edition (1773); and two appendixes presenting facsimile reproductions of manuscript material (never before generally available to scholars). The editors rightly claim that "this group of writings has never appeared in a single volume before"—although the more important ones have certainly appeared together in many editions.

The Kolb–DeMaria plan was excellent: collect the pieces, provide scholarly introductions, carefully note the variations among editions, and annotate the pieces with references to Johnsonian definitions, quotations from Johnson's correspondence, and other relevant materials.

Adapted from *Essays in Criticism* (Mar. 2007).

Yes, the plan was excellent. But the execution is flawed—so much so that this first printing is unworthy of becoming the standard work in the field. What we have here is a marginally acceptable sixth draft of what should have been a ten-draft work.

Nowhere is the misbegotten execution more apparent than in the grossly inadequate credit given to James Sledd, one of the most distinguished linguists of the 20th century. Although the commentary in the book is said to be "unprecedented," an enigmatic footnote to the editors' 21-page introduction to Johnson's plan for his dictionary explains that "unless otherwise noted, the present discussion is drawn from Sledd–Kolb." That's a 1955 book: James Sledd and Gwin J. Kolb, *Dr. Johnson's Dictionary: Essays in the Biography of a Book*. And so it is, often word for word.

This massive borrowing leads to several problems. If the Kolb–DeMaria introduction to the plan is in fact mostly a reprint of the Sledd–Kolb chapter of 1955, what has happened to the Sledd attributions? He is absent from the five long paragraphs of acknowledgments. Having died in 2003, Sledd is most conspicuously absent from the specific paragraph devoted to the "several scholars and friends whose deaths have deprived us of some of the pleasure we have in presenting this publication." Nor is Sledd even given his full name in this book—not in the text, not even in the footnotes—except in the table of short titles and the index. Every reference is to "Sledd–Kolb," mostly in footnotes, and there are only 13 of them (unlucky Sledd!) in this 506-page book.

This is no small matter. It appears that the better part of a 38-page chapter of Sledd–Kolb (published by the University of Chicago Press) has been appropriated into this Yale Edition, with grossly inadequate attribution to a coauthor. How much of that chapter was Sledd's and how much was Kolb's?

Other problems are present. If the better part of a 38-page chapter of Sledd–Kolb has been reproduced here—and that's 35% of the Kolb–DeMaria commentary—what happens to the claim that the commentary in this volume is "unprecedented"? Much of it has been taken almost wholesale from a 1955 volume.

There are still more problems. The copyright to the Sledd–Kolb book was registered in the name of the University of Chicago Press, not in Sledd's name or Kolb's. Did anyone obtain copyright permission to reprint the bulk of a 38-page chapter? Not according to the acknowledgments and not according to the copyright page. And not according to the permissions editor at the University of Chicago Press, either. A permission request to the University of Chicago might have resulted in Sledd's getting proper attribution.

Then there are the editorial shortcomings. Kolb and DeMaria are far too tentative as scholars and historical investigators in two respects.

First, they repeatedly labor the obvious. For example, after noting that Johnson cut a long paragraph from the final version of the "Scheme" for the *Dictionary*, they add that "he apparently decided not to use it." One conjectures so. But then they add even more: "The reasons for his decision can only be surmised, but perhaps . . ." (p. 11). Of course it's all a matter of surmise. Another example: they explain that Johnson traveled to Oxford in 1754 to visit Thomas Warton with the avowed purpose of working on the "History of the English Language" for the *Dictionary*. Our editors then go out on this bathetic limb: "We are . . . confident that during his 1754 visit to Oxford, Johnson's talks with Warton embraced the *Dictionary* (including the History)—the cause, after all, of Johnson's visit" (p. 119). Well, of course. Finally, consider this naively explicit statement: "Before his death in 1784, [Johnson] was surely aware . . . of the abridgment's much greater popularity than that of the original work" (p. 365). One imagines that he was: lexicographers tend to know which of their books are selling best. And notice the supernal redundancy in "before his death in 1784." The editors do not venture a guess on what knowledge Johnson might have had in an afterlife.

Second, the editors blanch from making reasonable deductions from the evidence. In a long passage, they note striking similarities between Johnson's preface and that of Ephraim Chambers's *Cyclopaedia* (1728): (1) both express the lowly reputation of lexicographers; (2) both discuss the pains involved in writing a dictionary; (3) both refer to Julius Caesar Scaliger's poem on the subject of painful work; (4) both discuss their inevitable failures; (5) both suggest the heroism involved in their work in light of the fact that other countries had assigned whole academies to carry out comparable assignments; (6) both reject the idea of an English academy; (7) both express the importance of shunning foreign words; (8) both revere what they called "intellectual history" and link it directly to lexicography; (9) both refer to lexicographers as "pioneers"; and (10) both mention "shops" and "mines" as being sources of legitimate vocabulary. Add to this Johnson's known familiarity with Chambers's work—Johnson cited it some 150 times in the first three letters of the *Dictionary* proper—and the similarities appear more than just coincidences.

So are the editors willing to suggest that Chambers almost certainly influenced Johnson? Astoundingly, no. Each of those ten correspondences can be found scattered in the lexicographic literature that existed in 1755, so they think it's just as likely that Johnson found each of these correspondences in one of those many other sources. Are the editors even willing to say that Chambers *probably* influenced Johnson? No. Instead, here's what they conclude: "The most that can reasonably be claimed is that Chambers is an important member of the tradition of lexicographical writings on which Johnson drew" (p. xxxiii). How, one wonders, are they defining *reasonably*?

Because the editors are weak in exposition, they habitually resort to repetition. On page 16 of their introduction to the plan, they say: "As R.W. Chapman noted long ago, signature A was set once and then completely reset." Then, on page 24, we're given the same information in much more detail—with the attribution "as R.W. Chapman pointed out many years ago." This kind of repetition suggests poor organization. But it's hardly a surprise, given the editors' weak grasp of chronological narrative. In one place, they tell a story by starting in 1755, moving then to 1658, then to 1617, and finally to 1587 and 1561 (pp. xxix–xxx). The reverse chronology only confuses. But then sometimes the poor organization is manifest, as when the editors begin a section by saying: "As stated above [where, exactly?], five early partial or complete versions of the *Plan* are extant. They include, to repeat . . . ," followed by another 194 words to complete the sentence (p. 22).

The paragraphing is sometimes odd. In a paragraph on favorable remarks about Johnson's preface, the editors list nine sources in a string of citations, quoting from three (p. 70). The last one, though, doesn't fit into the collection of plaudits. Without any signal such as "But cf.," "But see," or the like comes this unheralded rebuke of Johnson from James Thomson Callender: "that whole preface is a piece of the most profound nonsense, which ever insulted the common sense of the world." One feels a little the same way about that whole paragraph.

Although some of the footnotes are genuinely useful, others suggest that little effort went into the editors' scholarship. For example, in his plan, Johnson wrote: "It will be . . . sometimes proper to trace back the orthography of different ages, and shew by what gradations the word departed from its original" (p. 37). In a footnote, the editors state: "Our search—certainly not exhaustive—has disclosed no example of such 'tracing' in *Dictionary*" (p. 37 n.8). But Johnson himself gave *gibberish* as an example (and so it is). A brief troll through the first edition of the *Dictionary* will quickly turn up other examples: Johnson's entries for *abbess*, *account*, *blend*, *chymistry*, *ferrier*, *moble*, and *mungrel* all contain such tracing.

Often when one wants a footnote, there is none. For instance, in his *Grammar*, we find SJ writing: "The English verbs were divided by Ben Johnson into four conjugations" (p. 324). One suspects a typographical error in *Ben Johnson* for *Ben Jonson*. But a quick check of the first, second, and third editions of the *Dictionary* shows that all three contain the spelling *Johnson*. Is that the spelling that SJ always used in reference to Ben Jonson? A note here would have been helpful.

At many other points, marginalia would have been useful, if only to help the editors double-check their work. True enough, the editors often take Johnson's words and annotate them with his definitions in the *Dictionary*. But they don't do this consistently. For example, in the preface to Johnson's 1756 octavo abridgment of the *Dictionary*, the Yale Edition uses the spelling *ennumerated* (p. 368). The editors might have noted this unetymological spelling, yet no such note appears.

But wait: it gets worse. My two copies of the octavo edition (1760, 1766) both show *enumerated* properly spelled—not *ennumerated*. In an annotated edition that expressly purports to collate every printing of the octavo edition, with all variations noted, this is a serious fault. A little scholarly checking into the anomalous *ennumerated* (surely just their own typist's misspelling) would have revealed the error.

The scholarly impedimenta are inconsistent in other ways. One note lists "*eccentrick* [sic]" and "*phlegmatick*" (no [sic]) (p. 107). A long quotation from Allen Reddick has no direct attribution (p. 363), and one is left to wonder whether a later attribution—48 words later, on the next page—is meant to cover the first quotation as well as the second. In one place, we're told that Nathan Bailey's octavo edition of his *Universal Etymological English Dictionary* (1721) is, in someone's words, the "most popular of all dictionaries antedating Johnson" (p. 364). Who, precisely, is being quoted remains a mystery.

Kolb and DeMaria generally translate Latin (e.g., pp. xxiv, 43 n.8, 183 n.2), but not always (e.g., p. 325 n.1). Yet they routinely expect their readers to know 18th-century French (e.g., pp. xxv, xxviii [twice], xxx, 17–18). One puzzles over what the editors mean when they state that their goal is to "satisfy the scholar while erecting few barriers to the pleasure of the literate reader" (p. xi n.4). One imagines many readers—admittedly not as literate as they might like to be—struggling with the French and the untranslated Latin.

The editors are hardly believable in this claim about Johnson's abbreviations: "Johnson employed combinations of diagonal lines and consonants which we could not duplicate" (p. 123). Editors in 2005 couldn't reproduce abbreviations made in 1755? This sort of reproduction is easier today than it ever has been.

The editors' command of grammar and usage is shaky. They use unparallel constructions with correlative conjunctions (e.g., *both in our introductions and our notes* [p. xi]); they use the false subjunctive for a point of plausible historical fact, not something that is contrary to fact (Taylor sounds *as though he were on terms of easy familiarity with the author* [he may well have been, and the appropriate verb is *was*—p. 5]); they engage in noun plague (referring to *the conclusion of the discussion of definition* [p. 10]); they're fond of the needless *and/or* (*passim*); they use *former* (and, by implication, *latter*) without any grammatical antecedent (p. 20); and so on.

There are typographical errors, too. The misspelling *orthopoeist* (for *orthoepist*) infects one note (p. 305 n.3), and it's so far off as to be genuinely troubling. Then there are notes like this one, in which *as accurate* should probably read *inaccurate* or *as inaccurate*: "Many slightly inaccurate quotations suggest SJ's use of his memory in supplying illustrative quotations, but since he is often as accurate as a copyist, it is impossible to say how much he relied on his memory" (p. 99 n.2). What's the sense here? The line is one that later scholars may want to quote—but to what effect?

Even what should have been conscious editorial choices get muddled. The notes about Johnson constantly shift between present tense (e.g., *SJ does, SJ believes* [both p. 42 n.4]) and past tense (e.g., *SJ used* [p. 42 n.5], *SJ corrected* [p. 79 n.4]). The possibility that the editors were distinguishing between the authorial Johnson and terrestrial Johnson doesn't hold up to scrutiny.

In the moving peroration of his *Preface*, Johnson alludes to "those whom I wished to please, [who] have sunk into the grave" (p. 113). The editors' note to this line states: "SJ refers particularly to the death of his wife Elizabeth (Tetty)." No, he doesn't. He certainly alludes to it, but he doesn't "refer particularly" to it. The editors continue: "but he may also have in mind his dear friend Gilbert Walmesley." Why *but*? Why not *and*? Johnson's allusion was to *those* who *have sunk,* in the plural. Yet the editors seem to suggest otherwise. This inattentiveness to words is prevalent in the notes, and it is particularly troubling in an edition of the works of Samuel Johnson.

From an editorial standpoint, much remained to be done before this book should have gone to press. Many existing footnotes could have been fruitfully amplified. The editors' prose could have undergone a thorough edit to pare down the verbosity and repetition and to correct the inaccuracies and usage errors. Most important, a book in which 35% of the commentary comes straight from a 50-year-old book shouldn't have been passed off as "unprecedented"—and without adequate authorial acknowledgment. On close inspection, the book has a distinctly unfinished look.

ઋ   ઋ   ઋ

Not Your Father's Fowler

The New Fowler's Modern English Usage. Edited by Robert W. Burchfield
(Oxford & New York: Oxford University Press 2000). Pp. xxi, 873.

MAYBE IT'S UNFAIR to compare Burchfield's revision with Fowler's 1926
classic[1] or with Gowers's excellent second edition of 1965.[2] Burchfield,
you see, isn't really a Fowlerian. In fact, he seems to hold Fowler—as
many other descriptive linguists do—in contempt. In his preface, Burchfield confesses that he doesn't understand the book's long-standing appeal:
"The mystery remains: why has this schoolmasterly, quixotic, idiosyn-
cratic, and somewhat vulnerable book, in a form only lightly revised
once, in 1965, by Ernest Gowers, retained its hold on the imagination of
all but professional linguistic scholars for just on 70 years?"[3] He never
really tries to answer that critical question.

William Safire tried to answer it in his *New York Times* column on
December 1, 1996. Here's what he said: "In an age of semantic shift and
grammatical drift, this has been a book that offers moorings."[4]

But surely there's more to it than that. Here's what I'd say. Fowler
had four great qualities that no other grammarian or usage critic has had
in equal measure.

First, he was the ideal scholar–critic. He was a lexicographer, true,
but he was also a literary critic. He wasn't exclusively one or the other.
His interests were those of the professional editor more than of the pro-
fessional linguist. He shared that quality with Theodore Bernstein[5] and
Wilson Follett,[6] but he knew more about linguistics than either man.
That knowledge was something he had in common with Bergen and
Cornelia Evans,[7] but he had better literary and editorial judgment than
they, and he was confident in exercising that judgment. No one else has

---

Adapted from *Gleanings of the H.W. Fowler Society* (Spring 1997).

[1] H.W. Fowler, *A Dictionary of Modern English Usage* (1926) (*MEU1*).

[2] H.W. Fowler, *A Dictionary of Modern English Usage* (Ernest Gowers ed., 2d rev. ed.
1965).

[3] *The New Fowler's Modern English Usage* ix (R.W. Burchfield ed., 3d rev. ed. 1996)
(*MEU3*)

[4] William Safire, *On Language*, N.Y. Times, 1 Dec. 1996, § 6 (Magazine), at 34.

[5] *See* Theodore M. Bernstein, *The Careful Writer* (1965).

[6] *See* Wilson Follett, *Modern American Usage* (1966).

[7] *See* Bergen Evans & Cornelia Evans, *A Dictionary of Contemporary American Usage* (1957).

quite matched Fowler's blend of interests and talents: he was the most formidable prescriptive grammarian of the 20th century.

Second, Fowler was superb at insightfully categorizing linguistic phenomena and developing pithy names for them. To him we owe such important notions as "differentiation," "needless variants," "elegant variation," and "slipshod extension." A linguist might describe these phenomena in clinical detail—without judging a pair of words on the merits—but an editor wants to know what to do about an editorial dilemma. An editor needs to make a quick decision and yearns for guidance. Fowler gave that guidance and rarely disappointed even the most knowledgeable editors.

Third, although Fowler could occasionally be opaque (see his entry under *exception*), he generally wrote exceedingly well. Consider just the opening sentence for his essay on "Purism": "Now & then a person may be heard to 'confess,' in the pride that apes humility, to being 'a bit of a purist'; but *purist* & *purism* are for the most part missile words, which we all of us fling at anyone who insults us by finding not good enough for him some manner of speech that is good enough for us."[8] I count four genuine insights in that one sentence: (1) that people tend to "confess" this quality, but they're really proud of it; (2) that pride often manifests itself in feigned humility; (3) that *purist* is a "missile word"; and (4) that we tend to use that word out of insecurity.

So he loaded too much into one sentence? Quite the contrary. You wouldn't want four sentences for those ideas: Fowler used subordination well in achieving a tight style.

Fourth, Fowler was boldly original. He brought a fresh, critical mind to the language and therefore commented on words and phrases that no one before had thought noteworthy. And in the process, he created a new genre: the dictionary of usage. Before 1926, there were a few books on misused words, but nothing like a usage dictionary. If you want a glimpse of just how innovative Fowler was, compare *MEU1* to its contemporary American counterpart, George Philip Krapp's *Comprehensive Guide to Good English* (1927).

Dozens of usage dictionaries have now appeared, of course, but no other author of such a book has equaled Fowler's brilliance.

Perhaps the biggest mistake was calling Burchfield's book *Fowler's*. It isn't Fowler's—not H.W. Fowler's—not even 1% of it. The book is new, front to back. The author isn't particularly fond of Fowler. As both

---

[8] *MEU1*, note 1, at 474–75.

The New York Times and *The New Yorker* noted, Burchfield came to bury Fowler, not to praise him.[9]

So why was it called Fowler?

I can't give a definitive answer to that question, but I can propose what I think is a helpful analogy. Imagine a modern Jungian psychoanalyst—the foremost living one—becoming the editor of *The Complete Works of Sigmund Freud*. Of course, he fundamentally disagrees with Freud on myriad points, and so he radically alters the text. In fact, he rewrites the papers from beginning to end to coincide more with modern learning and with the Jungian doctrines to which he adheres. The set is then issued as *The New Freud*.

If we take the book as "Burchfield," not as Fowler, then it's much easier to admire. Perhaps the main comparison should be not between Burchfield and Fowler, but between Burchfield and *Webster's Dictionary of English Usage* (1989). These are the two usage books most recently produced by major dictionary publishers, *WDEU* being American and Burchfield (of course) being British.

The British win in this contest because Burchfield is at least willing to use his judgment. Where *WDEU* seeks primarily to show that every usage critic to date is a dunderhead and that "the evidence" suggests that almost any usage is acceptable, Burchfield occasionally takes a firm stand. Thus, *WDEU* takes almost three pages to say it's okay to say *deprecate* when you mean *depreciate*. But Burchfield says in one sentence what the doctrinaire *WDEU* could never say: "It is important to bear in mind that *deprecate* (from L *dēprecārī* 'to try to avert by prayer') is in origin an antonym of *pray* (from L *precārī* 'to pray'); and that *depreciate* (from L *dēpretiāre* 'to lower in value,' f. *pretium* price) is in origin an antonym of *appreciate, increase in value*."[10] The sentence is parenthetically encumbered, to be sure, but it's a finer statement than you'll find in the original Fowler.

Again and again, one finds useful information in Burchfield. And often it's memorably expressed:

- "These verbs [*affect* and *effect*] are not synonyms requiring differentiation, but words of totally different meaning neither of which can ever be substituted for the other."[11]

---

[9] *See* Christopher Lehmann-Haupt, *Not Only to Praise Fowler, but Also to Bury Him*, N.Y. Times, 26 Dec. 1996, at B2; John Updike, *Fine Points*, New Yorker, 23 & 30 Dec. 1996, at 142 ("Burchfield in his preface has come not to praise but to bury his fabled predecessor.").

[10] *MEU3* at 206.

[11] *Id.* at 31.

- "Lower the flag in sorrow whenever you see the word *idiosyncrasy* misspelt."[12]
- "The now widespread use in American publications of *reign* (instead of *rein*) in the phr. *give (free) reign to* is deeply regrettable."[13]
- "It is impossible to draw a firm line between hackneyed phrases and clichés: they are genera of the same species. [Interestingly put, but is that possible?] They are at the same time endearing and irreplaceable, and maddening and replaceable. . . . In passages that already lack any element of excitement or real interest they are unendurable. In obituaries they flourish like moss."[14]

In short, when you compare Burchfield to *WDEU*, he consistently wins the day.

Thus far, Burchfield has been better received in Britain than in the U.S. Perhaps that's because H.W. Fowler has been revered much more in the U.S. It is largely attributable to Fowler's influence, for example, that American editors follow his recommendations on *that* and *which*. British editors ignore them, and Burchfield himself often uses *which* where Fowler would have insisted on *that*.

Is it possible that, among professional writers and editors, American and British views on language are simply too divergent to be treated in a single work? Americans seem more conservative in their views than the British, and Fowler gave us an enlightened conservatism. Perhaps we'll need a second American edition of Fowler: a revision of Margaret Nicholson's sturdy American edition of 1957[15]—a book that everybody seems to ignore when talking about the history of Fowler.

My own forthcoming *Dictionary of Modern American Usage* is no such book, by the way: it's Garner, not Fowler. But I do think it would be possible to continue the American lineage that Nicholson started, with a book that remains 75% Fowler.

Meanwhile, Burchfield—as Burchfield, and within his own frame of reference—gives us much to be thankful for. And he deserves the accolades he's getting in the better reviews.

---

[12] *Id.* at 375.

[13] *Id.* at 664.

[14] *Id.* at 346.

[15] Margaret Nicholson, *A Dictionary of American-English Usage* (1957).

ॐ ॐ ॐ

Don't Know Much About Punctuation
Notes on a Stickler Wannabe

Lynne Truss, *Eats, Shoots & Leaves: The Zero[-]Tolerance Approach to Punctuation.* (London: Profile Books 2003). Pp. xxvii, 209.

ANY EXPERIENCED EDITOR who spends much time in both Britain and America will probably conclude that, on the whole, British standards of punctuation are somewhat lower than American ones.

Take, for example, the renowned legal scholar Peter Birks's obituary in *The Times* last summer. Written by an Oxford don, it was riddled with the most elementary punctuation errors: many missing commas, wrongly inserted commas, a superfluous hyphen, missing hyphens, and a missing apostrophe (omitted from *master's degree*)—not to mention a couple of grammatical bungles.[1] These weren't what professional editors would call discretionary errors; they were outright errors—11 inarguable ones. Regular readers of *The New York Times*, our closest analogous publication to *The Times*, would find it unthinkable for such sloppy work to appear in its own obit pages.[2]

Or take Britain's fatal attraction to dropping apostrophes. British store names such as *Harrods* and *Selfridges* lost their apostrophes long before similar names in America started losing them. In 1979, *Garners Steakhouse* could be seen prominently in London—yet the proprietor, I came to find out, was someone named Garner, not Garners. I couldn't help asking, and I wasn't the only American in my group driven to distraction over the point.

Small wonder that the late Robert W. Burchfield, editor in chief of the *Oxford Dictionary Supplement*, predicted that the apostrophe would disappear from English.[3] He was preceded by George Bernard Shaw, who

---

Adapted from *Texas Law Review* (Apr. 2005).

[1] *Professor Peter Birks*, The Times (London), 9 July 2004, at 34.

[2] That's not to say that *The New York Times* is unimpeachable. In *Garner's Modern American Usage* (2d ed. 2003) (*GMAU*), I cite that paper more frequently for grammatical and word-choice blunders than any other—some 450 times.

[3] Robert W. Burchfield, *The English Language* 25 (1985) ("The prevalence of incorrect instances of apostrophes at the present time, even in the work of otherwise reasonably well-educated people . . . , suggests that the time is close at hand when this moderately useful device should be abandoned.").

in 1902 wrote that "[t]here is not the faintest reason for persisting in the ugly and silly trick of peppering pages with these uncouth bacilli."[4]

Yes, the Brits (not *Brit's*) have long needed help in punctuation.[5] Not that Americans can't use some as well, but the British need it even more. In fact, it's fair to say that in edited prose, American standards of usage—not just punctuation—are generally higher than British ones. That may seem hard to substantiate, but 25 years of close professional observation, and voluminous research and writing on the subject, make it pretty clear to me.

So it's heartening to think that a British book on punctuation could become a best seller. No punctuation book before Lynne Truss's *Eats, Shoots & Leaves*[6] ever did that. Even in the early 19th century—when the American Lindley Murray become known as "the father of English grammar"[7] on both sides of the Atlantic, and his grammar books sold more than 15 million copies[8]—contemporaneous punctuation books probably fared poorly. After all, Murray's 1795 *English Grammar* contained just 15 pages on the subject, and that treatment probably struck most readers as adequate.

One imagines that the soon-to-appear books on punctuation didn't sell so very well, either. There was Cecil Hartley's 1818 *Principles of Punctuation*,[9] followed a few decades later by John Wilson's 1856 book entitled *The Elements of Punctuation*,[10] which by 1899 had appeared in its 31st

---

[4] George Bernard Shaw, "Notes on the Clarendon Press Rules for Compositors and Readers" (1902), *in George Bernard Shaw on Language* 26–27 (Abraham Tauber ed., 1963). *See* Ronald Wardhaugh, *Proper English: Myths and Misunderstandings About Language* 101 (1999) ("If we did not have an apostrophe in the written language, what would we lose? Probably very little."); Steven T. Byington, *Certain Fashions in Commas and Apostrophes*, 20 Am. Speech 22, 27 (1945) ("The fact is, the apostrophe is a morbid growth in English orthography, and our language would be none the worse for its abolition."). *But see* Edward N. Teall, *Putting Words to Work* 144 (1940) (lamenting the "sheer cussedness" of those who see the apostrophe as a "black beast," and attributing this benighted view to a "failure to understand what the apostrophe is and does, and a dodging of the issue").

[5] *Cf.* Louis Menand, *Bad Comma: Lynne Truss's Strange Grammar*, New Yorker, 28 June 2004, at 102 ("An Englishwoman lecturing Americans on semicolons is a little like an American lecturing the French on sauces.").

[6] Lynne Truss, *Eats, Shoots & Leaves: The Zero Tolerance Approach to Punctuation* (2003) (*ES&L*).

[7] Sir Paul Harvey, *The Oxford Companion to English Literature* 342 (2d ed. 1937).

[8] Charles Monaghan, *The Murrays of Murray Hill* 135 (1998); *see* Garner, "Lindley Murray," in *Invisible Giants: Fifty Americans Who Shaped the Nation but Missed the History Books* 209 (Mark Carnes ed., 2002).

[9] Cecil Hartley, *Principles of Punctuation: or, the Art of Pointing* (London: Effingham Wilson 1818).

[10] Boston: Crosby, Nichols & Co.

edition (the printings were likely small).[11] There was Adams Sherman Hill's 1878 booklet called *General Rules for Punctuation*,[12] abstracted from his excellent *Principles of Rhetoric*.[13] Marshall Bigelow's *Punctuation and Other Orthographical Matters*[14] appeared three years later. Then in 1893, Edmund Shaftesbury's *One Hundred Lessons in Punctuation*[15] was published. That book opens with stupendously grandiose hyperbole: "Probably the science and art of punctuation involve more departments of human learning than any other one branch of study."[16] That's the kind of overearnestness that helped give punctuation books a bad name—to the extent that they had any name at all.

Fast-forward 90 years—past the splendid, instructive works of Robert M. Gay,[17] G.V. Carey,[18] and Eric Partridge[19]—and we find our first near-best seller: Karen Elizabeth Gordon's *The Well-Tempered Sentence*.[20] Still, its sales in the 1980s must have been paltry by comparison with the current Truss phenomenon.

Surely Hartley, Wilson, Hill, Bigelow, Shaftesbury, Gay, Carey, and Partridge would have been astonished—and Gordon, since she is still with us, must indeed be astonished—to know that a punctuation book could have sales of more than two million copies[21] and counting.

Astonished, and none too pleased. Although the public seems enraptured by the book, linguistic pros are mostly aghast. In brief telephone interviews on December 29, 2004, four language pundits told me of their puzzlement and contempt. James J. Kilpatrick, the syndicated language columnist and author of such books as *The Writer's Art*[22] and *Fine Print*,[23] was bothered by Truss's sloppiness: "Parts of it were lightweight, and it was not well-edited—there were syntactical errors and outright typographical errors. Calling it a frivolous book is not quite fair, but it

---

[11] New York: American Book Co.

[12] Cambridge: Charles W. Sever.

[13] Adams S. Hill, *Principles of Rhetoric and Their Application* (New York: Harper & Bros. 1878).

[14] Boston: Lee & Shepard 1881.

[15] Washington, D.C.

[16] *Id.* at i.

[17] Robert M. Gay, *Stops: A Handbook for Those Who Know Their Punctuation and for Those Who Aren't Quite Sure* (1941).

[18] G.V. Carey, *Mind the Stop* (rev. ed. 1958).

[19] *You Have a Point There* (London: Hamish Hamilton 1953).

[20] Boston: Houghton Mifflin 1983.

[21] Graeme Hammond, *Chill Out with Summer's Hot Books*, Sunday Herald Sun, 19 Dec. 2004, at 92.

[22] James J. Kilpatrick, *The Writer's Art* (1984).

[23] James J. Kilpatrick, *Fine Print: Reflections on the Writer's Art* (1993).

certainly is lightweight." Barbara Wallraff, the author of *Word Court*[24] and *Your Own Words*,[25] found the book humorous but ridden with errors: "Though it made me laugh, it also made me cringe, because on page after page Truss says things that are ill-informed or even completely wrong." Bill Walsh, author of *Lapsing into a Comma*[26] and *The Elephants of Style*,[27] was struck that people could be taken in by Truss's blustery tone: "I was really surprised at the success of the book. It's less a useful tool than a rant on misplaced apostrophes." Patricia T. O'Conner, the author of *Woe Is I*[28] and *Words Fail Me*,[29] sees the whole enterprise as a major setback: "The misinformation in this book [*Eats, Shoots & Leaves*] could set good English back 200 years. In the name of correctness, Lynne Truss encourages bad punctuation, bad usage, bad sentence structure, bad spelling, and bad grammar. She's not even *consistently* wrong!"

The most searching review of the book was a devastating one by Louis Menand in *The New Yorker*.[30] It exposes Truss's tendency to be fussy about some punctuation matters but inattentive to others—a damning flaw in a book whose subtitle touts its "zero-tolerance approach to punctuation."

Well, that's what the subtitle should say. But instead of hyphenating *zero-tolerance*, as just about every punctuation authority would require,[31]

---

[24] Barbara Wallraff, *Word Court* (2000).

[25] Barbara Wallraff, *Your Own Words* (2004).

[26] Bill Walsh, *Lapsing into a Comma* (2000).

[27] Bill Walsh, *The Elephants of Style: A Trunkload of Tips on the Big Issues and Gray Areas of Contemporary American English* (2004).

[28] *Woe Is I: The Grammarphobe's Guide to Better English in Plain English* (rev. ed. 2003).

[29] Patricia T. O'Conner, *Words Fail Me: What Everyone Who Writes Should Know About Writing* (1999).

[30] Louis Menand, *Bad Comma: Lynne Truss's Strange Grammar* New Yorker, 28 June 2004, at 102.

[31] *GMAU*, note 2, at 604 ("When a phrase functions as an adjective preceding the noun it modifies—an increasingly frequent phenomenon in 20th- and 21st-century English—the phrase should ordinarily be hyphenated."); Paul R. Martin, *Wall Street Journal Guide to Business Style and Usage* 118 (2002) ("The hyphen is helpful to quick understanding even in some frequently used compound modifiers: *high-school students, real-estate dealers, stock-market rally, federal-funds rate.*"); Christopher Lasch, *Plain Style* 61 (Stewart Weaver ed., 2002) ("*Middle class* . . . should be written without a hyphen when it appears as a noun, but it should be hyphenated when it appears as an adjective."); John R. Trimble, *Writing with Style* 129 (2d ed. 2000) ("By itself, the phrase will rarely call for any hyphens, but put it in front of a noun and suddenly hyphens are essential. Why? To show that the phrase is now functioning as a *unit*. And why is that important? Because it can prevent confusion—anything from a momentary 'Huh?' to total bafflement."); Lyn Dupré, *Bugs in Writing: A Guide to Debugging Your Prose* 134 (rev. ed. 1998) ("The most important use of the hyphen is to tie together two words that modify a third, when the third word follows the first two. If you learn how to use hyphens in such compound adjectives, you will be able to tell your reader what you intend to modify what, and that is useful information. Without the hyphens, compound adjectives are ambiguous.");

Truss omits the hyphen.[32] Meanwhile, her dust-jacket photograph shows her impishly adding an apostrophe to the billboard for the 2002 movie *Two Weeks Notice*. She's right that it should have been *Two Weeks' Notice*. But if her arsenal of weapons in the zero-tolerance approach to punctuation includes countless apostrophes, couldn't she find room in there for a few hyphens to use in phrasal adjectives?

You'd think so, given her zealot's prose style. She writes about the "satanic sprinkling of redundant apostrophes"[33] in this "world of plummeting punctuation standards."[34] She laments that "the stickler's exquisite sensibilities are assaulted from all sides"[35] and, somewhat redundantly on the same page, that "[e]verywhere one looks, there are signs of ignorance and indifference."[36] She does, in fact, manage some terrific aperçus:

- "[T]he illiterate default punctuation mark is nowadays the comma."[37]
- "If you've . . . always wanted to know where to use an apostrophe, it means you never will, doesn't it? If only because it's so extremely easy to find out."[38]

Garner, *A Dictionary of Modern Legal Usage* 657 (2d ed. 1995) ("When a phrase functions as an adjective—an increasingly frequent phenomenon in late-20th-century English—the phrase should ordinarily be hyphenated. Seemingly everyone in the literary world knows this except lawyers. For some unfathomable reason—perhaps because they are accustomed to slow, dull, heavy reading—lawyers resist these hyphens."); Wilson Follett, *Modern American Usage* 428 (1966) ("The first and by far the greatest help to reading is the compulsory hyphening that makes a single adjective out of two words before a noun: *eighteenth-century painting / fleet-footed Achilles / tumbled-down shack / Morse-code noises / single-stick expert*. Nothing gives away the incompetent amateur more quickly than the typescript that neglects this mark of punctuation . . . ."); Carey, note 18, at 119 ("In general, writers, editors, and proof-readers need to be more alive to the *double entendre* that may result from omission of a hyphen."); Teall, note 4, at 15 ("The hyphen is useful. We can string nouns together to make a complex name for what is almost indescribable in a single word, and we can use the hyphen to make the relationship clear when mere juxtaposition does not do so.").

[32] *But cf.*, inconsistently enough, *ES&L*, note 6, at 172–73 ("[T]here is a rule that when a noun phrase such as 'stainless steel' is used to qualify another noun, it is hyphenated, as 'stainless-steel kitchen'. Thus you have corrugated iron, but a corrugated-iron roof. The match has a second half, but lots of second-half excitement. *Tom Jones* was written in the 18th century, but is an 18th-century novel. [Most punctuation authorities would omit the comma in the preceding sentence because *is* appears in the second half.] The train leaves at seven o'clock; it is the seven-o'clock train.").

[33] *Id.* at 1.

[34] *Id.*

[35] *Id.* at 2.

[36] *Id.*

[37] *Id.* at 35.

[38] *Id.* at 33.

- "[L]egal English, with its highfalutin efforts to cover everything, nearly always ends up leaving itself semantically wide open."[39]
- "The trouble with all of these grammar books is that they are read principally by keen foreigners; meanwhile, native English-speakers who require their help are the last people who will make an effort to buy and read them."[40]

And she's clearly having fun here, as when she lets fly with colorful Britishisms such as *Lawks-a-mussy!*[41] and *Argy-bargy!*[42]

But these appealing features are hardly enough to compensate for the book's many gaffes. I confine to this paragraph a sampling of Truss's benightedness. She tosses in—as a joke—the most inflammatory racial slur in the language.[43] She misuses *thankfully*[44] and *transpire*,[45] and she uses the nonword *ellipted*[46] for *elided*.[47] She uses *as yet* for *yet*,[48] *no one . . . their*,[49] and the redundant *join together*,[50] as well as erroneously lowercasing E.E. Cummings's name.[51] She mentions parentheses as "paired bracketing devices"[52] but then enumerates with an unpaired parenthesis: a), b), c), etc.[53] She mistakenly says that American editors prefer *1980's* over

---

[39] *Id.* at 102.

[40] *Id.* at 33.

[41] *Id.* at 22.

[42] *Id.* at 29.

[43] *Id.* at 51.

[44] *Id.* at 36.

[45] *Id.* at 102; *see GMAU*, note 2, at 781.

[46] The word does not appear in the *Oxford English Dictionary* (2d ed. 1989), *The New Shorter Oxford English Dictionary* (5th ed. 2002), or the *Chambers 21st Century Dictionary* (1996). Nor does it appear in even the most up-to-date American dictionaries, such as *Merriam-Webster's Collegiate Dictionary* (11th ed. 2003); *The New Oxford American Dictionary* (2001); *Webster's New World Dictionary* (3d coll. ed. 1994). It must have been ellipted out of them all. Or perhaps it resulted from a mistranscription of Tiger Woods's exclamation when his partner barely missed a putt (e.g., "He lipped it out!"). *Cf. GMAU*, note 2, at 552 (s.v. "Nonwords"). Never mind that the word ill-advisedly appears in Sidney Greenbaum, *The Oxford English Grammar* § 6.1, at 311 (1996) ("they cannot be analysed as elliptical clauses because we cannot be sure what has been ellipted").

[47] *ES&L*, note 6, at 81.

[48] *Id.* at 103; *see GMAU*, note 2, at 71.

[49] *ES&L*, note 6, at 127; *see GMAU*, note 2, at 175, 643, 718.

[50] *ES&L*, note 6, at 169; *see GMAU*, note 2, at 475.

[51] *ES&L*, note 6, at 23; *see GMAU*, note 2, at 213.

[52] *ES&L*, note 6, at 91.

[53] *Id.* at 39. *See* Garner, *The Redbook: A Manual on Legal Style* § 1.36(b) (2d ed. 2006) ("Use a set of parentheses—not a single end-parenthesis—around a number or letter used in a list.").

1980s[54] when in fact they generally prefer omitting the apostrophe.[55] She consistently prints ellipsis dots unspaced,[56] contrary to the established convention on both sides of the Atlantic.[57] At some points, she inexplicably puts her ellipsis dots within brackets in a quotation.[58] She consistently uses en-dashes in place of em-dashes, without explaining why until the end of the book, and even then there's not so much an explanation as a glib assertion.[59] She claims that "lawyers eschew the comma as far as possible,"[60] whereas in fact it's only the British lawyers of whom this has been true.[61] In opposing the serial comma,[62] she puts

---

[54] *ES&L*, note 6, at 46.

[55] *The Chicago Manual of Style* § 9.37, at 389 (15th ed. 2003) ("No apostrophe appears between the year and the *s.*"); *GMAU*, note 2, at 222 ("When referring to decades, most professional writers today omit the apostrophe: hence, *2010s* instead of *2010's*."); *Texas Law Review Manual on Usage, Style, and Editing* § B:1:5, at 11 (9th ed. 2002) ("Do not use an apostrophe and s to make numbers . . . plural; simply add s."); Paul R. Martin, *The Wall Street Journal Guide to Business Style and Usage* (2002) ("show plurals by adding the letter 's': *the 1890s*"); *The Associated Press Stylebook and Briefing on Media Law* (Norm Goldstein ed., rev. ed. 2002) ("show plural by adding the letter *s: the 1890s*"); *U.S. News & World Report Stylebook* 64 (9th ed. 2001) (recommending *1950s*); Joseph Gibaldi, *MLA Style Manual and Guide to Scholarly Publishing* 118 (2d ed. 1998) (recommending *1990s*); *The New York Public Library Writer's Guide to Style and Usage* 438 (1994) (recommending *1970s* and *1980s*); *Publication Manual of the American Psychological Association* § 3.49, at 105 (1994) ("To form the plural of numbers, whether expressed as figures or as words, add *s* or *es* alone, without an apostrophe."); *United Press International Stylebook* 80 (3d ed. 1995) ("show plural by adding *s: the 1890s*"); *Words into Type* 128 (3d ed. 1974) ("In referring to decades, *the sixties* or *the 1960s* is generally preferred."); *contra* Allan M. Siegal & William G. Connolly, *New York Times Manual of Style and Usage* 103 (rev. ed. 1999) (recommending *1990's*).

[56] *E.g., ES&L*, note 6, at 52, 106, 165 (four times).

[57] *See* Pam Peters, *The Cambridge Guide to English Usage* 177 (2004) (noting that, in British practice, the dots have "an equal space on either side of them"); R.M. Ritter, *The Oxford Guide to Style* § 8.4.1, at 197 (2002) (calling an ellipsis "three spaced points of omission"); *The Chicago Manual of Style*, note 55, § 11.51, at 458 (calling ellipsis points "three spaced periods").

[58] *ES&L*, note 6, at 144, 155. *But see* Ritter, note 57, § 8.4.1, at 197 (2002) (calling this "Continental practice" and suggesting that it's not normal British practice).

[59] *See ES&L*, note 6, at 189 ("Dashes which [read *that*] were once of differing lengths for different occasions [not specified] are now generally shorter, of uniform length, and set between spaces." [Note the unparallel phrasing.]).

[60] *Id.* at 81.

[61] *See generally* Richard C. Wydick, *Should Lawyers Punctuate?* 1 Scribes J. Legal Writing 7 (1990).

[62] *ES&L*, note 6, at 85.

herself at odds with the vast multitude of punctuation authorities, who favor it.[63] She routinely misplaces the word *only*.[64] She misuses *which* for *that* in restrictive clauses,[65] as the British seem forever wont to do.[66] She perpetrates this run-on sentence: "[Y]ou have to give initial capitals to the words Biro and Hoover otherwise you automatically get tedious letters from solicitors."[67] She mistakenly asserts that "American grammari-

---

[63] *See The Chicago Manual of Style*, note 55, § 6.19, at 245 ("Chicago strongly recommends this widely practiced usage, blessed by Fowler and other authorities, since it prevents ambiguity."); *GMAU*, note 2, at 654 ("Although newspaper journalists typically omit the serial comma as a space-saving device, virtually all writing authorities outside that field recommend keeping it."); *Texas Law Review Manual on Usage, Style & Editing*, note 55, § B:4:2, at 15 ("In a series of three or more terms with a single conjunction, use a comma after each term before the conjunction."—But note the ampersand exception, which comes into play in the title of that exalted work.); Lasch, note 31, at 55 ("Use a comma before the last item in a series. This practice is now almost universally preferred, at least in the United States, to the older practice, which omits the comma when the last two items in a series are joined by a conjunction."); Ritter, note 57, at 121 ("If the last item in a list has emphasis equal to the previous ones, it needs a comma to create a pause of equal weight to those that came before."); *U.S. News & World Report Stylebook*, note 55, at 41 (Grover ed., 9th ed. 2001) ("Items in a series are divided by commas: *On his farm he grew soybeans, peanuts, and corn.*"); *U.S. Government Printing Office Style Manual* § 8.42, at 131 (2000) ("The comma is used after each member within a series of three or more words, phrases, letters, or figures used with *and, or,* or *nor.*"); Trimble, note 31, at 116 ("The beauty of the serial comma is that it instantly signals our arrival at the last item. Without it, we might not be able to determine what the writer means—or might even be seduced into a misreading."); William A. Sabin, *The Gregg Reference Manual* § 123b, at 15 (9th ed. 1999) ("Some writers prefer to omit the comma before *and, or,* or *nor* in a series, but the customary practice in business is to retain the comma before the conjunction."); Gibaldi, note 55, § 3.4.2b, at 67 ("Use a comma to separate words, phrases, and clauses in a series."); Edgar A. Alward & Jean A. Alward, *Punctuation Plain and Simple* 36 (1997) ("A comma is preferred after the next-to-last item."); O'Conner, note 28, at 137 ("[M]y advice is to stick with using the final comma."); *Scientific Style and Format* § 4.15.6, at 49 (6th ed. 1994) ("[R]outine use of this comma saves having to take time to consider possible ambiguities."); Howard Lauther, *Lauther's Complete Punctuation Thesaurus of the English Language* § 4.5, at 12 (1991) ("Omitting the comma before the conjunction [in a series] is simply a bad habit [that] can lead to a lack of clarity."); Robert Brittain, *A Pocket Guide to Correct Punctuation* 19 (2d ed. 1990) ("[I]t seems to be better to insert the extra single comma between the last two elements in a series."); Joan I. Miller & Bruce J. Taylor, *The Punctuation Handbook* 21 (1989) ("Nothing is gained by omitting the final comma in a list, while clarity can be lost in some cases through misreading."); Kate L. Turabian, *A Manual for Writers of Term Papers, Theses, and Dissertations* §§ 3.68, 3.70, at 50–51 (5th ed. 1987) ("A series of three or more words, phrases, or clauses (like this) takes a comma between each of the elements and before a conjunction separating the last two."); *Words into Type*, note 55, at 187–88 ("In a series of the form *a, b, and c* or *red, white, and blue* most publishers prefer a comma (sometimes called the serial comma)

ans insist[ ] that, if a sentence ends with a phrase in inverted commas [quotation marks], all the terminal punctuation for the sentence must come tidily inside the speech marks, even when this doesn't make sense."[68] Actually, American grammarians have always excluded two such marks—exclamation marks and question marks—if they're not part of what's being quoted.[69] She hyphenates *full-time editors*,[70] but in the preceding sentence she omits the obligatory hyphen from *movie-heist gangs*.[71] On and on I could go, but I have zero tolerance for it.

---

before the conjunction, whether the items of the series are words, phrases, or clauses. The consistent use of this comma is recommended, for in many sentences it is essential for clarity."); Follett, note 31, at 398, 401 ("The recommendation here is that [the writer] use the comma between *all* members of a series, including the last two, on the common-sense ground that to do so will preclude ambiguities and annoyances at a negligible cost."); Harry Shaw, *Punctuate It Right* 68 (1963) ("Greater clarity—the main purpose of punctuation—is usually achieved by the comma with the conjunction. For this reason it is recommended."); Gay, note 17, at 13 ("Present usage calls for a comma before 'and' or 'or' joining the last two members of a series."); H.W. Fowler, *A Dictionary of Modern English Usage* 24 (1926) ("The only rule that will obviate . . . uncertainties is that after every item, including the last unless a heavier stop is needed for independent reasons, the comma should be used . . . ."); George Summey Jr., *Modern Punctuation: Its Utilities and Conventions* 123 (1919) ("Nearly all textbooks on rhetoric or punctuation specify the use of the comma before the conjunction [in a series]; and this style is customarily followed in many periodicals and books, especially by writers who are careful of their pointing."); William Livingston Klein, *Why We Punctuate* 23 (2d ed. 1916) ("[T]he use of the comma before the final 'and' in every series is *helpful* punctuation . . . . [I]t is well to make the punctuation of every series uniform."); John F. Genung, *Outlines of Rhetoric* 190 (1894) ("If *and* occurs with the last member of the series, the comma should precede it just the same."). *Contra The Associated Press Stylebook* 329–30 (Norm Goldstein ed., rev. ed. 2002). For a discussion of the lopsided alignment of authorities, see Garner, *The Winning Brief* 293–95 (2d ed. 2004).

[64] *E.g.*, *ES&L*, note 6, at 88, 93, 138. *See GMAU*, note 2, at 574.

[65] *E.g.*, *ES&L*, note 6, at 4, 101.

[66] *See* Peters, note 57, at 469 (noting that "American editors and writers more often seem to be exponents of [the Fowlerian ideal] than their counterparts elsewhere"); *GMAU*, note 2, at 782 (noting that "British writers have utterly bollixed the distinction between restrictive and nonrestrictive relative pronouns").

[67] *ES&L*, note 6, at 58.

[68] *Id.* at 152–53.

[69] *See, e.g., GMAU*, note 2, at 659 (observing that American and English practices are the same "with respect to question marks and exclamation marks . . . [as] they're either inside or outside the ending question mark depending on whether they're part of what's being quoted").

[70] *ES&L*, note 6, at 31.

[71] *Id.*

Many months before the book's release in the United States, the *Wall Street Journal* ran a front-page (not *front page*) story about its marketing blitz.[72] The strategy was brilliant: Truss wrote an op-ed piece in a British newspaper in which she mentioned that she was writing a punctuation book and invited readers to e-mail their pet peeves to her. A thousand or so responded. The publisher then offered all these people a discounted, signed edition, and some 70% took the firm up on the offer. That got things rolling, and the initial print run of 15,000 turned into sales of more than 500,000 long before the book was released in the United States. Extraordinary. The marketing savvy that went into the grassroots U.S. campaign must have been every bit as clever.

The success of the title itself comes as a surprise. Every language expert I've talked to had thought it a clunker—until it proved otherwise. It's based on a joke. A panda walks into a cafe, eats a sandwich, fires a gun, and then walks out. Someone says, "Why'd you do that?" The panda replies, "Go look it up." In the dictionary is an entry that says: "Panda. A large black-and-white bear-like mammal, native to China, that eats shoots and leaves." (One version of the joke has an extraneous comma after *eats*. That's the version Truss uses. She'd probably also change the *that* in the definition to a *which*.) A pretty clever joke. But tying the title of a book on punctuation to a punning punch line seems unappealingly esoteric.

Yet people find it memorable. In the fall of 2004, while walking past my young daughter, Alexandra, who was parked at her computer, I glanced at her screen. She was instant-messaging some of her classmates, and I saw the words *panda* and *cafe*. "Are you telling a joke?" I asked. "Sure, Dad, I'm telling the panda joke." "Where in the world did you hear that?" I asked, astounded that Truss's book had permeated the world of middle-schoolers. She reminded me that I'd played a Lynne Truss audiotape[73] in the car some three weeks before, as I prepared to write this review.

Surprised that she had remembered the joke, I asked her to repeat it, and she recounted it exactly. Then I asked her how her preteen friends had reacted to it. "We all think it's funny, Dad."

---

[72] Charles Goldsmith, *A Period Piece Punctuates Fear of Elliptical in U.K.*, Wall St. J., 15 Dec. 2003, at A9.

[73] On Amazon.com, the tape is marketed as the audiobook for *Eats, Shoots & Leaves*. In fact, it's Truss's earlier BBC series called *Cutting a Dash*, in which she interviews linguists and others about punctuation. That series apparently gave her the idea for the book.

So I won't criticize the main title of the book. But the book itself is a different matter. When people have asked me what I think of it, I've usually responded by summing up Truss's entire message in this way: "Don't know much about punctuation, but wouldn't it be nice if people could sort out their apostrophes?"

There lies the real answer to the question, Why do the experts uniformly disparage a punctuation book that appeals so much to the popular mind? It turns out that many people like to think they're sticklers when they're not. And Lynne Truss happens to be one of them. She's taken a leaf from Karl Marx in proclaiming that her rallying cry is "Sticklers of the world, unite!"[74] That's exactly what they're doing, but hardly as she intended. The true sticklers of the world are uniting against Lynne Truss.

---

[74] See Lynne Truss, *Sticklers of the World, Unite!*, Financial Times, 19 Dec. 2003, at 17.

ð ð ð

Conjugational Infidelity

Steven Pinker, *Words and Rules: The Ingredients of Language*. (New York: Basic Books 1999). Pp. xi, 348.

EVERY DICTIONARY HAS THEM, and anyone who has studied a foreign language knows what an ordeal they can be: the verbs that simply don't obey neat rules of conjugation with predictable endings and forms. Mastering the past perfect of, say, the French verb *aller* (to go) has sunk many an earnest student otherwise ready for Paris. The English language, too, has its vexing verbs. They've been slung around for more than a millennium.

Back in the early 1600s, Ben Jonson, the playwright and grammarian, issued a call to pens, hoping that other writers would help figure out the irregular verbs in English: "in tolling this bell," he wrote, "I may draw others to a deeper consideration of the matter." As for himself, "after much painful churning," Jonson conceded defeat. He found 120 irregular verbs, "or thereabouts," but didn't know quite how they came to be.

Some centuries later, Steven Pinker has answered Jonson's call with *Words and Rules*. Pinker's verb count comes to 164, or thereabouts— though unfortunately he doesn't provide a list. (On one page of the book, he says 164; on another, 165.) The real significance of Pinker's work is the theory he posits: Regular verb forms ending in -*ed* are generated by rules, he says, while irregular verbs are retrieved from memory. Teachers of yore knew this much, of course. That's why they endlessly drilled students on irregular verbs, while telling them simply to add -*ed* to all the others. Linguists, on the other hand, have come up with arcane theories about these matters.

Pinker explains precisely how people blunder with irregular verbs by applying rules that haven't traditionally applied to those verbs. We all know that children will say, "I breaked it." In an elementary way, they're doing precisely the same thing that adults do when they say *spitted* instead of *spat*. There are subtle implications discernible from these gaffes (which, of course, over time, may become standard). Pinker explores these implications in intimate detail, suggesting how the human brain is hardwired for language.

Adapted from *The Wall Street Journal* (20 Dec. 1999).

You do have to remember the irregulars: *go–went–gone, come–came–come, sink–sank–sunk*, and so on. Beyond the common ones, people start feeling uneasy. Many people today under the age of 45, for example, will give you a quizzical look if you say, "Have you drunk any of this tea yet?" Believe it or not, they prefer *drank* in that sentence. Perhaps they've become too accustomed to hearing the past-participial adjective *drunk* (as in Mothers Against Drunk Driving).

Inconsistently enough, when it comes to the verb *shrink*, people do remember the participial *shrunk*. Indeed, they remember it so well that they substitute it for the proper past-tense form: *shrank*. Hence the solecism in the 1989 Disney movie title, *Honey, I Shrunk the Kids!* Maybe the correct form would have put moviegoers off. Who, after all, wants a punctilious protagonist?

Pinker takes us through a kaleidoscope of blunders and double-takes with irregulars, arrayed in the form of comic strips, quotations, and anecdotes. These add to the appeal of a book that devotes a good deal of ink to debunking the famous linguist Noam Chomsky, who, according to Pinker, believes that all verb conjugations derive from rules, not memorized patterns. Pinker also quarrels with another school of linguists—"connectionists"—who believe that irregulars are governed largely by word associations. On the whole, Pinker seems to get the better of his linguist-adversaries.

As in his earlier book, *The Language Instinct* (1994), Pinker casts aspersions on what he calls "language mavens," meaning various language commentators who are neither linguists nor psychologists. Pinker tries to but doesn't really get the better of them, mostly because they're coming at language from a completely different vantage point.

Three points of caution here.

First, whether you're a language maven or (like Pinker) a director of a center for cognitive neuroscience at MIT, you ought to get your facts straight. It's a gross inaccuracy to say that "before Samuel Johnson standardized English orthography, people spelled more or less as they pleased, trying to capture the sounds of language as they heard them." There were, in fact, many lexicographers and orthographers who preceded Johnson (Cawdrey, Bullokar, Cockeram, and many others). As Albert Baugh and Thomas Cable state in their *History of the English Language*, "our spelling in its modern form had been practically established by about 1650." Johnson published his famous *Dictionary* more than 100 years later, in 1755.

Second, for a scientist, Pinker is rather unscientific in places. For example, he condemns Theodore Bernstein, the estimable author of *The Careful Writer*, for his 1965 preference for the past-tense *broadcast* over

broadcasted. Pinker says that this preference "had long been a losing battle," and quotes H.L. Mencken in support of *broadcasted.* Back in 1936,
Mencken said that *broadcasted* "is what one commonly hears."

Yet with only five minutes' work on the Westlaw database, it's possible to show that in modern print, the ratio is staggeringly in favor of
broadcast (19,805 sources) and not *broadcasted* (86) as a past form. Bernstein
was right in 1965, and Pinker should have known better than to rely on
a 1936 quotation as his sole evidence against Bernstein—whom he
snidely accuses of "hectoring people into sticking with the irregular."

Third, Pinker seems to have strange notions of what constitutes
"standard" usage. In one place, he says: "I have been advised that *tooken*
has become standard in Generation X circles . . . ." In another: "*I seen it*
and *A man come into the bar* are absolutely standard outside the upper and
middle classes . . . ." Two generations ago these things were called "substandard." A generation ago they were more gently labeled "nonstan-
dard." Now, apparently, Pinker would have us call them "standard outside
the upper and middle classes."

There are several missed opportunities in this book. For instance,
Pinker doesn't say anything about pedagogy. How should children learn
irregular verbs—especially the less common ones? Or should we abstain
from drilling students on them and allow linguistic natural selection to
take its course? If we did that, irregulars would probably become regu-
larized: e.g., *thriven* and *stridden*, proper but rare past participles, would
probably disappear altogether in favor of *thrived* and *strided*. And further
drift would eliminate the simple-past forms *stank* and *shrank*, among
others. What does Pinker think schoolteachers should do?

"The steady erosion of distinctions in English inflection," he writes,
"helps us understand why we continue to be confused" by irregular
verbs. But shouldn't we aspire to something more than a mere understanding of our continuing confusion?

With its many interesting examples of how language works, *Words
and Rules* is certainly worth reading and pondering. Just keep your critical wits about you. You won't wish you'd forborne.

ॐ ॐ ॐ

Internetese: Dialect of the Web Tribe

Constance Hale & Jessie Scanlon, *Wired Style: Principles of English Usage for the Digital Age* (2d ed., New York: Broadway Books 1999). Pp. vii, 198.

WHEN LINGUISTS TALK OF DIALECTS, they typically refer exclusively to the spoken word. But the Internet seems to have created a highly unusual beast: a written dialect in which punctuation is abandoned, uppercasing is largely unknown (unless you're shouting), and all sorts of acronyms replace phrases. Hence *BTW* means "by the way," *IMHO* means "in my humble opinion," *OTOH* means "on the other hand," *w/e* means "whatever" (in the slangy dismissive sense), and so on. Knowing these shorthand expressions—and using them—gives one a sense of belonging to the group. Yet the dialect doesn't really exist except through the written word, and the "group" to which one belongs exists only in cyberspace.

Parents and teachers sometimes ask me whether all this will affect standard American English. The answer is that it's bound to, although predicting the effect would be more difficult than predicting the outcome of a presidential election. In the main, though, it appears likely that these aspects of Internet style—the punctuationless, generally lowercase style riddled with acronyms—will largely remain confined to the Internet. To what extent children might face greater obstacles in learning to write what we now know as standard American English is a difficult question.

Yet people yearn for guidance, and the online folks have a style manual: three years ago Constance Hale and Jessie Scanlon—two editors at *Wired* magazine—produced *Wired Style*, which has just appeared in its second edition. The book is long on attitude and short on principles: "Think blunt bursts and sentence fragments. Writing that is on-the-fly—even frantic." This immediately raises an interesting question: If that's how writers are supposed to be thinking, then why would they stop to consult a style manual? How could they?

And, of course, there's the question of what guidance will they find if they *do* look at the manual. "Spelling and punctuation are loose and playful. (No one reads email with red pen in hand.)" "Write the way people talk. Don't insist on 'standard' English." "Appreciate unruliness."

Adapted from *The New York Times* ("'Wired' Style Captures Netspeak, But It Refuses to Be Reined In," 21 Mar. 2000, at E3).

"Welcome inconsistency." The authors do many of these things themselves. For example, they seem to welcome inconsistency by using *media*
as a singular on page 13 and as a plural on page 16. Yet on page 115,
they seem to endorse the singular.

The authors embrace the jargon of the digerati, and they even praise
the use of jargon. But the discussion stays superficial: they keep it light
and quick, presumably because their readers are on the fly (or *on-the-fly*,
as the authors incorrectly hyphenate the phrase).

A certain amount of their advice is sound. Internet English is surely
relaxed and playful and creative. The "smileys" made from ASCII characters—from the commonplace :-) for someone smiling to >:D for someone laughing demonically—show a delightful imagination at work. And
the pace of modern communication demands a saving of keystrokes,
however much the old-schoolers will lament the lack of reflection that
often goes into instant messaging.

But the authors are stingy with their advice: only a fifth of the 198-
page text is devoted to the "principles of English usage" promised in the
subtitle. The bulk of the book is a list of definitions for Internet terms.
Even the heavily dated ones, like WYSIWYG (= what you see is what
you get), are treated as though they were fully current. There's precious
little guidance about real usage problems in the A–Z listing.

Maybe that's understandable. How do you write a usage guide for
the unruly? The answer, judging from this book, is that you don't. Your
doctrine becomes linguistic libertarianism, in which the only dogmatic
judgments you make are to put down the standard authorities like *The
Chicago Manual of Style* and Strunk and White's *Elements of Style*—while
proclaiming on the front and back covers, and in press materials, that
your book has attained a status equal to those classics.

This raises a pervasive ambiguity. The authors don't quite say whether
they mean for their suggestions to apply to all writing in the "digital
age," or only to Internet writing. Even if their suggestions are limited to
Internet writing, are websites on the same footing as chat rooms when it
comes to rejecting standard English? Consider again the subtitle: principles for the digital *age*, not merely for digital technology. It's a chilling
thought.

Interestingly, the book has received a kinder reception from the general press than from Internet users. Although *Newsweek* and *Entertainment
Weekly* provided terrific cover blurbs, online reviewers have largely panned
the book: at Amazon.com and Barnesandnoble.com, the two largest
online bookstores, the book gets an average rating of two and a half stars
out of five. Some of the reviewers' repeated criticisms are both damning
and true: (1) the book's content is underdeveloped (still another exam-

ple: only a few of the countless smileys are given); (2) the glossary is hard to use because of insufficient cross-references; and (3) the main use of the book is as an Internet glossary, yet other such glossaries are better.

As a professional usage critic, I mainly wanted to know two things when I first picked up the book. What do the authors say about *e-mail* vs. *E-mail* vs. *email*? And what do they recommend as the plural for *mouse*? You see, I'm on record in support of *e-mail* and *mouses*. House style for the *Times* requires *e-mail* and *mice*. *Wired Style* favors *email* and *mouses*.

Little battles have been pitched over these points. We'll have to wait a few years to see whether the hyphen persists in *e-mail*. But the more interesting skirmish is over computer *mouses*. Some Internet users are agitating vehemently in favor of *mice*. IMHO, it's their dialect, so they can do as they please. OTOH, they might consider how the metaphorical use of *louse* (= a scoundrel) becomes *louses*—a useful analogue (BTW, not *analog* in this sense). w/e.

CHIEF JUSTICE WILLIAM H. REHNQUIST

ஃ CHAPTER SEVENTEEN

Chronicles of Grammar, Usage, and Writing

2004

January

WRITING IN THE *Skeptical Inquirer* on New Year's Day, Jennifer Sherwood Olathe opined that the ambiguity of Nostradamus's predictions "comes from his frankly poor grammar, particularly his scanty knowledge of Latin grammar"; one might have thought, to the contrary, that the ambiguities were purposeful and have made his predictions more durable. • In the *New Scientist*, Adrian Barnett reported that in the Amazonian language of Tariana, which is in danger of dying, it is a grammatical error to report a fact without citing your source; imagine how a switch to that language might affect American journalism and politics. • In the journal *Marketing*, a press-release writer for a major company wrote this self-proving sentence: "Grammar and writing is not one of my strong points." • Merriam-Webster reached the one-million mark in hard-copy sales of the 11th edition of its *Collegiate Dictionary*, published in the summer of 2003. The University of Chicago reached the 100,000 mark in sales of the 15th edition of *The Chicago Manual of Style*. Meanwhile, Oxford University Press reported that individual subscriptions to the *Oxford English Dictionary* (at $29 per month) were the most rapidly growing subscription type for the *OED* online; sales of the 20-volume hard copy, never especially brisk, had fallen off sharply.

Adapted from *The Green Bag* (Winter 2005).

February

A two-year study by the American Diploma Project reported that an American high-school diploma represents "little more than a certificate of attendance," according to one of its authors, Michael Cohen. Employers told researchers that high-school graduates lack basic skills in grammar, writing, and math; colleges told them that about half the entering freshmen needed remedial education before they were ready for college-level work. • In a 50-year retrospective, the (London) *Times Educational Supplement* reprinted a snippet from a February 1954 report in which college examiners said of the papers they graded: "The evidence of ignorance about the most elementary points of English was frightful and frightening." • Tiger Woods's father, Earl, took up cudgels for standard English in *Golf Digest*: "My mother insisted that I speak in good, clear English. No sloughing off my e's, f's, and t's. Learn good grammar. If I had said 'ax' when I meant 'ask,' she would have been all over my case. Today, I concur with Thurgood Marshall—there is nothing wrong with speaking the language of your culture when you're within that culture. But to be upwardly mobile in society, one must learn to speak the best English that one can." • A conservative group in San Francisco asked a judge to issue an order barring gay marriages, but the judge refused because the proposed order contained a semicolon where the word "or" should have been used. Because of the error, the judge had no authority to issue the order.

March

While talking about the findings in his latest book, *America Behind the Color Line: Dialogues with African Americans*, Harvard scholar Henry Louis Gates Jr. remarked on a poll in which "black kids were asked to list the things they considered 'acting white.' The top three things were: making straight A's, speaking standard English and going to the Smithsonian." Then Gates added: "If anybody had said anything like that when we were growing up in the '50s, first, your mother would smack you upside the head and second, they'd check you into a mental institution." • Barbara Wallraff published her second book, *Your Own Words*, a reference work about reference works; it compares dictionaries, usage and style manuals, and online sources, and teaches readers how to answer novel language questions for themselves. • *The Elephants of Style*, the second usage book by Bill Walsh, a *Washington Post* editor, arrived on bookshelves; though its advice is generally sound, Walsh missteps on page 60, where he states that "Whom will it be" is "technically correct." • In London, the *Times Higher Education Supplement* reported that straight-A students show a shaky grasp of the nuts and bolts of English; senior English tutors asserted that undergraduates lacked the basics for intellectual communication, often misusing commas and apostrophes and frequently botching their spelling. • The American Political Network reported that President George W. Bush's mispronunciation of *nuclear* "has become a flashpoint for his critics." In the *Chicago Daily Herald*, Norma S. Hass speculated: "President Bush knows perfectly well how the word 'nuclear' should be pronounced. He says it wrong on purpose, to seem less like the patrician he is and more like a regular feller. He wants to sound like a real guy's guy, not some effeminate liberal who cares about prissy, schoolmarmish things like correct pronunciation."

April

Jan Edwards, Mary Beckman, and Benjamin Munson reported, in an article for *The Journal of Speech, Language, and Hearing Research*: "Traditional models of grammar posit that phonological knowledge is instantiated in the form of rules or constraints operating on abstract mental representations of words." They failed to cite any traditional grammarians who said anything like this. • Cambridge University Press released a thorough but quite permissive usage guide by the Australian linguist Pam Peters, *The Cambridge Guide to English Usage*; it's the British English answer to America's ultrapermissive "guide," *Merriam-Webster's Dictionary of English Usage* (1989). • Lynne Truss's British best seller about punctuation, *Eats, Shoots & Leaves*, was released in the United States with an initial print run of 133,000; aficionados of fastidious punctuation were puzzled by the mispunctuated subtitle (*A Zero Tolerance* [read *Zero-Tolerance*] *Approach to Punctuation*), along with many other errors in the book. • New evidence about how much poor writing can cost: U.S. Magistrate Judge Jacob Hart reduced attorney Brian Puricelli's court-awarded fees by $31,450 for submitting briefs and motions that were "careless," "full of typographical errors," and "nearly unintelligible."

May

On May 15, Professor Christopher Ricks of Boston University—formerly Regius Chair in English Literature at Cambridge—was elected the Oxford Professor of Poetry by a majority of the 531 Oxford graduates who showed up to vote; over the next five years, Ricks will give talks at Oxford with the idea of "generally encouraging the art of poetry in the University," extolling the merits of not just Milton and Tennyson but also Bob Dylan. • In the *Journal of Teacher Education*, Carla R. Monroe and Jennifer E. Obidah reported disapprovingly that cultural biases in the classroom often take the form of "corrections for incorrect grammar usage." Do

Monroe and Obidah correct their own mistakes? They'd better: the journal *Technical Communication* reported the heartening news that in online courses, students "quickly lose respect for instructors whose online communications are filled with misspellings and grammatical errors."

June

The eighth edition of *Black's Law Dictionary* was released by West Group; compiled by the small team at LawProse (which I head), the book contains more than 17,000 terms new to this edition. • *Better Homes and Gardens* recommended that parents teach their children online manners, including obeying this command: "Use good grammar when writing to authority figures." • In her usage column in *The Spectator*, Dot Wordsworth pointed out that "sentence after sentence in the so-called Authorized Version of the Bible begins with *and*," adding: "The *Oxford English Dictionary* gives a tantalizingly short collection of quotations to illustrate the history of the usage, from the 9th century onwards." And she made a similar point about *but*, perhaps emboldening thousands of readers to reject the century-old superstition to the contrary. But don't hold your breath.

July

Bill Cosby drew cheers and jeers for criticizing the speech of black youths: "I can't even talk the way these people talk. 'Why you ain't,' 'Where you is' . . . and I blamed the kid until I heard the mother talk. And then I heard the father talk . . . . Everybody knows it's important to speak English except these knuckleheads. You can't be a doctor with that kind of crap coming out of your mouth." • Robert W. Burchfield, the greatest English-language lexicographer of the latter 20th century and the chief editor of the *OED Supplement*, died at home in Sutton Courtenay, England, at the age of 81. • William Safire marked the 26th anniversary of his *New York Times* "On Language" column with the publication of *The Right Word in the Right Place at the Right Time*—his 16th book on linguistic matters. • The British journal *Accountancy Age* conducted a survey and reported that in business communications, "the trend for texting means that spelling and punctuation mistakes are common" and that the "correct use of apostrophes and commas falls by the wayside"; one in three survey respondents reported using such abbreviations as "cd" for *could*, "cu" for *see you*, "2" for *to* or *too*.

August

The *Times Higher Education Supplement* reported that British children did worse in spelling in 1996 than in 1976, as far as the two years could be compared; most disappointingly, research showed that a majority of children in East Tilbury, in Essex, preferred to spell *thing* as *fing* and *nothing* as *nuffing.* • The College Board announced that the new SAT, to be launched in March 2005, would test grammar, word choice, and usage in a 35-minute segment of multiple-choice questions, together with a 25-minute essay. In response, according to the *Sarasota Herald Tribune*, school administrators around the country declared that high schools would begin to pay more attention to grammar. In *U.S. News and World Report*, Edward B. Biske and Bruce G. Hammond, authors of an SAT prep guide, wrote that "the rules of grammar and usage . . . can be easily learned (or relearned) without great difficulty"; as for the new SAT essay, these authors said that "the essay will be a standard state-an-opinion-and-back-it-up-with-evidence deal." That's the best kind of deal. • *Kirkus Reviews* released its review of David Crystal's new book about the glories of dialectal varieties, summing up the book with this sentence: "A celebrated linguist argues that all versions of English are created equal and that the reign of Emily Post-prescriptivists who insist that Standard English is 'right' and all the rest 'wrong' is nearing its end"; yet in the 584-page book itself, Crystal cites no modern prescriptivists who supposedly take this "Emily Post" position, and he cites only three allegedly prescriptivist bugaboos—namely, "the use of *and* at the beginning of a sentence [not really a bugaboo at all, since prescriptivists defend this usage], split infinitives [okayed to some degree by every reputable prescriptivist], and end-placed prepositions [ditto]" (p. 483). What is actually coming to an end is prescriptivists' patience with descriptivists' misrepresentations of their positions with the same old cliché shibboleths.

September

In *The New Yorker*, Philip Gourevitch argued that President Bush "is grossly underestimated as an orator by those who presume that good grammar, rigorous logic, and a solid command of the facts are the essential ingredients of political persuasion." • In *National Review*, Sidney Goldberg took the writers and editors at *The New York Times* to task for "an ignorance of orthography and grammar," particularly for not knowing the inflection of the verb *to lead*: "Almost as often as not, the Timesmen spell the past tense as 'lead,' when 'lead' can only be the present tense . . . or the name of the heavy metal . . . . I don't think a day passes without the *Times* getting it wrong." • Barbara Wallraff announced her resignation as editor in chief of *Copy Editor*, which under her editorship had become the most informative and lively periodical about grammar and usage. • The Hawaii department of education announced that sixth-graders there are expected to know how to "write and revise pieces several times for clearer meaning, more convincing language, stronger voice, and accurate grammar and usage." • City officials in Livermore, California, were red-faced over the $40,000 mural they had commissioned for the city's beautiful new library. The mural depicts the names and likenesses of 175 icons of arts (e.g., Michelangelo) and sciences (e.g., Einstein). The only problem was that 11 of the names were misspelled (e.g., *Michaelangelo*, *Eistein*), and the city had to fork over another $6,000 plus expenses to get the artist, Maria Alquilar, to correct her work. She had refused to do so, claiming that "words" were not important to her art.

October

In the first of three presidential debates, Senator John Kerry charged that President Bush had left America's alliances "in shatters across the globe," when he undoubtedly meant "in tatters"; the media didn't remark on his gaffe. • In the journal *Technology & Learning*, Saul Rockman reported that high-school students' attitudes toward writing have improved: 76% of students say they prefer writing on laptops as opposed to on paper, 80% say that laptops make rewriting and revision easier, and 73% say that they earn better grades for laptop work; meanwhile, Rockman reported that laptops have done nothing to improve performance on standardized achievement tests. • Adverbial inflation continues apace: *Forbes Global* reported that "in current English usage, it's not enough to say someone is rich; he must be 'seriously rich.'" • *The 9/11 Commission Report*, writ-ten by 80 staffers and 10 commissioners, was chosen as a nonfiction finalist for the National Book Award. Successfully avoiding the tendency for such reports to sound bland and bureaucratic, the writers gave their book the tone of a thriller, amazingly free of acronyms. Staffers joked that they were not allowed to use an acronym without the personal sign-off of vice-chair Lee H. Hamilton. • The *National Law Journal* reported that law firms had begun expunging commas from their names; Daniel Joseph, a partner at Akin Gump Strauss Hauer & Feld, argued that "to put in commas is to divide"—and apparently many others agree. As a market-ing matter, perhaps the comma is going the way of the apostrophe—and punctuation generally may be slowly going the way of diacritical marks.

November

William Safire, 74, announced that he would end his political column at *The New York Times* in January 2005 but would continue his weekly lan-guage column. • The *St. Petersburg Times* reported that a 2004 survey of the largest U.S. corporations found "widespread dissatisfaction with employee writing skills"; 40% of the companies said that they had to offer additional training in writing. In his *San Diego Union-Tribune* column,

Michael Kinsman reported that American businesses spend $3 billion annually to upgrade the writing skills of workers; two-thirds of salaried employees depend on those skills, and "an inability to write can severely limit workers as they try to climb into supervisory and management jobs." • But not, apparently, if they're in advertising: Wichita, Kansas, set off a grammatical furor with its PR slogan, "We got the goods"; Raleigh Drennon, the advertising consultant who invented the slogan, said that *We got* is sassier and more energetic than *We've got* (which he called "stuffy," "overly proper," and "overly literal"). Interviewed by the local newspaper, the chair of the Wichita State University English Department expressed resignation: "Generally, I wish I could carry an apostrophe around in my car and put it where it belongs, but who cares? It's hopeless."

December

NBC broadcast the Office Depot Father/Son Challenge golf tournament, in which veteran golfer Bob Charles and his son David were top contenders; the NBC scoreboard consistently labeled the team not the *Charleses* (as they should have been), but the *Charles'*. This is yet one more sign that (1) most people are increasingly ignorant of the only approved way of pluralizing names, and (2) NBC apparently believes that "most people" are qualified to prepare their scoreboards. • Michelle Trute, the cooking columnist for the *Courier Mail* in Queensland, Australia, acknowledged that her favorite dessert is pumpkin pie, but she recommended not using commercial pumpkin-pie mix: "just substitute mashed pumpkin for the same quantity of tinned; use butternut or a good grammar, as they are nice and sweet and not too watery." It would be interesting to try each of the two proposed recipes—since many grammars are known to be unpleasant and sour and rather dry. • In Wellington, New Zealand, the *Dominion Post* reported that many first-year university students there are failing basic writing and academic-skills tests; only 77% of the physics, computer-science, and engineering students passed a basic literacy test earlier in the year. • Laura Vanderkam wrote in *USA Today* that good writing skills are increasingly important in the American workplace, but that "grown-up Johnny can't write because young Johnny writes little beyond short book reports or haiku—and he rarely revises his work." Vanderkam proposed two reforms to the No Child Left Behind Act to improve students' writing: (1) require schools to boost the writing regimens of students, and (2) "pay to make grading fly," i.e., let teachers demand and correct three drafts of each paper, and get the teachers some grading help in the form of free-lance writers and grad students looking for cash. Meanwhile, reports Vanderkam, high-school students' college-admission cover letters "sag with needless words, fuzzy logic, and grammatical mistakes."

෨ ෨ ෨

2005

January

BILL O'REILLY interviewed Robert MacNeil, the journalist, on "The
O'Reilly Factor." When MacNeil mentioned the colloquial dropping of
the -g sound in participles such as *doin'*, O'Reilly (a former English
teacher) commented: "Those gerunds. We've got to get rid of those
gerunds. You know what I'm talking about, Mr. MacNeil? They've just
destroyed the language." He then ended the interview, as he does almost
all interviews, with a fused participle: "Mr. MacNeil, we appreciate you
taking the time." • In answer to the question, "Does anyone really care
about style and grammar anymore?", the *International Herald Tribune*
reported this answer: "Google does. Taking the stance that slang and
unorthodox usage and punctuation create a less straightforward searching experience, Google's AdWords division, which is responsible for the
contextual ads that appear alongside search results, insists on standard
English and punctilious punctuation." Good for Google. • The *Economist*
reported that linguists are increasingly using the Internet as a corpus for
formal research, citing a study finding that Web searches for rare two-
word phrases correlated well with the frequency found in traditional
corpora. The conclusion: "The easy availability of the Web also serves
another purpose: to democratise the way linguists work. Allowing anyone to conduct his own impromptu linguistic research, some linguists
hope, will do more to popularise their notion of studying the intricacy
and charm of language as it really exists, not as killjoy prescriptivists think
it should be." But of course, two nonkilljoy prescriptivists—Barbara Wallraff and I—have been using the Internet for years to assess both the language as it really exists and the language as it's best used • The *Standard*,
published in English in China, reported: "Hong Kong is losing out to
the mainland because of a decline in English standards in recent years."
It quoted former chief secretary for administration Anson Chan: "We are
told often by businessmen who have businesses in Shanghai how much
better English is spoken in Shanghai than Hong Kong." • In Cleveland,
the *Plain Dealer* reported that onomasticians are baffled by the origins of
the proper noun *Ohio* and how it was originally pronounced. In the

---

Adapted from *2006 Green Bag Almanac.*

1600s, Indians in the region told French explorers about a mighty river that sounded like "wauregan." Others spoke of "olighin," and still others of "oyo" or "ohiyo." All these words meant "good and beautiful" in the indigenous American languages. Somehow, between the Indians, the French, and the English, things got muddled. "Ohiyo" seems to have been taken from the Seneca Indians, and "wauregan" and "olighin" got morphed into *Oregon*—which apparently is etymologically identical. And all this made news in January 2005.

February

Linguistic researchers in Watertown, Wisconsin, dispelled the idea that broadcast communications would eventually kill regional differences in American speech. Tom Purnell, a University of Wisconsin linguist, was quoted in the *Wisconsin State Journal* as saying that "American English is becoming even more regionally distinct" over time. Some of the grammatical oddities found in heavily German areas of the state are "Come here once," "We have time yet," "We had dinner by Matt's," and "Are you coming with?" • But the evidence is mixed on the question whether dialects are thriving. The *Washington Post* reported that the native dialects, accents, and vocabularies of the Chesapeake Bay area are disappearing as expanding suburbs bring in newcomers. A native complained, "They're just smotherin' us. We're getting yuppitized." But researchers also found that, at least on Smith Island, Maryland, young people actually had stronger accents than their parents. • *The New York Times* published an article about Paul Topping, a pronunciation expert who works for Recorded Books. Topping researches the correct or preferred pronunciations for everything from foreign expressions and medical maladies to initialisms and words that don't exist (as in science-fiction books). Using a phonetic language of 30 characters that he invented (most dictionaries use about 60 characters), he then spells out the words phonetically for the audiobook narrators. Proper pronunication is a serious topic among audiobook publishers; Blackstone Audiobooks had to re-record a book that was soundly criticized for its mispronounced Hebrew and Arabic. (The new recording was praised, so the publisher wasn't a meshugganer.)

March

Accountancy Age reported research showing that 15–20% of all job applicants are immediately weeded out because of misspellings, poor grammar, and wordiness in their résumés. • In an article in *International Angiology*, the four authors of an article on oxygen pressure in the ankle during exercise were at some pains to thank one Mrs. Boye for "her help in improving grammar and style of the manuscript." Their lead sentence: "Even in patients with arterial disease proved by usual non-invasive techniques such as Doppler recordings and/or ankle/brachial index, the presence of associated disease of non vascular origin (musculo-skeletal or respiratory) may sometimes question the contribution of vascular disease in the symptoms of intermittent claudication." One pities Mrs. Boye for the manuscript with which she must have grappled. • In the *St. Petersburg Times*, Stephen Nohlgren wrote about the dysphemisms for old age, citing a study by the National Council on Aging finding that half the people from 65 to 74 thought of themselves as middle-aged—as did a third of the people 75 and older. The article quotes Janice Wassel, a gerontologist and amateur linguist, who believes that society's frequent avoidance of the word *old* leads to a "contorted language that can anger the very people it is intended to soothe." Wassel has found that almost all the English words denoting people before middle age are positive, whereas almost all the words for people in middle age or after are pejorative.

April

My review of Lynne Truss's *Eats, Shoots & Leaves* appeared in *Texas Law Review*; the review documents manifold errors and inconsistencies in the book and pointedly addresses the missing hyphen in the subtitle's "Zero Tolerance Approach." Included are quotations from interviews with fellow language mavens James J. Kilpatrick, Barbara Wallraff, Patricia T. O'Conner, and Bill Walsh, all of whom disparaged the book for its many pratfalls. • A study in the *Roeper Review* reported that "early social competence has a snowballing effect, and linguistic research shows specifically what the effects are" for verbally precocious children ages two to seven: (1) eliciting more and more-effective vocabulary-learning experiences from adults; (2) inducing rich speech environments that accelerate their development; (3) enhancing socialization skills because adults find them more interesting to talk to; and (4) improving their planning, monitoring, and outcome-checking skills as they seek to solve problems.

May

The *Charleston Gazette* reported that Les Perelman, a writing director at MIT, had studied the recently "improved" SAT, with its requirement for written essays, and found that the graders were giving top scores based solely on the length of the essays, not on their quality. He said he could predict the score of essays based on length with 90% accuracy. Particularly disturbing: "Some results implied that errors don't matter—even really disturbing ones, like putting the American Revolution in the wrong century." • Stanley Fish, recently retired as a professor of English at the University of Illinois at Chicago, claimed that most American high-school and college graduates are unable to write coherent sentences because they aren't taught what a sentence is. In an article for the *The New York Times*, Fish described how he made his students focus on understanding the structure of language, emphasizing form over content, and working on a semester-long project in which groups of students create unique languages with a syntax, a lexicon, a text, rules for translation, and strategies for teaching the languages to others. • In England, the Court of Appeal used linguistic evidence to overturn a man's 1976 conviction for attempted murder. The then-15-year-old defendant had written out a confession that was later used at his trial. An analysis of the language used in the statement and the structure of the sentences revealed that the police officers had been significantly involved in wording the "confession," making it unreliable and inadmissible.

June

Steven McCormack, writing in the *Independent* (London), reported that almost 40% of 11-year-olds in England fail to reach the writing standards set by their schools. The reason, according to McCormack, is that "teachers don't teach children grammar and punctuation . . . because they don't understand it themselves . . . . School teachers have such a shaky grasp of basic grammar that, at best, they fail to notice and correct their pupils' mistakes, and at worst they pass on their misconceptions." • Language columnist James J. Kilpatrick, shortly before the 85th anniversary of his birth, held firm on the meaning of *anniversary*: "A decent respect for the old ways should preserve 'anniversary' in its pristine meaning of yearly. The *American Heritage Dictionary* has it right: 'the annually recurring date of a past event.' *Random House* concurs. *Webster's New World* concurs. *Encarta* concurs. *Oxford* concurs. Everybody is in step on this one except the free spirits at *Merriam-Webster's Dictionary of English Usage*. Without the slightest blush, apology, or sigh, they cite 'a six-month anniversary' as acceptable usage. Bah! And humbug, too!"

July

A seminal article in *Linguistics*, an "interdisciplinary journal," reported a startling conclusion: "the development of possessive classifiers into benefactive markers in Oceanic languages" involves a "diachronic string comparison," so that "this change episode will then be demonstrated to involve structural scope increase contrary to the widely held assumption that scope decrease is a manifestation of grammaticalization." The article also reports surprising new developments in "clines" relating to "syntac-ticization," "morphologization," and "demorphemicization." Must read-ing for all language enthusiasts. • The *Irish Independent* reported that, after decades of attempts to revive the Irish language in Ireland, a new group Stad! (Stop!) has been formed to campaign against what it regards as a waste of millions in taxpayers' money in duplicating advertisements that Irish speakers can understand perfectly well in English. • In the *Contra Costa Times* (California), Randy Cohen opined in his "Ethicist" column that a printer has no obligation to improve literary blunders: "You should do your job according to the usual professional standards, ensuring that the printing isn't blurry and the ink doesn't run in the rain. You have no obligation to provide extra services—correcting the customer's sole-cisms, improving his prose, painting his house. He employs you to per-form a skilled mechanical operation, not to be his literary collaborator."

August

The New Yorker's "Talk of the Town" reported on an "independent inves-tigator" who found a copyright trap in *The New Oxford American Dictio-nary*. The dictionary's current editor, Erin McKean, confirmed that *esquiva-lience* was the invention of NOAD's Christine Lindberg and was included in the dictionary to spot copycats. "Talk" reported that Dictionary.com had indeed included the word in its database (it has since been removed). The column features a short introduction to these copyright traps, which it calls *mountweazels* after a fake entry in the 1975 *New Columbia Ency-clopedia* on "Lillian Virginia Mountweazel, a fountain designer turned photographer who was celebrated for a collection of photographs of rural American mailboxes." • The *Daily Mail* (U.K.) reported that exam-iners for GCSE (General Certificate of Secondary Education) literature papers have been banned from penalizing poor spelling and grammar; they were given explicit instructions to ignore grammatical shortcom-ings and concentrate only on the "ideas expressed." Examiners said they had been forced to award "ludicrously high marks" to candidates whose command of grammar and sentence construction was "simply nonexis-tent." • The *Independent* reported that Cockney speech is being greatly influenced by Indian languages because of immigration patterns in Lon-don. *Nang*, meaning "excellent" or "cool," comes from Bangladeshi immi-grants, and so perhaps does the invariable question tag *innit* (as in, "We're going to the shops, innit?"). Traditional rhyming Cockney slang persists only as a "rearguard action." • Michael Vestey, writing in the *Spectator*, editorialized that the BBC, which "once invented a form of speech, received pronunciation, . . . is now bent on destroying it." Hence BBC journalists are now allowed to use *innit?* (from *isn't it?*, but meaning also *don't we?, aren't we?*, etc.), *fink* (for *think*), *bovver* (for *bother*), etc. Vestey argues that it is hardly wonderful when "no one outside your immediate circle can understand what you're saying." ● The *Daily Express* reported on an incident to be recounted in a forthcoming biography of Sir John Mortimer, author of the series of Rumpole novels. Apparently when his daughter had trouble writing a story about fairies for one of her classes, Mortimer wrote it for her, and he became "furious when a teacher sent it back with the brutal comment that it 'lacked imagination.'" ● In Allentown, Pennsylvania, a writer for the *Morning Call* pointed out the newspaper's own howler of a misplaced modifier: "Anna Schutl, who has lived in the downtown neighborhood where the victim was shot for more than 40 years, said she's there to stay." ● Perhaps following in the bad-punctuation tradition of the 2002 Warner Bros. movie *Two Weeks Notice* (rather than the grammatically correct *Two Weeks' Notice*), Universal Pictures released *The 40 Year-Old Virgin. Editor & Publisher* reported that copyeditors split over how to handle the half-hyphenated phrasal adjective. Many reviewers followed the title, including those from the *Atlanta Journal-Constitution*, the *Los Angeles Times*, the *Sacramento Bee*, and *Rolling Stone* magazine. Others distinguished themselves by silently correcting the Hollywood howler, making it *The 40-Year-Old Virgin.* These included the Associated Press, the *Boston Globe*, the *Chicago Sun-Times*, and *Newsday*. In the end, even the studio seemed unsure of itself: The movie's official website showed the title as it originally appeared, but it also offered the DVD—which correctly adds the missing hyphen.

September

Chief Justice William H. Rehnquist—who on his second day as chief berated an advocate for using the nonword *irregardless*, and who would later occasionally correct lawyers' grammar from the bench—died on September 3. ● Hurricane Katrina forced thousands of New Orleans residents from their homes to seek shelter. But although the general definition of *refugee* is "one who flees to shelter"—and *refuge* is synonymous with *shelter*—referring to the storm victims as *refugees* unleashed a storm of its own. In his take on the controversy, William Safire of the *New York Times* agreed that the Rev. Jesse Jackson and others who objected to the word had a point: since 1685, *refugee* has had a connotation of "one who seeks refuge or asylum in a foreign country to escape religious or political persecution." Over a single weekend almost every TV news outlet switched to *evacuees*, as did most print media (the Associated Press held out). Word.com reported that *refugee* set a monthly record for online lookups, beating out *tsunami*. President George W. Bush added his own opprobrium when a reporter used the suddenly stigmatized word, saying,

"They are Americans." The President himself uses *displaced citizens.* It could always be worse: to the United Nations, they do not qualify as *refugees,* but instead are *internally displaced people.* Or "IDPs," of course. • Writing in the *Times Higher Education Supplement,* Tony Thorne argued that professional linguists in the U.K. refuse to study the slang and colloquialisms of students for no other reason than social prejudice.

October

The venerable writing guide *The Elements of Style*—written by William Strunk Jr. in 1918 and expanded by his student E.B. White in 1959—got a colorful facelift. The new edition, *The Elements of Style Illustrated,* features art by Maira Kalman, whose other work includes *The New Yorker* magazine covers and children's books. To mark the occasion, composer Nico Muhly gave the premiere of his operatic salute at the New York Public Library. "The Elements of Style: Nine Songs" was performed by the Omit Needless Words Orchestra. • Among fans of Supreme Court nominee Judge John Roberts's style and rigor was *The New York Times,* which reported that his writings in the Reagan administration "reflect his unwavering penchant for caution—and precision—in language and thought. He corrected misuses of the words 'which' and 'that' in draft White House documents. And reviewing a proposed economic message in 1986 in which Mr. Reagan was to say 'I just turned 75 today, but remember that's only 30 Celsius,' Mr. Roberts noted that 75 Fahrenheit is actually 23.9 Celsius." • In Turkey, courts cracked down on the public display of signs bearing the letters Q, W, or X. Reuters reported that 20 protesters were fined about $75 under a law that outlawed the use of letters that are not in the Turkish alphabet. Those fined had been holding up signs at a new year's celebration. The signs were written in Kurdish, which does use the banned letters. • The *Daily Telegraph* reported on the perils of writing and typing Japanese, a language with 2,000 often intricate kanji characters, many of which require over a dozen pen strokes. Word-processing software has simplified writing considerably, allowing users to type in words phonetically on an English-style keyboard and then select the kanji from several offered by the computer. But hilarious errors can result if typists are poor or inattentive spellers: one woman who intended to write "I started living overseas this year" reportedly ended up saying, "Shellfish started inhabiting my stomach this year." • On October 27, Harriet Miers bowed out of the confirmation process for her Supreme Court nomination. According to the *Worcester Telegram & Gazette,* her "dearth of substance and plodding prose, spiked with cringe-worthy grammatical lapses, were disparaged by pundits on the left and right and lampooned on late-night TV." During the controversy leading up to Miers's withdrawal, David Brooks of *The New York Times* drew the most negative attention to her bad prose style, concluding: "The quality of thought and writing doesn't even rise to the level of pedestrian." Passages that Brooks called typical of her "vapid abstractions" included this: "More and more, the intractable problems in our society have one answer: broad-based intolerance of unacceptable conditions and a commitment by many to fix problems." • The paperback edition of Lynne Truss's *Eats, Shoots & Leaves* appeared in the U.K., including a "punctuation repair kit" consisting of stickers (big punctuation marks) to enable people to correct everyday examples of wayward commas and unnecessary apostrophes. No magic marker was included to stick a hyphen in the book's subtitle—nor is it clear that Truss would want people in bookstores defacing the cover of her book the way she encourages people to deface mispunctuated signs. • Angus McIntosh, the Edinburgh linguist who made so many contributions to the study of the Scottish tongue—the greatest being the monumental, large-format, four-volume *Linguistic Atlas of Late Medieval English*—died at the age of 91. • On October 30, the *Sunday Times* reported on Scottish students' writing as follows: "Standards are now so low that even Higher students lack fundamental skills. The Scottish Qualifications Authority has slammed the quality of teaching in English, saying reading and writing ability is 'rather alarming.' More than 40% of 13-year-olds in Scottish schools are missing literacy targets, and few children grasp the simplest rules of punctuation." • The next day, on Halloween, the *Times* of London reported on a two-year Cambridge University study finding that "the writing ability of 16-year-olds has never been higher." The study found that although "teenagers are ten times more likely to use nonstandard English in written exams than in 1980," today's teenagers use "far more complex sentence structures" as well as a wider vocabulary, and have a better command of capitalization, punctuation, and spelling. Oddly enough, the sentence in which that very finding was reported in the *Times* was plagued with a nonsensically unparallel structure. The report seemed more like a trick than a treat. • Also on Halloween, it was widely reported that researchers at Princeton have found that writers who needlessly use big words are perceived as being less intelligent than those who write plainly.

November

Writing in the *New Zealand Herald*, Stephen Ross, a "Cambridge-educated English teacher" with a B.A. in English and linguistics, opined that "most people say proNOUNciation," arguing that "you can't legislate language" and "you can't issue a decree about the way people speak." He added that "the fundamental purpose of language is to communicate ideas and to be understood," omitting any reference to the lack of credibility that attaches to those who mispronounce the word *pronunciation*. • A column in the *St. Paul Pioneer Press* noted a curious job description in the want ads: "Applicants must be able to tolerate walking, climbing, stooping, kneeling, crouching, reaching, standing, pushing, pulling, lifting, fingering, grasping, feeling, talking, hearing, seeing, and repetitive motion. Good hand/eye coordination is real important." Unable to tolerate that last part, the columnist asked: "More or less important than good grammar?" • The *Globe and Mail* reported that Canadian judges were making great strides toward a more comprehensible writing style. The Supreme Court had recently eradicated *infra* and *supra* from its decisions. All new Canadian judges are encouraged to enroll in writing courses. Among the positive examples of judicial writing cited in the article was this, from Madam Justice Denise Bellamy of the Ontario Superior Court: "[The city budget chief] drifted from lie to lie in a performance worthy of Pinocchio."

December

Fifty years after the publication of his first *Miscellany-at-Law* in 1955, Sir Robert Megarry (now age 95) saw the third and final volume in the trilogy appear after decades of work on it. (The second came out in 1973.) It is full of uproarious accounts of legal-linguistic problems in recent centuries, with individual chapters devoted to the foibles of legislative drafting, law reports, legal language generally, maxims, and *andorandororand*. In a chapter on sex, Sir Robert addresses the fascinating question—a mixed question of law and fact—whether it is possible to have sexual relations on a "without prejudice" basis. • *Hospital Case Management* reported that although hospitals may have error-disclosure policies in place and physicians may talk to their patients about errors, "patients may be none the wiser that an error is at the base of his or her problem." Instead of using words like *error*, *mistake*, and *harm*, doctors tend to speak of *complications* and *incidents*. • *Affilia*, a journal about women and social work, reported that U.S. natives who speak primarily a language other than English have more mental-health problems than immigrants and migrants in the same linguistic position do. • In Australia, the *National Observer* reported on a controversy involving pro-al-Qaeda comments made in 2004 by Sheikh Hilaly of New South Wales. According to translations of a Hilaly speech, the sheikh called for jihad and suicide bombers, and he praised the September 11 terrorists as engaging in God's work. When that caused a firestorm in the press, Sheikh Hilaly repeatedly used a lost-in-translation defense, arguing that his "poetic" language had been misunderstood. Hilaly said: "They [reporters] cannot understand my high level of expression." Hilaly's two daughters blamed the complexities of the Arabic language, saying: "You cannot just interpret it, just word by word."

Significant Anniversaries

It has been 250 years since the first publication of Samuel Johnson's monumental *Dictionary of the English Language*; 150 years since the publication of Richard Chenevix Trench's *English, Past and Present*; and 25 years since the publication of William Safire's first book on language, entitled *On Language*, as well as of John Simon's *Paradigms Lost*.

ஜ ஜ ஜ

2006

January

THE *Chronicle Herald* of Nova Scotia reported that Sali Tagliamonte, a Toronto linguist, declared American teenage girls to be the most powerful influence on the English language today. They routinely coin new words and phrases such as *prostitot* (= a child dressed as a raunchy pop star) and *muffin top* (= the bulge of flesh over the top of too-tight, low-cut jeans). According to Tagliamonte, California Valley Girl dialect is particularly influential because it is used on popular TV programs such as *The OC*. Gag us all with a spoon. • In Scotland, efforts to make plain English mandatory in drafting government regulations were stymied by the Executive (the government branch that executes legislation) on grounds that it is too difficult to combine consistency, legal clarity, and understandability, particularly in the English versions of European regulations. Och, 'tis hard but nae impossible! • The *Sacramento Bee* reported that an appreciation of grammar and language is becoming trendy, at least among those concerned about career success. The unconvincing evidence: (1) bookstores devote many shelves to books on grammar and writing; and (2) bloggers receive complaints from readers irked by sloppy language and poor spelling. If there is such a trend, it hardly threatens to become a national pastime. • Dr. Darin Howe, a linguistics professor at the University of Calgary, studied African-American dialect by listening to rap music. Among other things, he identified the systems for using multiple negatives and replacing *didn't* with *ain't*. He also noted that white rappers who try to imitate black speech often get it wrong. They should be more punctilious. • Peter Ladefoged, one of the world's foremost linguistic phoneticians, died January 24. He pioneered the use of electronic equipment in fieldwork; was one of the first to model the relationship between speech acoustics and the positions of the tongue, lips, and other articulators responsible for producing speech sounds; and encouraged the recording of languages but not their preservation. He was the phonetics consultant for the 1964 movie *My Fair Lady*, responsible for coaching Rex Harrison on how to behave like a phonetician, advising on the lab equipment, and providing the phonetic transcriptions. His voice is heard in the movie on the humorous recordings of vowel sounds that Professor Higgins plays for Eliza Doolittle.

Adapted from *2007 Green Bag Almanac.*

February

The *Sunday Times* reported that the English language has approached one million words, in part due to the increase in local forms in ethnic hybridized dialects such as Hinglish (Hindi and English), Chinglish (Chinese and English), and Spanglish (Spanish and English). Professor David Crystal mused on the possible future of English: "Does it splinter into a loosely connected family of English languages, which become mutually incomprehensible again, like old Latin, or do we develop a standard global English that can be understood by all? We don't know what will happen." • According to *Proceedings of the National Academy of Sciences*, scientists at the University of Rochester have found evidence that humans are hardwired for fundamental characteristics of human-language systems. Focusing on the grammatical concept of subject—because it is used in much the same form in languages throughout the world—researchers studied three children who were deaf from birth, had no education, and had never been exposed to formal sign language. The children, each from a different home, communicated using a household-specific form of sign language. Despite never having heard language and having not been formally taught the grammatical concept, each child was able to use subjects grammatically. • A four-disc boxed set of "The Best of The Electric Company" brought back 20 episodes of the PBS classic for today's kids. Celebrities such as Bill Cosby, Rita Moreno, Morgan Freeman, and Mel Brooks made the show a great complement to "Sesame Street." The show taught young fans the basics of grammar and spelling by osmosis: memorable characters such as Fargo North, Otto the director, and the Spellbinder made the show fun without being preachy. After all, who could forget Tom Lehrer's lyrics: "He turned a dam—ala kazaam!—into a dame. / But my friend Sam stayed just the same." It's elementary for Silent E. • British Sign Language has been formally recognized as a modern language by a British university. The University of Central Lancashire offered only two courses in BSL before developing a three-year program leading to a bachelor of arts degree. It's the first of its kind in the U.K. In the U.S., more than 20 colleges and universities offer a similar degree.

March

Dan Brown, American author of *The Da Vinci Code*, was accused of infringing the copyright of a British book, *The Holy Blood and the Holy Grail*. Testimony centered on the differences in British and American punctuation and spelling, and on the similarity of passages in both books.

Brown admitted that he had "reworked" some, but denied copying: "I'm not crazy about the word *copied* . . . . Copying implies it is identical. It's not identical." There were also many questions about whether the word *savior* or *saviour* had been used in an unfinished version of the book and whether it had been taken from a British source. • Peter Millar, a book critic for the *Times* of London, commented on Brown's poor research skills by pointing to a gross error in the 1998 book *The Digital Fortress*: "a hero uses the words *without wax* as code for *sincere*, because 'the English word evolved from the Spanish *sin cera*,' a term used by sculptors to describe works where they had not cheated by patching marble with wax. Sorry, Dan, *sincere* comes from the Latin *sincerus*, meaning 'clean, pure or sound.' Next time, include the *OED* in your 'detailed research.'" • The *Times* reported that British students who speak English as a native language are less proficient in its grammar, particularly in writing, than foreign students who acquire English as a second or third language. A study found that foreign teachers of English were less tolerant of errors than British teachers. It's unlikely that British students will catch up to their foreign peers anytime soon: the *Times* also noted that many of today's English-language teachers were educated in the freewheeling 1970s and do not themselves know the rules of English grammar or spelling. • Cambridge University Press released the permissive *Cambridge Grammar of English: A Comprehensive Guide* by professors Ronald Carter and Michael McCarthy. The 973-page volume got mixed reviews as less a guide to grammar than an utterly descriptivist study devoid of value judgments (except, of course, the value judgment that all value judgments must be forsworn). Among the tidbits included is that *you know* is the 57th most common lexical item in English. Irked by the apparent professorial approval of the trite phrase, a columnist for the *Daily Telegraph* griped, "To use [*you know*] so often is not being creative. It is to keep the motor of the tongue idling between thoughts." • Political correctness has trickled down to nursery-schoolers. In Oxfordshire, England, teachers are required to alter nursery rhymes so they won't offend or upset anyone. They must recite "Baa, Baa, Rainbow Sheep." Snow White lives with seven height-challenged roommates. And the children can rejoice because Humpty Dumpty is no longer beyond being fixed with super glue. • Those prone to linguistic faux pas when trying to speak foreign words might benefit from the 2006 compilation by a British linguist, Philip Gooden, titled *Faux Pas? A No-Nonsense Guide to Words and Phrases from Other Languages*. The book gives not only pronunciations and meanings, but also a unique "pretentiousness index" that rates foreignisms from the commonplace (e.g., *haiku*) to the snooty (e.g., *au contraire*). Anyone for solipsistic weltschmerz?

April

The *Oxford English Dictionary's* language-research database, the Oxford English Corpus, reached a total of 1 billion words. Launched in 2000 and focusing on 21st-century English, the database is a collection not merely of different words, but of contextual examples of usage and spellings. Erin McKean, editor in chief for American dictionaries for Oxford University Press, explained: "The word *the* is 50 million of that billion. Those are 50 million different contexts. Think of it like this: There's an ocean filled with fish, and each fish is a different species. You don't just study one of each kind of fish. You want to know how they interact with each other. We're looking at the whole ecosystem of words." • In London, the *Da Vinci Code* case ended with a ruling that it did not infringe any copyrights. The 71-page opinion included a series of strange italicizations, which astute readers realized were a coded message. When asked about it, Mr. Justice Smith commented, "I don't see why a judgment should not be a matter of fun." It took code-breakers several weeks to solve The Smith J. Code. • There appears to be a connection between literacy and oral communication. According to the International Reading Association, a study at the Centre for Neuroscience in Education at the University of Cambridge has found that children grasp larger elements of language, such as syllables, onsets, and rhymes, through listening and speaking. But they don't become aware of other elements, such as phonemes, until they are taught to read. Differences in phonological and orthographic elements also had an effect on literacy. In orthographically consistent languages, such as Greek, Spanish, and German, most children can read accurately by the middle of first grade. For languages with inconsistent spellings or readings, accuracy drops. For French, Finnish, and Portuguese, the accuracy rate is 70%. English is at the bottom of the chart, with only 40%; the poor performance is attributed to the many anomalies in English spelling and pronunciation.

May

The BBC began broadcasting a weekly program called "Never Mind the Full Stops," described as "a quiz show about English, its speakers' foibles, and its innumerable heffalump-traps." According to the *Daily Telegraph*, four guests each week will punctuate paragraphs, divine dialects, translate text messages, invent mnemonics, spot euphemisms, and vent odd bits of spleen. Early reports suggest that the show is popular. • Plagiarism doesn't pay. In fact, it cuts pay. William Swanson, CEO of Raytheon, wrote a short management guide containing uncredited passages from a 1944 book, *The Unwritten Laws of Engineering.* After a blogger exposed the plagiarism,

Raytheon's board canceled Swanson's pay raise and reduced his stock options, worth a total of almost $800,000. • Grant Barrett, a lexicographer for the Oxford University Press, published the *Official Dictionary of Unofficial English*, offering 750 neologisms that are currently in use but not yet in any formal dictionaries. Its subtitle, *A Crunk Omnibus for Thrillionaires and Bampots for the Ecozoic Age*, gives a clue to the contents. Barrett admits that many of the terms will not thrive or survive long enough to be recorded in established dictionaries, but word-lovers will be happy to have this snapshot of the evanescent words. • Lawmaking is famously compared to sausage-making, and political jargon is every bit as lively as slaughterhouse slang. In Phoenix, Jim Small collected some samples for the *Arizona Capital Times*, including *the box* (= discretionary funds in the budget), *feed bill* (= appropriations for state agencies), and FTSE /**fuut**-see/ (= full-time student equivalent, used to set funding for colleges). He reports that in Arizona, a bill gets *dropped* (filed with the clerk), goes through the *COW* (Committee of the Whole), and always faces the threat of a *striker* (an amendment striking its entire contents).

June

On the heels of two great spelling-bee movies—*Spellbound* (2002) and *Akeelah and the Bee* (2006)—people got excited about the National Spelling Bee this year. A report about the winner even appeared on the Major League Baseball website, providing baseball-oriented sentences containing some of the words used in the final rounds. The two finalists battled for seven rounds until 13-year-old Katherine Close clinched the victory by correctly spelling *ursprache* (= a deductively reconstructed language). Close reportedly memorized 99% of the 23,000 words on an expert spelling-bee list before winning the national contest. It took her five years. • The revised 11th edition of the *Concise Oxford English Dictionary* was published, including a section ranking the most common words in the English language. As expected, the simple ones dominated—*the*, *to*, and *of*—but the list also held a few surprises. The top noun was *time*, followed by *person* and *year*. *Man* was seventh, *woman* fourteenth. *War* was forty-ninth, but *peace* didn't make the top 100. Angus Stevenson, project manager for Oxford University Press, noted, "The thing that struck me when I put together this list was that 90% of the top 100 words were one syllable, and that a large proportion were actually from Old English, meaning the basic words we use all the time in basic sentences are from before the Norman Conquest." Beneficial vocables persist. No: good words last. • According to the *Virginian-Pilot* (Norfolk, Va.), an elementary-school teacher and an English professor have collaborated to advocate a new way of teaching standard English to children who speak dialects.

They advocate using what linguists have long called "code switching," rather than correction. When a child says something in dialect, rather than responding by restating the sentence in standard English, the teacher is supposed to remind the child that everyone uses a different language in school and then to ask the child to restate the idea in standard English. The technique supposedly stresses awareness of the similarities and differences between dialect and standard English and encourages the use of both in the appropriate times and places. • For the first time, the U.K. Parliament presented a draft bill containing an explanation of the bill's purpose and provisions in plain English. The explanation wasn't perfectly clear, probably because it was written by the parliamentary drafters who had prepared the bill. Yet ordinary people reportedly could understand most of the bill's effects. With time and practice, perhaps Parliament's drafters will incorporate more plain English into their actual bills. • A reporter at *The New York Times* was unusually coy about using the Provençal name for the classic dish gnocchi niçois: *merda de can*. Apparently he confused *merda* with *merde* and believed that writing *merda de can* would have caused something to hit the fan. But *merde* has appeared at least 13 times in the *The New York Times*, twice in columns by William Safire. • An errant comma cost a Canadian telecom $2.13 million when government regulators interpreted its contract for stringing lines on utility poles in the maritime provinces. The relevant sentence allowed the deal to "continue in force for a period of five years from the date it is made, and thereafter for successive five-year terms, unless and until terminated by one year prior notice." Rogers Communications thought it could count on the contract rates for the first five years—and it would have been right if not for that pesky second comma. The grammatically savvy agency saw that the second comma made the *unless*-clause modify the entire term of the agreement.

July

According to the American Literacy Council, English has 42 sounds spelled 400 ways. So what's been done about it? A century ago this month, the Simplified Spelling Board was founded to promote simplification of English spellings and immediately offered a list of 300 words. President Teddy Roosevelt soon ordered the Government Printing Office to use the Board's spellings in all government publications, but Congress quickly blocked that order. Today, spelling reform seems much less likely than it did a century ago. • Noah Webster published *A Compendious Dictionary of the English Language* 200 years ago this month. It wasn't a big book, only 6 inches by 4 inches and containing just 37,000 entries. But 5,000 of those entries were words frequently used by Americans yet unrecorded in British dictionaries. Webster's dictionary was the first to record words such as *chowder, surf, hickory,* and *skunk.* But that wasn't all Webster did. He also promoted change in American English spelling. *Music, public,* and *fabric* lost their trailing *k*'s. Words such as *color, humor,* and *labor* dropped the silent *u* before the *r.* Not all of his Americanized spellings caught on: *ake, soop, tung,* and *wimmen* are among the flops. But no matter. Webster's little book thrived and grew. One of its descendants, the 11th edition of *Merriam-Webster's Collegiate Dictionary,* has 225,000 entries. ● Gwon Jae-il, a linguist at Seoul National University, reported in *Hankyoren* (Seoul) that more than 1,000 languages are on the verge of extinction. There are some 6,000 languages worldwide, but almost 23% are spoken by fewer than 1,000 people. In North America alone, about 165 native languages are declining; almost half are spoken by only a few elderly people. In South America, more than 100 languages are endangered. In Europe, Celtic languages, particularly Scots Gaelic and Irish, are attempting to stage a comeback, but few households use them as a first language.

August

Hazleton, Pennsylvania, enacted an ordinance that made English the city's official language and required all official business to be conducted in that language. It was promptly sued. Among other arguments, the plaintiffs noted that in Pennsylvania, public services have historically "been available in their native languages to speakers of German, Polish, Russian, Yiddish, Italian, Hungarian, and a variety of other languages." They also cited an 1837 law that "required school instruction in both German and English." The case is to be heard in 2007. ● According to the *Globe and Mail,* researchers at the University of Toronto reported on their study of teens' language in instant messaging. Among their findings: teens combine both formal and informal language in their messages, sometimes using a higher degree of formality than they would in speech. For instance, while teens might use *was like* for *said* in speech, *said* was more common in text messaging. On the other hand, text messages often used acronyms uncommon in speech, such as *rofl* (= rolling on floor laughing). ● Other researchers, at the University of Leicester, are studying the language and patterns in individuals' text messages as a means of identifying the sender. According to a BBC report, the scientists think that individual texting strategies and vocabulary are likely to remain relatively constant, so the technique of pattern analysis can be useful in many ways, including criminal investigations. In England, an analyst studied two text messages supposedly sent by a missing girl and compared them with messages she had sent before her disappearance. Differences in spelling established that she had not sent the later messages—and also helped identify the person who had. • To google or not to google? The *Oxford English Dictionary* added *Google* to its pages in June. And in July, *Merriam-Webster's Collegiate Dictionary* included it (with a small *g*) as a verb. But the Google company took exception, on the grounds that its trademark had been threatened. Its lawyers fired off letters to media organizations, warning them not to use *Google* as a verb, lest the term undergo what intellectual-property lawyers call *genericide*. So far, no formal legal action to protect the trademark has been taken. • Just in time for the Emmy Awards, the Global Language Monitor named the top TV buzzwords of 2006: *truthiness* and *wikiality*, both "Colbert Report" coinages. Next in line were *Katrina, Katie* (Couric), and *Dr. McDreamy* (from "Grey's Anatomy"). GLM is a San Diego company that tracks word frequencies and connotative contextual clues.

September

National Punctuation Day didn't make much of a mark on the public. Despite being described as "a celebration of the lowly comma, correctly used quotes and other proper uses of periods, semicolons, and the ever-mysterious ellipsis," it was largely uncelebrated. Angus Lind, a columnist with the *Times-Picayune* in New Orleans, gave readers suggestions on how to participate: "Read a newspaper and, with a red pen, circle all of the punctuation errors you find, or think you find but aren't sure. You can skip red-penning this column because it will be the pinnacle of punctuation perfection." • The linguist David Crystal blasted Lynne Truss, author of the error-riddled book *Eats, Shoots & Leaves*. Crystal criticized not the book's many factual blunders but instead its zero tolerance of errors, calling it "misconceived" and "deeply unnerving." He added, "Zero tolerance does not allow for flexibility. It is prescriptivism taken to extremes. It suggests that language is in a state where all the rules are established with 100% certainty. The suggestion is false. We do not know what all the rules of punctuation are." John Humphrys, author of *Lost for Words*, responded: "I think David Crystal is making a fundamental mistake when he says rules don't matter that much. I say they matter enormously. Take the example we always use on both sides of the debate: the apostrophe. It is either right or wrong. We wouldn't accept something being wrong in any other walk of life, would we?" • *Science* reported that what appears to be the earliest written language in the Western Hemisphere is on a stone carving in Mexico. Archaeologists date it to about 900 B.C. and identify it as Olmec, the first major civilization in Central America. It's the first carving containing enough text to establish conclusively that the characters are not merely decorative but actually part of a syntactical or organized language system meant to communicate more than just imagery. • In the United Kingdom, there was more bad news about the English-language skills of native English-speaking students. Test results showed that only 66% of 14-year-olds were able to read at grade level. There was also a pronounced gender difference: for boys, the figure was only 59%, compared to 74% for girls. Steve Sinnott, general secretary of the National Union of Teachers, warned that teenagers were just reading "less and less" and blamed "the impact of peer pressure, technological innovation, and just being a teenager in an ever-changing world." • The English language got yet another genderless third-person singular pronoun when a Johns Hopkins writing instructor, D.N. DeLuna, edited a book of essays about a political historian, J.G.A. Pocock. She calls her newfangled pronoun the *Hopkins hu* (on the pattern, one supposes, of the Oxford comma). She told the *Chronicle of Higher Education* that it's pronounced like *huh*, but with less aspiration. It's not just sexless, either—it's a caseless libertine, too, freely swinging from nominative to objective to possessive with not so much as a blush. DeLuna hopes it fares better than the 100 or so other epicene forms suggested over the last 150 years, most memorably the onomatopoeic *s/he/it*.

October

According to *The Washington Post*, more and more U.S. students prefer to type rather than write in longhand—and this preference is affecting their ability to write in cursive. Nearly 1.5 million students wrote essays for the SAT this year. Only 15% used cursive; the rest printed in block letters. Interestingly, the essays written in cursive received slightly higher scores. Most educators are unconcerned by the decline in cursive, opining that penmanship is an antiquated subject in a technological age, and the time once spent on it is better devoted to other subjects. But researchers who specialize in writing acquisition counter that children without proficient handwriting skills also write poorly, almost always producing shorter, cruder compositions than those with strong handwriting skills. And historical researchers plaintively note that handwriting is an important aspect in determining the authenticity of documents, such as the unpublished Robert Frost poem recently discovered stuck in a book donated to the University of Virginia. • Rogers Communications filed its appeal in the Two-Million-Dollar Comma case. (See June.) After two months of searching, it found a French-language version of the same contract. The punctuation is different in the French version and, Rogers argues, supports its interpretation of the English version. The appeal is to be heard in 2007. • A new book entitled *I Smirt, You Stooze, They Krump* records odd slang words and terms, many of them portmanteau words. Some are creative insults, such as *celebutard* (= a celebrity noted for public acts of stupidity) and *tanorexic* (= a person obsessed with indoor tanning). • A new issue has split the Supreme Court of the United States, according to an analysis by Jonathan Starble in *Legal Times*: how to form the possessive of a singular noun ending in *-s*. In *Kansas v. Marsh*, Starble notes, five justices (Alito, Kennedy, Roberts, Scalia, and Thomas, JJ.) embraced the journalistic apostrophe-only rule (*Kansas'*). In opposition to that liberal bloc stood the conservatives Breyer, Ginsburg, Souter, and Stevens JJ., true to the first rule of *Strunk and White* and making it *Kansas's*. • A Michigan County spent an extra $40,000 on its general election when the first press run of 170,000 ballots contained a common but embarrassing typo. One proposition to amend the state constitution used the word *public* six times, and the letter *l* appeared properly only five times. The Ottawa County clerk said that several staffers had proofed the ballot, but even after being told about the error they had a hard time spotting it. Only the crotchety ones found it.

November

OMG! The *Chicago Sun-Times* reported that national-exam graders in New Zealand will allow students to write next year's essays in the style of text-messaging as long as the meaning of what they say is accurate. Fortunately, they still score more points for quoting *Hamlet* in Shakespeare's English rather than "2B or nt 2B." Presumably, graders will consult one of the online TXTIN DXNREs. • A study by researchers at Wake Forest University Baptist Medical Center showed a connection between poor reading skills and suicidal tendencies. The researchers measured other factors, such as psychiatric disorders, but confirmed that reading difficulties are a distinct factor leading to suicide attempts. The study concluded that poor readers are three times as likely as average readers to attempt suicide. • Thomas Pynchon's newly published novel, *Against the Day*, contains a dramatization against prescriptive grammar on the very first page. An excited boy riding in a balloon exclaims, "I can't hardly wait!" Offended by the boy's informal usage, the airship's second-in-command hangs the boy overboard by his ankles, "proceeding to lecture him on the many evils of looseness in one's expression, not least among them being the ease with which it may lead to profanity, and worse." Meanwhile, Pynchon writes that since the solecistic character being dangled so precariously "was screaming in terror, it is doubtful how many of the useful sentiments actually found their mark." One wonders what childhood linguistic trauma led Pynchon to create this scene. • In Chile, a native tribe is suing Microsoft for translating its software into the tribe's language without permission. The theory underlying the lawsuit seems to be that language can be owned as property by the people who speak it. • In Canada, Norman Spector, a talk-radio pundit, called a member of Parliament a "bitch." He defended himself against the MP's ire by claiming that he had used the term correctly in the sense of "a treacherous or malicious woman," citing the *Oxford English Dictionary*. While covering the flap, the *Vancouver Sun* reported that it could not find such a sense in the *OED*, implying that Spector had lied. A writer at the *Toronto Star* likewise failed to find such a definition. Both reporters obviously failed to read sense 2a in the great reference book. Spector is now suing the *Sun* for libel. • What's in an e-mail sign-off? Standards are evolving quickly, according to *The New York Times*. A sign-off can imply cordiality and warmth, or aloofness and edginess. For instance, many people regard a curt closing, such as "Best" or "Sincerely," as cool and formal, whereas "Warmest regards" and similar expressions are perceived as warm and friendly but still professional. Choosing an inappropriate sign-off can result in a mixed message. When you write a complaint about a defective product or shoddy service, closing with "Warmly" suggests that you aren't really very upset. And ending an e-mail to a casual acquaintance or stranger with an "XOXO" suggests intimacy, real or imagined, and almost ensures that you won't get an answer. • Is it better to "gift" than receive? The *Wall Street Journal* reported on the trendy use of *gift* as a verb. Some people defend that usage, pointing out that many dictionaries, including the *Oxford English Dictionary*, define *gift* as a transitive verb. The *OED* traces its use in that sense to the 17th century. One commentator added, "It's nice to have a word that specifically means 'to give as a gift.'" And it has become more common than ever before in advertising ("go ahead, gift her a diamond"), supposedly witty headlines ("Thanksgifting"), and entertainment-related stories ("Each star was gifted with fabulous goodie bags"). The credit or blame for the faddish use of *gift* may go to a 1995 "Seinfeld" episode that introduced the word *regifting* (= to make a gift of something that one received as a gift) to popular culture. But many deride the verb *gift* as one they hardly wanted.

December

Voters in Arizona passed Proposition 203 on November 7, but as the *Arizona Republic* reported, nobody was sure quite what it did until this month. The initiative sought to raise the state's cigarette tax by 80 cents a pack. The draft wording that its backers presented had that as "$.80."

But the printed ballot, drafted by the Secretary of State's office and approved by the Attorney General's office, specified the increase as ".08 cents"—less than a penny a carton. The proposition passed anyway, but for a while it looked as if the snafu might cost the state's early-childhood health and education budget about $186 million. Then, on December 1, Attorney General Terry Goddard released a decidedly nontextualist opinion that the misprint should not thwart the declared intention of the well-publicized campaign. He also noted that the technical ballot language indicated that the hike would amount to 4 cents per cigarette: that's 80 cents for a pack of 20. Despite the AG's ruling, litigation doubtless looms. • An Associated Press business writer reported that more business schools are taking notice of the erosive effects of e-mail and instant messaging on business prose. By hitting the "send" button without adequate editing or even proofing, people "send messages they don't intend," said Jim O'Rourke, director of Notre Dame's Fanning Center for Business Communication. To counter the effects, Dave Carpenter reported, more business schools are adding or expanding writing classes. Others are citing examples of bad writing as cautionary tales to students. One example from a Fortune 500 company: "It is my job to ensure proper process deployment activities take place to support process institutionalization and sustainment. Business process management is the core deliverable of my role, which requires that I identify process competency gaps and fill those gaps." Carpenter's translation: "I'm the training director." Another example is the infamous RadioShack ax-by-e-mail: "The work force reduction notification is currently in progress. Unfortunately your position is one that has been eliminated." Carpenter quoted Peter Handal, head of Dale Carnegie Training, as attributing the failure to speed trumping accuracy: "People are just so happy to get the communications going that they aren't spending the time on how to communicate." In other words, blame irrational exuberance. • Jonathan Harrington, professor of phonetics at the University of Munich, studied Queen Elizabeth II's Christmas broadcasts to the Commonwealth from 1952 to 2005. In an article published in the *Journal of Phonetics*, he concluded that the royal vowel sounds have steadily shifted from Upper Received Pronunciation toward Standard Received Pronunciation or Estuary English. He noted that in the 1950s, class demarcations were clear. But they began blurring in the 1960s, and the queen has unconsciously altered her speech over time. As the *Chicago Sun Times* put it, she would now say "that man in the black hat" instead of "thet men in the bleck het," "dutee" instead of "dutay," and "home" instead of "hame." Still, she won't be chatting with commoners in the local pub anytime soon, said Harrington. "She may be drifting slowly downstream towards Estuary, but she has a very, very long way to go before she gets anywhere near the open sea." • Even as English emerges as the global language, thanks largely to international commerce and the Internet, England's traditional role as teacher of that language to visiting nonnative speakers has fallen sharply. The job has been outsourced, you might say. The *Guardian* of London reported that more people are traveling to closer locales such as Australia, New Zealand, even Malta to learn English. The British Council says that although the U.K. still dominates the field, it may not be the market leader for long. Among the 100 million people seeking to learn English, demand is reportedly strongest where global markets are growing, as in China and Vietnam. But as those countries' economies grow, so does their ability to provide English-language courses at home—often from other nonnative speakers. Indeed, nonnative speakers teach more English classes than native speakers do. They're getting better at it, too. The *Guardian* said that in some Middle Eastern and Asian countries, English is taught to young children "as a basic skill alongside the child's native language, mathematics, and IT." After the U.K., the United States is second in providing the most instruction in English as a second language. Australia and New Zealand teach the most Asian students, especially from China, Japan, and Thailand. The Mediterranean island nation of Malta is also a player, with more than 55,000 visiting students, mostly Europeans. A British study called Malta "a holiday and language opportunity with low prices, but not necessarily a serious academic destination." • The *Observer* reported that globalism has had another effect on the English language: Anglophones seem to have a harder time communicating with nonnative speakers than speakers of other languages do—even when they're also conversing in English. What's needed, Jean-Paul Nerriere contends, is English without idioms. To that end, he has developed the rudiments of a language he calls Globish /**glohb**-ish/. It's not pidgin English, he insists. It's just a simplified version, sort of "decaffeinated English or English-lite." Don't think it's another Esperanto, either, Nerriere said, because it's not a made-up language. It uses English words and grammar. Without idioms, Globish can be a bit wordier than the prose native speakers use. He gives as example *chat*, which might be phrased "speak casually to each other," or *kitchen*, which might translate into "room in which you cook your food."

Significant Anniversaries

It has been 200 years since Noah Webster published the first American lexicon, *A Compendious Dictionary of the English Language*; 100 years since H.W. and F.G. Fowler published *The King's English*; 80 years since H.W.

Fowler published *A Dictionary of Modern English Usage*; 50 years since J.N. Hook and E.G. Matthews published *Modern American Grammar and Usage*; 40 years since Wilson Follett published *Modern American Usage: A Guide*; 30 years since Edwin Newman published *A Civil Tongue*; 20 years since Robert W. Burchfield completed his massive four-volume *Supplement* to the *Oxford English Dictionary*, Jacques Barzun published *A Word or Two Before You Go*, and William Safire published *Take My Word for It*; and 10 years since William F. Buckley published *The Right Word*, Robert W. Burchfield published *The New Fowler's Modern English Usage*, and Patricia T. O'Conner published *Woe Is I: The Grammarphobe's Guide to Better English*.

ૠ ૠ ૠ

2007

January

WRITING IN *Childhood Education*, three scholars (Kristen Cuthrell, Carolyn Ledford, and Joy Stapleton) canvassed the literature on poverty and reminded readers of this enduring truth: "One of poverty's most deleterious impacts is on children's linguistic development. Impoverished students are far more likely than their classmates to enter school linguistically disadvantaged because they do not have the experiences that will promote literacy and reading-readiness." • *The Guardian* ran an obituary of Carlo Ponti, the late husband of Sophia Loren. Some readers questioned whether the newspaper's phrasing cast doubt on Ponti's sexual orientation. The piece said that in his early career Ponti was "already a man with a good eye for pretty actors." The next day, the newspaper ran a sheepish correction: "This was one of those occasions when the word 'actresses' might have been used." • The American Dialect Society announced its 17th annual Word of the Year (for 2006). It came down to a runoff between *plutoed* ("demoted or devalued," inspired by the planet Pluto when the General Assembly of the International Astronomical Union decided that Pluto no longer met the definition of a planet) and *climate canary* ("an organism or species whose poor health or declining numbers hint at a larger environmental catastrophe on the horizon"). The winner, despite its meaning, was *plutoed*. • The *Milwaukee Journal Sentinel* published Lake Superior State University's annual "List of Words and Phrases Banished from the Queen's English for Mis-Use, Over-Use and General Uselessness." More than 4,500 words and phrases were nominated, but only 16 made the ignominious cut. Among the banished are *i*-anything ("tech companies everywhere have picked this apple to the core") and *ask your doctor* ("the chewable vitamin morphine of marketing"). Tom Pink, a university official, conceded that since the list began in 1976, no dictionary-makers have been persuaded to participate in the banishment. • In the "Modern Morals" column in *The Times* of London, a reader queried whether, being "full of do-gooding zeal," he should correct people for "the spelling mistakes and grammatical errors on websites of friends and family." The columnist, Joe Joseph, responded: "Think of it as the visual equivalent of listening to Arnold Schwarzenegger speaking English yet being able to grasp what he is trying to say . . . . [Y]ou could certainly offer to correct spelling and grammar errors on websites that vex you. But don't be surprised if the site owners respond by offering to gvie u a bg salp in yuor fcae." • *The Times* of London also reported that the editors of the *Oxford English Dictionary* were turning to the public for help in solving some mysteries related to common 20th-century words and phrases. For instance, the *OED* has tentatively defined *dogging* as "the practice of watching people engage in sexual acts in a public space." But it still needs to confirm whether the word was actually coined by police officers to describe the activities of amorous suspects who, when caught, claimed they were "just walking the dog." • *The American Scholar*, the quarterly journal of literature, science, and culture published by the Phi Beta Kappa Society, marked its 75th anniversary.

February

The Times of London cited a National Literacy Trust study showing that baby strollers that face away from the caregiver can hamper a child's communication skills. According to the research, 90% of nursery workers worry that speech difficulties among preschoolers are increasing, partly because parents don't talk to their children enough. Hence the Trust has started a campaign (talktoyourbaby.org.uk) for increased awareness of the benefits of parent-facing strollers, which allow parents to see and talk to their children. • Cleveland's *Plain Dealer* ran a Sunday-edition front-page story saying "it's gonna get cruelly cold outside." A reader objected, asking whether the newspaper's stylebook now includes "gonna" as a substitute for "going to" in straight text (as opposed to a quote). Doug Clifton, an editor at the paper, formally apologized: "While I believe newspapers should speak in approachable language, I also believe we have an obligation to uphold linguistic standards. I think we abdicated on this one." • *Publisher's Weekly* reported that some librarians have banned *The Higher Power of Lucky* by Susan Patron because it contains the word "scrotum" on the first page, in reference to an injured dog. Although the book won the Newbery Medal, the most prestigious award in children's literature, one of the banishing librarians sniffed, "I don't want to start an issue about censorship, but you won't find men's genitalia in quality literature. At least not for children." Relying on a single word, the librarians seem to have bollixed this one. • Writing in *Slate*, Ben Yagoda bemoaned the disregard for interjections shown by grammarians and lexicographers. He argues that although interjections aren't easily defined or categorized, they are entitled to more attention and respect as part of the language than they have been given because they pervade our casual speech and writing. Yagoda admits that some interjections are nebulous, such as *meh*, which has 173 definitions in the online urbandictionary.com. But many have commonly understood meanings. For example: *Duh!* ("You've stated something obvious."), *Not!* ("What I just said? Reverse it."), and *Ka-ching!* ("That's a good idea. You might even make some money off it."). So will interjections ever get respect? Meh. • On the heels of last term's U.S. Supreme Court decision overruling *Strunk & White* (declaring 5-to-4 in *Kansas v. Marsh*, albeit in dicta, that the possessive of *Kansas* is *Kansas'*, not *Kansas's*), the Arkansas General Assembly mandated a different rule in that state. The *Arkansas Democrat-Gazette* reported on Rep. Steve Harrelson's resolution that "whereas confusion has arisen concerning the appropriate spelling of the name of our state," the possessive should henceforth and forevermore be *Arkansas's*. After Harrelson apologized several times for giving columnists and commentators nationwide fodder for items to the effect that the legislature had too much time on its hands, the matter went out for public deliberation. The Clinton School of Public Service even hosted a debate on the question, and the dean agreed with the state's governor, attorney general, and secretary of state that "apostrophe-s" is proper. With the Senate's approval, the nonbinding resolution entered the books in March. Historically, the controversy actually goes back to 1881, when the legislature distanced the state from the syllabically challenged Kansas by declaring its final *-s* to be officially silent. • The *Independent on Sunday* (London) reported that Lynne Truss, author of the best-selling, error-riddled guide to grammar *Eats, Shoots & Leaves*, was furiously sniping about works that parody her book, such as *Eats, Shites & Leaves: Crap English and How to Use It*, and *Doctor Whom*, a *Doctor Who* send-up about poor grammar acting as a catalyst for universal entropy. Truss declared that the latter had "no literary merit whatsoever" before admitting she had not read the book. Adam Roberts, author of *Doctor Whom* and a professor of literature at London University, responded: "I'm impressed at her ability to intuit the dreadfulness of *Dr Whom* without having read it. It might be that the point of parody is not whether it's original but whether it's funny." Truss also blasted the Vegetarian Society's cookery booklet, *Eat Shoots and Leaves? More Interesting Cuisine from the Cordon Vert School*. Truss didn't say whether she has tried any of the recipes. • *The Times* of London reported on the Academie Française's new campaign to establish French as the controlling language of the law in the European Union. The Academie argues, "The Italian language is the language of song, German is good for philosophy and English for poetry. French is best at precision, it has a rigor to it. It is the safest language for legal purposes." To support its position, the Academie points out that European Union law is based on civil-law norms drawn from Roman law, that French is related to Latin (in which Roman law was written), and that French is the language of the Napoleonic Code (the basis of modern French law). Other members of the E.U. aren't buying the arguments. One representative said anonymously, "They don't want to say it, but they are raising the alarm on English getting more and more predominant in the institutions." Zut alors!

March

In the March/April issue of *Child Development*, new findings on child-care centers were reported. Among them: the higher the quality of non-maternal care that children experience before starting school, the larger their vocabularies through fifth grade, around age 11. Writing in *Pediatrics for Parents*, Jay Belsky (Ph.D.) relied on these findings to pose an important question: "In a day and age when more and more chidren, at younger and younger ages, spend more and more time in childcare centers (and other arrangements), often of limited quality, what is the consequence for larger social systems?" • In the Indian publication *Business Line*, a writer named D. Murali contributed an article entitled "A Cardinal Sin Called Overconfidence," in which this good-grammar admonition appeared in reference to excellence in cold-calling: "When you speak in English which is full of grammatical errors, the other person is bound to slam the phone on your face." • The Internet word *wiki* (literally a Hawaiian word meaning "quick") was introduced into the *Oxford English Dictionary*, which defines it as "a type of web page designed so that its content can be edited by anyone who accesses it, using a simplified markup language." • The *Winnipeg Free Press* reported on the progress that Stefan Dollinger is making in revising the *Dictionary of Canadianisms on Historical Principles*, published by the University of Victoria. The first edition, published in 1967, was 927 pages long, containing 10,000 words of significance to Canada; the length of the second edition is yet to be known. If all goes well, it will appear in 2013. The revisers started their work not with A, but with C—for *Canuck*. • In a letter to the *Los Angeles Times*, Derek Drinon noted the effort of McDonald's Corporation to change various dictionaries' definition of *McJob* to "a job that is stimulating, rewarding, and offers genuine opportunities for career progression and skills that last a lifetime." Drinon opines that McDonald's "should leave the lexicographers alone and stop wasting their McTime." • The BBC reported that 5% of applicants to Oxford and Cambridge universities cheated on the personal-statement section of their applications by copying or adapting dramatic or eye-catching accounts from the Internet. Eight hundred applicants, mostly to science-related programs, incorporated language or took inspiration from three sample statements on a single website (www.studential.com)—370 sentences began with "a fascination for how the human body works," 234 related a dramatic incident involving burning a hole in their pajamas at age eight, and 175 referred to "an elderly or infirm grandfather." • John "McHardy" Sinclair, a Scottish linguist and lexicographer, died on March 13 at 73. A professor at Birmingham University from 1965 to 2000, he was the first to lay out a systematic scheme of discourse analysis in his 1975 book, *Towards the Analysis of Discourse*, cowritten by Malcolm Coulthard. Sinclair went on to make groundbreaking contributions in lexicography, including the concept of building a large corpus to show how the arrangement of words ("collocation") affect their meanings. He used that technique in a project called "Cobuild" (corpus-based) and used it as the chief adviser to *Collins' Cobuild English Language Dictionary*. In later years he founded the Tuscan Word Centre, dedicated to training linguists and conducting corpus-based research.

April

In the *Bergen County Record*, Evelyn Shih wrote an interesting article about how foul words can gradually become fair. The question is what happens when loaded words shift in meaning so that their less offensive secondary senses come into vogue. Among the examples of once-taboo but now not-so-taboo words are *ho*, *bitch*, *gay*, *retarded*, and *queer*. Keen listeners are aware that even the most taboo words are being heard with greater regularity in all sorts of circumstances. • The *Worcester Telegram & Gazette* reported on a talk that John Morse, president and publisher of Merriam-Webster, gave to high-school kids. Morse opined that although more people pay for Internet access to the unabridged dictionary than buy the print version, he is confident that there will always be a demand for dictionaries in print. The most common electronic searches at Merriam-Webster's website are for *effect* and *affect*. • In the *Boston Globe*, language columnist Jan Freeman reviewed Ben Yagoda's newly published book *When You Catch an Adjective, Kill It*, in which Yagoda characterizes descriptivist linguists as "a group whose motto, borrowed from Alexander Pope, is 'Whatever is, is right.'" So Freeman decided to ask some notable descriptivists what prescriptive norms they cherish, and she concluded that "language pros are not so different from you and me." Item: Geoffrey Pullum dislikes the phrase *people of color*. Item: Steven Pinker hews to the rule that you "put quantifiers like *only* and *not* as close to the quantified element as possible." Item: Geoffrey Nunberg "can't abide *author* and *dialogue* as verbs, *methodology* for *method*, *minority* and *elite* to refer to individuals ('many elites in the entertainment industry')." • The *Pittsburgh Post-Gazette* reported that *snuck* is sneaking up on *sneaked* in Standard English: although 61% of the American Heritage usage panel prefers *sneaked* in written English, *snuck* is gaining ground. On Google, according to the report, "*snuck* rules, with 3 million hits to just 1.6 million for *sneaked*." • In the *Irish Times*, the chief examiner in Ireland's Department of Education opined that text messaging and e-mails are taking a toll on students' ability to write because they encourage phonetic writing while discouraging proper spelling and punctuation. Commenting on the quality of high-level and honors papers submitted in a national exam, he said that many students "failed to display much knowledge of the subject, preferring to give minimal answers in short sentences, simple tenses and a limited vocabulary." • Prospective Oxbridge students aren't the only ones who plagiarize interesting expressions (see March). According to *New Scientist*, many science journals are also receiving papers that contain phrasings and even whole paragraphs taken from published materials without attribution. Editors for the journal *Biomaterials* discovered that their own words had been recycled in two separate submissions. David Williams, the editor in chief, noted that the offenders held posts at prestigious institutions. • The *Irish Independent* reported that a village in Ireland symbolically welcomed the return of its long-missing harlot when it gained official approval to change its name from An Dun back to Dun Bleisce. In modern Irish Gaelic, the word *bleisce* is derogatory and refers to "a woman of ill repute." That's likely the reason why the Minister for Community, Rural, and Gaeltacht Affairs changed the village's name in 2003—without the residents' consent. But in ancient Irish, according to Dun Bleisce Councillor Mary Jackman, "It would have meant that the woman was a strong or powerful woman in the locality." Given that *dun* means "fortress," the historical *bleisce* for whom the village was named must have been a powerful woman indeed. • When Prince William of England broke up with Kate Middleton, the *Guardian* (London), the *Independent* (London), and even the *Los Angeles Times* speculated that Kate's mother, Carole Middleton, was just too middle class to be a royal's mother-in-law. They dissected social markers in her speech patterns and verbal faux pas, noting how these markers rigidly cemented her comparatively low status in British society. Mrs. Middleton was mocked for using words such as *toilet* instead of *lavatory*; for saying, among other things, *Pardon?* when she hadn't heard something clearly instead of the posh *What?*; and for greeting the queen with *Pleased to meet you* instead of the correct *Hello, Ma'am.* • Will museum crawls replace pub crawls? The *Washington Post* reported that lectures, debates, book readings, and even spelling bees may be displacing raves, bars, and discos as the date-night venue of choice for thirtysomethings in New York, Washington, and Boston. As the reporter Anthony Faiola put it, "gray matter is the new black of the hip social scene." Call it *intellidating*, a welcome neologism coined in 2002 by British entrepreneurs who put on a series of popular debates on provocative topics. But spelling bees? Yes, Faiola wrote, "even spelling-bee nights have popped up as a romantic twist for the chic, unmarried and grammatically gifted."

May

HRMagazine, published by the Society for Human Resource Management, recommended ways to handle "millennials" in the workplace—those born since 1985. The recommendations were introduced with this warning: "Many millennials may lack basic spelling and writing skills because they have come to rely on spell check. Moreover, some millennials have become so accustomed to using IM abbreviations, such as 'b/c' for 'because,' that some don't know how to spell it correctly." Robert M. Wendover, director of a Colorado research and training company, recommended "asking candidates to write a letter from scratch without the benefits of grammar or spell check. 'Then, you'll know what their writing skills are.'" • May 28 marked the 165th anniversary of Noah Webster's death in New Haven. • In the May 12 municipal election, voters in tiny Forest Hill, Texas, were asked if they wanted to correct typographical and grammatical errors in the city charter. The *Dallas Morning News* reported that the proposition passed handily. But for reasons unknown, 15% of the electorate opposed it. • "What is consult a guide to grammar?" During the final round of the 2007 Jeopardy College Championship, this $2,000 answer appeared: "You may find 'awk' for 'awkward' next to this type of ambiguous modifier, like 'shake before using.'" The response sought by the Jeopardy writers was "What is a dangling modifier?" But there's no dangler in the example, which may be why none of the contestants responded. • The Library of Congress and the Law Library of Congress announced the winners of the Burton Awards for Legal Achievement. This year, the Reform in Law award, which is given to a public body for outstanding writing or rewriting of public documents, went to the project to clarify the Federal Rules of Civil Procedure. The project's members, including federal judges, practicing lawyers, law professors, and two drafting consultants, worked from 1992 to 1994 and from 2003 to 2007 to completely rewrite the 300 pages of rules for the first time since they were first promulgated in 1937.

June

In an article entitled "Canadians Don't Know Squat," the *Waterloo Chronicle* reported a recent discovery by the editors of the *Canadian Oxford Dictionary*: 90% of Canadians had no idea that butter tarts are a uniquely Canadian food. According to the editor in chief, "'Eh' is all

very well, but there is so much more to us than that." Hence the Canadianisms *date squares* (wedding cake), *all-dressed chips* (pizza), *Gravol* (Dra-
mamine), and *Joe job* (second job). • In the *Boston Globe*, language critic
Jan Freeman commented on the simultaneous appreciation and depreci-
ation of *swarthy*. Its traditional meaning is "having dark skin, dusky," but
Freeman reported that many people take it to mean "shady, greasy,
untrustworthy, sketchy, or pirate-like." Meanwhile, others think it means
"hearty, rich, gutsy, strong, maybe even macho." Amid this confusion, she
predicts that lexicographers are likely to have a hard time with this word
in future decades. • The *Philadelphia Inquirer* covered a mock funeral,
complete with a hearse, coffin, funeral program, and prayer, held by the
students of the NAACP Philadelphia Youth Council. The purpose was to
symbolically bury the word *nigger* and to grieve—not for the word but
for all the historical and current harm associated with it. Jacque Whaum-
bush, the 17-year-old president of the Youth Council, declared, "People
who think it's cool to use it are ignorant of history. I'm going to stop
buying music with the n-word in it, and I'm going to encourage my
friends to do the same. We're tired of being degraded. It's not going to
change overnight, but we can do it." The event was repeated in July at
the NAACP national convention in Detroit. • Dahlia Lithwick reported
in *Slate* that a Nebraska state-court judge banned the use of the words
rape, *sexual assault*, *victim*, *assailant*, and *sexual-assault kit* from a trial in
which the defendant was charged with acquaintance rape. But the judge
allowed the words *sex* and *intercourse*. He defended his actions on the
grounds that the banned words are so loaded that they present a danger
of "unfair prejudice, confusion of the issues, or misleading the jury." But
Lithwick pointed out that *sex* and *intercourse* are also loaded: both words
can connote consent and pleasure. Lithwick mused, "If the complaining
witness in a rape trial has to describe herself as having had 'intercourse'
with the defendant, should the complaining witness in a mugging be
forced to testify that he was merely giving his attacker a loan?"

July

The *Pittsburgh Post-Gazette* sponsored a wretched-writing contest among
its readers. Jay Speyerer of Mount Lebanon submitted this doozy: "It
goes without saying that we must prioritize our paradigms with an end
to leveraging the value-added synergy to our best advantage. That's half
the battle when opening that can of worms. For continued success moving forward, we must downsize our liabilities, upsize our skill sets, and
supersize our viable alternatives. I want to spend quality time picking
your brain re: belt-tightening in relation to our at-risk human resources.
Let's touch base and plan some face time to craft a mission statement for

getting these tasks in the pipeline." • The online journal *Science Daily* announced the results of a study by Northwestern University's Feinberg School of Medicine that found a direct link between literacy and health—and even with mortality rates. The researchers were surprised to find that the study's participants with low literacy scores suffered a 50% higher mortality rate than participants with at least average reading skills. The conclusion was that people who have poor or no reading skills are unable to read and comprehend basic health-related information. That means they're less likely to learn when to seek medical care, how to care for themselves when they are ill, and when and how to use medications. • In an article entitled "Linguists Seek a Time When We Spoke as One," the *Christian Science Monitor* described the international Evolution of Human Languages project. A multidisciplinary team is developing an etymological database of the world's languages, which will be freely accessible to researchers. As part of the project, EHL linguists are attempting to reconstruct extinct ancestral languages for comparison with one another, with the final goal of reconstructing a theoretical ancient common language. The hypothesis that such a language existed is not new; in the 18th century, Sir William Jones first postulated that ancient Greek, Latin, and Sanskrit had a common ancestor. The recognition of Indo-European as a language family is based on Jones's observations. But many linguists regard the reconstruction project as a fringe movement because, they insist, languages change so much they cannot be studied much further back than 8,000 years.

August

The distress is perennial: the *Times Educational Supplement* reported that complaints of slipping standards span the generations and are nothing new. The head of a UK exam board unearthed a 1954 report that said: "All eight examiners, independently, reported that a very high proportion (of candidates) presented the fruits of their study of acknowledged English classics in a written form that was, to some serious degree, illiterate. The widespread ignorance or indifference about the most elementary points of reputable English usage was distressing." • In a London courtroom, a homeless man pleaded guilty to attacking a painting of Samuel Johnson. The man, Mark Paton, was arrested after using a hammer on Joshua Reynolds's famous portrait of Johnson. The National Portrait Gallery reported that the painting, valued at $3.4 million, can be repaired. • In his monthly column, William Safire issued some particularly sage advice about *adviser* vs. *advisor*: "The word started out in 1611 spelled as *adviser* and was challenged in 1899 by *advisor*; though preferred in politics a half-century ago with the *e*, lately the *o* has been coming on strong. Lexicographers, wet fingers to the linguistic breeze, take no position; their foxy advice is 'you decide; we report.' Although President Andrew Jackson was reported to have said, 'It's a damn poor mind, indeed, which can't think of at least two ways to spell a word,' my advice is to stick with *adviser* until overruled by your supervisor." • Whither (or wither) literacy? According to an Associated Press–Ipsos poll of American adults, 27% of the respondents claimed they hadn't read a single book in the past year. For the other 73%, the median number of books read was only four. Women read more than men: nine books to five. People from the West and Midwest were most likely to have read at least one book in the past year. Although Southerners were the least likely to have read any books at all, those who do read are more likely to have read more copiously than those in any other region. Whites read more than minorities, and nonreligious people read twice as much as regular churchgoers. Yet the Bible and religious works were the most popular reading category, followed by popular fiction, histories, biographies, and mysteries. About 20% of those surveyed read romances. Fewer than 5% read classical literature, poetry, or books about politics. • The *Los Angeles Times* reported that the German language has been "officially reformed." The governments of Germany, Austria, and Switzerland have embraced new, simplified grammar rules that will be mandatory in textbooks from now on. Expert grammarians worked for almost ten years to reduce grammar rules from 212 to 112. Formerly, 52 rules governed the use of commas; now just nine will do. The changes will affect only schoolchildren and will apply mainly to written grammar—students will not be graded on whether they use the new or old rules in speech. Germans themselves, the *Times* reported, overwhelmingly "detest the 'reforms,'" and previous efforts to the same effect have failed to parse muster. • According to *Science Daily*, researchers at the University of South Carolina have found that pronouns aren't good just for varying sentences. They also help the brain speed up comprehension. Every time a person hears a noun—especially a proper name—the brain responds by creating a complex representation of that person, place, or thing. To do so, it must integrate visual images, sounds, relationships, and other associated information. That can disrupt the brain's processing of ongoing speech. But pronouns, when used in the right context, don't cause those representations to be regenerated, suggesting that a listener experiences less mental disruption and can move more easily from one thought to the next. • McDonald's Corporation bore down on its lexicographic lobbying (see March). In York, England, journalist Julian Cole reported that McDonald's had been pressuring the editors of the *Oxford English Dictionary* to change its unflattering definition of *McJob*, which currently stands as "an unstimulating, low-paid job with few prospects, especially one created by the expansion of the service sector." A petition was circulated at a local McDonald's. But Cole wrote: "You won't find my name on there. Had someone asked, I would have suggested they put their McPetition where the McSun don't shine."

September

Oxford University Press issued the sixth edition of the *Shorter Oxford English Dictionary*, the two-volume abridgment of the massive 20-volume *Oxford English Dictionary*. The editors appear to have followed a trend long apparent in American English: they've dropped more than 16,000 hyphens, solidifying such words as *bumblebee*, *crybaby*, and *pigeonhole*. The *New York Times* quoted the editor, Angus Stevenson, as saying, "People are not confident about using hyphens anymore. They're not really sure what they're for." • An article in *China Daily* succinctly illustrated the importance of careful spelling on Internet search engines. A family from Norway thought they had booked a vacation on the Greek island of Rhodes. So they were surprised when their flight delivered them to southern France for a sojourn in the small ancient town of Rodez. Airport authorities in Rodez said that about ten tourists make the same mistake each year. • Oxford University Press released a new much-expanded edition of *A Dictionary of Euphemisms: How Not to Say What You Mean*. R.W. Holder compiled hundreds of new entries, such as *couldn't be reached* ("was avoiding questioning"), *negative patient-care outcome* ("death"), and *taskforce* ("committee hastily summoned to deflect criticism"). Readers will get a chuckle from many of Holder's comments and the published examples that accompany the definitions, such as "*abuse a bed*—to cuckold. Not just to leap about on it: 'See the hell of having a false woman. My bed shall be abused.' (Shakespeare, *Merry Wives of Windsor*)." • The slangy phrase *like, totally* is, like, totally not a Valley Girl thing anymore. The *Chicago Tribune* reported on a University of Pennsylvania linguist's study that found the phrase to be about as common among males as females. Mark Lieberman said it's also as common among 40- to 59-year-olds as those aged 20–39. It even got President Bush's implied endorsement in August: "The impression you get from people who are reporting out of Iraq is that it's like totally dysfunctional." Another linguist, Carmen Fought, defended the phrase's usefulness as connoting that what follows *like, totally* is, in the speaker's opinion, exaggerated or even flat wrong. • Alex, a celebrated African gray parrot with remarkable communication skills, died at 31. *The Economist* reported that Alex had a vocabulary of 150 words and could identify 50 objects along with their shapes, colors, and textures. He could also count objects up to six (including zero). Skeptics suspected "the Clever Hans effect," referring to a horse whose "counting" was exposed as governed by its trainer's subtle cues. But Alex carried on the interaction with strangers as well. In the end, *The Economist* reported, he "convinced most in the field that birds as well as mammals can evolve complex and sophisticated cognition, and communicate the results to others." ● In a related story, Jonah Lehrer (author of *Proust Was a Neuroscientist*) reported in the *Boston Globe* that scientists studying the songs of sparrows have identified grammatical structures in their compositions. As a UC-San Diego neurologist, Timothy Gentner, put it, male sparrows "make their songs more and more complex in order to impress the females. The ability to learn these grammatical patterns grew out of that. It's like a cognitive version of the peacock's tail."

October

Oxford University Press released *The Myth of Mars and Venus* by Deborah Cameron (not to be confused with Deborah Tannen, author of *You Just Don't Understand: Men and Women in Conversation*). Cameron, the Rupert Murdoch professor of language and communication at Oxford University, skewers such pop-language books as Tannen's and John Gray's *Men Are from Mars, Women Are from Venus*. She explodes three important myths: the available scientific evidence demonstrates that (1) men and women don't communicate differently (there's a 99.75% overlap in the way they communicate—any differences are infinitesimal); (2) women don't talk more than men (both sexes use about 16,000 words a day); and (3) men in general don't interrupt more than women (how people interrupt is much more about power and social relations than about genetic makeup of the sexes). Quoted in the *Sunday Times*, Cameron called the myth that women are sympathetic communicators while men are autistic, inarticulate Neanderthals a "a cheap way for women to feel good." ● The *Boston Globe* announced that Houghton Mifflin would begin promoting American Heritage dictionaries at various bookstores by holding live-action competitions, known as "Define-a-Thons," in which 16 contestants participate in a "lexicographic scrum" by matching correct definitions with words. Admission is free. Steve Kleinedler, supervising editor at American Heritage, is the host. He has a tattoo of the phonetic vowel chart on his back, partly to demonstrate that the business of making dictionaries is sexy. ("It's unique," he says. "It's about the size of an index card on my shoulder.") He wants to debunk the notion that lexicographers are, in his words, "gray-haired people hunched over a drafting table who never see the light of day." ● By official decree, Brazil's Federal District Governor Jose Roberto Arruda banished the use of the present participle in government documents. The reason for the ban is to promote efficiency and end the common practice of using the present participle to make vague promises and unclear statements. For example, bureaucrats will no long be allowed to say such things as "We'll be taking steps" or "The study of the problem is ongoing," and instead would have to say expressly who will take what steps, or what progress the study has made. But Dario Borim, chair of the Department of Portuguese at the University of Massachusetts Dartmouth, scoffed at the governor's decree: "I find it somewhat ludicrous. It's a matter for linguists to discuss, not for politicians." • Writing in the *Daily News* (N.Y.), Michael O'Keeffe reported on how the NFL used—and still uses—a single letter of the alphabet to deny retirement and disability benefits to former NFL players. Until the early 1990s, the NFL's disability plan granted full benefits to players who suffered total and permanent disability caused by "a football injury." Players who became disabled because of multiple football injuries did not qualify because the NFL successfully argued that *a* meant the disability had to result from only one injury, not the cumulative effects of several. Although the report appears in the sports section, it's an interesting look at how a single word can affect a document's interpretation.

November

Writing in the journal *Nature*, Harvard scientists posited a formula for understanding how irregular English verbs evolve and homogenize at a rate inversely proportional to their prevalence. They conclude that the rule that an *-ed* suffix is added to simple-past and past-participial forms contributes to the evolutionary decay of irregular English verbs according to a specific mathematical function: it regularizes them at a rate that is inversely proportional to the square root of their usage frequency. So a verb used only 1% as often as another will evolve 10 times as fast. Hence some common verbs have long half-lives (*be*, 38,800 years; *think*, 14,400 years), but less frequent ones have short half-lives (*shrive*, 300 years; *smite*, 700 years). • In West Hartford, Connecticut, city officials opened Blue Back Square—a mixed-use development that includes stores, restaurants, a movie theater, condos, apartments, and public spaces. It's named after Noah Webster's famous "blue-backed speller," Webster having been the most famous citizen of West Hartford. A huge sign at the square directs passersby to "Old Center Cemetary"—yes, *-ary* instead of *-ery*—where Noah Webster's parents, Noah Sr. and Mercy, are buried (not to say rolling over). • Environmental neologisms abound. The editors of the *New Oxford American Dictionary* named *locavore* as their 2007 Word of the Year. It denotes a person who tries to eat only locally produced foods.

Meanwhile, the editors of *Webster's New World College Dictionary* named *grass station*, a pun that reflects America's growing love affair with hybrid cars and vegetable-based fuels. • The number and variety of online dictionaries has expanded. YourDictionary.com (www.yourdictionary.com) announced that it would add the fourth edition of *Webster's New World College Dictionary* to its database. HarperCollins Publishers announced that its *Collins English Dictionary Pro* would now be available in both hard copy and online formats (www.collinslanguage.com). And Merriam-Webster and QA International announced a joint project, the Visual Dictionary Online (www.visualdictionaryonline.com). • In his syndicated language column, the venerable James J. Kilpatrick posed the question whether someone who is electrocuted necessarily ends up dead. He looked into the dictionaries and reported as follows: "The vote is 4–2. To be electrocuted is invariably fatal in Merriam-Webster, American Heritage, New World, and Random House. In the Oxford and Encarta dictionaries, death takes a holiday. Their easygoing editors say a victim of electrocution may be merely injured. It's a shocking act of lexicographic clemency."

December

In the op-ed pages of the *New York Times*, Harry Mount, author of *Carpe Diem: Put a Little Latin in Your Life*, bemoaned the fact that "none of the leading presidential candidates majored in Latin." The shame, he said, is that "the professionalization of politics—which encourages budding politicians to think of education as mere career preparation—has occurred during an age of weak rhetoric, shifting moral values, clumsy grammar, and a terror of historical references and eternal values that the Romans could teach us a thing or two about." • The *Christian Science Monitor* reported on a vocabulary-quiz website that John Breen of Indiana developed initially to help his son prepare for the SAT. Some half a million people daily visit the "feel-good" website (freerice.com), where every time a player selects the correct definition for a particular word, 20 grains of rice are donated to the UN World Food Program. As of December 3, some 4 billion grains (160 metric tons) had been donated. • The BBC reported that publication of a hardcover edition of *The Harry Potter Lexicon*, an encyclopedic dictionary, has been blocked on the grounds that it violates copyright law and infringes trademarks. J.K. Rowling asserted that the book, which she has not seen, would draw too heavily from her works and would also prevent her from publishing a planned Harry Potter encyclopedia of her own. The Fair Use Project at Stanford University's Center for Internet and Society responded, on behalf of the publisher, that U.S. rules have long granted "the right to create reference guides that discuss literary works, comment on them and make them more accessible." The lexicon already exists in a fan-created online forum (www.hp-lexicon.org), and Rowling has not objected to it. • Merriam-Webster announced that the Word of the Year for 2007 is *w00t* (= yay), written with letters and numerals. Participants in the online survey at M-W's website made the dubious choice. As with the 2006 winner, *truthiness*, no major dictionary—including those published by Merriam-Webster—includes *w00t*. John Morse, M-W's president, told the Associated Press that the selection of *w00t* "shows a really interesting thing that's going on in language. It's a term that's arrived only because we're now communicating electronically with each other." But Allan Metcalf of the American Dialect Society disagreed, saying that the term is "amusing, but it's limited to a small community and unlikely to spread and unlikely to last." Even techies are less than enthusiastic. Nate Anderson, a writer for Ars Technica, derided *w00t* as "an expression so likely to die off in the near future that I can just about see its pallbearers lining up down the hall." • The Library of Congress unveiled "America's baptismal document" as part of its permanent collection: a map produced in 1507 by an obscure German cartographer, Martin Waldseemuller. The map includes the first known use of the name "America," which derives from the name of Amerigo Vespucci, the 15th-century explorer who was erroneously credited with having discovered America.

Robert E. Keeton

The Last Word

A Farewell Message

WE ALL EXPRESS our commitment to good legal writing in different ways. I do it by lecturing and writing on the subject. Others do it by lecturing and writing about any number of other law-related subjects. Some do it as publishers. Some do it as reporters of decisions, and still others as journal editors. And—as a symbol of how dramatically the field of legal writing has changed over the past half-century—many now teach legal writing full-time in our law schools.

Although there is ample cause for pessimism about the future of legal writing, there is also cause for optimism. I'd like to focus here on several positive developments.

First, dramatic changes have occurred in legal education. Over the past decade, law schools have begun to recognize the need for full-time professionals to teach legal writing. For many years, schools limited legal-writing instructors to a specified number of years—typically two—in their posts. Then they had to move on. Now fully two-thirds of American law schools have eliminated this time bomb, so that a sizable corps of legal-writing specialists has emerged. And increasingly, the most talented and the most senior members among them are enjoying tenured or tenure-track positions.

No law school has yet established an endowed chair or professorship in legal writing—at least, not on a par with those for torts and contracts and procedure. But I predict that such posts will become fairly common in the first few decades of the 21st century.

Second, the most influential members of the bar are coming to recognize that writing is a skill constantly in need of honing. The days are

CHAPTER EIGHTEEN

almost behind us when anyone would be so naive as to lament that judges need judicial-writing seminars, that litigators need brief-writing seminars, and that transactional lawyers need contract-drafting seminars. There is a vast body of knowledge on effective judicial opinions, briefs, and contracts, and no one could possibly expect grade schools and high schools to expose students to it.

Gradually, the profession has come to realize that learning how to write well goes well beyond memorizing rules of grammar and punctuation. It involves much larger issues of rhetoric and persuasion.

Third, all this consciousness-raising has resulted in practical applications that might be taken as harbingers:

- As president of the American Law Institute, Charles Alan Wright saw to it that the ALI's bylaws and council rules were redrafted in clearer English. And Michael Greenwald, deputy director of the ALI, has prepared a drafting manual that will improve the style of the ALI's influential Restatements.

- As chair of the Standing Committee on Rules of Practice and Procedure, Judge Robert E. Keeton created a Style Subcommittee to improve the drafting of federal rules. The Subcommittee has been in place since 1991, and its most important revisions to date—the restyled Federal Rules of Appellate Procedure, Criminal Procedure and Civil Procedure—are now in effect.

- Many states are now rewriting rules and jury instructions, traditionally phrased in an abominable style, in better English. California, Delaware, and Texas are all working on ambitious projects of this kind.

- The ABA and the ALI have jointly produced a revision of Articles 2 and 9 of the UCC, using plain-English drafting methods that will make the law more accessible than ever before.

- The SEC now requires plain English for certain parts of prospectuses. Despite much carping from some sectors, leading members of the securities bar have embraced the reform.

- The federal government has begun rewarding federal employees who redraft documents in plain English.

In short, momentum is on the side of the betterment of legal writing. We'll all need to be steadfast in our efforts, though, because any of these progressive strides might be undone in short order. The greatest enemies are the linguistically unsophisticated: those who think style unimportant, proudly boasting that they concern themselves solely with "matters of substance." If their ranks swell, we could all be in trouble. But with so many people involved in spreading knowledge and enlightenment, it's hard to imagine how that would come to pass.

SIR ROBERT MEGARRY

CHAPTER NINETEEN

Recommended Sources on Language and Writing

FOR MORE THAN 30 YEARS, I've collected and avidly read books about all facets of language and writing. What follows is a select bibliography of my favorites in the various subfields. Although it may not seem like it, most categories could easily be expanded tenfold. In each category, look especially for the one to three sources with an asterisk instead of a bullet; they're the most highly recommended. If no book in a category bears an asterisk, take your choice.

You can buy most in-print books from Amazon.com or Barnesand-noble.com with minimal hassle. For an out-of-print book, try Abebooks .com or Bookfinder.com. You'll probably find the book you want there if it's for sale anywhere in the world. But don't forget that you often needn't buy the books. Try your local library first.

Many of the books are released in new editions from time to time. Usually the most current version is best.

1	General Reference	7	Word-Loving
2	Writing	8	Linguistics
3	Editing	9	Public Speaking
4	Grammar	10	Reading
5	Usage	11	Law
6	Logic and Rhetoric	12	Subscriptions

Contents

1 General Reference

1.1 For a good desktop dictionary (buy a current edition):
- *The American Heritage Dictionary of the English Language* (thorough, with good usage notes).
- * *Merriam-Webster's Collegiate Dictionary* (used by most book publishers, but be wary of its permissive usage notes).
- *The New Oxford American Dictionary* (thorough, with good usage notes).

- *Random House Webster's College Dictionary* (sound for now, but Random House laid off its lexicographers a few years ago and may not be keeping up to date as well as its competitors).
* *Webster's New World College Dictionary* (used by most newspapers).

1.2 For a sound unabridged dictionary:
* *The Random House Dictionary of the English Language* (Stuart Berg Flexner ed., 2d ed. 1987).
* *The Shorter Oxford English Dictionary* (5th ed. 2002).
- *Webster's Second New International Dictionary* (William Allan Neilson ed., 1934) (still quite sound on historical matters, and exhaustive on traditional legal and literary terms).
- *Webster's Third New International Dictionary* (Philip B. Gove ed., 1961) (scholarly but infamously permissive in neglecting to include accurate usage tags, so use it discriminatingly).

1.3 For the mother of all dictionaries:
- Online edition of the *Oxford English Dictionary* (see www.oup.com) (useful mainly as a historical resource, not as a general-purpose dictionary; if the online version is beyond your means, try your local public library's website).

1.4 For a good desktop thesaurus:
* *The Oxford American Writer's Thesaurus* (Christine A. Lindberg ed., 2004).
- J.I. Rodale, *The Synonym Finder* (Laurence Urdang ed., rev. ed. 1986).
- *Roget's International Thesaurus* (Robert L. Chapman ed., 1992).
- *Roget's Thesaurus of English Words and Phrases* (George Davidson ed., 2006).
- *Roget's II: The New Thesaurus* (American Heritage Dictionary eds., 3d ed. 2003).

1.5 For a book of quotations:
- John Bartlett, *Bartlett's Familiar Quotations* (Justin Kaplan ed., 17th ed. 2002).
- *The Oxford Dictionary of Quotations* (Elizabeth Knowles ed., 6th ed. 2004).
* Fred Shapiro, *The Yale Book of Quotations* (2006).

1.6 For a compilation of similes:
* Elyse Sommer & Mike Sommer, *Similes Dictionary* (1998).
- Frank J. Wilstach, *A Dictionary of Similes* (new rev. ed. 1990).

1.7 For an authoritative reference on the origins of English words:
  • John Ayto, *Dictionary of Word Origins* (1980).
  * *The Barnhart Dictionary of Etymology* (Robert K. Barnhart ed., 1988).
  • *The Merriam-Webster New Book of Word Histories* (1991).
  • Eric Partridge, *Origins: A Short Etymological Dictionary of Modern English* (1958).
  • Adrian Room, *Dictionary of True Etymologies* (1986).
  • Walter W. Skeat, *An Etymological Dictionary of the English Language* (4th ed. 1910).

1.8 For learning how dictionaries are made:
  • Jonathon Green, *Chasing the Sun: Dictionary Makers and the Dictionaries They Made* (1996).
  * Sidney I. Landau, *Dictionaries: The Art and Craft of Lexicography* (2d ed. 2001).

1.9 For the fascinating story behind the *Oxford English Dictionary*:
  • Donna Lee Berg, *A Guide to the Oxford English Dictionary* (1993).
  • Lynda Mugglestone, *Lost for Words: The Hidden History of the Oxford English Dictionary* (2005).
  • K.M. Elisabeth Murray, *Caught in the Web of Words: James Murray and The Oxford English Dictionary* (1977).
  • John Willinsky, *Empire of Words: The Reign of the OED* (1994).
  * Simon Winchester, *The Meaning of Everything: The Story of the Oxford English Dictionary* (2003).

1.10 For the closest analogous American story:
  • *Dictionaries and That Dictionary* (James Sledd & Wilma R. Ebbitt eds., 1962).
  * Herbert C. Morton, *The Story of Webster's Third: Philip Gove's Controversial Dictionary and Its Critics* (1994).

2 Writing

2.1 For general guidance that will help novices and pros alike:
  • Henry Seidel Canby, *Better Writing* (1926) (unjustly overlooked).
  • Sidney Cox, *Indirections for Those Who Want to Write* (1947).
  • John Fairfax & John Moat, *The Way to Write* (1981) (mostly about fiction).
  • Charles W. Ferguson, *Say It with Words* (1959).
  • Rudolf Flesch, *The Art of Readable Writing* (1949).
  • Robert Graves & Alan Hodge, *The Reader over Your Shoulder* (2d ed. 1947).

- James J. Kilpatrick, *The Writer's Art* (1984).
- David Lambuth, *The Golden Book on Writing* (1964).
- Betsy Lerner, *The Forest for the Trees: An Editor's Advice to Writers* (2000).
- Richard Marius, *A Writer's Companion* (1985).
- Gorham Munson, *The Written Word: How to Write Readable Prose* (1949).
- Lucille Vaughan Payne, *The Lively Art of Writing* (1965).
* William Strunk & E.B. White, *The Elements of Style* (4th ed. 2000) (the most famous of all writing guides).
* John R. Trimble, *Writing with Style: Conversations on the Art of Writing* (2d ed. 2000) (a liberating, tip-filled guide to expository writing).
- Stephen Wilbers, *Keys to Great Writing* (2000).
- William Zinsser, *On Writing Well* (6th ed. 2006).

2.2 For guidance on the writing process:
* Kenneth Atchity, *A Writer's Time* (rev. ed. 1995).
- Peter Elbow, *Writing with Power* (1981).
- Bonnie Friedman, *Writing Past Dark: Envy, Fear, Distraction, and Other Dilemmas in the Writer's Life* (1994).
- Natalie Goldberg, *Wild Mind: Living the Writer's Life* (1990).
- Natalie Goldberg, *Writing Down the Bones: Freeing the Writer Within* (2005).
- Sanford Kaye, *Writing Under Pressure* (1989).
- Henriette Anne Klauser, *Writing on Both Sides of the Brain* (1987).
- Kevin Mack & Eric Skjei, *Overcoming Writer's Block* (1979).
* Herbert E. Meyer & Jill M. Meyer, *How to Write* (rev. ed. 1993).
- Gabrielle Lusser Rico, *Writing the Natural Way* (rev. sub. ed. 2000).

2.3 For guidance on writing by major writers:
- Kingsley Amis, *The King's English: A Guide to Modern Usage* (1997).
- Jacques Barzun, *Simple and Direct: A Rhetoric for Writers* (1975).
- Stephen Vincent Benét, *On Writing* (1964).
- Ambrose Bierce, *Write It Right: A Little Blacklist of Literary Faults* (1909).
- Dorothea Brande, *Becoming a Writer* (1934).
- Van Wyck Brooks, *From a Writer's Notebook* (1958).
- Van Wyck Brooks, *The Opinions of Oliver Allston* (1941) (in which "Oliver Allston" is Brooks's alter ego).
- William F. Buckley, *The Right Word* (1996).
- Raymond Chandler, *The Notebooks of Raymond Chandler* (Frank Macshane ed., 1976).

- Raymond Chandler, *Raymond Chandler Speaking* (Dorothy Gardiner & Kathrine Sorley Walker eds., 1977).
- Thomas De Quincey, *De Quincey's Writings*, vol. 10 (David Masson ed., 1889–1890) (a volume devoted mostly to writing style).
- E.M. Forster, *Aspects of the Novel* (1927) (really a book of literary criticism, but quite educational).
- Robert Frost, *Robert Frost on Writing* (Elaine Barry ed., 1963).
- John Gardner, *The Art of Fiction* (1984).
- John Gardner, *On Becoming a Novelist* (1983).
- John Gardner, *On Writers and Writing* (1994).
- Elizabeth George, *Write Away: One Novelist's Approach to Fiction and the Writing Life* (2004).
- Maxim Gorky, Vladimir Mayakovsky, Alexei Tolstoy, & Konstantin Fedin, *On the Art and Craft of Writing* (1972) (published in English in Moscow and stupendously good).
- Donald Hall, *Writing Well* (9th ed. 1998) (with Sven Birkerts).
- Ernest Hemingway, *Ernest Hemingway on Writing* (Larry W. Phillips ed., 1999).
- Paul Horgan, *Approaches to Writing* (2d ed. 1988).
- Stephen King, *On Writing: A Memoir of the Craft* (2000).
- Ursula K. Le Guin, *Steering the Craft: Exercises and Discussions on Story Writing for the Lone Navigator or the Mutinous Crew* (1998).
- David Lodge, *The Art of Fiction* (1992).
- David Lodge, *The Practice of Writing* (1997).
- Percy Lubbock, *The Craft of Fiction* (1921).
- Norman Mailer, *The Spooky Art: Some Thoughts on Writing* (2003).
- André Maurois, *The Art of Writing* (Gerard Hopkins trans., 1960).
- James A. Michener, *James A. Michener's Writer's Handbook* (1992).
- Henry Miller, *Henry Miller on Writing* (Thomas H. Moore ed., 1964).
- C.E. Montague, *A Writer's Notes on His Trade* (1946).
- Wright Morris, *About Fiction* (1975).
- V.S. Naipaul, *Reading and Writing: A Personal Account* (2000).
- Joyce Carol Oates, *The Faith of a Writer* (2003).
- Mary Pipher, *Writing to Change the World* (2006).
- Arthur Quiller-Couch, *On the Art of Writing* (1916).
- Walter Raleigh, *On Writers and Writing* (George Gordon ed., 1926).
- Ayn Rand, *The Art of Nonfiction* (Robert Mayhew ed., 2001) (published posthumously from lectures given in 1969).
- Richard Rhodes, *How to Write* (1995).
- Bertrand Russell, "How I Write" (1954), in *The Basic Writings of Bertrand Russell: 1903–1959*, at 63–65 (1961).
- Jean-Paul Sartre, *The Words* (Bernard Frechtman trans., 1964).

- Sol Stein, *Stein on Writing* (1995).
* Robert Louis Stevenson, *Learning to Write* (1920) (published posthumously).
- James Thurber, *Collecting Himself: James Thurber on Writing and Writers, Humor, and Himself* (Michael J. Rosen ed., 1989).
- Mark Twain, "Cooper's Prose Style," in *Letters from the Earth* (Bernard DeVoto ed., 1962).
- Mark Twain, *Mark My Words: Mark Twain on Writing* (Mark Dawidziak ed., 1996).
- Angus Wilson, *The Wild Garden or Speaking of Writing* (1963).

2.4 For interviews with major writers:
- Jo Brans, *Listen to the Voices: Conversations with Contemporary Writers* (1988) (with Saul Bellow, John Cheever, William Gass, Iris Murdoch, Eudora Welty, and others).
* Harvey Breit, *The Writer Observed* (1956) (with T.S. Eliot, William Faulkner, Ernest Hemingway, Norman Mailer, Carl Sandburg, and others).
- *Critical Intellectuals on Writing* (Gary A. Olson & Lynn Worsham eds., 2003) (with Judith Butler, Noam Chomsky, Jacques Derrida, Stanley Fish, Gayatri Spivak, and others).
- Naomi Epel, *Writers Dreaming* (1993) (with Isabel Allende, Maya Angelou, John Barth, Elmore Leonard, Maurice Sendak, and Amy Tan).
- *On Being a Writer* (Bill Strickland ed., 1989) (interviews with 31 writers).
- Philip Roth, *Shop Talk: A Writer and His Colleagues and Their Work* (2001) (with Milan Kundera, Primo Levi, Isaac Bashevis Singer, and others).
- Charles Ruas, *Conversations with American Writers* (1984) (with William Burroughs, Truman Capote, E.L. Doctorow, Joseph Heller, Norman Mailer, Susan Sontag, Gore Vidal, and Eudora Welty).
- Dorothy Scura, *Conversations with Tom Wolfe* (1990).
- Robert van Gelder, *Writers and Writing* (1946) (with Pearl Buck, Sinclair Lewis, H.L. Mencken, Katherine Anne Porter, William Saroyan, Rex Stout, E.B. White, and others).
- Kurt Vonnegut & Lee Stringer, *Like Shaking Hands with God: A Conversation About Writing* (1999).
* *Writers at Work: The* Paris Review *Interviews* (1st–8th series [8 vols.], 1958–1988) (with a vast assortment of major and minor 20th-century writers).

- *The Writer's Place: Interviews on the Literary Situation in Contemporary Britain* (Peter Firchow ed., 1974) (with Kingsley Amis, Margaret Drabble, V.S. Pritchett, William Trevor, John Wain, Angus Wilson, and others).
- * *The Writer's World* (Elizabeth Janeway ed., 1969) (with Louis Auchincloss, Robert Graves, Isaac Bashevis Singer, Susan Sontag, William Styron, Gay Talese, Barbara Tuchman, Robert Penn Warren, and others).

2.5 For anthologies of essays and lectures on the art of writing:
- Miriam Allott, *Novelists on the Novel* (1959) (with Jane Austen, Charlotte Brontë, Joseph Conrad, Daniel Defoe, Charles Dickens, Gustave Flaubert, Aldous Huxley, Samuel Richardson, George Sand, Walter Scott, Anthony Trollope, and Virginia Woolf).
- * *The Art of the Writer* (Lane Cooper ed., rev. ed. 1952) (with Goethe, Arthur Schopenhauer, Henry David Thoreau, Voltaire, and others).
- * *Best Advice on How to Write* (Gorham Munson ed., 1952) (with Arnold Bennett, Rudolf Flesch, Kenneth Payson Kempton, Manuel Komroff, Dorothy McCleary, Arthur Schopenhauer, Anthony Trollope, David Woodbury, and others).
- *The Best Writing on Writing*, vol. 1 (Jack Heffron ed., 1994) (with James Fenton, Bonnie Friedman, Donald Hall, William Kittredge, Tony Kushner, Nancy Mairs, James Michener, Donald M. Murray, Ben Nyberg, and others).
- *The Best Writing on Writing*, vol. 2 (Jack Heffron ed., 1995) (with Edward Albee, Dorothy Allison, Margaret Atwood, James Michener, Joyce Carol Oates, and others).
- *Classics in Composition* (Donald E. Hayden ed., 1969) (with Cicero, Joseph Conrad, David Hume, Charles Lamb, W. Somerset Maugham, Walter Pater, Jonathan Swift, Virginia Woolf, and others).
- *The Eleventh Draft: Craft and the Writing Life from the Iowa Writers' Workshop* (Frank Conroy ed., 1999) (with Ethan Canin, Justin Cronin, Deborah Eisenberg, Doris Grumbach, Francine Prose, Geoffrey Wolff, and others).
- *The Foundations of English Style* (Paul M. Fulcher ed., 1927) (with Comte de Buffon, Samuel Taylor Coleridge, Remy de Gourmont, Thomas De Quincey, G.H. Lewes, Jonathan Swift, Henry David Thoreau, and others).
- *Letters to a Fiction Writer* (Frederick Busch ed., 1999) (with Ann Beattie, Ray Bradbury, Raymond Carver, Malcolm Cowley, Shelby Foote, Lewis Lapham, John Updike, Tobias Wolff, and others).

- *Modern Essays on Writing and Style* (Paul C. Wermuth ed., 2d ed. 1969) (with Cyril Connolly, Bonamy Dobrée, Walker Gibson, Aldous Huxley, F.L. Lucas, George Orwell, Herbert Read, Robert Waddell, and others).
- *The Modern Writer's Art* (Theodore J. Gates & Robert E. Galbraith eds., 1936) (with Branch Cabell, Elizabeth Hartman, H.L. Mencken, Henry Van Dyke, Jack Woodford, Virginia Woolf, and others).
- *Perspectives on Style* (Frederick Candelaria ed., 1968) (with Joseph Addison, Sheridan Baker, Northrup Frye, William Hazlitt, Samuel Johnson, Leo Kirschbaum, W. Somerset Maugham, J. Middleton Murry, Edgar Allan Poe, and others).
- *The Scribes Journal of Legal Writing* (the "How I Write Issue"), vol. 4 (1993) (with Lawrence M. Friedman, Thomas Gibbs Gee, Geoffrey C. Hazard Jr., Edith Hollan Jones, James W. McElhaney, Richard A. Posner, Patricia M. Wald, Elizabeth Warren, John Minor Wisdom, and Charles Alan Wright).
- *Telling True Stories: A Nonfiction Writer's Guide* (Mark Kramer & Wendy Call eds., 2007) (with Nora Ephron, Malcolm Gladwell, David Halberstam, Jack Hart, Tracy Kidder, Phillip Lopate, Tom Wolfe, and others).
- *What Is a Book? Thoughts About Writing* (Dale Warren ed., 1935) (with Gertrude Atherton, Havelock Ellis, Esther Forbes, John Livingston Lowes, Archibald MacLeish, George Fort Mitten, Harold Nicolson, Edward J. O'Brien, and others).
- *Why I Write: Thoughts on the Craft of Fiction* (Will Blythe ed., 1998) (with Pat Conroy, Norman Mailer, Terry McMillan, Rick Moody, James Salter, David Foster Wallace, and others).
- *The Writer and His Craft* (Roy W. Cowden ed., 1954) (with Struthers Burt, Norman Cousins, Max Eastman, Zona Gale, Horace Gregory, Henry Hazlitt, Christopher Morley, John Crowe Ransom, Carl Van Doren, and others).
- *The Writer's Book* (Helen Hull ed., 1950) (with Jacques Barzun, Pearl Buck, Winston Churchill, Arthur Koestler, Thomas Mann, James Michener, Lionel Trilling, and others).
- *The Writer's Home Companion: An Anthology of the World's Best Writing Advice, from Keats to Kunitz* (Joan Bolker ed., 1997) (with Peter Elbow, Gail Godwin, Natalie Goldberg, Stanley Kunitz, Ursula Le Guin, B.F. Skinner, and others).
- *Writers on Writing: A Bread Loaf Anthology* (Robert Pack & Jay Parini eds., 1991) (with John Irving, Erica Jong, Philip Levine, Joyce Carol Oates, Nancy Willard, and others).

- *Writers on Writing: Collected Essays from* The New York Times, vol. 1 (2001) (with Saul Bellow, David Mamet, Annie Proulx, Carol Shields, Kurt Vonnegut Jr., Paul West, and others).
- *Writers on Writing: Collected Essays from* The New York Times, vol. 2 (2003) (with Ann Beattie, Stephen Fry, Elmore Leonard, Elinor Lipman, David Shields, and others).
- *Writer's Roundtable* (Helen Hull & Michael Drury eds., 1959) (with Pearl Buck, Loretta Burrough, Margaret Cousins, Babette Deutsch, Daphne du Maurier, William L. Shirer, Rex Stout, and others).
- *The Writing Art: Authorship as Experienced and Expressed by the Great Writers* (Bertha W. Smith & Virginia C. Lincoln eds., 1931) (with Henry Ward Beecher, Charlotte Brontë, Gustave Flaubert, Benjamin Franklin, Nathaniel Hawthorne, Washington Irving, Henry Wadsworth Longfellow, John Milton, John Ruskin, Walt Whitman, and others).
- *Writing Creative Nonfiction: Instruction and Insights from Teachers of the Associated Writing Programs* (Philip Gerard & Carolyn Forché eds., 2001) (with essays by Annie Dillard, Lee Gutkind, Phillip Lopate, Barry Lopez, Laura Wexler, Terry Tempest Williams, and others).
- *Writing for Love or Money* (Norman Cousins ed., 1949) (with Conrad Aiken, Henry Seidel Canby, Stephen Leacock, W. Somerset Maugham, Rex Stout, Thomas Wolfe, and others).
- *Writing in America* (John Fischer & Robert B. Silvers eds., 1960) (with Kingsley Amis, Robert Brustein, Alfred Kazin, Archibald MacLeish, Budd Schulberg, C.P. Snow, and others).

2.6 For writerly memoirs:
- James Baldwin, *The Fire Next Time* (1963 [much reprinted]).
- James Baldwin, *Notes of a Native Son* (1963 [much reprinted]).
- Ingmar Bergman, *The Magic Lantern: An Autobiography* (1988 [much reprinted]).
- Gardner Botsford, *A Life of Privilege, Mostly: A Memoir* (2003).
- Arthur Gelb, *City Room* (2003).
- Gail Gilliland, *Being a Minor Writer* (1994).
- Alfred Kazin, *A Lifetime Burning at Every Moment* (1996).
- Primo Levi, *The Reawakening* (1965 [much reprinted]).
- H.L. Mencken, *My Life as Author and Editor* (1993).
- Arthur Miller, *Timebends: A Life* (1987).
- Willie Morris, *New York Days* (1993).
- Vladimir Nabokov, *Speak, Memory* (1951; rev. ed. 1966 [much reprinted]).

- George Orwell, *Homage to Catalonia* (1938 [much reprinted]).
- Anna Quindlen, *Thinking Out Loud* (1993).
- Richard Rodriguez, *Brown: The Last Discovery of America* (2002).
- Richard Rodriguez, *Hunger of Memory: The Education of Richard Rodriguez* (1982).
- Gay Talese, *A Writer's Life* (2006).
- Amy Tan, *The Opposite of Fate: Memories of a Writing Life* (2003).
- Thomas Wolfe, *The Story of a Novel* (1936) (about the difficulty of approaching a second novel).
- C. Vann Woodward, *Thinking Back: The Perils of Writing History* (1986).

2.7 On the writing life:
  - Vera Brittain, *On Being a Writer* (1947).
  - Van Wyck Brooks, *The Writer in America* (1953).
  - Annie Dillard, *Living by Fiction* (1988).
  * Annie Dillard, *The Writing Life* (1990).
  - Cecil Hunt, *Living by the Pen* (1936).
  * Larry L. King, *None but a Blockhead: On Being a Writer* (1986).
  - Lu Chi, *Wen Fu: The Art of Writing* (Sam Hamill trans., 1987) (written ca. A.D. 303).
  - William H. Nolte, *H.L. Mencken, Literary Critic* (1966).
  - Brenda Ueland, *If You Want to Write* (2d ed. 1987).
  - Jack Woodford, *The Loud Literary Lamas of New York* (1950).

2.8 For literary anecdotes:
  - Clifton Fadiman & André Bernard, *Bartlett's Book of Anecdotes* (rev. ed. 2000).
  * John Gross, *The New Oxford Book of Literary Anecdotes* (2006).
  - Robert Hendrickson, *American Literary Anecdotes* (1990).
  - Robert Hendrickson, *British Literary Anecdotes* (1990).
  - Jack Hodges, *The Genius of Writers* (1992).
  - John Nichols, *Literary Anecdotes of the Eighteenth Century* (1967).

2.9 For quotations on writing:
  - James Charlton, *The Writer's Quotation Book* (4th rev. exp. ed. 1997).
  * *Good Advice on Writing* (William Safire & Leonard Safir eds., 1992).
  - *The Quotable Writer* (William A. Gordon ed., 2000).
  - *The Writer on His Art* (Walter Allen ed., 1949) (reissued in paperback as *Writers on Writing*).
  - *The Writer's Chapbook* (George Plimpton ed., 1989) (selected from the *Paris Review* interviews).
  - *Writers on Writers* (Graham Tarrant ed., 1995).
  * *Writers on Writing* (Jon Winokur ed., 3d ed. 1990).

- *The Writer's Quotebook: 500 Authors on Creativity, Craft, and the Writing Life* (Jim Fisher ed., 2006).

2.10 For books on prose style generally:
- * F.L. Lucas, *Style* (4th ed. 1958).
- J. Middleton Murry, *The Problem of Style* (1922).
- James R. Sutherland, *On English Prose* (1957).
- * Ben Yagoda, *The Sound of the Page* (2004).

2.11 For guidance on plain English:
- Martin Cutts, *The Oxford Guide to Plain English* (2d ed. 2004).
- Robert D. Eagleson, *Writing in Plain English* (1990).
- * Rudolf Flesch, *How to Write Plain English* (1979).
- * Ernest Gowers, *The Complete Plain Words* (Sidney Greenbaum & Janet Whitcut eds., 3d ed. 1986).

2.12 On the practicalities of getting published:
- Judith Appelbaum & Nancy Evans, *How to Get Happily Published: A Complete and Candid Guide* (1978).
- *The Beginning Writer's Answer Book* (Kirk Polking et al. eds., rev. ed. 1994).
- John Boswell, *The Insider's Guide to Getting Published* (1997).
- Thomas Clark, *Queries & Submissions* (1995).
- Oscar Collier & Frances Spatz Leighton, *How to Write and Sell Your First Nonfiction Book* (3d ed. 1997).
- Arielle Eckstut & David Henry Sterry, *Putting Your Passion into Print* (2005).
- Larston D. Farrar, *Successful Writers and How They Work* (1959).
- * William Germano, *Getting It Published: A Guide for Scholars and Anyone Else Serious About Serious Books* (2001).
- Michael Legat, *Dear Author . . .* (rev. ed. 1989).
- Susan Rabiner & Alfred Fortunato, *Thinking Like Your Editor* (2002).
- Esther L. Schwartz, *How to Become a Professional Writer* (1939).
- Michael Seidman, *Fiction: The Art and Craft of Writing and Getting Published* (1999).
- Eva Shaw, *Writing the Nonfiction Book* (1999).
- * Jack Woodford, *How to Write for Money* (1944).

2.13 For guidance on literary research:
- Richard D. Altick, *The Art of Literary Research* (John J. Fenstermaker et al. eds., 4th ed. 1981).
- * Jacques Barzun & Henry F. Graff, *The Modern Researcher* (6th ed. 2004).
- F.W. Bateson, *The Scholar-Critic* (1972).

2.14 For literary allusions:
* * *Brewer's Dictionary of Phrase and Fable* (John Ayto ed., 17th ed. 2000).
* • *Brewer's Dictionary of Twentieth-Century Phrase and Fable* (David Pickering et al. eds., 1992).
* • *Merriam-Webster's Dictionary of Allusions* (Elizabeth Webber & Mike Feinsilber eds., 1999).
* • *The Oxford Dictionary of Phrase and Fable* (Elizabeth Knowles ed., 2d ed. 2005).

2.15 For guidance on writing novels:
* • John Braine, *Writing a Novel* (1974).
* • Janet Burroway, *Writing Fiction: A Guide to Narrative Craft* (7th ed. 2006).
* • R.V. Cassill, *Writing Fiction* (2d ed. 1975).
* • Michael H. Cohen, *Creative Writing for Lawyers* (1991).
* • Oakley Hall, *The Art and Craft of Novel Writing* (1989).
* • Clayton Hamilton, *The Art of Fiction* (rev. ed. 1939) (with a foreword by Booth Tarkington and an introduction by Brander Matthews).
* • Stephen Koch, *The Modern Writer's Workshop: A Guide to the Craft of Fiction* (2003).
* * Anne Lamott, *Bird by Bird: Some Instructions on Writing and Life* (1995).
* • *Paths of Resistance: The Art and Craft of the Political Novel* (William Zinsser ed., 1989) (with Isabel Allende, Charles McCarry, Marge Piercy, Robert Stone, and Gore Vidal).
* • Sol Stein, *Stein on Writing* (1995) (mostly on fiction but some on nonfiction).
* • Dick Winfield, *One Way to Write Your Novel* (1969).
* * Jack Woodford, *Why Write a Novel?* (1943).
* • Writers Mentor Group, *How to Write an Uncommonly Good Novel* (1990).

2.16 For guidance on writing short stories:
* * Paul Darcy Boles, *Storycrafting* (1984).
* • Hallie Burnett, *On Writing the Short Story* (1983).
* • Rust Hills, *Writing in General and the Short Story in Particular* (rev. ed. 1987).
* * Cecil Hunt, *Short Stories: How to Write Them* (rev. ed. 1950).
* • Robert C. Meredith & John D. Fitzgerald, *The Professional Story Writer and His Art* (1963).
* • Ben Nyberg, *One Great Way to Write Short Stories* (1988).

- Earl Reed Silvers, *How to Write Short Stories That Editors Buy* (1943).
- Ray B. West Jr., *The Art of Writing Fiction* (1968) (mostly on short stories but some on novels).
- *The Writer's Digest Handbook of Short Story Writing*, vol. 1 (Frank A. Dickson & Sandra Smythe eds., 1981).
- *The Writer's Digest Handbook of Short Story Writing*, vol. 2 (Jean M. Fredette ed., 1988).

2.17 For guidance on writing nonfiction:
- Theodore Cheney, *Writing Creative Nonfiction* (1987).
- Jon Franklin, *Writing for Story: Craft Secrets of Dramatic Nonfiction* (1994).
- Lee Gutkind, *The Art of Creative Nonfiction* (1997).
- Patsy Sims, *Literary Nonfiction: Learning by Example* (2001).
- James B. Stewart, *Follow the Story* (1998).
- Barry Tarshis, *How to Write Like a Pro: A Guide to Effective Nonfiction Writing* (1982).

2.18 For guidance on writing biographies and autobiographies:
- E. Stuart Bates, *Inside Out: An Introduction to Autobiography* (1937).
- *Extraordinary Lives: The Art and Craft of American Biography* (William Zinsser ed., 1986) (with Robert A. Caro, David McCullough, Paul C. Nagel, Richard B. Sewall, Ronald Steel, and Jean Strouse).
- Michael Holroyd, *Works on Paper: The Craft of Biography and Autobiography* (2002).
- Mary Jane Moffat, *The Times of Our Lives: A Guide to Writing Autobiography and Memoir* (1989).

2.19 For guidance on writing about history:
- Anthony Brundage, *Going to the Sources: A Guide to Historical Research and Writing* (3d ed. 2002).
- Martha C. Howell & Walter Prevenier, *From Reliable Sources: An Introduction to Historical Methods* (2001).
- Sherman Kent, *Writing History* (1941).
- * Richard Marius & Melvin E. Page, *A Short Guide to Writing About History* (6th ed. 2006).
- Louis O'Brien, *The Writing of History* (1935).
- William K. Storey, *Writing History: A Guide for Students* (1996).

2.20 For guidance on writing book reviews:
- * *Book Reviewing* (Sylvia E. Kamerman ed., 1978).
- John E. Drewry, *Book Reviewing* (1945).
- Wayne Gard, *Book Reviewing* (1927).

- Llewellyn Jones, *How to Criticize Books* (1928).
- Evelyn Oppenheimer, *Book Reviewing for an Audience: A Practical Guide in Techniques for Lecture and Broadcast* (1962).

2.21 For guidance on writing op-ed pieces:
  * Conrad C. Fink, *Writing Opinion for Impact* (2d ed. 2004).
  - Curtis D. MacDougall, *Principles of Editorial Writing* (1973).
  - Harry W. Stonecipher, *Editorial and Persuasive Writing* (2d ed. 1990).

2.22 For the best advice on essay-writing:
  - Sheridan Baker, *The Essayist* (5th ed. 1985).
  - Sheridan Baker, *The Practical Stylist* (8th ed. 1997).
  - Lydia Fakundiny, *The Art of the Essay* (1991) (mostly an anthology of essays).
  - Elizabeth Penfield, *Short Takes* (6th ed. 1999).
  - Peter Redman, *Good Essay Writing* (3d ed. 2006).

2.23 For guidance on serious journalism:
  - Mervin Block, *Writing Broadcast News: Shorter, Sharper, Stronger* (1987).
  - William E. Blundell, *The Art and Craft of Feature Writing* (1988).
  - *The Complete Book of Feature Writing* (Leonard Witt ed., 1991).
  - Brendan Hennessy, *Writing Feature Articles* (3d ed. 1997).
  - Bill Kovach & Tom Rosenthal, *The Elements of Journalism* (rev. upd. ed. 2007).
  - John M. Wilson, *The Complete Guide to Magazine Article Writing* (1993).
  * William Zinsser, *Speaking of Journalism* (1994).

2.24 For guidance on understanding and writing poetry:
  - Anne Hamilton, *How to Revise Your Own Poems: A Primer for Poets* (1945).
  - Anne Hamilton, *The Seven Principles of Poetry* (1940).
  - Mary Kinzie, *A Poet's Guide to Poetry* (1999).
  - Steve Kowit, *In the Palm of Your Hand: The Poet's Portable Workshop* (1995).
  - *Poets on Poetry* (Charles Norman ed., 1962) (with essays and comments by T.S. Eliot, Ralph Waldo Emerson, Samuel Johnson, Edgar Allan Poe, Ezra Pound, Allen Tate, William Wordsworth, and others).
  - See especially 10.4.

2.25 For guidance on writing plays and screenplays:
  - Irwin R. Blacker, *The Elements of Screenwriting* (1986).
  - John Brady, *The Craft of the Screenwriter* (1981).

- Lajos Egri, *The Art of Dramatic Writing* (1946).
- St. John Ervine, *How to Write a Play* (rev. 2d ed. 1936).
- William Froug, *The Screenwriter Looks at the Screenwriter* (1972).
- Bernard Grebanier, *Playwriting: How to Write for the Theater* (1961).
- Jeffrey Hatcher, *The Art and Craft of Playwriting* (2000).
- Walter Kerr, *How Not to Write a Play* (1955).
- John Masefield, "Play-Writing," in *Recent Prose* (1924).
- * Josefina Niggli, *New Pointers on Playwriting* (1967).
- *Playwrights and Playwriting* (Toby Cole ed., 1960).
- * *The Playwrights Speak* (Walter Wager ed., 1967).

2.26 For guidance on writing about philosophy:
- A.P. Martinich, *Philosophical Writing* (3d ed. 2005).

2.27 For guidance on scientific writing:
- Robert Barrass, *Scientists Must Write* (2d ed. 2002).
- Robert A. Day, *How to Write and Publish a Scientific Paper* (6th ed. 2006).
- Robert A. Day, *Scientific English: A Guide for Scientists and Other Professionals* (2d ed. 1995).
- * Lester S. King, *Why Not Say It Clearly* (2d ed. 1991).
- M. O'Connor & F.P. Woodward, *Writing Scientific Papers in English* (1978).
- Alan D. Sokal & Jean Bricmout, *Fashionable Nonsense: Postmodern Intellectuals' Abuse of Science* (1998).

2.28 For guidance on writing in the social sciences:
- Howard S. Becker, *Writing for Social Scientists* (1986).
- Arthur W. Biddle & Kenneth M. Holland, *Writer's Guide: Political Science* (1987).

2.29 For guidance on writing e-mail messages:
- Patricia T. O'Conner & Stewart Kellerman, *You Send Me: Getting It Right When You Write Online* (2002).
- David Shipley & Will Schwalbe, *Send: The Essential Guide to E-mail for Office and Home* (2007).

2.30 For models of good letters:
- Diana Booher, *To the Letter: A Handbook of Model Letters for the Busy Executive* (1988).
- * Corey Sandler & Janie Keefe, *1001 Letters for All Occasions* (2004).

2.31 For guidance on business correspondence:
- * Earle A. Buckley, *How to Write Better Business Letters* (4th rev. ed. 1971).
- L.E. Frailey, *Handbook of Business Letters* (rev. ed. 1965).
- Ellis Gladwin, *The Letters You Write* (1969).

2.32 For business writing generally:
- Gary Blake, *Quick Tips for Better Business Writing* (1995).
- Gary Blake & Robert W. Bly, *The Elements of Business Writing* (1991).
- Diana Booher, *Would You Put That in Writing?* (rev. ed. 1992).
- David W. Ewing, *Writing for Results* (2d ed. 1979).
- Rudolf Flesch, *On Business Communications* (1972).
- Robert Gunning & Richard A. Kallan, *How to Take the Fog out of Business Writing* (1994).
- Richard A. Lanham, *Revising Business Prose* (4th ed. 1999).
- * Royal Bank of Canada, *The Communication of Ideas* (rev. ed. 1972) (an amazingly good little book).
- * William Sabin, *The Gregg Reference Manual* (10th ed. 2004).

2.33 For guidance on writing reports and memos:
- Bruce Ross-Larson, *Riveting Reports* (1999).
- Norman B. Sigband, *Effective Report Writing* (1960).
- * Patricia H. Westheimer, *The Perfect Memo* (1988).

2.34 For guidance on business proposals:
- * Richard C. Freed, Shervin Freed & Joseph D. Romano, *Writing Winning Business Proposals* (rev. ed. 2003).
- Joseph R. Mancuso, *How to Prepare and Present a Business Plan* (1983).
- Tom Sant, *Persuasive Business Proposals* (2d ed. 2004).

2.35 For help in writing employee evaluations:
- * James E. Neal, *Effective Phrases for Performance Appraisals* (2006).
- Glenn Shepard, *How to Make Performance Evaluations Really Work* (2005).

2.36 For guidance on résumés:
- * Scott Bennett, *The Elements of Résumé Style* (2005).
- Nancy Schuman & William Lewis, *Revising Your Résumé* (1987).

2.37 For ideas on keeping a diary:
- Thomas Mallom, *A Book of One's Own* (1995).
- Tristine Rainer, *The New Diary* (1978).
- Charles B. Wright, *The Making of Note-Books* (1928).

2.38 For guidance on what to avoid putting in writing:
- Edward P. Ahrens Jr., *The Perils of Imprudent Writing* (2d rev. ed. 1999).

2.39 On teaching writing and literature:
- *Cross-Talk in Comp Theory* (Victor Villanueva Jr. ed., 2d ed. 2003).
- G.B. Harrison, *Profession of English* (1962).

* E.D. Hirsch, *The Philosophy of Composition* (1981).
* Alfred M. Hitchcock, *Bread Loaf Talks on Teaching Composition* (1927).
* Robert C. Pooley, *The Teaching of English Usage* (2d ed. 1974).
* Mina Shaughnessey, *Errors and Expectations* (1977).
* *Teaching Composition: Twelve Bibliographical Essays* (rev. ed. 1987).
* *The Teaching of English* (Incorporated Association of Assistant Masters in Secondary Schools ed., 1952).
* Jane Tompkins, *A Life in School: What the Teacher Learned* (1996).

2.40 For guidance on student papers:
* Joseph Gibaldi, *MLA Handbook for Writers of Research Papers* (6th ed. 2004).
* Charles Lipson, *How to Write a B.A. Thesis* (2005).
* Lee J. Martin & Harry P. Kroitor, *The 500-Word Theme* (5th ed. 1993).
* David B. Pirie, *How to Write Critical Essays* (1985).
* Kate L. Turabian et al., *A Manual for Writers of Research Papers, Theses, and Dissertations* (7th ed. 2007).
* Stephen Weidenborner & Domenick Caruso, *Writing Research Papers* (6th ed. 2000).

2.41 For guidance on the graphic element in conveying information:
* Susan Hilligoss & Tharon Howard, *Visual Communication: A Writer's Guide* (2d ed. 2002).
* Edward Tufte, *Beautiful Evidence* (2006).
* Edward Tufte, *Envisioning Information* (1990).

2.42 For development of the idea that writers make wonderful friends:
* E.B. White, *Charlotte's Web* (1952).

3 Editing

3.1 For guidance on revising and editing:
* Jacques Barzun, *A Word or Two Before You Go* (1986) (see esp. the essays "A Copy Editor's Anthology" and "Dialogue in C-Sharp").
* Jacques Barzun, *On Writing, Editing, and Publishing* (2d ed. 1986) (see esp. the essay "Behind the Blue Pencil," which appears only in the second ed.).
* Renni Browne & David King, *Self-Editing for Fiction Writers* (2d ed. 2004).
* Claire Kehrwald Cook, *Line by Line: How to Edit Your Own Writing* (1985).
* Richard A. Lanham, *Revising Prose* (5th ed. 2006).

- Bruce Ross-Larson, *Edit Yourself: A Manual for Everyone Who Works with Words* (rev. ed. 1996).
- Donald M. Murray, *The Craft of Revision* (5th ed. 2003).
- Arthur Plotnik, *The Elements of Editing: A Modern Guide for Editors and Journalists* (1982).
- Michael Seidman, *The Complete Guide to Editing Your Fiction* (2d ed. 2002).
- Leslie Sharpe & Irene Gunther, *Editing Fact and Fiction: A Concise Guide to Book Editing* (1994).
- Barry Tarshis, *How to Be Your Own Best Editor* (1998).

3.2 For copyediting guidance:
- Judith Butcher, *Butcher's Copy-Editing: The Cambridge Handbook for Editors, Authors, and Publishers* (4th ed. 2006) (the classic British text).
- * *The Chicago Manual of Style* (15th ed. 2003) (the classic American text).
- Amy Einsohn, *The Copyeditor's Handbook: A Guide for Book Publishing and Corporate Communications* (2d ed. 2005).
- Karen Judd, *Copyediting: A Practical Guide* (3d ed. 2001).
- William Sabin, *The Gregg Reference Manual* (10th ed. 2004).
- *Words into Type* (3d ed. 1974).

3.3 For an anthology of essays on editing:
- Marjorie E. Skillin & Robert M. Gay, *Editors on Editing* (Gerald Gross ed., 3d ed. 1993).

4 Grammar

4.1 For a clear, step-by-step explanation of English grammar:
- * George O. Curme, *A Grammar of the English Language* (1935 [much reprinted]) (2 vols.).
- * Bryan A. Garner, "Grammar and Usage," ch. 5 of *The Chicago Manual of Style* (15th ed. 2003) (a 92-page restatement of English grammar).
- Otto Jespersen, *Essentials of English Grammar* (1933).
- Edward D. Johnson, *The Handbook of Good English* (1982).
- Martha Kolln, *Rhetorical Grammar* (4th ed. 2003).
- John B. Opdycke, *Harper's English Grammar* (Stewart Benedict ed., 1965).

4.2 For a light, entertaining guide to English grammar:
- Hugh Sykes Davies, *Grammar Without Tears* (1951).

* Patricia T. O'Conner, *Woe Is I: The Grammarphobe's Guide to Better English in Plain English* (rev. ed. 2003).
• Ben Yagoda, *When You Catch an Adjective, Kill It! The Parts of Speech for Better and/or Worse* (2006).

4.3 For a guide to grammar in the form of a high-school or college handbook:
• Diana Hacker, *Rules for Writers* (5th ed. 2003).
* Diana Hacker, *A Writer's Reference* (5th ed. 2003).
• Maxine Hairston & John Ruszkiewicz, *The Scott Foresman Handbook for Writers* (7th ed. 2003).
• James A. Heffernan, John E. Lincoln & Janet Atwill, *Writing: A College Handbook* (5th ed. 2000).
• John E. Warriner, *English Composition and Grammar: Complete Course* (1988).

4.4 If you're a native speaker of a non–Indo-European language and you're having difficulty with *a*, *an*, and *the* in English:
• Elizabeth Claire & Richard Greenwood, *Three Little Words: A, An, and The* (1991).

5 Usage

5.1 For guidance on virtually any tricky question of grammar, word choice, punctuation, or pronunciation, in a dictionary format:
• Mark Davidson, *Right, Wrong, and Risky: A Dictionary of Today's American English Usage* (2006).
• Bryan A. Garner, *Garner's Modern American Usage* (2d ed. 2003).

5.2 For a discursive treatment of English usage:
• Barbara Wallraff, *Word Court: Wherein Verbal Virtue Is Rewarded, Crimes Against the Language Are Punished, and Poetic Justice Is Done* (2001).

5.3 For journalistic guidance on matters of form and style:
* *The Associated Press Stylebook and Briefing on Media Law* (Norm Goldstein ed., rev. ed. 2007).
• *The New York Times Manual of Style and Usage* (Allan M. Siegal & William G. Connolly eds., rev. ed. 2002).
• Bill Walsh, *The Elephants of Style* (2004).
* Bill Walsh, *Lapsing into a Comma* (2000).

5.4 For guidance on gauging English-usage questions for yourself:
• Barbara Wallraff, *Your Own Words* (2004).

5.5 For a daily usage tip by e-mail:
- Garner's Usage Tip of the Day (see www.lawprose.org to sign up).

5.6 For somewhat dated but classic guides to English usage:
* Theodore M. Bernstein, *The Careful Writer: A Modern Guide to English Usage* (1965).
- Bergen Evans & Cornelia Evans, *A Dictionary of Contemporary American Usage* (1957).
- Wilson Follett, *Modern American Usage: A Guide* (1966).
* H.W. Fowler, *A Dictionary of Modern English Usage* (Ernest Gowers ed., 2d ed. 1965).
- H.W. Fowler & F.G. Fowler, *The King's English* (3d ed. 1931).
- Eric Partridge, *Usage and Abusage* (1942).

5.7 For the nonnative speaker who wants to learn about English usage:
- Michael Swan, *Practical English Usage* (3d ed. 2005).

5.8 For a thesaurus that distinguishes between synonyms:
- S.I. Hayakawa, *Use the Right Word* (1968 [occasionally reprinted]).
- *Webster's Dictionary of Synonyms* (1942 [occasionally reprinted]).

5.9 For the nonnative speaker who wants to learn English idioms:
- *Longman Dictionary of American English: A Dictionary for Learners of English* (3d ed. 2004).

5.10 For entertaining, informative guides to punctuation:
* Karen Elizabeth Gordon, *The New Well-Tempered Sentence* (rev. ed. 1993).
- Richard Lederer & John Shore, *Comma Sense: A FUNdamental Guide to Punctuation* (2005).
- *Oxford Advanced Learner's Dictionary* (7th ed. 2005).
- Eric Partridge, *You Have a Point There: A Guide to Punctuation and Its Allies* (1953).

5.11 For a punctuation guide that is entertaining but error-ridden, beloved by amateurs but scorned by connoisseurs:
- Lynne Truss, *Eats, Shoots & Leaves* (2004) (see my review at 83 Tex. L. Rev. 1443–52 (2005) or in Chapter Sixteen of this book).

5.12 For in-depth treatment of preferred pronunciations in American English, assuming you don't mind being told that some of your cherished pronunciations are wrong:
- Charles Harrington Elster, *The Big Book of Beastly Mispronunciations* (2d ed. 2006).

6 Logic and Rhetoric

6.1 For guides to classical rhetoric:
- William J. Brandt, *The Rhetoric of Argumentation* (1970).
- Edward P.J. Corbett, *Classical Rhetoric for the Modern Student* (4th ed. 1998).
- Winifred Bryan Horner, *Rhetoric in the Classical Tradition* (1988).
- Brian Vickers, *Classical Rhetoric in English Poetry* (rev. ed. 1989).
- * Brian Vickers, *In Defense of Rhetoric* (1988).
- Richard M. Weaver, *The Ethics of Rhetoric* (1985).

6.2 For seminal texts on classical rhetoric, without an intermediary:
- * Aristotle, *The Art of Rhetoric* (H.C. Lawson-Tancred trans., rev. ed. 2004), *or* Aristotle, *Rhetoric* (Lane Cooper trans., 1932).
- Cicero, *On Oratory and Orators* (J.S. Watson trans., 1986).
- Demetrius of Phalerum, *On Style* (ca. 300 B.C.; T.A. Moxon trans., 1943).
- *The Rhetoric of Blair, Campbell, and Whately* (James L. Golden & Edward P.J. Corbett eds., 1990).

6.3 For rhetorical terminology (see also 8.7):
- Richard A. Lanham, *A Handlist of Rhetorical Terms* (2d ed. 1991).
- Arthur Quinn, *Figures of Speech* (1982).

6.4 For guidance on critical thinking:
- * Monroe C. Beardsley, *Thinking Straight* (4th ed. 1975).
- Neil Browne & Stuart Keeley, *Asking the Right Questions: A Guide to Critical Thinking* (8th ed. 2006).
- Edward de Bono, *De Bono's Thinking Course* (rev. ed. 1994).
- Alec Fisher, *The Logic of Real Arguments* (2d ed. 2004).
- Antony Flew, *How to Think Straight* (2d ed. 1998).
- Dominic A. Infante, *Arguing Constructively* (1988).
- Robert Pirsig, *Zen and the Art of Motorcycle Maintenance* (1974).
- Lionel Ruby, *The Art of Making Sense: A Guide to Logical Thinking* (3d ed. 1974).

7 Word-Loving

7.1 For basic vocabulary-building books:
- * Charles Harrington Elster, *Verbal Advantage* (2000).
- Bergen Evans, *The Word-a-Day Vocabulary Builder* (rev. upd. ed. 1982).
- Norman Lewis, *New Power with Words* (2d ed. 1974).

    * Maxwell Nurnberg & Morris Rosenblum, *How to Build a Better Vocabulary* (1949 [much reprinted]).

7.2 For more advanced vocabulary-building books:
- Norman W. Schur, *2000 Most Challenging and Obscure Words* (1994).

7.3 For guidance on English idioms and their origins:
    * Charles Earle Funk, *2107 Curious Word Origins, Sayings and Expressions* (1993) (actually a combination of four Funk books: *A Hog on Ice* [1948], *Thereby Hangs a Tale* [1950], *Heavens to Betsy!* [1955], and *Horsefeathers* [1958]).
- Webb B. Garrison, *What's in a Word?* (1965).
- Webb B. Garrison, *Why You Say It* (1955).

7.4 If you're interested in wordplay:
- Gyles Brandreth, *The Joy of Lex* (1980).
- Gyles Brandreth, *More Joy of Lex* (1982).
- Willard Espy, *The Game of Words* (1973).
    * Richard Lederer, *Crazy English* (1989; repr. 1998).
- Richard Lederer, *The Play of Words* (1990).
- Richard Lederer, *Word Circus* (rev. ed. 1998).

7.5 For unusual English words:
- Josefa Heifetz Byrne, *Mrs. Byrne's Dictionary of Unusual, Obscure, and Preposterous Words* (rev. ed. 1994).
- Charles Harrington Elster, *There's a Word for It: A Grandiloquent Guide to Life* (1996).
- Erin McKean, *Weird and Wonderful Words* (2002).
- Erin McKean, *More Weird and Wonderful Words* (2003).

7.6 For literary terminology (see also 7.3):
    * Chris Baldick, *The Concise Oxford Dictionary of Literary Terms* (1990).
- Sylvan Barnet, Morton Berman & William Burto, *A Dictionary of Literary Terms* (1960).
- Northrup Frye, Sheridan Baker, George Perkins & Barbara M. Perkins, *The Harper Handbook to Literature* (1997).
- *The New Princeton Encyclopedia of Poetry and Poetics* (Alex Preminger & T.V.F. Brogan eds., 3d ed. 1993).

7.7 For a good dictionary of slang (not for the prudish):
- Tom Dalzell, *The Slang of Sin* (1998).
    * Eric Partridge, *A Dictionary of Slang and Unconventional English* (8th ed. 2002).

- Richard A. Spears, *NTC's Dictionary of American Slang and Colloquial Expressions* (3d ed. 2000).

7.8 For insights into foul language:
  - * Geoffrey Hughes, *Swearing* (1991).
  - Hugh Rawson, *Wicked Words* (1989).
  - Ruth Wajnryb, *Expletive Deleted* (2005).

8 Linguistics

8.1 If you're interested in English linguistics:
  - * Anthony Burgess, *A Mouthful of Air* (1992).
  - *Introductory Readings on Language* (Wallace L. Anderson & Norman C. Stageberg eds., 4th ed. 1975).
  - *A Language Reader for Writers* (James R. Gaskin & Jack Suberman eds., 1966).
  - *Readings in Applied Linguistics* (Harold B. Allen ed., 3d ed. 1982).
  - R.L. Trask, *Language: The Basics* (2d ed. 1999).
  - R.L. Trask & Bill Mayblin, *Introducing Linguistics* (2000).

8.2 For encyclopedias of the English language:
  - *The Cambridge Encyclopedia of the English Language* (David Crystal ed., 2d ed. 2002).
  - * *The Oxford Companion to the English Language* (Tom McArthur ed., 1992).

8.3 For encyclopedias about language generally:
  - * *The Cambridge Encyclopedia of Language* (David Crystal ed., 2d ed. 1997).
  - *International Encyclopedia of Linguistics*, 4 vols. (William J. Frawley ed., 2d ed. 2003).
  - *The Linguistics Encyclopedia* (Kirsten Malmkjaer ed., 2d ed. 2004).

8.4 For dictionaries of linguistics:
  - * David Crystal, *A Dictionary of Language* (2d ed. 1999) (originally published as *An Encyclopedic Dictionary of Language and Languages*).
  - Andrew MacLeish, *A Glossary of Grammar and Linguistics* (1972).
  - P.H. Matthews, *The Concise Oxford Dictionary of Linguistics* (2d ed. 2007).
  - R.L. Trask, *A Dictionary of Grammatical Terms in Linguistics* (1993).

8.5 For a book of quotations on language and languages:
  - David Crystal & Hilary Crystal, *Words on Words* (2000).

8.6 To learn about general semantics, namely, the study of how symbols and reality interrelate:
- Stuart Chase, *The Tyranny of Words* (1938 [much reprinted]).
* S.I. Hayakawa & Alan R. Hayakawa, *Language in Thought and Action* (5th ed. 1991).

8.7 For a brief overview of the English language:
- Robert W. Burchfield, *The English Language* (1985).
- Robert W. Burchfield, *Unlocking the English Language* (1991).
* Simeon Potter, *Our Language* (rev. ed. 1966).
- Logan Pearsall Smith, *The English Language* (3d ed. 1966).
- Ernest Weekley, *The English Language* (1952).

8.8 For a scholarly history of the English language:
* Albert C. Baugh & Thomas Cable, *A History of the English Language* (5th ed. 2002).
- G.L. Brook, *A History of the English Language* (1958).

8.9 For a popular, nonscholarly history of the English language:
- Lincoln Barnett, *The Treasure of Our Tongue* (1962).
- Melvyn Bragg, *The Adventure of English* (2003).
* Bill Bryson, *The Mother Tongue: English and How It Got That Way* (1990).

8.10 For an anthology of readings about the English language:
- *The Play of Language* (Leonard F. Dean et al. eds., 1971) (earlier editions were called *Essays on Language and Usage*) (with essays by Margaret M. Bryant, Robert Frost, Raven I. McDavid, James Sledd, Thorstein Veblen, Kurt Vonnegut Jr., and others).
* *The State of the Language* (Christopher Ricks & Leonard Michaels eds., 1980) (with essays by Kingsley Amis, Robert W. Burchfield, Angela Carter, Maxine Hong Kingston, David Lodge, J. Enoch Powell, Randolph Quirk, John Simon, Edmund White, and others).
* *The State of the Language* (Christopher Ricks & Leonard Michaels eds., 1990) (with essays by John Algeo, Robert W. Burchfield, Bryan A. Garner, Henry Louis Gates Jr., Roy Harris, Ted Hughes, Hermione Lee, Martha Minow, Geoffrey Nunberg, and others).
- *The Ways of Language: A Reader* (Raymond J. Pflug ed., 1967) (with essays by Mortimer Adler, Albert C. Baugh, Wilson Follett, Charlton Laird, Donald J. Lloyd, Mitford M. Mathews, James Thurber, and others).

8.11 For studies of American English:
- H.L. Mencken, *The American Language* (4th ed. 1936) (an original volume plus two supplements).
- Thomas Pyles, *Words and Ways of American English* (1952).

8.12 For reading about American dialects:
- John Baugh, *Black Street Speech: Its History, Structure, and Survival* (1983).
- Craig M. Carver, *American Regional Dialects: A Word Geography* (1987).
- Raven I. McDavid Jr., *Varieties of American English* (1980).
- * John McWhorter, *Spreading the Word: Language and Dialect in America* (2000).
- Carroll E. Reed, *Dialects of American English* (rev. ed. 1977).
- Walt Wolfram, *Dialects and American English* (1991).

8.13 If you're interested in English worldwide:
- David Crystal, *English as a Global Language* (2d ed. 2003).
- * Tom McArthur, *The Oxford Guide to World English* (2002).

8.14 For understanding the great debate between prescriptivists and descriptivists:
- David Crystal, *Who Cares About English Usage?* (2d rev. ed. 2000) (for a descriptivist view).
- Wilson Follett, "On Usage, Purism, and Pedantry," in *Modern American Usage: A Guide* (Jacques Barzun ed., 1966) (for a prescriptivist view).
- Bryan A. Garner, "Making Peace in the Language Wars," in *Garner's Modern American Usage* (2d ed. 2003) (for an evenhanded view).
- Mark Halpern, *Language and Human Nature* (2006) (by a self-described "linguistic activist").
- James Sledd, *Eloquent Dissent* (Richard D. Freed ed., 1996) (for a descriptivist view).
- * David Foster Wallace, "Authority and American Usage," in *Consider the Lobster and Other Essays* (2006) (for a moderately prescriptivist view).

8.15 If you're interested in language and social class:
- * Paul Fussell, *Class* (1983).
- *Noblesse Oblige* (Nancy Mitford ed., 1956).
- Alan S.C. Ross, *Don't Say It* (1973).
- *U and Non-U Revisited* (Richard Buckle ed., 1978).

8.16 For insights into sociolinguistics:
- Ralph Fasold, *The Sociolinguistics of Language* (1990).
- Ralph Fasold, *The Sociolinguistics of Society* (1984).
- R.A. Hudson, *Sociolinguistics* (2d ed. 1996).
- Peter Trudgill, *A Glossary of Sociolinguistics* (2003).

* Peter Trudgill, *Sociolinguistics: An Introduction to Language and Society* (4th ed. 2001).
• Ronald Wardhaugh, *An Introduction to Sociolinguistics* (3d ed. 1978).

8.17 For insights into psycholinguistics:
• Roger Brown, *Psycholinguistics* (1970).
* Jean Caron, *An Introduction to Psycholinguistics* (Tim Pownall trans., 1992).
• Judith Greene, *Psycholinguistics: Chomsky and Psychology* (1972).
• Steven Pinker, *The Language Instinct* (1994).
• Steven Pinker, *Words and Rules: The Ingredients of Language* (1999).
• *Psycholinguistics: A Book of Readings* (Sol Saporta ed., 1961).
• Thomas Scovel, *Psycholinguistics* (1998).

8.18 For insights into linguistic sexism:
• Dennis Baron, *Grammar and Gender* (1986).
• Val Dumond, *The Elements of Nonsexist Usage* (1990).
• Casey Miller & Kate Swift, *The Handbook of Nonsexist Writing* (2d ed. 2001).
* Dale Spender, *Man Made Language* (2d ed. 1998).

8.19 For insights into bilingualism and bilingual education:
• James Crawford, *Hold Your Tongue: Bilingualism and the Politics of "English Only"* (1992).

8.20 If you're interested in how children acquire language:
• David Crystal, *Listen to Your Child: A Parent's Guide to Children's Language* (1986).

8.21 For information on language disorders:
• Benson Bobrick, *Knotted Tongues: Stuttering in History and the Quest for a Cure* (1995).
• Vicki A. Reed, *An Introduction to Children with Language Disorders* (3d ed. 2004).

9 Public Speaking

9.1 For guidance on public speaking:
• Mortimer J. Adler, *How to Speak, How to Write* (1983).
• Reid Buckley, *Speaking in Public* (1988).
• Dale Carnegie, *The Quick and Easy Way to Effective Speaking* (1962 [much reprinted]).
* Ron Hoff, *I Can See You Naked* (1992).
• Louis Nizer, *Thinking on Your Feet* (1940).

* Peggy Noonan, *Simply Speaking* (1998).
• Charles Osgood, *Osgood on Speaking* (1988).
• Jack Valenti, *Speak Up with Confidence* (2002).

10 Reading

10.1 For guidance on developing literary taste:
• Montgomery Belgion, *Reading for Profit* (1950).
* Arnold Bennett, *Literary Taste: How to Form It* (1911) (dated but still valuable).
• F.H. Pritchard, *Training in Literary Appreciation* (1924).
• Robert E. Rogers, *The Fine Art of Reading* (1929).
• C. Alphonse Smith, *What Can Literature Do for Me?* (rev. ed. 1932).

10.2 For guidance on critical reading:
* Mortimer Adler, *How to Read a Book* (rev. ed. 1972).
• Harold Bloom, *How to Read and Why* (2000).
• William Empson, *Seven Types of Ambiguity* (1st U.S. ed. 1947).
• Richard A. Lanham, *Analyzing Prose* (2003).
• Ezra Pound, *ABC of Reading* (1934).
• I.A. Richards, *How to Read a Page* (1942).

10.3 For guidance on reading fiction:
• Cleanth Brooks Jr. & Robert Penn Warren, *Understanding Fiction* (3d ed. 1979).
• Thomas C. Foster, *How to Read Literature Like a Professor* (2003).
• Caroline Gordon, *How to Read a Novel* (1964).
* Francine Prose, *Reading Like a Writer* (2006).
• *Rereadings* (Anne Fadiman ed., 2005) (with Sven Birkerts, Pico Iyer, Arthur Krystal, Phillip Lopate, and others).

10.4 For guidance on appreciating poetry:
* Cleanth Brooks Jr. & Robert Penn Warren, *Understanding Poetry* (4th ed. 1976).
• Paul Fussell, *Poetic Meter and Poetic Form* (1979).
• Robert Graves, *Poetic Craft and Principle* (1967).
• John Hollander, *Rhyme's Reason: A Guide to English Verse* (3d ed. 2001).
• Robert Pinsky, *The Sounds of Poetry: A Brief Guide* (1999).
* Christopher Ricks, *The Force of Poetry* (1995).
• Christopher Ricks, *Poems and Critics* (1972).
• Jon Stallworthy, "Essay on Versification," in *The Norton Anthology of Poetry* (Margaret Ferguson et al. eds., 5th ed. 2004).
• John Hall Wheelock, *What Is Poetry?* (1963).

10.5 For good reading generally (examples of first-rate writers at work):
Magazines and newspapers:

- *The American Scholar*
- *The Atlantic Monthly*
- *Commentary*
* *The Economist*
- *Harper's*
- *The New Republic*
* *The New Yorker*
- *The New York Review of Books*
- *The New York Times*
- *The Wall Street Journal*

Nonfiction:

- James Agee, *Let Us Now Praise Famous Men* (1941).
- Christopher Alexander et al., *A Pattern Language: Towns, Buildings, Construction* (1977).
- Stephen E. Ambrose, *Undaunted Courage* (1996).
- Barbara Armstrong, *A History of God: The 4000-Year Quest of Judaism, Christianity, and Islam* (2004).
- Jacques Barzun, *From Dawn to Decadence: 1500 to the Present* (2000).
- Jeremy Bernstein, *The Life It Begins: One Physicist's Beginnings* (1997).
- G.L. Brook, *Books and Book-Collecting* (1980).
- E. Janet Browne, *Charles Darwin: Voyaging* (1995).
- Bill Bryson, *Notes from a Small Island* (1995).
- Anthony Burgess, *Little Wilson and Big God: Being the First Part of the Autobiography* (1986).
- Anthony Burgess, *You've Had Your Time: The Second Part of the Confessions* (1990).
- Roy Campbell, *Broken Record* (1934).
- Roy Campbell, *Light on a Dark Horse* (1952).
- Robert A. Caro, *Master of the Senate* (2003).
- Robert A. Caro, *Means of Ascent* (1991).
- Robert A. Caro, *The Path to Power* (1990).
- Winston Churchill, *My Early Years: A Roving Commission* (1930).
- Michael Crichton, *Travels* (1988).
- Robert Dallek, *An Unfinished Life: John F. Kennedy, 1917–1963* (2003).

- Will Durant, *On the Meaning of Life* (1932).
- Barbara Ehrenreich, *Nickel and Dimed: On (Not) Getting by in America* (2001).
- Nora Ephron, *Crazy Salad: Some Things About Women* (2000).
- Joseph Epstein, *The Middle of My Tether* (1983).
- Joseph Epstein, *Once More Around the Block* (1987).
- Joseph Epstein, *Snobbery: The American Version* (2002).
- Anne Fadiman, *Ex Libris: Confessions of a Common Reader* (1998).
- Paul Fussell, *Bad, or the Dumbing of America* (1991).
- Brendan Gill, *Here at the* New Yorker (1975).
- Doris Kearns Goodwin, *No Ordinary Time: Franklin and Eleanor Roosevelt* (1994).
- Doris Kearns Goodwin, *Wait Till Next Year* (1997).
- Christopher Hitchens, *Why Orwell Matters* (2002).
- Karen Horney, *Neurosis and Human Growth* (1950).
- Pico Iyer, *Sun After Dark: Flights into the Foreign* (2004).
- Clive James, *Cultural Amnesia: Necessary Memories from History and the Arts* (2007).
- Randall Jarrell, *A Sad Heart at the Supermarket* (1962).
- Elia Kazan, *Elia Kazan: A Life* (1988).
- Tracy Kidder, *House* (1985).
- David Laskin, *The Children's Blizzard* (2005).
- Nicholas Lemann, *The Big Test: The Secret History of the American Meritocracy* (2000).
- C.S. Lewis, *Surprised by Joy* (1956).
- Dwight Macdonald, *Against the Grain: Essays on the Effects of Mass Culture* (1962).
- Dwight Macdonald, *Memoirs of a Revolutionist: Essays in Political Criticism* (1960).
- Dwight Macdonald, *The Responsibility of Peoples: An Essay on War Guilt* (1944).
- Peter Mayle, *A Year in Provence* (1990).
- David McCullough, *Truman* (1992).
- John McPhee, *The John McPhee Reader* (1982).
- John McPhee, *Rising from the Plains* (1986).
- John McPhee, *The Second John McPhee Reader* (1996).
- H.L. Mencken, *A Mencken Chrestomathy* (1949).
- Richard Mitchell, *Less than Words Can Say: The Underground Grammarian* (1979).

- Jessica Mitford, *The American Way of Death Revisited* (2000).
- Vladimir Nabokov, *Lectures on Literature* (1980).
- Richard E. Neustadt & Ernest R. May, *Thinking in Time: The Uses of History for Decision-Makers* (1986).
- Peggy Noonan, *What I Saw at the Revolution: A Political Life in the Reagan Era* (1990).
- Cynthia Ozick, *Fame and Folly* (1996).
- George Plimpton, *Paper Lion* (1964).
- Richard Rhodes, *The Making of the Atomic Bomb* (1986).
- Rainer Maria Rilke, *Letters on Life* (Ulrich Baer trans., 2006).
- Andrew A. Rooney, *The Most of Andy Rooney* (1986).
- Andrew A. Rooney, *Word for Word* (1986).
- Andrew A. Rooney, *Years of Minutes* (2003).
- Bertrand Russell, *Skeptical Essays* (1961).
- Witold Rybczynski, *Home: A Short History of an Idea* (1986).
- Oliver Sacks, *Uncle Tungsten: Memories of a Chemical Boyhood* (2001).
- Carl Sagan, *Demon-Haunted World: Science as a Candle in the Dark* (1995).
- Charles Scribner Jr., *In the Company of Writers* (1990).
- David Sedaris, *Me Talk Pretty One Day* (2000).
- Eric Sevareid, *Not So Wild a Dream* (1946).
- John Simon, *Paradigms Lost* (1980).
- Ron Suskind, *A Hope in the Unseen: An American Odyssey from the Inner City to the Ivy League* (1998).
- Virgil Thomson, *Virgil Thomson* (1966).
- Calvin Trillin, *Messages from My Father* (1996).
- Henri Troyat, *Tolstoy* (1967).
- Barbara Tuchman, *A Distant Mirror* (1978).
- Barbara Tuchman, *The Guns of August* (1962).
- Barbara Tuchman, *Practicing History: Selected Essays* (1982).
- John Updike, *More Matter: Essays and Criticism* (1999).
- John Updike, *Self-Consciousness: Memoirs* (1989).
- David Foster Wallace, *Consider the Lobster and Other Essays* (2006).
- David Foster Wallace, *A Supposedly Fun Thing I'll Never Do Again: Essays and Arguments* (1998).
- E.B. White, *Essays of E.B. White* (1977).
- E.B. White, *Letters of E.B. White* (rev. ed. 2006).
- Tom Wolfe, *From Bauhaus to Our House* (1981).

- Tom Wolfe, *The Painted Word* (1976).
- Alexander Woollcott, *The Letters of Alexander Woollcott* (1944).

Fiction:

- James Agee, *A Death in the Family* (1957).
- Isabel Allende, *The House of the Spirits* (1985).
- Isabel Allende, *Portrait in Sepia* (2001).
- Kingsley Amis, *Lucky Jim* (1954).
- Kingsley Amis, *The Old Devils* (1987).
- John Ashbury, *Self-Portrait in a Convex Mirror* (1990).
- Paul Bowles, *Collected Stories 1939–1976* (1979).
- Paul Bowles, *The Sheltering Sky* (1949).
- Paul Bowles, *The Spider's House* (1955).
- Ray Bradbury, *The Martian Chronicles* (1950).
- Raymond Carver, *Where I'm Calling From: New and Selected Stories* (1998).
- Anton Pavlovich Chekhov, *The Essential Tales of Chekhov* (1998).
- Michael Crichton, *The Great Train Robbery* (1976).
- Louise Erdrich, *The Last Report on the Miracles at Little No Horse* (2001).
- F. Scott Fitzgerald, *The Great Gatsby* (1925).
- Thomas Hardy, *The Mayor of Casterbridge* (1886).
- Thomas Hardy, *Tess of the d'Urbervilles* (1891).
- Thomas Hardy, *The Woodlanders* (1887).
- Ernest Hemingway, *A Moveable Feast* (1964).
- Ernest Hemingway, *The Sun Also Rises* (1926).
- Kazuo Ishiguro, *The Remains of the Day* (1989).
- Franz Kafka, *The Trial* (1925).
- Barbara Kingsolver, *Animal Dreams* (1990).
- Barbara Kingsolver, *Poisonwood Bible* (1998).
- Harper Lee, *To Kill a Mockingbird* (1960).
- Rosamond Lehman, *Dusty Answer* (1927).
- C.S. Lewis, *The Screwtape Letters* (1942).
- Alan Lightman, *Einstein's Dreams* (2004).
- David Lodge, *The British Museum Is Falling Down* (1965).
- David Lodge, *A David Lodge Trilogy* (1993) (containing *Changing Places*, *Small World*, and *Nice Work*).
- David Lodge, *Thinks . . .* (2001).

- Gabriel Garcia Márquez, *One Hundred Years of Solitude* (Gregory Rabassa trans., 1998).
- Cormac McCarthy, *Blood Meridian* (1985).
- Cormac McCarthy, *The Road* (2006).
- Larry McMurtry, *Lonesome Dove* (1985).
- Larry McMurtry, *Texasville* (1986).
- George Meredith, *Diana of the Crossways* (1885).
- George Meredith, *The Ordeal of Richard Feverel* (1859).
- Brian Moore, *The Lonely Passion of Judith Hearne* (1955).
- Toni Morrison, *Beloved* (1987).
- Vladimir Nabokov, *Pale Fire* (1962).
- Cynthia Ozick, *The Cannibal Galaxy* (1983).
- Cynthia Ozick, *Heir to the Glimmering World* (2004).
- Cynthia Ozick, *The Puttermesser Papers* (1997).
- Ann Patchett, *Bel Canto* (2001).
- T.R. Pearson, *A Short History of a Small Place* (1986).
- J.D. Salinger, *Franny & Zooey* (1961).
- Betty Smith, *A Tree Grows in Brooklyn* (1943).
- Susan Sontag, *In America* (1999).
- Susan Sontag, *The Volcano Lover* (1992).
- Robert Louis Stevenson, *Fables* (1916).
- William Styron, *Sophie's Choice* (1979).
- Leo Tolstoy, *Anna Karenina* (1877 [much retranslated & reprinted]).
- Leo Tolstoy, *Hadji Murat* (1912).
- Su Tong, *Raise the Red Lantern* (1996).
- Edmund Wilson, *Galahad: I Thought of Daisy* (1967).
- Edmund Wilson, *The Higher Jazz* (1998).
- Edmund Wilson, *Memoirs of Hecate County* (1946).

11 Law

11.1 For a law dictionary:
- *Black's Law Dictionary* (Bryan A. Garner ed., 8th ed. 2004) (a thorough revision adding more than 17,000 terms).

11.2 For a legal thesaurus:
- William C. Burton, *Burton's Legal Thesaurus* (4th ed. 2006).

11.3 For quick but in-depth guidance on questions of legal usage, such as whether to use *attorney's fees*, *attorneys' fees*, or *attorney fees*:
- Bryan A. Garner, *A Dictionary of Modern Legal Usage* (2d ed. 1995).

11.4 For improving legal style:
- Bryan A. Garner, *The Elements of Legal Style* (2d ed. 2002) (for style mostly in the larger rhetorical sense).
- Bryan A. Garner, *The Redbook: A Manual on Legal Style* (2d ed. 2006) (with Jeff Newman and Tiger Jackson) (for style mostly in the sense of punctuation minutiae, etc.).
- Irving Younger, *Persuasive Writing* (1990) (Younger's *ABA Journal* essays collected edited posthumously).

11.5 For practical guidance on minimizing legal jargon:
- Bryan A. Garner, *Legal Writing in Plain English* (2001).
- Joseph Kimble, *Lifting the Fog of Legalese* (2006).
- Richard C. Wydick, *Plain English for Lawyers* (5th ed. 2005).

11.6 For a scholarly treatment of legal language and its fascinating history:
- * David Mellinkoff, *The Language of the Law* (1963).
- Peter M. Tiersma, *Legal Language* (1999).

11.7 For watching first-rate legal minds address practical legal problems:
- Lon L. Fuller, *Anatomy of the Law* (1968).
- Grant Gilmore, *The Death of Contract* (2d ed. 1995).
- Grant Gilmore & Charles L. Black, *The Law of Admiralty* (2d ed. 1975).
- Tony Honoré, *Responsibility and Fault* (1999).
- Charles Alan Wright, *The Law of Federal Courts* (5th ed. 1994) (the final edition by Wright himself).

11.8 For improving your transactional-drafting skills:
- Scott J. Burnham, *The Contract Drafting Guidebook* (1992).
- *Drafting Contracts and Commercial Instruments* (Research & Documentation Corp. ed., 1971).
- Carl Felsenfeld & Alan Siegel, *Writing Contracts in Plain English* (1981).
- Bryan A. Garner, *Securities Disclosure in Plain English* (1999).

11.9 For guidance on oral arguments:
- David C. Frederick, *Supreme Court and Appellate Advocacy: Mastering Oral Argument* (2003).
- Bryan A. Garner, *The Winning Oral Argument* (2007).

11.10 For guidance on drafting legislation and rules:
- Peter Butt & Richard Castle, *Modern Legal Drafting* (2d ed. 2006).
- Reed Dickerson, *The Fundamentals of Legal Drafting* (2d ed. 1986).
- Bryan A. Garner, *Guidelines for Drafting and Editing Court Rules* (1996).
- Joseph Kimble, *How to Mangle Court Rules and Jury Instructions*, 8 Scribes J. Legal Writing 39 (2001–2002).

11.11 For reading about judges and judging:
- Erwin N. Griswold, *The Judicial Process* (1973).
- Donald Dale Jackson, *Judges* (1974).
- Robert E. Keeton, *Keeton on Judging in the American Legal System* (1999).
- Karl N. Llewellyn, *The Common Law Tradition: Deciding Appeals* (1960).
- David Pannick, *Judges* (1987).
- *Judicial Decision-Making* (Glendon Schubert ed., 1963).
- Lawrence M. Solan, *The Language of Judges* (1993).
- Charles E. Wyzanski Jr., *Whereas: A Judge's Premises* (1965).

11.12 For detailed guidance on brief-writing:
- Bryan A. Garner, *The Winning Brief* (2d ed. 2004).
- Girvan Peck, *Writing Persuasive Briefs* (1984).
- Frederick B. Wiener, *Briefing and Arguing Federal Appeals* (rev. ed. 1967).

11.13 For guidance on writing judicial opinions, and examples of good ones:
- Ruggero J. Aldisert, *Opinion Writing* (1999).
- *The Dissenting Opinions of Mr. Justice Holmes* (Alfred Lief ed., 1931).
- Bryan A. Garner, "Opinions, Style of," in *The Oxford Companion to the Supreme Court of the United States* (2d. ed. 2005).
- Joyce J. George, *Judicial Opinion Writing Handbook* (4th ed. 2000).
- Joseph Kimble, *The Straight Skinny on Better Judicial Opinions*, 9 Scribes J. Legal Writing 2 (2003–2004).
- *Representative Opinions of Mr. Justice Holmes* (Alfred Lief ed., 1929).
- Antonin Scalia, *Scalia Dissents* (Kevin A. Ring ed., 2004).

11.14 For up-to-date guidance on legal citations:
- *The Bluebook: A Uniform System of Citation* (18th ed. 2005).
- Darby Dickerson, *The ALWD Citation Manual* (3d ed. 2005).

11.15 For legal humor:
  - *Amicus Humoriae* (Robert M. Jarvis et al. eds., 2003).
  - Peter Hay, *A Book of Legal Anecdotes* (1989).
  - * R.E. Megarry, *Miscellany-at-Law: A Diversion for Lawyers and Others* (1955).
  - R.E. Megarry, *A Second Miscellany-at-Law: A Further Diversion for Lawyers and Others* (1973).
  - * R.E. Megarry, *A New Miscellany-at-Law: Yet Another Diversion for Lawyers and Others* (Bryan A. Garner ed., 2005).
  - William Prosser, *The Judicial Humorist* (1952).

11.16 For guidance on legal reasoning:
  - * Wilson Huhn, *The Five Types of Legal Argument* (2002).
  - Edward H. Levi, *An Introduction to Legal Reasoning* (1949).
  - Douglas Lind, *Logic and Legal Reasoning* (2001).
  - * Clarence Morris, *How Lawyers Think* (1937).

11.17 For a book of legal quotations:
  - Fred R. Shapiro, *The Oxford Dictionary of American Legal Quotations* (1993).

12 Subscriptions

12.1 For the best law journal:
  - *The Green Bag* (www.greenbag.org).

12.2 For the best journal on legal writing:
  - *The Scribes Journal of Legal Writing* (www.scribes.org).

12.3 For the best newsletter on copyediting:
  - *Copyediting* (www.mcmurry.com/copy/).

12.4 For the best language-related journals:
  - *American Speech* (Duke University Press, Journals Fulfillment, Box 90660, Durham, NC 27708-0660, 1-888-651-0122).
  - *English Today* (Cambridge University Press, 40 W. 20th St., New York, NY, 10011-4211).

Table of Cases Cited

Index